FIFTH EDITION

Personality Theories

Development, Growth, and Diversity

Bem P. Allen
Western Illinois University

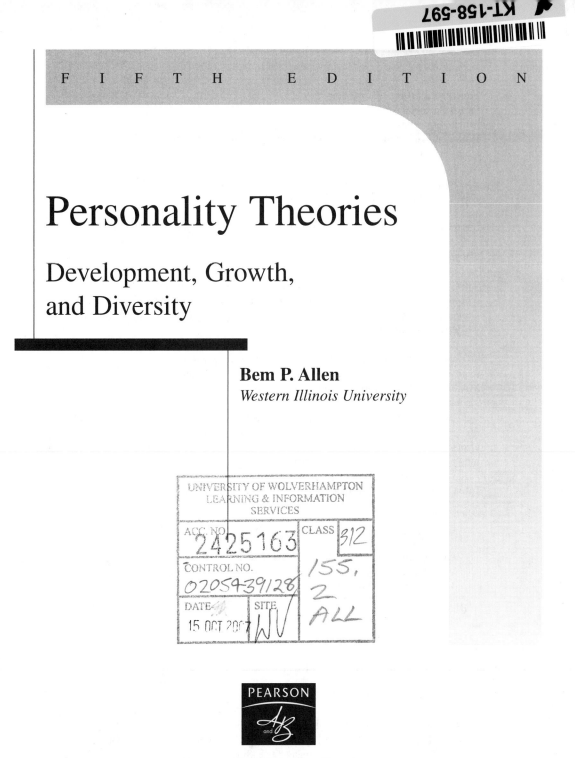

PEARSON

Boston   New York   San Francisco
Mexico City   Montreal   Toronto   London   Madrid   Munich   Paris
Hong Kong   Singapore   Tokyo   Cape Town   Sydney

Executive Editor: *Karon Bowers*
Series Editorial Assistant: *Lara Torsky*
Marketing Manager: *Pamela Laskey*
Editorial Production Service: *Omegatype Typography, Inc.*
Composition Buyer: *Linda Cox*
Manufacturing Buyer: *JoAnne Sweeney*
Electronic Composition: *Omegatype Typography, Inc.*
Cover Administrator: *Linda Knowles*

For related titles and support materials, visit our online catalog at www.ablongman.com.

Between the time website information is gathered and then published, it is not unusual for some sites to have closed. Also, the transcription of URLs can result in typographical errors. The publisher would appreciate notification where these errors occur so that they may be corrected in subsequent editions.

Library of Congress Cataloging-in-Publication Data

Allen, Bem P.
    Personality theories : development, growth, and diversity / Bem P. Allen.—5th ed.
        p.   cm.
    Includes bibliographical references and index.
    ISBN 0-205-43912-8 (casebound)
    1. Personality—Textbooks.   I. Title.

    BF698 .A3614 2006
    155.2—dc22

                                                                2005043007

Printed in the United States of America

10 9 8 7 6 5 4 3 2   10 09 08 07 06

Photo credits: pp. 21, 56: National Library of Medicine; p. 78: The Granger Collection; p. 101, © Bettman/CORBIS; p. 127, The Granger Collection; p. 149, © Bettman/CORBIS; p. 173, Library of Congress; p. 197, © Bettman/CORBIS; p. 221, © Bettman/CORBIS; p.239, Corbis; p. 245, Lyrl Ahern; p. 270, Walter Mischel; p. 287, Julian Rotter; p. 299, Albert Bandura/Stanford; p. 323 (left), Corbis; p. 323 (right), © CORBIS; p. 328, AP/Wide World; p. 355, AP/Wide World; p. 369, Bem P. Allen; p. 381, Raymond P. Cattrall; p. 399, Hans Jurgen Eysenck; p. 414, © Bettman/CORBIS; p. 417, © Reuters/CORBIS.

To Paula and our children,
Bem III, Kathleen, and Margaret,
and granddaughters Courtney, Emma, Kaitlyn, and Kelly

Brief Contents

Contents

4 *Overcoming Inferiority and Striving for Superiority:*
Alfred Adler   *78*

5 *Moving toward, away from, and against Others:*
Karen Horney   *101*

8 *The Sociopsychological Approach to Personality:*
Erich Fromm   *173*

9 *Every Person Is to Be Prized: Carl Rogers*   *197*

18   *Where Is Personality Theory Going?*   *452*

Preface

In terms of human personality development, almost all texts, including previous editions of *Personality Theories: Development, Growth, and Diversity,* recognize the contribution of Freud's and Erikson's stage theories. More uncommon is the coverage of developmental stages and other aspects of development found in this book's treatment of Jung, Adler, Horney, Sullivan, Kelly, Skinner, and Allport. Jung, Sullivan, and Allport present stage theories that are well covered in the current edition, but neglected elsewhere. Horney's, Kelly's, and Skinner's theories have strong implications for personality development that are explicit in the writings of Horney (e.g., basic anxiety) and Kelly (e.g., dependency constructs), but must be "read between the lines" of Skinner's writings. All of these contributions to understanding personality development are "writ large" in the pages of this text. Further, some other contributions are teased from the writings of additional theorists (e.g., Mischel's "delay of gratification").

The humanistic perspective and its orientation to growth are central foci of this edition. Horney's alleged early pessimism about humans has been de-emphasized in favor of accentuating her later humanistic inclination, reflected in the notion of "real self." Fromm's role as a pioneer in the humanistic movement is highlighted in this edition of *Personality Theories.* Allport's humanism is also brought more into focus, especially in regard to his concern for religious issues (religion itself is more often mentioned). Finally, existentialism, a key plank in the floorboards of the humanistic house, receives considerable attention. It is introduced in the Fromm chapter with special reference to the ideas of Rollo May. Coverage continues in the Rogers and Maslow chapters and appears again in the Allport chapter. All in all, there is emphasis on what people can become.

Diversity is still quite a buzzword these days. Text authors are regularly injecting it into their books. To me it is much more than that. Beginning almost twenty years ago, a few colleagues and I started to develop a diversity curriculum at our university. Through persistence, we have overcome initial resistance and have instituted a diversity requirement for all our students. In the process, we have developed a core diversity course, which I have taught for nearly fifteen years. I have also written several articles about diversity and have made presentations at several national, state, and local diversity conventions.

Obviously, I believe diversity is here to stay. In fact, it is my belief that our students' ability to prosper in the future depends, in part, on their grasp of diversity issues. This position has also been adopted by the University of Michigan and supported recently in their partially successful case before the U.S. Supreme Court. Accordingly, every chapter devotes significant space to diversity. Students should come away from this book-long consideration knowing what diversity *is* (no single definition, even one several pages long, can do justice to the term) and what *it is not* (it is not something just for "minorities" and women; it is for everyone).

But, one may still wonder, "Why all this emphasis on diversity in a personality theories book?" Given that "individual differences" is a core personality consideration (it obviously is), "diversity" is a natural companion to the study of personality theories. Actually, I cannot think of a better place to put coverage of diversity issues.

Of the theories attempting to explain psychological phenomena, those applied to understanding personality are among psychology's oldest and most enduring sets of theories, with origins dating to the ancient Greeks and to Eastern philosophies. Despite being "long in the tooth," these venerable points of view are still being pursued by modern theorists, researchers, and practitioners. In fact, few groups of theories focused on a single, complex phenomenon have survived so well as theories of personality. For example, while some personality theories have gained many new advocates, theories of conditioning (instrumental and classical) have recruited relatively few.

Why the longevity of these notions? They have served psychology well in terms of generating fruitful new ideas, leading to means of helping people with psychological problems, and providing the grist for psychological researchers' scientific mills. Thus, one basic assumption behind this book is that personality theories are central to psychological thinking. I have woven this assumption into the fabric of the text.

A second basic assumption is wrapped up in the answer to the question, "At what level of difficulty can a broad range of college students be expected to function successfully?" Personality theories do not have the reputation for difficulty and arcane structure by which physicists' theories of time and space are known. They do, however, involve complexities and abstractions that can be quite challenging. Nevertheless, the question can be answered in an optimistic fashion: Typical students attending every kind of school, including community colleges and Ivy League universities, can learn even intricate and daunting material, provided it is presented in a manner that will excite their imaginations and relate to their lives. Therefore, I have worked hard to make each personality theory come alive by showing how it relates to the personality of the individual who composed it, by indicating how solutions to life's puzzles may be better approximated through understanding it, and by using it to inspire some insightful thoughts that most students have yet to think.

A third basic assumption of *Personality Theories* involves notions of objectivity. Although perfect objectivity is almost certainly unobtainable, even-handedness can be achieved. *Personality Theories* assumes that students should come away from a thorough consideration of personality theories with a sense that each has its merits and deficiencies and none can be reasonably called "the best" or "the worst." Allowing students to achieve this goal entails taking the perspective of each theorist as I write about her or his theory, while also maintaining an informed, balanced point of view so that merits and deficiencies are seen in relation to the field of personality as a whole. These two complementary orientations allow me to write about theorists' major contributions with great enthusiasm, sometimes bordering on zealousness. At the same time I step back and caution students about the apparent weaknesses of even the most laudable ideas and about holes in theories left by failures to entertain important matters of personality.

Audience

Personality Theories is designed for undergraduate students, regardless of level. It is written to be easily read. However, it does include sentences of moderate complexity and length that contain uncommon words. Although some students may be advised to occasionally use a dictionary, care is taken so that context usually defines uncommon words. These practices ensure that students who are unintimidated by any readings, even the most difficult, will find that *Personality Theories* holds their interest. At the same time, students who are not so widely read can manage this text without undue trouble and can improve their ability to read more challenging literature.

Organization

The organization of the chapters in *Personality Theories* is unique and consistent throughout the book. All chapters are written using basically the same format, allowing students to quickly learn what to look for, a lesson that will make reading more comfortable and rapid. I have seen many comments about the earlier editions by students at my university, and by students at many other colleges and universities. They clearly indicate great appreciation for *Personality Theories'* organization (more generally, student reaction to the text has been very favorable). Because the organization is so important to students, it is detailed in the first chapter where they will not miss it. Here, I have provided only a brief rationale for the various chapter sections constituting the organization. (Readers who want more information should see Chapter 1.)

An Introductory Statement, designed to link a given chapter to preceding ones, is followed by a biography of the theorist under consideration. Here each theorist is humanized and groundwork is laid for linking his or her personality and personal history to the theory in question. These biographies provide students with "memory hooks" on which to hang components of each theory.

A View of the Person section follows and orients students by providing them with the philosophical underpinnings of each theory. This section answers such questions as "To what degree is the theory scientific?", "Does the theory attempt to understand the person by reference to the past, present, or future?", "Are external or internal determinants of psychological functioning emphasized?", and "Do inborn or acquired determinants explain personality?" If I had to name one section that is crucial to student understanding this is it. A new chapter of this book pursues issues raised in "view of the person."

The Basic Concepts section lays out the fundamental constructs of each theory. These critical elements are linked so that students may understand their interrelationships and, where possible, are organized according to some familiar schema. For example, if a theory includes a series of developmental steps, its concepts are presented within the framework of sequential stages. In any event, an effort is made to begin with more global concepts, where they can be identified, and proceed to more specific ones.

Evaluation of each theory is organized into "contributions" and "limitations" subsections. Two broad categories of criteria applicable to both subsections are used to assess aspects of each theory. A given criterion may be used for one theory to illuminate contributions, and for another to point out limitations. Alternatively, a theory may meet a given criterion to some degree, therefore revealing a contribution, or fail to meet the criterion to some degree, indicating a limitation. None of these criteria is relevant to every theory; thus, a given one may be used to evaluate one theory but not another. One of these broad categories is "science criteria." These criteria address such questions as "Is the theory constructed in logical fashion?", "Are the concepts well interrelated?", "Do the concepts tend to be distinct or are they overlapping?", "Are common labels for concepts used or are obscure labels used?", "Does each label give precise meaning to its concept or does it have multiple meanings?", "Do concepts imply testable predictions?", and "Do research studies support the validity of concepts?" "Non-science criteria," the other category, raise such questions as "Does the theory inspire psychologists to experience new insights and clarify their thinking?", "Does the theory lead to a useful method of therapy?", and "Have the theorist's writings been interesting and helpful to laypeople?" Some of these issues are taken up in a new chapter of the book.

Content and Chapter Organization

Personality Theories is comprehensive. A first step in developing a plan for the book was to informally survey the range of theories apparently deemed most central to instructors of personality theory. Every theory that has been of interest to even a substantial minority of personality instructors is included in this text. Few texts, if any, cover as many theories, and none covers a better representation of mainstream theories. It is, therefore, likely that most personality instructors will find the theories they want to cover within the pages of *Personality Theories*. Furthermore, coverage of modern research on personality is so extensive that this new edition qualifies as a general personality text. However, the discussion of research is succinct and straightforward so that any student can easily grasp it.

The chapters are grouped in representative clusters and ordered within clusters in popular fashion. For example, Chapters 3 through 8 are devoted to theorists who use Freud's perspective (Chapter 2) as a point of departure for developing their own theories. Theorists most closely linked to Freud are considered in early chapters of this cluster (Jung and Adler), and those more removed from direct influence by him are considered in later chapters (Horney, Sullivan, Erikson, and Fromm). Consideration of Fromm, who should be regarded as an early humanist, provides a bridge to the second cluster, the two chapters on the modern humanists, Rogers and Maslow. Again, existentialism receives significant attention. A chapter on the cognitive approach (Kelly) is followed by chapters on the social–cognitive point of view (Mischel/Rotter and Bandura). Next comes the ideas of self-proclaimed anticognitive theorist, Skinner. Then a chapter on Murray's theory links early chapter traditions to the humanistic, cognitive, and behavioral orientations, and lays the groundwork for the trait theories. Cattell's and Eysenck's theories are next and emphasis is on modern approaches to the study of traits. A chapter devoted to Allport's more humanistic and socially flavored theory of traits, focused on personality development and prejudice is next. By popular demand, "Where Is Personality Theory Going?" has become the final chapter that ties the others together and projects personality theory into the future.

Alternative Uses of Personality Theories

I have always found comprehensive texts more attractive than ones with specialized content because they invariably include the chapters I want to cover. Only some of them, however, are written so that I can "unplug" the chapters I want to consider without concern that I have eliminated material essential for understanding covered chapters. In composing *Personality Theories,* I have taken great care to interrelate chapters, while, at the same time, making sure that each chapter can stand alone should a given instructor wish to consider only a subset of all chapters. I believe that personality instructors will find they can readily skip some chapters of *Personality Theories* and focus on others without fear that students will be unduly troubled by lack of exposure to eliminated material. Actually, with 18 chapters, averaging less than 25 pages each, rather than dropping some chapters, or in addition to dropping some, one could consider a growing trend in psychology: the modular approach. Select some portions of some chapters. For example, drop the research sections, or pick and choose pages from chapters. That is what I do.

Special Features

Each chapter begins with "teaser questions" that are designed to alert students to critical issues considered in the chapter and to arouse their curiosity regarding the theory. The presence of these questions at the beginning of each chapter primes students to entertain new material that is dissimilar to that discussed in previous chapters. The questions are always answered in the text of the chapter.

Immediately following the text for each chapter, students will find some Summary Points that will allow them a quick review of the chapter. These points are synopses of ten major considerations. They are not an attempt to reiterate the entire chapter. Students can expect that the points will trigger their memories concerning major issues in the chapter and the details surrounding them, **if they have carefully read the text.** The points are not a substitute for perusal of the chapter.

All too often, some students will read a chapter—or, more likely, a set of chapters over which they are to be tested—and then forget about chapter content as soon as they will no longer be evaluated based on their knowledge of it. The Running Comparison that follows the Summary Points is constructed so that students are continually reminded of material in earlier chapters. This goal is accomplished by comparing the theory currently under consideration with theories covered in previous chapters. Also, the comparison helps students anticipate future theories by occasionally comparing the current theory with ones yet to be considered. Should instructors wish to give a comprehensive final exam, the comparison will help students greatly because it will ensure that they are continually reviewing material from all chapters. In addition, the comparison further sharpens students' understanding of a given theory by contrasting it with other theories.

The next section in each chapter is designed to promote critical thinking. While these *Critical Thinking* questions can be used as essay-test items, alternatively, they can also be used as a basis for class discussions. In addition, they are good review questions. More importantly, they can be used by students to expand their thinking by suggesting the implications of theories that reach far beyond the text. Many of these questions will be challenging even to the best students, partly because they require analysis, not rote memory. These truly are questions that go beyond the text and cannot be answered based solely on the text.

A complete Glossary of all concepts composing covered theories is presented at the end of the book. The listing is alphabetical, and each entry clearly specifies its concept. I have simplified many of the glossary definitions and eliminated some entries that were peripheral. Concepts are also listed (with text page numbers) under each theorist's name in the subject index. I have had my students make multiple copies of the subject index so they can more easily prepare for essay questions that ask them to compare theorists.

The last section of each chapter is a listing of questions students can address to me personally via e-mail. Of course, they may also send me their own questions. The goal is for individual students to satisfy their curiosity. Of course, instructors are encouraged to contact me as well. I hope adopters of this book will encourage students to interact with me in this modern way, not just for their further education in personality, but also because they will benefit by using a mode of communication that will characterize their future. I look forward to relating to student-users of my book in a more personal way than is allowed by most text authors. My experience with many hundreds of student readers tells me that students learn from and enjoy interactions with the text author.

A comprehensive test-item file is available. Multiple-choice items thoroughly cover each chapter's material. Many of these items have been thoroughly tested. Having used them for my own tests, I have been able to eliminate questionable items, rewrite others for clarity, and create new ones that are easily understood by today's students. There are an average of about 100 items per chapter providing instructors with approximately 1,700 items, more than enough for several during-the-semester tests and a final exam. This includes some extra items at the end of each item file so that adopters will have a separate pool for make-up tests and finals. As I have years of experience in contributing multiple-choice items to test manuals, instructors can be assured that items are carefully and professionally done. Alternatives such as "all of the above," "none of the above," and "both a and b" are avoided because they confuse students. Each item, therefore, has only one correct alternative. All incorrect alternatives are written to be highly plausible so that students must make thoughtful choices. They are often statements true of other aspects of a theory, but incorrect in terms of the main body of the question. These alternatives require students to discriminate among concepts of a theory. Concepts from other theories are also sometimes used so that inter-theory discrimination can be assessed.

I have always believed that tests are learning experiences, not just occasions for evaluation. Accordingly, items are written to engage students in analytic thinking. Most require that students employ their reasoning powers, rather than merely recognize the correct alternative. Items are written so that correct alternatives follow logically from main bodies of questions, a process that will sharpen students' logical thinking. They are also written to be interesting in and of themselves. A computerized test bank is available through your sales representative.

The Instructor's Manual accompanying this text is constructed so that instructors can initiate interesting and edifying classroom discussions and exercises to complement the lectures. As a member of a national college teacher's organization, and a frequent participant in its conventions, I have become convinced that spending the entire class period lecturing is not ideal either for students or instructors. Students can obtain basic information from the text. Class time can be used to get students excited about the course content, to go over difficult material, to provide the latest hot-off-the-press information about course content, and to cover issues about which the instructor is expert in greater depth than text space allows.

The Instructor's Manual section for each chapter also contains an outline of the chapter so instructors can orient themselves regarding chapter content, chapter objectives (which may provide further orientation and can be passed on to students), a list of readings for lecture support, and a list of readings for students that can be placed on library reserve lists. Also, the Instructor's Manual contains a film/video list and the Case of Estella Monroe, an additional experience in diversity that will allow instructors to engage students in the application of all theories to a single case history (the case of Estella Monroe is considered further in Chapter 1). I often ask essay questions based on the Estella case.

Other Materials

The many case histories presented in the book include some about "people I've known" who illustrate critical concepts. Examples include "the good mother" (Chapter 6), "the narcissistic personality" (Chapters 1 and 2), "the mature person" (Chapter 17), "the self-actualized person" (Chapter 10), and a case of identity change (Chapter 7), the hippie protester who became a conservative.

The Freud chapter contains his famous case histories and critiques of them. Among them is a recently discovered case of a U.S. woman and little-known cases such as The Gingerbread Man and The Milk Man. Classic cases—the Wolf Man and the Rat Man, as well as Little Hans, Dora, and Anna O—are extensively considered. They hit at the heart of Freud's support for his theory. Other innovations include a Web site student guide with practice test items and links to interesting materials (go to my site www.wiu.edu/users/mfbpa/bemjr.html for a link to the student guide site or www.ablongman.com/allen5e). My Web site also contains many links to a broader consideration of personality and other psychological issues. Finally, Web sites for the theorists are listed under their pictures.

Occasional mnemonics are added to text headings to help students remember concepts (e.g., "FITS" for Jung's feeling, intuiting, thinking, and sensing psychological functions). Ask students to look for these and encourage them to e-mail me additional candidates. I will pass the good ones on to other students and give the student authors credit. Exciting, relatively new topics include evolutionary theory applied to jealousy (and other issues), how to take the Jung-related version of the Myers-Briggs Type Indicator on the Web (it is among the links found on my home page), the "repressed memories" controversy, the eugenics scandal that cost Raymond Cattell a prestigious award, and a discussion of the currently popular "Emotional Intelligence."

This edition includes a final chapter that not only pulls together the theories covered in the book, but also makes some predictions about where personality theory is going in the future. It considers basic assumptions of the various theorists, their critical concepts, and their methodologies so that what has worked can be separated from what has not. The result is a synthesis of covered theorists' notions that suggests new directions theorists might take during the twenty-first century. This section should be particularly interesting to advanced undergraduate students and graduate students.

A final note: students in classes using this book will be learning *in detail* about more of the top figures in psychology than are featured in just about any book available today (Haggbloom et al., 2002). Each chapter will provide evidence to support this assertion. Each theorist's rank on the psychological professional journal citations lists (25 places), introductory textbook citations list (25 places), survey of contemporary psychologists (25 places), and overall list (100 places) will be given near the end of his or her chapter.

Acknowledgments

I offer sincere thanks to Executive Editor Karon Bowers and her assistant Lara Torsky for their conscientiousness and support. I would also like to thank the following reviewers for their comments on the manuscript: Joy Patricia Burke, Central Missouri State University; Vicki Dretchen, Volunteer State Community College; Jean W. Hunt, Cumberland College; Bonnie Moradi, University of Florida; Dan Segrist, Southwestern Illinois College; and Jerome Tobacyk, Louisiana Tech.

CHAPTER 1

Introduction

- How is personality defined and measured?
- Are personality researchers scientists?
- What kinds of tests do personality psychologists use?

One goal of this first chapter is to answer the question "What is personality?" by providing a preliminary definition. Another is to consider how personality is studied and the kinds of tests *personologists*—personality psychologists—use. A final goal is to lay out the logic behind the structure of chapters.

Preliminary Definition of Personality

The preliminary definition of personality has several facets: individual differences, behavioral dimensions, and traits. **Individual differences** refers to the observation that people differ in a variety of ways. In the study of personality, the important differences involve **personality traits,** internally based psychological characteristics that often correspond to adjectives such as *shy, kind, mean, outgoing, dominant,* and so forth.

Each trait corresponds to one end of a **behavioral dimension,** a continuum of behavior analogous to a yardstick. Just as one end of a yardstick is anchored by 0 inches and the other end by 36 inches, one end of a behavioral dimension is anchored by one behavioral extreme and the other end by the opposite extreme. For example, affiliativeness, anxiousness, and conscientiousness are labels for behavioral dimensions. The following example shows the extremes for conscientiousness:

conscientious:1:2:3:4:5:6:7:unconscientious

One end of the assertiveness dimension is anchored by *conscientious,* the tendency to be neat, well organized, on time, efficient, and effective. The other end is anchored by *unconscientious,* the tendency not to defend one's rights and to say "yes" when one wants to say "no." For the sake of convenience and simplicity, the example has only seven degrees. In reality, the number of degrees of a dimension is difficult or impossible to determine. In any case, only behaviors falling near the extremes of dimensions have much meaning for personality. Only if a person's behavior can be represented on the assertiveness dimension by a degree close to the anchor assertive can it be inferred that he or she possesses the trait *conscientious*. A *trait dimension* may be seen as the internal representation of a behavioral dimension.

Putting the facets together, an individual's **personality** is a set of degrees falling along many behavioral dimensions, each degree corresponding to a trait. Note that, although some people may share a particular trait, there are individual differences in possession of the trait. Some people have it and others do not. However, sharing does not apply to entire personalities. There are individual differences in the sets of traits that people possess such that no two personalities are exactly alike. Figure 1.1 shows the personality of Oprah, a favorite of students. The line drawn from each degree (trait level) to each other degree is her personality profile. Given enough dimensions, every person's profile will be different from that of every other person. The line connecting degrees on dimensions is the "personality profile line." For the middle-of-the-scale entries, Oprah is not extreme enough to be "traited" on these dimensions. Thus, she has neither trait represented by the ends of these dimensions.

Implications and Cautions

There is a coincidence of personologists' beliefs about personality and the common sense notions held by nonprofessionals or laypersons. First, many personologists and laypersons believe that an individual is quite consistent across different situations (his or her behavior is at about the same point or degree along the assertiveness behavioral dimension in one situation as it is in the next). This point of view constitutes the most basic assumption of our preliminary definition of *personality*. Second, where single dimensions are involved, individuals can be very similar or even identical. That is, two or more people can, on the average, exhibit about the same degree of a behavior, and, thus, possess the same trait. Third, the overriding agreement between personologists and the people they study is the shared belief in individual differences (Lamiell, 1981). Because there are individual differences along every behavioral dimension, given enough dimensions, personalities must differ. One respected estimate puts the number of traits and corresponding dimensions at over 17,000, thereby guaranteeing that each individual's personality is different from that of each other person and, thus, that each person has a unique personality (Allport and Odbert, 1936).

Unfortunately, some people mindlessly assume that "individual differences" are immutable. If we view our positions on various dimensions—whether they are personality or intellectual dimensions—as "innate" and, thus, assumed to be unchangeable, our lives will be very limited. In an insightful article, Robert A. Bjork (2000) challenges the assumption that individual differences are set in stone. Basically, he takes on the widely held belief that we have or do not have valued characteristics the day we are born. That is, we tend to assume that our behaviors fall at the positive or the negative end of various behavioral dimensions, and, if the latter, that there is nothing we can do about it. If, according to one of Bjork's examples, we fail a standardized math test early in elementary school, we assume that we are no good at math and should give up on it. "The role of [innate] aptitude is over-appreciated and the role of experience, effort, and practice are under-appreciated" (p. 3). We assume that we cannot, by our own devices, develop science aptitude, conscientiousness or the ability to appreciate others' emotions, so we don't try. Further, if we do assume

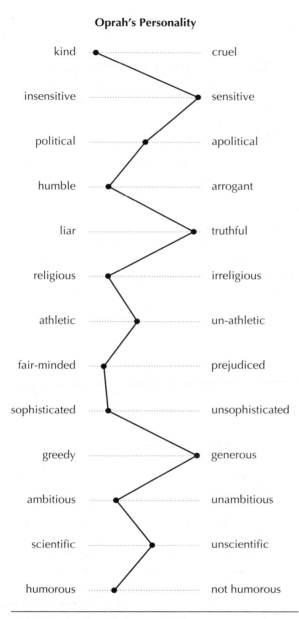

Oprah's Personality

kind	cruel
insensitive	sensitive
political	apolitical
humble	arrogant
liar	truthful
religious	irreligious
athletic	un-athletic
fair-minded	prejudiced
sophisticated	unsophisticated
greedy	generous
ambitious	unambitious
scientific	unscientific
humorous	not humorous

FIGURE 1.1 *Oprah's Personality*

that our behaviors occupy the "good" end of important dimensions, we are careful not to accept challenges, risk mistakes, or "think outside the box" lest we disprove our assumption that we are inherently gifted. I've known some honors students who assumed they were inherently smart, then avoided challenges and "out of the box" thinking lest they prove their assumption wrong. The result was mediocre work. I would add to Bjork's points that the *burning need to know* may be more important to mastering some pursuit than all the "innate intelligence" we can claim for ourselves. Murray (2002) echos Bjork's rejection of over-attention to "natural ability" and inattention to experience.

My experience as a personality researcher, reviewer of articles submitted to personality journals, and reader of personality publications tells me that the preliminary definition is implicitly, if not explicitly, adopted by more personologists than any other. It fits the theories of Murray, Cattell, Eysenck, and Allport rather well. All of them to some degree, at least implicitly, adopt its most basic assumption: a person behaves consistently from one situation to the next. These "trait theorists" must make the consistency assumption. Otherwise they would not be able to infer a trait from observations of a person's behaviors. They reason if a person is assertive in one situation and not in the next, how could anyone draw an inference about whether he or she has the trait *conscientious*?

The consistency assumption, while widely adopted, is nevertheless not without its critics. Some theorists, such as Rotter and Mischel, reject it outright. I also have serious reservations about it. Other deficiencies of our preliminary definition include inattention to physiological and developmental processes. In view of these shortcomings, consider the preliminary definition to be a frame of reference against which definitions of the theorists covered in this book can be considered. You will find that each theorist has her or his own definition, in some cases fitting the preliminary definition fairly well, but not always.

Methods of Studying Personality

First, a set of criteria for evaluating methods of studying personality must be specified. As in other fields of psychology, science is a main source of standards. The minimum requirement for a research method to be called **scientific** is that it involve unbiased observations that are quantified so that systematic analyses can be performed (Allen, 2001). Methods can properly be called "scientific" if (1) they allow researchers to make observations without regard to their personal biases, and (2) they permit the assignment of numbers to those observations so that systematic analysis is possible. By contrast, users of unscientific methods base selection of observations on convenience—whatever happens to be handy is observed—or personal bias—the researchers arbitrarily believe that selected observations are more important than other observations they might make. In addition, users of unscientific methods may draw conclusions about what they have observed without reference to theory or previous research. However important such efforts may be for some purposes, the methods involved do not ordinarily qualify as scientific.

The Case History Method

The **case history method** involves collecting background data about and making intensive observations of a single individual in order to discover how to treat that person or to obtain information that may apply to other people (Rosenhan & Seligman, 1995). It may be scientific in that observations can be unbiased. After all, it is possible for psychologists to lay aside their own personal biases about personality. However, unbiased observations may be difficult for them because the person under observation may be a patient with whom the psychologists are personally involved. Also, observations made on a single individual may not be applicable to other persons. A given individual may be quite unusual and, therefore, not at all representative of other people. Further, although it may be possible to assign numbers to observations, systematic analysis may be difficult or impossible. For example, a psychologist may give personality tests to an individual and then derive some scores. Still, systematic analysis may be difficult because scores from more than one person are ordinarily needed to conduct a meaningful analysis.

Despite these shortcomings, case histories may sometimes qualify as scientific. It is possible to give the subject of a case history personality tests and then compare her or his scores to norms or average scores derived by testing large populations of people. In this way, how the case history subject's scores compare to those of "people in general" can be determined and, thus, whether his or her score is unusual or like most people's can be stated. Further, there have even been whole books written using a single case as the source of data for a statistical analysis in a scientific study (Davidson & Costello, 1969). Charles Potkay and I have actually used a single case to illustrate research results for our entire sample of research subjects (Allen & Potkay, 1973a, 1977).

While the case history method does not typically qualify as scientific, information derived from it may be useful in many ways. Reports based on observations of single individuals often are valuable as illustrations of personality functioning. While lamenting a lack of publications featuring case histories, Masling (1997) mused, " . . . it is a pity, because a good, carefully written and clearly documented case can be more instructive, and usually more interesting, than any number of research papers" (p. 261).

At a number of points in this text, many real and some contrived cases will be used to concretely illustrate some aspect of personality functioning. Box 1.1 contains an example that relates to a criticism of the working definition of personality: personality is not set in stone; it can change. Bearing these cases in mind will help you remember some of the important patterns that relate to personality theories.

Among this book's case histories are some that you may find especially interesting: the Rat Man and the Wolf Man (and others, Chapter 2); characters in horror movies, delightful and mischievous Little Anna, and Bill Cosby (Chapter 3); an analysis of Frankenstein and his monster, based on the actual story by Mary Shelley (Chapter 4); the cases of Clare, a clingy, dependent woman madly in love with a self-centered man, and of the controller (Chapter 5); the good mother (Chapter 6); a hippie rebel turned conservative (Chapter 7); Hitler as a necrophilous (death-loving) character (Chapter 8); Becky and Dennis, Catholic and Protestant, coming to know one another in war-torn Northern Ireland (Chapter 9); a self-actualized person (Chapter 10); Jim and Joan, two college friends trying to resolve Jim's conflict with a professor, and a cognitively simple person (Chapter 11); a person with an external orientation (Chapter 12); resilience in the face of defeat displayed by famous people (Chapter 13); a baby reared in a box (Chapter 14); dreams about the kidnapping and murder of the Lindbergh baby and an analysis of a disturbed college student (Chapter 15); a schoolgirl case of mass hysteria (Chapter 16); and the cases of Rinehart and Jenny and the mature person (Chapter 17). In addition, every theorist's life story constitutes an often fascinating case history that begins every chapter.

In addition, your professor and you have a comprehensive case history in the Instructor's Manual and in the Student Guide that accompanies *Personality Theories* (for the student guide see my Web site: www.wiu.edu/users/mfbpa/bemjr.html). The case history subject, Estella Monroe, is a young Latina mother who has survived a divorce and is

BOX 1.1 • *George Foreman: From Angry and Depressed to Joyful and Successful*

I remember the earlier George Foreman well. I was and am a big Muhammad Ali fan, but at the time of the "rumble in the Jungle" (Zaire, Africa, 1974) Ali was past his prime and George Foreman was at his peak. Foreman appeared to be unbeatable. Joe Frazier had beaten Ali and Foreman "knocked Frazier down six times in two rounds" (Dahlberg, 2003, p. c4). Foreman was more than big, fast, and tough. He was constantly angry and apparently depressed. He threatened people and seemed never to smile or laugh except in a hostile way. Further, he was irreligious.

During the pre-fight hype in Zaire, Ali carefully nurtured World Champion Foreman's rage. He stuck verbal needles into Foreman at every opportunity. By fight time Foreman was vowing to pound the life out of Ali. And pound he did for many rounds. Ali performed his famous "rope a dope" maneuver, leaning against the ropes and taking Foreman's sledgehammer blows. Perhaps Ali's Parkinson's disease stems partly from this fight. Finally, in the eighth round Foreman was exhausted and Ali emerged from his defensive crouch to knock the Champ down and out. Afterwards, Foreman described himself as "the most boring man in the world."

Following another loss in 1977 he had an "out of body experience" and accepted Christ (Dahlberg, 2003). When he emerged as a contender again in 1986 he was a different man: the joyful, gregarious, at-peace man you may have seen on CBS's *60 Minutes* and surely have see in commercials for his "George Foreman Grill." Now a devout minister who shed around 100 pounds—and fathered five boys also named George—Foreman is a millionaire, far more successful and maybe better known than he was in his fighting days. He now makes $27,000,000 per annum from his endorsements, compared to a peak of 12.5 million for a 1991 unsuccessful comeback fight against then champ Evander Holyfield (Dahlberg, 2003). Today Foreman oozes happiness, love for others, and contentment. He has come 180° from the snarling, self-deprecating man whose anger and resentment cost him his most important fight. George Foreman is living proof that personality can change over time. Writing in psychology's most respected personality journal, Srivastava, John, Gosling, and Potter (2003) report research that confirms change in personality even during adulthood. One's personality is not written in stone.

"moving up the corporate ladder." Estella's relations with her son, her ex-husband, her new romantic partner, her coworkers, and her parents reveal material suitable for analysis by all the theories covered in this book.

The Correlational Method

The correlational method involves variables. The term **variable** refers to a variation in quantity specified by numbers. The numbers associated with a variable are called "values." Weight is a variable because it can take on different values. Some people weigh 100 lbs, some weigh 200 lbs, others 140 lbs, and still others 250 lbs. For adults, weight can vary from well under 100 lbs to well over 500 lbs. Likewise, height is a variable. Adults vary in height from under three feet to well over seven feet. Anxiety, intelligence, and kindness are also variables. In each case, observations can assume values that vary over some range.

The correlational method is used to determine whether variations in certain variables tend to occur together. Any two variables are said to be **correlated** if variations in one correspond to some degree with variations in the other.

To illustrate the correlational method, consider an example. Suppose a psychological researcher has subjects report their levels of stress daily by completing a questionnaire with scales like those used to measure assertiveness (for example, seven-point scales having anchors like "stressed-out" and "relaxed," "hurried" and "time to spare," and "anxious" and "calm"). As she wishes to correlate stress level with amount of upper respiratory congestion, she has her subjects visit cooperating physicians daily who record amount of congestion, an index of viral infection (e.g., the common cold). After a month she finds that, as daily stress goes up, congestion goes up; as stress goes down so does congestion. When high values on one variable correspond to high values on another variable, and low values on one variable correspond to low values on the other, the variables are said to be **positively correlated.** This correlational relationship is represented by a **correlation coefficient,** the index of degree of correlation. The obtained coefficient, symbolized by *r,* is .67. Because positive correlations range from 0.00 to 1.00, the researcher has found a rather strong relationship. In fact, research of this sort has caused the medical profession to finally recognize that psychological factors like stress can influence various medical conditions (Cohen, Tyrrell, & Smith, 1993).

In the case of a **negative correlation,** as values on one variable go up values on another variable go down. Psychological investigations have shown that, as noise levels go up, performance on various cognitive tasks (reading, arithmetic, and problem solving) goes down (e.g., Cohen, Evans, Krantz, & Stokols, 1980). Negative correlation coefficients range from 0.00 to –1.00. If a correlation is nil, there is no relationship between variables and *r* is near zero. Contrary to popular belief, you will learn from the chapter on Adler that the relationship between birth order—whether one is born first, second, third, or last—and various personality traits is virtually nil.

While the correlational method can readily qualify as scientific, like the other methods it has its problems. Chief among them is the fact that, while it can indicate whether there is a relationship between two variables, it cannot indicate whether one variable determines variation in another. This weakness is best expressed in the statement "correlation is not causation." That is, just because two variables are correlated does not mean one "caused" variation in the other. A few examples will illustrate the point. There is a high positive correlation between the inseam length of pants and the height of wearers, but buying longer jeans will not not make a person taller, nor will increases in height cause jeans to grow. Similarly, a researcher once found a high positive correlation between the amount of rainfall in Arizona and the rate of suicide in Canada. Obviously, no one was willing to argue that rain in Arizona "causes" suicides in Canada, or vice versa. The research literature continues to report that the experimental approach is superior to the correlational method for testing causal hypotheses (Enzel & Wohl, 2002). However, correlational research also has convincing supporters (Farr, 2002; Jussim, 2002).

It often happens that, when one of two correlated variables seems to have caused variation in the other, a third or fourth variable actually is a more likely candidate as the "cause." One winter in another country, there was a high correlation between the presence of storks on roofs and the births of babies the following summer and fall. Assuming that storks do not bring babies, something else accounted for the obtained relationship. Consider this alternative account: The storks roosted on the roofs near chimneys to keep warm, and the people, having no TV and tiring of card games, resorted to other forms of evening recreation. "Escaping the cold" both led the storks to the chimneys and confined the people inside where the possibilities for enjoyable entertainment were limited.

Even with new sophisticated techniques, it is accurate to say that the correlational method generally cannot tell us what variables determine variation in what other variables (Chapter 18 takes up this issue; see the Other Materials section of the Preface). Nevertheless, the correlational method can be very useful. First, sometimes it does not matter which of two variables "causes" variation in the other. If intelligence is highly, positively correlated with doing well in school, college recruiters will not care whether high intelligence "causes" doing well in school or doing well in school "causes" high intelligence. They may go about the business of recruiting those who score high on some intelligence test and rest easy in the belief that these people will succeed in college. Second, correlational methods may suggest a causal relationship between variables, thereby alerting researchers to apply other methods to confirm causality. The persistent positive correlation between cigarette smoking and lung cancer certainly suggests that smoking causes lung cancer. Use of another kind of method has confirmed that, indeed, cigarette smoking is a primary cause of lung cancer. Chapter 18 reconsiders correlational methods and causation.

That method is considered next, but first it is worth mentioning that a sophisticated technique built on correlation—called "factor analysis"—is very important to the study of personality. It will receive considerable attention in the chapter on Raymond Cattell and Hans Eysenck (and in Chapter 18).

The Experimental Method

The variables that psychologists deal with when they use the experimental method are classified into two categories. **Independent variables** have variation that is arranged by the person who uses the experimental method, called the "experimenter." Through certain manipulations, the experimenter assigns values (numbers) to independent variables, thereby dictating their variation. **Dependent variables** have values that are free to vary so that they are open to influence by the independent variables. The experimental method involves performing an **experiment,** a procedure whereby an experimenter first sets the variation in some independent variable(s) and then ascertains whether variation in some dependent variable(s) is influenced. In contrast to correlation, with use of the experimental method it may be possible to assert that, when variation in two variables corresponds, variation in one determined or "caused" variation in the other. The claim is possible because the experimenter, not some third variable, dictated the variation in the independent variable that, in turn, corresponds with variation in the dependent variable. With the correlational method, there is no prior manipulation of one variable followed by verification of whether the other variable was influenced.

An interesting experiment by William Perry and colleagues Sprock, Schaible, McDougall, Minassian, Jenkins, and Braff (1995) illustrates the experimental method. These researchers wanted to find out whether the famous Rorschach (1942/1951) inkblot test would be sensitive enough to detect anxiety generated by a drug. This familiar test consists of ten cards on which there are inkblots, five in black and white and five in color. Each inkblot was originally created by spilling some ink onto the middle of a sheet of paper and then folding the paper in half. This technique produced random configurations that can be interpreted in an indefinite number of ways (see Figure 1.2; this test is described further in a later section).

FIGURE 1.2 *Inkblot*

The experimenters created variation in the independent variable by giving three different doses of a drug known to cause anxiety-like symptoms—dextro-amphetamine—to three different groups of subjects. One group got a mild dose of amphetamine (16.5 mg). Subjects in a second group received a mild-to-moderate dose (29.2 mg). A third group got capsules that looked like those ingested by subjects receiving amphetamine, but their capsules contained only an inert substance (zero mg). Please note that the mg numbers are averages for each of the two groups of subjects receiving amphetamine, as each subject's dose was adjusted to fit his or her body weight.

The Rorschach inkblots were presented to subjects three hours after amphetamine capsules were ingested, enough time to ensure that the amphetamine had reached maximum levels in subjects' blood (those receiving the inert substance also waited three hours). Subjects looked at the inkblots and described what they saw (on seeing the blots, people often make simple responses like "butterfly" or "flower" and then they elaborate). These responses were scored for anxiety content. Results showed that there was no difference between the two amphetamine groups in the amount of anxiety imagery reflected in their responses. However, the difference between anxiety shown by subjects receiving some amphetamine and anxiety displayed by those who got no amphetamine was **statistically significant:** the difference between groups was so large that it was unlikely to occur solely by chance. Thus, experimenter-generated variation in the independent variable, number of mgs of amphetamine ingested, was related to variance in the dependent variable, amount of anxiety imagery reflected in responses to Rorschach inkblots. It is legitimate to state that amphetamine determines anxiety reflected in responses to Rorschach inkblots.

While the experimental method may be the most powerful scientific procedure, it, too, has its problems. Its most serious fault may be that, in order to have the control researchers need to carry out manipulations of independent variables, experiments must be performed in laboratories or other artificial settings. As a result, experimental outcomes must be generalized to real life with considerable caution. Experiments conducted under stale laboratory conditions may sometimes tell us little about how real people behave, feel, and think in real life. Consistent with this complaint against experimentation, and indirectly against an overemphasis on science, some of this book's theorists have condemned the experimental method. Murray must have had it in mind when he blasted "scientism," as did Cattell when he derogated "brass instrument" psychology. Many humanists also have grave reservations about "science" as represented by the experimental method.

Personality Tests: Personologists' Tools

Reliability and Validity

Like other scientists, personologists also have their instruments. Their tools, or assessment tests, come in a variety of forms, all of which are evaluated on two important dimensions. First, tests must demonstrate **reliability,** the degree to which test results are repeatable. When people take a test on one occasion and then again a short time thereafter, *test-retest reliability* is demonstrated if the scores on the two occasions are highly similar. Should people score similarly on two forms of the same test, *reliability of parallel forms* is demonstrated. Second, tests must demonstrate **validity,** the degree to which a test measures what it was designed to measure. A test can be said to have *content validity* if its items actually sample the behaviors of interest. A test of arithmetical skill has content validity if some of its items involve adding, some involve multiplication, and some involve division. *Predictive validity* refers to a test's capacity to make predictions about people's behavior. A test of the trait aggressiveness in children that accurately predicts pushing and shoving on the playground would have this kind of validity. *Construct validity* is the degree to which a test measures a defined concept. If a test measures the construct honesty, several of its items should be highly intercorrelated and, together, represent honesty. Example items would be "I frequently lie," "I never cheat on tests," and "I never steal," all rated on agree–disagree scales. Finally, a valid personality trait test should correlate positively with tests of dissimilar format that assess the same trait (*convergent validity*), but not at all with tests of similar format that assess different traits (*divergent validity*). A multiple-choice test of "helpfulness" and a true/false test of the same trait should be positively correlated, but two true/false tests, one measuring "helpfulness" and the other "ambition," should be uncorrelated.

Projective and Objective Tests

Most personality tests fall into one of two categories. **Projective tests** present people with test items that are unstructured, ambiguous, or open-ended, thus allowing them a wide range of freedom in making responses. The inkblots used in the amphetamine experiment are a prime example of the projective test (Rorschach, 1942/1951). Because the inkblots result from spilling some ink in the middle of sheets of paper and then folding the sheets together, they are inherently unstructured, ambiguous, and, thus, interpretable in various ways (see Figure 1.2). People "project" their psychological selves onto the "blank screens" represented by the inkblots, thereby revealing their individual backgrounds, perceptions, thoughts, feelings, and fantasies (Frank, 1939). Responses are scored in several ways, based on what an individual said about the inkblot: what part of it is emphasized, what shape is seen, whether the individual's response is typical of what other people say or original, how organized responses are, how the individual uses color, and whether what the individual says about the blots relates to factors like anxiety. Historically, scoring has been rather subjective: it is up to the peculiar interpretation of the particular psychologist who looks at responses.

The Thematic Apperception Test (TAT) developed by Henry A. Murray, one of the theorists covered in this book, has also been popular. Because the TAT is considered in detail later, for now it is sufficient to say that the test consists of 20 cards, each containing a black-and-white drawing, painting, or photograph of a human situation, such as a boy playing a violin. An individual is asked to look at each card and make up a short story about it, which the personologist writes down. These stories are analyzed to identify dominant themes that are important for understanding the individual's personality and relate to inner needs and external pressures. In other kinds of projective tests, respondents are asked to complete partial sentences, add an ending to a story, or draw a picture of a house or a human figure.

Recent extensive scrutiny of projective tests under the microscope of scientific evaluation produced results that are quite discouraging (Lilienfeld, Wood, & Garb, 2000a, b). Although different tests faired differently, the much revered Rorschach clearly failed to meet users' expectations. For example, Rorschach testers' great confidence in John Exner's Comprehensive System (CS) for administering and scoring the test was found to be unjustified. Lilienfeld's team reported that the sample of people whose responses to the inkblots constituted the norms for the CS were unrepresentative of the U.S. population. The normative sample must have been composed of extremely well-adjusted or otherwise unusual people, because, compared to them, normal people look pathological. Further, Exner's CS appears to be inappropriately applied when test-takers are people of color or non-U.S. people. Finally, reliability and validity were found to be much lower than previously assumed and rather poor in an absolute sense. The Lilienfeld group also reported that the human-figure drawing tests performed at least as poorly as the Rorschach. While the TAT faired better, it showed some important weaknesses. However, a consideration of TAT's shortcomings, and its strengths, is reserved for the Murray chapter.

Recently Hibbard (2003) published a spirited reply to Lilienfeld and colleagues in which he found many errors, omissions, and misinterpretations in their report. Thus, the issue of projective test reliability and validity is still open.

The second category is **objective tests,** highly structured paper-and-pencil questionnaires, usually true/false or multiple-choice, each with a single score-key, reflecting the fact that there is general agreement on scores. They are considered "structured" because they allow people very little freedom of response in answering items. People typically are instructed to read a number of statements and indicate which best applies to them or which are true of them and which are false. A sample item on an objective personality test might be, "When I go to a party (check the statement that best applies to you) (1) "I am a wallflower"; (2) "I am the life of the party"; (3) "I just blend in with the others"; (4) "I tend to throw a wet blanket on other people's fun." Alternatively, an item might simply be, "I am the life of the parties I attend (indicate true of you or false)." There is a way to appreciate the difference between objective and projective techniques that will be familiar to you. Contrast true/false and multiple-choice tests with essay exams in terms of format and freedom to chose your own responses.

The scoring of objective tests is straightforward. Each possible response can be regarded as factually correct or not. Thus, an item can be assigned some numerical value and the values of items are totaled to yield an overall score. Because objective tests, being highly structured, can be quantified in a concrete, nonarbitrary fashion, they show high reliability and validity relative to projective tests. There are several examples of objective personality tests in this book.

Objective tests, like projective tests, have shortcomings. Because what is being measured is usually obvious, objective test-takers can fake answers (check the socially desirable end of each scale; Masling, 1997). Compared to women, men show low "dependency" with their objective test responses, but display the same level of "dependency" on projective tests (Masling, 1997). Finally, objective tests predict behavior better than projective tests in the short term, especially if a very specific behavior is to be performed in a restricted situation. However, Masling (1997) points to evidence that projective tests predict broader behavior in the long term better than objective tests.

Testing and Theorizing about Personality in a World of Human Diversity

Human diversity refers to the numerous cultures, along with gender and sexual orientations, that characterize the population in the United States and other countries. There has always been great diversity in the United States and Canada. Diversity now characterizes much of Europe. Always, more than half of these populations have been female. Always gays, lesbians, bisexuals, and indigenous people have been present. In Canada and the United States, people from Asia are present in increasing numbers and people of African heritage have been present for hundreds of years. Diversity is here. We need to acknowledge and embrace it if we are to survive and prosper at work, at school, and in our neighborhoods.

Diversity considerations are prominent in *Personality Theories*. This emphasis seems particularly appropriate because personality theories, and the tests that arise out of them, have been based primarily on observations of European-American males. Usually, the theories can be readily generalized to other groups, such as females and Latinos. However, in many cases it is spontaneously suspected, or entirely obvious, that some theories and some tests do not apply well to some groups. That is partly because some groups, for example, East Asians and Westerners, don't think in the same way (Nisbett, 2003).

Progress has recently been made in addressing how diversity relates to personality theory and testing. For example, Whitworth and McBlaine (1993) have shown that the famous objective personality test, the MMPI and its successor the MMPI-2, yield similar scores for Anglos and Latinos. However, they found that the two groups did respond differently on four scales. Rogers, Flores, Ustad, and Sewell (1995) compared the Spanish Personality Assessment Inventory (PAI) with the corresponding English version, using some bilingual Mexican-Americans and some who spoke only Spanish. Bilingual subjects' responses to the Spanish and English versions corresponded reasonably well and two administrations of the Spanish version revealed good test-retest reliability. However, there was evidence of variation in responding across the two language forms and across administrations of a form. Hibbard, Tang, and Latko (2000) compared Asians and whites on scores and scale validity of TAT responses as interpreted by use of the Defense Mechanism Manual. Asians scored lower on Denial than whites, but there were no differences on Projection, Identification, and total scores. Validity coefficients were, on average, higher for Asians. Zhang and Norvilitis (2002) found smaller gender differences on four personality scales for Chinese subjects than for American subjects. Only Americans were likely to score higher on socially desirable scales (e.g., self-esteem) than undesirable dimensions (e.g., suicidal ideation). Tiemann (2001) found that fluent bilinguals did not differ in their Spanish and English descriptions of TAT cards, but their Spanish and English descriptions of Rorschach cards did differ. Wasti's and Cortina's (2002) report on ethnic differences in reactions to sexual harassment indicated that Turkish and Hispanic women engaged in more avoidance ("stayed out of his way") than white Americans, while Hispanics used more denial ("tried to forget it") and less advocacy seeking ("filed a grievance") than others.

Despite these recent efforts, inattention to diversity when personality theories and tests are considered remains a problem. Thus, when diversity issues are explicitly mentioned in the present edition, or simply implied, you can help your classmates and your professor by initiating or promoting discussion. The more we take diversity into account, the better our tests and theories will be and, more importantly, the richer and more successful our social and professional lives will be. For more information on diversity, follow the instruction for finding my Web page at www.wiu.edu/users/mfbpa/bemjr.html. Scan down until you get to "Diversity" and "Multiculturalism" (or substitute "multicultural" or "diversityweb" for "bemjr" in the above URL). Under the latter you can find Web pages relating to your ethnic group.

A Final Word about "Science"

All this talk of science should not leave you with the impression that it is good and other approaches are bad. It is neither good nor necessarily better than other orientations; science just is. However, because personologists generally claim that their theories are in the realm of science, it is reasonable to use scientific criteria to evaluate them. Some covered theories will successfully meet scientific criteria. Those that fail will be subjected to appropriate criticism. But no theories will be dismissed solely on the basis of failure to be scientifically sound. There are good reasons to include theories that do not meet scientific criteria well. In fact, strengths in the nonscientific realm may make these theories more valuable than some more scientific theories. Sometimes a well-thought-out philosophical position, though it is too abstract to be tested scientifically, can have more merit than a "hard science" point of view. For these reasons, nonscience criteria will also be used to evaluate theories.

Chapter Sections

The chapters of this book have virtually the same sections. After you have read a few chapters, you will know what to expect from the rest. The remainder of this introduction is devoted to familiarizing you with the chapter format.

Introductory Statement

Brief introductory sections at the beginning of each chapter are designed to provide a transition from the previous chapters to the current one. Contrasts between previous theorists and their theories and the theorist/theory presently under consideration will allow you to "shift gears" in preparation for a new orientation. How you may expect to benefit from the chapter is also often a part of this first section.

The Person: Biographies

Just as oppression suffered during his youth led former Supreme Court Justice Thurgood Marshall to pursue racial justice throughout his illustrious career, psychological interests born of theorists' peculiar backgrounds have influenced the development of their personality theories. Some theorists covered in this book suffered hardships during their formative years that influenced which personality issues interested them. Others had highly positive experiences that drew them to certain personality issues rather than others. In turn, how they framed their ideas about those issues was determined by their own reactions to their important experiences. Knowing about a theorist's life can tell you something truly meaningful about where that person "is coming from."

There are two new features relevant to the biography section. First, under each theorist's picture is his or her web address. Second, a new survey and literature search is used to pinpoint the remarkably high status this book's theorists have attained among all psychologists of the 20th century (see Preface for details).

In addition, knowing about the life of a theorist can transform a sometimes alien name and a curious picture in the text into an image of a fascinating person. Indeed, by any standard, many of the theorists covered in this text are remarkable individuals. Some have overcome enormous obstacles to win fame and make lasting contributions. Others are notable for devoting themselves to making other people's lives better, not only through their theories, but also through their personal efforts. Some theorists have escaped from territories controlled by the Nazis, others have overcome the handicap of poverty, and still others have conquered psychological disorders or the aftermath of childhood trauma.

All this information will provide you with "memory hooks." Many people have no trouble remembering details of individuals' personal lives, but sometimes do have some difficulty remembering abstract theories. After grasping a theorist's personal background and how it may relate to her or his theory, you can more easily get a grip on that person's basic ideas. Ideas are like articles of clothing that lie around in disarray if there is nothing to "hang them on," but become easy to organize and relate one to another if an "apparel rack" is available with hooks of various sizes and shapes. Extending the analogy to advances in brain science, if you have a "neurological network" for information about computers, it is a memory rack with many hooks on which you can "hang" newly encountered ideas relating to computers. Should you lack such a network, you are forced to use cumbersome and inefficient rote memory. To provide further memory help, occasionally mnemonics are placed in parentheses next to headings in chapters.

Memory hooks come from more than just details of theorists' lives. Very often the personalities of theorists are important determinants of their theories and, thus, can provide additional memory hooks. For example, one theorist's personality may dictate the assumption that conflict in interpersonal relations is the rule, but another's may yield the assumption that harmony characterizes interpersonal relations. Visit Web sites for more information about theorists (example sites are listed under their pictures). Also, go to my Web site, then scan down to and click the picture of Gordon Allport. There you will find almost anything you want to know about personality. In addition, a student guide with hints for studying, multiple-choice questions, and more Web sites has the same address as my Web site, but substituting "personalityguide" for "bemjr."

View of the Person: General Philosophical Orientation

Before getting into theorists' basic concepts, it is beneficial to consider their underlying assumptions. Without knowing theorists' orientation to people and how their personalities function it is difficult to understand their basic concepts. Trying to absorb a theory without grasping the theorist's orientation is a little like going to the polling booth without knowing politicians' positions on critical issues.

Answers to a number of questions must be forthcoming before a theorist's orientation can be understood. Is a theory founded on the belief that all people can solve their own problems if offered adequate support? Is a theory predicated on the presumption that normal and abnormal personality are on the same continuum or that the two are quite separate, so that the theory deals with one or the other, or both? Does the theorist believe in free will or determinism? Is the theorist a "scientist" who quantifies personality data so that correlational and experimental methods can be used or a "nonscientist" who relies solely on intuition and qualitative information? Does the theorist look to the person's *past* in attempting to understand her or his personality or to the *present* (or to the *future*)? Does the theory assume that personality can be understood only by examining circumstances *outside* the person or by looking at processes *inside* the individual? Does genetic coding determine personality, or do events after birth shape personality? The *view of the person section* will tackle these and other questions so that you can get into the mind of the theorist you are considering before you entertain his or her theoretical concepts. These issues are reconsidered in Chapter 18.

Basic Concepts: The Heart and Soul of a Theory

The Basic Concepts section is the centerpiece of each chapter. It contains a presentation of a theory's elements fitted into the structure of the theory. Whenever possible, the theory's framework, which may take the form of trait categories or stages of personality development, is used to organize concepts. If appropriate, the description of a given theory is constructed pyramid fashion, with more global concepts at the top and more elemental concepts forming the foundation. In any case, connections among concepts are emphasized so that understanding relations among them is the learning mode, not memorizing disconnected ideas.

Evaluation: Placing a Theory in Perspective

Each evaluation section is divided into contributions and limitations subsections. It is sort of a pluses and minuses organization. Various criteria are used to evaluate theories. Because not all of them are relevant to all theories, only some are used in the examination of a given theory. These criteria are organized into two categories.

Science Criteria.   For a theory to be scientific, it must be structured in a logical fashion. Concepts must bear a definite relationship to one another; however, some may be seen as more central than others and some may build on others. Thus, one criterion can be stated: "Is the theory coherent, so that the relationship among concepts is clear and overlap among them is minimal or is the theory chaotic so that some concepts are disconnected from others while some overlap?" Some theories may be tightly bound networks with each concept having a definite place relative to others. Conversely, some may be a collection of isolated concepts or a group of mini-theories, each not well related to the other.

Are labels for concepts common terms, each with several meanings, or are they words, common or not, that have precise and specific meanings? Words with several meanings, such as *hot, cool,* or *gay,* are a nuisance when used as labels for concepts. When trying to relate such labels to those of other concepts, the irrelevant meanings get in the way. By contrast, words with precise and specific meanings are easy to grasp and relate one to another because there are no irrelevant meanings that one must attempt to ignore.

Words that can be easily given different meanings by different people can also be problematic. *Experience,* a word often used by personologists, may be a confusing label for a concept because, invariably, each theorist defines it differently. Also, nonprofessional people use it in different ways. *Competency,* on the other hand, is a helpful word because it always refers in some way to a person's skills, talents, or abilities.

Generally, the fewer the concepts the better. This is the first rule of parsimony. The essence of efficient explanatory power is simplicity. Whenever redundant terms can be collapsed into one another, a helpful act of parsimony has been performed.

Another axiom of science is that, if two notions account for something equally well, choose the simpler one. This is the second rule of parsimony. Concepts with short definitions that are "given away" by their labels are to be preferred to those with lengthy definitions seemingly unrelated to their labels. *Positive self-regard* is an example of a label preferable to *sizothymia.* The latter word roughly means 'reserved,' though most people would not know why. *Sizothymia* brings up another issue. Theorists may resort to Greek or Latin words to avoid multiple meanings, but, in so doing, enshroud their concepts in unnecessary mystery. A well-known word is best, so long as it does not have surplus meaning.

Do concepts imply definite predictions that can be confirmed or disconfirmed by some method or another, or do they yield no clear expectations that can be evaluated through systematic observation? If a theory cannot be falsified as well as supported, it is not scientific. On the one hand, high self-efficacy refers to confidence in one's ability to perform some feat and predicts enhanced performance. If one has high self-efficacy for handling a snake, it is predicted that one can unhesitatingly pick up the reptile and, perhaps, even hold it close. On the other hand, *proprium* is "me as felt and known," but what predictions can be derived from the concept?

Does a theory have a body of data to support it, or is there little observable evidence to confirm implications of its concepts? To modify the second rule of parsimony offered earlier, if two theories are equally coherent and equally simple, choose the one that is most strongly supported by evidence. Some of the theorists covered in this book have inspired many researchers to produce much current data that supports their theories, but others' theories suffer from lack of evidential support. Those theories that catch the attention of each new generation of researchers are more likely than the others to maintain a place in future books like this one. The Running Comparison section of each chapter is designed to allow comparison of theories on these and other criteria.

Non-Science Criteria.   Science is not everything. There are criteria for evaluating theories that are not strictly scientific. Theorists may inspire not just researchers, but others as well. If second-generation theorists or practitioners make careers of pursuing a given theory, the long-term impact of the theory will be ensured. Some theories covered in this book have failed to stimulate a great deal of research. Still, among them are theories of such great interest to professionals that they have generated a lively discourse in journals devoted solely to them. Psychotherapies derived from some of these same theories have been embraced by thousands of practitioners.

In turn, these same practitioners have used the theory-based therapies to help thousands of people. Nevertheless, therapies arising from theories are not the only ways that theorists' ideas may have positive impacts on people. There are personality theorists who have written books that have been read by thousands and thousands of people, many of whom have experienced increased understanding of themselves and increased fulfillment. Some theorists covered in this book have a large following among laypeople, if not among researchers and other theorists.

Occasional Sections

Aside from the sections that occur in every chapter, there are a couple that appear only in some chapters. A separate section entitled Supporting Evidence will appear in chapters devoted to theories that have generated important current research. Some theories merit a separate section on Personality Development because they include especially strong ideas relating to that issue.

Conclusions Section

If a theory did not have more positive than negative features, it would not have the following that dictates its representation in books like this one. The conclusions section states why entries in the evaluative ledger are writ large in the assets column, even if not more frequently recorded there.

E-mail Interaction Section

Sometimes it is hard to sit down and write someone a letter. We feel that we have to "say" quite a lot and write at least a page. However, as most of you who use e-mail can testify, we tend not to show "writing inhibition" when we resort to e-mail. It takes an instant to type in someone's e-mail address and only a moment more to rattle off a message a few sentences long. It is kind of like leaving a note for a friend. We don't worry so much about how much or what we write.

So why not e-mail the text author? All you have to do is type in b-allen@wiu.edu (or mfbpa@wiu.edu). You can ask anything or state whatever is on your mind. Not only is it OK for the message to be short, brevity is preferred. And, be assured, I certainly will not look at your message with an English teacher's eye.

Just in case you want to say something, but cannot think of what to say, at the end of each chapter I will list a few possible questions or statements you may wish to forward. My e-mail address will be there also, so you will not have to look it up. Alter my suggested questions and statements in any way you wish, or, perhaps, one of them will inspire an original response on your part. Whatever, just do it. I promise to respond, although sometimes it may take a while.

Summary Points

1. The working definition of *personality* is based on the notion of individual differences: People may score at different points on behavioral dimensions. *Personality,* therefore, is a set of points falling along several behavioral dimensions, each corresponding to a trait. Unfortunately, "individual differences" has been taken to mean that one's place on a dimension is "written in stone," but the case of George Foreman defies this assumption.

2. The scientific method involves quantification of observations. The case study method involves intensive observations of a single person. Unbiased observations may be difficult because the observer is frequently involved with the observed. Also, the observed may be atypical and a meaningful analysis is difficult to conduct on the data of one person. Nevertheless, case histories illustrate important aspects of theories. The case of Estella Monroe relates to all the theories.

3. A variable assumes different values. Two variables are correlated if variation in one closely corresponds to variation in the other. They are positively correlated when high values on one correspond to high values on the other; they are negatively correlated when high values on one correspond to low values on the other. When the relationship between variables reflects neither of the two patterns, it is called "nil." The correlational method can be scientific, but correlation does not mean causation, though it has its defenders.

4. In an experiment, variation in an independent variable(s) is set, and it is ascertained whether variation in a dependent variable(s) is influenced. Perry and colleagues gave subjects two different doses of amphetamine or no dose (independent variable) and observed what effect their manipulation had on anxiety as reflected in subjects' responses to Rorschach inkblots (dependent variable).

5. Personality tests must demonstrate reliability and validity. Reliability can be determined by the test-retest or the parallel forms techniques. Methods for determining validity include content validity and convergent versus divergent validity. On projective tests, people respond to ambiguous, unstructured, or open-ended stimuli. With the Rorschach test, people describe what they see in some inkblots. Scoring is rather subjective, so reliability and validity are difficult to demonstrate. With use of the TAT, people view ambiguous pictures and tell stories about them. Recent work indicates that projective tests show lower reliability and validity than was previously attributed to them.

6. Objective tests employ multiple-choice or true/false formats. They have relatively high reliability and validity as well as advantages and disadvantages relative to projective tests. Testing and theorizing must take diversity into account, people's ethnicity, gender, and sexual orientation. Evidence indicates that test results may vary across genders and across certain ethnic groups. The several sections of each chapter include a biography section that forms a link between a theorist's personality and background and her or his theory. Knowing about the lives of theorists makes them real. It also provides "memory hooks" on which to hang theoretical principles.

7. The philosophical orientation of a theorist lays the groundwork for understanding his or her basic concepts. Does the theorist believe people can solve their own problems? Is she or he scientific or intuitive? Does she or he believe in free will? Is what matters "inside" or the "outside"? Is nature more important or nurture? With answers to these questions, basic concepts can be fitted into a theoretical framework such as stages of development.

8. Scientific criteria for evaluating a theory include: Do labels for concepts each have many common meanings, or highly specific meanings? Do the labels "give away" the meanings of the concepts? Are the rules of parsimony obeyed? Have theorists' ideas inspired researchers to produce supportive data?

9. Nonscientific criteria include: Have second-generation theorists and practitioners been inspired to pursue the theory? Have lay-readers of books about the theory embraced its principles to the betterment of their lives? Conclusions sections state the overall merit of each theory. An e-mail interaction section contains questions and statements to send the author.

Essay/Critical Thinking Questions

1. What did the term *personality* mean to you before you encountered the preliminary definition?

2. Prior to encountering a formal definition of *scientific,* what did it mean to you?

3. Could you do a case study of someone you know well?

4. If you developed a personality test, how would you go about showing that it was reliable and valid?

5. Could you conceive of a novel situation in which a projective test would be more informative than an objective test?

E-mail Interaction

Write the author at b-allen@wiu.edu. Forward one of the following questions or send one of your own.

1. What did your training in psychology emphasize?

2. Why did you decide to write the book?

3. Will this book help me solve my problems?

The Psychoanalytic Legacy: Sigmund Freud

Sigmund Freud
http://Lcweb.loc.gov/
exhibits/Freud

- Is the relationship between boy and mother special?
- How much of what we call our "minds" is unconscious?
- Is the unconscious revealed in our dreams?

When asked about personality, Sigmund Freud responded in a tone usually reserved for the revelation of timeless truths. Some of his answers are important contributions to understanding personality. Others, offered with equal certainty, are less helpful. However, Freud clung to all of his ideas with great tenacity. He was suspicious of those who disagreed with any of his notions. Carl Jung, and many other early followers, soon split with Freud as their ideas began to deviate from his. Nevertheless, all were influenced by him, whether they admitted it or not.

Freud, the Person

Sigmund Freud was born on May 6, 1856, in Moravia, a Germanic area that is now a part of the new Czech Republic. He was the oldest of Amalie and Jakob Freud's eight children. Amalie, Jakob's second wife, 20 years his junior, bore her "golden Sigi" at age 21. She had a lively personality and was sharp-witted. Jakob, a wool merchant, had a good sense of humor and was a liberal thinker. They were Jewish.

Sigmund was scarcely 10 when he entered high school and only 17 when he entered medical school at the University of Vienna, where he used his photographic memory to excel as a student of neurology (1994 materials from the Freud Museum, Vienna). Young Freud was most influenced by Professor Ernst Brucke, a respected and disciplined physiologist with an uncompromising spirit and a stare that could petrify students.

During medical school, Freud was preoccupied with becoming well known and eco-nomically secure by making some important discoveries (Jones, 1953; Parisi, 1987). His research as a student included: (1) dissecting 400 male eels to show, for the first time, that they had testes; (2) discovering new characteristics of neurons (nerve cells) in fish; and (3) developing the first gold-chloride technique of staining nerve tissue. It is also note-worthy that Freud's notion of "contact barriers" anticipated the concept "synapse," the space between neurons (Parisi, 1987). Using himself as a subject, he discovered that co-caine was an effective anesthetic (Parisi, 1987). However, contrary to still-circulating ru-mors, he was not a lifelong cocaine user. Nevertheless, he did once recommend the widespread use of cocaine, even by injection (McCullough, 2001). He was 25 when he re-ceived his MD degree (1994 materials from the Freud Museum, Vienna).

Freud lived 78 years of his life in Vienna, Austria, where he established a private practice for the treatment of nervous disorders (1994 materials from the Freud Museum, Vienna). His home and offices were located at Berggasse 19, now a world-famous museum in his honor, where he enjoyed his role as father to three girls and three boys (1994 mate-rials from the Freud Museum, Vienna). Anna, the youngest, became an important child psy-choanalyst. Shortly after the German invasion in 1938, Freud was persuaded to leave Vienna because the Nazi harassment of Austrian Jews began immediately. In fact, he was never an avid believer in Judaism, considering all religions illusions used by civilization to cope with feelings of infantile helplessness. At the time of his departure, the Gestapo (Nazi secret police) attempted to obtain an endorsement from him. Freud declined. Nevertheless, they allowed him to immigrate to England on June 4, 1938, probably because to do other-wise would have adversely affected world opinion of Hitler's regime.

Freud died from cancer of the jaw and mouth on September 23, 1939, only a year and a summer after he migrated to London. The malignancy undoubtedly stemmed from his life-long addiction to cigars, which he chain-smoked from early morning to late evening. You may find this addiction quite interesting when you read about Freud's theory of orality.

During his last years he experienced pain, fatigue, and difficulties in speaking and eating caused by repeated surgery and a mechanical device that separated his nasal cavity from his mouth. Essayist Stefan Zweig (1962), who delivered one of several eulogies of-fered at Freud's funeral, wrote of Freud's "gloomy" perspective, which became all the more evident during the autumn of his years: "So long and so abundantly has Sigmund Freud been a physician that he has gradually come to look upon mankind at large as ail-ing. His first impression, therefore, when he looks forth from his consulting-room into the outer world, is a pessimistic one . . . " (p. 208). However, Freud valiantly fought his dis-ability and the Grim Reaper: "I prefer a mechanical jaw to no jaw at all. I still prefer exis-tence to extinction" (quoted in Golub, 1981, p. 195). However, eventually, the pain of cancer and the continual operations became too much. On September 21, 1939, Freud asked his personal physician to continually administer morphine to him until he died (*Mon-itor on Psychology,* September, 1998, p. 10). Two days later the morphine ended his life.

Freud's View of the Person

Freud painted a vivid portrait depicting human nature under the dictatorship of instinctual, unconscious, and irrational forces. To him, the human organism is a selfish being existing in a state of external and internal turmoil. Even during the supposed innocence of childhood, it displays aggressive and sexual excesses. Dominated by forces outside of conscious control, people are covered with a thin crust of civilization, but exist in a constant state of frustration. These aspects of people's nature preempt free will: humans were considered incapable of dealing with their own psychological problems. They turn to religion in the vain hope of gaining some control over their wanton urges and of procuring absolution for their compulsive pursuit of pleasure. But their efforts to gain control, or explain the lack of it, come to naught.

Throughout his life, Freud never ceased self-analysis. Arguably his most important book, *The Interpretation of Dreams* (1900/1958), was based in large part on analyses of his own dreams. Freud believed that dreams allow people to experience the wish fulfillments that elude them in real life (Dement, 1976). His *Psychopathology of Everyday Life* (1901/1965) also was derived from self-analysis and dealt with the psychological meanings of apparent "mistakes" in memory, speech, reading, and writing. Both works assumed the influence of **psychological determinism,** a belief that nothing about human behavior occurs by accident or chance. For Freud, everything about personality is "determined" or has a psychological cause. One need only uncover these causes and examine them. However, he was not an advocate of rigid biological determinism (Parisi, 1987). In fact, in attempting to discover why people do what they do, Freud often emphasized psychological rather than biological determinism. He wrote, "consciousness knows nothing of . . . neurons" (quoted in Parisi, 1987, p. 240). He meant that, while consciousness could not exist without nerve cells, what emerges from the neurons transcends them and cannot be explained solely by reference to them.

During his self-analyses, Freud traced his behaviors back to their hidden origins. He explored the closeness of his relationship with his mother, as well as hostile feelings toward his father. In fact, those personal explorations of his own childhood experiences were important contributors to his belief that boys want to "kill" their fathers in order to "marry" their mothers. Among Freud's earliest memories, "one was of penetrating into his parents' bedroom out of [sexual] curiosity and being ordered out by an irate father" (Jones, 1953, p. 7). Consistent with his theory, these feelings toward his father created guilt when Jakob died during Freud's fortieth year. About the time of the funeral, he wrote his friend Wilhelm Fliess: "By one of those dark pathways behind the official consciousness the old man's death has affected me deeply. . . . I now feel quite uprooted" (quoted in Bronfen, 1989, p. 963).

Basic Concepts: Freud

Personality Structure: Three Interacting Systems (SIDE)

For Freud, personality has three basic components. One can be cast as the personality's biological side, a second represents the psychological side, and a third reflects society's contribution to personality. These are not "parts" of personality in a physical sense, nor do they have any specific, physical location in the person. Rather, they are processes or systems of the mind: they organize mental life and dynamically interact with one another.

Id.   The id is the origin of personality, the most basic of the three systems. **Id** is beyond conscious awareness and is composed of whatever is present at birth, including elements relating to the satisfaction of physical drives, such as sex and hunger, or primitive psychological needs, such as comfort and protection from danger. Id operates according to the **pleasure principle,** the achievement of pleasurable feelings as quickly and immediately as possible through the reduction of discomfort, pain, or tension. Id satisfies its needs through the **primary process,** a continual flow of infantile images and wishes that demand immediate and direct satisfaction. Id demands satisfaction of its needs without consideration of what is right or wrong or "good" for the person. Primary process thinking characterizes the unconscious (Brakel, Kliensorge, Snodgrass, & Shevrin, 2000).

Id is the reservoir of **instincts,** inborn forces with characteristics that are both physical (bodily needs) and psychological (wishes). Along with the other two systems, id is powered by **libido,** an energy variously described as "psychical desire," "erotic tendencies," "sexual desire in the broadest sense," and the "motive forces of sexual life" (Freud, quoted in Rychlak, 1981, p. 54). Freud (1940/1949) assumed only two basic categories of instincts, those of life and those of death. Instincts toward life, called **Eros,** represent energy for preserving oneself (love of self) and one's species (love of others). He eventually subsumed the several meanings of *libido* under "love," thereby tying libidinal energy to Eros.

Thanatos is the instinct toward destructiveness and death that is aimed at returning living things to their original lifeless state. Aggressiveness is the most important function of Thanatos. Life and death instincts may fuse together or work against each other, giving rise to "vicissitudes" or frequent changes in a personality, as well as to individual differences among personalities.

Behaviors of a newborn baby reflect the id's operations. It sleeps, it awakens, it makes sucking sounds, it squirms to keep warm, and it urinates and defecates. However, it does nothing for anyone, at least not intentionally. Because the baby's personality is dominated by id, its preoccupation is with itself and its primarily physical needs and comforts.

Ego.   The infant behaviors are focused on inner states of tension because id has no means of directly establishing contact with the world outside itself. While able to detect changes in internal tension, such as hunger or cold, it has no way of relieving them. It experiences only pain/discomfort and pleasure or unpleasure, but it is isolated from external sources of relief and satisfaction.

It should be obvious that humans equipped only with ids would have difficulty surviving. It is dangerous to satisfy a need as soon as it arises with whatever apparently gratifying object happens to be available. For example, hungry babies will stuff apparently edible objects into their mouths, including poisonous or otherwise dangerous objects. There is a clear need for another structure that will satisfy id needs without getting the baby in trouble (Freud, 1961).

Ego is a coherent organization of mental processes that develops out of id energy, has access to consciousness, and is devoted to contacting reality for the purpose of satisfying id needs. Id is subjective, directed internally toward itself in its wants and demands. In contrast, ego is objective, or directed outside itself. Ego has the task of satisfying id needs in a manner that promotes self-preservation. The term has evolved to be the "I" or "me" that gets things done in the best interest of oneself.

Ego operates according to the **reality principle:** ego has the capacity to delay satisfaction of id's demands until an appropriate object is found that will allow gratification without harmful side effects. Ego is guided by a higher level of mental functioning, called **secondary process:** intellectual operations such as thinking, evaluating, planning, and decision making that test reality to determine whether certain behaviors are beneficial. Ego thus serves as a bridge to reality. It plans for actions in the real world that will satisfy id. Unlike id, ego has the capacity to appreciate the difference between food-producing breasts or bottles and ineffective objects such as thumbs or dangerous ones such as poisons. Ego processes increase the likelihood that id will experience satisfaction of its demands without harmful side effects.

While ego has contact with reality, it is not totally conscious (see Figure 2.1). It also "suffers" from secondary status: It is an arm of the id rather than an entirely independent entity. On both conscious and unconscious levels, ego's operations, along with its secondary status, make it vulnerable to both internal and external dangers. For this reason, ego is constantly walking a tight rope. External dangers include insufficient food, water, and physical comfort as well as threats of physical or psychological injury and loss of parental love. Internal dangers include uncontrollable increases of instinctual energies, particularly sex and aggression. Freud (1923/1961b) used the horse and rider metaphor: the superior strength of the horse (id) must be held in check by its rider (ego).

Ego's reaction to threatening surges of instincts is to experience **anxiety,** a state of extremely unpleasant emotional discomfort. To minimize anxiety, ego calls on various **defense mechanisms,** which are internal, unconscious, and automatic psychological strategies for coping with or regaining control over threatening id instincts. Defense mechanisms keep unacceptable urges or ideas from reaching conscious awareness.

The first listed mechanism was entirely due to Freud, but Anna Freud played a major role in developing the others. **Repression** is a selective type of memory mode in which threatening material is unavailable for recall because it has been pressed down into the unconscious. It protects the personality by allowing ego to be conscious only of those

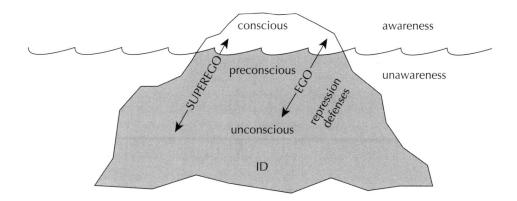

FIGURE 2.1 *Personality as an iceberg: only the tip of the psychic iceberg is above the waterline, which represents the part of the psyche that is available to awareness. Some of the psyche below the waterline is available with effort—the preconscious—but most is unavailable—the unconscious.*

thoughts and urges that do not relate too closely to threatening material. **Projection** protects us from threat by allowing us to see our unacceptable characteristics only in other people—"Those filthy Abagarians; unlike me, all they can think about is sex!" There is some support for this defense mechanism in that subjects told that they showed dishonesty and subsequently allowed to project dishonesty onto another person, thereafter reported low dishonesty (Schimel, Greenberg, & Martens, 2003). **Rationalization** allows us to excuse our destructive and unacceptable behavior and thoughts—"So what if I stole from my employer; they don't pay me enough." **Denial** allows us to avoid whatever is too hard to bear by refusing to think about it or otherwise address it. We **intellectualize** when we talk and think at an academic rather than an emotional level about what we do or contemplate that is threatening to us. (The smoker says, "The link between cancer and smoking is unproven; I've seen the studies.") We may also attempt **undoing** "bad" behavior by displaying behavior designed to reverse the effects of the undesirable acts. ("Forgive me for hitting you! Let me grovel at your feet, proclaim my undying love for you, and buy you flowers.")

Freud believed that exaggerated use of such defense mechanisms is associated with **neuroses,** anxiety-driven patterns of abnormal behavior related to over-control of instincts. One such pattern is **hysterical neurosis** in which a person develops symptoms of a disorder to avoid experiences too painful or threatening for conscious consideration, though physical evidence of the disorder is absent (the root word for "hysteria" means "womb"). For example, a person who feels angry may develop a "paralyzed" arm to lessen the chances of hitting someone. These neuroses often assume metaphorical form (White, 1989). One of Freud's patients who felt "stabbed in the heart" by important persons in her life developed chest pains in the heart region. Another, who experienced lack of feeling in the face, declared that her husband's remarks were " . . . like a slap in the face" (p. 1042).

Superego.   The third major force in personality is **superego,** the representation of society in personality that incorporates the norms and standards of the surrounding culture. Children strive to **identify** with and, thereby, become like their parents, a process considered later. During identification they adopt their parents' renditions of their society's rules, regulations, and codes of right and wrong. The specific mechanism through which superego receives its content is called **introjection,** a process by which the personality incorporates the norms and standards of its culture through identification with parents or other admired persons in society.

The superego may be thought of as operating according to a **morality principle,** a code that concerns society's values regarding right and wrong. One of its aspects is equivalent to **conscience,** the internal agent that punishes us when we do wrong. Like ego, superego develops from id energy. Superego's most important function is to help control id impulses by directing energy toward entirely inhibiting id's expression of its sexual, aggressive, and other antisocial instincts. Thus, the superego, like the ego, addresses id needs, but the superego seeks to suppress those needs rather than satisfy them.

Superego can become a relatively independent and dominating force that makes the personality conform to social norms excessively. This tendency results in patterns of anxiety-driven behavior such as striving for 100 percent perfection in absolutely everything one does. Superego can observe and influence ego directly, taking it to task, giving it orders, or correcting it. It can also threaten ego with unpleasant emotional experiences when perfectionistic, parental standards—represented by its "conscience" aspect—are not being met. These unpleasant emotions include **guilt,** an intense feeling of regret over having done something wrong and evaluations of oneself as an undeserving, inadequate person. It is as if the maturing personality never outgrows the role "child of one's parents." As young children grow toward maturity they gradually replace the verbal punishment once meted out by parents with internal self-scolding: "That's wrong! Always do what's right. Be perfect in everything." Through this process, the voices of one's parents, speaking of right and wrong, move inside oneself and become one's own inner call to righteousness.

On the other hand, superego can offer the personality favorable emotional experiences when another of its aspects comes into play. The superego can result in feelings of pride and self-respect through the influence of the **ego ideal,** positive standards in the form of internal representations of idealized parental figures (Freud, 1977; Macmillan, 1997). These favorable feelings can take the form of statements about oneself that substitute for parental statements: "You're a good child. You make your parents proud and happy. They love you."

Freud conceived of personality as an internal battleground where the combatants are id, ego, and superego, each constantly struggling with the others to dominate the personality. One of the spoils of this war is energy captured from one of the three systems by another. The victor can use this plundered fuel for its own purposes. Sometimes there is a temporary truce: one system forms an alliance with another. The ego may "say," in effect, "Superego, let me satisfy this aggressive need; then you may have your revenge." Table 2.1 compares the three major structural systems of personality identified by Freud.

TABLE 2.1 *Comparisons of Freud's Three Systems of Personality*

	Id	*Ego*	*Superego*
Nature	Represents biological aspect	Represents psychological aspect	Represents societal aspect
Contribution	Instincts	Selfness	Conscience
Time Orientation	Immediate present	Present	Past
Level	Unconscious	Conscious and unconscious	Conscious and unconscious
Principle	Pleasure	Reality	Morality
Purpose	Seek pleasure; Avoid discomfort	Adapt to reality; Know true and false	Represent right and wrong
Aim	Immediate gratification	Safety and compromise	Perfection
Process	Irrational	Rational	Illogical
Reality	Subjective	Objective	Subjective

The Five Stages of Personality Development
(*Old Aunt Pamela Loves Gorillas*)

Development, processes by which something grows from a beginning state to a later one, is seen in plants, animals, and even solar systems. Personality also develops over time from an immature beginning state to a later mature state. Freud hypothesized a series of five sequential stages of personality development. Four of the stages are closely associated with **erogenous zones:** sensitive areas of the body from which instinctual satisfactions can be obtained (Freud, 1920/1977). These zones, in chronological order of appearance, are the mouth, anus, penis or clitoris, and penis or vagina. Freud assumed the clitoris to be a miniature penis because both structures are outer sexual organs that become erect during sexual stimulation.

Freud defined *sexual* very generally to encompass any pleasurable feeling associated with stimulation of any one of the erogenous zones. One example of libidinous satisfaction is stimulation of the lips and tongue during sucking. Given this general view of sexuality, it is easy to see why Freud referred to the developmental epochs as **psychosexual stages,** phases that are "sexual" only in the broadest sense of the word, because some stages involve organs ordinarily seen as "sexual" and others organs not popularly regarded as "sexual." Freud believed that people's basic personalities are established by age five and remain essentially the same throughout life.

Oral Stage: Phase One.   During the **oral** or **narcissistic (self-centered) stage** that begins at birth, the organism's psychic activity focuses on satisfying the needs of the mouth and digestive tract, including the tongue and lips (Freud, 1920/1977, 1977). Narcissus is a Greek mythological figure who, on seeing his reflection in a pool of water, fell in love with himself.

Eros's aim of self-preservation is facilitated by the production of energy, made possible by nourishment received orally. Whatever promotes self-preservation is likely to generate pleasure. Likewise, whatever is related to the self-preservation promotion process, even if it is not a direct contributor, produces pleasure. Thus, sucking, in and of itself, provides infantile pleasure. "Thumbsucking shows that the pleasure gained from breast or bottle is based not alone on the gratification of hunger but on the stimulation of the erogenous oral mucous membrane as well; otherwise the infant would disappointedly remove his thumb, since it produces no milk" (Fenichel, 1945, p. 63). Box 2.1 explores narcissism further.

The importance of stages in understanding adult personality is manifested in Freud's concept of **fixation:** the impairment of development at a particular stage because its satisfactions are frustrated, resulting in permanent investment of libidinal energy in the stage. When under stress the fixated person is likely to show **regression,** retreating to behaviors, feelings, and thoughts characteristic of the earlier fixated stage (a 12-year-old frightened by a dog begins to suck his thumb).

Freud referred to two personality types related to fixation at the oral stage that become fully developed by adulthood. The **oral-receptive** personality type results from childhood pleasurable experiences of food in the mouth and of ingestion. This type is especially suggestible and gullible (willing to "swallow" anything) and forms relationships characterized

BOX 2.1 • *Developing a Narcissistic Person with Little Social Interest*

Long ago I knew a person who fit "narcissistic" well. This person almost immediately displayed signs of high intelligence and strong athletic abilities. He walked and talked very early and was reading and performing arithmetic before entering school. His parents idealized him, declared him a genius, and pampered him. He learned that he could do no wrong and that he was "special." Later when siblings were born, he was unthreatened, because his parents continued to lavish attention and praise on him. Meanwhile his siblings were, at best, viewed as ordinary and deserving of no special consideration. In fact, at first the parents thought the second born was retarded because the younger sibling walked and talked at the normal time, much later than their genius. These siblings appeared to become playthings for their special child. Because they always lagged behind their older brother in all categories of skills, they obediently followed him about, doing his bidding. As you will discover in Chapter 4, these circumstances were ideal for stifling the development of social interest. The family's chosen one was well on his way to "leading" others, but rarely truly cooperating with them or investing in them.

In elementary, junior high, and high school he excelled both academically and in sports. His family regarded his accomplishments as "no big deal," just what one would expect of a superior person. Almost effortlessly, he outperformed all of his peers and basked in the admiration of everyone he knew. Not surprisingly, he was given to braggadocio, but somehow managed not to offend others with his self-praise. He was so matter of fact and low key in stating the case for his own greatness that others tended to believe him. Baseball great Dizzy Dean put it this way: "It ain't bragging if you done it." And this young man had done it.

The family hero, now apparently the community hero, passed up a chance to play college football, because, in so doing, he could obtain a high-tech degree at a prestigious university in the shortest possible time. Not satisfied, he also acquired an advanced degree from yet another prestigious university. Hired by a top firm, he was the darling of the new recruits. To this point his life was one effortless triumph after another. Friends adored him and so did the women he encountered.

He was working on his second marriage engagement. Then things began to come unraveled. He was now in the real world where effortless accomplishment was hard to come by and where cooperation with others was essential. His failure to "produce" and his insensitivity to the needs of others soon cost him his job and his fiancée. When last I heard of him, he was playing with life as if he were still a teenager.

Modern research confirms many of the notions about narcissistic people outlined above. Gabriel, Critelli, and Ee (1994) examined positive illusions of intelligence and physical attractiveness among people administered the Narcissism Test. Positive illusions were excess self-perceptions of intelligence and attractiveness after actual intelligence and attractiveness were measured and statistically removed. High narcissism was associated with high positive illusions of intelligence and attractiveness for both males and females. Males tended to significantly overestimate both their intelligence and attractiveness, but females significantly overestimated only their intelligence. Males tended to be higher than females on narcissism. Consistent with this observation, they showed greater positive illusions of attractiveness and intelligence than females.

Not all of narcissistic people's characteristics are as relatively benign as those chronicled above. In Chapter 15 you will encounter another narcissistic person: personality theorist Henry A. Murray. Although he was a fine human being in many ways, Murray was sometimes arrogant in his interactions with others and often dismissive of "lesser persons" (almost everyone he encountered).

Fitting Murray rather well is the tendency to a game-playing love style (ludus). Campbell, Foster, and Finkel (2002) found that people who scored high on a narcissism scale showed the game-playing style by endorsing such items as "I

(continued)

BOX 2.1   Continued

try to keep my romantic partner a little uncertain about my commitment to him/her" and "I enjoy playing the 'game of love' with a number of different partners" (p. 343).

Narcissistic people have such a grandiose self-image that it must be difficult to maintain (Mc-Cullough, Emmons, Kilpatrick, & Mooney, 2003). Even narcissists themselves must know that their god-like self-views are difficult to support, because they tend to be almost paranoid in their defense of their self-grandiosity. In a study that included a test of narcissism, compared to other participants, high narcissistic scorers may have protected their self-grandiosity by claiming in their daily diaries that others transgressed against them very often (Mc-Cullough et al., 2003). It was as if they were saying, "Should I appear less wonderful than I am, it's because others try to pull me down." This tendency was especially true of narcissists who scored high on the "exploitiveness/entitlement" dimension of the narcissistic scale. Also this perception that others are "out to get me" may allow narcissists to justify their exploitation of others and expectation of privilege relative to others by believing that others transgress against them regularly. Consistent with these findings, Baumeister, Campbell, Krueger,

and Vohs (2003) refer to results showing that narcissistic people were more aggressive than others when provoked by an insult.

Bushman, Bonacci, Dijk, and Baumeister (2003) have documented an even more alarming disposition of narcissistic people. High narcissistic participants in their study showed low empathy for rape victims and a greater tendency to believe rape myths (e.g., "women want to be raped") compared to other male participants. Also, compared to low narcissistic men, they enjoyed a filmed rape scene involving both sexual assault and pre-rape affection displayed toward the rapist by the victim. They also found the affection-then-rape film more entertaining and sexually arousing than did low narcissistic males. Because high narcissistic men in this study identified with the male actor playing the rapist, it is possible that they viewed the affection shown the rapist as being reflected toward them.

These recent findings suggest that narcissism is and will continue to be under the psychological research microscope. In fact, researchers report that narcissism is on the rise and apparently will continue to increase in the future (Hibbard, 2003).

by dependency on others. Such people are also interested in receiving information, acquiring material goods, and are especially fond of sweets, smoking, and oral sex. To Freud, obesity stems from oral-receptiveness.

The **oral-aggressive** type is also derived from childhood pleasures associated with the mouth, food, and eating, but with emphasis on chewing and biting (Freud, 1977). Persons of this type would be expected to favor rock candy to marshmallows and hard-stemmed pipes to cigarettes. They are orally aggressive in their relationships with others, may be put-down artists, and their manner of talking is sarcastic and argumentative. They also seek to hold firmly onto others, as if to possess them or even swallow them whole.

Anal Stage: Phase Two.   During the **anal stage** (beginning at approximate age 1½ years) sexual gratification occurs when defecation relieves the tension of a full bowel and simultaneously stimulates the anus. "There are many people who retain a voluptuous feeling in defecating all through their lives and describe it as being far from small" (Freud, 1920/1977, p. 316).

An important aspect of the anal stage is toilet training, which involves children and parents in matters of interpersonal conflict. From the parents' point of view, the issue is control: "Will my child 'go' on the toilet as I desire or not?" For the child, the issue is power: "Should I do what I want to do or what they want me to do?" Individual differences are shown in the way parents and children answer these questions. Some parents are rigid and demanding, expecting their child to "Go right here! Now!" These interactions can lead to a contest of wills, with the child experiencing frustration and pressure to perform for Father and Mother. Such experiences can carry over to later situations in life, even building to rebellion against other authority figures—schoolteachers, principals, police, and bosses. On the other hand, some parents are highly permissive in accepting their child's preferences and react supportively to the child's personal needs: "Take as long as you want. Oh, you did it! Good for you." Such reactions can foster positive self-esteem.

Fixation at the anal stage may produce types that fully bloom in adulthood. The **anal-retentive** personality type delays final satisfactions to the last possible moment and shows orderliness, stinginess, and stubbornness, a constipated orientation. This type constantly "saves" for the future, whether the reference is to money or gratification of some need. They delay gratification and retain objects for future use just as once, at the behest of their parents, they retained their feces until an appropriate receptacle was found.

In contrast, the **anal-expulsive** type is inclined to disregard widely accepted rules such as cleanliness, orderliness, and "appropriate behavior," a "diarrhetic" orientation. Anal-expulsive people react against others' attempts to restrict them by doing whatever they want, just as, during childhood, they defecated whenever and wherever they wanted. Characteristics of these people include messiness—their lifestyle is sloppy and slovenly. They may also show aggressive destructiveness, temper tantrums, explosive emotional outbursts, and even sadism.

Phallic Stage: Phase Three. During the **phallic stage** (beginning at approximately age 3; *phallic* means "penis"), satisfaction is gained primarily by stimulation of the penis or clitoris, through masturbation (Freud, 1920/1977). Physical and fantasy pleasures experienced through masturbation are important aspects of the phallic stage. However, satisfaction of libidinous needs is only one part of this phase, because the phallic stage is dominated by the realization that boys have penises whereas girls do not. The focus then becomes the significance of this anatomical difference as it is manifested in Freud's famous "complexes." Drawing an analogy to the mythological Oedipus Rex, who killed his father and married his mother, Freud theorized that boys have feelings of possessive love for their mothers and see their fathers as rivals. He termed this process the **Oedipus complex,** the constellation of feelings, desires, and strivings revolving around the boy's desires for his mother and his fearful/hateful orientation to his father. The corresponding dynamic for girls, involving love of father and hatred of mother, is called the **Electra complex** after the myth of Electra, who hated and participated in killing her mother. The parents cooperate in developing these complexes by providing "affection [that] bears the clearest characteristics of sexual activity . . . " (Freud, 1910/1977, p. 47). That Freud attached great significance to issues surrounding these mirror image complexes is seen in his assertion, "If psychoanalysis could boast of no other achievement than the discovery of the repressed

Oedipus complex, that alone would give it a claim to be counted among the precious new acquisitions of mankind" (1940/1949, p. 97).

And how does the difference in sex organs affect boys and girls? Freud saw boys as experiencing **castration anxiety,** a generalized fear that they might lose their highly prized penises (Freud, 1977). They "reason" that "if Father discovers I want to love Mother the way he does, he might cut 'it' off." Girls, on the other hand, display **penis envy,** feelings of inferiority over not having the male organ and compensatory wishes to someday obtain one of their own. They may blame their mothers for their lack of penises—"after all she doesn't have one either; maybe in a fit of jealousy she cut mine off."

At this point the foundations of socialization are set. The boy is faced with a fanta-sized dilemma: either he risks losing his penis or gives up his desire to have "Mama the way Daddy does" in favor of a safer but more indirect relationship to her. To some degree he chooses the latter. Boys react to the imagined threat of castration by accepting their fa-ther's dominant status and power. They identify with father, becoming "just like Dad." **Identification** is the process of becoming like the same-sex parent. Just as tigers attack members of other species, not their own, the boy reasons that, if he becomes like his fa-ther, his father will not attack him. Also, if he becomes like his father, it is almost as if he is his father. Therefore, when his father possesses and physically loves his mother, so does he. Finally, if he becomes like his father he will adopt the masculine characteristics that are apparently pleasing to his mother. This is how he embraces the masculine sex-role. In this process of becoming "like Dad," he also introjects his father's rendition of society's rights and wrongs—his superego begins to form—and thereby takes the final step toward resolving the Oedipal complex.

Failure to identify appropriately and, thus, failure to resolve the Oedipal complex has important implications for the mature male personality. The male who is fixated at the phal-lic stage may become a Don Juan as he matures into adulthood, devoting himself to promis-cuity in a quest for the sexual gratification denied him as a child. Alternatively, he may fail to take on the masculine characteristics due to weak identification with the father. The re-sult could be a feminine orientation and, possibly, attraction to men. Libidinous feelings toward mother, the first object of childhood phallic pleasure, must be entirely eliminated. Otherwise they will be kept buried in the unconscious by the defense mechanisms and re-main a threat.

Freud argued that, on the average, girls resolve their complex less completely than boys. Boys are motivated to work through their complex by castration anxiety, but girls, lacking a penis, lack the appropriate motivation. Girls do identify with the same-sex par-ent, thus promoting feminine sex-role development, and do so for roughly the same three purposes as boys. There are, however, two reasons why identification is more difficult for them. First, girls experience ambivalence toward their mothers. Pre-Phallic love may be eclipsed by Electra hostility, because the girl may blame her mother for "cutting off my penis" and devalue Mother for lacking a penis. Mothers, therefore, are not so attractive as objects of identification. The probability that daughters will identify with their mothers is further lowered by their jealousy of their mothers' closeness to their fathers. Second, the girl's Electra complex turns her toward father in the hope of indirectly obtaining the miss-ing penis from him, perhaps by having all of him for herself. This motivation also lowers the likelihood that girls will fully identify with their mothers. These difficulties in completing the process of identification led Freud to believe that females' superegos would, on average, develop less completely than males'. Further, fixation at the phallic stage accompanying incomplete resolution of the Electra complex ensures that women will have, on average, less **ego-strength,** the ability of the ego to successfully interact with reality on behalf of the id and inhibit id impulses until "safe" satisfactions are found (Freud, 1977). Deficient ego-strength results because fixation ties up libidinal energy, leaving less of it available to the ego for use in its attempts to deal with reality. The female's failure to identify fully with her mother may lead to masculine traits that predispose her to masculine pursuits and homosexuality.

Both ancient and modern culture appears to support Freud's Phallic Phase. Gray (1999) reports that the Tallensi people of Ghana openly recognize the Oedipus complex and incorporate control of it into their social organization. According to Levine-Ginsparg (2000), *Legends of the Fall* provides an excellent example of Oedipal conflict depicted in the movies. All three brothers fall in love with a woman who resembles their mother. The two oldest brothers are fierce rivals and the oldest is estranged from the father.

Reading about Freud's famous patients will help you understand the Phallic Stage processes (see Box 2.2).

Latency Period: The Fourth Phase. Freud's fourth phase is called a "period" because it is notable for its absence of a dominant erogenous zone and important events. **Latency** is a quiet period beginning around age six during which children repress their attraction to their parents and their other infantile urges. It is not the actual interactions with parents that are lost from consciousness (van der Kolk, 2000). Rather, it is libidinous instincts that are deeply buried in the unconscious. That they continue to exist can be seen in **sublimation,** a process that reorients instincts in new directions that are consistent with social norms. For example, an adolescent fixated at the anal stage might become interested in sculpting with clay, an acceptable substitute for earlier desires to play with his feces.

Genital Stage: The Fifth Phase. Freud's final phase is called **genital,** the period of mature sexual love that begins at puberty and includes directing both feelings of lust and of affection toward another person. The difference between this more mature stage and the first three stages revolves around **cathexes,** attachments of libidinous energy either to real external-world objects or to fantasized inner-world images. Pregenital-stage cathexes are typified by self-centered maximizing of bodily pleasures accompanied by "me first" relationships with parents or peers. In contrast, genital-stage cathexes are directed less toward bodily pleasures and self-enhancement and more toward relatively altruistic relating to others. While identifying with a person is to become like him or her, cathexing a person is to have her or him.

These externally directed energies are represented by two psychoanalytic ideals of mature, normal-personality functions: love and work. Thus, loving and caring relationships with others develop during adolescence and young adulthood, along with interests and activities related to productive, cooperative work. The successful pursuit of these goals contributes to the fulfillment of Eros' instinctual aim, preservation of self and species. People

BOX 2.2 • *Freud's Famous Case Histories*

Freud acknowledged that one of the case histories on which he relied heavily was not his (Freud, 1920/1977). Anna O, real name Bertha Pappenheim, was the patient of Josef Breuer, Freud's friend, colleague, and mentor. Because of his closeness to Breuer, Freud was privy to all the details of Anna O's case.

Anna O displayed a world-class laundry list of bizarre symptoms. Though intelligent, attractive, and the possessor of an appealing personality, Anna O was distorted, disoriented, and twisted in many ways (Jones, 1953). At one time or another, she displayed paralysis of the limbs including lack of normal sensations, as well as refusal to drink, inability to eat, a nervous cough, multiple personality, and, on occasion, communication only in English, though German was her native language. Sometimes her eye movements were abnormal, her vision restricted, and her head posture unusual (Freud, 1910/1977). She also periodically was in a state of "absence," withdrawal from reality or, as we might say today, "spaced out" (p. 10). Freud suspected that her symptoms were related to the circumstance of her sick father, whom she nursed and to whom she was devoted. Among her hallucinations was the image of an approaching snake against which she had no defense because of her paralysis. Anna O's case is critical to Freud's theory because it was the primary source of the critical questions that gave rise to the initial statement of the theory: Freud set as his task explaining "how . . . symptoms such as Anna O's . . . were isolated from . . . consciousness . . . [and] outside the patient's control" (Macmillan, 1997, p. 5).

If Anna O's case built the skeleton of Freud's theory, the case of Dora fleshed it out. While Anna O displayed numerous bizarre symptoms, Dora's life resembled a soap opera. At age 18, a reluctant Dora accepted treatment by Freud only at the insistence of her father. Her resistance was manifested in a "loss of consciousness, . . . with convulsion and deliria" (Macmillan, 1977, p. 249) following "words" with her father, presumably about therapy. Her earlier symptoms included labored breathing (dyspnea) beginning at age 8, which Freud (1977) interpreted as the heavy breathing of sexual intercourse, migrainous headaches at age 12, increasingly severe coughing at age 16 accompanied by loss of voice, continual fatigue, depression with suicidal ideation, and inability to concentrate. Also, allegedly, she was wetting her bed at a later age than is typical, which Freud took as evidence that she masturbated as a child. Further evidence came later when Freud witnessed Dora thrusting her finger into the opening of her small purse.

Dora was apparently "most tenderly" attached to her father, who had tuberculosis when she was 6, and, when she was 12, developed paralysis and mental disturbance attributable to syphilis (Macmillan, 1997, p. 249). Dora's mother, busy with domestic chores, was oblivious to Dora's problems and concerns. Thus, Dora turned to Frau K, whom she described as a "young and beautiful woman" (p. 250) in possession of an "adorable white body" (p. 251). Frau K, it seems, was having an affair with Dora's tubercular father while nursing him. Dora visited Frau K frequently in the company of her father. Herr K, in turn, was infatuated with Dora and, although she was but 14, he kissed and embraced her (Macmillan, 1997). Dora was "disgusted," but Freud surmised that Herr K had an erection that he pressed against Dora's clitoris through her clothing, greatly exciting her. Herr K denied this improper behavior and was backed up by Dora's father. When she was 16, Herr K propositioned Dora. Though the nature of the proposition was unclear, it is known that Dora slapped Herr K's face. Nevertheless, it was likely that Herr K was a philanderer as he did have an affair with his children's governess (Esterson, 1993).

Among Dora's significant dreams was one about a house on fire. On the night of the day Herr K made an advance, she dreamed that her father was standing by her bed as he rejected her mother's request by exclaiming, "I refuse to let myself and my two children be burnt for the sake of your jewel case" (Freud, quoted in Macmillan,

1997, p. 252). On waking from the dream, she smelled smoke, which Freud assumed indicated a desire to kiss Herr K ("There can be no smoke without fire"; Freud, quoted in Esterson, 1993, p. 43). The "jewel case" was a symbol for the female genitals and, significantly, its appearance was not limited to the dream: Herr K had given one to Dora. In a related memory, Dora recalled a parental dispute about her father's failure to give her mother some pearl drops (symbolic for semen; Macmillan, 1997). Freud thought this recollection meant Dora wished to give her father the sexual favors her mother denied him. The therapy ended when " . . . Dora disputed the facts [regarding Freud's insistent claim that she loved Herr K] no longer" (Freud, quoted in Esterson, 1997, p. 45). At the beginning of the next session she announced that she would return no more. Dora married, lived to the early 1950s, and died in New York (Macmillan, 1997).

The case of Dora was exceedingly important to Freud's theory because it began in 1900, the year *The Interpretation of Dreams* became widely distributed and was regarded by him as conclusive evidence in support of his theory. By the time a description of it was published in 1905, Freud was famous.

While the case of Dora was central to Freud's point of view, three other cases are probably better known. Little Hans was a five-year-old boy who was described by his father as fearful that a horse would bite him (Macmillan, 1997). This horse phobia involved the **displacement** defense mechanism: finding a new target for one's strong emotions that is less threatening than the original. From the boy's perspective the father was like a huge, powerful, scary horse. Hans ambivalently both loved and hated his father, the latter arising from the boy's Oedipal jealousy that Father possessed Mother (Freud, 1977). Having seen a horse fall down, Hans developed a wish that his father would fall down and hurt himself. The horse-bite terror was a fear that his "widdler" (penis) would be castrated by his hated and powerful horse-like father who may have been viewed as wishing to neutralize a budding young rival. Freud regarded this fear and hatred directed to the father as stemming from the inherited early experiences of humans with the all-powerful alpha-male, tribal chief.

A second well-known case, that of Serge Pankejeff, "The Wolf Man," centered on a critical dream and some family experiences of a wealthy Russian (Esterson, 1993). At age four, Serge dreamed that he saw "six or seven white wolves with big tails like foxes sitting very still in a large walnut tree facing . . . [his open bedroom] window" (p. 68). The wolf dream was related to a fairy tale in which a wolf had its long penis-like tail pulled off, but was actually inspired by seeing his parents copulating when he was 1½ years old (the *primal scene*). According to Freud's interpretation, devised during the adult Serge's therapy (1910–1914) for depression and intestinal disorders, the most important aspect of the boy's exposure to the primal scene was his rearview perspective that revealed his mother lacked a penis (Macmillan, 1997). Freud thought the boy suffered from a "negative Oedipus Complex": the meaning of the scene for the boy was that he "would have to be deprived of his penis if he were to gratify his feminine libidinal wish by satisfying his father sexually" (Macmillan, 1997, p. 482). Freud linked this interpretation to the dream by regarding the wolves as stand-ins for the parents (Esterson, 1993). The stillness of the wolves was the censored opposite of the violent activity typical of coitus. The whiteness of the wolves signified the parents' bed sheets and underclothes. That the wolves were facing the boy as if to stare at him was the censored opposite of the boy staring at his parents. The wolves with their long tails connoted the possibility of castration. Freud also surmised that it was "at least highly probable" that the boy's father played a childhood game in which he pretended to be a wolf, jokingly gobbling the boy up (Freud, 1977, p. 30).

The third well-known case was that of Ernst Lanzer, a young man with obsessional difficulties who saw Freud for seven months beginning October 1, 1907 (Jones, 1955; *Monitor on Psychology,* 1999). The patient was later dubbed "The Rat Man" because he was obsessed with a vision of rats eating their way into the anuses of his late father and the woman he was courting (Kerr, 1993).

(continued)

BOX 2.2   Continued

As the young man expressed a long-standing, intense affection for his father, Freud assumed the opposite was at least partly true: he hated his father (Esterson, 1993). Freud thought that this "actual" view of the father dated to a childhood incident in which the father, after beating the boy for masturbating, exclaimed "it would be the death of you" (Freud, quoted in Esterson, 1993, p. 65). Thus, the boy's hatred for his father arose from a grudge: the father had terminated his sexual pleasure and threatened him with castration.

Freud briefly noted a case similar to those of the Rat Man and the Wolf Man. One of his patients, a young American, related how he became sexually excited as a child by the story of "an Arab Chief who pursued a 'gingerbread man' so as to eat him up. He identified himself with the edible person and the Arab chief was recognizable as a father-substitute" (Freud, 1977, p. 31).

Obviously, the cases of Little Hans, the Wolf Man, and the Rat Man were crucial to the centerpiece of Freud's theory, the Oedipal Complex and its associated castration anxiety. It appears that cases relating to the other stages are more rare, although the Rat Man case has obvious implications regarding anal eroticism and anal sadism/masochism (desire to hurt, desire to be hurt; Esterson, 1993; Jones, 1955). Also, an interesting case of oral obsession has been reported, though the patient was not Freud's. Call this one the case of the milkman. Karl Abraham, a Freudian, "described an adult schizophrenic patient who drank milk heated to body temperature with a pronounced sucking action and who tended to wake up with strong sexual desires that were satisfied by drinking milk. . . . However, if the patient was unable to find milk, he would masturbate" (Macmillan, 1997, p. 543).

unable to avoid fixations at earlier stages will show abnormal personality patterns during this later stage: immaturity, sexual deviation, and neurosis.

Another characteristic of this stage is the final resolution of the phallic-stage identification difficulties theorized for women. Supposedly, to mature successfully, women must be able to accept the absence of a penis and identify with the vagina. With this change to "femininity," the clitoris "should wholly or in part hand over its sensitivity, and at the same time its importance, to the vagina" (Freud, 1901/1965, p. 118). This view supported Freud's belief in vaginal orgasm as the standard of mature, normal, sexual experience for women.

Table 2.2 summarizes the five stages of psychosexual development.

A Basic Diversity Issue: Freud's View of Females

Because of the different socialization processes for girls and boys, Freud believed girls are more dependent on repression. Further, because of their assumed weaker superego development, "for women the level of what is ethically normal is different from what it is in men" (Freud, 1925/1959, p. 196). That is, Freud thought that, on average, women function at a lower moral level than men and show a lesser ability to sublimate (Macmillan, 1997). The fact that this opinion is still around is evidenced by an unflagging interest in the work

TABLE 2.2   *Summary of Freud's Stages of Psychosexual Development*

Stages	Ages	Zones	Activities	Task
Pregenital (infantile)				
Oral	0–1½	Mouth	Sucking Biting	Weaning
Anal	1½–3	Anus	Expelling; Retaining	Toilet training
Phallic	3–6	Penis Clitoris	Masturbating	Identifying
Latency	6–13	none	Repressing	Sublimating
Genital	13+	Penis Vagina	Being sexually intimate; Sublimating	Loving another; Working

of leading moral development theorist Lawrence Kohlberg, who allegedly also consigned women to a relatively low level of moral functioning (Kohlberg, 1981). Continued interest in attempts by Carol Gilligan (1982) to defend female morality against the Freud/Kohlberg position also attests to the currency of this issue (see Allen, 2001). Further, to Freud, civilization was solely a male creation (Macmillan, 1997). Even worse, women, through their incessant sexual demands, allegedly retarded civilization's development by sapping libido reserved by men for cultural tasks (Macmillan, 1997). Freud's final pronouncement was that he refused "to be deflected from [my conclusions about women] by the denials of the feminists, who are anxious to force us to regard the two sexes as completely equal in position and worth" (1925/1959, p. 197).

Assume that gender bias is actually the source of Freud's conception of women, in that he viewed women from his masculine vantage point. It follows that it should be possible to rewrite his theory from a feminine perspective and preserve all its concepts and basic assumptions, except one. Male inferiority would replace female inferiority. Box 2.3 constructs that logical sequence.

Evaluation

Contributions

To talk of unconscious aspects of personality is one thing; to observe or measure such phenomena is quite another. How can psychologists possibly get at something that, by definition, is not directly available to consciousness? Freud suggested a number of avenues to the unconscious: free association, slips of the tongue, certain events occurring during psychoanalytic therapy, waking fantasy, and interpretation of dreams.

BOX 2.3 • *Phyllis Freud*

Journalist Gloria Steinem (1994) asked "What if Freud had been a woman?" Here is a summary of "Phyllis" Freud's biography, a tongue-in-cheek paraphrasing of Sigmund Freud's biography "with only first names, pronouns, and anything else related to gender changed in order to create a gender-reversed world" (p. 50). If you have attended a presentation of the *Vagina Monologues,* you may find it parallels some aspects of "Phyllis Freud."

When Phyllis was a girl in mid-1800s Vienna, women were considered superior due to the power inherent in the birth process. Thus, men were afflicted with womb envy. Women's right to dominate was at the heart of Western matriarchal society. Women of the day would argue that men could never be great artists, musicians, or poets, because they lacked the true source of creativity, the womb. They might manage family meals, but having only "odd, castrated breasts that created no sustenance" (p. 50), their deficient knowledge of nutrition precluded ever attaining the title "chef."

Men were allowed to design their own clothes, but a preference for certain patterns rendered their "creations" rather monotonous. "Thus, the open button-to-neck 'V' of men's jackets was a recapitulation of the 'V' of female genitalia; the knot in men's ties replicated the clitoris while the long ends of the tie took the shape of labia; men's bow ties were the clitoris erecta in all its glory" (p. 50). Every woman knew that men, not being subject to the monthly menses, were out of tune with time, the tides, the stars, and the seasons. Little wonder they were no good at mathematics, engineering, and science.

Phyllis Freud's timeless phrases like "womb envy" and "anatomy is destiny" were constantly on the lips of even uneducated men. One concept, however, was the source of special fascination. "Testyria" was particularly intriguing to people, because it is, in today's phraseology, weird. Men show mysterious symptoms—blindness though there is nothing wrong with their eyes—that seem traceable to the testes. After all, mostly men show these strange symptoms. There-

fore, they must be laid at the door of what is unique to men, the testicles (it could not be the penis, because women have that too, the clitoris). Early treatments in use before Freud developed her theory seem abhorrent to us now: " . . . electric shock . . . removal of the testicles . . . cauterization of the penis . . . " (p. 51). Shunning these barbaric measures, Freud, in collaboration with Dr. Josephine Breuer, used hypnosis. While in a trance, famous patient Arnie O "talked out" about what was later determined to be a fantasy of seduction by his mother. Even this more humane method had temporary effects. Undaunted, Freud marshalled the imposing forces of her legendary genius and discovered that if Testyrics "talked out" while fully awake, effects were permanent.

Among Freud's most endearing qualities was a rarity for women of her time. She was able to listen to men for hours on end and take them seriously. Even though laywomen and professionals alike marveled at this astonishing ability, masculinists, though not so shrill as the modern versions, nevertheless charged her with "androphobia" (p. 52). As long as she continued to insist that men's anatomy doomed them to inferiority, nothing Freud did could redeem her in the eyes of the masculinists.

When confronted with such irrationality, Freud always pointed to the scientific facts. For example, if harassed because she asserted "men possess a weaker sexual instinct" (p. 52), Freud reminded critics that only women were capable of multiple orgasms. She added, how could women's sexual superiority be doubted when the sexual act produces a pack of puny sperm all pathetically fighting for union with the massive ovum, only to be immediately swallowed up by it. And why is the clitoris superior? Obviously it has only a single function, while the penis is burdened with dividing its energies to accommodate dual function: "excretion of urine and sperm delivery" (p. 53). Not only was the duality of the penis a problem with regard to basic physiological functions, it also reared its ugly head on a more psychological level. "Immature penile orgasm had to be replaced by lingual or digital ones" (p. 54).

Of course, no account of Freud's theory would be complete without bringing up an early change of critical assumptions. When Freud first heard her young male patients claim they were sexually abused by their mothers, she may have been skeptical, but she soon experienced a revelation.

They had actually been seduced! However, after later allegedly reflecting on public reaction, and contemplating implications for mothers—even her own (Phyllis had brothers)—letters to very close friend Wilimina Fliess documented Freud's abrupt switch from the seduction theory. Some claim it was an honest change of heart; others doggedly continue to question her intellectual integrity.

Free Association. Freud's primary assessment technique for getting at the unconscious was **free association,** in which the person adopts a mental orientation that allows ideas, images, memories, and feelings to be expressed spontaneously. It allows patients to experience **catharsis,** a process by which inner feelings are openly expressed in words or behaviors that can lead to relief of tensions. If one idea—apple—suggests an associated idea—worms—one is free to pursue thoughts about worms. The fundamental rule of free association is to allow expression of anything and everything that comes to mind, no matter how senseless, illogical, trivial, embarrassing, unpleasant, or absurd it may seem. Free association is important because it provides Freudian therapists with clues about a person's unconscious. It is worth noting, however, that free association is not entirely free. Free association sessions often start with a topic suggested by the therapist (Macmillan, 1997). Also, Freudian therapists interrupt free association with suggestions as to which of the patient's thoughts should be elaborated further.

Interpretation of Dreams. According to Freud (1900/1958), dreams are "the royal road to . . . the unconscious . . . " (p. 608). It is not simply dreams per se that are important, but their interpretation, which rests in part on infantile wish fulfillments represented in them. Freud believed that the **manifest content** of dreams, what the dreamer remembers about the dream when awakened, is deceptive and should not be taken at face value. Dreams originate in unconscious, primary processes of the id. Id forces gain strength during sleep, when conscious suppression is less than during wakefulness. By using censorship and substitution of benign content, ego distorts and modifies id instinctual impulses and images that are represented in dreaming, thereby lessening the threat they pose. Consequently, the true content of dreams is seldom what it appears to be on the surface. Because everything is disguised and mysterious, skilled interpretation is required to get at **latent content,** the underlying meaning of each dream.

Freud assumed that every dream has a meaning that can be interpreted through decoding representations of unconscious materials. Symbolic interpretation focuses on replacing disguised manifest content with some reasonable latent parallel. For example, a dream of climbing stairs (manifest content) is actually about sexual intercourse (latent content).

A **dream symbol** is an element of dream content that represents some person, thing, or activity involved in unconscious processes. Freud believed that symbols can sometimes

TABLE 2.3 *Some Freudian Dream Symbols*

Dream contents	Symbolic meanings
Knife, umbrella, snake	Penis
Box, oven, ship	Uterus
Room, table with food	Woman
Staircase, ladder	Sexual intercourse
Water	Birth, mother
Baldness, tooth removal	Castration
Left (direction)	Crime, sexual deviation
Children playing	Masturbation
Fire	Bed-wetting
Robber	Father
Falling	Anxiety

have common meanings for people in general. Table 2.3 illustrates this point. However, he believed even more strongly that symbols are often highly personal rather than universal. He wrote, "The same piece of content may conceal a different meaning when it occurs in various people or in various contexts" (Freud, 1900/1958, p. 105).

Psychoanalysis.   Free association quickly became the basic technique of Freud's "talking treatment" (Breuer & Freud, 1895/1950). This technique was embedded in **psychoanalysis,** Freud's systematic procedures for providing a patient with the insight necessary to rid the personality of its neurotic conflicts. The eventual recall of childhood experiences is central to these procedures, especially recollections of sex and aggression involving one's parents. Through **insight,** unacceptable and socially "taboo" experiences buried in the person's unconscious can be made conscious. The experience of insight frees the patient from the grip of childhood traumas and, thereby, constitutes a "cure."

Free association substituted for Freud's earlier use of hypnosis as a treatment technique, which he tried before the turn of the century when working with Josef Breuer (Nathan & Harris, 1975). They showed that patients will abandon neurotic symptoms while in the hypnotic trance. However, Freud became discouraged with hypnosis when the symptoms often returned after the trance was removed. Free association was a more permanent solution.

Unlike the supposedly unconscious "trance" state, free association enabled patients to consciously comprehend everything they said while they were saying it. One reason Freud decided to have patients recline on a couch was that it helped them settle into the mental state needed for effective free association (see the picture of the couch in Chapter 17, p. 417). Use of the couch led patients to adopt a passive posture and relaxed attitude, which generated a more preconscious-like state than usually occurs during normal wakefulness. Freud sat behind his patients, away from their direct view, partly to minimize his influence on their psychological explorations. He wanted to be like a neutral or blank screen, so that his patients would feel free to verbalize their associations without looking for his facial reactions or fearing criticism and disapproval.

Patients would sometimes display **transference,** a condition in which patients relate to the psychoanalyst as if he or she were a significant person from their past about whom they were continuing to experience mixed feelings. The origin of these unrealistic transformations is the patient's unconscious. It is as if the patient needs to remake the analyst in the image of Father or Mother or some other significant person in order to work through the psychological problems left over from childhood. Reclining on the couch partly contributed to transference by fostering a dependent, child-like relationship with the parent-like psychoanalyst hovering in the background. **Countertransference** occurs when analysts project their own unconscious needs onto their patients. For example, the analyst may be sexually or romantically attracted to the patient as if the patient were the analyst's opposite-sexed parent.

Supporting Evidence: Older and More Current

Probably thousands of studies done over at least 70 years have addressed Freud's ideas. This section provides a summary of the older research and a few examples of the newer work. J Hunt (1979) assessed evidence from different lines of investigation flowing from Freud's ideas. He found that the studies "lent support" to Freud's general proposition about "the special importance of early experience" (p. 119), but not to the specific experiences hypothesized by Freud. Salvatore Maddi (1968) reviewed the research literature and concluded that there was qualified support for two Freudian concepts in the older literature. First, while not all behavior is defensive, he asserted that the general concept of ego defense is "tenable," supported by a "rather convincing" number of studies related to repression. Second, he claimed that "there is more evidence of castration anxiety among men than women" (p. 392).

Much research has attempted to support Freud's most central idea, the unconscious. Freud found evidence for the existence of the unconscious in **slips of the tongue,** verbal errors that seem to replace neutral words with ones that supposedly emanate from the unconscious. However, researcher Michael Motley, (1985, 1987) believes that most such slips are due to the misfirings of the brain and its verbal mechanisms. For example, consider the following scenario: young man approaches attractive women with whom he has plans to spend the evening and exclaims, "I'll pick you up at sex. . . . I mean six!" According to Motley, the most efficient and verifiable way to explain this error is in terms of word-retrieval mechanisms. The words *six* and *sex* share two of three letters, and are, thus, probably stored in connected neural networks. Therefore, the young man's brain "went looking for" the word *six,* but "found" *sex* instead, because their structural near-identity caused them to be stored "close to" one another.

Motley believes, however, that notions about the unconscious are not entirely without merit. In fact, his work has shown that sometimes the unconscious actually may rear its ugly head, much to our embarrassment. In one of his studies, he and his colleagues tested three groups of college men. The men in one group were fitted with electrodes and warned that they would receive an electric shock at some point in the experiment. A second group performed in the presence of a provocatively dressed female experimenter. Both groups and some control subjects were asked to speak a set of word pairs designed to elicit verbal foul-ups (spoonerisms) that Freud would interpret as spillover from the unconscious. Males threatened with electric shock tended to say "damn shock" for "sham dock" and "cursed wattage" for "worst cottage" rather than commit sexual slips. The group in the presence of the sexy female experimenter tended to make mistakes like "fast passion" for "past fashion" and "nude breasts" for "brood nests." Control subjects were no more likely to make sexual than electricity-related slips. Thus, when the environment contains cues relating to certain motivations that we tend to harbor in our unconscious minds, words that represent these forbidden motivations may pop out.

Freud's ideas about dreams have come under fire as mid-twentieth century research appeared to show that vivid dreams are controlled by a primitive lower brain stem area, the pons (Carpenter, 1999). Control by this area is consistent with the modern belief that dreams are no more than random bits of information sometimes assembled into wholes that seem to make sense. However, more recent research shows that the prefrontal cerebral cortex (just behind the forehead) is more important to dreaming than the pons (Carpenter, 1999; Solms, 1999). Normally, the prefrontal cortex reins in the emotional areas that lie behind it. However, during dreaming it is inhibited. This finding fits Freud's conception of dreams as irrational, disorganized, abstract, and, more importantly, libidinous. That the chains of control are stripped from the emotions, allowing them to be freely expressed in dreams, is just the evidence Freud was hoping for.

G. William Domhoff's (2003) review of J. Allan Hobson's new book entitled *Dreaming* provides both some good news and some bad news regarding Freud's view of dreaming. In concert with other dream experts, Hobson argues "that random signals from the brainstem force the cortex to make" (Domhoff, 2003, p. 1997) "the best of a bad job in producing even partially coherent dream imagery from the relatively noisy signals sent up to it from the brainstem" (Hobson quoted in Domhoff, 2003, p. 1997). According to Domhoff, Hobson's characterization of dreaming is designed to challenge "every aspect of Freudian theory" (Domhoff, p. 1997). Elsewhere in his book Hobson casts dreaming as "a psychotic state" or a state of "delirium" that amounts to an "organic brain dysfunction characterized by visual hallucinations, illogical thinking, loss of recent memory, and confabulation" (p. 1998). Further, Domhoff cites David Foulkes' research-based position that children's dreams are too "bland" and "static" until age 7 or 8 to fit Freudian interpretations. As you have already seen and will see again, it is crucial to Freud's theory that children have as-real-as-life dreams as early as one year of age. However, the news is not all bad. In criticism of *Dreaming,* Domhoff attributes to "cognitive psychologists" the research-based belief that "dreams are reasonably coherent simulations of the everyday world, which make good use of language and other waking cognitive abilities" (p. 1998).

It can now be asserted that there is an unconscious (see the *American Psychologist,* v. 47, #6, 1992). That unconscious, however, may not be the analytic, manipulative, and smart entity that Freud assumed. Instead, it may be simple, straightforward, and unanalytical compared to consciousness (Greenwald, 1992) and is revealed by the influence that what we catch unawares out of the corners of our eyes has on our subsequent behavior (e.g., the word *sexy* presented too quickly for conscious awareness would influence our subsequent ratings of pictures of people (Greenwald, Drain, & Abrams, 1996).

Limitations

The Uncertain Status of Psychoanalytic Theory (PT).   Taking into account the large number of attempts to support Psychoanalytic Theory (PT), it has shown little ability to predict future behavior. PT concepts work best when applied backward, accounting for an individual's past behavior after the facts have been gathered (Stanovich, 1989).

The primary setting for gathering data relevant to PT has been the clinic, not the laboratory. In the clinic, events that are irrelevant to diagnosis and treatment act on patients and analysts but cannot be controlled: interruptions, chance moods of patient and analyst, temporary health status of both, events in the setting (baby crying next door), and unknown events occurring just before the session (a lover's quarrel). One of Freud's patients, a psychiatrist, wrote that during treatment sessions Freud's dog was "sitting quietly . . . at the foot of the bed . . . a big chow" (Wortis, 1954, p. 23). Obviously, it did not occur to Freud that the presence of this possibly threatening, at least distracting, animal may have affected his patient's thoughts, verbalizations, and behaviors, and, in turn, Freud's interpretations. If Freud thought this patient's discomfort was due to touching on sensitive, unconscious material, he might have been incorrect.

The clinic subject–samples often used by Freud and his supporters are unrepresentative of people in general: unlike most people, clinic subjects are psychologically disturbed. Further, Freud's major case studies were of people seen in Victorian Vienna (nearly 100 percent) between the years 1889 and 1900 (50 percent) who showed abnormal behaviors (50 percent hysterical neuroses; Brody, 1970). Further, the sample was upper-class (nearly 100 percent) women (67 percent) between the ages of 18 and 20 (75 percent) who were single (75 percent). They could be described as YAVIs (young, attractive, verbally apt, intelligent). This selective sample may have biased theory development and limited how readily Freud's observations can be generalized.

Though Freud's ideas relied heavily on people's early childhood experiences, he actually had few child patients (Daly & Wilson, 1990). He obtained most of his information about children through everyday experience, reading, his own recollections of his childhood, the recollections of adult patients, and anecdotes provided by nonpatients.

The "evidence" for the validity of Freud's concepts is often very indirect, so much so that the data supplying that evidence may be better explained by other theories. As Kihlstrom (1994) implies, it is quite a stretch from the data of Anderson and colleagues Baum and Cole to transference involving analyst and patient (Anderson & Baum, 1994; Anderson & Cole, 1990). In some excellent work that is well explained by cognitive social principles, Anderson and Baum (1994) showed that a person supposedly in a room next to the subject's, who was described as similar to one of the subject's significant others, was remembered as more similar to the significant other than was in fact the case. We make people who resemble our significant others into clones of those important figures in our lives. However, the significant others chosen by subjects for use in the Anderson/Baum research rarely were relatives, much less parents. Thus, generalizing from feelings and recollections about nonrelatives "in the next room" to transference during therapy seems unwarranted.

The attack on Freud was exacerbated when Jeffrey Masson (1984) claimed that Freud thoughtlessly abandoned his initial "correct" observation that his early patients (1880s) had been sexually seduced during childhood. Allegedly, Freud's change of heart, only about nine months after he publicly announced his "seduction theory," was inspired by the incredulity with which the theory had been received (McCullough, 2001), his concern that the theory implicated his own father, and his fear that he would be condemned for suggesting that sexual abuse of children is widespread. The change from "child sexual abuse is common" to "no it isn't" may have severely damaged the credibility of perhaps millions of real child abuse victims.

Masson's charge carries less weight today because it has become widely accepted that Freud's early patients actually told Freud nothing reasonably interpretable as "stories of abuse" (Esterson, 1993; Macmillan, 1997; McCullough, 2001). Either Freud read too much into what his patients said to him or he made suggestions to them that elicited what he viewed as statements confirming the alleged seductions. Regarding the latter, Russell Powell and Douglas Boer (1994) presented evidence from Freud's own writings that he pressured patients to accept his suggestions that they had been abused: one patient was called "dishonest," another was threatened with being sent away, and others were literally subjected to pressure applied to their heads because they resisted his suggestions that they had been abused. The pressure was so great that patients would sometimes make comments like "Something has occurred to me now, but you [Freud] obviously put it into my head" (Freud, quoted in Powell & Boer, p. 1287). Finally, they cite a passage by Freud written many years later in which he seems to admit that he may have been guilty of forcing seduction scenarios onto his early patients: " . . . [memories of seduction] which I myself had perhaps forced on them" (Freud, quoted in Powell & Boer, p. 1286). It is evident that Freud's use of pressure to get patients to accept his suggested reasons for their psychological problems did not end with abandonment of the seduction theory (Esterson, 1993; Macmillan, 1997).

One may wonder, can "false memories" be implanted into people's heads to the point that they come to believe something happened to them which, in fact, never occurred, at least not in the way it has come to exist in their memories? Initially, Elizabeth Loftus's (1979) research showing that false memories can be successfully implanted was heavily criticized (e.g., Zaragoza & McCloskey, 1989). However, in more recent years it is clear that she was right all along: memories can be altered, mixed one with another, and it is even possible to create a memory about an event that never happened (Belli, Lindsay, Gales, & McCarthy, 1994; Ceci, Huffman, Smith, & Loftus, 1994b; Johnson, Hastroudi, & Lindsay, 1993; Lindsay, 1990; Loftus, 1993; Pezdek & Banks, 1996; Zaragoza & Mitchell, 1996). What we recall regarding an event can be shaped by what happened since the event, especially if another similar event occurs subsequent to the one we try to recall. If Kate says something to us at a party, and a similar friend Margaret says something similar to us at the same party, we may confuse sources of the comments: we may attribute to Kate what Margaret said to us (Johnson et al., 1993). If you witness a robbery and are later asked to recall what you saw, details from a TV-cop-show robbery you viewed subsequent to the actual robbery may intrude on your recollection. If the real robber was tall and the TV robber was short you may report to the police that the real robber was "short."

But what about suggestions of unconfirmed childhood sexual events such as Freud is accused of making to his clients (e.g., Dora)? Whereas in scientific research the witnessed event (analogous to an actual robbery) and the subsequent event (analogous to a TV robbery) are typically about the same kind of thing (a robbery), the therapeutic context is different from the alleged abuse context. Can what happens subsequent to a given event influence recollection of the event, even if the subsequent event is different? Preliminary evidence to support an affirmative answer was reported by Allen and Lindsay (1998). A recent study provides more convincing support. Lindsay, Allen, Chen, and Dahl (2004) showed that false memories about an event can occur as a result of exposure to subsequent events that are the same as, similar to, and very different from the original event. Whatever happens after a person witnesses an event, no matter whether it is similar to or different from what occurred in the witnessed event, can result in false memories about the event. Thus, suggestions by a therapist to an adult patient may falsify recollections of childhood events.

All in all, it is plausible to believe that even modern-day therapists may suggest to their patients that the source of their problems is sexual abuse suffered during childhood, even though no abuse occurred, and their patients may incorporate abuse into childhood memories (Pendergrast, 1995). Did Freud influence these so-called "recovered memory" therapists (McCullough, 2001)? I think so. First, one of Freud's most basic assumptions is that trauma far back in one's past is the "cause" of current problems, and the solution is to dredge up that awful past and reexperience the emotions and thoughts associated with it (Macmillan, 1997). But where did this assumption come from, scientific research or at least systematic observation by Freud or others? The answer is almost certainly "no." Freud reported no such research or observations. Instead, he got this basic assumption from Anna O, through Breuer, though he credits it to Breuer and Janet (Freud, 1920/1977, p. 257; Macmillan, 1997). In turn, she got it from the folklore of the time. In any case, modern evidence suggests that digging up past traumas may be fruitless or even harmful (Bonanno, 2004).

Further, there is additional evidence that modern therapists who believe that "recovered memories" are real memories were influenced by Freud. First, therapists who induce patients to recover memories during therapy may use many of the same suggestive techniques used by Freud (e.g., hypnosis). Second, some of the pressure techniques they use appear to be borrowed from Freud: they, like Freud, persist in attempts to persuade patients that they were abused as children until the patients appear to display memories of abuse (Pendergrast, 1995). Interestingly, at least one of Freud's patients never forgot a childhood experience that Freud insisted he had repressed (Macmillan, 1997). Third, they seem to have the same alarming attitude displayed by Freud: Part of Freud's legacy may be seen in the inclination by some modern psychoanalysts and recovered memory therapists toward disregarding the truth value of what they uncover in therapy as long as recovered material is deemed to have therapeutic value (Macmillan, 1997; Pendergrast, 1995).

Obviously, the "recovered memory" therapists share Freud's belief that childhood trauma has caused current problems and the solution is remembering and reexperiencing the trauma. Perhaps consideration of the more "here and now" theories covered later will convince you that Freud's "dig up the past" assumption is not necessarily a good one, and, in fact, may be detrimental. It may be best to let "sleeping dogs lie." Attempting to recall old horrors that may or may not have actually occurred may create new horrors or make those that really did occur seem even worse than they actually were.

A word of caution: that "false memories" can be relatively easily implanted into people's minds is still controversial in some quarters. For excellent treatment of this controversy, see Kathy Pezdek's book with William Banks (1996). If you are interested in allegations of real-life damage caused by the recovered memory movement see Pendergrast (1995).

Even more damning than Masson's and Powell/Boer's work is Allen Esterson's contention, in his fascinating book *Seductive Mirage* (1993), that whether Freud "changed his mind" or implanted suggestions is moot. Instead of early patients' comments interpretable as abuse stories, there were only Freud's preconceived analytic reconstructions that he tried to coerce patients into accepting. Esterson supports his position by showing that Freud's early "seduction" cases were not what he described them to be in writings published many years later. First, when Freud wrote about the Oedipus complex in 1925, he either suffered from such severe memory loss that his competency should have been questioned or he was disingenuous. At this later time Freud wrote that the early cases involved fathers seducing daughters, when in fact his early writings indicated that the "accused" had been mostly brothers or nonrelatives, not fathers. In a letter to Fliess, in which he announced his disenchantment with the seduction thesis, Freud indicated that "the father . . . *had to be accused,*" not that any fathers were being accused (Freud, quoted in Masson, 1984, p. 108, emphasis added). He must have known then, and later, that a preponderance of abusive fathers, whether parties to the early cases or fantasized as he asserted in 1925, did not exist. Second, Esterson argued that, no matter what patients may or may not have said in therapy, Freud typically concocted an interpretation that fit his current theory, whatever that happened to be.

Esterson notes that Freud loved and often used analogies, but those he constructed to support his theory were often faulty. For example, he used an analogy to imply that psychoanalysts could ignore patients' overt testimony in favor of other "evidence." He noted that a physician is able to look at a patient's symptoms and determine the patient's disorder, no matter what the patient says. By analogy, a psychoanalyst can look at a patient's symptoms and determine what his or her childhood trauma had been, regardless of what the patient might have said. Esterson sees a serious breach of scientific protocol in this line of "reasoning." Freud assumed the validity of his theory, then "collected evidence" by creating a fit between what his theory would dictate and what he attributed to the patient. The irony of ignoring what patients explicitly said in therapy, while acting as if their testimony was the primary basis of psychoanalytic interpretations, is seen in Freud's acknowledgments that patients often stubbornly refused to accept his interpretation of what they said to him.

If Esterson's (1993) critique was a logician's treatise on the illogic of Freudian thought, Macmillan's (1997) "evaluation of Freud," as he euphemistically called it, was a preemptive strike on Freud and all his ideas. Macmillan's massive book (750+ pages) reduces the Freudian theoretical structure to a gutted building left barely standing after an atomic blast (Crews, 1996). He uses Freud's own writings to show that few of the "master's" ideas hold up under close scrutiny. Obviously it is impossible to provide a reasonable summary of Macmillan's book, but I can give a few examples of the thoroughness with which he takes Freud to task.

In several places Macmillan points out that Freud is guilty of tautological or circular reasoning: observations give rise to a theory, which then is used to explain the observations. For example, convulsions of an hysterical person give rise to a theory of unconscious motivation, which is then used to explain the convulsions. Macmillan also charges that Freud often contradicted himself. A good example is Freud's reference to the primary process and its associated mechanism of repression as preventing the development or storage of structured thought. Yet analysis of dreams and symptoms, supposedly the result of repressed anxiety, revealed to Freud fully structured and organized but unconscious thoughts. Also, Freud was inconsistent in his explanations of various phenomena. A prime example requires some detail.

In the course of only a few years, Freud adopted three different points of view regarding homosexuality. When Freud analyzed Leonardo da Vinci, he wrote about the effect of the father's absence or the mother's ability to "push the father out of his proper place" (p. 338). With this kind of family situation in mind, Macmillan quoted Freud: "The boy represses his love for his mother: he puts himself in her place, identifies himself with her and takes his own person as a model in whose likeness he chooses the new object of his love. In this way he has become a homosexual. . . . He finds the objects of his love along the path of *narcissism*" (p. 338). That is, he becomes his mother, falls in love with himself as a woman, and, of course, becomes attracted to men. At another point, Freud assumed that the boy-child early on simply chooses his mother as a sexual object—she is the first object for all children—and never abandons that choice. When he discovers that his mother does not have a penis, he becomes attracted to effeminate males who are like women, but have penises. In his analysis of Schreber he took still another turn. Macmillan indicates that "Freud transform[s] narcissism from a method by which an object was chosen [as it was in the version inspired by Leonardo] to a stage in a developmental process" (p. 358). Now the boy becomes invested in his own body, especially his genitals, and chooses people with the same genitals. Freud's tendency to tautology, and his inclination to contradict himself and to be inconsistent, makes one wonder whether the Freud we know is the real Freud. Perhaps those who have written about Freud have so leveled, sharpened, and refocused Freud's ideas to deal with these three tendencies that Freud's thoughts are no longer his own.

It is worth noting that, since 1973, gay and lesbian orientation has not been officially classified as pathological (Carson, Butcher, & Mineka, 1996). The vast majority of clinical psychologists and psychiatrists now consider gays and lesbians to be as psychologically normal as any other group. All that can be said for sure about the "cause" of these orientations is that they show up early in life and, in the case of male homosexuality, there is a possibility of at least partial genetic determination.

Finally, other weaknesses uncovered by Macmillan are worth brief mention. Freud tended to change his definition of key terms. Examples are *repression* and *sublimation.* Taking the former, at one point *repression* is seen as a conscious process; at another it is seen as unconscious. Freud, according to convincing evidence gleaned from his writings and those of others, plagiarized from the works of other authors and out-and-out stole ideas from other therapists. For example, Freud took a therapeutic method from Frenchman J. R. L. Delboeuf without attribution and reported it as if he had invented it. Freud was ignorant of memory processes. For example, he had the Wolf Man, at age 1½, "remember," at least unconsciously, seeing his parents engaging in intercourse. It is now clear that it is virtually impossible to remember any event occurring that early (most people do not remember anything before age three, though they "recall" what parents and other older people have told them as if they remembered; Loftus, 1993). Also, it is clear that memories do not remain dormant for 10, 20, 30 years, after which they can be recalled in extraordinary detail as required by the recovery of repressed memories. Finally, Freud protested so many times that he did nothing in therapy that implanted suggested ideas into his patients' heads that one has to wonder whether he actually consciously recognized his unwarranted influence on his patients.

Given the devastating attacks by Macmillan and others, how does Macmillan account for the continued popularity of Freud and his theory? He offers five reasons: (1) most laypeople and many professionals think that Freud's relatively unchanged PT is beyond criticism (most do not know of the numerous criticisms); (2) psychoanalysis seems to allow for an extensive understanding of behavior and personality (post hoc or after the fact, Freud's theory seems to easily explain behavior and personality); (3) people are attracted to the irrational (at times, most people believe that they are at the mercy of forces beyond their understanding); (4) psychoanalysis deals with those things that are inherently interesting like sex (and weird dreams); (5) most people take it for granted that psychoanalytic therapy is uniquely and highly effective (they do not know that it is no more effective than other therapies and may be less effective than some). Box 2.4 illustrates many of these criticisms by revisiting Freud's famous cases. Finally, Freud and eleven others featured in this book are among the best-known figures in psychology (Haggbloom et al., 2002). Of all twentieth century psychologists, Freud was first in journal citations, first in introductory textbook citations, third most frequently named in a survey of psychologists, and third overall. Freud is alive and kicking. Befitting his continued high status, his works will again be published, but this time in handy, hip-pocket paperbacks that are accessible and affordable for everyone (Merkin, 2003).

Conclusions

The intensity, number, and, perhaps, convincingness of the assaults on Freud's theoretical fortress may seem to have increased so much over time that its walls appear sure to soon come tumbling down. However, there is another perspective. Detractors, though increasing in number, may be a mere platoon compared to the vast army of psychological professionals who either explicitly support Freud or imply support by making his ideas central to their own. Just as Freud was initially reviled by American psychologists, he came to be adored by so many of them that in 1999 his life works were the subject of a massive exhibit sponsored by the United States Library of Congress (Fancher, 2000). Some of his admirers currently are finding support for his concepts (Azar, 1996).

BOX 2.4 • *Revisiting Freud's Famous Case Histories*

Many of Freud's interpretations of "his" cases fit neither the facts about the cases or others' interpretations of them. First, consider the case of Anna O. Was she, as Freud claimed (Freud, 1920/1977, p. 257), ever cured by her own "talking out" method, which he later adopted along with her "dig it up and reexperience it" assumption? Anna O was treated from December 1880 to June of 1882 when Breuer declared her "cured" (Macmillan, 1997). By five weeks later she had suffered four lapses and on July 12, 1882 was committed to a sanitarium. She later spent five years in another sanitarium and did not show complete remission of symptoms until the end of the 1880s. Freud's ever sympathetic biographer, Ernest Jones (1953), acknowledged these facts and that Breuer shared them with Freud. He went on to point out that Anna O (Bertha Pappenheim) became the first social worker in Germany and founded "several institutes where she trained students" (p. 225). She also became a leading European feminist, and ultimately a victim of the Nazi Gestapo (www.bet-debora.de/2001/jewishfamily/konz.htm). Thus, Anna O returned to normalcy, but it is quite a stretch to say that it was because of psychoanalysis.

In a letter to a colleague, Freud's comments and interpretations concerning the case seemed to attribute Anna O's delayed recovery to psychoanalysis (Forrester & Cameron, 1999; Tolpin, 2000). It was argued that her close therapeutic relationship with Breuer created a residual effect that kicked in years later to generate a compensatory personality structure, which was enough to make Anna O functional. More likely, Anna O finally recovered because she got over a real neurological disorder that caused her great physical pain and left her addicted to morphine, originally provided by Breuer.

The main bone of contention between Dora and Freud is summed up in the query, "Was Dora in love with Herr K as Freud insisted, or did she actually regard him with a mixture of disgust and hate?" Part of Freud's "evidence" for the "love thesis" was that Herr K had an erection when he embraced and kissed the pubescent Dora and he rubbed it against her clitoris. Actually, there was not one shred of evidence for anything more than a hug and a kiss (Esterson, 1993; Macmillan, 1997). Except for Freud, no one, including Dora, ever said anything about Herr K rubbing his erection against Dora. Freud simply made it up because it fit his interpretation drawn from his theory. Actually, Freud was in the habit of manufacturing "evidence" for his theory even when there was evidence contrary to his own. For example, Freud said Dora masturbated; she vehemently denied it. His evidence? The finger in the purse incident. That thrusting a finger into a purse means a woman masturbated as a child is a logical leap of Olympian proportions. Notice that her denial did not deter him. In fact, to Freud, denials meant what was denied was actually true (Macmillan, 1997). If what was alleged was confessed that also meant it was true. In short, whatever a patient might say about an allegation was accepted by Freud as evidence that the allegation was true, even a noncommittal statement. When Freud pressed his case that Dora was in love with Herr K, he stated, "Dora replied in a depreciatory tone: 'Why has anything so very remarkable come out?'" (Freud, quoted in Esterson, 1993, p. 46). Freud took this question as confirmation that he was right about her love for Herr K.

Further, no association, no matter how remote, was overlooked by Freud when he was in pursuit of "evidence" for his theory. You may wonder, how does "smelling smoke" mean one wants a kiss? When Freud suggested that meaning to Dora she pointed out that both her father and Herr K "smelled up the place" smoking tobacco. Undaunted, Freud asserted, it could "scarcely mean anything else than the longing for a kiss, which, with a smoker, would necessarily smell of smoke" (Freud, quoted by Esterson, 1993, p. 44). In addition, as Freud was himself a smoker, it occurred to him that she also wanted to kiss him (alleged transference and actual countertransference)!

(continued)

BOX 2.4   Continued

And what of the jewel box and the pearl drops? By some stretch of the imagination, one might see a jewel box as a symbol for female genitalia, and pearl drops as symbolic of semen. If so, a mosquito is a good symbol for a whale. What about the bizarre interpretations Freud wove into his explanations of patients' symptoms? Were they the only ones possible? No. Several commentators have offered equally bizarre and equally (im)plausible interpretations (Macmillan, 1997).

A very pertinent question is, "Was Freud's behavior in the best interest of Dora?" Dora was probably reduced to the low state of needing therapy by the lewd advances of Herr K, a man old enough to be her father (Esterson, 1993). And what does she get from Freud?: The allegation that she loved the man who was molesting her. It would have been more sensitive, therapeutic, and humane to assume from the onset that, indeed, she hated Herr K and was genuinely disgusted by him.

Little Hans was actually no psychological professional's patient, unless one counts Freud's long-distance relationship. Hans was seen briefly by Freud on one occasion (Macmillan, 1997). Almost all of the information Freud had about Hans came from the boy's father, who was strongly biased toward Freud's theory. As for the horse phobia, it first occurred shortly after the boy became anxious, probably because he had been separated from his mother. While the phobia was real, Freud had no facts to support his fabricated story about the father being symbolized by the horse and about the boy's hostility and desire that his father be harmed for posing a castration threat and monopolizing his mother. Further, the castration threat was also apparently real (the boy was told that his widdler might be cut off because he played with it too much; Freud, 1909/1963). But the timing of the threat was such that it was not a plausible cause of the phobia or Hans's anxiety (the threat occurred months before the phobia appeared, Macmillan, 1997). Finally, Freud believed that Hans was primed to hate, fear, and wish to harm and replace his father by experiences inherited from humans' past. To support this belief, Freud relied on the theory of Chavalier de Lamarck which he knew had been discredited (there is more about Lamarck in the next chapter). In fact, Freud clung to theories he knew to be wrong because he needed them to support his theory (Macmillan, 1997). The cases of Leonardo and Schreber were also not about patients Freud actually had in therapy. Both were taken from books. In the case of Leonardo, Freud got the facts of the great artist's life wrong in many instances (Macmillan, 1997). Recent revelations are also damning. Rudnytsky (1999) reports that Freud sent Hans a rocking horse for his birthday and recommended that he be raised as a Jew, which meant he would be circumcised. Was Freud creating a self-fulfilling prophesy to make his hypothesis about Hans seem valid?

The Wolf Man's case is exceptional in that Lanzer lived to old age, was interviewed, and wrote his memoirs. Esterson (1993, pp. 69–70) relates the following instances in which Lanzer contradicted Freud: (1) Freud claimed the Wolf Man was incapacitated at the beginning of psychoanalysis; the Wolf Man claimed he was much improved before psychoanalysis. (2) Freud indicated the Wolf Man's intestinal troubles had a psychological source; the Wolf Man asserted that inappropriate medicine prescribed by a country doctor caused the troubles. (3) Freud claimed psychoanalysis cleared up the intestinal troubles; the Wolf Man stated that the troubles lasted his whole life long. (4) Freud claimed the primal scene supposedly witnessed by the boy was not a product of *recollection* during treatment, but was constructed during analysis. Yet Freud reported details of the relevant events "recalled" by the Wolf Man during therapy. The Wolf man reported no recollection of seeing his parents having intercourse. (5) Freud claimed that the Wolf Man envisioned wolves as a boy; a later report instead described Spitz dogs with pointed ears and bushy tails (at one point in the case history Freud indicated that the wolves were really sheep dogs!). (6) Freud wrote that the Wolf Man's sister tormented him with a picture of a wolf, which caused him to exclaim that he feared a wolf would eat him. The Wolf Man countered that his sister promised a picture of a pretty girl, but instead she displayed a picture of Little Red Riding Hood about to be gobbled up by the Wolf. As a result, he became angry at the teasing, not fearful of the wolf (the Wolf Man went on wolf hunts as a youngster and reports nothing about a wolf phobia in his memoirs). Macmillan (1997) adds that the Wolf Man's sister seduced him, a fact, acknowledged by Freud, which may have partly accounted for the Wolf Man's problems. In addition, Jones (1957, Vol. 3) revealed former Freudian Otto Rank's contention that the Wolf Man hoodwinked Freud: the Wolf Man got the idea for the six or seven wolves from pictures of six members of Freud's committee that hung on his treatment room wall. And it is worth adding that the "father plays wolf gobbling up the boy" tale was one of Freud's frequent unsupported guesses about patients' childhoods (Freud, 1977, p. 30).

One of the most noteworthy aspects of the Rat Man case is the allegation, reported by Esterson (1993), that a researcher found a discrepancy between Freud's published account of the case and his original notes found after his death. It seems that Freud may have reported a longer treatment period in his publication than in his notes in order to make it appear that the Rat Man's therapy was very extensive. Further, at about the same time Freud's publication claimed the Rat Man's symptoms had disappeared, his notes indicated the Rat Man was complaining of rats gnawing at his anus.

The alleged beating for childhood masturbation "was administered" by Freud, not the Rat Man's father. Freud made up his masturbation story *before* he had any supporting evidence, including the Rat Man's mother's recollection that his father had once beaten him. As soon as the mother reported the beating to Freud, he appropriated it to support his story, even though she did not mention masturbation (the Rat Man did not remember the event; Macmillan, 1997). In fact, later, the mother said that the beating was for biting someone (Esterson, 1993). Once again Freud invented a story and presented it as "fact" supporting his theory.

Three of Freud's global conceptions have had profound impact on psychology. First, more than anyone else, Freud has taught us not to take literally people's behaviors and their expressions of thoughts and emotions. Rather, we can understand people better if we look beyond the blatantly obvious to the more challenging and meaningful subtleties. And maybe he wasn't so wrong about repression into the unconscious. Exploring certain neurological control mechanisms covered later in Chapter 17, Anderson and colleagues (2004) show how control centers work with the premier memory organ of the brain to allow suppression of unwanted memories. Second, his ideas about the identification process through which children become like their parents have influenced most theories of human development (Mussen, Conger, & Kagan, 1979). Third, while it may not be quite what Freud thought it was, even some of the most tough-minded experimental psychologists now acknowledge the existence of Freud's most central idea, the unconscious. Further, they assign a significant role to the unconscious in the lives of people (*American Psychologist*, vol. 47, #6, 1992).

While Freud's PT may not be scientific, he was in the vanguard of early psychologists who sought to make a science of psychology (Andreasen, 1997). His faith that psychology could become a science contributed greatly to its current scientific status. As for PT, even if it cannot be regarded as a scientific discipline, it can exist as a kind of philosophical position (Kihlstrom, 1994).

Freud's vast writings are still being mined to discover new fuel for thought. For example, Freud was ahead of his time with regard to attitudes toward gay people. Years ago he wrote: "We surely ought not to forget that . . . the sensual love of a man for a man, was not only tolerated by a people so far our superiors in cultivation as were the Greeks, but was actually entrusted by them with important social functions" (quoted in Young-Breuhl, 1990, p. 14). Although Freud has been gone for more than sixty years, we still have much to learn from him. One cannot claim to be an educated person without possessing knowledge of Freudian thought. Box 2.5 shows Freud's willingness to help all who called on him.

Summary Points

1. Freud was born (1856) of Jewish parents in the Germanic area of Moravia. He made a number of notable discoveries while a young medical student. *Interpretation of Dreams* (1900) set the tone for later breakthrough concepts, such as libido. Freud was banished from Vienna by the Nazis and died in London of cancer in 1939.

2. Freud pictured humans as under the control of instincts that fall into two categories: Eros and Thanatos. He posed a primitive first structure of personality, id, that operates according to the pleasure principle and the primary process. Ego holds the id in check with its reality principle and secondary process. It protects itself with defense mechanisms. The superego, a product of introjection, operates according to the morality principle.

3. The oral stage involves pleasure from stimulating the mouth area. Fixation can lead to either oral-receptive or oral-aggressive mature personality types. Narcissism is a growing phenomenon associated with irritating and dangerous behaviors. During the anal stage, pleasure is achieved by dispelling the feces. Toilet training can lead to fixation and anal-retentive or anal-expulsive personalities.

4. During the phallic stages, boys lust after their mothers. Fear of their fathers takes the form of castration anxiety. They resolve their Oedipal complexes by identifying with their fathers, a process that leads to superego development if it succeeds and overuse of defense mechanisms as well as adult promiscuity or feminization if it fails. Freud's famous cases, such as Anna O, Dora, Hans, and the animal men, reveal how he provided support for his theory. Some modern and ancient cultures reflect the complex.

5. The girl lusts after her father and hates her mother, but her lack of castration anxiety, due to lack of a penis (penis envy), makes resolution of her Electra complex difficult. As a result she may have lowered ego-strength and superego development relative to males. An apologist for Freud contends that he did not intend to degrade women but his own words contradict that contention.

6. The latency stage involves no focal genital area, but entails the process of sublimation. The genital stage involves cathexes that are more altruistic and less self-centered than earlier ones. Freud's psychoanalytic free association technique depended on use of a couch that induced patients to cathartically pursue insight. It replaced hypnosis and involved

BOX 2.5 • *An American Woman Asks Freud for Help*

Recently Ludy Benjamin and David Dixon (1996) discovered a previously unknown case of a young American woman who wrote Freud for advice. That he answered her may seem remarkable, but Benjamin and Dixon reveal that Freud, who spoke and wrote well in English, attempted to answer all of his mail, even if it meant working deep into the night.

This well-educated, widely read, and well-to-do woman was having a conflict with her conventional and apparently bigoted parents over her right to see a young Catholic man of Italian descent. She herself claimed to be unprejudiced. Her primary concern was that Freud help her understand a dream in which she found herself in an unfamiliar house with furnishings of unaccustomed poor quality. Her father and her uncle were on the front porch talking and fanning themselves as it was a hot day. When she answered a knock on the door, she found the brother of the young Italian, but her father and uncle had disappeared. He was dressed in modern clothing, but was wearing a sombrero. After a congenial conversation, the brother handed her a letter from her boyfriend and promised to visit her again, along with some male friends. To her horror, on opening the letter she read that her young man had married a Mildred Dowl (the authors found no record of the name). Grabbing a large brass knife nearby, she stabbed herself in the heart. When the knife passed through her body she experienced an "eternal thrill" (p. 464). She fell to the floor "dead" still holding the knife. On awakening, she discovered herself in the same position as she left herself in the dream but with tears streaming down her face. That day she was blue and dejected.

Freud's prompt response, dated only 22 days later (Dec. 2, 1927), opened with kind words: "I found your letter charming . . . " (Freud, quoted in Benjamin & Dixon, 1996, p. 465), but he went on to say that "Dream interpretation is a difficult affair" and he could not provide a trustworthy interpretation of the dream without knowing the source of the name Mildred Dowl. He continued that she must have heard the name somewhere:

" . . . a dream never creates, it only repeats or puts together." It was unfortunate that she was not in Vienna where they could talk. He did go on to say that he sensed her feelings about the young Italian were mixed and conflicted. These emotions were covered up by her love for the man and " . . . your resistance against your parents." Further, he indicated that, if her " . . . parents did not dislike the boy," she would be aware of " . . . the splitting of your feelings." He saw the dream as a " . . . way out of the maze" and he was sure that she would not desert the young man. "But if he drops you this is a solution." Freud closed with, "I guess that is the meaning of the dream . . . ," the content of which was the result "of the repressed antagonism which yet is active in your soul."

A couple of points are noteworthy. First, Freud shows a level of kindness and sensitivity that is rarely attributed to him. Second, he is cautious not to overinterpret the dream without further information. This kind of reluctance to provide an interpretation based on limited information is not consistent with the allegations against him.

Not only did Freud generously offer aid to people outside the therapy context, his writings have contributed to people's understanding of themselves. Robin Maltz (2002) found Freud's "case of a homosexual woman" (1920/1955) to be a helpful parallel to her own life circumstances. Freud's patient was a young woman who grew to hate her father, and eventually all men, because he impregnated her rival-mother, when the patient "should have" borne his child. This young woman infuriated her father by publicly fawning over an older women. This "Lady," as she was called, was a known bisexual who initially rejected Freud's patient, instigating a genuine but unsuccessful suicide attempt. In parallel, Maltz fell for early TV personality Shari of "Lamb Chop" fame. Like the "Lady," Shari was a strong mother figure, who manipulated the hand puppet "Lamb Chop" and gently scolded her for minor infractions. The recollection of Shari, and parallel appreciation of Freud's patient, helped Maltz to come to grips with her own sexual identity.

transference and countertransference. Freud examined dreams for both manifest and latent content. Recent neuroscience results support his view of dreams in some ways and contradict it in others.

7. Some research results that support Freud include evidence for the importance of early experience, and evidence confirming defenses, narcissistic tendencies, and the operation of the unconscious when cued by the environment. Problems with his psychoanalytic theory include relatively low predictive validity, use of uncontrolled clinical settings, sampling bias, and limited experience with children. Research results appearing to support his concepts (e.g., transference) must be stretched to fit.

8. Challenges to Freud's ideas in recent years include Masson's accusation that Freud, for personal reasons, abandoned an earlier seduction theory in favor of a fantasy position. Powell and Boer charge that Freud suggested seduction scenarios to patients who may have incorporated them into memory. Freud's assumption that the past must be dug up may have contributed to the current "recovered memory movement," which is based on misunderstandings of memory processes (suggestions during therapy may falsify recollections of early life) and may be detrimental. Esterson asserted that patients' reports to Freud contained nothing regarding seduction; Freud invented the seduction scenarios.

9. Macmillan showed that Freud capriciously changed his position and was inconsistent, self-contradictory, and tautological. He also borrowed ideas from others and supported his theory by inventing evidence. His change regarding homosexuality illustrates inconsistency. Reexamination of Freud's case histories shows that he did not actually have some case subjects in therapy, he made up childhood traumas for some case subjects, he turned failed cases into successes (Anna O), he directly intervened to influence cases (Hans), and he misrepresented the efficacy of his therapy.

10. Freud continues to have strong supporters. He ranks third among twentieth century psychologists and his work was the subject of a 1999 U.S. exhibit. His timeless contributions include inspiring us to look beyond the obvious, the identification process, the unconscious, and the promotion of psychology as a science. Because Freud's writings are so vast, he may yet teach us more. The case of his U.S. patient shows his sensitivity and unwillingness to make hasty judgments. His "case of a homosexual woman" helped a modern woman understand herself.

Essay/Critical Thinking Questions

1. What was it about the era in which Freud lived that so shaped his point of view?

2. Name two hysterical neuroses not discussed in the text.

3. How do suggestions made during therapy affect recollections of early life?

4. Defend Freud's interpretations of one of his most controversial case histories.

5. Paint a picture of a narcissistic person you know (no IDs, please).

E-mail Interaction _____

Write the author at b-allen@wiu.edu. Forward any of the following or write your own:

1. Do you think that Freud lied?

2. Did Freud really believe that females are inferior?

3. Tell me what to concentrate on in my studies of Freud.

Personality's Ancestral Foundation: Carl Jung

- Did you inherit your mind?
- Are you an introvert or an extravert?
- Feeling, intuiting, thinking, sensing, judging, perceiving, which is you?

Carl Jung
www.cgjungpage.org

On the occasion of his former mentor's death, Carl Jung described Freud's work as "surely the boldest attempt ever made . . . to master the riddle of the unconscious psyche. For us young psychiatrists, it was a source of enlightenment . . ." (quoted in Wehr, 1989, p. 29). These words were written despite the fact that Freud's view of Jung had changed from that of a loving father to one of a betrayed patriarch. In the early years of their collaboration, Freud pleaded with Jung: "My dear Jung, promise me never to abandon the sexual theory. That is the most essential thing of all. You see, we must make a dogma of it, an unshakable bulwark" (p. 34). Later he wrote, to his "number one man, the 'crown prince' " (p. 34). "I therefore don once more my horn-rimmed paternal spectacles and warn my dear son to keep a cool head . . . I also shake my wise gray locks . . . and think: Well, that is how the young folks are; they really enjoy things only when they need not drag us along with them . . . " (p. 36). But, unfortunately for Freud, Jung could not endorse dogma nor could he drag along someone else's theoretical baggage. He had his own ideas, including a conception of an unconscious that is dominated by the ancestral past of humans, not sexuality.

Hints of trouble in the Freud–Jung relationship appeared early (*Monitor on Psychology,* 1999). In 1909 Freud fainted and Jung attributed his collapse to their just completed conversation about corpses. Freud, in turn, interpreted Jung's account of the fainting spell as a wish that Freud were dead. On another occasion, Jung's interest in paranormal phenomena led him to declare his "father" wrong. While in Freud's presence, Jung had a curious sensation in his diaphragm that was followed by a loud "detonation" in a nearby bookcase. When he labeled the experience a "catalytic exteriorization phenomenon" and Freud responded "sheer bosh," Jung exclaimed "You are mistaken Herr Professor" (p. 35). Then Jung proceeded to add insult to injury by successfully predicting a second "detonation."

From Freud's perspective, by 1913 the personal and professional gap between the two psychiatrists had become too great to bridge. He wrote Jung, suggesting "that we give up our private relationship altogether. I lose nothing by this, since . . . I have been bound to you only by the thin thread of . . . previously experienced disappointments. . . . Assume complete freedom and spare me the supposed 'duties of friendship' " (p. 39). Jung wondered whether he was ever really a student of Freud.

Jung, the Person

Carl Gustav Jung (1875–1961) was born in Kesswil, Switzerland, the son of a pastor in the Swiss Reformed Church and the grandson of a professor and a clergyman (Kim, 2002; Wehr, 1989). One of those grandfathers was rumored to be the bastard son of Goethe, the famed German author of *Faust,* a play about a magician who sold his soul to the devil in return for magic powers (Lebowitz, 1990). Jung nurtured this rumor because, at the time, he liked to view himself as a person with ties to mysticism and to famous people.

Jung suffered through some painful childhood experiences that were accompanied by numerous "visions" (Feldman, 1992). Reflecting on this time, he recalled a dark and dreary funeral during which men in black clerical gowns lowered a coffin into a deep hole and repeated the phrase "Lord Jesus" over and over. This phrase scared him thereafter. A recurrent dream, also involving a dark hole, haunted Jung for years.

> I ran forward and peered into it . . . I saw a stone stairway . . . At the bottom was a doorway . . . closed off by a green curtain . . . I pushed it aside [and] saw a rectangular chamber . . . a red carpet ran from the entrance to a low platform. On this platform stood a . . . golden throne . . . Something was standing on it . . . It was a huge thing, reaching almost to the ceiling. . . . It was made of skin and flesh, and on the top was something like a rounded head with no face and no hair. On the very top of the head was a single eye, gazing motionlessly upward (Lebowitz, 1990, p. 13).

One can only wonder whether the obvious phallic symbolism of this dream so intrigued Jung that it lead him to Freud's door.

Partly because his mother was absent for a time—possibly confined to a mental hospital—Jung spent much of his youth by himself, in "extreme loneliness." He comforted himself by talking out his innermost thoughts to a small mannequin he had carved and secreted away under the floorboards of the family's "forbidden attic" (Jung, 1963, p. 42).

> I am a solitary, because I know things and must hint at things which other people do not know, and usually do not even want to know. Loneliness does not come from having no people about one, but from being unable to communicate the things that seem important to oneself, or from holding certain views which others find inadmissible (p. 356).

Following medical training at the University of Basel, Jung became aware of Freud's work and began to defend him against critics (Wehr, 1989). When Jung's *Studies in Word Association* was published in 1905, he sent a copy to Freud, only to be informed that the famous psychoanalyst had, "out of impatience," already acquired a copy. Freud's blunt message arrived in April of 1906. Seven years later, the two had exchanged 350 letters. Freud had looked on Jung as heir apparent to the psychoanalytic throne. Had Jung succeeded Freud, an intolerant world would have been assured that psychoanalysis was not a "Jewish movement." Around the time Freud ended their relationship, Jung experienced a period of soul-searching and psychological upheaval. Visions of apocalypse overwhelmed him. "I saw a monstrous flood covering all the northern low-lying lands between the North Sea and the Alps. . . . I realized that a frightful catastrophe was in progress. I saw the mighty yellow waves, the floating rubble of civilization, and the drowned bodies of uncounted thousands. Then the whole sea turned to blood" (Wehr, 1989, p. 41). That was October 1913. The next year, World War I broke out.

The "bloody war" premonition must have shaken Jung, because it was followed by, in his words, a struggle with the "building blocks of psychosis" (p. 44). The turmoil within him would not cease. His mind was flooded with images, many of them mythological symbols and figures. One day, when gripped with the feeling that he was in the "land of the dead," Jung glimpsed two human forms (p. 45). One was an elderly sage, "Elijah," and the other was a blind, seductive beauty who called herself "Salome." It was the beginning of his unique conception of the unconscious.

Jung's View of the Person

Jung and Freud did share ideas and even theoretical concepts. Like Freud, Jung wrote about the psyche, ego, consciousness, and unconsciousness. Jung's theory included analogies to id and "insight." Their theories even shared some of the same shortcomings. But the common ground ended there. Jung threw out Freud's definitions of the concepts they shared and substituted his own. Further, Jung viewed dream content quite differently than did Freud. He also believed that the human organism's physical and psychological functions were more *teleological*—characterized by purpose—than did Freud: "Life is teleology par excellence; it is the intrinsic striving toward a goal, and the living organism is a system of directed aims which seek to fulfill themselves" (Jung, quoted in Rychlak, 1981, p. 196). Finally, Jung's rejection of Freud's sexualism guaranteed that his theory would be fundamentally different.

Jung's orientation to people was different not only from Freud's but also from that of other theorists covered in this book. Freud was authoritarian as a therapist in comparison to Jung, who sometimes participated in therapy sessions as a partner with the patient, much like Carl Rogers. Freud never did, but he would allow patients to "free associate." In contrast, Jung frequently offered less freedom during association sessions and, in some ways, provided more structure. On some occasions, Jung would even suggest what patients should think and talk about.

Jung's trust in people's ability to contribute to their own "cure" is seen in his suggestion that they "self-analyze." His greater trust in other points of view was reflected in his occasional use of other people's ideas and methods. Further, he felt that people's minds were not limited by the size of their craniums, but could expand beyond their skulls into the mental spaces of other people. He believed that there is connectedness between the minds of people and that minds could communicate with other minds. In addition, as implied by Jung's claims to have anticipated "detonations," minds can communicate with nonhuman entities. Little wonder that Jung was labeled a "mystic," which lowered his status among colleagues, but may have raised it among the public.

Perhaps the label "mystic" was not entirely misapplied. Despite the existence of Christian religious figures among his ancestors, Jung may have felt ideologically closer to the Eastern religions. Oriental religious notions of transcendence above materialism and reincarnation resonated with Jungian thought. In fact, a comparison of Nesbett's (2003) assessment of East Asian modes of thought and Jung's ideas shows the two coincide rather well.

To Jung, humans are multifaceted beings who, if they wish to be whole beings, have to accept all aspects of themselves, the unsavory as well as the pristine, the selfish as well as the altruistic, and the physical as well as the spiritual. We have to reconcile the opposing forces in our psyches. In fact, the very essence of human mentality is the clash of opposites. Jung believed that, for every facet of our mental life, there is a contrasting face. In every male there is femaleness; in every female there is maleness. Consciousness opposes unconsciousness and feeling opposes thinking. A nonviolent person will dream of violence; a chaste person will dream of sexual wantonness. If we acknowledge these opposing forces and coordinate their expression, we can become fulfilled, complete people who can relate more fully to others and to realms of experience that are beyond our restricted and meager physical reality. Further, not only is this view consistent with Eastern modes of thought, Africans often cast reality in terms of opposing sides. In "The Half Boy," an African tale, a right-side-only boy encounters a left-side-only boy and they tumble into a river as they fight. They emerge as a whole boy and return to their village, where their completeness is celebrated (this story is courtesy of G. Kwame Scruggs). Thus, opposing sides can unite, which is also a Jungian theme.

Basic Concepts: Jung

Consciousness and Unconsciousness

For Jung, unconsciousness refers to two distinct entities. His **personal unconscious,** which "is made up essentially of contents [that] have at one time been conscious but which have disappeared from consciousness through having been forgotten or repressed . . . ," did bear some resemblance to Freud's unconscious (Jung, 1959a, p. 42). Each individual's personal unconscious is constituted by experiences occurring during his or her lifetime. However, he devoted a lion's share of his attention to the **collective unconscious,** a storehouse of ancestral experiences dating to the dawn of humankind and common to all humans. This unconscious belongs to the collective, not just to a single person. It has "never been in consciousness, and therefore [has] never been individually acquired, but owe[s its] existence exclusively to heredity" (p. 42).

Jung's conception of the collective unconscious crystallized as he pursued scholarly interests in a variety of fields: archeology, history, religion, mythology, and even the long-discredited predecessor to chemical science, alchemy. In addition, his affinity for anthropology led him to the United States for explorations of American Indian culture. During these pursuits he was struck by the remarkable consistency with which certain themes emerged from a colossal array of cultures, religions, literary works, and art forms. Despite differences in time, geography, culture, and historical development, people everywhere seemed to express their life experiences in highly similar ways in terms, attitudes, ideas, feelings, actions, fantasies, and dreams. Jung saw much of human experience as being communicated through common, age-old symbols, artistic figures, myths, legends, fairy tales, and folklore. These images would crop up century after century, even among cultures isolated from those that had previously displayed them. Jung attributed the consistent appearance and reappearance of these ancient motifs and figures to the mechanisms of the collective unconscious. In a series of 1937 lectures at Yale University, Jung asserted that religion comes from the collective unconscious (Kim, 2002). In addition, the core of religion is not "doctrine, creed, or traditions, but religious experience" (p. 421). Putting these two ideas together, religion comes from the believers' internal experience, not from external institutions. The collective unconscious stimulates internal experiences that are expressed in religious beliefs and practices. In normal people, these expressions are at most merely cast in terms of institutionalized religious doctrine. Religious experience happens to people because elements of the collective unconscious seize them, not because of their own volition. Jung saw viable, beneficial religion as fluid and dynamic, not static and rigid. In anticipation of modern events like the September 11, 2001, terrorist attacks and their aftermath, he condemned the absolutism of extreme religious dogmatism. Historically, religious extremism has fueled the persecution of one religious sect by another and violence against anyone who deviates a millimeter from extremists' views.

Like Freud, Jung wrote of a **psyche,** or total mentality, all of consciousness and unconsciousness. But **ego** is what one thinks of oneself, the genuine "me," and is the "centre of the total field of consciousness" (Jung, 1959b, p. 3). While not Freud's servant of unconscious urges, the ego does have communion with the collective unconscious.

That Jung's ego is not entirely equivalent to consciousness is confirmed by the existence of another facet of consciousness, **persona,** or mask, the identities we assume because of the socially prescribed roles we play. Jung wrote:

> Every calling or profession . . . has its own characteristic persona. It is easy to study these things nowadays, when the photographs of public personalities so frequently appear in the press. A certain kind of behavior is forced on them by the world and professional people endeavour to come up to these expectations. Only the danger is that they become identical with their personas, the professor with his text-book, the tenor with his voice (Jung 1959a, pp. 122–123).

Rychlak (1981) dubbed persona the "collective conscious" because we all share knowledge of the prescribed behaviors that are associated with the various roles people play. In a sense, personas are stereotypes associated with various roles: the dumb jock, the nerdy student, the straightlaced accountant.

Consciousness and unconsciousness may be welded into a unified whole by the development of the **self,** the "total personality," the unifying core of the psyche that ensures a balance of conscious and unconscious forces (Jung, 1959b, p. 5). This balancing is also typical of East Asian thought (yin and yang; Nisbett, 2003). When properly and fully developed, self is a fulcrum located at the center of the psyche, balancing conscious and unconscious like the centered device that balances the playground teeter-totter. However, the self is a potentiality that may not become actual. In the poorly developed self, the balance of the conscious and unconscious is disrupted. The result could be various psychological ills.

Jung often wrote in terms of balancing opposing forces or opposites. Like Freud, he referred to **libido**—psychic energy—which he imbued with less sexual meaning than Freud. Libido is subject to the principle of **equivalence**—energy consumed to accommodate one intention, "be benevolent," is balanced by energy fueling an opposite intention, "be hostile." **Entropy** is the equalization of differences in order to bring about a balance or equilibrium. Balancing maleness with femaleness is an example. Box 3.1 shows that Jung was very much in tune with diversity.

Archetypes

The contents of the collective unconscious are called **archetypes** or ancient types, pre-existent forms that are innate and represent psychic predispositions that lead people to

BOX 3.1 • *A Theory That Revels in Diversity*

If there is a virtue that Jung's theory exudes, it is panculturalism. Jungian psychology applies to all cultures. If it were to favor some cultures more than others, it would be drawn to the pejoratively labeled "primitive" cultures. People indigenous to various areas of the world, such as American Indians and Australian Aborigines, who have somehow managed not to be assimilated, may be regarded as closer to the basic humanity embedded in the collective unconscious. The artifacts of their cultures as well as their rituals and customs reflect more openly and clearly such basic human themes as an awestruck reverence for nature, the life/death/rebirth cycle, and the transitions of every human life. In contrast, it would not favor so-called "civilized" cultures, as these more recent cultures have submerged or lost contact with ancient propensities and expressions.

Given Jungian theory's recognition of each culture's uniqueness, as well as the commonality of cultures, participants in any culture could embrace Jung's ideas as a means of communication with their culture. People of African heritage could examine Egyptian culture in search of its unique expressions of all humanity's basic themes. Does the perfect geometry of the pyramids reflect the inherent attraction of humans to numerical precision? G. Kwame Scruggs (personal communication, 2003) believes that Jungian ideas help illuminate African modes of thinking. People of American Indian heritage could examine the ancient Pueblos of the Southwest for implications regarding humans' sense of community. Those of Chinese ancestry could examine the recently unearthed precise ranks of ancient horsemen for evidence pertaining to the orderliness of human relations. People of Northern European ancestry could investigate their Viking past for evidence of humans' need to explore beyond the confines of their own locales.

apprehend, experience, and respond to the world in certain ways (Jung, 1959a). Jung believed that the existence of archetypes is due exclusively to heredity. Therefore, the mind of the newborn infant is not a tabula rasa, or blank slate, but is imprinted with forms from the past experience of humans. What is inherited are not specific ideas or images but predispositions to recognize and appreciate certain general ideas and images. They are potentials rather than actuals. They often may be cast in terms of human or animal forms, but many are most accurately perceived by the mind's eye if pictured as nonliving symbols, such as numbers representing "order." They may be thought of as magnets that attract ancestral experiences that all relate to a common theme. For example, the mother archetype draws together ancient experiences common to all humans such as nurturance, warmth, love, protection, and others related to motherness.

One prominent archetype comes as close to Freud's id as Jung gets. The **shadow** is the underside of the personality, the inferiorities of the person that are emotional in nature and too unpleasant to willingly reveal (Jung, 1959a). Jung believed that the shadow is a moral problem for the ego because it may resist moral control. This resistance may be bound up in projection—a person sees some of her or his unsavory qualities in other people. From an African perspective, this kind of projection may be rather common (G. Kwame Scruggs, 2003, personal communication). Jung was sometimes evasive when writing about the shadow. Although he refused to clearly indicate that its contents included Freud's primitive biological instincts, it does apparently contain the physical urges. However, there is more to it. The shadow is manifested as the crude, bumbling, immature, incomplete side of us. It is the worst of us; it is what causes us to do what we do when "the devil made us do it." But the shadow is important. If the self is to evolve from potential to actual, it must fully acknowledge and deal with the contents of the shadow, as well as the ego and persona.

The archetype **anima** is the representation of woman in man. It is the accumulation of men's ancestral experiences of relating to women. Jung conceived of this archetype in terms of genetics as it existed in his day. "It is a well-known fact that sex is determined by a majority of male or female genes, as the case may be. But the minority of genes belonging to the other sex does not simply disappear. A man therefore has in him a feminine side, an unconscious feminine figure—a fact of which he is generally quite unaware" (Jung, 1959a, p. 284). **Animus** is the corresponding man in woman. It is a constellation of ancestral experiences concerning women relating to men. Anima is to Eros (sexual allure) as animus is to Logos (rational thinking). In women, animus may "show up" in argumentativeness, opinionatedness, and insinuation. In men, anima may appear in the form of faithlessness, sentimentality, and resentment. When the two archetypes "meet," they clash: "the animus draws his sword of power and the anima ejects her poison of illusion and seduction" (Jung, 1959b, p. 15). Ageless assumptions about differences between the genders are evident in these archetypes. Also implied is the more modern assumption regarding the prevalence of androgyny: a mix of masculinity and femininity exists within many, maybe most, people.

The result of a man's anima meeting a woman's animus can be humorous. Initially the man, under the influence of anima, may be seductive. When the woman, at the behest of animus, counters with arguments, he may become resentful. In turn, she may make insinuations. According to Jung, "no man can converse with an animus for five minutes without becoming the victim of his own anima. Anyone who still had enough sense of humour to listen objectively to the ensuing dialogue would be staggered by the vast number of commonplace, . . . misapplied truisms [and] cliches . . . " (p. 15). On the positive side, anima gives men a sense of relatedness to others that may help them interact with people more smoothly. Animus provides women with the capacity to reflect and deliberate, which may help them understand their natural surroundings. By extrapolation, it seems reasonable to assume that the presence of woman in man and man in woman allows each to better understand the other.

While Jung believed that there may be an indefinite number of archetypes, he focused on several in addition to shadow, anima, and animus. Table 3.1 lists a sample of these and some Japanese archetypes.

Jung likened the process by which archetypes affect us to the experience of "love at first sight." Love "can suddenly seize you." Imagine that a person has been carrying "a certain image" of a potential partner, without necessarily knowing it. Another person then appears who fits that inner image and "instantly you get the seizure; you are caught" (Jung, quoted in Evans, 1964, p. 51). Archetypes may seize you in a similar fashion. You may find yourself in their clutches when you are strolling through a museum and happen on a suit of armor that was worn by a medieval warrior. One may sink its talons into you as you show unusual interest in a pregnant woman. You may experience the vise-like grip of an

TABLE 3.1   *Some Jungian and Japanese Archetypes*

Name	Qualities
Jungian Archetypes	
Trickster (also clown)	Characterized by unconsciousness and ability to change forms
Child	Beginning and the end; invincible
Mother	Sacred motherness (as in the Virgin Mary)
Father	Dynamism, form and energy; like the cerebrum
Wotan	Warrior-god
Animal	Horse or snake
Quarternity	Squared circle with cross: fourfold division of ideal completeness
Order	Number; the numbers 3, 4
Hermaphrodite	Union of opposites
Japanese Archetypes	
Lion	Pride
Monkey	One's children
Sheep	Friendship
Cow	Basic needs
Horse	One's passion

archetype when you gaze at a symbol rendered in stone or wood—such as a representation of the quarternity—even though you have never encountered it before. It will be déjà vu: you will feel that you have been there before. Indeed, Jung would say you have, or rather your ancestors have. Thus, the roots of your shared experience are embedded in your collective unconscious in some archetypal form.

Jung (1978) speculated that twentieth-century interest in saucer-like unidentified flying objects (UFOs) may reflect the workings of the archetype for wholeness or totality. He noted that the sightings of flying saucers were frequent toward the end of World War II, a time of intense conflict and strife. The psychic basis of these sightings is a splitting apart. The opposite of splitting apart is wholeness, as symbolized by a **mandala** or magic circle, a round object often including an inner spiral that draws the eyes to the center of its surface. Wholeness, as opposed to fragmentation, is the basis of East Asian thought (Nisbett, 2003). Therefore, the "many thousands of individual testimonies" involving round flying bodies illustrate how the collective unconscious seeks to bring about order and "heal the split in our apocalyptic age by means of the symbol of the circle" (Jung, 1964, p. 285). UFOs are often reported as luminous disks that come from another planet (the unconscious) and contain strange creatures (archetypes) (Hall & Nordby, 1973).

Archetypes are not merely invoked to explain perceptions of alien presence. They creep into even the most modern expressions of culture, including the movies. James Iaccino (1994) has produced an enjoyable and edifying book on archetypes in horror movies. His argument seems to be that the horror movie genre is inspired by, even founded on, archetypes and would not exist without them. Examples are plentiful. Mother archetypes are often the theme of horror movies. In *Aliens,* "a gigantic Queen Bee protect(s) her revolting larvae" (p. 5). The mother archetype also rears its sometimes ugly head by forming the core of a "mother complex" that, in turn, plagues a movie's central character. Norman Bates, of the classic *Psycho* movies, is an outstanding example. Manifestations of the "invincible" child archetype abound as well. *The Exorcist, Omen,* and *Children of the Corn,* as well as other Steven King works, center on children possessed by evil and endowed with the power to make the devil reign. Shadow archetypes in movies are so numerous that Iaccino breaks them down into categories. He places Dr. Jekyll and Mr. Hyde in a category of disguised forms. Here the shadow is masked, but reveals itself periodically (often when the moon is full). Obviously, the various werewolf and Dracula movies fit: normal people become shadowy monsters after dark. Shadow motifs can become inflated to "bigger than big" (p. 8), a second category. *Them!* and the *King Kong* movies are examples. A more recent example is a sensitive man turning into the raging Hulk. Irrational, avenging shadows form the third class. Monsters in this case are the dead coming back to life. *Night of the Living Dead* and *Tales from the Crypt* show zombi-like creatures reeking havoc on the living.

Animus manifestations are seen in any movie wherein women show masculine aggressiveness and dominance. The *Bride of Frankenstein, The Cat People, Fatal Attraction,* and *She-Wolf of London* provide good illustrations. Anima, cases in which the woman in men comes out, are amply represented in the classic *Some Like It Hot* and the maybe classic *Mrs. Doubtfire.*

Other archetypes include the mad magician, fully exploited by the *Frankenstein* movies, and the wise old man, manifested by the Merlin character in the King Arthur movies and Obi-Wan Kenobi of the *Star Wars* series. Salome, the temptress, is well illustrated in

American Beauty. Finally, any of the shapeshifting movies would fit the trickster archetype. The *Howling* series is illustrative, as well as the more contemporary Mystique from the X-Men movies.

Archetypes seem present always and everywhere in the psyche. While predominantly emotional, they also have intellectual elements. However, no archetype has itself ever been present in any individual's consciousness (Jung, 1959a). Archetypes manifest themselves only secondarily, through symbols, images, and behavior. Their pure form is not concrete. They exist as potentials, similar to genetic dispositions. When they are manifested in consciousness, they are not themselves, but some representation of themselves that is manufactured by consciousness. For example, if one has a dream or daydream of the Christ Child, the archetype of the child has not entered consciousness. Rather, a manifestation of it has been developed by consciousness into a recognizable form. It is possible for archetypes to become so powerful that they give rise to a separate personality system, as sometimes occurs in certain mental disorders. Box 3.2 illustrates archetypes.

An archetype may manifest itself in one's experience and, at about the same time, in an external event. To explain this phenomenon, Jung introduced **synchronicity,** the simultaneous occurrence of two happenings that are correlated but have no direct cause-and-effect connection. Jung sought to understand coincidences and connections that are meaningful because each forms a pattern that cuts across chains of causally linked events. There is the appearance of communication between external and internal events, not causal connection. He used the concept of synchronicity to explain simultaneous occurrences of inner images and outer events relating to some archetype. Inner images may be manifested in dreams, visions, forebodings, and hunches. Outer events may include any observable occurrences from the past, present, or future. Here are a few everyday examples: "It's weird that you telephoned about the birth of your baby, because I was talking about babies with my wife"; "Grandfather had flashbacks of his World War I experiences just as he turned on the radio to hear that World War II had begun"; "I dreamed of the Devil last week and the next day a friend offered me her copy of *Faust.*"

Jung also linked synchronicity to *parapsychology,* a subfield of psychology in search of acceptable scientific explanations for extrasensory perception (ESP) phenomena such as mental telepathy and clairvoyance. That he made this connection is not surprising in view of the fact that parapsychological roots run deep in his family history (Las Heres, 1992). You may be experiencing ESP when you have the same thought as someone else (telepathy; "I was thinking about Christopher Reeve just as his death was announced") or successfully predict a future event (clairvoyance; you have a feeling that a relative is coming to visit and he or she shows up shortly thereafter).

Dreams as Messengers from a Wise Unconscious

Jung was highly respectful of dreams and fantasies. Dreams were among the primary tools used in his approach to therapy. "I have spent more than half a century in investigating natural symbols, and I have come to the conclusion that dreams and their symbols are not stupid and meaningless" (Jung, 1964, p. 93). He was convinced that dreams contained important messages from the "wise" unconscious. The task was to decipher these messages, a job that was much more straightforward than Freud thought.

BOX 3.2 • *The Case of Little Anna*

"About the time when Freud published his report on the case of 'Little Hans,' I received from a father who was acquainted with psychoanalysis a series of observations concerning his little daughter, then four years old" (Jung, 1954, p. 8). So Jung introduced his analysis of a bright little girl who, in anticipation of the birth of a sibling, was obsessed with what the casual observer might view as the age-old childhood question, "where do babies come from?"

Before Anna was told that her brother had been born, she was asked, "What would you say if you got a little brother tonight?" She promptly answered, "I would kill it." This "shocking" response might have been interpreted by Freud as indicating that Anna was showing natural jealousy of her new brother's anatomy, or "worse," if he were dead, maybe she could take his penis. However, Jung characteristically had a much milder interpretation: Anna did not mean "kill it" literally, but "just get rid of it," perhaps because she was jealous of the attention it would receive or maybe because it was something new and new "things" are nuisances with which one must cope.

Some of Anna's behaviors and experiences did seem "Freudian." She saw some carpenters working and then dreamed that one of them cut off her genitals. A game she played in the tool house involved "getting rid of mother." Seeing the gardeners and her father urinating outdoors made her very curious. Jung's response to the "sliced genitals" comment was a reference to Anna's curiosity regarding the purpose of her genitals. "Getting rid of mother" was merely to keep her from interfering with the children's games (they enjoyed defecating in the corner of the tool house, a practice that Mother wished to terminate). However, watching the men urinate had greater significance, but not in the Freudian sense.

To Jung, Anna was curious about the men urinating because she had a burning interest in how babies are formed, how they "get out" of mothers, and, more relevant to the present concern, what role fathers play in all of this. She wanted to know "what fathers do" that contributes to the birth of babies. The interest was not mere childish curiosity. Anna's collective unconscious was at work. The ancient, never-ending cycle of birth, death, and rebirth was manifesting itself.

Anna was fond of her uncle and once asked if she could sleep with him (think of what Freud would make of that!). While making this request she was clinging to her father's arm as her mother often did. Later she dreamed that she crept into her uncle's and aunt's bedroom and peeked under the covers to discover that " . . . Uncle lay on his stomach, and joggled up and down on it" (p. 31). Still later she frequently crawled into her father's bed, lay on her stomach—arms and legs stretched out—and joggled back and forth while exclaiming, "this is what father does" (p. 32). According to Jung, all this was in pursuit of knowledge concerning what "father does" in the process of birth.

Evidence of rumblings in the unconscious regarding the life/death/rebirth cycle were more clearly displayed when Anna asked whether her mother would die when the baby was born. This question suggests that death is exchanged for life. The cycle is also evident in a conversation Anna had with her grandmother:

"Granny, why are your eyes so dim?"

"Because I am old."

"But you will become young again?"

"Oh dear, no. I shall become older and older, and then I shall die."

"And what then?"

"Then I shall be an angel."

"And then you will be a baby again?" (p. 9)

To Jung, many childhood games have meaning related to the collective unconscious. When Anna stuffed pillows under her clothes and incessantly queried adults about "where do babies come out?" she was not just playing games or satisfying childish curiosity. Nor was she being controlled by psychosexual urges when she spoke of "joggling back and forth" in bed like "father does." She was under the spell of the collective unconscious.

Jung did not distinguish between "manifest" and "latent" content of dreams as did Freud. He wrote: "The 'manifest' dream-picture is the dream itself and contains the whole meaning of the dream. What Freud calls the 'dream-facade' is the dream's obscurity, and this is really only a projection of our own lack of understanding" (Jung, quoted in Rychlak, 1981, p. 246). In dreams, the symbols of the collective unconscious are undisguised, ready for interpretation. But interpretation may be difficult because of the complex and abstract nature of the symbols, each of which has at least two meanings. Nevertheless, one need not dig through some protective crust to get at those symbols. They are naked, out in the open, and in plain sight.

Compensation is the balancing of a conscious experience with an opposing unconscious representation, as in observations that a dream's meaning is often just the opposite of the person's conscious experience. In this sense, the collective unconscious represents the second of "two sides to every story," each side reflecting an autonomous function that compensates for the other. As you have seen and will see again, the balance of opposites is a constant theme in Jung's writings. Jacobi (1962) offers an example and interpretation of a compensation dream:

> Someone dreams that it is spring, but that his favorite tree in the garden has only dry branches. This year it bears no leaves or blossoms. What the dream is trying to communicate is this: Can you see yourself in this tree? That is how you are, although you don't want to recognize it. Your nature has dried up, no green grows within you. Such dreams are a lesson to persons whose consciousness has become autonomous and overemphasized. Of course the dreams of an unusually unconscious person, living entirely by his instincts, would correspondingly emphasize his "other side." Irresponsible scoundrels often have moralizing dreams while paragons of virtue frequently have immoral dream images (p. 76).

Another type of message is **prospective,** or anticipatory, through which dreams may "foretell" future events and outcomes. My closest friend dreamed he was riding a bicycle, with his brother on the handlebars, when a hole suddenly opened in the street, toppling both of them. Two days later, the mishap of the dream occurred in real life. Jung's favorite example illustrates how dreams may prepare a person for the future . . . if they pay attention to dream-meaning. A friend of Jung's described a dream about climbing a steep mountain and experiencing exhilaration on reaching the top. When Jung advised caution in the future, the friend scoffed. Later he fell to his death during a climb.

Personality Typology

Two Psychological Attitudes: Extraversion and Introversion. After 20 years of observing people "of all classes from all the great nations," Jung theorized that human beings tend toward one of "two fundamentally different general attitudes," extraversion and introversion (Jung, 1921/1971, p. 549). He defined **attitude** as "a readiness of the psyche to act or react [to experience] in a certain way" (p. 414). He defined **type** as a habitual attitude, or a person's "characteristic way."

According to his theory (1921/1971), **extraversion** is an "outward-turning" of libido that involves a positive movement of interest away from one's inner experience toward outer experience. The extravert is characterized by interest in the external object, responsiveness, and a ready acceptance of external happenings, a desire to influence and be influenced by events, a need to join in . . . the capacity to endure [and even enjoy] bustle and noise of every kind . . . constant attention to the surrounding world, the cultivation of friends and acquaintances, none too carefully selected, and . . . a strong tendency to make a show of oneself (p. 549).

Introversion is an "inward-turning" of psychic energy and involves a negative movement or withdrawal of subjective interest away from outer objects and toward one's inner experience. Jung, a well-documented (Dolliver, 1994) and self-acknowledged introvert, believed that introverts have more problems with social relations than extraverts (Lebowitz, 1989). The introvert

holds aloof from external happenings, does not join in, has a distinct dislike of . . . [being] among too many people. In a large gathering he feels lonely and lost. The more crowded it is, the greater becomes his resistance. . . . He is apt to appear awkward . . . [and] inhibited . . . His own world is a safe harbour, a . . . walled-in garden, closed to the public and hidden from prying eyes. His own company is the best. He feels at home in his world, where the only changes are made by himself. His best work is done with his own resources, on his own initiative . . . (Jung, 1921/1971, p. 550).

Four Psychological Functions: Feeling, Intuiting, Thinking, Sensing (FITS).   Jung's four psychological functions, when combined with introversion/extraversion, make eight possible combinations. **Feeling** evaluates how experiences strike us, whether they are suitable to us or not; it is a kind of judgment that is entirely subjective. Feeling imparts a definite value, of acceptance–rejection or of like–dislike. It also includes mood. **Intuiting** suggests where something seems to have come from and where it may be going. It is a kind of "instinctive apprehension" having an unconscious origin and no tangible basis. You display intuition when you understand something but cannot explain how or why you understand. **Thinking** determines what is present and interprets its meaning; it connects ideas with one another to form intellectual concepts or reach solutions. **Sensing** determines that something is present; it is the same as sensory perceptions of sight, sound, smell, taste, and touch. The sensation function is especially characteristic of children.

Personality Development

Individuation.   For Jung, the direction of personality development is **individuation,** "the process by which a person becomes a psychological 'in-dividual,' that is, a separate, indivisible unity or 'whole' " (Jung, 1959a, p. 275). It is a process of self-realization in which the totality called "self" is differentiated from the various parts of the personality, including the collective unconscious. It is the union of opposites represented by the archetype Hermaphrodite. It is confronting what we are not as well as what we are. Through individuation animus is balanced with anima and conscious with unconscious.

At first, people refuse to accept the unconscious, "projecting" it outside the self, onto others. But later it may become an integral part of their personalities. In this process, personality development is expressed through the archetypes, as people come to terms with each (Hogan, 1976). The proposed steps are as follows: (1) the persona dissolves when the person recognizes the artificiality of society's goals; (2) the shadow is integrated with other psychic units when there is awareness of one's selfish and destructive "dark side"; (3) acceptance of the anima or animus is achieved by recognition of opposite-sex components in one's personality; and (4) commitment to an archetype that is symbolic of spiritual or creative meaning allows one to tackle the final stage of individuation.

The process of individuation proceeds slowly, in stages that cover the entire life span. The fulfillment of individuation is "a favor that must be paid for dearly." Archetypes need to be recognized every step of the way, which is no easy task. However, the process is not simply one of struggling with the collective unconscious, but a continuing adaptation to it. In its ultimate adult form, individuation shows characteristics not found during childhood: definiteness, completeness, and maturity. As you will see, the notion of individuation of the self anticipates Carl Rogers's ideas about self-acceptance and Abraham Maslow's thoughts about self-actualization.

Four Stages of Life-span Development.   *Childhood* (0 to 13 years) is a relatively problem-free period that is dominated by instincts, dependency, and an atmosphere provided by parents (Hall & Nordby, 1973). Development of an ego occurs gradually, as does one's separation from the protective "psychic womb" of home that occurs when schooling starts. The infant has no real ego and is totally dependent on its parents. Its unconscious is collective, not personal.

Youth (14 to 21 years) begins with physiological changes at puberty and heralds "psychic revolution." Life's demands determine decisions and youth find it difficult to abandon illusions and fantasies of childhood. "Psychic birth" occurs as the psyche begins to take on its own character and youth establish vocational, marital, and community roles. A turning outward and engaging life is the hallmark of this time (Kelleher, 1992).

Middle age (40 to old age) begins the construction of a whole personality. Jung witnessed adult patients struggling with loss of zest and meaning. They oriented to inner, spiritual values, in contrast to the earlier external and materialistic inclinations. Maturity's main goal is achieving an integrated personality by relating conscious and unconscious aspects of the self (Kelleher, 1992). Contemplation becomes more important than activity. Opposite psychological processes, such as feeling–thinking, may be synthesized. This blending process involves a symbol of the spirit rising above worldly matters. For example, yin and yang may be seen as symbolizing female-like and male-like forces in nature. Appreciation of this symbol may lead to a synthesis of the male and female aspects of people.

Old age parallels childhood because of a return to submersion in the unconscious. The figure of a snake biting its own tail is symbolic of life coming full circle. Death is as important as birth. Belief in a hereafter was so universal that Jung considered it a manifestation of the collective unconscious (Kim, 2002; see Campbell, 1975). Perhaps psychic life does not end with bodily death because the psyche is reincarnated in some form. This theme is in tune with Jung's greater affinity for Eastern religion and its more wholistic, bipolar (yin and yang), and intuitive rather than logical orientation (Nisbett, 2003).

Evaluation

Contributions

Jung's Psychological Types.   Later in this book I will return to introversion/extraversion and the hundreds of studies that support this important contribution initiated by Jung. Here the concentration is on the combination of this central dimension with the four functions.

The most popular psychological measure of Jung's typology is the Myers Briggs Type Indicator (MBTI) (Myers, 1962), a widely used self-report questionnaire (Carlyn, 1977; Carskadon, 1978). Strong interest in the MBTI and issues related to it has continued (Harvey & Murry, 1994). Carskadon (1978) used the MBTI to predict the quality of contributions made by students to discussions in undergraduate psychology classes. He noticed that self-described MBTI extraverts made "very infrequent discussion contributions," whereas introverts made "frequent and thought-provoking contributions." However, this pattern seemed to be related less to the extraversion–introversion dimension than to the sensation–intuition dimension. At the end of the semester, students were rated on the quality of their discussion contributions. Students with high intuitive scores obtained the highest discussion ratings; high sensation scorers obtained the lowest ratings. By way of general advice to instructors, Carskadon noted, "Too many extraverts can give all action but little thought; too many introverts all thought and no action. Too many thinking types can use all logic and no human values; too many feeling types, all subjective values and no critical analysis" (p. 141). Box 3.3 discusses use of the MBTI today.

Jung's Analytic Psychotherapy.   Jung's approach to therapy was flexible. He used whatever methods seemed most workable with individual patients (Hall & Nordby, 1973). Freud's and other theorists' methods were used right along with his own (Rychlak, 1981). He was even known to send his Catholic patients to confession as he thought their knowledge of that "method" might lead them to use it effectively in ferreting out unconscious influences.

Jung "successfully pioneered short-term psychotherapy" and promoted the development of such self-help programs as Alcoholics Anonymous (Roazen, 1974, p. 284). Initially he might see patients four times a week. Then he would cut back to one to two hours a week. Finally, he would encourage patients to do self-analysis and would serve only as their consultant (Rychlak, 1981).

A pioneer in the use of projective tests, Jung often encouraged patients to express their experiences through drawings, a technique adopted by others, especially child therapists. His waking-imagery techniques are popular with professionals who work with terminally ill cancer patients (Achterberg & Lawlis, 1978; Simonton & Simonton, 1975).

Because Jung tended to see older patients than Freud (Rychlak, 1981), a main therapeutic goal was to promote individuation and development of the self. Often, however, these mature achievements were blocked by **complexes:** mental contents in the psyche that agglutinate or stick together like the clumping of red blood cells and eventually take up residence in the personal unconscious. For example, a person's strong religious faith may lead to the agglutination of religious beliefs into a complex that may overwhelm the identity of the person. Complexes may be thought of as clogs in the pipeline of the psyche that block commerce between the conscious and the collective unconscious. A frequent goal of Jungian analytic psychotherapy was to identify these complexes and "dissolve them"—in

BOX 3.3 • *The MBTI Today*

Researchers have added two functions to the four provided by Jung (Thorne & Gough, 1991): judging and perceiving. While feeling is evaluative in an emotional sense, judging appears to be evaluative in a more ideological sense. People high on "judging" tend to be conservative and moralistic and, at the same time, rather plodding, "work for its own sake" kind of people. The "perceiving" addition is more puzzling. In psychology, sensation and perception are part and parcel of the same thing: sensations are the elements that make up perceptions (Matlin & Foley, 1997). However, "perceiving," as it is used in the MBTI, is not positively related to sensing. In fact, people who are high on the perceiving function are rebellious, unpredictable, and desirous of rudimentary sensory experiences, such as touch, taste, and smell, while sensing people are somewhat the opposite (conventional, narrow, practical, and plagued with uncertainty).

I will use myself to illustrate the new MBTI, which has 16 combinations. I came out as E(extraverted) N(intuitive) F(feeling) J(judging). ENFJs are responsive as well as responsible and are concerned about what other people think and want. They are sensitive to other people's feelings and are at ease in a social situation. When I looked up "Joe Butt" with a Web search engine, like people who fit any of the combinations, I found myself in good company. He lists Dick Van Dyke, Abraham Maslow, and Abraham Lincoln as public figures who share the ENFJ orientation.

Using public figures is a good way to pursue the construction of case histories that illustrate some personality type. Take, for example, ENTP Bill Cosby. ENTPs are ingenious, logical, stimulating company, outspoken, dislike routine tasks, like to play the "devil's advocate," pursue one new interest after another, and are quick witted. The description fits Bill Cosby very well. He is certainly outspoken. Witness his crusade against the media's ubiquitous display of casual sex, violence, and disrespect for women. It is hard to imagine him doing anything routine. Instead he moves with ease from one creative project to another: from *I Spy,* a comedy thriller, to *The Cosby Show,* about parent–child relationships, to the *Cosby* show, which finds humor in the adventures of an older couple coping with retirement and their grown children. He is also clearly ingenious and quick witted. His performance at my university before an audience of parents and their college-aged children had people falling out into the aisles, they were laughing so hard. It was the single best comic performance I have ever seen. Apparently it was all right off the top of his head.

the sense of decentralizing them—so that the conscious and collective unconscious might better relate to one another. An illustrative case involves a mother complex (Jung, 1959a), the core of which might be the mother archetype. As the complex develops it migrates from the collective unconscious, the realm of the archetype, to the personal unconscious, where experiences with the individual's mother agglutinate to it. A boy with this complex may unconsciously seek his mother in every woman he encounters.

The existence of the mother complex may be confirmed by one of the first personality tests used in clinical settings, Jung's (1910) **Word Association Test,** which involves instructing people to say the first word that comes to mind after hearing each of 100 words from a standardized list (Cramer, 1968). People's associations with list words are then analyzed according to content, commonness or uniqueness, time lapse between list word presentation and patient's response, later recall, and accompanying behavior (facial expressions, postural shifts, voice changes, laughing, crying). Jung paid particular attention to emotional reactions. Strong reactions to the word *mother* would imply that a mother complex exists. That revelation, however, may do little to solve the patient's problem. For dissolution of the complex to occur, the patient must have *insight*. This critical event will likely require deeper probing all the way to the heart of the matter, in this case, the mother archetype. Other techniques are needed for this plunge into the depths of the collective unconscious.

Interpreting Dreams in a Series.   Unlike Freud, Jung generally saw dreams as having little to do with worldly concerns and much to do with the meaning of life. Jung's approach to dream interpretation was one of **amplification,** broadening and enriching dream or other image content through a process of directed association (Rychlak, 1981). Jung's interpretations were guided by images and analogies related to the dream's emotional nucleus or hub. His method differed from Freud's free association in three ways: (1) Instead of deducing meaning by working backward from present to past, Jung sought meaning by progressing forward, from present to future; (2) Jung provided dreamers with knowledge of universal archetypal symbols and meanings, orienting them in certain directions and actively guiding their interpretations (in our example, he would introduce the patient to symbols of "mother"); and (3) Jung offered his own associations to dream content, sometimes simultaneously engaging in the association process with the patient. The goal was to aid patients in deriving the meanings of symbols. Once acquired, those meanings led to dissolution of troublesome complexes. Aside from dream analysis, amplification could be helpful in wide-awake exchanges between patient and analyst. Jung's dream analysis was highly individualized, taking into account different personalities, circumstances, and contexts. For example, while, for some individuals, sex may signify lust, for others it may symbolize union with another human being. He enhanced patients' ability to analyze dreams by having them keep a dream-diary so they could pursue their own interpretations.

Jung was the first theorist to investigate large numbers of dreams in succession, or **dream series** (Jacobi, 1962). He did not find interpretations of single dreams generally representative of the dreamer, but he did find later dreams helpful in correcting misinterpretations of earlier ones. He also recognized that the meaning of dreams in a sequence is not necessarily chronological, but radial. Imagine a wagon wheel and the spokes that extend outward from its central hub. Different dreams would be represented by the spokes, but all would be related to the hub, which could be a complex of the dreamer.

Waking-dream Fantasy.   Another of Jung's useful techniques was **active imagination,** through which patients are encouraged to simulate dream experiences by actively engaging in imagination while fully awake (Watkins, 1976). For example, with her eyes closed, a patient is asked to imagine herself descending a succession of stairways (symbolically going down into the unconscious), and to report the sensations, perceptions, thoughts, and behaviors she experiences. She may find herself near water, perhaps a lake, the most common symbol of unconscious psychological spirit. To pursue our example further, "deep water" is a mother symbol.

Limitations

Many of Jung's concepts are not amenable to scientific testing. It is difficult to get a handle on a Jungian symbol because each symbol has at least two meanings. Further, some of Jung's notions seem mixed up with others, for example, the shadow and the trickster. In fact, his writing is sometimes perplexing: some concepts are never clearly defined—*complex* is a case in point—and others are defined in obscure fashion or defined differently in different writings—*individuation* is an illustration (Rychlak, 1981). Even the central concept, "collective unconscious," is sometimes treated ambiguously. It is not entirely clear whether there is initially anything in the collective unconscious except archetypes. Jung (1959a) does mention simple unconscious elements in the collective unconscious—such as fire and water—but does not make it clear whether these elements stand alone or exist only as parts of archetypes.

These problems are relatively minor compared to Jung's ideas concerning how the collective unconscious comes into being. Like Freud, Jung was influenced by Charles Darwin's predecessor, Chavalier de Lamarck, who believed that animals and plants can change their forms during their lifetimes in adapting to their environments, and these changes can be passed on to future generations. In other words, Lamarck believed in the inheritance of acquired characteristics: for example, if a seagoing animal loses its front feet, that condition might be passed on to future generations. Unfortunately Lamarck's ideas are not scientifically sound.

Broadly speaking, the "mind" (Psyche) can be thought of as composed of "ideas" (ideas can include thoughts and feelings relating to experiences). There are problems with associating "inheritance" and the "mind." First, inheritable traits are usually thought of as physical, but the mind and its contents are not physical. Second, "ideas" are acquired during people's lifetimes and, in view of the way the scientific community regards Lamarck's infamous notion, are not properly thought of as inheritable.

There is a strong flavor of "inherited ideas" in Jung's notion that the collective unconscious consists of elements that originated in the experiences of ancient humans and then were genetically passed to the present generation. According to Jung's view, ancient humans developed ideas resulting from their experiences, then these ideas became parts of their collective unconscious. He writes, "We must assume that [mythological types] correspond to certain collective (and not personal) structural elements of the human psyche in general, and, like the morphological elements of the human body, are inherited" (Jung, 1959a, p. 155). Jung knew the claim that any characteristic can be acquired during a lifetime and then passed on to future generations was discredited along with its advocate, Lamarck. In an attempt to defend the acquisition of collective unconscious content against the "acquired characteristics" charge, Jung argued that what is inherited are not ideas per se and certainly nothing concrete, but "experiences" that are merely dispositions. These dispositions may ready a person for certain experiences, but never are present themselves in any observable form (remember, archetypes appear in consciousness only as transformed representations). Yet, the problem remains: an experience, however defined, occurs to somebody at some point in time, and anything occurring during a lifetime would rarely if ever qualify as "inherited." Jung was never able to get around this problem. Accordingly, the stigma of "inheritance of acquired characteristics" remains branded on notions of the collective unconscious and may be the most serious weakness of Jung's theory.

At barely more than twenty years of age, Jung delivered several largely ignored lectures. In retrospect, these speeches appear to lay the foundation for his future theory and its reliance on unconventional science and mysticism (Grivet-Shillito, 1999). In these lectures, he endorsed *Spirtism*—the belief that living organisms, most especially humans,

Chapter 3

cannot be reduced to physical material. Humans have consciousness, self-consciousness, and yes, souls, which allow them to transcend their physical constitutions. According to Grivet-Shillito (1999), the endorsement of spiritism came directly from the Reverend Mr. Jung, Carl's father with whom he was strongly identified. Spiritism led to parapsychological experiences in which the youthful Jung willingly participated. Between 1895 and 1899, he "regularly attended séances in his family environment" (p. 93). There he participated in telepathy, clairvoyance, and in premonitory dreams and visions. During this period Jung also questioned the tenets of science, including its assumption that every phenomenon must be explained at a physical level and nothing at a spiritual level. Thus, Jung came honestly by his affinity for Lamarckism, parapsychology, mysticism, and other positions that were beyond the pale of science in his time and today.

Like Freud, Jung's character and intellectual integrity have been attacked. From time to time Jung has been accused of being anti-Semitic and sympathetic with the Nazi movement (Neuman, 1991; Samuels, 1993). He has also been accused of "lying" about the scientific origins of the collective unconscious (New York Times Service, 1995). Richard Noll, in his book *The Jung Cult: Origins of a Charismatic Movement* (1994), contends that Jung's account of the "scientific" origins of the collective unconscious is suspect. According to Noll, Jung claimed he collected his first objective data supporting the collective unconscious from the hallucinations reported by one of his patients during some 1906 therapy sessions. This patient had visions of the Sun Phallus: an image of the sun with an erect penis extending from its surface. A book published in 1910 confirmed that the Sun Phallus was indeed a symbol from humans' ancient history as told in mythology. Because the Sun Phallus Man, as he was dubbed, had his visions before the book's publication, Jung argued that his patient could have had no prior knowledge of the Sun Phallus. Thus, Jung claimed the Sun Phallus visions must have come from the patient's collective unconscious. But Noll charges that Jung prevaricated about some important facts. First, the patient was not his, but was in the charge of his student, Honegger. Second, Honegger did not begin working with the patient and recording the Sun Phallus visions until 1909. Third, the 1910 book was clearly marked as a second edition; the first edition was published in 1903, making it the possible source of the Sun Phallus Man's visions. Further, contrary to Jung's elitist belief, uneducated people like the Sun Phallus Man had access to the symbols of mythology through the popular press of the day. Given that these allegations are true, Jung based the existence of the collective unconscious on tainted evidence. While these charges are serious, they are neither as long-lived nor forceful as those lodged against Freud. Only time will tell whether they are sufficiently valid to be a matter of great concern.

The guru of American parapsychology was J. B. Rhine. The fact that Rhine and Jung corresponded regarding their beliefs has lead to speculations about the relationship between parapsychology and synchronicity. Norman Don's (1999) examination of an article concerning the meaning of the Jung–Rhine letters and their related writings led him to conclude that both parapsychology and synchronicity involve only correlation, not causation. If true, this conclusion would have been no comfort to Jung, who did not want his ideas mistaken for parapsychology, a mystical pursuit. Rhine would also not likely be pleased as his work seemed to show that telepathy, for example, involves real connections between the thoughts of people.

Conclusions

Jung's contributions to the psychology of personality have had less impact than those of Freud. Nevertheless, Jung is certainly one of the all-time great psychologists. Hagbloom and colleagues (2002) rank Jung 23rd overall, just above I. P. Pavlov, famous for classical conditioning of dogs. He was 50th on the journal citation list, 40th on the textbook citation list, and tied for 40th on the survey of psychologists.

If one lays aside scientific criteria and views Jung's theory as more philosophical, many of its problems evaporate. Regardless of the "science" question, it was Jung who introduced the timeless notion of introversion/extraversion—now a part of our language—and popularized the central idea "self." Further, as you will see in subsequent chapters, his openness to the use of many different kinds of procedures in therapy and his willingness to participate in therapy with patients set precedents that are still being followed today. More specifically, other theorists have endorsed Jung's assumptions regarding the holistic nature of human experience (Rogers, 1961), and the biological origin of spiritual meaning (Maslow, 1967).

Unlike Freud, Jung worked more with normal people and his clientele covered the full range of the lifespan, including adults undergoing midlife crises. Also, his disturbed patients were not limited to neurotics, but included some seriously mentally ill people. Thus, ideas derived from his clinical experience have the aura of more general representativeness than those of Freud. In addition, thanks in part to the great variety of patients contributing to his clinical experience, his theoretical notions are broader, spanning not just childhood and adolescence, but also adulthood and old age. As you have seen and will see again, there is support for Jung's concepts of introversion and extraversion, the four functions. A journal devoted to his view, *The Journal of Analytical Psychology,* has a U.S. as well as a British version.

Jung's 20-volume collected works contain many undiscovered insights. His orientation to the mystical and to the past history of humans may have more appeal to young people of today than to the youth of Jung's own time. That you can expect increased interest in Jung during the next century is evidenced by the observation that Jungian therapists are thriving and Jung's ideas are moving into the sphere of popular literature (DeAngelis, 1994). As proof of the latter, witness the success of Latina author and Jungian therapist Clarissa Pinkola Estes's *Women Who Run With Wolves,* an exploration of the wild woman archetype. Surfing the Web may also convince you of his resurgence. Few, if any, other theorists covered in this book are better represented in cyberspace.

Summary Points

1. Jung was born (1875) in Kesswil, Switzerland, the son of a minister, and was possibly the great-grandson of Goethe. As a lonely, reclusive boy, he had many visions. This mysticism was reinforced in his twenties and carried over into adulthood. His interest in Eastern religions matched his endorsement of East Asian and African modes of thinking. His break with Freud was traumatic, but was associated with creative visions and experiences. He believed in the balance of opposites. Jung's theory is pancultural and can be embraced by people of any culture.

2. Jung's view of religion endorses openness and flexibility and rejects fanaticism. Jung's personal unconscious is different for different people, but his collective unconscious is the same for all people. The ego is associated with consciousness. Persona is a mask that corresponds to one of society's roles. The self is the core of the psyche. The collective unconscious contains the archetypes.

3. Jung emphasized the archetypes shadow, anima, and animus. Archetypes can suddenly "seize you," and have been used to explain reports of UFOs. Archetypes are plentiful in horror movies and may be manifested in synchrony with external events. Synchronicity is a concept in tune with ESP.

4. Jung discounted Freudian explanations in favor of Little Anna's archetypical obsession with the cycle of birth and rebirth. Unlike Freud, Jung did not distinguish between latent and manifest dream content; the symbols of the collective unconscious and its archetypes are displayed directly in dreams. Dreams anticipate the future and compensate for a conscious process by manifesting its unconscious opposite.

5. Jung's most enduring contributions are extraversion/introversion along with his four psychological functions. Individuation is the process by which a person becomes a psychological "in-dividual." It differentiates the self from the rest of the psyche with the aid of the transcendental function. Jung postulated four stages of development.

6. Some research regarding Jung's psychological types seems to indicate clearer support for extraversion than introversion and stronger support for his four functions than for introversion/extraversion. Jung's analytic psychotherapy is unique in that patient and therapist have relatively equal status, therapy tends to be relatively short-term, and different techniques are seen as equivalent. The MBTI, with the addition of perceiving and judging, has become very popular.

7. Jung pioneered use of projective tests and helped popularize the concept "complex." Dissolving troublesome complexes was a main goal of psychotherapy. Jungian therapeutic and diagnostic techniques include the Word Association Test, dream and waking amplification, dream series analysis, and active imagination.

8. Jung's limitations include some concepts that are poorly or ambiguously defined, concepts that are mixed up with others, concepts that are defined differently in different writings, and unclear specification of the contents of the collective unconscious. The association of synchronicity with parapsychology further lowers his scientific credibility. This tendency to mysticism was founded in young adult Jung's endorsement of spiritism.

9. The most serious problem with Jung's point of view is that assumptions behind the collective unconscious have the flavor of "inheritance of acquired characteristics." Jung has been accused of prevaricating in regard to his claims for evidence in support of the collective unconscious. Jung's impact may have been less than Freud's because he stood in the "master's" shadow and was identified with mysticism. Still he is highly ranked among twentieth century psychologists.

10. Jung's innovations, such as extraversion/introversion and self, as well as his flexibility and contribution to others' theories, make him a major contributor. Undoubtedly, Jung's vast writings will yield new insights when they are more fully examined. In the meantime, his more mystical point of view may receive increased attention as time passes. He is even moving into the sphere of popular literature and the Web.

Running Comparison

Theorist	Jung in Comparison
Freud	Jung also used psyche, ego, consciousness, unconsciousness, id, and insight, but rejected sexualism, and the distinction between latent and manifest dream content.
Carl Rogers	Anticipated Rogers's concern with self-acceptance and equal-status relations with patients.
Abraham Maslow	Jung anticipated Maslow's concern for self-actualization.

Essay/Critical Thinking Questions

1. List and describe three personas that are not mentioned in this text.

2. Write a one-page story including the Japanese archetypes (Table 3.1).

3. Reconsider the case of Little Hans and reinterpret it in Jungian terms.

4. Write four items for a test of introversion/extraversion, two that would be endorsed by introverts and two that would be endorsed by extraverts.

5. Describe a series of your own dreams, then analyze them in Jungian terms.

E-mail Interaction

Write the author at b-allen@wiu.edu. Ask any of these or phrase your own.

1. Do you believe in parapsychology?

2. Do strange beings visit from other planets or from the collective unconscious?

3. Are you an introvert or an extravert?

CHAPTER 4

Overcoming Inferiority and Striving for Superiority: Alfred Adler

- Does almost everyone feel inferior, deep down?
- Does it matter whether you are born first, second, middle, last, or are an only child?
- Was Dr. Frankenstein spoiled as a child?

Alfred Adler
http://ourworld.compuserve.
com/homepages/hstein/
homepage.htm

Some of Freud's followers adhered closely to his beliefs (Deutsch, 1945; Fenichel, 1945). Others, like Jung, shared many ideas with Freud, but deviated from his position. Still others developed entirely new concepts. They questioned and even abandoned some of his tenets. These *neo-Freudians* include the theorists covered in this and two subsequent chapters: Alfred Adler, Karen Horney, and Harry Stack Sullivan. That Erik Erikson and Erich Fromm were also neo-Freudian is questionable because they ventured too far from Freudian thought. In fact, you may have difficulty seeing Horney, Sullivan, and, perhaps, especially Adler, as neo-Freudian. Although these theorists were influenced by Freud, they reacted against his ideas in developing their own. All abandoned Freud's emphasis on infantile sexuality in favor of parent–child relationships and social experiences.

Jung's split with Freud was painful and not really desired by either party. In contrast, Alfred Adler's fatal rift with Freud was more due to a clash of wills. When Adler brazenly refused to embrace Freud's sexual instinct, he came to be regarded as a renegade. Adler even saw Jung as deviating little from Freud's "sexualism" (Kaiser, 1994). At the urging of his close followers, Freud decided to force Adler out of the psychoanalytic camp. As both were editors of a key psychoanalytic journal, Freud wrote the journal staff a "him or me letter": he would resign if Adler remained on the editorial board.

Adler promptly quit and thereafter became the enemy. During the period that followed, some of Freud's communications with Jung were diatribes against Adler.

•

Adler, the Person

Alfred Adler was born in Vienna in 1870 to a middle-class Jewish family. Because he did not grow up in a Jewish neighborhood, he never developed a strong identity as a Jew. Accordingly, he converted to Protestantism in his youth and thereafter considered himself a Christian.

The fact that he was the second of six children was to have a profound effect on Adlcr. He felt that he would always be in the shadow of his successful older brother. Further, he was plagued with childhood illnesses: he suffered from rickets during infancy and nearly died of pneumonia at age five. Following a miraculous recovery, young Adler vowed to become a physician and save others. Later he was to theorize about being an invalid and conclude that it was an asset.

In a lecture given when he was more than 60 years old, Adler talked about the importance of his early physical ailments:

> I was born a very weak child suffering from . . . rickets which prevented me from moving very well. Despite this obstacle, now, nearly at the end of my life, I am standing before you in America. You can see how I have overcome this difficulty. Also, I could not speak very well early in my life; . . . [Now] though you are probably not aware of it in my English, I am supposed to be a very good orator in German (Stepansky, 1983, p. 9).

Because, during childhood, Adler was close to his father but rather distant from his mother, as an adult he was predisposed to reject Freud's belief that boys wish their fathers would disappear so they can possess their mothers.

Adler did not distinguish himself as a student. In grade school he was average. The University of Vienna did grant him a medical degree in 1895, but he failed to impress any professor enough to develop the close mentor–student relationship that Freud experienced. During this period, he flirted with Marxism and became something of a student revolutionary. Among the rebellious youths who shared his socialist inclinations was an intellectual from a wealthy Russian family who especially interested him. She eventually became Raissa Adler.

Adler began his medical career as a general practitioner. Among his typically impoverished patients were some who showed outstanding physical abilities such as acrobatics. That some of these strong performers had earlier suffered disability intrigued Adler: they, like himself, may have developed adult proficiencies to compensate for childhood deficiencies.

Adler had a strong social conscience. His tendency to support the underdog may explain his initial defense of Freud. Despite the irreconcilable differences they developed, Adler never totally rejected Freudianism. Even after his break with Freud, Adler recommended that his students become thoroughly acquainted with Freud's "meritorious" theory of dreams (Adler, 1964). Like Jung, he was more open to Freud than Freud was to him.

Unlike Jung, the formation of Adler's major ideas followed rather than preceded his split with Freud. It was after serving as an army physician during World War I that

Adler framed what is, perhaps, his most useful concept. During this period, he witnessed firsthand the suffering of wounded soldiers and the despair of children damaged by war. These human tragedies and some people's altruistic responses to them led him to theorize about *Gemeinschaftsgefuhl,* development of a deep-seated concern for others and a need to associate with them (Ionedes, 1989).

Adler endured rebellion among the socially conscious radicals he attracted. He also suffered the deprivations that came with serving the "common folk" rather than the well-to-do who gathered in Freud's waiting room. These difficulties increased his interest in overcoming adversity and his identification with victims of calamities. As vicechairman of the workers committee in Vienna, Adler was able to install mental health clinics in the thirty state-run schools of Vienna. These Adlerian facilities prospered from 1921 until 1934 when they were closed by the Nazis. Adler counted a drop in the Viennese delinquency rate during this 13-year period as one of the clinics' successes.

After enjoying a first visit in 1926, the United States became his home in 1934 when he and his wife fled Nazi-infested Austria. Here Adler became known as an "indefatigable lecturer" to parents and teachers, as well as a "constant advisor" to child-guidance clinics (Alexander & Selesnick, 1966). These characteristics clearly confirm his tendency to extraversion, especially relative to Freud and Jung (Dolliver, 1994). His devotion to parenting was reflected in the fact that two of his four children, Alexandra and Kurt, became psychiatrists in their father's tradition. Later you will learn that he had significant influence on many other personologists.

Adler's View of the Person

Basic Orientation

Adler refused to think of humans as collections of ids, egos, and complexes. He saw each person as a whole individual with aspects that are too interconnected for meaningful examination apart from one another. The lives of people were seen as flowing from immaturity to maturity without the discrete breaks that characterized Freud's psychosexual stages. From his perspective, people decide for themselves what direction their lives take, sometimes wisely, sometimes not. Whatever their direction, Adler saw them as striving for "perfection" as they conceived of it.

At first Adler emphasized natural feelings of inferiority that appear very early in life and require compensation thereafter (Ansbacher & Ansbacher, 1964). However, Eva Dreidurs Ferguson (1989) argued that Adler evolved toward greater emphasis on striving for power and superiority. Near the end of his career, "Adler made it explicit that humans as a species strive to belong and that the goal . . . is to contribute to human welfare" (p. 354).

Dinkmeyer and Sherman (1989) list five principles that might be regarded as basic Adlerian assumptions about people and their psychological functioning.

1. *All behavior has social meaning.* A group, such as a family, has its own social system, including methods of relating and ways to communicate power. "All behavior has meaning inside this social context . . ." (p. 148). The emphasis was psychosocial rather than psychosexual (Mansanger & Gold, 2000).

2. *All behavior has a purpose and is goal-directed.* Adler held that behavior is *teleological,* performed with a purpose, and that people are always moving toward a significant *goal* that is the key to understanding them.
3. *Unity and pattern.* Adler saw people as unified, indivisible wholes, each with a unique pattern of behaviors designed to reach a goal (Watts, 2000).
4. *Behavior is designed to overcome feelings of inferiority and to move toward feelings of superiority.* "We are continuously working from a feeling of being less, toward a feeling of being more. This is the striving for significance" (p. 149).
5. *Behavior is a result of our subjective perceptions.* "We actually create our script, produce, direct, act and act out our roles" (p. 149). We develop our own unique perspectives from which we see ourselves in relation to others.

These principles may seem to embrace conflicting goals. On the one hand, individuals strive to perfect themselves. On the other hand, they are supposedly embedded in and dedicated to the social group. How does one devote oneself to the group and at the same time pursue personal goals? Kurt Adler (1994) answers that, when a person develops well, he or she forms such a strong synthesis of self-interest and social interest that whatever is done for the group is also done for the individual.

Humanitarianism: Diversity as It Concerns Women and People Everywhere

A section of the *Psychologists for Social Responsibility Newsletter* was devoted to Adler's contribution to the cause of world peace and just treatment of all people. Rudman and Ansbacher (1989) declared that "Adler was a social activist in theory and practice. He opposed violence of all forms and promoted social interest in the individual and in the group. To him mental health implied 'socially affirmative action' . . . and social responsibility was fundamental to the practice of psychology . . . " (p. 8). Adler wrote:

> The honest psychologist cannot shut his eyes to social conditions which prevent the child from becoming a part of the community and from feeling at home in the world, and which allow him to grow up as though he lived in enemy country. Thus, the psychologist must work against nationalism . . . against wars . . . against unemployment which plunges people into hopelessness; and against all other obstacles which interfere with the spreading of social interest in the family, the school, and society at large" (Adler, quoted in Rudman & Ansbacher, 1989, p. 8).

In 1928 Adler, along with such notables as Mohandas Gandhi, contributed an article to *Violence and Non-violence: A Handbook of Active Pacifism,* edited by Franz Kobler. In this piece he proved to be ahead of his time in appreciating diversity. Believing that people who are different from those in power should not be subjected to oppression made him an early male advocate of women's rights. Rudman and Ansbacher (1989, p. 8) summarized his position on women: "He theorized that it was war, with its high valuation on physical strength, that led to the original subjugation of women, and he claimed that the 'inequality of women is greater in warlike countries.' " Adler's pursuit of social equality and acceptance of differences among people predated today's multiculturalism (Watts, 2000).

Though a socialist, Adler was vehemently anticommunist. His main reason for hating the Communists was the arrest of his daughter Valentine during the Stalinist purges of 1937 (she had fled to the Russia of her mother to escape the Nazis). In April of the same year, he wrote that "Vali" caused him sleepless nights and that he did not know whether he could endure the thought of her incarceration. Later, when he had exhausted all means of freeing Vali, he reported that he could neither eat nor sleep for worrying about her. At about this time he was on a trip to Scotland as a part of his 1937 speaking tour. While on an after-breakfast walk he suffered a fatal heart attack.

Basic Concepts: Adler

Developing Social Feeling: Society, Work, and Love

Alfred Adler's commitment to "individual differences" is seen in the label he affixed to his point of view, **individual psychology,** an attempt to conceive of a unique human being as an interconnected whole, biologically, philosophically, and psychologically (Adler, 1929/ 1971). Given this uniqueness and wholeness, the same situations, experiences, and life problems have different meanings for and effects on different people. While recognizing the existence of inborn differences among people, Adler warned against overstressing them: the important thing is "not what one is born with, but what use one makes of that equipment" (1956, p. 176). He viewed the basis of individual differences as more psychosocial than hereditary. The psychosocial factor of ultimate importance to civilization is **social feeling,** concern for the community and need to associate/cooperate with people (Adler, 1964).

The cornerstone of individual psychology is Adler's belief that there are three unavoidable tasks each person must address in life: society, work, and love. The pursuit of these tasks requires childhood preparation for development of **social interest (Gemeinschaftsgefuhl)**—individuals' efforts to develop social feeling (Rychlak, 1981). Although *social feeling* is a potential and *social interest* involves efforts to make it actual, Adler often used the terms interchangeably (Rychlak, 1981).

First, the relevance of social feeling to society is revealed in the individual's capacity to develop and maintain friendships, cooperate in school and in sports, and make a choice of a partner. Also the development of interest in state, country, and humanity is involved. Second, the individual must show an ability to be interested in work. Here social feeling takes the form of cooperative activity for the benefit of others. Individuals who perform useful work not only provide themselves with a livelihood but obtain a sense of what society values, for example, industry over laziness. It is through work that individuals assist in the progress of their developing community. Third, social feeling relates to love, the ability to be more concerned for a partner than for oneself. Here social feeling is focused on a task that requires the cooperation of two people, as both help perpetuate the human species by caring for offspring. Prerequisites of love include childhood preparation for a two-person task, continuing consciousness of the equal worth of both partners, and a capacity for mutual devotion.

Some 30 years ago it was proposed that "spirituality" and "self" be added to society, work, and love. However, Mansanger and Gold (2000), after noting that the proposed additions had not caught on and having examined them carefully, declared them possibly important for counseling, but not real "life tasks."

Style of Life

An individual's attitudes toward society, work, and love are summarized in a **style of life,** the individual's unique but consistent movement toward self-created goals and ideals developed beginning in childhood (Adler, 1964). The style of life is an original psychological orientation that contains the individual's relatively permanent **law of movement**—the direction taken by the person that originates in his or her ability to exercise free choice in fully exploiting personal capabilities and resources (Adler, 1933a). You have likely noticed the coincidence of style of life and *lifestyle,* a currently popular word that was probably suggested by Adler's key phrase. It is another example of how our language has been influenced by the major personality theorists.

Adler illustrated style of life by reference to a couple of pine trees, one growing in a valley and one growing on a mountaintop. Although they are of the same species, each shows a distinct style of life, with individuality "expressing itself and molding itself in [a unique] environment" (1956, p. 173). In human terms, the style of life is the medium through which each of us interprets the facts of our existence and through which our lives unfold. It dominates personal experience and guides dreams, fantasies, games, and recollections of childhood.

Style of life guides personality development. Personality results from the activity of the **creative power of the individual,** the process by which we each make original conceptions of ourselves and our world as we develop a style of life for pursuing the three great tasks (Adler, 1932). Thus, each of us is the sculptor of our personality. Childhood beliefs, typically developed between the ages of three and five, are particularly influential in the process that nurtures the developing style of life. Once these beliefs have become entrenched, experiences out of tune with them have little influence.

Future Goals versus Past Events

It is also during childhood that each person establishes a **prototype,** the "complete goal" of the style of life that is a fiction conceived as a means of adapting to life and includes a strategy for its achievement (Rychlak, 1981, p. 128). Adler also conceived of *fictional finalism,* which became virtually synonymous with *prototype* (Adler, 1933b). Eventually Adler discarded fictional finalism, although some of his modern-day followers cling to it (Watts & Holden, 1994).

A goal orients the individual's personality toward future expectations, not the past. It provides direction for promised security, power, and perfection, and awakens feelings consistent with one's anticipations. Freudian instincts, impulses, and childhood traumas pale by comparison to the importance of Adlerian teleology or purposiveness.

The attitude we adopt toward pursuing the three great tasks is necessarily reflected in our personalities. Because personality is a unity, the nature of our capacity for living life in common with others is manifested even in the slightest of our expressive movements. Our beliefs, misconceptions, social interest—or failure to achieve it—characterize all forms of personal expression, including our memories, dreams, bodily postures, and physical ailments. Further, an individual's style of life is best seen in new situations, especially those involving difficulties. This is because one's stylistic "gait"—whether it is best characterized as a trot, a canter, or a gallop—is more clearly displayed during crises than during untroubled times.

A type of psychological **shock** may be experienced when a person's fiction runs head-on into reality. It results in a narrowing of the person's field of action or path of advance, an exclusion of threatening tasks, and a retreat from problems for which the person is not prepared. Disillusionment, disappointment, and isolation may occur. In fact, Adler defines **neurosis** as an extreme form of reaction to shock, "a person's automatic, unknowing exploitation of the symptoms resulting from the effects of a shock" (1964, p. 180).

The general level of social interest is not high among neurotics, who likely have been pampered as children. At the lowest level, negative personality traits such as shyness, anxiety, and pessimism indicate a "defective inclination and preparation of the whole personality" in its relations with other people (p. 112). The goal of Adlerian therapy is to increase the neurotic's awareness of this lack of manifested social feeling. Adler found it helpful to bring out the "courage" and "optimism" aspects of social interest still existing within the neurotic personality.

Overcoming Inferiority

Adler believed that to be human means to feel inferior, insufficient, and helpless. Though this orientation is de-emphasized in his later writing, if one considers his writings as a whole, it is quite central. The universal human experience of inferiority generates a struggle for perfection. Individuals are "always possessed and spurred on by a feeling of inferiority," brought about by their perpetual comparisons of themselves with unattainable ideals of perfection (Adler, 1964, p. 37). As in evolution, there is a "great upward drive" toward perfection or a "compulsion" to carry out a better adaptation. In essence, all personality develops from **inferiority,** the persistent feeling that one does not measure up to society's ideals or to one's own fictional standards (1964). The individual's movement in life is from a minus to a plus condition. **Inferiority complex** is Adler's term for the consequences of an exaggerated, persistent form of inadequacy that is partly explained by a deficiency in social interest (Adler, 1964). Three childhood handicaps contribute to inferior feelings and a resultant lack of social interest (Adler, 1933a).

Inferior Physical Organs.   To Adler, an "organ" could be any physical attribute. His study of organ inferiority led him to conclude that feelings of psychological inferiority are due, in many cases, to physical limitations (Adler, 1907/1917). This is because children born with organ weaknesses are necessarily required to **compensate,** to overcome their weaknesses by striving to become superior in some way (Adler, 1929/1971). They may even **overcompensate,** bend over backwards to do or become whatever their weaknesses have denied them. The ancient Greek Demosthenes had frail lungs and a weak voice, yet he became a famous orator. Pianist Klara Schumann overcame childhood hearing problems. James Earl Jones (Darth Vader), Geraldo Rivera, and ABC *20/20*'s John Stossell all overcame stuttering to become noted for their fine speaking ability. Adler saw human development as "blessed with inferior organs" (1930, p. 395) because of the achievements that can be traced to the efforts aimed at overcoming physical inferiorities.

Parental Neglect: The Unwanted or Hated Child.   The neglected child does not experience love, cooperation, or friendship, and seldom finds a trustworthy other-person. Throughout life, problems are "too difficult" and problem-solving resources are "too limited." Neglected children may be described as cold, suspicious, untrusting, hard, envious, and hateful.

Parental Overindulgence: A Harmful Practice That Often Produces a Pampered or Spoiled Child.   Adler proposed *overindulgence* as an alternative to Freud's sexual interpretations of observations that led him to the Oedipus complex (Adler, 1964). Symptoms that have been attributed to the "unresolved Oedipus Complex" are rare and, when they occur, actually result from overindulgence by the child's opposite-sex parent. The basic pattern is one in which the pampered child is allowed contact mainly with the person doing the spoiling, thereby excluding others. The result of this pattern is a child who feels superficially superior and expects homage from others. The case history in Chapter 2 of the spoiled child who becomes a narcissistic adult fits well.

Striving for Superiority and the Superiority Complex

During the transition from emphasizing inferiority to stressing service to society, Adler wrote of **striving for superiority,** a universal psychological phenomenon that parallels physical growth and involves the goal of bringing about perfection, security, and strength. Specific paths to perfection differ in a multitude of ways, just as do the chosen goals. **Superiority complex** is Adler's term for an exaggerated, abnormal form of striving for superiority that involves overcompensation for personal weakness. Like other severe psychological problems, this one is partly explained by a deficiency in social interest development. The neurotic person may present a false front of superiority as a method of escaping from social difficulties. Normal people do not have superiority complexes. Their strivings for superiority are aimed at common ambitions for success, expressed through work, love, and cooperation in society. In this light, striving for superiority is a positive pursuit akin to "self-actualization" as discussed in the Rogers and Maslow chapters. By contrast, a superiority complex "invariably" stands in opposition to social cooperation.

Adler's theory has something to say about braggarts, people who may irritate us with their constant claims of superiority. Many of us probably assume that braggarts believe themselves to be superior. However, Adlerians would be inclined to a different interpretation. The more people brag about themselves, the more an Adlerian might see them as just compensating for unresolved feelings of inferiority. That is, braggarts may actually be people who feel inferior and are boasting to compensate.

"Low self-esteem" is a modern phrase meaning "feelings of inferiority." On the other side of the coin "high self-esteem" bears a striking resemblance to "superiority complex." Box 4.1 shows that Adler's "superiority" and "inferiority" notions anticipated some modern research findings on high and low self-esteem.

BOX 4.1 • *Self-esteem: May Not Be What You Think*

If one describes oneself as "happy, kind, loving, thoughtful, and helpful" one is using highly positive terms. Thus, high self-esteem is expressed. However, the description "sad, mean, deceptive, angry, and selfish" connotes low self-esteem. Until recently it has been assumed that high self-esteem is "good," and, therefore, everyone should have it. Allegedly, school administrators, especially those in California, have been taking this assumption so much to heart that teachers are encouraged to praise children no matter what they do. Former American Psychological Association President Martin Seligman caused quite a stir both within psychology (Polce-Lynch & Lynch, 1998) and outside of psychology (Begley, 1998) when he asserted that praising children to raise their self-esteem does *not* boost them academically or otherwise and may even be harmful. Several other psychologists stepped forward to support Seligman's contention.

Self-esteem expert Roy Baumeister (1996, 1999) suggested there is no evidence that low self-esteem is behind aggression. Colleague Ervin Staub (1999) agreed. Baumeister, Campbell, Krueger, and Vohs (2003) report that high self-esteem does not cause improved academic performance or interpersonal success. However, high self-esteem may contribute to happiness and may,

if properly qualified (e.g., girls only), act as a determinant of healthier lifestyles for some factors related to health (e.g., smoking). They also cite research results revealing no relationship between levels of self-esteem (high, medium, or low) and levels of aggression.

Both Baumeister (1996) and Barbara Learner (1996) argue that a disconnect between self-esteem and real accomplishments, such as occurs when children are praised for no reason, can generate vacuous self-esteem that can even be dangerous. When vacuous self-esteem is challenged, defensiveness or even explosive aggression can occur. It now seems clear that raised self-esteem should be based on real accomplishments. If the arenas for accomplishment are equally highly valued (for example, music, math, athletic, and artistic skills equally valued) it should not be hard to maintain children's self-esteem at reasonable levels. It is also clear that promoting high self-esteem based on empty praise should be abandoned.

Thus, vacuous "high self-esteem," based on nothing, is like the "superiority complex": neither entail real superiority as both are defensive reactions to perceived personal weaknesses. It's opposite, "low self-esteem," doesn't predict very much in the outcomes domain.

Family Influences on Personality Development

"Mother" is the most important family influence on personality development (Adler, 1964). Contact with her probably makes the largest contribution to the social interest of the child. Two tasks are involved. One is encouraging social feeling by providing the deepest and most genuine love and fellowship the child will ever experience. Another is spreading this connectedness, trust, and friendship to others in the form of displaying a cooperative attitude when interacting with them. Adlerian therapists perform these tasks for patients who are deficient in social interest. Fathers, who are second in importance, may contribute to their children's development by allowing them freedom to speak and ask questions, by being supportive, by encouraging the pursuit of personal interests, by avoiding ridicule and belittlement, and by not seeking to supplant the mother.

Third in importance is **birth order,** the child's birth position relative to other siblings (Adler, 1964; see Table 4.1). In addition to birth order in and of itself, Adler's theory ad-

TABLE 4.1   *Some Adlerian Hypotheses about Birth Order*

Birth Order	% of Population*	Hypotheses
Only child	5	The center of attention, dominant, often spoiled because of excessive parental timidity and anxiety
Firstborn	28	Dethroned from a central position, has negative attitudes and feelings toward the second child, and a passion for domination, but protective and helpful toward others
Secondborn	28	Actively struggling to surpass others, with success related to competition with the firstborn; restless
Lastborn	18	The most pampered (the smallest and weakest), not unhappy, able to excel over others by being different, often a problem child
Only girl/boy		Extreme feminine or masculine orientation

*From Simpson, Bloom, Newlon, & Arminio (1994); percentages do not add to 100 because a "middle-born" category used by Simpson et al. is not included.

dresses the impact of family size and sex of siblings on personality. He deemed it a "superstition" to believe that a given family situation is the same for each individual child. This qualification helps to account for cases for which circumstances may be psychologically similar for children in different birth order positions. Thus, it is not birth order itself that accounts for differences among siblings, but the psychological situation resulting from it. Table 4.1 summarizes Adler's view of birth order.

The "birth order" factor has been heavily researched in the decades since it was posed by Adler (Falbo & Polit, 1986). For example, reviews of the literature indicate a total of 391 studies on birth order between 1963 and 1971 alone (Miley, 1969; Vockell, Felker, & Miley, 1973). I recently searched the literature and found 1780 birth order references dating from 2003 on back in time. Birth order was also the sole topic of the May 1977 issue of *Individual Psychology.* After all these investigations, it is now clear that most of the differences, insofar as they exist, are between firstborn (or only) and laterborn individuals. Research suggests that firstborns and only children are higher than laterborns in achievement motivation and actual success. Such may be the case because their environment contains only adults, mature people who are capable of creating an achievement-oriented atmosphere. On the other hand, laterborns have an atmosphere that is less mature, because it is composed of children as well as adults (Zajonc & Markus, 1975). Thus, one is more likely to find firstborns rather than laterborns in the U.S. Senate or the executive board room. However, firstborns are not better in every way. For example, laterborns are less self-centered (Falbo, 1981).

Robert Zajonc and his colleagues have focused on the dilution of the home intellectual atmosphere by mixing laterborn children with firstborns and the adults who constitute the firstborn's mature environment. Zajonc and Markus (1975) related family size to intellectual development. Using data on nearly 400,000 Dutch 19-year-old males, they found larger family size detrimental to intellectual development. They explained this result by reasoning that each laterborn child added to a family of increasing size dilutes the intellectual atmosphere for all children. Further, the larger the family, the more compressed the spacing between children, which leads to a decline in average age of family members, and, in turn, a more immature intellectual atmosphere for each child. Large families immerse children in a laterborn intellectual atmosphere, one created by cognitively primitive people, a sharp contrast to the adult atmosphere that exists for firstborns. For example, if the intelligence level (IL) of parents is set at 100, the average atmosphere for the first born is 100 (100 [for mother] + 100 [for father] = 200/2 = 100). However, if a secondborn arrives when the firstborn is 9 months old (it's IL is set at 10), the intellectual atmosphere for the laterborn declines to 70 (100 [for mother] + 100 [for father] + 10 [for firstborn] = 210/3 = 70).

Despite the pessimism regarding birth order chronicled in earlier editions, since then, if anything, there has been an increase in birth order research activity. Researchers simply will not give up on the concept.

Some research results seem to support traditional hypotheses about birth order. For example, Knight and colleagues (2000) investigated the relationship between birth order and *connected knowing*, "knowers take the perspective of others in an attempt to understand their ideas," or *separate knowing*, "knowers distance themselves from the ideas of others, preferring to challenge and doubt" (p. 230). As many sources paint a picture of firstborns as somewhat disagreeable, independent, and self-sufficient, while laterborns are the opposite (e.g., Sulloway, 1996), firstborns were expected and found to be higher on separate knowing. Because Adler, Sulloway, and others view laterborns as more rebellious, Zweigenhaft and von Ammon (2000) predicted, and found, that students who had been arrested (some of them for protesting) were more likely be laterborns. In an interesting article on how learning can be specific to the context in which it occurs, J. R. Harris (2000) presents argument and evidence to support her position that birth order effects are specific to the family context. Laterborns, for example, act as Sulloway and others would expect while around their parents and siblings, but not in other contexts. The family context is where they learned to act like laterborns. This point of view would partially explain why birth order research results have been mixed and would save birth order by limiting its effects to the family context.

While these results may be good news for those who ascribe great power to the birth order variable, other outcomes may yet kill interest in research on birth order. Since Sulloway's (1996) best-selling book seems to have revived the traditional view of birth order, it has been under heavy scrutiny. Freese, Powell, and Steelman (1999) note that Sulloway's evidence comes from "historical data": he searched the historical record for famous first- and laterborn figures to see if they differed as expected. And they did. For example, Freud was a typical ambitious, high achieving firstborn, while laterborn Adler was a rebellious socialist and advocate for human rights. As should have been obvious, Freese and colleagues pointed out that Sulloway's "sample" was terribly biased: it was small and consisted of long-dead, elite public figures, such as Voltaire, Darwin, and Martin Luther. To make their point, Freese and colleagues examined the attitudinal record of nearly 2000 modern, ordinary people who participated in a national opinion survey. To sum across the many attitudinal variables they investigated with a representative and large sample of today's people, they found that firstborns were not more conservative and laterborns were not more liberal.

Other discouraging results come from Rodgers, Cleveland, van den Oord, and Rowe (2000), who noted that most studies supporting popular notions about birth order have been *cross-sectional:* a group of firstborns who were reared in various families are compared at the same point in time to a group of laterborns who are reared in a second, different set of families. Almost never are birth order studies *longitudinal:* the course of change in birth order effects is examined as more children are born within the same families. Rodgers and colleagues tested the Zajonc hypothesis that bigger families generate children with lower average IQ scores. They looked within families to see what happens when more and more children are added. Both the IQ scores of children and of mothers were examined. The Rodgers' group summarized their results straightforwardly: " . . . low IQ parents make large families . . . large families do not make low-IQ children" (p. 607). Guo and Van Wey (1999a, 1999b) found much the same thing when they also looked at longitudinal, rather than cross-sectional, data. By and large, these and the other studies covered here took spacing among children into account.

Thus, reexamination of the attitudinal and IQ evidence using longitudinal data shows that Sulloway's and others' beliefs about differences between first- and laterborns are not supported. What about personality and birth order? Beer and Horn (2000) noted that previous birth order and personality studies had confounded biological birth order with rearing order. All of the earlier studies had used children who were both biologically first- (or later-) born and reared first (or later), because the child subjects were the natural children of parents (none was adopted). Obviously, earlier researchers have believed that rearing position should affect the personalities of children (reared first or later), not biological position (born first or later). With the inclusion of adopted children who were all biologically firstborns, but were reared in various ordinal positions (first or later), Beer and Horn examined rearing position separated from biological position. If Sulloway and like-minded researchers are correct, scores on Cattell's 16PF should reveal that laterborns are more "warm," firstborns more "dominant," laterborns more "tender-minded," firstborns more "suspicious," laterborns more "experimenting," and firstborns more "conscientious." However, they were incorrect. Except for some evidence supporting the last-listed expectation, relationships between rearing order and personality traits were very weak and such was the case for both cross-sectional and longitudinal portions of the research. Despite these criticisms, Adler's ideas about firstborns continue to capture people's imagination, as seen in Box 4.2.

Evaluation

Contributions

Early Recollections: A Prediction of the Present.   Adler employed a simple method to assess aspects of people's lifestyles (Adler, 1956). **Early recollections (ERs)** indicate how a person views her- or himself and other people and reveal what the person strives for in

BOX 4.2 • *Frankenstein and His Monster Reconsidered: An Adlerian Analysis*

When R. John Huber, Joan Widdifield, and Charles Johnson (1989) took another look at Mary Shelley's (1965) classic novel about a brilliant scientist who creates life in the laboratory, they noted remarkably clear illustrations of Adler's major principles and conceptions. Huber and colleagues contend that Frankenstein was not a scientist interested in advancing his discipline and benefiting humanity who was victimized by laboratory manipulations gone wrong. Rather, he was a man overwhelmed with compensatory strivings for godlike superiority because of inferior feelings dating to his pampered childhood. Further, his "monster" began life with human qualities, including the desire to be a loved member of the community, and might have developed his natural propensity to social feeling had it not been for the neglect of his "father," Frankenstein. An examination of the two main characters in Shelley's misunderstood novel provides helpful illustrations of Adler's most critical concepts.

Victor Frankenstein: The pampered child becomes the adult seeker of grandiosity

For the first five years of his life, only-child Victor Frankenstein was the recipient of his parents' "inexhaustible stores of affection from a very mine of love" (Shelley, 1965, p. 32). He was his parents' "innocent and helpless creature bestowed on them by heaven," their "plaything and idol," and their "only care" (p. 32). When his parents adopted a daughter, Frankenstein was not threatened. His new sister was presented to him as his "pretty present." He came to regard her as a possession. During what was for him an idyllic childhood, Frankenstein had only his family and one friend, all of whom regarded him as the center of the universe. However, at maturity, having ventured forth from his privileged realm and arrived at the university, he felt immediately alienated from the other students, a sure sign of deficient social interest. Neither did he seek the help and cooperation of his professors. Frankenstein earned his own way into the halls of science. Throughout his early adult years, he yearned only for those who had

pampered him during childhood. Finally, the longing became so strong that he partially transferred his childhood universe to his new galaxy by marrying his adopted sister!

You may wonder how a pampered child harbors feelings of inferiority and resultant exaggerated strivings for superiority as Adler has claimed and as Huber and colleagues extrapolated to Frankenstein. Pampering may promote inferiority because coddled children do not recognize their feelings of inferiority, much less feel the need to struggle with those basic emotions. Rather, they respond to exaggerated attention by assuming their superiority and letting close relatives grapple with their problems. Consistent with these ideas, Frankenstein grew to adulthood laboring under the delusion that he was a superior being.

Then, suddenly, he was at the university, facing the shock of being surrounded by people who, by their inattention, challenged the fiction of his genius. His response to shock was withdrawal into plans to rise above all students, all people. Through the creation of life, Frankenstein expected to transcend mere mortals. Instead he suffered the fate of all those who are dominated by the superiority complex, self-destruction.

Frankenstein's creation: Unsupported attempts to develop social feeling yield monstrous results

In complete contradiction to movie depictions, Frankenstein's "monster" began life with clear signs of social interest. His "life" is a profound testimony to the truth of Adler's belief that social feeling is a potential common to us all that may or may not become actual. The "monster," whose strength and intelligence were extraordinary, showed the need for upward striving by immediately displaying an intense desire to learn. In particular, he strove to learn language, a definite sign of emerging social feeling. A still clearer mark of social interest was his need for companionship and desire to relate to others. He peered from his miserable hovel at the villagers as they passed by and longed to become one of them. When they were joyful so was he; when they were unhappy he was depressed. "The creation wept with sensitivity when he observed displays of affection, heard of injustices to mankind, or heard beautiful music" (Huber et al., 1989, p. 275).

Despite this evidence that social interest was blooming in the "monster," events began to remind him of his inferiority. When he visited a blind priest from whom he expected sympathy, all went well until others arrived on the scene and recoiled in horror at his appearance. It was the first time that others' abhorrence of his organ inferiority fully registered on him. When he saw his own image in a pool of water for the first time, he was able to understand their revulsion at the mere sight of him. The final blow was struck when "The Creation" read an abandoned copy of *Paradise Lost* and contrasted his own existence with that of Adam. Adam was loved; Adam had a mate; he did not. When he revealed the agony of his loneliness to his creator and pleaded for a mate, Frankenstein at first expressed intentions to sculpt a wife for him. But when the scientist began what was to be his second creation, he was overcome with guilt and concern. If the monster had a mate, they would have offspring that might terrorize the world. Was this concern a vestige of social interest? Huber and colleagues think so. Was his guilt a sign of his genuine affinity for people and love of community? The authors thought not. His display of guilt was merely an attempt to appear more sensitive and thoughtful than others.

Extreme strivings for superiority end in self-destruction

When guilt led Frankenstein to destroy his laboratory, and thereby end the possibility of a female creation, the monster realized that his "father" had abandoned him. At the same time, the scientist's rash act made him apprehend that the life he had created in his lab would visit catastrophe on the world rather than heap glory on himself. His creation, on accepting that his desire for companionship and membership in the community had been dashed forever, declared " . . . if I cannot inspire love, I will cause fear" (Shelley, 1965, p. 147). Truly there is no hatred so intense as that born of unrequited love. The enraged monster went on an unmerciful rampage. He stalked Frankenstein, leaving the mangled bodies of the scientist's loved ones in his wake. Finally, they adopted a mutual goal: destroy the other. In the end, Frankenstein's desperate striving to overcome inferiority due to a pampered childhood, and the monster's struggle to compensate for the repulsive appearance that constituted his organ defect, led to the demise of both. Each was a victim of failure to develop social feeling.

life, what he or she anticipates, and, more generally, his or her conception of life itself. ERs also index present attitudes, beliefs, and motives. That is, ERs are more important for what they say about a person as she or he is now than for what the person was like as a child.

Collecting ERs was dear to Adler. He would invariably ask patients for their first memories, which he considered a most trustworthy way of exploring their personalities. ERs are an introduction to personality that is closely tied to the individual's current style of life.

Adler's reliance on ERs reflects his special brand of determinism: *the present determines the past,* exactly the opposite of Freud's determinism. According to Adler, the individual's *current* style of life forces him or her to select precisely those events from the past that best represent its contemporary condition. One has little choice in the matter. Also, it makes no difference whether the events constituting an ER actually occurred as the patient reports them. Patients may report certain aspects of an early event, neglect others, embellish some details, and, perhaps, invent still other details, whatever is in line with their current style of life. Obviously Adler, unlike Freud, knew that recollections of early life were at least partly fabrications influenced by current circumstances. He anticipated the "false memory" phenomenon by arguing that current events can influence recollections of past events.

One of my earliest memories reflects selective and embellished recollection. I attended early elementary school in a Texas town of 800. My school had about two hundred students, first grade through high school, spread across several classes, many containing more than one grade level. One day during recess, I climbed a log that was leaning next to a window at about a 45-degree angle against a wall of a utility building. The log slipped and my arm rammed through a window pane. When I yanked it back through the window the jagged pane ripped a four-inch gash in my forearm. What did I recall when first asked "Where did you get that scar"? Not the pain, not the blood, not the fear. Instead, I remember being held up in front of the entire student body while they gawked at me and I smiled back. That day I basked in the warm glow of center stage.

Adler's reverence for ERs is seen in the following.

> Among all psychological expressions, some of the most revealing are the individual's memories. . . . There are no "chance memories": out of the incalculable number of impressions which meet an individual, he chooses to remember only those which he feels, however darkly, to have a bearing on his situation. . . . Memories can never run counter to the style of life (Adler, 1956, p. 351).

Sanitioso, Kunda, and Fong (1990) produced results consistent with Adler's belief that people's current conceptions of themselves influence their recollections of the past. These researchers first informed some subjects that it is better to be introverted. Others were told that being extroverted is better. It can be assumed that subjects in the first group would come to see themselves as introverted, and those in the second group would see themselves as extroverted. Then subjects read a message on a personal computer screen and pressed a key to signify "yes" as soon as they had a memory related to the message. Each message pertained to introversion or to extroversion. Subjects who were made to feel "introverted" were quicker to come up with a memory when cued by an introverted message than those who were led to feel "extroverted." The analogous results occurred for those led to feel extroverted. Thus, as Adler would have predicted, individuals whose current conception of themselves was "extrovert" were relatively quick to retrieve extroverted memories and those whose conceptions were "introvert" were relatively quick to recollect introverted memories.

Two examples of ERs follow, accompanied by Adler's (1956) interpretations of them.

> #1. When I was three years old, my father purchased for us a pair of ponies. He brought them by the halters to the house. My sister took one strap and led her pony triumphantly down the street. My own pony, hurrying after the other, went too fast for me and trailed me face downward in the dirt. It was an ignominious end to an experience which had been gloriously anticipated. The fact that I later surpassed my sister as a horsewoman has never mellowed this disappointment in the least (pp. 354–355).

Adler opined that the girl was unable to keep up with her triumphant older sister who may have been the mother's favorite. She believed she must be careful or her older sister would always win and she would always be left behind "in the dirt," defeated. The girl's attitude conveyed in the ER is "If anyone is ahead of me, I am endangered. I must always be first."

> #2. When I was about four years old I sat at the window and watched some workmen building a house on the opposite side of the street, while my mother knitted stockings (p. 356).

This memory was provided by a 32-year-old man, an eldest sibling whom Adler identified as the "spoiled son of a widow." His life was characterized by severe anxiety attacks, except when he was at home. Past school and professional pursuits had proved difficult for him. While good-natured, he had found it difficult to make social contact with others. His recollection of a solicitous mother in the background, probably knitting his stockings, supports the possibility that he was a pampered child. More importantly, playing the role of the onlooker characterized his childhood preparation for life: "he looks on while other people work." Adler proposed exploitation of the man's natural inclination to observe. He recommended a business dealing with art objects.

Adler's measure of ERs has received much attention and proven quite useful (Mosak, 1969). Olson, in 1979, estimated that 100 articles have been written about ERs. By 1992, Watkins counted another 30 written between 1981 and 1990. Using ERs, Burnell and Solomon (1964) were able to predict success or failure in basic military training of Air Force recruits. Jackson and Sechrest (1962) reported more ER themes of fear in anxiety-neurotics, of abandonment in depressed clients, and of illness in psychosomatic patients. In a study by Hafner, Fakouri, and Labrentz (1982), more alcoholics than nonalcoholics remembered threatening situations and showed themes of being controlled *externally* rather than *internally* (see next section). Hyer, Woods, and Boudewyns (1989) report ER evidence that Vietnam veterans suffering from Posttraumatic Stress Disorder (PTSD) are low in social interest, pursue goals in a devious manner, are manipulated by others, and pursue negative outcomes and themes.

Of the 30 studies reviewed by Watkins (1992), the great majority produced statistically significant and strong results. Watkins drew four substantive conclusions. First, there was consistency between ERs and current interpersonal behavior. Second, compared to normal control subjects, psychiatric patients' ERs tended to be more negative in emotional tone, showed more fear/anxiety themes, and reflected greater feelings of control by external factors like *fate* and *luck*. Third, psychiatric patients' ERs showed changes over the course of treatment: ER content became more positive as favorable life changes occurred. Fourth, male delinquents and criminals, in comparison with controls, showed memories that reflected more negative emotionality, injury or illness, rule breaking, victimization, and having been alone in an unpleasant situation.

Social Interest Research and Application.   Previous editions of this book reported that measures of social interest showed good reliability and validity. I recently searched the literature and found three representative articles that (1) further demonstrate the validity of Adler's "social interest," (2) introduce concepts to be considered later in the book by relating them to social interest, and (3) show the usefulness of social interest in understanding cases of severe mental disturbance.

Ashby, Kottman, and Draper (2002) related James Crandall's social interest scale to a measure of internal–external locus of control (I–E). As will be considered later in a section on Julian Rotter (Chapter 12), "I" refers to believing that one's outcomes are controlled by [I]nternal factors, such as ability and effort and "E" means believing that one's outcomes are controlled by [E]xternal factors such as luck, chance, and powerful others. The I–E measure included sub-scales measuring "external locus of control by powerful others" and "external control by chance." The former, but neither the latter nor "internal locus of control," predicted levels of social interest: "external locus of control by powerful others" was significantly, inversely related to social interest. Consistent with Adler's conception of social interest, the more subjects believed that they were controlled by powerful others the lower their social interest.

Christopher, Manaster, Campbell, and Weinfeld (2002) related social interest measured by Crandall's and Tavis's social interest scales to Eugene Mathes's "peak experiences" scale (Maslow, Chapter 10). "Peak experiences" are intense mystical personal episodes accompanied by feelings of powerfulness, helplessness, ecstasy, and wonder. As "social interest" implies openness to a wide variety of experiences, particularly those involving others, it would be expected to relate positively to "peak experiences." Results confirmed this expectation, but only for Crandall's and Tavis's social interest scales.

Leeper, Carwile, and Huber (2002) examined events in the life of Theodore Kaczynski, the infamous "Unabomber" in relation to the Adlerian concepts "style of life" and "social interest." They concluded that Kaczynski compensated for feelings of inferiority by nurturing a false feeling of superiority. Like Frankenstein, this subversion of "striving for superiority" led Kaczynski to grandiose perceptions of controlling life, by causing people to die in the Unabomber's case. More generally, his faulty style of life, reflected in his destructive behavior, precluded development of social interest.

Adlerian Therapy.   While the psychoanalytic brand of therapy developed by Freud may be fading in popularity, it appears that Adlerian therapy is gaining advocates. An entire journal devoted to Adlerian theory and therapy, *Individual Psychology,* has been thriving for years.

Counselors have adapted the Adlerian approach to their arena. Kern and Watts (1993) point to basic Adlerian assumptions that are important to success during counseling: (1) the social context in which a behavior occurs must be considered; (2) persons are best viewed as wholes rather than parts interacting with one another (the *holistic* approach); and (3) behavior changes in relation to life situations and long-term goals.

One practical problem with some therapies, such as psychoanalysis, is the large number of sessions assumed to be required. The greater the number of sessions, the more the time and money invested. In light of this problem, Adlerian therapy may be superior to some other therapies, because it is easy to adapt Adler's methods to the **brief therapy approach,** techniques that are able to address and solve clients' problems in a specifiable and relatively small number of sessions.

Carlson (1989) illustrates brief therapy of the Adlerian type in the case of a patient, Jim, who wished to stop smoking. Jim did not learn that his stepfather was not his "real" father until age nine. Up to that point he had been a rather typical child. Thereafter he became a "hellraiser," perhaps in response to feelings of inferiority born of the perception that being abandoned by the real father meant rejection by him.

Jim's background information revealed that he had a 20-year smoking history in which he consumed about 150,000 cigarettes at an estimated cost of $15,000. His addiction to cigarettes can be viewed as similar to an organ defect. Despite drinking about 10 cups of coffee a day, and, in the past, too much alcohol, Jim's general health was good. His two lifestyle priorities, perfectionism and being a victim, were revealed by his responses to the Kern Life-style Scale (Kern, 1986). ER data indicated that Jim was a thrill seeker and bent on oral gratification. At age six he recalled running down a hill toward the ocean, too enthralled by the roar of the water to heed his mother's terrified pleas for him to stop. At age seven Jim recalled being at a large family gathering during which someone pushed him off a tree stump, breaking his arm. He ran around howling in pain, unable to stop even when others attempted to comfort him. In both cases an Adlerian point of focus, the social context, is evident.

Putting together the test data and the fact that Jim remained thin and beat alcohol, Carlson declared Jim "an excellent candidate to stop smoking" (p. 222). Jim was told to work on his *self-efficacy,* the perception of one's ability to perform a specific task, in this case smoking cessation. To increase self-efficacy is to improve mastery over one's circumstances, a key Adlerian principle.

The first step in therapy is the education phase. In response to Carlson's query, "Why do you want to stop smoking?" Jim referred to the state of his health. He was experiencing morning coughing and shortness of breath. Also, smoking offended his friends whose "kidding" made him hide in the bathroom when smoking, further evidence of inferior feelings. Finally, Jim wrote his reasons for not smoking on a card to which he could refer when the urge to smoke arose.

Second, Jim's diet was addressed: when in need of a smoke, he was advised to eat sunflower seeds. Because they are botanically related to the tobacco plant, the sunflower seeds curb the urge to smoke. Carlson's third suggestion referred to the fact that nicotine raises the alkaline level in the body, thus shifting the *PH balance:* the alkaline and acidic levels relative to one another. When an individual stops smoking, the PH balance is shifted again. The changed PH balance after smoking cessation is corrected by the consumption of fruits and vegetables: Jim agreed to eat more apples and oranges. Also, Jim agreed to cut down on meat, eggs, sugar, and caffeine, substances that make smoking cessation difficult. To lower caffeine intake, Jim agreed to use a smaller mug and mix in decaffeinated coffee. Finally, Jim was asked to consider taking vitamins C and B, which are typically deficient in smokers.

Carlson outlined a simple, "diaphragmatic breathing" method that combats the stress of smoking cessation: one hand is placed on the belly, one on the chest, and the patient is told to practice breathing such that the hand on the belly moves, not the one on the chest. Jim was also encouraged to continue his walking and recently initiated bicycling. Again striving for superiority, in the form of pursuing self-efficacy, is illustrated. To elude situations that elicit smoking behavior, Jim was instructed to avoid the chair he typically sat in while smoking, to discard ashtrays, to clean the cigarette smells from his car, to seek professional teeth cleaning, and to brush regularly. Jim was also given an audiotaped hypnosis routine that reinforced Carlson's initial suggestions. These are also self-efficacy endeavors.

True to Adler's orientation, Carlson focused on Jim's present problems. In contrast to psychoanalysis, Jim was not just encouraged to "talk things out in order to gain insight"; in line with striving for superiority, he was given some tasks to do. Also, consistent with Adler's focus on the need to enhance self-esteem, Jim was encouraged to build his self-efficacy. Finally, Jim was encouraged to fulfill his need to accommodate his friends at work, a community concern involving an opportunity to show social interest. The brief therapeutic method had equipped Jim to handle his smoking problem on his own. Thereafter Carlson merely checked his progress a few times. Carlson reported that 70 percent of research patients who adopted suggested activity changes were still not smoking one year after initial sessions.

Limitations

Birth Order Research: A Big Boondoggle?   The numerous investigations of birth order are beginning to create more confusion than enlightenment. Contradictory findings are more the rule than the exception, and often result from the absence of a coherent theoretical rationale and inattention to sex of siblings (MacDonald, 1971; Schooler, 1972). As you have seen, results of more recent studies imply that the birth order variable should be abandoned altogether (Freese et al., 1999). Also, when rearing order substitutes for birth order, relationships with personality characteristics evaporate (Beer & Horn, 2000).

Discouragement with the birth order effect has become epidemic, even spreading to the popular literature. Kohn (1990) interviewed leading researchers on the topic and concluded that birth order probably matters only if parents take it seriously. One researcher, Toni Falbo, conceded that "Birth order doesn't really explain a whole lot . . . But people like it. It's much like astrology. It says, 'I'm not to blame for the way I am' " (Kohn, p. 34).

Much criticism has been aimed at the Zajonc and Markus (1975) assertion that large family size, which produces large numbers of close-spaced laterborns, has a negative effect on intellectual development. Several excellent research articles have all but laid the birth order/family size/IQ issue to rest (e.g., Rodgers et al., 2000; but see the June/July, 2001 issue of the *American Psychologist*).

For a more general view of progress, or lack thereof, in birth order research, I reviewed a sample of studies on the topic published during 2002–2003. Largely, nothing had changed: birth order effects were usually either weak or nonexistent. However, interestingly, a study of people's beliefs about birth order revealed that the public continues to endorse the conceptions of birth order effects outlined in Table 4.1 and surrounding text (Herrera, Zajonc, Wieczorkowksa, & Bogdan, 2003). For example, participants believe that different birth order ranks are associated with different personalities and those high in birth order rank are more intelligently and occupationally successful. This finding and the continued publication of books on birth order (e.g., Leman, 2002) suggest that concern for birth order will continue indefinitely. However, Box 4.3 indicates that "birth order" may have scientific merit for some purposes.

BOX 4.3 • *Sibling Rivalry: An Alternative to the Birth Order View*

Sibling rivalry is an "obvious" implication of birth order theory that was rarely explicitly considered until recently (Sulloway, 1996). Laterborns try to compete with firstborns, but it is difficult as the firstborn is always ahead in skills and enjoys the advantage of having had mature models longer. Because of their competitive disadvantage, laterborns may give up their rivalry with the firstborn and pursue goals at variance with the family traditions that are so well manifested in the firstborn's accomplishments. Thus, firstborns may continue to "best" laterborns throughout childhood and, perhaps, beyond.

Evolutionary theory provides an alternative explanation of sibling rivalry. Darwin's point of view has been extrapolated to psychological matters, including personality (Buss & Shackelford, 1997; Sulloway, 1996). This extension of evolutionary theory assumes that people's most basic motivation is to propagate their genes: pass their genes on to future generations. Whatever traits promote survival to sexual maturity and the birth of many viable offspring will be well represented in the human gene pool. One

of these traits would be the ability to control many *maternal resources,* all of those endowments of caretakers—such as nourishment, comfort, and security—that contribute to survival and prosperity of offspring. Obviously maternal resources are limited and must be shared among offspring. The more children there are the more maternal resources are spread thin, and the less are available to each child. The firstborn commands all resources until other children are born. Then resources must be shared. The firstborn will continue to horde as many resources as possible, just as laterborns will struggle for their share. While the firstborn has the advantage of mature skills, laterborns can capture resources by displays of helplessness or neediness. One can postulate many traits that would be useful in gaining maternal resources, such as ability to express emotions, especially affection, and verbal proficiency. Whoever possesses these traits will experience more success in overcoming sibling rivals in the struggle for limited maternal resources. Related expectations of evolutionary theory will be considered later in this book.

ERs Revisited.   While ERs are interesting, they are also open-ended and abstract, thus, subject to various interpretations (Carlson, 1989). Because of their nature, they are also difficult to quantify. As a case in point, Hyer and colleagues (1989) attempted to quantify some subjects' ERs and relate them to several personality measures. Their results were notable for displaying an almost complete lack of relationship between ER variables and many different personality factors. Watkins (1992) also found nil or weak ER/other-variable relationships in a few of the studies he reviewed. Finally, a recent search of the literature turned up only twelve articles on "early recollections," the most current of which was published in 1999.

Is Adlerian Theory and Therapy Dying?   Arthur Freeman (1999) lamented the possible demise of Adlerian psychology as members of the national society of Adlerian psychologists age and membership in the society dwindles. He asserted that the mission of the society is unclear, ties to non-Adlerians practicing similar forms of therapy have not been established, the Adlerian approach needs to be more inclusive of other approaches, and a stronger research base for Adlerian psychology is needed. Without these changes, Freeman believes that Adlerian psychology faces a bleak future.

Conclusions

In the chapters ahead you will find that Alfred Adler's influence on other theorists is very great, if not widely recognized. His effect on others was not just in terms of theory or the practice of psychotherapy. Freeman (1999) notes that such important psychology figures as Carl Rogers, Albert Ellis, Aaron T. Beck, Arnold Lazarus, Harry S. Sullivan, and Karen Horney were personally as well as professionally influenced by Adler. Adler was a model of the responsible, humanitarian professional. As a person who fervently sought world peace and fought for more humane treatment of people, especially children and women, he almost certainly had impact on the senses of moral responsibility of the psychologists who followed him.

There are several other ways in which he influenced psychological theorists both in his time and currently. He advocated a holistic approach, shunning the view that people could be thought of as a collection of pieces loosely connected and remotely interacting with one another. In so doing, he anticipated Rogers, Maslow, and Murray. He also was among the first to focus on the present and the future, rather than the past. Finally, his brief therapeutic approaches are being mimicked today. Judging by the apparent increase in the number of research articles and published commentaries appearing from the early to the late 1990s, Adler may well overtake some of his contemporaries. Like Jung, Adler's presence on the Web is significant. The existence of Adlerian institutes for training therapists in Adler's methods also attests to his continuing influence. Although not on the journal citation, text citation, or survey lists of top twentieth century psychologists, Adler was ranked sixty-seventh overall (Highbloom et al., 2002).

Summary Points

1. Adler was born (1870) the second of six children. He was a "father's son" who overcame childhood weaknesses. At school he was average. Adler met his wife, Raissa, among the rebellious company he kept as a young man. During his early medical career, he treated mostly poor patients. During a minor political career, he established children's clinics. After these were closed by the Nazis, he fled to the United States.

2. Adler viewed the person as an indivisible whole. Late in his career, he deemphasized inferiority in favor of striving for superiority. His basic assumptions included: behavior has social meaning and purpose and is goal-directed; behavior has unity and pattern; behavior is a result of our subjective perceptions. Adler set the stage for today's diversity-driven attention to the needs of disadvantaged children, women, and other oppressed people and the elimination of war.

3. Adler's most useful concept, social interest, the development of social feeling, is directed to the solution of three life tasks: society, work, and love. "Spirituality" and "self" might be added. Individuals' unique movements toward self-created goals are their styles of life. Their "laws of movement" are the directions taken in exercising free choice and exploiting their skills. The "creative power of the individual" is the process by which each person makes original conceptions of him- or herself.

4. During childhood we develop prototypes, fictional goals, a teleological notion. Shock occurs when the individual's fiction runs head-on into reality. An extreme reaction to inferiority is the inferiority complex that may require overcompensation, rather than the more usual compensation. Inferiority takes different forms, depending on whether the person has been neglected or overindulged during childhood.

5. Striving for superiority is a reaction to inferiority and can lead to the superiority complex. People with this complex may brag to cover up inferiority. Mothers are most important in the development of their children, but fathers are important, too. High and low self-esteem is not necessarily related to outcomes and traits. Adler believed that only children tend to be dominant and are often spoiled. Firstborns are disturbed by a new arrival and strive for domination. Secondborns struggle to surpass others, and lastborns are pampered.

6. Earlier research suggested that differences between first-only and laterborns do exist. However, recent research shows that Sulloway's historical evidence is not replicated by current data from a representative sample. Also, Zajonc's family size hypothesis is confirmed only in cross-sectional data, not in longitudinal data. Frankenstein and his misunderstood "monster" illustrate Adlerian principles.

7. An ER simply involves recalling an early childhood event. Adler believed that ERs are indexes of a person's present conceptions of self and style of life. Sanitioso and colleagues did a memory study that confirmed Adler's view. Supportive studies show ERs' ability to make predictions in various arenas (e.g., military training). Thirty recent studies point to additional ER/other-variable relationships.

8. External locus of control by powerful others was inversely related to social interest. In other recent work "peak experiences" were positively related to social interest. Finally, lack of social interest development aids understanding the Unabomber. In an illustration of many Adlerian principles, Carlson led "Jim" to quit smoking by developing self-efficacy, changing his diet, using deep breathing, cleaning out traces of cigarettes from his life, and using hypnosis and exercise.

9. Limitations of Adlerian theory and practice include that birth order hypotheses have failed to be supported by recent research results. However, people's beliefs in birth order continue to be strong. ER measures have also been questioned, but continue to be used. Evolutionary theory provides a different perspective on sibling rivalry.

10. Arthur Freeman expressed fear that Adlerian psychology will die if more flexibility is not embraced and new advocates are not recruited. Despite these limitations, Adler will long be remembered, especially when psychologists reflect on the roots of their social activism and the source of many of their ideas, including holism, optimism, present/future orientation, and brief therapy. The list of famous psychologists who have been influenced by Alder is impressively long. Adler is ranked sixty-seventh among all twentieth century psychologists.

Running Comparison

Theorist	*Adler in Comparison*
Freud	He rejected sexualism and focused on community (social) factors, rather than intrapsychic ones. Consciousness, the present, and holism were more emphasized than in psychoanalytic theory (PT). He believed that people are pulled by goals rather than pushed by instincts.
Abraham Maslow and Carl Rogers	Striving for superiority has the flavor of "self-actualization." Adler was holistic like these two.
Albert Bandura	Like Bandura, he stressed that anticipations of the future, rather than motivations rooted in the past, determine behavior. Self-efficacy and striving for superiority have much in common.
Murray	Murray also endorsed holism and believed that people are pulled by goals rather than pushed by instincts. Unlike PT, personality was viewed holistically and people have freedom of choice.

Essay/Critical Thinking Questions _____

1. Contrast Freud and Adler in terms of the individuals they were.
2. Using Adler's definition of the term, indicate the clearest instance of *shock* occurring to you.
3. How do healthy and unhealthy "striving for superiority" differ?
4. List child-rearing techniques that create a spoiled child.
5. What could Frankenstein have done to make a.super good human being of his creation?

E-mail Interaction _____

Write the author at b-allen@wiu.edu. Forward any of the following or write your own.

1. Tell me why you paint a kinder gentler picture of Adler than of Freud and of Jung.
2. How do I know if I was spoiled?
3. Tell me what is the most important information I need to know about Adler's theory.

Moving toward, away from, and against Others: Karen Horney

Karen Horney
www.ship.edu/~cgboeree/
horney.html

- How basic is anxiety?
- What makes people jealous?
- If some women are "castrating," why are they?
- What is your orientation to others, toward them, away from them, or against them?

Freud saw personality largely as a function of instinctive influences. Jung's "collective unconscious" was intimately tied to humans' ancestral past, and Adler's point of view was anchored by present strivings for superiority. In contrast, Karen Horney's most central concepts emerge from explorations of parent–child relationships, especially during early childhood. Interactions between parents and children are the focus, not repressed attraction to the opposite-sex parent, early experiences with remnants of humans' ancestral past, or early childhood strivings to overcome inferiority. Nevertheless, Horney used Freud's theory as a reference point beyond which she ventured to build a new, more socially oriented theory that revamped Freud's conception of females and reformulated his hypotheses about parent–child relationships.

Horney, the Person

Karen Clementina Theodora Danielsen was born on September 15, 1885, in Eilbek, Germany, a community near Hamburg (Quinn, 1988), but was not really German. Her father, Berndt Henrik Wackels Danielsen, was a Norwegian sea captain working for a Hamburg-based shipping line. Her mother, Clothilde Marie Van Ronzelen, was born to a well-regarded Dutch-German family. Clothilde, called Sonni, was the beautiful and commanding daughter of Dutch architect Jacob Van Ronzelen, born during the second of his three marriages. Sonni's mother died giving birth to her and she was reared by Van Ronzelen's third wife.

Captain Danielsen was 18 years older than Sonni and had four children by a previous marriage. Karen, the second child of his second marriage, admired her father, but he was stern, a man of strong religious fervor who attempted to control her life. There was a time when she felt attracted to men like her father, "brutal and . . . forceful men" (Quinn, 1988, p. 160). Perhaps to establish some bond with him, she even claimed that they made an extended sea voyage together, but Quinn has doubts. However, Karen also expressed loathing for him and they had many conflicts, especially over her education.

Because Karen was very bright, and early on expressed an interest in pursuing an advanced education, the Captain's belief that education was "for men" predicted a clash. When the inevitable happened, Karen's mother stood by her. While Sonni's support was important, Karen's determination to be an educated person may have come from knowledge of her maternal stepgrandmother's unusual childhood. Wilhelmine Lorentz-Mayer Van Ronzelen, or Minna, who reared Sonni as her own, was educated by her father along with her seven brothers, very unusual treatment at that time (Quinn, 1988). Fortunately, Captain Danielsen was at sea so often that he proved a paper barrier in Karen's path to academic success. Having thus escaped from under the thumb of her father, she submitted to the protection of her mother, which undermined her sense of security. A self-perceived lack of beauty made matters worse (Quinn, 1988). As a remedy, Horney immersed herself in her studies as if to say "Since I cannot be beautiful, I will be smart."

Horney's adolescent diaries began to overtly display a concern for human relationships and the role of women. "I think very highly of men who can bear to love a woman just as she is without demanding that she be in one certain uniform" (Horney, 1980, p. 177). By age 14 Horney resolved to be a physician, though "woman physician" was an oxymoron in her day. Fortunately, social changes then occurring in Germany increased opportunities for women to pursue "male careers." In 1905, at age 20, she became one of a very few women immersed in a sea of first-year, male, medical students at the University of Freiburg. She stood out in her long skirt and fluffy blouse when she posed for a picture surrounded by male medical students carrying swords. During the first semester, she met Oscar Horney, with whom she maintained a lively correspondence after he left almost immediately to pursue a law degree (Quinn, 1988). Four years later she married Oscar and, during the second part of her medical training, she became pregnant with the first of three daughters. While Oscar was moving up the managerial ladder of an investment firm, Karen was trying to balance mother, homemaker, and medical student roles. In 1915, she managed to complete the final requirements for her M.D. degree.

Possibly stresses involved with her protean lifestyle explain Horney's depression and alleged suicide attempt during her years in medical school. In turn, by 1910, these psychiatric conditions apparently led her into therapy with Freudian Dr. Karl Abraham. Eventually she attended meetings on psychoanalysis at Abraham's house and he became her mentor, the same role he played for Erich Fromm. The Berlin Psychoanalytic Institute emerged from these meetings, with Horney among its early members. The meetings also planted the seeds of doubt in Horney's mind regarding Freud's point of view.

Horney's early letters to Oscar revealed deep inner exploration and self-questioning. Adler's concepts of inferiority and striving for superiority, especially regarding women in social relationships, were prominent in Horney's thinking at this time. When her marriage began to dissolve in 1926, writing in search of the "truth" became her passion. She could think of nothing more unbearable than "disappearing quietly in the great mass of the average" (Horney, 1980, p. 245).

Horney emigrated to the United States in 1932, perhaps to escape the possibility that the Nazis would seize power and probably to escape the remnants of her marriage. Almost immediately she became associated with the American Psychoanalytic Institute. Although she was more positive about Freud than vice versa, she did not accept all of his ideas (Horney, 2000). After its members criticized her for questioning Freud, she and her followers resigned and founded the Association for the Advancement of Psychoanalysis (Frosch, 1991; Horney, 2000) and the American Institute of Psychoanalysis, a training facility. Horney was a founding editor of the Association's official organ, the *American Journal of Psychoanalysis.* Her U.S. colleagues included Fromm, Harry Stack Sullivan, and Margaret Mead. Horney and the first two were members of the Zodiac Club, colleagues who believed "in the importance of interpersonal fractors in human development" (Cresti, 2003, p. 196). She lived in the United States until she died of cancer in 1952.

Horney's View of the Person

> I realized . . . that my search for a better understanding had led me in directions that were at variance with Freud. If so many factors that Freud regarded as instinctual were culturally determined, if so much that Freud considered libidinal was a neurotic need for affection, provoked by anxiety and aimed at feeling safe with others, then the libido theory was no longer tenable. Childhood experiences remained important, but the influence they exerted on our lives appeared in a new light (Horney, 1945, p. 13).

Anxiety became a central aspect of Horney's theory, accounting for the personality's defensive and security operations. Though, like Freud, she dealt with anxiety neuroses, she discarded Freud's theory of instincts as the explanation of anxiety-related behavior. She also pointed out that oral, anal, and genital drives do not exist in all human beings (1937). For her, the aim of compulsive drives is not to satisfy sexual instincts but to provide safety from feelings of isolation, helplessness, fear, and hostility. The "Oedipus complex" was declared not universal and not central to understanding personality. In fact, she rejected Freud's sexual emphasis: "But the . . . emphasis Freud [gave] sexual factors may tempt many people to single them out above others . . . To be straight in sexual questions is necessary; but to be straight only with them is not enough" (1942, p. 295). Psychosexuality is relevant only to a few cases of neurotic jealousy in parent/child relationships (Horney, 1937).

Horney focused on Freud's biased postulations about women, especially his concept "penis envy" (Eckardt, 1991). Freud's extrapolation from his perception of his own culture to all other cultures showed his ignorance. While Horney acknowledged that in some cultures women may be jealous of men's anatomy, in other cultures it is the reverse (1937). Even in European-American culture, envy of male anatomy may be limited to neurotic women. Women's alleged "castrating tendencies," often associated with Freud's "penis envy," supposedly derive from women's need to take from men what women lack. To the contrary, "Much of what in psychoanalytic literature is regarded as castrative tendencies in women and is traced back to penis envy is . . . the result of a wish to humiliate men," not the desire to take their penises (Horney, 1937, p. 199). Freud not only ignored other cultures, he showed a "total" disregard for the influence of cultural factors on personality.

Further, Freud's view was contrary to social experience. When Horney (1945) first came to the United States, she noted important differences between the behaviors of people in this country and in some European countries that "only the difference in civilizations" could account for. In response to Freud's neglect of culture, Horney developed alternative, socially oriented concepts. The real forces motivating human attitudes and actions were social: dependency, cooperation, interpersonal anxiety, hostility, love, jealousy, greed, competitiveness, and inferiority. Even a newborn's first experience, feeding, is one of social cooperation. Like Adler, she emphasized human interactions in cultural contexts: exchanges with parents, siblings, peers, and significant others.

In general, Horney focused on conscious processes. Thus, id influences recede into the background, but influence of superego remains important. However, it is tied to the process of **socialization,** learning one's particular culture, not just "identification." The primary vehicle of socialization, the family, derives its importance from passing society's culture to future generations, not from acting as a psychosexual agent. Miletic (2002) notes that Horney criticized Freud for neglecting the importance of motherhood. Also, to Horney, the boy's problem is that his penis is too small to accommodate his mother's genitals, not that he suffers from castration anxiety. Horney's unconventional views are further examined in Box 5.1.

Basic Concepts: Horney

Basic Anxiety: Infantile Helplessness in a Hostile World

According to Horney (1950), normal personality development occurs when factors in the social environment allow children to develop basic confidence in themselves and other people. Confidence is most likely to result when parents display genuine and predictable warmth, interest, and respect for their children. Abnormal development occurs when environmental conditions obstruct a child's natural psychological growth. In this case, confidence is replaced by **basic anxiety,** "an insidiously increasing, all-pervading feeling of being lonely and helpless in a hostile world" (Horney, 1937, p. 89). The child feels "small, insignificant, helpless, deserted, endangered, in a world that is out to abuse, cheat, attack, humiliate, betray, envy" (Horney, 1937, p. 92). Basic anxiety is an irrational emotional experience involving a pervasive, unpleasant feeling of extreme discomfort.

A wide range of factors in the family environment contribute to this fundamental insecurity: parental domination, belittling attitudes, indifference, unkept promises, overprotection, a hostile home atmosphere, encouraging the child to take sides in parental disagreements, isolation from other children, and lack of respect for the child's individual needs (Horney, 1945). Perhaps Horney's sensitivity to these conditions comes from the observation that some of them existed in her own childhood home. However, "the basic evil

BOX 5.1 • *Horney on Adult Sexuality and Sexual Orientation*

Although Horney largely bypassed Freud's psychosexuality, she had much to say about adult sexuality, an unusual propensity for a woman of her era. Horney regarded masturbation as normal. However, individuals who masturbate compulsively—frequently, without the ability to stop—are attempting to release anxiety through a sexual "safety-value" (Horney, 1937, p. 52). In the realm of sexual relations, Horney saw four types of troubled people, all of whom primarily seek sex for reasons other than physical gratification. The first type crave sexual interaction because it allows them to establish human contact. Unfortunately, malevolent motivation lies behind their desire for relations with others: " . . . it is not so much a need for affection as a striving to conquer, or more accurately, to subdue others" (1937, p. 154).

The second type " . . . are prone to yield to sexual advances from either sex, [and] are driven by an unending need for affection, especially by a fear of losing another person through refusing a sexual request, or through daring to defend themselves against any requests made upon them, whether just or unjust" (p. 154). However, Horney is quick to point out that such people are not genuine bisexuals, people who have a real attraction to both sexes. Rather, they have interpersonal problems that go far beyond sexuality. They become the slaves of others because they cannot bear the thought of losing them.

For the third type, sexual excitement " . . . is an outlet for anxiety and for pent-up psychic tensions" (p. 155). When these individuals find themselves in a context that provokes their anxiety, they become attracted to the most prominent individual present. When in therapy, they may become passionately attracted to their psychotherapists. Alternatively, they may be highly aloof, unconsciously preferring to transfer the need for sexual closeness to an "outside" person who resembles the therapist. Finally, they may manifest their need for sexual contact with the therapist only in dreams. Ironically they have a "deep disbelief in any kind of genuine affection" and feel that the analyst is interested in them only for "ulterior motives" (p. 156).

The fourth type, homosexuality of the neurotic variety, is due to fear of competitiveness. This type (1) withdraws from attempts to attract the opposite sex so that he or she may avoid competition with individuals of his or her sex, and (2) deals with the anxiety born of competitiveness with the same sex by seeking the reassurance that only affection from the same sex can provide. Apparently these individuals stand in contrast to genuine homosexuals who are as normal as heterosexuals (Bailey, Gaulin, Agyei, & Gladue, 1994; Friedman & Downey, 1994). Horney (2000) mentions what could be a subtype of this category. Repressed female homosexuals are not overtly sexual, but are attracted to women and constantly seek their company.

Horney dismisses the Freudian allegation that women are masochistic: desire to be hurt, even physically, a probable source of the myth that women wish to be raped (Allen, 2001). She issued a general statement that makes no reference to gender: "Masochistic drives are neither an essentially sexual phenomenon nor the result of biologically determined processes, but originate in personality conflicts" (1937, p. 280). Other commentators cite Horney when they attribute masochistic behavior in women to culture, not biology (Shafter, 1992).

Horney also addressed women's alleged sexual frigidity by first acknowledging that, with the close of the Victorian era, frigidity was no longer considered a "normal condition in women" (1937, p. 199). Still, it may occur as a "deficiency" for two reasons. First, women may display frigidity, not because they have no sexual desire, but because they wish to humiliate the men in their lives (Horney, 2000). This explanation is especially applicable if their men have a neurotic fear of being humiliated by women. Second, women may display frigidity because of " . . . a feeling of being abused, degraded and humiliated by sexual relations." Sex was, and to some degree still is, something that was done to them, even against their wills, as implied by the popular male inquiry, "Did you make her?" In the past, marriage gave women license to have sex, but even

(continued)

BOX 5.1   Continued

today some still feel the need to be frigid in order to avoid the feeling that they are willingly submitting to humiliation.

Horney felt comfortable with her own sexuality. To her sex was a normal, natural, and enjoyable experience. She was known to have had meaningful affairs before, during, and after her marriage to Oscar Horney (Quinn, 1988).

In sum, Horney reminds us that sexual activity is rarely, if ever, just to achieve physical orgasm. Almost always there are psychological reasons behind sexual expression that are far more important than physical gratification. In turn, we are reminded that any sexual interaction is complex, a human relationship not to be taken lightly or to be engaged in thoughtlessly.

is invariably a lack of genuine warmth and affection" because of the parents' own incapacity to give it (Horney, 1937, p. 80). In the final analysis, disturbances in human relationships are expressed in **neuroses,** "psychic disturbance[s] brought about by fears and defenses against these fears, and by attempts to find compromise solutions for conflicting tendencies" (1937, pp. 28–29). Horney thought that neurotic people require excessive reassurance and are incapable of loving.

Coping with Ten Neurotic Needs

The child's methods of adjusting to basic anxiety form enduring motivational patterns. These patterns are called **neurotic needs,** the coping techniques that are initiated in childhood and composed of excessive, insatiable, and unrealistic demands developed in response to the basic anxiety that dominates the person (Horney, 1950). These needs crystallize into important aspects of personality. Their aim is not instinctual satisfaction, as Freud believed, but security.

Needs are considered neurotic (1) when a person adheres to them more rigidly than do other people in the culture, and (2) when there is a discrepancy between the person's potentialities and actual accomplishments. Neurotic people lack flexibility in reacting to different situations. For example, most people are likely to react indecisively or suspiciously when they have to make a difficult choice or when they respond to evidence of insincerity from another person. However, neurotic individuals tend to be unable to make up their minds, or repeatedly indicate how impossible it is to trust anyone because "everyone" is out to get whatever they can. Further, even though they may seem to have everything going for them, they display inappropriate feelings of inferiority and unhappiness. They sense that they stand in their own way. Table 5.1 presents Horney's ten neurotic needs, together with some illustrative behaviors.

Moving toward, against, and away from People

According to Horney, identifying the characteristics of an individual's dominant needs can reveal the direction the person is likely to take in relationships with other people. The over-

TABLE 5.1   *Ten Neurotic Needs Identified by Horney*

	Excessive needs for	*Shown in behaviors*
T **O** **W** **A** **R** **D**	**1.** Affection and approval	Striving to be liked and pleasing to others, to live up to the expectations of others; dreading self-assertion and hostility
	2. Having a "partner"	Seeking to be taken over by another, through "love"; dreading being left alone
	3. Narrowly restricting one's life	Trying to be inconspicuous, undemanding, and modest; contented with little
A **G** **A** **I** **N** **S** **T**	**4.** Power	Seeking domination and control over others; dreading weakness
	5. Exploiting others	Taking advantage of others, using others, dreading being "stupid"
	6. Social recognition or prestige	Seeking public acceptance; dreading "humiliation"
	7. Personal achievement	Striving to be best; defeating others; ambitious; dreading failure
A **W** **A** **Y**	**8.** Personal admiration	Self-inflating; not seeking social recognition, but admiration for their idealized self-image (I'm a saint)
	9. Self-sufficiency and independence	Trying to not need others; maintaining distance, dreading closeness
	10. Perfection and unassailability	Being driven toward superiority; dreading flaws and criticism

all pattern of needs also suggests the form that intrapsychic conflict is likely to take. For Horney (1945), contradictory dispositions toward other people constitute a critically important form of conflict.

Conflict is an essential aspect of Horney's description of neurosis. All normal people experience conflict; however, conflict of neurotic proportions is an excessive deviation from the cultural norm. Eventually, neurotic conflict comes to involve contradictory orientations to the self that pervade the entire personality. Horney (1945) discussed three generalized trends that individuals may show in regard to others and themselves. These trends may be thought of as a synthesis of the neurotic needs. Each trend is "a whole way of life" and each encompasses a subgroup of the ten needs summarized in Table 5.1.

Moving toward people reflects neurotic needs for a partner and for affection; it also involves compulsive modesty. This trend is associated with the first three needs listed in Table 5.1. Predominant characteristics are helplessness and compliance. Such people accept their own helplessness, and, despite their estrangement and fears, try to win the affection of others and to lean on them. Only in this way can they feel safe with other people. If there is conflict in their personal community, they will attach themselves to the most powerful person or group. By complying with sources of power, they gain a feeling of belonging and support that makes them feel less weak and less isolated.

A neurotic solution to anxiety often adopted by people extreme in this orientation is called **self-effacing,** a mode of responding to others in which the person will seek accommodation at any price including backing down whenever there is an interpersonal conflict in order to avoid loss of friendship, support, or love of others (Horney, 2000; Muller, 1993). It is modesty gone awry. Individuals displaying this characterological profile will sabotage their own best interest, deny their own points of view, and derogate themselves publicly if it seems necessary in order to keep the affections and attentions of others.

Moving against people reflects compulsive, exaggerated cravings for power and prestige, as well as personal ambition (needs 4, 5, 6, and 7 in Table 5.1). There is such an overemphasis on hostility that these people may be thought of as suffering from "basic hostility." In this case, people accept and take for granted the hostility around them, and determine, consciously or unconsciously, to fight. They implicitly distrust the feelings and intentions of others toward themselves and rebel in whatever ways are available. They want to be the stronger and defeat others, partly for protection, partly for revenge.

The extreme neurotic solution in this case is called **expansive,** to be "in control," to not admit that one is incorrect (or another person is correct), and to never give an inch in a conflict (Muller, 1993). These people are invested in avoiding the "horror" of being the "controlled" rather than the "controller." They must always determine who does what in a setting, never letting others determine behavioral outcomes. They are also afflicted with **hyper-competitiveness,** the indiscriminate need of individuals to compete and win (and avoid losing) at any cost as a means of maintaining or enhancing feelings of self-worth. To them, winning is everything; how the game is played is nothing.

Moving away from people reflects a person's concern with self, as seen in needs for admiration and perfectionism (needs 8, 9, and 10 in Table 5.1). The predominant characteristic is seeking isolation. This type "wants neither to belong nor to fight, but keeps apart. He feels he has not much in common with them, they do not understand him . . . He builds up a world of his own—with nature, with his dolls, his books, his dreams" (p 43). Box 5.2 illustrates the dangers of extreme adherence to these orientations.

In this case, the neurotic solution is termed **resignation,** which is to free oneself from the risks involved in approaching or attacking others by being an onlooker, a non-competitor, an avoider, and a reactive person who is hypersensitive to influence attempts (Horney, 1950; Muller, 1993). He or she literally resigns from social discourse. When conflict arises, these people are inclined to say "What difference does it make?" (Muller, 1993, p. 266). Muller has also pointed out that people showing this syndrome resemble the "borderline" personality type as classified in the American Psychiatric Association's manual of abnormal behaviors.

These orientations can exist within a single person. **Basic conflict** involves contradictory orientations to move toward, away from, and against others, all existing within a neurotic. Likewise, a single person can show, at times, elements of self-effacement, expansiveness, and resignation.

Developing an Idealized versus a Real Image of Self

Once firmly established, basic anxiety gives rise to additional feelings of alienation from one's real self and growing self-hatred. Genuine realization of the self is sacrificed to an

BOX 5.2 • *The Controllers*

The present case is a composite of those considered in the media, but has a particular case at its core. Randall and Jullianne had been "going steady" since their junior year in high school. Rarely was one seen without the other. If Randall was observed alone in public, it was a good bet that Jullianne was home with her parents. Neither had many friends, especially Jullianne. Her friends had long since given up trying to spend time with her. If they wanted to see her, Randall had to be there and his cold surveillance of their interactions made the experience too uncomfortable. When they were seen in public, Randall always had a hand on Jullianne. Typically, he had his fingers around her upper arm, or placed a hand at the junction of her neck and back as if to steer her. People joked that she was really a puppet and he a master puppeteer. No one noticed that, when a young and handsome man happened to pass them, Jullianne averted her eyes.

After high school, Jullianne's insistence that they finish college before marrying met with such an angry escalation of Randall's controlling behavior that she threatened to break off their relationship. His response was much more of the same. He would literally stand between her and other people with whom she was attempting to converse. When another man approached as if to speak to her, his cold stare lapsed into a snarl. Jullianne fled such scenes quickly lest a fight ensue.

Overwhelmed finally, Jullianne broke off the relationship. Randall's incessant calls to her house were answered with "She isn't home." Assuming the truth of these statements, he went looking for her. Occasionally he found her driving around or walking into a store and shadowed her. Once he threatened a male clerk with whom she was conversing. However, his behavior remained a mere nuisance until Jullianne begin to date other men. One Saturday Randall could no longer bear the thought of her being with another man. He followed Jullianne and her date to a bar, and slipped in after them. As soon as they were seated, he approached, began to shout at them, and abruptly punched the date. After the bouncer tossed him from the bar, he waited in his car for Jullianne and the date to emerge. As they were getting into the date's car, he gunned his engine, slipped his foot off the brake pedal, and, with the squealing sound of spinning tires, the car lunged toward the helpless couple. The date was clear of the point of impact and sustained minor injuries, but Jullianne was crushed and died instantly. Randall suffered head and spinal injuries. He is now free: the court declared that his mental deficiency made him no longer a threat. In the months during which he seemed profoundly retarded when he appeared in court, he was doing very well in college.

idealized image of self, an artificial pride system that the person creates to give the personality a sense of unity that does not exist. For example, imagine a heavyset, middle-aged adult looking in a mirror and seeing a trim, young adult (Horney, 1945). Such an idealized image serves five functions: (1) it substitutes for the absence of realistic self-confidence and pride, through an inflated but unsupported feeling of significance and power; (2) it counteracts the presence of real inner weakness and self-contempt by allowing the individual to feign being more worthy than others; (3) it compensates for a lack of genuine ideals, without the presumption of which the individual would feel lost; (4) it represents an idealized, private mirror on which to rely so that one's most blatant shortcomings disappear or take on an attractive coloration; and (5) it offers the appearance but not the actual reconciliation of conflicts and inconsistencies within the individual's personality. By contrast, the **real self** is the potential for growth beyond the artificial idealized image of self. It is the self one can become if all the potentialities that one has are fully developed (Cresti, 2003). *Self-realization* is the process of real self development.

Creation of an idealized self takes place unconsciously. It also may be accompanied by other forms of pretense, such as **externalization,** the tendency to experience internal processes as if they occurred outside oneself and to hold these "exterior" factors responsible for one's difficulties. Externalization serves to eliminate oneself as the cause of personal problems by projecting or shifting blame onto entities "outside" oneself, especially other people. Externalization is not just shifting responsibility. "Not only one's faults are experienced in others but to a greater or lesser degree all feelings" (1945, p. 116). Thus, externalization is much broader than Freud's defense mechanism, projection.

"Another inevitable product of externalization is a gnawing sense of emptiness and shallowness" (p. 117). Along with it comes an externalization of self-contempt in which one either despises others or feels "that it is others who look down upon oneself" (p. 118). Finally, rage results and is itself externalized in three ways. First, anger is "thrust outward" either as general irritability or as "specific irritation directed at the very faults in others that the person hates in himself" (p. 120). Second, rage is externalized in the form of an ever-present expectation that the faults "which are intolerable to oneself will infuriate others" (p. 121). Horney's former patient whose idealized self-image was as saintly as the priest in Victor Hugo's *Les Misérables* is a good example. The patient expected that others would have contempt for her as she was, so she hid behind a "holier than thou" facade. When she deviated from this angelic image and became angry, she was amazed to find that others liked her better. The third way to externalize rage is to channel it into physical ills, which involves incessant complaining about various vague maladies, from headaches to fatigue.

"The discrepancy between *a neurotic's actual behavior* and his *idealized picture of himself* can be so blatant that one wonders how he himself can help seeing it" (Horney, 1945, p. 132; emphasis added). Here Horney refers to the **actual self,** who one currently is, which stands in contrast to the idealized self, who one should be, and real self, who one could be. The inevitable trauma of the brutal collision between the idealized and actual selves is akin to Adler's shock. This destructive clash can be postponed by resorting to one or more of seven defenses (Horney, 1945).

A **blind spot** is an area of contradiction about which the individual manages to remain unaware. One of Horney's patients never saw the contradiction between his "game" of figuratively killing colleagues at a meeting by "gunning them down" with an index finger and the "Christlike" idealized image he maintained. In **compartmentalization,** individuals separate key aspects of themselves and their life situations into "logic-tight" compartments. "There is a section for friends and one for enemies, one for the family and one for outsiders, one for professional and one for personal life . . . what happens in one compartment does not appear to the neurotic to contradict what happens in another" (p. 133).

Rationalization "may be defined as self-deception by reasoning" (p. 135). By performing mental gymnastics, the individual makes despicable behavior into benevolent deportment. For example, someone who sees himself as helping another, when, in fact, "strong tendencies to dominate are present" (p. 135). **Excessive self-control** arises in reaction to a flood of contradictory emotions and involves holding feelings and behavior in a vise-grip. "Persons who exert such control will not allow themselves to be carried away, whether by enthusiasm, sexual excitement, self-pity, or rage" (p. 136). **Arbitrary right-**

ness is the strategy of people who see life as a merciless battle and, therefore, feel they must be definite and "right" about everything lest "foreign influence" control them. For these people, doubt is a dangerous weakness. In the event of a conflict, they can feel "in control" only if they can declare themselves "in the right."

Elusiveness is the ability to slither away from conflicts by refusing to ever take an identifiable stand. Elusive people "resemble those characters in fairy tales who when pursued turn into fish; if not safe in this guise, they turn into deer; if the hunter catches up with them they fly away as birds. You can never pin them down to any statement" (p. 138). If one of their pronouncements is challenged, they deny having said whatever they said, say they did not really mean it, or reinterpret it. **Cynicism** is "the denying or deriding of moral values" because of a deep-seated uncertainty with regard to morality (p. 139). These people's response to moral uncertainty is skepticism about morality. They twist wrong into right and vice versa. All that matters is doing what they please and looking good in the process. Those who reason and behave otherwise are thought to be either hypocrites or stupid.

A Basic Diversity Issue: The Psychology of Women

Women lived for centuries in a world that kept them away from economic and political responsibilities and restricted them to a private emotional sphere. They did carry responsibility and had to work, but their work was done within the confines of the family and, thus, was based on emotional rather than practical interpersonal relations. Love and devotion came to be regarded as specifically feminine ideals and virtues. To women, because their relations to men and children were their only path to happiness, security, and prestige, love represented a realistic value. In men's sphere it was earning capacity. Thus, only emotional pursuits were encouraged. Other pursuits were of secondary importance in women's minds.

Horney made significant contributions to the psychology of women by criticizing Freud and his "boy's eye" view of anatomy as the basis of psychological differences between men and women. Horney challenged Freud's speculations that lacking male anatomy led women to (1) envy men for their penises (Symonds, 1991); (2) feel shame over biological "deficiency"; (3) blame this deficiency on their mothers; (4) overvalue relationships with men; (5) become jealous of other women as competitors for anatomically superior men; (6) prefer stimulation of the clitoris because it is penis-like; and (7) strive to be submissive, dependent, and masochistic because "these traits are natural to women" (Eldredge, 1989).

Horney also challenged Freud's underlying assumptions about gender. First, she considered it illogical that persons built for specific biological functions should be obsessed with obtaining the biological attributes of the other sex. Second, cross-cultural investigations have failed to demonstrate the universality of Freud's speculation about females' wish for male anatomy. In fact, there are societies whose males show "womb envy." Third, Horney (1926) asserted that a psychological theory "written" by a man may not be wholly relevant to women. In fact, the masculine point of view pervades science and most of European and European-American thought. "Like all sciences and all valuations, the psychology of women has hitherto been considered only from the point of view of men" (Horney, 1967, p. 56).

Women have been enmeshed in social systems that have forced them into political, economic, and psychological dependency on men (Eldredge, 1989). Women have been socialized to seek "love" relationships, based on the belief "I must have a man" (1942). This belief motivated women to unconsciously conform to the demands of men and then assume, erroneously, that the behavior and feelings they adopt represent true feminine nature.

Evaluation

Contributions

Help with Everyday Problems.   Horney often worked with neurotics, but, because she had much concern for the everyday problems of normal people, she promoted self-exploration in her popular books. Her books are filled with discussions of ambition, depression, self-confidence, dependency, and greed. Her purpose was not to offer clear-cut solutions to neurotic conflicts, but to provide information useful for self-examination. Her books include *The Neurotic Personality of Our Time* (1937), *Self-Analysis* (1942), *Our Inner Conflicts* (1945), and *Are You Considering Psychoanalysis?* (1946). Her adolescent diary is still studied today (Seiffge-Krenke & Kirsch, 2002).

Among the everyday concerns featured in Horney's books was **jealousy,** the fear of losing a relationship that is seen as the best available means of satisfying an insatiable need for affection and incessant demands for unconditional love (Horney, 1937). She recognized that jealousy is evident even in early childhood. A child can be jealous of siblings or of a parent who seems to be receiving more attention from the other parent than is the child. Furthermore, Horney acknowledged that Oedipal jealousy may also exist: a child may be jealous of the parent of the same sex for monopolizing the physical (sexual) and emotional attention of the opposite-sex parent.

Some degree of jealousy is true of all of us and may be a quite reasonable reaction to the real but generally remote possibility that an important love relationship may end. However, the kind of jealousy Horney considered is exaggerated beyond the bounds of reason. The fear of these people is so great that any of the loved one's interests not revolving around themselves is a threat to them. "This kind of jealousy may appear in every human relation—on the part of parents toward their children who want to make friends or to marry; on the part of children toward their parents; between marriage partners . . ." (1937, p. 129).

Morbid adult jealousy can be a carryover from childhood neurosis: both involve an insatiable appetite for love arising from unresolved basic anxiety. In recognizing a possible tie between jealousy involving childhood relationships and jealousy in adult relationships, Horney was ahead of her time. Philip Shaver and his colleagues have established a link between the way children relate to their parents and how they later relate to important people in their adult lives, most especially lovers (see Shaver and Hazan, 1987). As adults, certain insecure people whose childhood needs were not consistently met show the same kind of insatiable need for unconditional love to which Horney alluded. Because they cannot get enough assurance of love, they are morbidly jealous of anyone who is a rival for the attentions of their loved ones. Box 5.3 contains information relevant to Shaver's theory and also a jealousy scale. Read and follow the instructions in the box before returning here.

DeAngelis (1994) reported on additional work by Shaver and colleagues. Shaver's first category, secure people, are high on interpersonal sensitivity, but low on compulsive, obligatory caregiving. Anxious-ambivalent adults, the second category, display exactly the opposite pattern. Avoidant individuals, the third category, tend toward "one-night stands" and find pleasure in sex without love. Secure adults enjoy experimenting sexually with all kinds of physical contact, from hugs to oral sex, but only within the context of a continuing relationship. By contrast, avoidant types like only sexual forms of physical contact. Anxious-ambivalent types like the more nurturing kinds of physical contact, but were not overly enthralled with sexual contact. Shaver wondered whether the 40,000 people who wrote Ann Landers proclaiming a preference for hugs over intercourse were predominantly anxious types.

To answer "What is it about parents that promotes development of one style or another in their children?" Levy, Blatt, and Shaver (1998) had subjects write a description of each parent. Consistent with expectations, the descriptions of anxious-ambivalent men's mothers were more ambivalent (a mix of positive and negative attributions) than descriptions of other style/gender combinations. Unexpectedly, avoidant women's descriptions of their mothers were greater in ambivalence than even anxious-ambivalent women. Secure subjects described both mothers and fathers at a higher conceptual level (more complex and abstract descriptions) than subjects with other styles, but avoidant women also described mothers and fathers at a high conceptual level. Thus, not only anxious-ambivalent types, but also avoidant women, had mixed conceptions of their mothers. They also gave conceptually complex descriptions of both parents. Perhaps because their parents sometimes rejected them during childhood, but not always, these women's parents are still heavy on their minds.

In an Internet study of 5,248 responses to questions about romantic relationship breakups, Davis, Shaver, and Vernon (2003) uncovered a laundry list of negative cognitions, emotions, and behaviors associated with attachment-related anxiety: heightened preoccupation with the lost partner, enhanced physical and emotional distress, exaggerated attempts to reestablish the relationship, increased anger and vengeful behavior, and dysfunctional coping strategies. Although attachment-related avoidance was positively related to avoidant and self-reliant coping strategies, attachment-related security was positively related to relying on friends and family for comfort.

In other recent work, Mikulincer (1998) found that secure people showed low anger proneness and dealt with angry encounters in a more even-handed, positive, and adaptive way. In contrast, anxious-ambivalent people displayed lack of anger control and a tendency to "mentally ruminate or stew over anger feelings without expressing them overtly" (p. 514). Avoidant people were high in hostility and displayed a lack of awareness of their anger, as well as attempts to deny and escape anger episodes. In the context of participation in group tasks, Rom and Mikulincer (2003) investigated attachment anxiety and attachment avoidance in relation to "closeness goals" (love), "distance goals" (self-reliance), instrumental functioning (IF) during a group task ("I took the task seriously"), and social emotional functioning (SEF) during a group task ("I helped group members work together"). Attachment anxiety was negatively related to IF and attachment avoidance was negatively related to both IF and SEF. Attachment anxiety was positively related to close-ness goals and attachment avoidance was positively related to distance goals.

In recent years, there have been many studies which, like Mikulincer's, show that attachment processes are complex. For example, Cook (2000) found that attachment security level can be relationship-specific (attachments to mother, father, and lover could all be different), attachment security is affected by the person(s) to whom one attaches, and attachment security is reciprocated (when people feel comfortable depending on others, others feel comfortable depending on them). Students often ask me, "Can attachment styles change?" The answer is a qualified "yes." Davila and Cobb (2003) found sufficient changes in attachment styles over a one-year period to allow for meaningful associations of attachment change with several variables. Farley (2002) found low attachment instability (relatively little change) from age one to age six, but moderate to modest instability (appreciable change) for four other age ranges, including age 1 to age 19. Attachment styles are related to jealousy in Box 5.3.

Anticipating Research on Concepts of Interest to the Public.   "Jealousy" was only one of Horney's ideas that was ahead of its time. She anticipated many beliefs of the humanists (Chapters 9 and 10). Like Adler, Horney's therapy was not just for gaining what Freud called "insight." It was for growth (Cresti, 2003). Another of Horney's notions anticipated a popular idea of psychotherapist Albert Ellis, the psychologist who is known for his assumption that people are basically irrational (Allen, 2001). As reflected in Ellis' concept "musturbation," Horney believed that some people are subject to the **tyranny of the shoulds,** the belief that one should do this and that, whatever a good person *should do,* whatever is expected by others, rather than what one feels it is his or her nature to do. People afflicted with this malady think of themselves as miserable worms who must forever wriggle forth in pursuit of the elusive perfection that eludes them. Horney wrote, "Forget about the disgraceful creature you actually *are*; this is how you *should* be; and to be this idealized self is all that matters. You should be able to endure everything, to understand everything, to like everybody, to be always productive . . . " (Horney, 1950, pp. 64–65). The shoulds dominate the individual, so that not to do what one "should" generates anxiety and guilt. "He should be the utmost of honesty, generosity, considerateness. . . . He should be the perfect lover, husband, teacher . . . he should love his parents, his wife, his country . . . he should never feel hurt, and he should always be serene and unruffled" (p. 65). He should be whatever others deem to be the "right kind of person," never himself. Needless to say, many of us are bound by the chains of the "shoulds." Horney believed that the first step in escaping this bondage is to recognize the tyrant who has tied us up. Then we may begin to acknowledge that the ideal of perfection we pursue is impossible to obtain, and, in fact, deters us from being who we could become.

Developing New Clinical Techniques: Self-analysis.   Horney's therapeutic approach involves trust, confidence, respect for each person's individual uniqueness and constructive resources, and adherence to the principle that exploration precedes explanation. The goal is to seek the real self, not to discover some awful problem and somehow correct it (Cresti, 2003).

BOX 5.3 • *Attachment Styles and Jealousy*

First read the three descriptions of attachment styles and choose the one that fits you best. Then respond to Mathes's Interpersonal Jealousy Scale. Finally, refer to the information at the end of the box to learn of the relationship between the two exercises.

Part 1: Attachment Styles

An attachment style is the mode of relating to important people in your life that you developed through your relationships with your parents. Now follow the instructions.

Shaver's Attachment Styles. Read the statements below and simply check the one that is most applicable to you. If you are not sure, check the statement that is more applicable than the others.

1. I find it relatively easy to get close to others and am comfortable depending on them and having them depend on me. I don't often worry about being abandoned or about someone getting too close to me.
2. I find that others are reluctant to get as close as I would like. I often worry that my partner doesn't really love me or won't want to stay with me. I want to merge completely with another person, and this desire sometimes scares people away.
3. I am somewhat uncomfortable being close to others; I find it difficult to trust them completely, difficult to allow myself to depend on them. I am nervous when anyone gets too close, and often, love partners want me to be more intimate than I feel comfortable being.

Quoted from Shaver (1986, p. 31), with permission.

Part 2: The Interpersonal Jealousy Scale

In responding to each item, place the name of your current romantic partner in the blank of each item. If you have no romantic partner at present, use the name of a person from a past relationship. If you are married, use your spouse's name. Then,

use the scale below to express your feelings concerning the truth of the item. For example, if you feel the item is "absolutely true" of you, place a 9 to the left of the item number. If it is only definitely true, place an 8 beside the item, and so on.

9 = absolutely true; agree completely
8 = definitely true
7 = true
6 = slightly true
5 = neither true nor false
4 = slightly false
3 = false
2 = definitely false
1 = absolutely false; disagree completely

(Gay and Lesbian individuals, please forgive and ignore the reference to "opposite sex"; place your current or past partner's name in the blanks.)

1. If _____ were to see an old friend of the opposite sex and respond with a great deal of happiness, I would be annoyed.
2. If _____ went out with same sex friends, I would feel compelled to know what he/she did.
3. If _____ admired someone of the opposite sex I would feel irritated.
4. If _____ were to help someone of the opposite sex with his/her homework, I would feel suspicious.
5. When _____ likes one of my friends I am pleased.
6. If _____ were to go away for the weekend without me, my only concern would be with whether he/she had a good time.
7. If _____ were helpful to someone of the opposite sex, I would feel jealous.
8. When _____ talks of happy experiences of his/her past, I feel sad that I wasn't part of it.
9. If _____ were to become displeased about the time I spend with others, I would be flattered.

(continued)

BOX 5.3   Continued

10. If _____ and I went to a party and I lost sight of him/her, I would become uncomfortable.
11. I want _____ to remain good friends with the people he/she used to date.
12. If _____ were to date others I would feel unhappy.
13. When I notice that _____ and a person of the opposite sex have something in common, I am envious.
14. If _____ were to become very close to someone of the opposite sex, I would feel very unhappy and/or angry.
15. I would like _____ to be faithful to me.
16. I don't think it would bother me if _____ flirted with someone of the opposite sex.
17. If someone of the opposite sex were to compliment _____, I would feel that the person was trying to take _____ away from me.
18. I feel good when _____ makes a new friend.
19. If _____ were to spend the night comforting a friend of the opposite sex who had just had a tragic experience, _____'s compassion would please me.
20. If someone of the opposite sex were to pay attention to _____, I would become possessive of him/her.
21. If _____ was to become exuberant and hug someone of the opposite sex, it would make me feel good that he/she was expressing his/her feelings openly.
22. The thought of _____ kissing someone else drives me up the wall.
23. If someone of the opposite sex lit up at the sight of _____, I would become uneasy.
24. I like to find fault with _____'s old dates.
25. I feel possessive toward _____.
26. If _____ had previously been married, I would feel resentment towards the ex-wife/husband.

27. If I saw a picture of _____ and an old date I would feel unhappy.
28. If _____ were to accidentally call me by the wrong name, I would become furious.

Note: To calculate your score, put minuses in front of the scale numbers you assigned to items 5, 6, 11, 16, 18, 19, and 21, then add these numbers. Next add the numbers for the other items. Your score is this total minus the negative total. The higher it is, the more the jealousy. Reprinted with permission of Eugene Mathes.

Part 3: Relationship between the Exercises

About the same percentage of newspaper respondents checked a given attachment style statement as university students. About 56 percent of all respondents checked the first statement, thereby indicating secure attachment, 19 percent endorsed the anxious-ambivalent statement listed second, and 25 percent checked the third statement, identifying them as tending toward avoidant attachment. More recently, Mickelson, Kessler, and Shaver (1997) found the percentages to be 59, 11.3, and 25.2, respectively (4.5 percent were unclassified because their three ratings were equal). The last two statements indicate insecure attachment styles. People with these two styles, especially the anxious-ambivalent style, are expected to be unusually jealous. Notice that Shaver's second statement indicates high need for assurance of love. It could have been made by one of Horney's patients with "an insatiable need for affection" (moving toward). The third statement has the flavor of moving away. "Moving against" is not represented, but isn't it easy to imagine an attachment style of the controlling kind?

Assume that scores on Mathes's jealousy scale of 100 or above indicate high jealousy, and scores of 25 or below indicate low jealousy. However, here are a couple of points to remember in evaluating your responses to the two exercises and the relationship between them. First, both the research associated with Shaver's statements and Mathes's scale are oriented to romantic involvements, but Horney's point of view relates to a broader range of relationships (see Mathes, Adams, & Davies, 1985). Thus, whether or not your attachment style choice matched your jealousy score reflects only partially on Horney's theory. Second, much more information about you would be needed before solid conclusions could be drawn concerning whether or not you are a particularly

jealous person and concerning what your attachment style might be.

Before leaving this box, go back to Mathes's jealousy scale one more time and look for items that fit Horney's conception of jealousy well. For example, items 7 and 17 are clear examples of what Horney meant by "morbid jealousy."

One of her relatively ignored contributions is **self-analysis,** a process whereby people come to understand themselves better through their own efforts, often outside the context of psychotherapy (Horney, 1942). It is apparently rare that people are trusted to probe their own psyches in the hope of self-discovery without their psychologist, psychiatrist, or counselor being present. But Horney regularly did what others rarely dared to do.

In Horney's view, self-analysis is certainly not the same as "self-help," which is typically done by people with no assistance, except that provided by a popular book. Rather, it is a step that a person takes in the direction of **self-recognition,** coming to know one's neuroses, idealized self-image, and real self, including positive and negative attributes. It is also a step taken under supervision. The patients described in Horney's 1942 book may have tried "self-analysis" (the book title) outside of therapy, but they had received therapy and would have it again.

I have chosen the case of Clare to illustrate self-analysis, because, of the several case histories covered in *Self Analysis,* it is the most detailed. Reading the summary of Clare's case will tell you something about self-analysis and partially reiterate Horney's theory. Clare was unwanted by her mother, who unsuccessfully attempted to abort her. Her father simply was uninterested in any of the children. However, Clare was intelligent and received a good education. By the time she entered therapy at age 30, she had been married—her husband died—and had become a successful magazine editor. During analysis she was involved with Peter, a businessman and the focus of her problems. Clare was morbidly dependent, lacking in self-confidence, and gripped by an insatiable need for reassurances of love. This account concentrates on instances of self-recognition that occurred to Clare.

Clare's whole life was wrapped up in Peter. She wanted to be with him all the time. When he failed to keep a promised date with her, which happened often, she was devastated. A lightbulb went on for Clare and illuminated both herself and her relationship with Peter when she awoke on a Sunday morning intensely irritated at an author who broke his promise to submit an article for her magazine. While reflecting on this puzzling incident, it occurred to Clare that she was not really angry with the author nor at people who fail to keep promises. Rather, she was angry because Peter had frustrated her desire to be with him by failing to show up on that weekend as promised. This realization caused her to remember the heroine of a novel who lost her feelings for her husband while he was away at war. In turn, she wondered whether she wanted to sever her emotional ties with Peter, but dismissed the thought "because I love him so much" (p. 194). Thus, despite correctly recognizing that she was really angry with Peter, she lost an important opportunity to break Peter's hold on her.

Clare "managed to shake off the whole problem" and fell back to sleep (p. 196). She dreamed of being lost in a foreign city where people spoke an unknown language and that she had left her luggage and money at the train station. Then she was at a fair where there was gambling and a freak show. Reflecting on this dream, she realized that counting on the unreliable Peter was a "crap shoot," and that he was something of a freak. This shallow analysis was, however, as far as she was able to go. She missed the symbolism of being lost without luggage and money: she had "invested" everything in Peter and it all had been lost.

One morning a notice of a shipwreck brought back a dream in which she was adrift on the waves, in danger of drowning, but a "strong man put his arms around her and saved her" (p. 202). She had a feeling of belonging and of endless protection. "He would always hold her in his arms and never leave her" (p. 202). This dream reminded her of Bruce, an older writer who had promised to be her mentor. He was a "hero" whose interest in her was described as a "blessing." These experiences moved Clare closer to recognizing that she wanted everlasting love and protection. Though she also realized that Bruce was not as brilliant as her dream implied, she did not generalize her revelation about him to the "superior" man in her life, Peter. It was to be some time before she fully acknowledged Peter's many deficiencies. Nevertheless, it was the first time she truly recognized that Peter was not giving her what she wanted and that she was dissatisfied with the relationship.

Clare's mood hinged on every nuance of Peter's behavior. An instance of his lateness plunged her into deep depression. The smallest favor generated disproportionate joy. When he gave her a scarf, she reacted as if he had presented her with the Hope diamond. If he relented and went out with her after all, she was as grateful as a condemned man granted a last-minute pardon. Later Clare recalled a dream of a large bird flying away. It was glorious in color and grace, not unlike Peter who was handsome and a fine dancer. It meant that Peter, under whose "wing" she wanted to hide, had flown away, or was about to.

Eventually, Clare recognized that she desperately needed Peter for the protection and reassurance that she hoped he would provide, not because he was a great hero or because she had true affection for him. Fortunately she was in the process of weaning herself from him when the rumor mill told her he was having an affair. When he subsequently wrote her asking for a separation, she averted the emotional collapse that would have occurred earlier. Instead she got through the crisis and later came to recognize that her problem was broader than Peter: "her picture of herself was determined entirely by . . . evaluation[s] by others" (p. 245). The revelation almost made her faint. Later, back in therapy, Clare executed the final incision to excise Peter from her psyche, but Horney asserts she likely could have done it on her own in continued self-analysis.

While self-analysis is valuable, Horney acknowledged its several shortcomings. During self-analysis, patients: (1) may perceive something about themselves that is not true, but see it as accurate; (2) may come up with correct information about themselves, but misinterpret it; (3) may have a partial and accurate recognition regarding themselves, but fail to extend it to core personality dispositions; and (4) may analyze an incident correctly with regard to its implications for themselves, but not know what to do with the result. These are all reasons why self-analysis should be done under supervision, as was always true of Horney's patients. Clare made all four errors.

Some Research Support

While research support for Horney's theory has been relatively meager, hypercompetitiveness has been significantly investigated. This "moving against" orientation is accompanied by a need to manipulate and denigrate others in a variety of situations. Ryckman, Thornton, and Butler (1994) related their index of hypercompetitiveness to several measures suggested by Horney's writings concerning the constellation of characteristics that embody hypercompetitiveness. The first of these measures was based on Horney's belief that hypercompetitive individuals are prone to be narcissistic. They are overtly self-laudatory, but beneath the bravado they feel inferior as well as powerless and insignificant.

Based on Horney's contention that hypercompetitive individuals tend to be exhibitionistic and unconventional, they should attain high scores on a second measure, Sensation Seeking. A third measure assessed a tendency to be "everything to everybody" (p. 86), a Horney-inspired disposition that is indexed by the Type E scale. Type E's, who want to be the best at everything, habitually take on multiple roles leading to overload and conflict. Hypercompetitors are also Machiavellians, a reference to Italian Prince Niccolo Machiavelli, a master of the fine art of manipulation and exploitation. Machiavellians lie and cheat, whatever it takes to beat their enemies, who are numerous, as they dislike almost everyone. The best predictors of hypercompetitiveness were narcissism, followed by Type E orientation and some measures of sensation seeking. Although not a strong predictor of hypercompetitiveness, Machiavellianism was positively correlated with it.

Ryckman, Libby, van den Borne, Gold, and Lindner (1997) compared hypercompetitiveness with individual development competitiveness. While hypercompetitiveness involves narcissistic individualism, personal development competitiveness entails no sharp boundaries between self and others. Personal development competitors endorse "I enjoy competition because it brings me and my competitors closer as human beings" while hypercompetitors endorse "It's a dog-eat-dog world. If you don't get the better of others, they will surely get the better of you" (p. 277). Both types showed values encompassing selfcontained individualism—achievement, hedonism, striving for an exciting and challenging life—but only hypercompetitors endorsed "power and control over others." Only personal development competitors valued respecting, caring for, and being concerned about the well-being of others. Burckle, Ryckman, Gold, Thornton, and Audesse (1999) found that "hypercompetitiveness" is strongly, positively related to eating disorder symptoms, but "personal development competitiveness" is not. Further, they reported that eating disorder symptoms are related to "motivation to achieve in appearance" but not to "motivation to achieve academically."

Some Application: Group Therapy

Horney was quite critical of group therapy. Among her complaints was that its outcomes were difficult to evaluate, it may generate superficial improvements "of a behavioral rather than structural nature" (Cresti, 2003, p. 196), it may generate overwhelming anxiety (possibly due to revelations of deficiencies in front of a group), and it would not be suitable for all patients. Still, Cresti (2003) saw many applications of Horney's ideas to group therapy. The support of group members fuels true self-fulfillment. If interpersonal relations in the group are respectful and accepting, growth of self is likely. Insofar as the group climate promotes an "ethic of sympathy" (p. 197), the capacities of the true self will unfold. Growth-bolstering intimacy development can be cultivated in the group context. Finally, the group can be a "warm cocoon" (p. 197) in which intimacy and trust can foster the expression of the self's potential.

Unfortunately, Horney's insights into group therapy have been largely ignored, as have her ideas about jealousy. Box 5.4 looks at how jealousy has been treated by evolutionary psychologists.

Limitations

The scarcity of scientific support for Horney's theory can, in part, be traced to the difficulty of measuring her concepts. Neurotic needs, externalization, the real self, and other concepts are too abstract to be measured reliably. She, like the others covered so far, was trained as a physician–psychiatrist, not a psychological scientist. All were simply not equipped to conduct the scientific research that might have confirmed or disconfirmed their points of view. Further, none of these theorists seemed able to recognize contradictions to their theories found in their own writings. For example, according to Horney's notions of "need for assurance of love" and "jealousy," Clare ought to have been an especially jealous person. In fact, there are few, if any, lines in the description of her case that can be clearly interpreted as references to jealousy.

Conclusions

Although some of Horney's concepts are too broad and general "to get a handle on," most of them are quite specific and defined in crystal clear fashion. While other theorists are evasive, Horney is refreshingly straightforward. In fact, Horney is a superb writer, probably the best among the theorists covered in this book. Unlike the books of other theorists, I can recommend hers as both an enjoyable read and a useful source of information. Further, she, more than some others, addressed the considerations that are of interest to normal people. Her intuitively optimistic "growth approach" is a refreshing contrast to the gloomy view of the psychoanalysts (Rubin, 1991). She was known to be optimistic as a therapist (Cresti, 2003).

The alleged untestability of her concepts may also be overstated. Because she defined her concepts clearly, many should be testable. Her notions about jealousy in relation to need for reassurances of love are quite testable. Horney's ideas on attachment clearly predated those of modern researchers. Shaver tested some of her ideas, though he does not credit her. Attachment research might be advanced if a "controlling" (moving against) style were added to the others. Given that Horney's ideas are more testable than the lack of research on them implies, one may ask why they have not often been subjected to scientific scrutiny. The answer may well be that the only woman theorist taken seriously by modern personality psychologists is taken less seriously than male theorists. Her name is omitted from the four lists of outstanding twentieth century psychologists (Haggbloom et al., 2002). A reconsideration of Horney's writings seems in order.

BOX 5.4 • *Evolutionary Theory and Jealousy*

Evolutionary theory offers alternatives to Horney's and Shaver's notions of jealousy. In the struggle to propagate their genes, men and women face different adaptive problems. She knows that the fetus she carries has her own genes by the simple fact that it is inside her. However, he can never be absolutely sure that the fetus his mate carries is his own and, thus, is a vessel transporting his genes into the next generation. He suffers from "paternity uncertainty," an issue that is irrelevant to her. It follows that he will be very concerned about sexual infidelity: he must exercise high surveillance over her lest she have sex with another man and he risk the ultimate disaster, wasting his precious *resources* on another man's genes (Buss, Larsen, Westen, & Semmelroth, 1992). On the other hand, she will be more concerned about emotional infidelity: that he may have sex with another woman does not matter so much relative to an emotional bond he may make with another woman who may then command his resources. Buss and colleagues (1992) conducted several simple studies to support the evolutionary point of view. Their male and female subjects were asked to choose which would bother them the most, sexual infidelity or emotional infidelity. Women showed more emotional jealousy: they were most concerned about their mates' possible emotional infidelity. Men displayed more sexual jealousy: they were most upset by the possibility of their mates' sexual infidelity. Buunk, Angleitner, Oubaid, and Buss (1996) impressively replicated these results in the United States, Germany, and the Netherlands, though the difference between men and women on sexual jealousy was somewhat smaller in the European samples. The evolutionary position also has been supported using other methods (Buss & Shackelford, 1997; Shackelford & Buss, 1997; Mason, 1997; Wilson & Daly, 1996).

However, some researchers have objected (Harris, 2004). Both Harris, and Christenfeld (1996) and DeSteno and Salovey (1996) have supported the "double shot hypothesis": cultural beliefs dictate that, sometimes, sexual infidelity

may *also* imply emotional infidelity or emotional infidelity may *also* imply sexual infidelity. Harris and Christenfeld found that if a man is in love with another woman it is implied that they are having sex (double shot), but if he is having sex with another woman it does not necessarily imply he's in love (single shot). Little wonder she is not so concerned about sexual infidelity: it does not necessarily mean he is in love (emotionally involved) with someone else. On the other hand, if a woman is having sex with another man, it means she is in love (emotionally involved; double shot). Maybe his real concern is that she is in love with someone else. He attends more to sexual infidelity only because it is a sure indicator of emotional infidelity which has few other concrete, easy-to-detect manifestations. He would also attend to emotional infidelity. In fact, Harris (2003) refers to results supporting these possibilities. Consistent with Harris's and Christenfeld's and DeSteno's and Salovey's view, the latter (1996) found the less male and female subjects believed that sexual infidelity implies emotional infidelity, the less likely they were to select sexual infidelity as more distressing.

DeSteno, Bartlett, and Salovey (2002) took the issue to another level by showing that if the Buss and colleagues' forced-choice format (subjects were forced to choose between emotional and sexual infidelity as most upsetting) were replaced with Likert scales (hurt 1: 2: 3: 4: 5: 6: 7 not hurt) the gender difference disappeared. In its place, sexual infidelity elicited the most jealousy on the part of both genders. However, Buss and colleagues opened a big hole in the "double-shot hypothesis" by showing that the sex difference they had reported persisted even when questions to subjects were rephrased to prevent one kind of jealousy (sexual) from implying another (emotional) (Benson, 2002). Thus, DeSteno and colleagues (2002) resorted to a different strategy in a second study. They reasoned that if the gender difference in jealousy is accounted for by an evolutionary process dating to ancient humans, it should be branded in the reptilian brain (lower

(continued)

BOX 5.4 Continued

brain). Thus, it should be automatic (Harris, 2004). To test this expectation, some subjects acted under "cognitive load"—they had to remember a string of digits presented before each question. If Buss's gender difference hypothesis is correct, "load" subjects should show the difference as strongly or more strongly than subjects responding to questions without the load. Buss's gender difference was shown in the no-load condition, but in the load condition almost two-thirds of the women and nearly all of the men chose sexual infidelity as most upsetting. Buss and colleagues' expectations were not supported.

Additional research either does not entirely support evolutionary theory or qualifies it. Harris (2000) connected male and female subjects to equipment that measured their physiological reactivity (similar to that used in lie detection) while they imagined the Buss "sexual infidelity" and "emotional infidelity" scenarios. As expected, it was men who reacted more strongly to the "sexual infidelity" scenario. However, males also reacted more strongly to a sexual than to an emotional scenario when infidelity was not involved. Harris took these results to mean that men are generally prone to sexuality reactivity, regardless of the context in which it occurs. It is sexual obsession, more than sexual jealousy, that drives men to seek frequent sex with a variety of partners.

Pratto and Hegarty (2000) granted that evolutionary imperatives play a role in gender differences regarding reproductive behavior, but they felt that it was not the whole story. They showed that men's suspiciousness concerning sexual infidelity, their concern that they not invest in others' children, and their greater tendency to exercise surveillance over their partners were related to Social Dominance Orientation (SDO). SDO is a social power factor associated with endorsement of inequality among people. Likewise, women's desire for high status and economically powerful mates who would have many resources was related to SDO. Thus, a social factor, SDO, was part of the story about men's and women's reproductive behavior.

"Gender differences in sexual strategies" is another expectation of Buss and colleagues' evolutionary theory. Under this theory, men are programmed to have as much sex as possible with as many women as possible to maximize the odds of passing on their genes. In contrast, women can only become pregnant once every nine months. Having sex with one man who will provide resources for her children is the best strategy for passing along her genes. Mathes and Smith (1999) reported results consistent with the proposed difference in sexual strategies under conditions that rendered the parental uncertainty hypothesis moot. In their study, only men were less willing to give up sex with their partners than emotional warmth from their partners.

Buss and Schmitt (1993) refer to results consistent with their hypothesized difference between the genders in sexual strategies. The data they reported seemed to show that men pursue short-term sexual relationships with many women, while women seemed to seek long-term relationships that would necessarily involve few men. However, Miller, Putcha-Bhagavatula, and Pedersen (2002) challenged the Buss and Schmitt data in two ways. First, Miller and colleagues noted that the Buss and Schmitt data for men involved different measures of long- and short-term relationship preferences than the measures used for woman. When Miller and colleagues used the same measures for both genders, they failed to support gender differences in preferences for short- and long-term relationships. Second, if human males are so obsessed with having short-term sexual relationships with many women (promiscuous) they should show rather large testicle size relative to body size. Promiscuous males need to unload much sperm with each sexual encounter in order to ensure that they achieve pregnancy. After all, they are not likely to have a second chance with a given female (at least not before other males beat them to her). In contrast, males who are monogamous or have sex with only a few females (polygynous) can survive with smaller testicles relative to body weight, because they have many opportunities with the single or few females in their lives. First, Miller and colleagues report that human males show a rather small testicle size to body size ratio compared with other primates. Second, human male testicle size ratio is much closer to that of monogamous (gibbons) and polygynous primates (gorillas and orangutans) than to the ratio of the highly promiscuous male chimpanzees. Human males fail to measure up to the testicular size requirements demanded by Buss and colleagues' view of them seen through the lens of their sexual strategies hypothesis. Not so incidentally, it appears that sexual potency is a function of testicle size, not penis size. So, "well hung" takes on new meaning.

Even more damaging to Buss and colleagues is Christine Harris's (2003; and see 2004) extensive review of the evolutionary psychology data. First, she showed that, indeed, when the forced choice format is used to test the gender difference in sexual jealousy hypothesis, it is supported. However, in other cases, such as using Likert scales or investigating actual rather than imagined infidelity, the hypothesis is not supported. Second, she reported that when physiological measures are used, as in her study, support for evolutionary psychology hypotheses declines. Third, she challenges the "real life" data that seems to support the gender difference in sexual jealousy. Homicide statistics and data on assault of women seemed to fit the sexual jealousy hypothesis. Supposedly men beat and kill women out of sexual jealousy. After an impressively extensive and sophisticated analysis of the homicide literature, she concluded " . . . there is no evidence for a systematic sex difference in the role of jealousy . . . in murders, with the trend running . . . opposite [to the evolutionary hypothesis] (p. 110; and see Harris, 2004). As to spousal abuse, Harris

refers to recent evidence that women admit to instigating family violence at about the same rate as men. Further, new evidence indicates "that women report slapping, hitting, or kicking their mates about as often as men" (p. 115). Though the evidence is meager regarding the motivations behind attacking spouses, Harris refers to a Dutch study in which almost all the women, but only about two-thirds of the men, indicated that they would physically attack an unfaithful mate. Women in this study also scored "much higher" than men in sexual jealousy. If there is a gender difference in sexual jealousy, future research may show that women are more jealous.

Harris (2004) resorts to Social Cognitive Theory (see Chapter 13) to explain people's jealousy. As infants we become anxious when maternal attention turns to another child (even if it's just a doll, as it was in one study). We become jealous when a cognitive appraisal of the threat posed by a rival leads us to perceive that disruption of an important relationship may occur. The relationship can be sexual or not. A threat to any important relationship may lead to jealousy.

Finally, Levy and Kelly (reported in Anderson, 2002) bring us full circle. They looked at gender differences in jealousy and differences among subjects in attachment styles. Results showed that attachment styles were much more potent in predicting jealousy than gender differences. It mattered more whether subjects were anxious types (highly jealous) or a secure type (low jealousy) than whether they were male or female.

Putting the new evidence presented here together with the evidence reported in earlier editions of this text, it now seems that the pendulum has swung away from the evolutionary psychologists, led by Buss and colleagues, in the direction of their critics. But stay tuned.

Finally, Karen Horney was a fascinating person. Even as an adolescent she wrote extraordinarily candid, literate, and often poetic lines about herself and others close to her. If she seemed to be more troubled during her early life than other theorists, it may be because she was more self-disclosing than the others. Reading her adolescent diaries (1980) and her life story (Quinn, 1988) is more than perusing biographies of a famous figure. It will allow you to get under the skin of an interesting human being and also to follow the development of a significant contributor to understanding the human condition.

Summary Points

1. Karen Clementina Theodora Danielsen was born to Norwegian and Dutch-German parents near Hamburg, Germany. Her father, a sea captain, was often gone, but dominated her life when he could. Despite paternal resistance, Karen received a good education and entered medical school. There she met her eventual husband, Oscar Horney. Balancing school with typical homemaker "obligations" was stressful. Depression led to therapy, where she was exposed to psychoanalysis.

2. Horney questioned Freud's sexual instincts, Oedipal theory, his view of gender differences, and the psychosexual stages. Penis envy was deemed not generally true and, in this culture, is confined to neurotic women. "Castrating tendencies" were also snubbed and Freud's inattention to social matters criticized.

3. Horney regarded masturbation as normal and identified several sexually troubled types. She also dismissed the Freudian allegation of female masochism and frigidity. Basic anxiety is due to a number of family-background factors. Horney's neurotic needs include affection and approval, having a "partner," narrowly restricting one's life, power, exploiting others, social recognition or prestige, personal admiration, personal achievement, self-sufficiency and independence, and perfection and unassailability.

4. The three orientations are moving toward people (self-effacing), moving against people (expansive, hypercompetitive, and controlling), and moving away from people (resignation). The idealized image of self is an artificial pride system. It stands in contrast to the actual self, who one currently is, and the real self, who one could become. The inevitable clash between actual behavior and idealized self can be postponed by resorting to such mechanisms as blind spots, externalization, excessive self-control, elusiveness, and cynicism.

5. Horney threw out the Freudian assumption that women long for male anatomy and the several implications of that alleged need. She noted the illogical nature of women's alleged desire for male anatomy, the lack of evidence for the universality of Freud's assumptions about the genders, the irrelevance to women of a theory written by men for men, and false belief "I must have a man." Finally, Horney condemned male selection processes that create a self-fulfilling prophesy.

6. Horney wrote plain-language books for everybody. She also showed an unusual interest in concepts that are important to rank-and-file people. Morbidly jealous people show fear of losing someone's love that is way out of proportion to the actual danger. Their excessive jealousy, which may be a holdover from childhood, is due to an insatiable need for love caused by unresolved basic anxiety.

7. Horney's views of jealousy anticipated the work of Philip Shaver, who proposed three attachment styles dating to parent–child interactions, two of which predict inordinate jealousy.

He and others reported differences among secure, anxious-ambivalent, and avoidant people on interpersonal sensitivity, caregiving, sexual attitudes/behavior, and anger-proneness. Anxious people show a laundry list of negative psychological symptoms. Other work revealed that avoidance was negatively related to instrumental functioning and emotional functioning. Recent work reflects the complexity of attachment security: it is relationship-specific, affected by with whom one attaches, and is reciprocated. Recent research shows that attachment styles can change.

8. Mathes's jealousy scale may relate to the attachment styles. Horney's the tyranny of the shoulds paints a vivid picture of people who feel they should do this and that, whatever is demanded by the idealized self. Horney also reoriented therapy, making it more concerned with "being a better person." She uniquely recommended self-analysis, during which one can begin to gain self-recognition.

9. Clare, a self-analysis case, was unwanted by her parents and grew to be a dependent, assurance-seeking adult. She was morbidly dependent on unreliable Peter. Several dreams gave Clare insight into what lay behind her dependency. Work by Ryckman and colleagues showed that Horney's concept, hypercompetitiveness, is related to narcissism, Type E orientation, and Sensation Seeking. Eating disorder symptoms were related to "hypercompetitiveness" but not to "personal development competitiveness." In terms of application, Horney's theory supports the efficacy of group therapy.

10. Evolutionary theory has been challenged by alternative explanations, such as the "double shot" hypothesis. DeSteno and colleagues showed that Buss's jealousy effect disappears when Likert scales are used and is not as automatic as it should be. Miller and colleagues showed the sexual strategy effect fails if the same measures are used for both genders and human male testicle size doesn't support the sexual strategy theory. Harris reports that physiological data fails to support Buss's jealousy theory; so do gender differences in relationship violence. It may be that attachment styles predict jealously more than gender. A lack of scientific training limited Horney's ability to test her theory, but others' neglect of scientific attention to her ideas may be due to their lack of respect for her gender. Horney was a fascinating person whose writings should be reconsidered and who is well worth reading. But she is not listed among twentieth century psychology greats.

Running Comparison

Theorist	Horney in Comparison
Freud	Disagreed with him about libido, sexual motivation, Oedipus complex, penis envy, culture, consciousness, and women.
Adler	She agreed with him on social cooperation and her discovery of conflict between the idealized and real self is akin to his "shock."
Rogers and Maslow	Her "real self" matches their recognition of people's endless potential for positive growth.
Jung	She also encouraged patients to do self-analysis, but more formally than Jung.

Essay/Critical Thinking Questions _____

1. What made U.S. psychoanalysts so upset with Horney's criticisms of Freud?

2. What is a parent to do in order to be a good parent in Horney's eyes?

3. Transform one of Horney's three directions so that it would be adaptive.

4. Write a paragraph describing a person who fits Horney's jealous type.

5. Isolate instances in which you have been victimized by the "tyranny of the shoulds."

E-mail Interaction _____

Write the author at b-allen@wiu.edu. Forward one of the following or phrase your own.

1. Tell me which of Horney's contributions is her most important.

2. What is wrong with doing what you *should* do?

3. If my mate is insanely jealous, does that mean she or he really loves me?

6

Personality from the Interpersonal Perspective: Harry Stack Sullivan

- Can a person with severe psychological problems give useful advice to others?
- Was your mother or father a "good parent" or a "bad parent" (or neither)?
- Are there just four ways to classify the sexual orientations of people?

Harry Stack Sullivan
www.haverford.edu/psych/
ddavis/sullivan.html

The chapters in the first half of this book may be thought of as starting with Freud and withdrawing from him gradually. Jung maintained a relationship with Freud longer than any former pupil. Adler disagreed with Freud, but his theory was in part a response to Freud's. Horney never had personal contact with Freud, but his theory was a launching pad for hers. Harry Stack Sullivan also had no personal relationship with Freud. One of his mentors even warned him against Freud (Perry, 1982). Yet Sullivan was heavily influenced by Freud, and, like Horney, used the framework of psychoanalytic theory to build his own point of view. Nevertheless, he joined the others in deserting the sexual emphasis. To Sullivan, the critical consideration in attempts to understand personality is *interpersonal relations,* the relationships between a person and each other important person in his or her life. These crucial twosomes, or dyads, were behind many of the concepts that distinguish Sullivan's theory.

Sullivan, the Person

Born in 1892 to a recent Irish immigrant family in the rural New York town of Norwich and raised on a nearby farm, Sullivan was traditionally American and clearly entitled to be called

"America's Psychiatrist" (Perry, 1982). He grew up with "farm folk" who came to the United States to better themselves and were advocates of the Protestant work ethic. However, in some ways they led lives that did not fit the idyllic image of the rural United States. The surrounding region was known for its high depression and suicide rate, with isolated farm wives most often taking their own lives, and sometimes taking their children with them.

Sullivan was an only child, worshiped by his mother, Ella Stack, but considered by his father "no good to work, for he has his nose stuck in a book all the time" (Perry, 1982, p. 85). Although Harry was prone to greatly overstate their accomplishments, the Stack family was well regarded in the community. The same could not be said for the Sullivans. This comparison is an example of the "social law of relativity": the Stacks had relatively high status in a very humble community compared to the Sullivans. In fact, Sullivan's family background is among the most pedestrian of the theorists covered in this book. Horney's name on her mother's side, Ronzelen, began with *Van,* a mark of nobility. By contrast, the Sullivans were pretty much "fresh off the boat" and working-class. One of the factors that pushed Sullivan to succeed may have been his desire to rise above his background. Alternatively, his delusions about the accomplishments of mother Ella Stack's family may have driven him to "live up to her standards." The vacillations of name change that he displayed may support the contention that Ella's influence was behind his drive to achieve. When he entered medical school, he was Harry Francis Sullivan, or H. F. Sullivan (Francis was given to him at age thirteen, on his confirmation). Later he used a variety of combinations, for example, Harry F. Sullivan and just plain Harry Sullivan. But eventually Francis was dropped out in favor of the maternal surname, Stack. He shared this identity confusion with Erik Erikson.

As a person, Sullivan was lonely, somewhat reserved, fatalistic about his health, and a user of alcohol "to combat anxiety" (Perry, 1982, p. 175). Not only did he imbibe alcohol himself, he gave it to patients to loosen them up before therapy (Le Doux, 2002). He had the vulnerable, haunted look of actor James Dean. These symptoms suggest depression. During childhood and preadolescence, Sullivan was a loner who conveyed a sense of ambiguous sexuality that lingered into adulthood. Supposedly he was involved in a homosexual relationship during preadolescence. He entered puberty late, possibly not until age seventeen.

In college he did report "lust" for a girl in one of his classes, but people close to the adult Sullivan were never quite sure about his sexual orientation (Perry, 1982). Some friends believed Sullivan had both male and female sexual partners. Whether these speculations were true or not, Sullivan was known to long for marriage and to lament his bachelorhood. Perry even suggests that Sullivan may have sent proposals of marriage to astounded women with whom he was merely acquainted. At one point, he was reported to be "attentive" to Karen Horney, but despite rumors, he was not sexually involved with colleague Clara Thompson (Perry, 1982, p. 335). Nevertheless, sustained love for women was probably directed exclusively to his mother and his Aunt Maggie. Whether Sullivan was gay, bisexual, or heterosexual probably will never be known. His were not the times in which people who were other than "straight" admitted as much in public.

Psychological turmoil characterized Sullivan's life. While a student at Cornell University, allegedly he was involved in "mail fraud," supposedly as a part of a "criminal gang" (Perry, 1982). Scant detail of the relevant incidents led Perry to speculate that Sullivan and "the gang" were using the mail to obtain "chemicals" from a drugstore (1982). Yet the penalty meted out to Sullivan was slight: he was suspended from Cornell for a year and could have returned to school (but he never did). Between his suspension in 1909 and his arrival at medical school in 1911, Sullivan disappeared. It was remotely possible that he was in jail; maybe he was "sprung" by his uncle, a judge. More likely, Sullivan suffered a psychotic break during this period and was receiving treatment. In any case, the youthful Sullivan was known to have had bouts of *schizophrenia,* withdrawal from reality, and disturbances in thoughts, feelings, and behaviors. These episodes probably explain his burning interest in the disorder.

Sullivan was admitted to the Chicago College of Medicine and Surgery (CCMS) despite the absence of credits from Cornell, where he did poorly as a physics student (Chapman, 1976; Perry, 1982). In effect, he went directly from high school to medical school without the benefit of a full college education. Though valedictorian honors in high school implied significant academic abilities, his record in medical school was dismal. While living in poverty and working as an elementary physics teacher and a Chicago Elevated Railway conductor, Sullivan received only one "A" at CCMS, but accumulated several "Ds" (Perry, 1982). This undistinguished performance was recorded at a school that may have been suspect in its time. Although Perry (1982) regarded CCMS as most likely average for its day, Chapman (1976) described it as one of many fly-by-night physician factories that sprung up around the turn of the century. Sullivan called it a "diploma mill" (Chapman, 1976). It was defunct by 1917, leaving no record of Sullivan's degree (his diploma was found among his effects after he died).

These aspersions cast on CCMS and Sullivan's performance there may seem to mean that he was mediocre as a scholar and intellect. To the contrary, he was a brilliant, original thinker who may well have "gone through the motions" during medical school to make himself eligible for what he really wanted to do, become a psychiatrist. Self-administered psychiatric training conducted at St. Elizabeth's Hospital in Washington, D.C. (Chapman, 1976) led him to make numerous erroneous statements about psychiatry and abnormal behavior, some of them in print (Chapman, 1976). Yet, having enlisted the help of his patients in teaching himself about psychiatry, rather than relying on the dogmatic psychiatric professors of the day, may have permitted the creative ideas that made him famous. Of the ironies that surround Sullivan's training, none is more profound than the observation that he is a central figure in the development of psychiatric training (Conci, 1993). Sullivan's most significant clinical work involved schizophrenic men, for whom he established a successful residential treatment program founded on interpersonal trust (Sullivan, 1927/1994).

Harry Stack Sullivan died under mysterious circumstances on January 14, 1949 (Perry, 1982). He was found in a Paris hotel room, sprawled on the floor, his heart medication scattered about him. Rumors of self-destruction circulated immediately, especially in the suicide-ridden rural community where he was reared. However, Perry was well acquainted with Sullivan's heart ailment and knew that the official cause of death, "meningeal hemorrhage," was entirely plausible in view of his medical condition. Still, she wondered whether certain thoughts that may have occurred to him on the day of his death had not contributed to his demise, or even caused it. When he arose on the day of the fatal attack, the fact that it was his deceased mother Ella's birthday must have been on his mind. It was also close to the anniversary of a dear friend's death, and he may have remembered that relative Leo Stack had died of a similar attack in a hotel room on a day in January. Finally, Sullivan's prediction, made in 1931, that he would die of a "rupture of the middle meningeal artery at the age of 57 . . . " was astoundingly accurate. Perhaps memories of these four events came together to hasten what was already inevitable. The mystery may never be solved, but psychiatry suffered from his early demise. Box 6.1 indicates that Sullivan's problems were his connection to diversity.

Sullivan's poor health and early death may be explained in part by his relatively low socioeconomic status (SES; Adler & Snibbe, 2003). Recent evidence indicates that the lower the SES the greater the likelihood of early death. Among the health liabilities of low SES are an increased likelihood of cardiovascular disease, such as that which killed Sullivan, and increased odds of becoming schizophrenic and depressed. While high levels of the personality factor *optimism* are known to positively affect health, low SES people tend toward pessimism. Higher education and income level appears to provide people with the information they need to pursue good health and the means to access the best health care. Although Sullivan's family may not have been poor, because it was an immigrant family, it probably had a history of poverty. Even if individuals move out of poverty, the more time spent in that state the greater the health deficits (Adler & Snibbe, 2003).

People of lower SES face more stressful environments. They are more likely to be subjected to social conflict, overcrowding, crime, and other sources of stress. Poor people may develop techniques to combat sources of stress that work in the short term, such as arming themselves against criminals. However, while these methods may create temporary feelings of security, the continued high vigilance needed to maintain security (preparations to fight criminals) likely will increase stress in the long term. Over time, the accumulation of adaptations to stressors, such as protecting oneself against criminals, increases wear and tear on physiological and psychological systems (called "allostatic load"). In turn, the accumulating stress load associated with relatively low SES takes such a heavy toll on physiological and psychological systems that health will almost surely suffer. The cardiovascular disease that killed Sullivan, and the schizophrenia and depression from which he suffered,

BOX 6.1 • *Sullivan: Diversity Incarnate*

When we think of diversity we often dwell on issues of race. There are, however, many more dimensions to diversity, religion, for example. Although neither Freud nor Adler was a devout Jew, being Jewish was an apparent source of insecurity for Freud. Sullivan's investment in religion was apparently minimal, but being Catholic may have had something to do with his family's immigration to the United States. In any case, that Sullivan was Irish almost certainly affected him. His was an era of prejudice against recent immigrants, including those from Ireland. It was the same time in which the Kennedy family battled anti-Irish bigotry.

That Sullivan was possibly gay or bisexual placed him on another dimension of diversity. Ambiguities surrounding his sexual orientation probably greatly affected his interpersonal relations. Finally, still another dimension, mental health status, probably shaped Sullivan's life to a degree. He may have suffered from the "schizophrenia" stigma most of his life.

must have in part been generated by a family history of relatively low SES and the stress he suffered in his rural community, at Cornell, and during his medical training.

Sullivan's View of the Person

Significant Others and the Self

Sullivan's theory revolves around the idea that a person's needs and developmental tasks are met in a series of two-person relationships, beginning with "a mothering one" and culminating in the selection of a sexual partner. While he believed we have as many personalities as we have interpersonal relationships, he formally defined **personality** as "the relatively enduring pattern of recurrent interpersonal situations which characterize a human life" (1953, pp. 110–111). This orientation is certainly different from that of Freud, but Sullivan did see himself as a psychoanalyst. Further, he used many of Freud's methods. Nevertheless, he backed away from Freud's underlying assumptions revolving around psychosexuality. Sullivan's orientation is, however, in the spirit of Adler's "social interest." It also bears some similarity to Horney's emphasis on anxiety dating to infancy and on relationships. Little wonder they were in sync.

      Significant others are those people who are most meaningful to us in our lives. In essence, personality does not exist in the absence of important other people. Without them, there can be no development of a **self-system,** "that part of personality which is born entirely out of the influences of significant others upon one's feeling of well-being" (Sullivan, 1954, p. 101). As most people know, our senses of self-esteem depend largely on the positive and negative evaluations we receive from other people. Interestingly, these relationships with others may be fantasized or real: we may relate to imaginary playmates, literary characters, and public figures. An example is John Hinckley's fantasized relationship with movie actress Jodie Foster, whom he tried to impress by attempting to assassinate Ronald Reagan.

A Need for Tenderness

Personality is derived from human experiences that involve the reduction of two kinds of tensions: like Freud, physical needs, and, in contrast with Freud, interpersonal anxiety. *Needs* seek *satisfactions:* " . . . all those end states which are rather closely connected with the bodily organization" such as relief from want of oxygen, water, food, body warmth, and so forth (Sullivan, 1947, p. 6). **Interpersonal anxiety** is a tension that is alleviated in relationships with significant others or in feelings of well-being.

      Like Horney, Sullivan saw infants as being totally powerless and at the mercy of other people for their security. However, Sullivan further theorized that the infant's nearly absolute dependency revolves around a **mothering one,** a " . . . significant, relatively adult personality whose cooperation is necessary to keep the infant alive" (1953, p. 54). This critically important individual addresses the infant's **need for tenderness** which, different from "love," refers to relief from various tensions (1953). Sullivan effectively captured the essence of the close connection between the infant and the mothering one: "The observed activity of the infant arising from the tension of needs induces tension in the mothering one, which . . . is experienced as tenderness and [leads] to activities [that provide] relief of the infant's needs" (1953, p. 39).

Basic Concepts: Sullivan

Empathy, Anxiety, and Security

"The tension of anxiety, when present in the mothering one, induces anxiety in the infant" (1953, p. 41). Anxiety may be transferred to the infant when it is subjected to unsympathetic behaviors by the mothering one that communicate something is "bad" or "disapproved," even though the origin of the mothering one's tension has no direct connection with the infant. It may be due to the caregiver's personality, uncertainty about the parenting role, or circumstances unrelated to the infant, such as parental illness, fatigue, or upset due to bad news. However, the infant has no way of knowing about these possibilities. She or he simply participates in the caregiver's tension or discomfort through **empathy,** "the term that we use to refer to the peculiar emotional linkage [that exists between the] infant [and] other significant people—the mother or the nurse" (1947, p. 8). It involves the reciprocal role-taking seen in the infant's expression of need for tenderness and the mother's motivation to provide tenderness (Hayes, 1994). Anxiety acquired by this and other means can interfere with the satisfaction of physical and tenderness needs. For example, the infant may cry or regurgitate, thereby disrupting critical behaviors such as feeding, which further increases both its own and the mothering one's anxiety. Because it has no effective means to remove, reduce, or escape from the anxiety, the infant is totally dependent on a caretaker for relief. Due to the infant's helpless condition, only the mothering one can provide relief in the form of **interpersonal security,** "relaxation of the tension of anxiety," which is experienced as a return to a tranquil, untroubled state (1953, p. 42). This unique experience is different from the satisfaction that occurs when physical needs are met.

Three Modes of Experience and Six Stages of Development

Sullivanian personality development encompasses six stages, spanning infancy through late adolescence, each centering on a unique kind of interpersonal relationship. Because three of the stages revolve around his rather abstract and complex "modes of experience," which are difficult to "put a finger on," it is best to consider them first.

Modes of Experience.   The **prototaxic** mode is the earliest (infancy), most primitive type of experience, a state of generalized sensation or feeling, in the absence of thought (Sullivan, 1953). The infant knows only what William James called a "big, blooming, buzzing confusion," vague perceptions of momentary states having no "before" or "after." There is no awareness of self as separate from the world. Sullivan, who often avoided formal definitions, is rescued by Patrick Mullahy's translation of *prototaxic:*

> The infant vaguely feels or 'prehends' earlier and later states without realizing any serial connection between them. . . . He has no awareness of himself as an entity separate from

the rest of the world. In other words, his felt experience is all of a piece, undifferentiated, without definite limits. It is as if his experiences were "cosmic" (Mullahy, 1948, in Sullivan, 1953, p. 28).

The **parataxic** mode is experienced as the infant becomes a child who begins to use speech, but still makes few logical connections within the sequence of its experiences (approximately the preschool years; Sullivan, 1953). Thinking and speech are disorganized and disjunctive as in a dream, and understanding remains minimal. There is a sense of "magic" in which things "just happen," as in seeing colorful Christmas lights suddenly appear with the simple flip of a switch. In adults, parataxic experience may serve as a rough basis for memories related to habits. Examples include routine activities that often occur without conscious thought: dressing, walking to class, eating, or doing repetitive arithmetic. Again, Mullahy comes to Sullivan's aid:

> As the infant develops . . . , the original undifferentiated wholeness of experience is broken. However, the 'parts' . . . are not related or connected in a logical fashion. . . . The child cannot yet relate them to one another or make logical distinctions among them. . . . Since no connections or relations are established, there is no logical movement of 'thought' from one idea to the next. The parataxic mode is not a step by step process (Mullahy, 1948, in Sullivan, 1953, p. 28).

In other words, the unbroken mass—like a glob of jelly—that was feeling and perception is now segmented into parts, like separate cubes of jelly. Nevertheless, the parts are disconnected and not logically related to one another.

The **syntaxic** mode becomes important when the meaning of words becomes shared with most other people so that experience, judgments, and observations can be shared (approximately the early elementary school years; Sullivan, 1953). The individual and another person can communicate syntaxic experiences because both define language symbols alike. This is the stage of "consensual validation" in which children learn to separate experiences they share with others from experiences peculiar to themselves, make their thoughts and feelings clear to others, and appreciate what others are thinking and feeling (Sullivan, 1953). Again, Mullahy provides clarity:

> The child gradually learns the . . . meaning of language. . . . These meanings have been acquired from group activities, interpersonal activities, social experience. Consensually validated symbol activity involves an appeal to principles which are accepted as true by the hearer (Mullahy, 1948, in Sullivan, 1953, p. 28).

When children acquire the syntaxic mode, others have taught them the shared rules of organizing thoughts so that thoughts and speech are no longer disconnected. The undifferentiated mass that became the unsystematically linked assortment of pieces has now become an assemblage of separate parts, each bearing some relationship to some of the others. The direction of development as reflected by the three modes is toward increased socialization. Over time, the "social majority" rules over personal interpretations.

Infancy: Prototaxic Feelings about "Good" and "Bad" Caregivers. The **infancy** stage starts at birth and continues until the appearance of speech (Sullivan, 1953). The development of personality begins with feeding, because the infant's initial interpersonal situation is "nipple-in-lips": the infant's mouth to the mother's breast or to the bottle. The experience integrates the infant's need for water, food, and contact, and the caregiver's need to show tenderness. The infant's accompanying hand and foot movements—touching, grasping, pushing, rubbing, and cuddling—become an increasingly important part of this first interpersonal situation.

As the infant begins to accumulate experiences, it forms **personifications,** investments of human attributes in persons or objects that do not actually possess the assigned traits, at least not in the degree to which they are applied. For example, if the infant's need for nourishment is accommodated by the willing presentation of a satisfying nipple, it forms the early personification "good nipple." When the infant's interactions with the mothering one are experienced as satisfying, warm, and comforting, it forms the personification "good mother." This empathic sensory image is not of the real mother, but of the infant's vague, prototaxic sense that feeding experiences are "good" because they result in relaxation of tensions. If the same caregiver interacts with the infant in ways that are "rough, sound unpleasant, hurt the baby, and generally discompose him," the infant will be led to form the "bad mother" personification, which entails the "nipple of anxiety" (Sullivan, 1953, pp. 116 and 87). Sullivan summarized these personifications: ". . . all relations with . . . people . . . [who] are a part of . . . satisfying . . . the infant's needs blend into a single personification which I call the good mother . . . all experience . . . which results in severe anxiety blends into a single personification which I call . . . the bad mother" (Sullivan, 1953, p. 120).

These personifications may endure in memory as "eidetic people": "illusory people," "imaginary people," or "past people" who are sometimes dredged up and matched to people in adult life (boss as "bad mother"). Personal personifications develop as well. The individual comes to know "me," "good me," "bad me," and "not me." Interestingly, Blechner (1994) has proposed a fifth category. "Maybe me" is a me under consideration, a potential me that involves some dissociated aspect of personality that the individual has yet to muster the courage to accept. The threatening, aggressive side of the infant is an example. Later the sexual facet of the child would fit the "maybe me."

You may wonder how the primitive prototaxic skills of the infant allow it to differentiate between "bad mother" and "good mother." The infant cannot understand what the mothering one says, nor can it interpret "appearances" (Sullivan, 1953). "Good" and "bad" mothers may look the same in basic physical appearance, including clothing. The "good nipple" and the "bad nipple" are identical in appearance. The signs the infant must read to tell "good" from "bad" are subtle. In the case of the "bad mother" they are **forbidding gestures,** negative, covert cues such as a wrinkled brow, a cold tone of voice, a too tight grasp, a hesitancy, reluctance, or even revulsion at having to interact with the infant. Sullivan put it this way:

> The discrimination of heard differences in the mother's vocalization and seen differences in the postural tensions of the mother's face, and perhaps later of differences in speed and rhythm of her gross bodily movements in coming toward the infant, presenting the bottle, changing the diapers . . . all these . . . discriminations . . . are frequently associated with . . . anxiety, including the nipple of anxiety . . . (Sullivan, 1953, pp. 86–87).

Early experiences with others allow the infant to begin differentiating its own self-system from the world around it. Experiences of positive satisfactions, in which the mothering one is pleased, are organized around a personification of "good me." In this case, interpersonal security prevails. On the other hand, experiences of anxiety in the parent–infant relationship are organized around a personification of "bad me," resulting in insecurity. Undifferentiated early experience begins to break down into parts. The infant learns to make some distinctions between itself and the world.

What creates "bad mothers?" Serbin and Karp (2003) believe that people's parenting styles result from observing behavior modeled by their parents and from their own behavioral orientations evidenced early in life. These researchers note that both current parents and the next generation of parents, their children, are influenced by environmental contexts such as poverty, foster care, and dangerous neighborhoods. Parental modeling of aggressive, belittling, rejecting behavior and harsh environmental contexts produce children who will grow up to be hostile, insensitive, punishing parents. This destructive process generates a vicious cycle of bad parenting that extends from generation to generation.

On the other hand, "good mothers" participate with their children in a *mutually responsive orientation* (MRO; Kodhanska, 2002). MRO involves parents who are responsive to their children's needs and who share their own "positive affect" with their children. They create a chronic positive mood in their children that binds their offspring to themselves. The "good mother" can read her children's most subtle "signals of distress, unhappiness, needs, bids for attention, or attempts to exert influence" (p. 192). Such a close bond develops that the child not only seeks to please the parent, but also strives to become like her. Among the positive attributes displayed by children of MRO relationships is a strong conscience. The MRO relationship is illustrated in Box 6.2.

Childhood: Parataxic Learning Applicable to Social Habits and Self.   The **childhood stage** emerges with articulate speech and ends with the appearance of the need for peers. A number of important developmental tasks are begun during this stage. First, the child is rapidly socialized regarding what is "proper." Children come to accept parents' lessons on feeding, toilet use, cleanliness, obedience, oughts, and musts. Second, language becomes a tool for manipulating the social world into alleviating the child's tensions. Third, there is continuing development of the self-system, which functions to minimize anxiety. As its ability to learn matures, the child becomes more skillful at reading the forbidding gestures of significant others. The self-system is partly like Freud's "ego" in that it seeks satisfaction in ways that avoid anxiety. The self-system minimizes anxiety through *selective inattention* to threatening events and by anticipating, and thereby avoiding, experiences that are incompatible with its past development. It sinks into maladjustment when it resorts to *dissociation,* severing any connection of the threatening events or experiences to the self. It is through our self-systems that we psychologically carry our parents around with us throughout our lives, as a continuing reminder of what is "approved" and "disapproved." Thus, the self-system is also similar to Freud's "superego."

Fourth, negative emotions such as disgust, shame, anger, and resentment are learned. The child also learns negative social interaction orientations such as *malevolence,* perhaps the most disastrous lesson taught during childhood personality development. Ironically, the child may develop malevolence while seeking tenderness.

BOX 6.2 • *The Good Mother*

Adam was Sara's first baby, but you wouldn't know it by watching them interact. There seems to be an invisible connection between the two, as if the umbilical cord were still intact, but incorporeal and infinitely stretchable. If Adam is in his room and Sara down the hall, he can make certain sounds that not only bring her to him, but also induce her to carry whatever he needs with her. She arrives promptly with a blanket, if he requires warmth, a bottle, if he needs nourishment, or a fresh diaper if he needs changing. When she picks him up, there isn't the awkward tensing and wriggling that some babies display. He tends to smile faintly, coo, and maintain his relaxed posture as she raises him to her shoulder. Once snugly against her, Adam shuffles his knees up and down and rubs his head against her in an apparent attempt to get even closer. If she should have to leave him for a time, he waits patiently, confident that she will appear when he needs her.

When Sara's friends come to visit he is comfortable with their presence. Drawn by the symphony of interpersonal harmony performed by mother and child, they show up regularly. He does not react when Sara leaves the room while they attend to him. In fact, he smiles sweetly when they murmur to him or playfully tickle him. But, even though he can't see her when she returns and despite the cacophony of voices, he spontaneously moves his head in her direction when she speaks. When she is ill or feeling down, he senses her mood and summons her to him as though he wishes to comfort her. Likewise, she knows when he is "coming down with something" before he gets it. Her pediatrician is amazed that Sara can spot Adam's medical problems before they show overt signs such as fever. Sara and Adam are two parts of one whole. Their interactions are a marvel of cooperation, coordination, and synchronous affection.

[M]any children . . . when they need tenderness, . . . are not only denied tenderness, but they are treated in a fashion to provoke anxiety. . . . A child may discover that . . . the need for tenderness toward the potent figures . . . leads . . . to his being . . . made anxious, . . . made fun of. . . . Under those circumstances, the developmental course changes [so] that the . . . need for tenderness brings a foresight of anxiety. . . . The child learns . . . that it is highly disadvantageous to show any need for tender cooperation from the . . . figures around him, in which case he shows . . . the basic malevolent attitude, the attitude that one really lives among enemies . . . (Sullivan, 1953, p. 214).

Having a strong interest in the processes by which children learn, Sullivan proposed five main avenues to acquiring new, useful information. Three of these are straightforward, commonsensical, and rather self-evident: (1) *trial and success* (behaviors that succeed are stamped into memory as habits); (2) *rewards and punishments;* and (3) *trial and error* (noting errors in order to avoid them). However, one of them is unique and innovative. Children may **learn by anxiety:** when anxiety is not severe, individuals may become acquainted with the situations in which it is present so that those circumstances may be avoided. Even infants can learn that some situation or object is not desirable, thus to be avoided. Later, with the arrival of language ability, such circumstances can be labeled as anxiety-provoking, making them easier to shun. A still higher plane of learning by anxiety involves the **anxiety gradient,** "learning to discriminate increasing from diminishing anxiety and to alter activity in the direction of the latter" (Sullivan, 1953, p. 452). Children must be able to monitor sometimes subtle changes in their feelings and become aware of the situations in which the changes occur. Then, when anxiety rises, they can move themselves to circumstances that will lower it. For example, the child might learn that playing with the genitals when the mothering one is present causes steadily rising anxiety. To change the gradient, when the mothering one is present the child must stop manipulating the genitals and apply its hands to a task that is associated with lowered anxiety. An example would be drawing pictures that please the mothering one.

Sullivan wrote about three contributions to *socialization* of the child—becoming a functional citizen of society. The *frequency* with which the child behaves can cue the child and trainers as to which behaviors are being acquired. Attention to frequency may allow cultivation of behaviors that are socially desirable and culling of those that are undesirable. *Consistency* is the "repetition of particular patterns of events." If the child behaves consistently, learned behaviors are being performed or behavioral acquisition is underway. *Sanity* is an attribute of parents who fully understand the assets and deficits of their children so that educational demands are reasonable and appropriate. Without sanity children may not discover what they are good at, and, thus, at later stages, they may be uncertain as to their worthiness (Bromberg, 1993). Box 6.3 allows you to experiment with learning processes.

BOX 6.3 • *What Learning Processes Were Involved in Your Childhood Training?*

Four of Sullivan's learning processes are arranged into two categories and each is briefly defined. For each of the four, pick a number between 0 and 100 to represent the percentage of your training—instituted by you or your parents—that employed the process in question. Your four numbers should add up to one hundred. For example, you might assign 10 to "learning by anxiety," 20 to "rewards and punishments," 40 to "trial and success," and 30 to "trial and error."

Positively Oriented Processes

Process	*Number out of 100*
Trial and success—attempting a behavior until it succeeds.	
Trial and error—observing own and others' behavior to profit by knowledge of mistakes.	

Negatively Oriented Processes

Process	*Number out of 100*
Learn by anxiety—individuals become acquainted with anxiety-provoking situations so that these may be avoided.	
Rewards and punishments—arranging for pleasure to encourage a behavior and punishment to discourage its undesirable counterpart.	

Note which process you assigned the largest number. If its assigned number is 40 or greater, you are indicating that it was clearly the primary training procedure in your learning history. Tally by category: add the two numbers in the positive category and the two in the negative category. If one of these two subtotals is 60 or more, you are indicating that you were primarily subjected to positively or negatively oriented processes, depending on the category to which the number applies.

Juvenile Era: Syntaxic Experiences of Finding Playmates and Questioning Parents.
The **juvenile era** is ushered in with the child's need for peer companions, or "playmates
rather like oneself." During the elementary school years, the child has many opportunities
to learn the ways of other children and show social subordination to new authority figures
such as teachers, coaches, and club leaders. During this time, children gain *compeers,* playmates who teach them more about their social capabilities and shield them from loneliness.

The juvenile develops an appreciation of certain variations in living never conceived
of before, some "right" and some "wrong." Ideas and social operations learned at home
may be inapplicable at school or with friends, and are reformulated. Authorities, including
one's parents, are reduced from godlike figures to people. Along with cooperation are experiences of competition, stereotyping, ostracism, and compromise. References are made
to "our team" and "our teacher." Social accommodation is partly motivated by peer pressure. A personally meaningful orientation to living takes form, based on a growing understanding of one's needs and future goals.

Preadolescence: Collaborating with a Chum.   The period of **preadolescence** is brief,
beginning with the need for interpersonal intimacy in the form of a close relationship with
another person "of comparable status." Somewhere between the ages of 8½ and 10, the
child "begins to develop a real sensitivity to what matters to another person" (Sullivan,
1953, p. 245). One's predominant interest is in establishing a relationship with a *chum,* a
particular member of the same sex who becomes a friend and confidant. Preadolescents
contribute to the happiness of their friends through collaboration. Each makes adjustments
aimed at providing mutual satisfactions. When two young people become important to
each other, the worth of both is supported by the process of consensual validation, in this
case, sharing beliefs. Preadolescents may spend hours in shared daydreaming. Participation in cliques or gangs may be traced to interlocking, two-person relationships in which
pair members A and B each also have relationships with pair members C and D. Loneliness resulting from the absence of close peers may be overcome by acting on an irresistible
need for cooperative companionship. This need is so powerful that people seek relations
with others despite fear of rejection.

Early Adolescence: Experiencing Lust toward a Sexual Partner.   **Early adolescence**
erupts at puberty when the need for intimacy evolves toward lustful feelings of closeness
and tenderness with a sexual partner. Interest in a member of one's own sex is usually replaced by interest in a member of the opposite sex, a person who is "very different." During this time, patterns of behavior emerge that satisfy **lust,** Sullivan's term for "certain
tensions of or pertaining to the genitals," culminating in orgasm (1953, p. 109). "Lust,"
along with *intimacy* needs, now become important.

Sullivan classified lust and intimacy needs into three categories: (1) orientation to
others on the basis of intimacy needs; (2) orientation to others on the basis of partner's status (self or other, same or different gender, human or not, alive or dead; lust); and (3) orientation to others on the basis of how the genitals are used during sexual interaction (lust).

Sullivan used the Greek root word "philos," meaning "loving," as the suffix for terms
referring to expressions of intimacy needs. In this category (1) he postulated choices of *intimacy expression* that correspond to three kinds of people. First, there is the **autophilic**

person, one who manifests no preadolescent development, because it has not occurred or was attempted without success, causing the continuation of self-directed love. This kind of person's intimacy expressions have the flavor of "narcissism." "An **isophilic person** has been unable to progress past preadolescence, and continues to regard as suitable for intimacy only people who are as like himself as possible . . . that is, members of his own sex" (Sullivan, 1953, p. 192). Finally, "A **heterophilic person** has . . . made the early adolescent change in which he has become intensely interested in achieving intimacy with members of . . . the other sex" (Sullivan, 1953, p. 192).

The "orientation to others according to status" category (2) is related to lust and contains mostly familiar entries. *Homosexuals* orient to the same sex, *heterosexuals* orient to the opposite sex, and *autosexuals* orient to themselves. Less familiar is the *katasexual,* who prefers nonhumans such as animals or dead people.

Lust regarding use of the genitals (3; *Oh Please Make Amends*) has four unique varieties. **Orthogenital** involves the integration of one's own genitals with the "natural receptor genitals" of the opposite sex, that is, heterosexual use of the genitals (p. 293). In **paragenital** use of the sex organs one acts to seek contact with genitals opposite one's own, but in such a way that impregnation will not occur. Rubbing one's own genitals against those of an opposite-sex person is an obvious example. **Metagenital** use does not involve one's own genitals, but another person's genitals are involved. Masturbating someone else or performing oral sex on another person are examples. **Amphigenital** refers to the case in which one or both members of a pair, who both may be homosexual or heterosexual, take on a role that is different from their usual role. For example, a woman straps on a penis-like device and uses it in sex with her partner. Two other varieties predate Sullivan: *mutual masturbation,* which is self-explanatory, or *onanism,* which refers to heterosexual intercourse that is terminated before orgasm occurs. Theories of homosexuality are further explored in Box 6.4.

Late Adolescence: Establishing Love Relationships.   What separates early and late adolescence is not so much biological as interpersonal maturation. Partially developed aspects of personality fall into place in the late stage. People are able to tolerate some previously avoided anxiety, which allows favorable changes to be made in the self-system. **Late adolescence** begins with the acknowledgment of an orientation to genital behavior and how to fit that revelation into the rest of life, then ends with "the establishment of a fully human or mature repertory of interpersonal relations" (Sullivan, 1953, p. 297). Being able to take first steps on adult legs, one can "establish relationships of love for some other person, in which relationship the other person is as significant, or nearly as significant, as one's self" (p. 34). Table 6.1 summarizes the six stages along with the corresponding benchmarks.

Evaluation

Contributions

Physical Contact and Peer Relationships.   Human infants show a need to have intimate physical contact with a parental figure, termed "primary object-clinging" by John

BOX 6.4 • *Theories of Homosexuality: More Sophisticated Than in Sullivan's Time*

One will not be surprised to find that there is no theory about homosexuality that most scientists accept. Theories of homosexuality come in two varieties. Some scientists think that it is learned during the course of growing up, while others believe that it is biologically determined. A modern example of the "learning" hypothesis has been offered by Michael Storms (1982). Supposedly, individuals who reach sexual maturity early direct their new sexual urges toward those who are most readily available, the same-sex friends with whom children their age exclusively associate. People who mature on time or late have already given up exclusive same-sex associations in favor of interaction with the opposite sex. Therefore, they direct their sexuality to people of the opposite sex. Storm's theory has faded in recent years for want of supporting data.

Daryl Bem's (Azar, 1997; Bem, 1996) "exotic is erotic" theory is similar in that early interactions with peers are crucial, but this time it is relating with the opposite gender that is important. Bem's view is that, if, for example, one is a boy who spends most of his time with girls and prefers girl-typical activities, he will see boys as different from himself. Because other boys are different, thus exotic, the same gender becomes sexually attractive.

Evidence relevant to gay male development is found in the typical male ring-finger-longer-than-the-index-finger configuration. Homosexual men show the longer ring finger configuration less than heterosexual men (Lippa, 2003). Other work indicates that lesbian and bisexual women are in-between heterosexual women and men in magnitude of the inner ear's response to a certain auditory click (Holden, 1998). Exposure to male hormones in the womb may be the causative factor. In multiple-pup rat litters, a female fetus surrounded by two male fetuses shows clear male physical characteristics and behaviors after it is born (Vanderbergh, 2003).

A neurological study of the hypothalamus, a brain body known to have sexual function, has revealed a difference between homosexual and heterosexual males. LeVay (1991) found differences between the structures of gay and "straight" men's hypothalamuses. However, some biological paths have been dead-ends. Initial enthusiasm for a gene on the maternal X chromosome that may predispose men to homosexuality has been dampened (Rice, Anderson, Risch, & Ebers, 1999).

TABLE 6.1 *Sullivan's Six Developmental Epochs*

Epochs	Characteristics	Capacities for
Infancy	Need for contact with caregiver; prototaxic experience	Beginning speech
Childhood	Need for adult participation in activities	Language
Juvenile Era	Parataxic experience	Compeer or playmate relationships;
Preadolescence	Need for acceptance by peers	Close, same-sex relationship–chum
Early Adolescence	Syntaxic experience	Close, opposite-sex relationships; patterning of lustful or genital behavior
Late Adolescence	Need for intimate exchange with a loved one	Mature and independent development of love relationships in which another person is as important as oneself

Bowlby (1969). In a 1951 report to the World Health Organization, Bowlby concluded that mental health in infants requires a warm, intimate, and continuous relationship with a maternal figure, not necessarily the biological mother. He indicated that infants placed in institutional settings, such as orphanages, who do not receive physical contact from a nurturing figure, show developmental and survival difficulties attributable to interpersonal deprivation.

To illustrate, Spitz (1946) observed symptoms of depression in 45 of 123 infants who had been placed in nursery homes following separation from their parents. Symptoms included loss of appetite, trouble sleeping, crying, slow motor movements, apathy, physical withdrawal such as turning toward a wall, vulnerability to infection, and slowed development. An extreme form of this reaction is *marasmus,* a syndrome of neglected infants who "waste away" in the absence of any physical cause (Bosselman, 1958). That marasmus is counteracted by daily physical contact with a particular adult caregiver has been translated into international prevention programs involving routine, daily "cuddling" of all babies in institutions. After the fall of the Communist regime in Rumania, many institutionalized infants and children were found to be suffering from a condition similar to that described by Spitz. During the 1990s, many U.S. citizens traveled to Rumania and Russia to bring children back with them, or stayed to provide the close and warm interaction that promotes survival.

Separation may elicit attachment behaviors, through which infants try to find the missing caregiver and reestablish physical contact. Also, infants, especially those subjected to more prolonged separation, may show detachment behaviors of indifference, protest, or despair (Bowlby, 1969; Suomi, Collins, Harlow, & Ruppenthal, 1976). Ainsworth (1979) linked personality adjustment in the first few years to what are now called secure and anxious-ambivalent attachment styles, finding that, in later years, the secure were better adjusted than the anxious ambivalent.

Harlow placed infant rhesus monkeys in individual cages containing two substitute or surrogate mothers (see Harlow, 1958). One "mother" was made of wire mesh equipped with a milk-supplying nipple. The other was made of terry cloth, and in some cases, also contained a nipple. Observations revealed that infant monkeys spent far more time clinging to the cloth-covered surrogate, regardless of whether it was the source of milk. When frightening stimuli were introduced into the cages, such as a mechanical teddy bear beating a drum, the infants immediately sought security by running to the cloth mothers.

Suomi and Harlow (1972) reported fascinating use of younger-age peers as "therapists" in successfully rehabilitating monkeys who previously had been socially isolated for six months. The supportive behaviors of the young monkey "therapists" that were caged with the former isolates may be analogous to the "trust" and the gradual "reeducation" characteristic of Sullivan's approaches to therapy with humans. It certainly is analogous to the benefits peers offer one another, as seen in the notions of "compeer" and "chum."

The "Psychiatric Interview": A Contribution to Helping People Achieve Psychological Adjustment. Sullivan's (1954) posthumous book, *The Psychiatric Interview,* is a classic text on the most widely used assessment technique, the interview of individuals with psychological problems. Sullivan saw the interview as an alternative to Freud's methods because it appears to work better with a wider range of patients, from the mildly to the seriously disturbed. His three contributions to interviewing encompass: (1) assumptions about the nature of interview data; (2) structural outlines for obtaining and organizing information; and (3) guidelines for interpreting the interview process and defining the roles of the participants.

To Sullivan (1954), two factors determine that "there are no purely objective data in psychiatry" (p. 3). First, much inference is required before the information people provide about themselves begins to make sense. Second, the interviewer directly influences the information people provide. In brief, data about the patient passes through the interviewer, who operates as a *participant observer:*

> the psychiatrist cannot stand off to one side and . . . [notice] what someone else does, without becoming personally implicated in the operation. His principal instrument of observation is his self—his personality, him as a person. The processes . . . that make up the data . . . subjected to scientific study occur, not in the subject person nor in the observer, but in the situation which is created between the observer and his subject (Sullivan, 1954, p. 3).

Sullivan's statement indicates an ironic circumstance, not fully recognized by Freud and others. Attempts to assess the personality of another individual inevitably involve the intrusion of the assessor's personality, which contaminates the data bearing on the interviewee's personality. Then one is stuck with a dilemma: to what degree does the data tell us about the interviewee's personality and to what degree does it inform us about the interviewer's personality? The heart and soul of the interview and major source of revelations about the personality is:

> a situation of primarily *vocal* communication in a *two-person* group . . . [which involves] a progressively unfolding expert–client . . . [relationship that illuminates] *characteristic patterns of living* [and offers the] . . . benefit[s] [that derive from learning about] . . . patterns he experiences as particularly troublesome or especially valuable (Sullivan, 1954, p. 4).

The first of four interview stages is called the *inception,* the formal reception of the client and inquiry about why he or she has come to the interviewer. Second, the *reconnaissance* stage "consists in obtaining a rough outline of the social or personal history of the patient" (p. 40). In the critically important third phase, *detailed inquiry,* in-depth exploration occurs that involves many "subtleties and complexities" of technique all employed in the interest of examining "another person's life" (p. 410). In the fourth phase, *interruption* signals that a particular interview session has come to an end, but other sessions are expected to occur, and *termination* means no further sessions are expected.

The detailed inquiry, the core of the psychiatric interview, begins with the therapist's attempts to gain an accurate impression of the patient. This pursuit is hindered by the patient's understandable concern about what the "doctor" thinks of him or her. Initially the patient attempts to avoid a bad impression if not to create a good one. At this point, the job of the therapist is to gain the patient's confidence so that he or she will make honest self-disclosures. This task may be accomplished by showing irritation-free tolerance for the patient's circuitous answers to questions, "walking around the obvious," as Sullivan put it (p. 98). Eventually, the patient will see that direct and forthright answers will be favorably received.

Beyond the initial game of cat and mouse played by interviewer and patient, there are two substantive issues addressed during the detailed inquiry phase. The interviewee may signal anxiety, the first issue, by abrupt changes or transitions in the course of the interview. The interviewer may take advantage of these changes to either lessen anxiety, for the comfort of the patient, or raise it, for the purpose of exploring it. Episodes of anxiety may be especially intense when the patient is concerned about the therapist's view of her or him. In any case, these episodes are uniformly unwanted. Unlike fear, which may sometimes attract us—we may attend a scary movie or ride a roller coaster—anxiety is never wanted. Thus, in therapy, as in everyday life, when anxiety is on the rise, patients do whatever is necessary to lower it. They may even sometimes "act . . . like asses" (Sullivan, 1954, p. 101). Episodes of anxiety during interviews cue interviewers that they have "hit a nerve."

The second substantive issue involves the self-system. During the later part of childhood, the individual refines **security operations,** skills that allow avoidance of forbidding gestures. When these skills are properly and successfully applied, the child can maintain a state of relative euphoria. Should these abilities fail—the self-system is unable to protect the person's feeling of well-being—a drop in euphoria occurs and is experienced as anxiety. Thus, protecting well-being or relative euphoria is a basic task of everyone from infant to adult and certainly is a major goal of the patient during the interview. The exercise of security operations gives the person better **foresight,** the capacity to look ahead in search of good experiences and in the interest of avoiding bad ones. Foresight is facilitated by looking constantly for signs of approval and disapproval in others.

What the patient needs from the interviewer are signals indicating that he or she is doing fine and is "approved." Absent or ambiguous signals from the therapist generate anxiety, which may reactivate the game of cat and mouse: "you are reading me and I look good . . . No! I'm coming across badly . . . I'll try to communicate another impression." All these signals and miscommunications are evidence that the self-system is "up and running." The job of the interviewer is then to help the patient tune the self-system, make it run right so that she or he can receive euphoria-maintaining signals.

These are the therapeutic tasks of the psychiatric interview, but what can patients do for themselves? Believing, like Adler, that troubled people must take action in their own behalf, Sullivan outlined three tasks for patients (Sullivan, 1947). First, the patient, and everyone else, can learn to **notice changes in the body** that signal decreases or increases in the tension signifying anxiety. By monitoring their bodies, patients can recognize when anxiety is rising or falling and the situations in which these events occur. Being aware of the situations associated with increases or decreases of anxiety is a kind of insight that precedes coping with anxiety.

Second, the patient—and the rest of us—can learn to **notice marginal thoughts,** thoughts that monitor, critique, and alter speech in terms of formation and grammar, and in terms of errors that may cause incomplete or misunderstood communications to others. There are two kinds of "critics." The first is called I_1 and is merely concerned with the mechanics of speech. We are often aware of this "rather unfriendly critic" (Sullivan, 1954, p. 99). It is an irritant that chastises us for our failures to speak correctly. By contrast, I_2, a "rather intelligent creature," is concerned with more central matters: how well we are presenting ourselves to other people. I_2 is a mirror that reflects the impression we are making on others back to us. We may pay attention to I_1 and, based on its feedback, correct ourselves as we go. However, I_2, because it deals with more threatening interpersonal matters, is likely to be beyond our conscious awareness and show up only in increased tensions. Should we be able to tune in to I_2, we would be taking the first step toward dealing with the interpersonal issues that face us, and, at the same time, move toward lowering tension.

The third action that all of us can take, patients or not, is to **make prompt statements of all that comes to mind,** a process that is enabled by trusting the "situation to the extent of expressing the thoughts that it provokes" (p. 100). Performing this feat is easier said than done, however, because of inhibitory factors. People are likely to be plagued with thoughts of past behavioral disasters. They may wonder whether they are creating a bad impression on the interviewer and, therefore, may be reluctant to "speak their minds" about whatever is being discussed. Instead they may provide "a circumstantial account of some insignificant current event, or an extravagant report of the marvelous good results that have . . . been achieved by exposure to the . . . " therapist (p. 100). Only when they learn to speak candidly about the current situation will they be able to provide the information that the interviewer needs to help them. The detailed inquiry phase may continue in any subsequent session. The interviewer's tasks, relating to anxiety and the self-system, and the three actions by the patient, jointly constitute the therapeutic benefits of the psychiatric interview. The interview is a productive "two-person group" partnership benefiting the patient.

Limitations

Formal science was not well understood nor highly valued by Sullivan, who was marginally trained as a physician and psychiatrist. Like Freud, Horney, Adler, and Jung, he was a clinician and theorist rather than a scientist. Sullivan declared the virtual impossibility of "doing science" with regard to personality and relied on informal methods of study such as clinical observation. More generally, unlike psychologists of Sullivan's day, psychiatrists of his time did not make "doing science" a major priority. They were strictly therapists who were more apt to be guided by nonscience concerns, such as addressing people's psychological problems. In view of these circumstances, it is little wonder that, to this day, there is a virtual absence of direct scientific support for Sullivan's theory. Although consistent with Sullivan's ideas, even the results of the "monkey" studies by Harlow were not directly inspired by Sullivanian theory. In fact, these studies support the ideas of Bowlby, as well as those of many other theorists including Horney, not just Sullivan. It seems that Sullivanians must look to other people for support of their ideas, as they have generated precious little of their own.

While many of Sullivan's concepts approached profundity, others bordered on the trivial and still others appeared to be borrowed from someone else. For example, "rewards and punishments" is a common sense notion familiar to everybody's grandmother, and "trial and success" appears borrowed from E. L. Thorndike, without credit. Sullivan seemed to theorize about everything, but it mattered little to him whether others had already thoroughly "covered the subject." Because Sullivan used many of Freud's concepts (free association, repression, and insight) one may wonder whether he was really a Freudian who developed a language that made him "sound" different. In any case, he may have gotten major orientations from other theorists. For example, did he originate the emphasis on anxiety, or did he get it from Horney, a theorist with whom he was personally familiar? Sullivan is not listed among the greatest psychologists of the twentieth century (Haggbloom et al., 2002).

Conclusions

It has been argued that some of what readers of Sullivan attribute to Freud is actually original Sullivanian thought that was not even inspired by Freud (Robbins, 1989). As you have seen, his theory and therapy bears only superficial resemblance to Freud's. He may also have sometimes written about trivia, but he certainly introduced some highly original and useful ideas, including "prototaxic, parataxic, and syntaxic," which originated with Sullivan and anticipated modern cognitive developmental theories. Also, one may wonder, who "stole" from whom? Maybe Horney was heavily influenced by Sullivan. Finally, some of his ideas laid a solid foundation for future theory and research. "Foresight"—being pulled by the future rather than being pushed by the past—was one of his creative ideas that has several modern advocates. Forbidding gestures, subtle signs often communicated without words, was an early consideration of what has become the currently fascinating field of "nonverbal communication."

Some individuals question the credibility of a disturbed psychiatrist who tried to offer the rest of us advice concerning our problems. However, one must remember that many creative contributors to the human condition, scientists, artists, and entertainers, were individuals who had "brilliant lights in the attic that sometimes blinked erratically." The revered artist Van Gogh was considerably off-center. Relativity theorist Albert Einstein and "the father of the atomic bomb," Robert Oppenheimer, were at least eccentric. Even extraordinary comedians, such as Lenny Bruce, Jonathan Winters, Robin Williams, and Richard Pryor led troubled lives (the Woody Allen you see on the screen could well be the real Woody). In fact, even profoundly disturbed people, such as schizophrenics, can be unusually creative (Carson & Butcher, 1992). Perhaps what some of us may view as "obscurity in Sullivan's writings" is creative thinking that is too unique and complex to be penetrated by less than deeply reflective contemplation. Perhaps we should reconsider Sullivan's works, this time with attention to what is "written between the lines."

Summary Points

1. Sullivan's family lived in rural New York. His achievements may have been spurred by a desire to rise above his background. His life reflects the diversity he represented: Irish, recent immigrant family, possibly gay or bisexual, Catholic, and probably schizophrenic. He suddenly disappeared from Cornell, possibly because he suffered a psychotic episode. When he surfaced, it was to enter a medical school of uncertain reputation where he performed poorly.

2. Without benefit of a formal residency, he became a psychiatrist interested in schizophrenia. His family history of low SES may have hastened his death. Sullivan died under mysterious circumstances. His family history of low SES may have hastened his death. Sullivan's definition of personality highlighted his "two persons at a time" approach. The core part of personality is the self-system. Sullivan postulated that people experience two kinds of tensions: (1) physical needs and (2) interpersonal anxiety. He believed the infant's tension induced tension in the mothering one, which is experienced as tenderness that meets the infant's needs.

3. "Empathy" is the mode through which the infant participates in the other person's tension. Anxiety aroused through the empathy mechanism can lead to disruptive behavior. Relief is provided by interpersonal security. Sullivan postulated three modes of experience: the infant's speechless prototaxic reality, the parataxic mode, involving speech but little logical connectiveness, and the syntaxic mode, entailing the advent of shared meanings.

4. In infancy "nipple-to-lips" contact with a mothering one becomes central. Personifications and the ability to read "forbidding gestures" occur at this time. The self-system is an example of the organizing, integrating process. "Bad mothering" may be passed down through generations and "good mothering" may operate through MRO. During the childhood stage, speech and the need for peers emerge. The self-system continues to develop greater facility at avoiding anxiety.

5. Manifestations of the need for tenderness become more complex: what once brought tenderness may now bring pain; because seeking tenderness may be disadvantageous, the child may develop a malevolent attitude. Sullivan posed five learning processes of which "learning by anxiety" is unique. Sullivan also pointed out the importance of frequency, consistency, and sanity in child training.

6. During the juvenile era, peers become central. Here, what the child has learned at home may not apply to life among peers. Parents lose their godlike aura and children begin to see themselves as members of groups and connected to nonfamily. During preadolescence, the child becomes genuinely sensitive to the needs of others and seeks a comparable status person for a close relationship. During early adolescence, lustful feelings arise and tenderness with a sexual partner is sought.

7. Expression of intimacy needs takes several different forms: (1) autophilic, intimacy need directed to self; (2) isophilic, directed to similar people; (3) heterophilic, directed to the opposite sex. The sexual orientations are autosexual, homosexual, or heterosexual. Genital use forms are: (1) orthogenital, integration with opposite sex person; (2) paragenital, sex without the risk of pregnancy; (3) metagenital, one's own genitals are not involved; and (4) amphigenital, pair members switch roles.

8. Modern theories of homosexuality include "early sexual maturity," "exotic is erotic," finger configuration, auditory click, hormonal exposure in the womb, and hypothalamic structure. Harlow's work with wire and cloth "monkey mothers" confirms the critical importance of close physical intimacy. Spitz showed that motherless infants develop severe depression. Other work indicates that separation from a mothering one may elicit attachment seeking in some infants and detachment in others. "Monkey therapists" improved the condition of socially isolated monkeys.

9. Limitations of the psychiatric interview are: (1) inference is required to interpret the information that people provide, and (2) the interviewer may influence what the interviewee provides. The four stages are: (1) inception; (2) reconnaissance; (3) detailed inquiry; and (4) interruption or termination. In Stage 3 patients are concerned with the impression they make. The self-system institutes security operations to maintain a state of relative euphoria. Patient contributions to the success of therapy are: (1) notice changes in the body that herald tension changes; (2) notice marginal thoughts, especially I_2; and (3) make prompt statements of all that comes to mind.

10. Because Sullivan was a clinician, not a scientist, there has been very little scientific research in direct support of his theory. Readers may have to scramble for additional information to interpret Sullivan's writings. He used so many of Freud's concepts that one wonders whether Sullivanian theory is actually Freudian. Nevertheless, many of Sullivan's ideas are highly original and extremely useful. Others, such as foresight and forbidding gestures, anticipated much modern theory and research. If he was a troubled person, disturbed individuals are often creative.

Running Comparison

Theorist	Sullivan in Comparison
Freud	He questioned Freud's "sexual instincts" but agreed on physical needs. He used "oral gratification," other Freudian terms. The self-system is somewhat ego-like and a little superego-like.
Adler	Some of his ideas had the flavor of social interest (compeer and chum) and he, like Adler, believed people must do for themselves.
Horney	They both showed interest in anxiety dating to infancy and in human relationships.
Fromm	The "katasexual" was somewhat like the necrophilous character of Fromm.
Carl Rogers	Both sought to make patients feel approved and both thought that patients could do much for themselves.

Essay/Critical Thinking Questions

1. Can a person's fears or perceptions that it is time to die hasten her or his death?

2. Can you develop an argument against Sullivan's two people at a time orientation?

3. What are the critical traits of a "mothering one"? Is gender an important factor?

4. Can you break up Sullivan's detailed inquiry stage into at least three parts?

5. Which modern theory of homosexuality fits Sullivan best?

E-mail Interaction _____

Write the author at b-allen@wiu.edu. Forward one of the following or phrase your own.

1. What is the central idea that distinguishes Sullivan from the other theorists covered so far?

2. What is the real truth about Sullivan's sexual orientation?

3. Why are researchers ignoring Sullivan's ideas?

The Seasons of Our Lives:
Erik Ericson

- Does everyone have an identity crisis?
- Does the development of human personality end with adolescence?
- Are the major tasks of life finished by retirement age?

Erik Erikson
http://facultyweb.cortland.edu/
~andersmd/erik/welcome.html

Erik Erikson is quite different from the other theorists covered in this book. He is the only one who had no advanced degree. In fact, Erikson never went beyond high school (Woodward, 1994), yet he made it all the way up the academic ladder to a professorship at Harvard. Because he lacked formal training, he was not so devoted to the usual academic traditions in psychology. His point of view is quite cross-disciplinary, mixing Freudian with anthropological language, but it was mostly unique. Some observers may regard his orientation as more philosophic than scientific. However, unlike Fromm and others who have migrated from psychological science to philosophy, some of Erikson's concepts have received scientific support.

Despite his devotion to Freud, Erikson's basic concepts are highly original and drawn from the common language rather than psychological jargon. This inclination makes his ideas not well related to most of the other theorists' concepts. His most creative idea is the "identity crisis." It is the vehicle on which he rode into a personality territory that was virtually unexplored. Gordon Allport did write about the "mature personality," but it was Erikson, more than anyone else, who popularized the idea that personality development does not end with adolescence. While Allport wrote of adult life without reference to stages, Erikson elaborated three stages of adult development. Just as he has broadened the vista of personality psychology, he will expand your view of the rest of your life.

Erikson, the Person

In 1902, Erik Homburger Erikson was born in the German town of Frankfurt to Danish parents (Stevens, 1983). His name, sans Homburger, meant "Erik son of Erik," an appellation taken from his father, whose only other legacy was a genetic gift contributed during a brief affair with his mother (Woodward, 1994). Abandoned by the senior Erik even before his birth, Erikson was nurtured by the Jewish pediatrician who married his mother when he was only a few years old (Stevens, 1983).

A look at Erikson's childhood makes it easy to see where his interest in "identity crises" originated. He was a child with an identity dilemma. As most boys are, he was pressured to pin his identity to his biological father, but it is almost impossible to tack anything onto a virtual void. Thus, he turned to his adopted father, who loved him and treated him well (Hall, 1983). Out of affection for his adopted father, Erikson initially chose Homburger as his surname. Even early in his career, including the period when he worked with Henry Murray, he went by Erik Homburger. Yet his ambivalence showed when later he relegated Homburger to a middle initial. This display of confusion about his stepfather was only a rare outward sign of the identity crises that occurred to him repeatedly. An ideal Aryan in appearance—he was tall and blond—Erikson faced taunts served up by the children at his father's synagogue. At the same time he was shunned by some of his German schoolmates because of his stepfather's religion. Later he toyed with the idea of following in his stepfather's professional footsteps, but threw it aside, along with other aspirations for an advanced education. The lack of an advanced degree was itself a source of identity conflict. Was he a full-fledged academic or not? A former colleague thought that the lack of the academic "union card"—the Ph.D.—haunted Erikson when he joined the faculty at Harvard (Keniston, 1983). Later in life Erikson aptly expressed how uncertainty about his identity affected him during his youth, "I was," he recalled, "morbidly sensitive" ("Erik Erikson," 1970, p. 87).

In lieu of college, young Erikson took up painting (Roazen, 1976). This career move paid off in 1927 when an old friend and director of a progressive school in Vienna invited Erikson to ply his trade in the Austrian capital. Sponsors of the friend's school included American Dorthy Burlingham, scion of the immensely rich and famous Tiffany family, who could well afford to commission portraits of her four children. It turned out that she also was undergoing psychoanalysis at the hands of the master himself, Freud. Through this connection, Burlingham became a friend of Freud's daughter Anna, who counted the four Tiffany heirs among her first child patients. Erikson experienced only brief interaction with the four children before Burlingham and Anna Freud began persuading him to become a child analyst. Though he was unfamiliar with this new speciality, Erikson was intrigued and agreed to undergo training analysis with Anna Freud. Soon he was drawn into the inner circle of the Vienna Psychoanalytic Society.

Owing to Erikson's shyness and the oral cancer that already plagued Freud, the two seldom conversed. Nevertheless, as a follower of Freud he reveled in the excitement of a secretive psychoanalytic movement that was forced underground by the disdain of the medical establishment. In the six years that Erikson remained in Vienna, he delivered his first paper before the Vienna Psychoanalytic Society, pursued an education in the Montessori method of schooling, and met his bride-to-be, a Canadian-born, U.S. student, Joan Serson.

A number of factors made Erikson view his time among the Vienna analysts as somewhat uncomfortable. Roazen (1976) thought that Erikson was "dissatisfied as one of Freud's younger disciples" (p. 4). As a newcomer, Erikson felt called on to be a "servant for the master" (p. 4). He was even known to drive Freud around in Burlingham's car. Also, his status as a non-M.D. "lay" analyst may have bothered him, but there were two reasons why he was at least reasonably well respected. First, being upset with the medical establishment for not openly accepting his point of view, Freud could readily overlook Erikson's and others' lack of "proper credentials." Second, it was deemed less essential for child analysts to have medical qualifications. Generally, Freud welcomed lay analysts in the hope of attracting a variety of people with broad backgrounds. Erikson was also attractive because he was one of the few men willing to pursue the fledgling profession of child analysis. Finally, he was Aryan.

Another source of discomfort was the constitution of the Vienna group, especially the child analysts. Freud had lost some of his most able male analysts and had surrounded himself with women, mostly recruited by Anna. "Erikson felt stifled by what he described as the maternalistic overprotection of the women analysts" (p. 6). Further, he, like the males who had abandoned Freud, felt the pressure to conform. He wrote about "a growing conservatism and especially a subtle yet pervasive interdiction of certain trends of thought. This concerned primarily any idea which might be reminiscent of the deviations perpetrated by those earliest and most brilliant of Freud's co-workers . . . " (quoted in Roazen, 1976, pp. 6–7).

Perhaps his disaffection with Freudian thought, which he never openly admitted, accounted for his quick response to Hitler's assumption of power in Germany during 1933. Erikson and his new wife first tried to establish citizenship in Denmark. When that effort failed, they migrated to the United States, where Erikson became the first child analyst in Boston (Stevens, 1983). There he was immediately accepted by the American Association of Psychoanalysis, despite his lack of credentials, because its members so revered the International Psychoanalytic Association to which Erikson belonged and were so in awe of anyone who had been close to Freud.

Erikson did try to do something about his deficient qualifications, but he failed at graduate work in the psychology program at nearby Harvard (Roazen, 1976). That apparently was his last effort at a formal, advanced education. His alliance with Harvard, however, did not end. Soon he was working on research leading to the book that made Murray famous. During this period he had the opportunity to work with children of both the wealthy and the poor (Stevens, 1983).

After a stint at Yale's Institute of Human Relations, during which he made a side trip to a Sioux Indian reservation, the Eriksons moved to California where, in 1939, Erik took a position at the University of California at Berkeley. His observations of the Sioux and the Yurok, a Northern California tribe who preserved many of their ancient traditions, changed his orientation profoundly. These experiences convinced him that Freud's sexual ideas were not universal. Rather, he discovered that a progression through stages of identity acquisition is generalizable across cultures (Evans, 1967).

After ten years on the West Coast working on a longitudinal child development program, analyzing Hitler's speeches during the war, and studying life aboard submarines, he took a teaching post at the University of California. Unfortunately it was short-lived. When confronted with the demand that he sign an anti-Communist loyalty oath, Erikson, who was not Communist, refused and resigned (Woodward, 1994). Returning to the East Coast, he received an appointment to a psychoanalytic center specializing in child psychiatry. Soon thereafter, *Childhood and Society* (1950) made him famous. This seminal work was followed by other popular successes: *Young Man Luther,* a psychobiography of religious rebel Martin Luther, the Pulitzer prize-winning *Gandhi's Truth,* and, finally, *Life Cycle Completed.*

By 1960, he was so well known and respected that he was appointed Professor of Human Development and lecturer in psychiatry at Harvard, an extraordinary development in view of his nonexistent academic credentials. After his retirement, he and his wife returned to the San Francisco area. Until his death on May 12, 1994, he remained active advocating rights for children as well as for the elderly, and campaigning for an emphasis on people rather than nations. A colleague summed up the respect that she and others have for this prophet who proclaimed that personality development never ends: "As they used to say of Gandhi, he was a mahatama, a great soul, very wise, [a] very wide-ranging humanist" (Diana Eck, quoted in *Peoria Journal Star,* 1994).

Erikson's View of the Person

Freudian?

Erikson has been counted among the Freudians (or neo-Freudians). Roazen (1976) asserted that he was a self-proclaimed Freudian and there is no question that he was devoted to Freud on a personal level. Having read everything Freud wrote, including his correspondence, Erikson could not resist citing Freud at every possible opportunity. His dedication to Freud seems to stem from his beliefs about "great leaders." During his study of Gandhi, his reflections on the Indian practitioner of nonviolent protest revealed his conception of the dilemma that followers of giants must resolve: " . . . who is the true representative of revolutionary advance—he who modestly continues the work of a giant and adapts it to less heroic circumstances, or he who continues to flex his muscles to see whether he may prove to have gigantic measurements himself" (Erikson, quoted in Roazen, 1976). It seems that Erikson came down on both sides, one explicitly and the other implicitly. Explicitly he pronounced himself a Freudian, often excusing the master's personal weaknesses (e.g., his railroad phobia) and his theoretical vulnerabilities (e.g., his conception of women). Erikson waved his hand at Freud's bizarre middle-aged abandonment of sexual relations and overlooked his nearly neurotic correspondence with Wilhelm Fliess. He felt obligated to dig for a seemingly appropriate Freudian citation with each mention of his own original ideas. In fact, Erikson credited some of his own ideas to Freud though they could be traced to his former mentor only by an enormous stretch of the imagination. Even Erikson's most original and important idea was laid at Freud's door. "Erikson's many citations of Freud's single mention of the concept of inner identity is an instance of a disciple trying to foist off an original idea onto [Freud]" (p. 12). As late as 1967, Erikson called himself a psychoanalyst. In terms of his explicit pronouncements, there is little question that Erikson was Freudian.

Accepting credit for one's own ideas is to abandon humility. Taking credit is also accepting blame. Erikson tacitly acknowledged that it is difficult for creative people to achieve "the courage of their own originality" (Erikson, quoted in Roazen, 1976, p. 12). "When I started to write extensively about twenty-five years ago, I really thought I was merely providing new illustrations for what I had learned from Sigmund and Anna Freud. I realized only gradually that any original observation already implies a change in theory. The scientific climate has changed so much that older and new theories cannot really be compared" (quoted in Evans, 1976, p. 292). Thus, Erikson implicitly acknowledges that his ideas are more his own than Freud's. Further, he deemphasizes sexual motivation in favor of the quest for identity. The unconscious takes a backseat to the ego, which, in Erikson's hands, becomes molded into a form of the self. The superego becomes akin to the conventional conscience. At times he seems more like Jung than Freud, as his interest in anthropological issues and ancient cultures appears to exceed his concern for the obsessions of current, Western society. His experiences with the Sioux and Yurok made him more an anthropologist/sociologist than a psychoanalyst. Also, it made him see that Freud's ideas were culture-bound, founded on European culture and thus not applicable to many other cultures.

He was more concerned with people's missions in life as these quests evolve through the life span than their struggles with unresolved traumas of childhood. In fact, he openly expressed his reservations about Freud's emphasis on cataclysmic events of early life: "If everything 'goes back' into childhood, then everything is somebody else's fault, and trust in one's own power of taking responsibility for oneself may be undermined" (quoted in Woodward, 1994, p. 56). In sum, despite the homage paid to Freud, he was certainly not a Freudian and maybe not a neo-Freudian. His theory was too much a mix of psychology, anthropology, and sociology to be "psychoanalytic." Box 7.1 shows that Erikson parted company with Freud regarding women.

BOX 7.1 • *Acknowledging Diversity: Erikson's Evolving View of Women*

Erikson not only used masculine pronouns in writing, which was common in his time, he also frequently couched his pronouncements in masculine terms: "Evolution has made man . . . ," "mature man," "Whatever chance man has to transcend the limitations of his self . . ." (Erikson, 1968a, p. 291). In writing about the sexuality of male and female children, he proclaimed, "In the boy, the sexual orientation is dominated by phallic-intrusion; in the girl, by inclusive modes of attractiveness and 'motherliness' " (p. 289). He felt "stifled" by the Vienna women with whom he worked. Yet, he was an open person who appears to have changed as he matured during the early stages of the women's movement. In almost no other area did he so closely approximate declaring that Freud was "wrong." In an interview he indicated (from Evans, 1976, pp. 294–300):

Obviously [Freud and I] would not agree today with all the generalizations which have been

made with regard to the Oedipus complex, least of all the female Oedipus complex. My feeling is that Freud's general judgment of the identity of women was probably the weakest part of his theory. Exactly what is to blame for that I don't know, except that he was a Victorian man, a patriarchal man. Freud's perception might also have been colored by the sexual mores of his time, which could not admit at first that an upper-class woman could have passionate and active sexual wishes and yet be refined and intelligent. At any rate, psychoanalytic literature tends to describe woman as an essentially passive and masochistic creature, who not only accepts the roles or identity assigned to her submissively, but needs all the masochism she can muster to appreciate the phallic male.

Erikson was flexible. He changed, and in so doing, moved further from Freud.

On the Tasks and Polarities of Life

The "tasks of life" theme is at the heart of Erikson's theory. At each succeeding stage of human development people have new tasks to master. Thus, life and its challenges are constantly evolving. Contrary to the way Freud thought of it, or even the way Allport conceived of it, maturity to Erikson is not something most people achieve or not. Instead, it is something that people approximate well or not so well.

How well people conquer the tasks of a given stage determines toward which of two poles they migrate, one representing positive development and the other negative development. The poles symbolize the horns of a dilemma. Parents, the individual's society, interactions with peers, and the individual's own skills determine how well the dilemma is resolved. In turn, resolution promotes the development of a new **strength,** a virtue arising from dominant movement toward the positive pole. With resolution comes the ability to face the challenges of the next stage.

Basic Concepts: Erikson

Erikson believed that people go through eight stages of psychosocial evolution that is termed **psychosocial development,** a union of physical yearnings and the cultural forces that act on the individual ("Erik Erikson," 1970). These phases include four childhood stages, one adolescent stage, and three adult stages. They are characterized by **epigenesis** (*epi* means "upon" and *genesis* means "emergence"): the stages literally emerge "one on top of another in space and time" (quoted in Evans, 1976, p. 294). Each is built on the other like each upper-level math course is built on lower-level courses. His most basic concepts are tied to the eight stages.

Like Jung, Erikson advocated a reality in which thesis and antithesis, the conflict of opposites, yielded synthesis, the resolution of conflict. Maturity and contentment result from synthesis; stagnation and maladjustment follow failure to resolve conflicts. The conflict at each stage is termed a "crisis." In effect, at each stage, the crisis that the individual experiences entails being stretched between the opposing positive and negative poles associated with the stage. Successful resolution of a crisis prepares the person for the next step in the quest for identity. As may have occurred to you, the popular phrase "identity crisis" originates in Erikson's conception of the psychosocial crises.

Erikson makes it clear that resolution of the crisis is never absolute. To approximate resolution people must experience **a favorable ratio,** the greater the magnitude of the pull to the positive pole relative to the pull of the negative pole the better (Erikson, 1968a). In turn, the more favorable the ratio, the more people manifest the strength available at a given stage. Lest the reader think that Erikson's repeated references to "crises" makes a pessimist of him, it is important to note that resolution of conflicts is normal and expected, and "crises" are turning points, not threats of catastrophe (Erikson, 1968a). Each resolution of a crisis brings with it progress toward a full and rich identity, an issue explored in Box 7.2.

BOX 7.2 • *What Are Your Own Sources of Identity?*

Exploring your own feelings of "identity" should help you get the flavor of Erikson's ideas on the subject. First, examine all of the "sources of identity" listed below. Then try to decide which are most important to you. It is a difficult task. Once Barbara Jordan, famous former Congresswoman and professor, was asked to choose between two prominent sources of identity, being Black and being a woman. This eloquent devotee of the U.S. Constitution paused to reflect for a moment. She did make a decision, but I do not recall what it was.

After examining the sources, rank them in order, giving the most important source a rank of one (1), the second most important a two (2), and so forth until all sources are ranked. Force your-self to make choices; the result of the ranking will tell you much about yourself. The choices are listed alphabetically. If you want to add other sources, do so before ranking.

career (specify present or anticipated career)
child of my parents
ethnic group (Black, White, Latino, Asian, or
    whatever applies)
friend to several people
gender (male or female)
hobbyist (sports, exercise, or whatever applies)
human being
parent
sibling (brother or sister)
[others of your own choosing]

Infancy: Trust and Distrust

Infants (first year) arrive with basic physiological needs that parents must be willing and able to meet. Parents usually satisfy needs, but the inevitable delay or neglect of satisfaction and the occurrence of weaning generates the first crisis. **Basic trust** results from the infant's sense that it can count on satisfaction of its needs (Erikson, 1968a); the world takes on the aura of a "trustworthy realm." Its opposite is **basic mistrust,** the feeling of abandonment and helpless rage that accompanies uncertainty of satisfaction. Trust is injected into the infant in different ways by different mothers. Each mother is unique and, thus, conveys trust in a unique way. "Moreover, mothers in different cultures and classes and races must teach this trusting in different ways, so it will fit their cultural version of the universe" (Erikson, quoted in Evans, 1976, p. 293).

Erikson makes a point of the observation that both trust and mistrust are learned. We all must learn trust if we are to be fully functional humans, "But to learn to mistrust is just as important" (Erikson, quoted in Evans, 1976, p. 293). Mistrust is part of life also, and we must become familiar with it. We can hope, however, that trust will outweigh mistrust in the ratio of the two orientations.

Basic trust lays the foundation for the first of the strengths, hope, the enduring belief in the attainability of basic satisfactions. "You see, **hope** is a very basic human strength without which we couldn't stay alive" (Erikson, quoted in Evans, 1976, p. 293). It is the foundation of faith, often manifested in adult religious practices (Hall, 1983). In fact, faith is protected by religion, its **institutional safeguard,** a cultural unit that protects and promotes products of crisis resolution. Failure to develop basic trust yields mistrust and hopelessness.

Early Childhood: Autonomy versus Shame and Doubt (SAD; Shame/Autonomy/Doubt)

During this second stage (age 2–3), the child develops motor skills that open up the first possibilities of independence (Erikson, 1968a). Part of the trauma the child experiences at this time is in the transition from the first to this more mature second stage. Just when the child has learned to trust its mother and the world, it must become self-willed. It must change from being the one-sided trusting soul to being also worthy of others' trust. Only by calling on others to trust it, rather than just trusting in others, can it exercise its will.

Children can now move to desired objects and thereby possess them without the aid of parents. The dawning of grasping ability allows children to experience the power of imprisoning an object within fingers, hands, and arms. Power also comes from letting go, but so does conflict. To hold can be destructive, as in restraining, or it can be positive, as in cuddling. Letting go has two additional meanings: giving up something desirable, or casually "letting it be." Here Erikson hints at Fromm's "dilemma of freedom": to let go of something is to be free of it, but also to lose it.

With the newly acquired muscular skills, the child experiences doing for herself. Unfortunately, she also knows the frustration generated by needing the help of others who can do more for her than she can do for herself. For Erikson as well as Allport, self-esteem derives from doing for oneself. Consistent with this orientation, the two poles of the crisis involve the themes of independence and the self-esteem that comes with it versus the self-estrangement that accompanies dependency. **Autonomy** is independence stemming from the reasonable self-control that allows children to hold rather than restrain, to let be rather than lose. **Shame and doubt** is the estrangement that results from the feeling of being controlled and of losing self-control. It is the precursor of neurosis, a desperate struggle for control of one's environment, and paranoia, a manifestation of feeling controlled by others. A child who is tentative and self-effacing is reflecting shame and doubt.

The strength that emerges from resolution during early childhood is **will power,** "the unbroken determination to exercise free choice as well as self-restraint in spite of the unavoidable experience of shame, doubt, and a certain rage over being controlled by others" (Erikson, 1968a, p. 288). The exercise of free choice has its institutional safeguard—the principles of law and order and of justice. However, Erikson argues that "law and order" when overblown can rob people of the very choice it is supposed to protect.

Erikson acknowledges that infants go through a Freudian "anal stage," but "we have to consider that the anal musculature is part of musculature in general" (quoted in Evans, 1976, p. 293). The task of the infant is to learn control of his musculature, including his sphincters. In contrast to Freud, culture is emphasized rather than universal physiology in achieving sphincter control.

Play Age: Initiative versus Guilt

In the fourth year, children become aware of the differences between the sexes. During this third stage, sex-role playing and sexual feelings occur for the boy. But to Erikson the girl plays the feminine role, trying to look attractive and to be nurturing, rather than being sexual. Conscience appears at this stage and forever places restraints on actions, thoughts, and fantasies. One of the poles at this stage is **initiative,** acting on one's desires, urges, and potentials. The other is **guilt,** the harness that restrains pursuit of desires, urges, and potentials, the exercise of an overzealous conscience. The boy learns that competition for a favored position with his mother leads to the inevitable fear of damage to his genitals. The result is guilt at having taken the initiative well beyond that which is permissible (Evans, 1967). Erikson turns further from Freud when he suggests that it is only natural for the boy to fall in love with his mother, because she is everything to him. She is the center of his life and his caretaker. Any fantasies a child may have will tend to focus on what is crucial to her or his survival and prosperity. Thus, the boy's fantasies, even those relating to his emerging genital urges, will likely center on his mother. The girl has problems relating to pursuit of her father's attentions. For both genders, guilt arises from a failure to demonstrate capability when the initiative is taken (Evans, 1967).

At first, children's play involves only wish fulfillment and fantasy rather than real purpose, but gradually it changes. "The child begins to envisage goals for which his locomotion and cognition have prepared him. The child also begins to think of being 'big' and to identify with people whose work or whose personality he can understand and appreciate" (Erikson, quoted in Evans, 1967, p. 25). That is, children's developing new strength is **purpose,** "the courage to envisage and pursue valued and tangible goals guided by conscience but not paralyzed by guilt and by fear of punishment" (Erikson, 1968a, p. 289). Failure at resolution leads to repression or inhibition and to adult pathology such as sexual impotence, overcompensation, and exhibitionism.

School Age: Industry versus Inferiority

At each stage, the child becomes a somewhat different person. At the school age, the fourth stage (ages 6 through 12), children evolve into intellectually curious people. They want to know, to learn. During this time, children begin to lay the groundwork for becoming parents. They play at the parental role to prepare themselves for the real thing. For the first time, they relate to the larger society and one of its core elements, work. They learn to apply themselves to tasks that have practical outcomes such as schoolwork for grades or housework for a "salary."

Erikson sometimes referred to the school age as asexual or the "latency period." He is quick to add, however, that Freud missed all the cognitive development that blossoms during the school age "because he was only concerned with what happens to sexual energy during that time" (Erikson, quoted in Evans, 1976, p. 295). One of the poles of the school age is **industry,** children's absorption in the "tool world" of their culture—the workaday world—which prepares them "for a hierarchy of learning experiences which [they] will undergo with the help of cooperative peers and instructive adults" (Erikson, 1968a, p. 289). Of course, school is the first productive situation that provides an inkling of the "tool culture." Here "work" is school performance. In other settings it may be athletic performance or group-play activities. In each case the child is learning adults' rules of work, as directly seen in playing "house" or "doctor." The other pole of the crisis, **inferiority,** occurs if children perceive their skills or status among peers to be inadequate. This perception arises because of failures at establishing competence in some specialized way, such as playing a game or spelling well. Race or ethnic background may become barriers that prevent children from experiencing success and the accompanying actualization of the will to learn. Inferiority can yield regression to the hopelessness of over-concern about the opposite-sex parent that characterized the previous stage. The triumph of inferiority leads to an obsession with work, which becomes the sole source of identity, a workaholic orientation. "If the overly conforming child accepts work as the only criterion of worthwhileness, sacrificing too readily his imagination and playfulness, he may [as an adult] . . . [become] a slave of his technology . . . " (Erikson, 1968a, p. 289).

Resolution of the crisis at the school age gives children critical experiences, including working beside and with others and "division of labor." From this resolution emerges the strength of **competence,** "the free exercise (unimpaired by an infantile sense of inferiority) of dexterity and intelligence in the completion of serious tasks" (Erikson, 1968a, pp. 289–290). With competence, children are ready for cooperative participation in some segment of the culture.

Adolescence: Identity versus Identity Confusion

The adolescent search for self represents the fulcrum on which the lifelong struggle for identity is balanced. Adolescence, the fifth stage (13–19), allows a synthesis of previous stages, but it is more than the mere sum of what developed earlier. It is also an extension into the future. One pole of the adolescent crisis is **identity,** accumulated confidence that the sameness and continuity one has previously cultivated are now appreciated by others, allowing, in turn, the promise of careers and lifestyles to come. *Continuity* is an important term in the conception of identity. "Identity means an integration of all previous identifications and self-images, including the negative ones" (Erikson, quoted in Evans, 1976, p. 297). Continuity ensures that one is all that one was, but also something new and something yet to be. The opposite of identity is **identity confusion,** the failure of previous identity developments to coalesce in such a way that it is clear what roles one is expected to play in the future. While all teens may change superficial identity periodically—Goth one month, hip-hop the next—repeated changes at short intervals may signal abnormal identity confusion. The victory of confusion predicts acute maladjustments due to a feeling of meaninglessness. Further, adolescent identity is not merely obtaining genital maturity. It is an ability to be concerned about others, because one's own problems relating to previous periods have been largely solved (Evans, 1976). Identity problems for teens are in part related to their personal histories and in part arise from identity pitfalls peculiar to their historical era. For example, today's teenage boys may be torn between the macho orientation that dominated their fathers' identities and the more gender-neutral identity that seems appropriate today.

In their struggle to answer the question "Who am I?" adolescents often form cliques. These clans bolster self-images and provide a mutual defense against "enemies" whose different characteristics challenge the "truth" of their own developing identities (Hall, 1983). If teens turn this condemnation of the "different" against society, delinquency can result. In fact, modern teen gangs can be viewed as Eriksonian clans formed to foster identity development. However, adolescent rebellion is not seen by Erikson as a necessarily negative force, at least when the larger culture is considered (Erikson, 1968a). Societies must be flexible, and Erikson sees adolescent challenges as a source of cultural rejuvenation. Youth, in their quest for identity, question the norms of their society, vigorously supporting those that meet the challenge and contributing to the demise of rules that cannot bear close scrutiny. Periods of unrest among the young attest to the sickness of a society failing to meet the promise of youth—that the best will rule and the rulers will bring out the best in people. The unrest of the 1960s was a response to a society whose leaders were not "bringing out the best." During such times, the mind of youth and that of society become one in the pursuit of ideological unification and return to coherent purpose.

The strength that comes from the adolescent period is **fidelity,** "the opportunity to fulfill personal potentialities . . . to be true to himself and true to significant others . . . [and to] sustain loyalties . . . in spite of inevitable contradictions of value systems" (Erikson, 1968a, p. 290). For Erikson, fidelity is the cornerstone of identity. It is, however, not devotion to a particular ideology, but loyalty to ideologies that are appropriate to the individual. As Erikson put it, "I would go further and claim that we have almost an instinct for fidelity—meaning that when you reach a certain age you can and must learn to be faithful to some ideological view . . . without the development of a capacity for fidelity the individual will either have . . . a weak ego, or look for a deviant group to be faithful to" (Erikson, quoted in Evans, 1976, p. 296).

The need to adopt ideologies, particularly a focal ideology, can be a trap that ensnares the impulsive teen. Erikson believed that "Adolescents are easily seduced by totalitarian [authoritarian] regimes and all kinds of totalistic fads" (Erikson, quoted in Evans, 1976, p. 297). Like Allport and Fromm, he was especially concerned because youth are prone to succumb to the siren song of "nationalism" (exclusive devotion to one's nation). The allure of nationalism is in its ideological simplicity and resultant promise to answer all questions and solve all problems. As far back as 1942, Erikson recognized the effect of the nationalistic narcotic on the "Hitler Youth" (Hoffman, 1993). Youth must somehow avoid impulsivity in responding to the almost instinctual demand of fidelity that one quickly adopt the most obvious ideology available. If they cannot, ideology may become the basis of their identities. Only with restraint will the magnetic force of simplistic ideologies like nationalism be resisted until broader ideologies are considered.

But what gets confused when "identity confusion" occurs? Box 7.3 suggests that young people who infrequently enjoy the presence and influence of their parents may resort to other models in their search for identity. However, research by Mashek, Aron, and Boncimino (2003) suggests identity confusion might be seen from a broader perspective than "parents versus other adult figures." Their results indicate that how close we feel toward others with whom we engage in some kind of relationship may explain identity confusion. The teenage to young adult participants in their research (mean age averaged across three studies, 19.6 years) first named people to whom they felt close, such as "best friend" and "father." In some studies, they also named people to whom they did not feel close: "familiar stranger" (Bill Clinton) and "non-familiar stranger" (Chelsea Clinton). Then they indicated the applicability of some trait words to themselves and, with different lists, ascribed trait words to close others (best friend) and non-close others (Bill Clinton). Finally, participants were given a memory test in which they tried to remember which trait words they had ascribed to themselves, close others, and non-close others. Results clearly showed that participants were more likely to confuse trait words ascribed to close others as having been applied to themselves than they were to confuse words ascribed to non-close others

BOX 7.3 • *How Do We Become Who We Are?*

One wonders whether, in these times, some parents have set aside sufficient time and effort to have a positive impact on their children. In this era of two-income families, commuting long distances to work, and multiple ways to spend recreational time—100+ TV channels, the Web, bigger and better movies, gigantic shopping malls, and increased interest in sports—some parents may not be present often enough to influence the identities of their children. So where do the children of such parents turn? One obvious answer is to the media. Another is to other people who are "there for them," such as teachers, coaches, clergy, and peers. In any case, it is hard to fashion an identity solely of our own choosing. We must have some influential figures in our lives who provide standards for shaping an identity.

But are our identities at adolescence and young adulthood our final identities? I once knew a college student who apparently had rejected his

rather conservative, middle-class parents and all they stood for. He was a campus radical of yesterday, the tumultuous late 1960s. We would now think of him as confirmation of the hippie, draft-dodging, antiestablishmentarian, rebel stereotype. His values were free living, prolove, antiviolence, and antiwar, like the hippies. He "practiced at being gay" so he could avoid military service (he never served). He made fun of the university administration who begged him to stay on campus during breaks and weekends so he could help them calm any "out-of-control" dissidents. He ridiculed the political establishment, especially then-President Nixon. He even engaged in some minor "dirty tricks" to stick a needle in the hide of "greedy Corporate America." He was brilliant, funny, and a catalyst for needed change. Where is he now? Unlike most former campus rebels, he has turned in the other direction. Now in his fifties, he is widely known for his conservative views.

as having been applied to themselves. When we show identity confusion, we are likely to confuse our own identities with the identities of the people in our lives to whom we feel close.

Young Adulthood: Intimacy versus Isolation

During previous stages, strengths allowed the genders to merge in cooperation and fruitful communication. When "falling in love," teenagers attach themselves to another person in an attempt to arrive at self-definition. Teens "in love" see themselves reflected in an "idealized other," but do not actively attempt to differentiate themselves from the other. Now, during the sixth stage (20–35), the biological differences come to the fore, so that the genders, similar in consciousness and language, become different in the mature quest for love and procreation. The two poles of this sixth stage are tied to the themes of attachment to and alienation from others. **Intimacy** "is really the ability to fuse your identity with somebody else's without fear that you're going to lose something yourself" (Erikson, quoted in Evans, 1967, p. 48). Fromm's view of intimate relations with others is similar. It is more than the mere physical intimacy that occurs in sexual exchanges (Hall, 1983). "Of course, I mean something more—I mean intimate relationships, such as friendship, love, sexual intimacy, even intimacy with oneself, one's inner resources, the range of one's excitements and commitments" (Erikson, quoted in Evans, 1976, p. 300). With this broader definition of intimacy in mind, Erikson anticipated modern theories of marital success (Allen, 2001). He asserted that intimacy is what makes meaningful marriage possible.

The other pole in the crisis for this stage is **isolation,** the failure to secure close and cooperative relationships with the same, and especially the opposite, gender such that partners' identities are important to, but distinct from, one's own. The triumph of isolation dooms the individual to infantile fixations and lasting immaturities that interfere with love and work. On the other hand, intimacy brings the strength of this period. **Love** "is the guardian of that elusive and yet all-pervasive power of cultural and personal style which binds . . . the affiliations of competition and cooperation, procreation and production" into a "way of life" (quoted in Evans, 1976, p. 291). Love is "a mutuality of devotion greater than the antagonisms inherent in [mates'] divided function[s]" (p. 291).

Middle Adulthood: Productivity versus Futility

During the first dozen years I've been doing this book, my own students and students at other colleges and universities have pointed out that longevity is not what it was when Erikson first composed his stages. The average longevity for women in Western societies is approaching 80 and it is around the mid-seventies for men (it is even greater elsewhere, e.g., Japan). As students have suggested, it is high time for an additional stage. I propose a new stage called "Middle Adulthood" that spans the ages 35–60.

One pole of this stage is **productivity,** people's perception that they are contributing to society through their careers and to their community through their personal involvement. People who develop productivity through resolution at this stage are doing what Adler would hope for. They are, through their labors, generating outcomes that they see as improving society. Obviously, school teachers, social workers, farmers, physicians, college teachers, nurses, clinical psychologists, and ministers are in a position to develop productivity. Others may also perceive that their vocations contribute to society: insurance agents, attorneys, refuse collectors, energy producers, and many others can be in a position to benefit society. Anyone can support perceptions of productivity in their communities by becoming involved. Everything, from just voting in local elections, through contributing money to local charities, to visiting shut-ins, qualifies as community involvement.

The other pole is **futility,** the perception that one is on the proverbial treadmill, merely keeping body and soul together, but doing nothing for the good of society or one's community. People who fail to resolve the conflict at this stage feel that they are producing nothing worthwhile, except sustenance for their own benefit. They view their jobs not as careers, but as useless work. Any of the careers listed under "productivity" could be listed here as well, because futility, like productivity, is in the eye of the beholder: if one does not see one's work as worthwhile, it is not. But could people see their contributions as having no value when, in fact, their efforts are highly valued? Not likely, because they would be getting positive feedback from others if their works were highly valued. In almost all cases, perceptions of futility are supported by negative feedback or by the absence of positive feedback. Futility guarantees alienation from society and from one's community. Society is seen as having no use for one's efforts. In the same vein, one can offer one's community nothing of value. Depression is likely to accompany futility.

The strength of this stage would be **contentment,** the perception that one's efforts result in the promotion of human well-being and that one is revered in the local community because of "good works." A contented person perceives that what he or she does is not mere labor. Instead it is a service to society that advances the culture by improving or enriching the lives of others and it is a concrete contribution to the local community that people can see and appreciate. Contentment comes with believing that one's efforts are valued by society and by one's neighbors. Box 7.4 is Erikson's take on cultural diversity in people's communities.

Mature Adulthood: Generativity versus Stagnation

"At this stage one begins to take one's place in society, and to help in the development and perfection of whatever [society] produces" (Erikson, quoted in Evans, 1976, pp. 301–302). Humans are not only "learning animals" they are teachers as well. It is during the maturity of adulthood (60–75) that the need to be needed and the accumulation of wisdom lead to assumption of the "teacher" role. Thus, during the seventh stage, people strive for **generativity,** "the concern with establishing and guiding the next generation" (Erikson, 1968a, p. 291). It is manifested in the advice that middle-aged people are inclined to offer younger individuals. Erikson admitted that *generativity* is "not an elegant word" (p. 301). He indicated that he might have used *creativity* instead of *generativity,* but the substitution would put "too much emphasis on the particular creativity which we ascribe to particular people" (p. 301). *Generativity* has a broader meaning that

BOX 7.4 • *Erikson on Cultural Diversity*

Except possibly for Jung, no other theorist covered so far has left her or his theoretical door more wide open to cultural diversity than did Erikson. He recognized that mothers from different cultures must teach trusting in ways that are consistent with their traditions. You can well imagine that, compared to North America, trust is imparted differently in South American societies and Asian societies, where babies are strapped for hours on the mother's back facing away from her. It is also taught differently in African societies, where "it takes a whole village to rear a child." Although he believed that people of different cultures passed through the same developmental stages, his studies of non-Western cultures led him to acknowledge that the ways his stages were manifested were different for different cultures. For example, during the "school age," the "adult rules of work"

that children learn, and the role-teaching games they play, are different for different cultures. For example, Masai (East Africa) children learn how to care for livestock and Maori (New Zealand) children learn wood and stone carving. Erikson recognized as well that during the school age avoidance of inferiority was more difficult for the children of oppressed social and ethnic groups than for others. As for the teen period, Erikson observed that youth are both the architects of the cultural evolution that occurs during troubled times and the victims of it. His popularity among 1960s youth arose from his recognition that U.S. society needed changing and that youth would be the catalysts for change. His writings predicted that youth would be in the forefront of the civil rights movement and of the campaign to end the U.S. role as the world's police.

is applicable to people in general: "everything that is generated from generation to generation: children, products, ideas, and works of art" (p. 301).

The failure of generativity leads to **stagnation,** the arrest of the ripening process that comes with inability to funnel previous development into the formation of the next generation. Boredom is the constant companion of stagnation, as is false intimacy and adult self-indulgence. Inevitably, the failure of generativity shows up in the next generation as the aggravation of estrangements in childhood, adolescence, and early adulthood.

Care, the strength of maturity, is "the broadening concern for what has been generated by love, necessity, or accident—a concern that overcome[s] . . . the narrowness of self-concern" (Erikson, 1968a, p. 291). Care is a major force behind utilization of "proven methods with which each generation meets the needs of the next" (Erikson, 1968a, p. 291). Erikson was at first concerned about the selection of *care* because of its multitude of connotations, including "anxious solicitude" (Evans, 1976). But he concluded that the word has evolved and now means " 'to care to do' something, to 'care for' somebody or something, to 'take care of' that which needs protection and attention, and 'to take care not to' do something destructive" (quoted in Evans, 1976, 301).

Old Age: Integrity versus Despair

Power in old age is wit in full bloom—a storehouse of knowledge, an inclusive understanding, and a maturity of judgment. These intellectual contributions provide a bridge to the next generation by reminding all that the knowledge of a given generation is not "truth," but a cog in the infinitely large and everturning wheel of human experience. Crisis at this time (75 until death) involves contributing to the continuity of the human condition versus distraction from that noble purpose by an obsession with death. The poles for this eighth stage revolve around wholeness and completeness versus disintegration and defeat. **Integrity** is "an emotional integration faithful to the image bearers of the past and ready to take (and eventually renounce) leadership in the present" (Erikson, 1968a, p. 291). Integrity is the continuity that comes from being solidly founded on a past that contributes to the present and projects into the future. My grandmother had it.

Lack of resolution leads to **despair,** a feeling that time is too short for the achievement of integrity and the accompanying contribution to the connection between generations. Despair can result in bitterness at not being able to extend oneself into the future and a losing battle with death, rather than a calm acceptance of it. Despair yields psychological death before the physical counterpart. The strength that comes from resolution of the eighth crisis is **wisdom,** a "detached and yet active concern with life in the face of death," not magical access to "higher knowledge" (Erikson, 1968a, p. 292; Hall, 1983). With wisdom, death is accepted, and one's role in the human drama is assured.

Erikson was not entirely satisfied with the term *wisdom* "because to some people it seems to mean a too strenuous achievement for each and every old person" (Erikson, quoted in Evans, 1976, p. 301). In fact, during old age people may show a renewal of infantile traits, even including senile childishness. *Wisdom* in any sense is not a necessity during old age. "The main point is again a developmental one: only in old age can true wisdom develop in those who are thus gifted. And, in old age, some wisdom must mature, if only in a sense that the old person comes to appreciate and to represent something of the wisdom of the ages, or plain old wit" (p. 301). Though he was not old when he died, wisdom is what Malcolm X had at the end of his life. Table 7.1 summarizes Erikson's eight stages, as well as my new middle adulthood stage, spanning ages 35–60, and the crisis of identity associated with each.

Theoretical and Empirical Support for Erikson's Point of View

Levinson: The Midlife Crisis

Daniel Levinson was in his mid-forties when he recruited a sample of middle-aged men (1978). Levinson's crisis, suffered at the midpoint of life, yielded creative conceptions. The *midlife transition* is a bridge between young adulthood and middle age, a time when indi-

TABLE 7.1   *Erikson's Eight Stages and a New Stage*

Stage	*Crisis*	*Resolution*	*Poor Resolution*	*Strength*
Infancy	Basic trust vs. mistrust	Confidence in satisfaction of needs	Rage due to uncertainty of satisfaction	Hope
Early childhood	Autonomy vs. shame and doubt	Independence stemming from self-control	Estrangement due to being controlled	Willpower
Play age	Initiative vs. guilt	Acting on desires, urges, potentials	Conscience restrains pursuits	Purpose
School age	Industry vs. inferiority	Absorbed in "tool world"	Skills and status inadequate	Competence
Adolescence	Identity vs. identity confusion	Confident that sameness seen by others	Previous identity developments fail	Fidelity
Young adulthood	Intimacy vs. isolation	Fusing identity with another	No close relationships	Love
Middle adulthood	Productivity vs. futility	Contributing to society and community	Feeling alienated	Contentment
Mature adulthood	Generativity vs. stagnation	Guiding the next generation	Arrest of the ripening process	Care
Old age	Integrity vs. despair	Emotional integration	"Time is short"	Wisdom

The middle adulthood stage is not one of Erikson's stages but has been added here by the author, given the increase in longevity since Erikson first composed his stages.

viduals look back at their previous successes and failures and look forward to future prospects (Levinson, 1978). Because of concern about mortality, people begin to reevaluate the past in order to use the future more wisely. They raise questions about their contributions to family and career and vice versa. The result usually is *de-illusionment,* a reduction of illusions, a recognition that assumptions and beliefs about self and the world are not true. Illusions have worked well in earlier life as fuel to drive ambitions and ideals. At midlife it is time to cast them aside in favor of objective assessment.

Reappraisal may take the form of major upheaval, the midlife crisis. The new lifestyle may replace family and career, or a simple reordering of priorities may occur. In any case, Jung's *individuation* begins, a process by which the relationship between a person's self and the external world is changed so that there is a clearer separation between self and the world. At midlife, progress to maturity defines a sharper distinction between self, family, and friends than occurs at earlier stages. Also, expectations that restrict behavior and thought are rejected. Generativity accompanies individuation.

Some people sail through the midlife transition with little questioning. Their lives may be sufficiently stable and satisfying that they do not experience severe crisis. Others accept the loss of some dreams and are able to face the future without pain. However, Levinson contends that most people's struggles with the self and the external world reach crisis proportions (80 percent in his sample). They display guilt, anguish, upset, new lifestyles, and personality changes reflected in clothing, hair styles, and use of language.

To accept middle age is to realize that life is partly over and that death must be considered. When functions decline at age 40 or so, people must think about the unthinkable. The possibility of death runs head on into our cherished assumption of immortality. The contradiction thus generated is not eliminated by giving up the illusion of immortality; instead, it is seen in a new light. If one leaves behind a *legacy,* material goods, wisdom for others to use, and examples for others to follow, one lives on despite the demise of the body.

Sheehy: Women Are Different

Gail Sheehy (1977) focused on the midlife crisis as it applies uniquely to women. Age 35 begins a dangerous period for women. It is when the last child is sent off to school, ending the period of intense child care. Now she has time to think and her thoughts may turn to her attractiveness. Fearing her beauty is fading, she uses it while it lasts. The biological clock is ticking and, as it winds down, opportunities to have children and, thus pass on her genes, begin to wane. An affair may result.

Intense child care ends about when women enter the workforce. Working outside the home is motivated by economics and a need to fill the child-care void. Once in the workforce, she is likely to stay. This move can be good or bad or both. She may be well educated and thereby equipped to succeed. If so, she will be frustrated to find that competitors for advancement, often men, are ahead of her by virtue of their greater experience. If she is poorly educated, she will soon realize that advancement is unlikely for her. Frustration caused by being behind or despair due to being stuck at a low-level job may cause a crisis.

Clay (2003) reports that researchers associated with the McArthur Foundation network have exploded some long-standing myths about "mid-life crises." For example,

David Almeida has found that it is the everyday stressors, such as fights with a spouse and work deadlines, that have the most impact on midlife, not rare events such as death of a loved one or a divorce. His work also shows that while younger adults experience more daily stressors, *overload stressors*—engaging in too many activities at the same time—are more often experienced by midlife people. However, there are gender differences. Compared to midlife men, midlife women experience more *crossover stressors*—simultaneous demands arising from several domains, such as work and family. Educational level is an additional factor: midlife people with little education report the same number of stressors as their more educated counterparts, but they rate them as more severe. Obviously, it may be the recurring relatively "small" stressors that shape midlife, not the astronomical, lifestyle changing crises that Levinson and Sheehy emphasized.

Empirical Support: Research Confirming Erikson's View

Ochse and Plug (1986) looked at trust, autonomy, initiative, industry, intimacy, and generativity among White and Black South Africans aged 15 to 50. The seven positive poles of the first seven stages were represented by questionnaire items, along with a measure of well-being. As expected, subjects' responses to the questionnaire indicated that, the more the positive poles were manifested in their responses, the higher their sense of well-being. Also, a factor analysis of these adults' data revealed factors corresponding only to adult poles: intimacy versus isolation and generativity versus stagnation.

In addition, it was expected that intercorrelations among the poles relating to crises that had already been passed—those of childhood—would be relatively strong. Such was the case for White women and to some degree for White men, but not for Blacks. In fact, the intercorrelations among the poles tended to be high regardless of whether subjects had yet passed crises. This result was taken to mean that "Erikson's personality components to some extent develop in parallel [rather one before another] and are interdependent even before the relevant crises are resolved" (p. 1246). This conclusion is contrary to "epigenesis": earlier crises must be resolved before later ones. However, Erikson "does suggest that all the components develop to some degree throughout life, even before their critical stages" (p. 1246).

The prediction that *intimacy* would be generally higher for women than for men was confirmed, but only for Whites. For Blacks, intimacy was higher for men than for women. This outcome was one of several where results for Blacks and Whites differed, with only Whites confirming predictions for Erikson's theory. It reminds us of a fact that Erikson acknowledged: theories derived by people of one culture may not apply to people of another culture. One would also predict that identity would become more highly related to intimacy in the early twenties than in the teens. Further, identity would become most highly related to generativity in middle age, when generativity becomes salient. But, continuing the cultural difference trend, Erikson's prediction was borne out only for White women. For White and Black men, only the prediction regarding generativity was supported. Other results showed that scores associated with poles of already-passed childhood stages showed declines with increases in age, but those associated with adult poles increased with age. Also, men showed stronger autonomy, initiative, and industry, as sex-role adoption would predict. Finally, and very importantly, factor analysis revealed a strong and overriding factor: "identity" in the global sense. This result suggests that the various crises at the several stages are indeed "identity crises."

Kowaz and Marcia (1991) developed a measure of "industry" for administration to school children, their parents, and teachers. It focused on three components: (1) cognitive (skills and knowledge); (2) behavioral (applications of skills and knowledge); and (3) affective (attitudes and experiences relating to the acquisition and application of skills and knowledge). Evidence for the validity of the concept "industry" was strong. Cognitive industry scores were positively correlated with achievement scores, whether measured by children's subjective judgments of school achievement or grades. An overall score on industry was also positively related to achievement test scores. For teachers' judgments, being on-task versus off-task was positively related to industry scores. Also, "level of reasoning" was positively related to the overall industry scores.

The researchers developed a measure of concern for the process involved in a task, as opposed to interest only in the task outcome. This measure was positively related to the overall measure of industry: the more the industry, the more the interest in the process versus the outcome. Finally, overall contentment was positively related to industry. Results showed that the concept "industry" strongly applies to the age-group that should orient to it, according to Erikson.

McAdams, Ruetzel, and Foley (1986) looked at a measure of generativity in relation to indexes of power and intimacy motivation as measured with use of the Thematic Apperception Test (TAT). Subjects were adults between the ages of 35 and 49. The index of generativity was taken from an interview in which subjects explored plans for the future. Two independent scorers looked for evidence indicating concern for guiding the next generation either directly—caring, giving, teaching, leading, mentoring—or indirectly—contributing in a literary, scientific, artistic, or altruistic sense. Results showed that TAT scores indexing power and intimacy motivation were positively associated with the measure of generativity: the greater the generativity, the greater those motives. The researchers interpreted this result to mean "that generativity calls on an adult's fundamental needs to feel close and to feel strong vis-à-vis others" (p. 806).

McAdams and Mansfield looked at the relationship between generativity and communion: being self-sacrificing and "one with" others (Mansfield & McAdams, 1996). They found that the higher the level of communion shown by subjects, the higher was the level of generativity. The same team plus de St. Aubin and Diamond (McAdams et al., 1997) collected life stories in a two to three hour interview with people high in generativity (e.g., school teachers involved in voluntary work) and a contrasting group who were less generative. The high generativity group was significantly higher on moral steadfastness, redemptive sequences (turning negative events into positive outcomes), prosocial future goals, and early family advantage (e.g., person singled out early by family as having a special talent).

McAdams, Reynolds, Lewis, Patten, and Bowman (2001) interviewed 74 adults, evenly split into high and low generativity groups, about events during their lives. Measures of redemption (bad outcomes turning into good ones) and contamination (good outcomes turning into bad) were derived from the interview data. Redemption was positively correlated with favorable traits (e.g., self-esteem) and negatively correlated with depression. The correlations for contamination were the opposite.

Pratt, Danso, Arnold, Norris, and Filyer (2001) used the generativity scale of McAdams and colleagues (1997) to study the relationship between generativity and parenting style. They found that generativity positively related to mothers' authoritative style (expecting mature behavior from their teens and enforcing reasonable rules). For mothers, generativity was positively related to positive, optimistic views of teen development. For fathers, no clear pattern emerged.

Peterson, Smirles, and Wentworth (1997) contrasted generativity with authoritarianism, the tendency toward closed-mindedness as well as overrespect of authority figures and the values they espouse. Subjects were college students and their parents who completed the same questionnaires. Generativity was positively related to political involvement, but negatively related to authoritarianism. For parents, generativity was highly positively related to openness to experience, but authoritarianism was strongly negatively related to openness. Conscientiousness and generativity were positively correlated for both students and their parents. Extraversion was positively related to generativity for both parents and offspring, but it was negatively related to authoritarianism. Parents' high authoritarianism was strongly linked to conflict with their offspring through their authoritarian parenting style (e.g., not permitting children to have input regarding rules). Thus, generative people, especially parents, are open, conscientious, extraverted and, as parents, tend to allow children input into the rules that govern family life. Authoritarians tended to be the opposite.

Peterson and Stewart (1993) derived TAT scores on achievement, affiliation-intimacy, and power. Generativity was separately indexed by scores on parenting involvement, personal productivity, and societal concern. For women, power motive related to parenting and achievement motive related to forms of generativity expression outside the home. Men showed the opposite tendency: power motive related to generativity outside the home and achievement motive related to parenting. It was concluded that differences in opportunities and expectations for men and women accounted for the gender difference. As the average age of subjects was 27.7, results also showed that people begin to develop generativity well before middle age.

Franz, McClelland, and Weinberger (1991) followed up research beginning in the early 1950s. Participants, aged about 41 by 1990, were 94 men and women who completed a questionnaire and submitted to an interview. The measure of generativity was taken from written details of "hopes and dreams for the future" submitted by subjects (p. 589). These plans were scored by two students using a method developed by McAdams. Results showed that psychosocial maturity—indexed by having close friends at midlife, a long, happy marriage, and children—was positively related to generativity.

McAdams (2000) pointed out that "care," the strength associated with generativity, is similar to but not the same as the "care" expressed by parents toward their children. Erikson's "care," associated with mature adulthood, is broader, encompassing volunteer activities and civic obligations, as well as family concerns. It also does not imply a power differential, or a dominant/dependent relationship, as in parent vis-à-vis child. He went on to suggest that the caregiver-dependent model of attachment fits parent–child relationships well, but not romantic relationships. If he is correct, Shaver's analogy between child–parent attachment and romantic attachment is weakened.

Evaluation

Contributions

Erikson's is a remarkable story. With only a high school education, he made it to the lofty status of Harvard professor. More importantly, he formulated a theory that has heavily influenced not only academics but also the public. Erikson was a hero during the 1960s because of his views regarding youth and rebellion. His assertion that people continue to grow and change in specifiable ways not only opened new vistas to millions of older people, it also revolutionized the study of personality. Prior to Erikson, it was becoming a dogma that personality is set in stone by the end of the teens at the latest. Erikson's unique and creative thoughts opened the eyes of other theorists to the possibility of personality growth at and after middle age. Never again will psychologists neglect older people or believe that everything currently happening in their lives was predetermined by events in their youth.

Like Adler, Horney, Fromm, Rogers, Bandura, and Allport, Erikson is important because of the person he is. Making it as an academic without academic credentials is somewhat akin to making it as a politician without the backing of the political power brokers. Like Adler and Murray, Erikson turned psychological deficiencies into ideas that not only helped him but are valuable to countless others as well. If we adopt his respect for the goals and aspirations of people of all ages, we will take an enormous stride in the direction of respecting all people everywhere.

Thanks to Erikson, there is now up-to-date evidence that people pass through something akin to Erikson's epigenic stages. Further, two of the ideas that he took off the top of his head have been supported by research: industry and generativity.

Limitations

While it is admirable that someone could gain the respect of academics without obtaining the academic union card, a doctorate, Erikson's lack of advanced training showed up in his thinking. There is a certain lack of logical consistency in his ideas. For example, it is not entirely clear why he chose the labels "autonomy versus shame and doubt" to characterize developments at early childhood. Likewise, why was "initiative versus guilt" chosen for the play age? While "autonomy" makes some logical sense, why is "shame and doubt" the other side of the coin representing the early childhood crisis? "Guilt" or "inferiority" or another label might fit just as well. The opposite of "autonomy" is "dependence" and the counterpart of "initiative" could be "dependence." "Competence" seems to fit as well at early childhood as "will power," which may be regarded as a cliché that has been adopted by everyone from frustrated dieters to Adolf Hitler. Erikson was openly dissatisfied with *wisdom.* Aside from the multiple meanings attached to the word, which he does mention, he might have added the fact that the word is so overused it has become trite. One could add, why eight stages?

"Fidelity" seems to be a particularly murky concept. The way Erikson defines it and the way he talks about it do not match well. If it is related to the adoption of ideologies, as Erikson indicates, one could wonder whether adolescence is the appropriate place for it.

Perhaps the seeds of ideological flowering are planted during the teens, but the blossoming may well occur during young adulthood or even later. College students led the protest movement of the 1960s.

While Erikson has inspired several researchers as well as many ordinary citizens, he has apparently failed to recruit notable followers to take up his cause. There are few if any Eriksonians around, at least among well-known psychologists. Perhaps it is because his theory has relatively little practical import compared to others. It has no therapy associated with it, and, unlike other theories, Erikson's theory has been relatively little used to solve real-world problems.

Conclusions

While Erikson's lack of academic training may be a fault that places limits on his theory, it may also be regarded as a virtue. One wonders whether he would have seen that personality development does not end at age 20 if he had been trained in the typical psychology department. As it is, his vision is characterized by greater acuity than most. He anticipated the "midlife" crisis and reminded us all that elderly people can be productive. Not only does he provide us with the possibility of productivity during old age, he points out creative tasks appropriate to the golden years.

Erikson's example reminds us that creative thoughts applicable to the lives of people are not the sole province of the highly educated. Not being encumbered by academic dogmas and methodologies, he was able to focus on what others had neglected. He brought an end to the overemphasis on youth just at the right time. As we enter the era of the "graying of the population," the thoughts of Erik Erikson will become more and more relevant. Erikson was 16th on the list of most frequently cited in journals, 11th on the list of those most frequently cited in textbooks, 17th most frequently named in the survey, and 12th overall (Haggbloom et al., 2002).

Summary Points

1. Erikson was born the son of Danish parents, but he was reared by a Jewish physician. As a young man, a job as a children's portrait painter proved to be his passport into Vienna's secretive psychoanalytic society. In the United States, he attempted graduate work and worked with Murray. He was a professor at Yale, the University of California, and Harvard.

2. Erikson was a Freudian in that he felt he owed allegiance to Freud. Most of his important concepts, however, are distinct from Freud's. He rejected Freud's unflattering view of women. At each successive phase of life, people find themselves on the horns of a new dilemma and confronted with new tasks.

3. Erikson believed that we pass through a series of eight psychosocial stages, each building on the earlier ones (epigenesis). Each stage brings a new crisis: people are caught between two new conflicting poles. The crisis thus represented is never fully resolved, but, hopefully, the ratio of orientation to the positive pole, relative to the negative pole, is favorable.

4. In the first stage, infancy, the poles are basic trust and basic mistrust. The strength of this period is hope. It is the foundation of faith, which is protected by the institutional safeguard, religion. Early childhood presents the poles autonomy versus shame and doubt. Its strength is will power.

5. The third stage involves initiative versus guilt. The boy does fantasize about his mother, but it is because she is central to his life, not solely because of genital urges. The strength of this period is purpose. At the school age, the horns of the dilemma are industry and inferiority. The child at this stage prepares for the "tool culture." The strength of this period is competence.

6. During adolescence the poles are identity versus identity confusion. At this stage previous identity developments either come together or not. It is a time of rebellion against the rules and norms of society. Fidelity is the strength: loyalty to self, others, and to personal ideologies. Ideologies must be adopted, but the danger is subordination of identity to ideology. Identity confusion involves confounding our identities with those of close others.

7. Erikson's theory is in sync with diversity because he acknowledged that his stages and dilemmas would manifest themselves differently in different cultures. In young adulthood, intimacy is fusion of one's identity with another's without loss to self. Love binds together competition and cooperation, procreation and production. In an additional stage, middle adulthood, the poles are productivity versus futility and the strength is contentment. In mature adulthood, generativity is concern for guiding the next generation. Stagnation is the negative pole and care is the strength of this period.

8. Research indicates that midlife is shaped by daily stressors—overload and crossover stressors—not life-changing traumas. In old age, integrity opposes despair: passing on power and leadership to the next generation versus failure to establish a connection between generations. The strength is wisdom, in the sense of "wisdom of the ages." Levinson's midlife transition entails a show of de-illusionment and individuation. We must give up our illusion of immortality and contemplate a legacy. Women's crisis begins at 35: lost children and lost attractiveness. Divorce, concern for "biological clocks," and job competition with men confront women.

9. The poles for young adulthood and adulthood were extracted from factor analysis, but the lack of appearance of the other poles suggests overlap among them. An overriding factor, "identity," was also extracted. Several predictions from Erikson's theory were supported, but usually for Whites, not Blacks. There were also some troublesome gender differences. In another study, measures of industry predicted achievement, grades, and being on- versus off-task. Studies by the McAdams group showed that generativity is related to communion, moral steadfastness, redemption, prosocial future goals, and early family advantage. McAdams pointed out that care associated with generativity is similar to but not the same as parental care.

10. Peterson's group found highly generative people more open, especially about family rules, as well as conscientious and extraverted compared to authoritarians. Other work found gender differences on power and achievement related to generativity. Erikson's theoretical and career accomplishments are remarkable given that he lacked a Ph.D. He was a hero to youth of the 1960s and a champion of the elderly. Research has mostly supported his view. Unfortunately, some of his concepts seem exchangeable across stages, some are trite in meaning, some, like "fidelity," are murky, and some have too many meanings. Research has turned up other problems and raised questions, such as "are eight stages enough?"

Running Comparison

Theorist	*Erikson in Comparison*
Freud	He de-emphasized the unconscious: he merely mentioned oral, anal, and phallic factors and the latency period, and he played down their physical–sexual side all in favor of psychosocial aspects. He came close to calling Freud "wrong" about women.
Gordon Allport	He agreed with Allport that self-esteem derives from doing for oneself. They both deplored nationalism.
Erich Fromm	He also considered the dilemma of freedom and they had similar notions about union with another and nationalism.
Sullivan and Horney	He was also concerned about early, faulty parent–child relationships.
Jung	Like Jung, he emphasized the polarities (opposites).

Essay/Critical Thinking Questions

1. What are the tasks of your life now and what do you expect them to be in ten years?

2. What are your major sources of identity?

3. Why have "industry" and "generativity" been singled out for special research attention?

4. Why do identity developments coalesce during adolescence? Why not at some other stage?

5. As a young adult, how can you "fuse your identity with somebody else's without losing" it?

E-mail Interaction

Write the author at b-allen@wiu.edu. Forward any of the following, or phrase your own.

1. Was Erikson a person with deep-seated inferior feelings?

2. Indicate Erikson's single most important contribution.

3. Was Erikson really sexist?

CHAPTER 8

The Sociopsychological Approach to Personality: Erich Fromm

- Are there basic needs rooted in the very essence of humans?
- Do some people love death?
- What can an investigation of life in a Mexican village tell us about personality?

Erich Fromm
www.ship.edu/~cgboeree/
Fromm.html

Erich Fromm stood at the crossroads of modern personality psychology. Similar to Erikson, some say that he came from the Freudian branch of the psychological tree. If so, he nurtured a new limb supporting a more broad-based personality theory. Fromm, compared to theorists covered earlier, described Freud's scientific contributions in glowing words: "... his discovery of unconscious processes of the dynamic nature of character traits is a unique contribution to the science of man which has altered the picture of man for all time" (Fromm, 1962, p. 12). Yet, when he compared Freud with social theorist Karl Marx, as he often did, Marx was the clear winner. "I consider Marx, the thinker, as being of much greater depth and scope than Freud" (p. 12). Further, Fromm's criticisms of Freud center on the claim that psychoanalysis "can define man scientifically" (Funk, 1982, p. 13). Indeed, Fromm believed that Freud's most basic notions are not amenable to scientific study.

Another reason that Fromm is pivotal in the history of personality theory derives from his academic training and background. He is the first of the theorists covered in this book who was trained in a university graduate school. Like Erikson, he had no medical school training, opting instead to study psychology, philosophy, and, especially, sociology. He received his Ph.D. from Heidelberg in 1922 following completion of "a dissertation on the sociopsychological structure of three Jewish Diaspora

173

communities . . . " (Funk, 1982, pp. 2–3). Quite naturally his orientation would be away from biological/medical matters toward a **sociopsychological orientation,** the sociological study of people that sheds light on their psychological nature. During his long career, Fromm held professorships in several departments of psychology, including those at Michigan, Michigan State, Yale, New York University, and the University of Mexico. Because his background was a mixture of sociology, political philosophy, and psychology, he was the prophet of things to come: personality research and theory were to be taken away from psychiatry/psychoanalysis and given over to psychology and allied sciences.

Fromm, the Person

Erich Fromm was born in Frankfurt, Germany, March 23, 1900, the only child of Orthodox Jewish parents. As a Jewish boy in a Christian community, he experienced feelings of "clannishness" on both sides, along with occasional episodes of anti-Semitism. He characterized his father, the owner of an independent business, and his mother, a homemaker, as "highly neurotic," and himself as an "unbearable, neurotic child" (Funk, 1982, p. 1). Fromm wrote that "an anxious and moody father and a depression-prone mother was enough to arouse my interest in the strange and mysterious reasons for human reactions" (Fromm, 1962, pp. 3–4).

Spurred by a deeply religious family, young Fromm became engrossed in the teachings of the Old Testament "which touched me and exhilarated me more than anything else I was exposed to" (Fromm, 1962, p. 5). He was enthralled by the tale of Adam's and Eve's disobedience, and by Jonah's mission to Nineveh. Isaiah, Amos, and Hosea moved him not so much by their prophesies of disaster as by their visions of the "end of days" when nations "shall beat their swords into plowshares and their spears into pruning hooks: nation shall not lift sword against nation, neither shall they learn war any more" (p. 5). These words were adopted by the international peace movement to which the adult Fromm was to contribute substantially.

Fromm developed his concepts in large part by reflecting on the thoughts of Freud and Marx, whose ideas he tried to synthesize (Fromm, 1962; Weiner, 2003). His early interest in psychoanalysis was triggered by an incident that occurred during his adolescence. A 25-year-old friend of the family killed herself following the death of her widowed father, with whom she had spent nearly all of her time.

> I had never heard of an Oedipus complex or of incestuous fixations between daughter and father. But I was deeply touched. I had been quite attracted to the young woman; I had loathed the unattractive father; never before had I known anyone to commit suicide. I was hit by the thought, "How is it possible?" How is it possible that a beautiful young woman should be so in love with her father, that she prefers to be buried with him to being alive to the pleasures of life. . . ? (Fromm, 1962, p. 4)

In 1929 Fromm began a psychoanalytic apprenticeship under the tutelage of Hans Sachs and Theodor Reik at the Berlin Institute, which also was the site of Karen Horney's training (Funk, 1982; Hausdorff, 1972). Like Horney, he had no direct exposure to Freud.

Because he lacked medical training, Fromm was suspect in some corners of the Freudian world. Although Freudian concepts were rather simplistic from a biological perspective, even for the time, many Freudians thought that one needed medical training to comprehend Freud's ideas. They probably believed that Fromm avoided Freud's biological notions because, lacking medical training, he could not understand them.

For a short time after his psychoanalytic training, Fromm appeared to be a devout Freudian (Hausdorff, 1972). *The Development of the Dogma of Christ* (1931) supported Freud's idea that religion is an illusion adopted in the interest of infantile gratification. But appearances can be deceiving. Although Fromm's Freudian period continued past his move to the United States in 1934, later he was to call himself at best, " . . . a very unorthodox Freudian" (Hausdorff, 1972, p. 3). Fromm's retreat from Freudianism may have begun during the writing of his highly successful book, *Escape from Freedom* (1941). This widely read declaration of independence from Freud advanced Fromm's unique ideas concerning how a totalitarian society and its ideology (e.g., Nazi Germany) can shape the thinking of its citizens. Needless to say, *Escape* was the right book at the right time: the United States was entering World War II against Japan and Germany, models of authoritarian societies.

Fromm, like Jung and Adler, declared that World War I was "the event that determined more than anything else my development" (Fromm, 1962, p. 6). Fromm was 14 when the war began and, at first, was confused by people's reactions to armed conflict. Prior to the outbreak of hostilities, his Latin teacher, who seemed peace-loving, proclaimed his favorite "law" to be, "if you want peace, prepare for war" (p. 6). In a show of true colors, when the war began the Latin instructor was obviously delighted. "How was it possible that a man who always seemed to have been so concerned with the preservation of peace should now be so jubilant about the war?" (p. 6).

Experiences in Fromm's English class helped him deal with the "armament preserves peace" paradox. He and other students were told to learn the heart of the British national anthem over the summer. However, by the time they returned to school, the British had become "the enemy" and the students proudly announced that they would not learn the anthem. Fromm's teacher answered their defiance with a calm, prophetic reminder: "Don't kid yourself; so far England has never lost a war" (p. 7). "Here was the voice of . . . realism in the midst of insane hatred—and it was the voice of a respected . . . teacher!" (p. 7). Never again would Fromm think it merely odd that "arms bring peace"; it was insane.

Amidst Orwellian doubletalk of "strategic retreats" and "victorious defenses," he found that a number of uncles, cousins, and schoolmates had been killed and he again asked himself, "How is it possible?" Fromm puzzled over the bugles of war-justification blaring from the headlines of German newspapers: "was Germany not fighting against the very embodiment of slavery and oppression—the Russian Czar?" (p. 7). When he read convincing evidence that Germanic nations were responsible for the war, his consternation deepened. But confusion became mixed with horror when he realized that young men were buying their country's propaganda and paying dearly for it. They were *not* sacrificing life and limb for peace, freedom, and justice. They were being maimed and killed because their governments had declared the other side "evil," just as the other side had denounced them. This projected-image view of mutually antagonistic groups persists today in the United States's views of adversaries in Afghanistan, Iraq, Iran, and North Korea and in their views of the United States; when one looks at the other, one sees what the other sees when look-ing at oneself, evil. He became "deeply suspicious of all official ideologies and declara-tions" (1962, p. 9).

Fromm was truly a citizen of the world. He received his academic training at the Uni-versities of Heidelberg, Frankfurt, and Munich, Germany. While in the United States, he lived in many locations. His last professorship was at the National Autonomous University of Mexico in Mexico City. Retirement in 1965 was followed by a blitz of professional ac-tivity: 20 percent of his books were completed, including the report on his monumental study of Mexican villagers. In 1976, the year his last book appeared, Fromm moved to the borders of beautiful Lake Maggiore, straddling the Swiss–Italian border. He died in the Swiss town of Muralto on March 18, 1980 (Funk, 1982).

Fromm's View of the Person

It was Fromm's search for answers regarding the ills of society that led him to Marx and Freud. Yet, in studying their theories he began to see flaws, defects in their attempts to be scientific and deficiencies in science itself. Eventually, he began "believing in the superior value of blending empirical observation with speculation (much of the trouble with mod-ern social science is that it often contains empirical observations without specula-tions) . . . I have . . . [been] guided by the observation of facts and have striven to revise my theories when the observation seemed to warrant it" (pp. 9–10). With these words, he adopted the scientific–empirical method and also assigned heavy weight to speculation.

Fromm's leftish inclinations began in childhood when he talked politics with a so-cialist who worked with his father (Fromm, 1962). Although he considered himself at the time "not suited for political activity," after he settled in New York City he became a mem-ber of the American Socialist Party (p. 10). During the Vietnam era, he supported the peace movement and its candidate Eugene McCarthy (Funk, 1982). Fromm was a cofounder of SANE (the Organization for a Sane Nuclear Policy).

Like Adler, though Fromm was a lifetime socialist, he had serious reservations about the Soviet brand of socialism (Funk, 1982). When Fromm was in his seventies, Hausdorff (1972) asked him to define himself. Fromm replied, "[I am] a socialist who is in opposi-tion to most Socialist and Communist parties . . . " (p. 3). He saw socialism from a hu-manistic perspective and was repelled by what he regarded as Communist attempts at subjugation of the human spirit in the interest of perpetuating the power of party officials. That he thought of Soviet Communism as a failed attempt at instituting the Marxist form of socialism is seen in his derisive reference to the "perversion of the Russian revolution" (Fromm, 1962, p. 11). Despite these reservations, Fromm's continued devotion to social-ism, even in its Communist form, is seen in his solution to the confused social order that existed in his time. To solve social ills he offered **humanistic communitarian socialism,** a political system embracing economic, social, and moral functions wherein ordinary cit-izens interact cooperatively and are actively involved in the various functions (Fromm, 1955, 1976). With this process of governing, the governed would participate in all facets of society. Each person would help to ensure that all people enjoy the products of society and none be exploited. The object would be "serve the people" not "make a profit."

Fromm considered a broad spectrum of social influences on personality including the feudal system of the Medieval Age, the Protestant Reformation, nineteenth century industrialization, and twentieth century Nazism, fascism, Communism, and capitalism. Despite the diversity of his writings on social matters, his terminology remained at least somewhat psychoanalytic and he advocated the Freudian unconscious (Pietikainen, 2004). Nevertheless, he was a practicing **humanistic psychoanalyst,** one who believes in the essential worth and dignity of each person, and in the importance of helping each person to do the most with what she or he has. Fromm was convinced that psychology cannot be divorced from philosophy, ethics, values, meaning, sociology, or economics. He saw psychology as having the potential to debunk false ethical judgments and build objective, valid rules of conduct.

Fromm was also influenced by **existentialism,** an approach to understanding each person's most immediate experience, the conditions of his or her existence, and the necessity of exercising freedom of choice in a chaotic world (Binswanger, 1963; Boss, 1963; Kierkegaard, 1954; May, 1958; Merleau-Ponty, 1963; van Kaam, 1963, 1965, 1969). Existentialists encourage psychologists to get inside each person's world, to understand how that person lives, moves, and experiences his or her "being-in-the-world" (Heidegger, 1949). The critical existential concept *being* refers to a condition that is unique to each entity, whether it is a person or a grain of sand, and that transcends the particular qualities of the entity (size, weight, color). Being cannot be assessed by the usual scientific or psychoanalytic methods. It can only be intuitively grasped.

Existentialists value consciousness and personal responsibility (Frankl, 1963). Human freedom is defined not as freedom *from* responsibility but freedom *to accept* responsibility. Thus, one cannot rely on upbringing, early experience, heredity, or present environment to shape oneself. One must make oneself. This rather total responsibility for oneself can be burdensome and even frightening (Sartre, 1957). For this reason, existentialists often write about nothingness, alienation, despair, absurdity, and anxiety. Although influenced by existentialism, Fromm's outlook is more positive. He stressed the unique capacities of each individual to create and love, not his or her despair, alienation, and anxiety. In reference to a basic dilemma, he asserted that the aim of each person's life is to *join* with others while remaining a *free* and separate being. The uniquely human aspects of experience were emphasized, including choosing life's direction and transcendental or spiritual experiences.

Basic Concepts: Fromm

Existential Needs

According to Fromm, people are alike in that they all experience the same dilemmas and contradictions that are heart and soul of human existence. These worrisome paradoxes and conundrums are grounded in opposites that are rooted in the very essence of humans, for example, freedom–subjugation (Fromm, 1973). Thus, all people find themselves joined with others, yet alone; living, yet dying; free, yet responsible; conscious of their potentialities, yet powerless over their limitations. People also are alike in sharing **existential needs,** needs that must be met if one's existence is to be meaningful, one's inner being is to be developed, one's talents are to be fully exploited, and abnormality is to be avoided. Fromm emphasized eight such needs.

Frame of Orientation and Object of Devotion.   People need a **frame of orientation,** a cognitive "map" of their natural and social worlds that enables them to organize and make sense of puzzling matters and allows them to operate in the arena of rational understanding. A frame of orientation is an important factor in a person's life whether it is "true" or "false." Thus, although they are falsehoods from an objective point of view, beliefs "in the power of a totem animal, in a rain god" or in the "superiority and destiny of [my] race" may function as frames of orientation (Fromm, 1959, p. 160). In fact, false or irrational ideologies may be particularly seductive when adopted as frames of orientation. Unlike their scientifically based counterparts, political and religious notions may seem to offer solutions to every problem. "The more an ideology pretends to give answers to all questions, the more attractive it is" (Fromm, 1973, p. 231).

In addition, people need some **object of devotion,** a *goal* that gives meaning to their existence and position in the world. Such an "ultimate concern" provides direction in life, reduces isolation, and permits transcendence beyond one's immediate self. Fromm (1973, pp. 231–232) wrote,

> The objects of man's devotion vary. He can be devoted to an idol which requires him to kill his children or to an ideal that makes him protect children; he can be devoted to growth of life or to its destruction. He can be devoted to the goal of amassing a fortune, of acquiring power, of destruction, or to that of loving and of being productive and courageous. He can be devoted to the most diverse goals . . . yet . . . the need for devotion itself is a primary, existential need demanding fulfillment regardless of how this need is fulfilled.

These two motivational forces together provide a synthesis of one's self and one's life circumstances (Grey, 1993). A way to deal with life's puzzles and a meaningful goal weld the self to life circumstances.

Relatedness.   Humans have an intense need for **relatedness,** "the necessity to unite with other living beings . . . [constitutes] an imperative need on the fulfillment of which man's sanity depends" (Fromm, 1955, p. 30). Among the ways that one can fulfill the relatedness need is by joining another person in a **symbiotic union,** a coupling of beings in which each meets the needs of the other while they "live 'together' " as "two, and yet one" (Fromm, 1956, p. 15). As birds feed on the pests that infest the crocodile and the rhinoceros, each member of a symbiotic pair serves the other.

There are two forms of the symbiotic union, both destructive. In the *passive* union, the person submits to the control of another person, institution, or substance that "directs him, guides him, protects him . . . is his life and his oxygen . . . " (Fromm, 1956, p. 16). Submission takes the form of masochism in that the person is used and abused by the power to which he or she has submitted. If one becomes subservient to another person, the other becomes an idol. Subjugation can involve the whole body, as in sexual submission. Horney's moving toward others is similar. Submission can be "to fate, to sickness, to rhythmic music, to the orgiastic state produced by drugs . . . —in all these instances, the person renounced his integrity, makes himself the instrument of somebody or something outside of himself . . . " (p. 16). If submission is to a country or society, the subservient person may show **automaton conformity,** the condition that occurs when the person, out of fear of aloneness, gives up freedom for union with society. And she or he bends over backwards to maintain the union by strict adherence to social norms and conventions. A rigid net of cultural values ensnares us so completely that we do what *it* dictates, never what *our* inner voices demand (Lesser, 1992).

In the *active* symbiotic fusion, the theme of the union is domination involving sadism, the opposite of masochism. The dominating individual seeks to escape from aloneness by making another person a part of him or her. People of this sort sadistically achieve self-inflation by incorporating another person who, in turn, masochistically worships them. Each is so dependent on the other that neither can live without the other. "The difference is only that the sadistic person commands, exploits, hurts, humiliates, and that the masochistic person is commanded, exploited, hurt, humiliated" (Fromm, 1956, p. 17). While the sadist and the masochist are different, they also are the same: they have fused with another at the sacrifice of their personal integrity. Not surprisingly, a given person can react both sadistically and masochistically, usually toward different objects. Hitler, for example, was sadistic toward the German people, who worshiped him as a god. But he was masochistic in regard to fate: he rode destiny wherever it carried him, from the glory of conquest to the ignominy of suicide.

In contrast to the tragedy of symbiotic union, **mature love** "is union under the condition of preserving one's integrity, one's individuality . . . [it] is an active power of man" (p. 17). The power of love demolishes the barriers that separate people. It overcomes isolation and separateness, yet it maintains personal integrity. Love is "becoming one and yet remaining two" (p. 17). There is no need to inflate either one's own or the other person's image and the need for illusions regarding the other person and oneself vanishes. Fromm believed that "In the act of loving, I am one with All, and yet I am myself, a unique, separate, limited, mortal human being" (Fromm, 1955, p. 32). When one truly loves another person, one loves all of humanity, and, therefore, oneself. These ideas are reminiscent of Erikson's identity resolution at the young adult stage.

Rootedness.   **Rootedness** is a deep craving to maintain one's natural ties and not be "separated" (Fromm, 1973). Without roots we would have to stand alone, in isolation and helplessness, not knowing who we are or where we are. Most people show progress in life by substituting new roots for old. When biological separation occurs, through birth and maturation, substitute attachments are sought, both symbolically (God, country) and emotionally (love, community). The more complete the original separation, the greater the need to form new roots that approximate the paradise of security represented by envelopment in the womb. The intensity of the craving for roots as deep and secure as the original ones can be so overwhelming that the individual may regress to a near infantile state in which dependence on some symbolic substitute for mother occurs. Such substitutes include "the soil," "nature," or "God." The healthy opposite to this regression toward a primitive state is finding new roots in "the brotherhood of man, and by freeing [oneself] from the power of the past" (Fromm, 1973, p. 233). A destructive "symbiotic" regression was illustrated by the young woman who committed suicide after her father's death. She was unable to separate herself from her father. An example of mature love is provided by Fromm himself in his marriage to Annis Freeman in 1953 (Hausdorff, 1982). He was truly one with her, but he clearly maintained his integrity, as reflected in the enormous productivity he showed during the years of their marriage. In sum, one can satisfy the need for roots through love, or one can take the destructive route by seeking a symbiotic relationship.

We can become detached from our roots, if, for example, we are identified as African American, Latino, Asian, or American Indian, and do not know the language, history, or traditions of our culture. Reattachment can be a powerful experience.

Identity.   **Identity** is the need to be aware of oneself as a separate entity, and to sense oneself as the subject of one's own actions (Fromm, 1955). The person is able to say and feel "I am I." This need also applies to seeing others as separate persons. Members of ancient clans sometimes are unable to see themselves as existing separately from the group, expressing their identity as "I am we." Throughout history, individuals have identified themselves with social roles. Medieval roles included "I am a peasant" or "I am a lord." These ideas are akin to "persona," Jung's mask concept. When the feudal system broke down, major uncertainties were created. Peasants and lords were unable to answer the questions "Who am I?" or "How do I know who I am?" They then turned to nation, class, religion, and occupation as substitutes for unique identity. People have sought to obtain a false sense of personal identity, security, or status by adhering to such social roles as "I am an American . . . a Protestant . . . an executive." Citizens living in the twentieth century also have sought to "Escape from Freedom" by giving up their individuality to totalitarian governments. Fromm maintained that we must stop this tragic and fruitless quest for identity. We must abandon "being" the roles we play or "being" as others want us to be. Instead, we must devote ourselves to "being" separate entities who can relate to others without dissolving into them. We may also wish to separate our own identities from those of people close to us as these identities may be confounded (Mashek et al., 2003).

Unity.   **Unity** is a sense of oneness within one's self and with the "natural and human world outside" (Fromm, 1973, p. 233). Unity can be approached through dressing in animal skins, in efforts to unite with the animal portion of nature. It can also be approached by subordinating one's energies to an all-consuming passion for power, fame, or property. Failures to achieve unity can evade consciousness if one anesthetizes oneself through alcohol, drugs, sexual orgies, trances, or cultist rituals. These tricks played on consciousness are attempts to restore unity within oneself. Indeed, when one is drugged or drunk one achieves a sense of unitary experience that is a kind of oneness. However, Fromm believed that this method has only temporary positive effects and is counterproductive in the long run. It damages those who use it, estranges them from others, twists their judgment, and makes them dependent on the substance or passion in which they have chosen to invest themselves. The true and certain path to unity lies in developing human reason and love. Religion can be the light to illuminate that path, but only if one participates in it, rather than passively submits to it. All the great religions of the world have a common goal: "to arrive at the experience of oneness, not by regressing to animal existence but by becoming fully human—oneness with man, oneness between man and nature, and oneness between man and other men" (Fromm, 1973, p. 234).

Transcendence.   **Transcendence** is the act of transforming one's accidental and passive role of "creature" into that of an active and purposeful "creator" (Fromm, 1955). As you will soon see, this idea is much like the humanistic notions of Carl Rogers and Abraham Maslow.

It can be accomplished through various means, in as simple a process as planting seeds and producing material goods or in as complicated a manner as creating art and ideas and loving others. By creative acts, humans can rise above the "creature" in them and ascend to new heights where purposefulness and freedom dwell. But "How . . . does man solve the problem of transcending himself, if he is not capable of creating, if he cannot love? There is another answer to this need for transcendence: if I cannot create life, I can destroy it. To destroy life makes me transcend it" (Fromm, 1955, p. 37). Because humans must transcend themselves, they are compelled to create or to destroy, to love or to hate. Both the destructive and the creative paths lead to transcendence. "However, the satisfaction of the need to create leads to happiness; destructiveness to suffering, most of all, for the destroyer himself" (Fromm, 1955, p. 38). It follows from this position that we must do all we can to foster creativity, a potential that exists in all of us, so that happiness prevails rather than destructiveness. Later you will read about how Carl Rogers and B. F. Skinner sought to promote creativity.

Effectiveness.   **Effectiveness** is the need to compensate for "being in a strange and over-powering world" by developing a sense of being able to do something that will "make a dent" in life (Fromm, 1973, p. 235). To be effective is to "get things done," "to accomplish," and to be a person "who has the capacity to do . . . something" (p. 235). It also offers some proof of one's existence and identity, based on the realization "I am, because I effect." People may experience joy by producing effects that are either positive or negative—making a noisy clatter, eliciting a smile from a loved one, doing what is forbidden, destroying property, or even causing terror in a victim. We first manifest effectiveness in child's play when we experience the "joy of being a cause" (p. 235). One of the earliest expressions of effectiveness is the child utterance "I do . . . I do." As you will see, Gordon Allport argued that, to be effective, to do for oneself, is a landmark developmental event. According to Fromm, effectiveness striving arises in part from being overwhelmed by parental power: " . . . to rule when one had to obey; to beat when one was beaten; to do what one was forced to suffer, or to do what was forbidden to do" become principal goals of the child (p. 236). As adults we are preoccupied with effects and are compelled to produce them. We must "elicit an expression of satisfaction from the baby being nursed, a smile from the loved person, sexual response from the lover, interest from the partner in conversation" in order to feel "I am because I effect" (pp. 235–236). As with Fromm's other concepts, this one has its downside. If we cannot by our actions elicit loving feelings in others, we can, like Shelley's Frankenstein monster, cause them fear and suffering. The choice between construction and destruction is, as always, ours to make.

Excitation and Stimulation.   **Excitation and stimulation** is the need for the nervous system to be "exercised," that is, to experience a certain amount of excitation (Fromm, 1973). The importance of this need is supported by research showing brain-generated dream activity during sleep, by the abnormal reactions of infants and monkeys reared in environments lacking varied sensory stimulation, and by studies of normal young adults exposed to environments lacking in sensory variation.

Consistent with Fromm's view, hundreds of studies on sleeping and dreaming demonstrate that the brain must be continuously stimulated, even during some phases of sleep (see Anch, Browman, Mitler, & Walsh, 1988). Because sensory stimulation is shut off during sleep, the brain, in effect, self-stimulates (Allen, 2001). During rapid eye movements (REM) associated with dreaming, the senses act as if they are functioning, even though they are receiving no information. Behind the eyes, ears, and other sense organs, the brain, even in terms of its electrical activity, operates almost as if it is awake and receiving sensory input. Thus, we can experience vivid, full-color dreams that are so real we may awake perspiring and in a state of terror (or ecstasy). When experimental subjects are deprived of dreams, by, for example, being awakened whenever their eyes move under their lids (REM), they appear to suffer difficulties in problem solving and may show at least short-term emotional disturbances (see Anch et al., 1988, for a cautionary note). Stimulation and excitation are ever-present needs.

The work of Canadian psychologist D. O. Hebb (1949) established that proper functioning of the brain requires continuously varied sensory stimulation. Primates, experimental monkeys or children in institutions, were reared in stale environments where there was little variation in what was seen or heard or felt (recall the Sullivan chapter). Compared to monkeys and children reared amid ever-changing sights and sounds, the deprived primates' brains were underdeveloped. Thus, their intellects and perceptual capabilities were blunted. Hebb's collaborators placed normal college students in an environment designed to eliminate variation in visual, auditory, and tactile stimulation (Heron, 1957). They wore diffusing goggles that let in light, but no pattern or form. Also, they were exposed to a fan that generated "white noise" (all the auditory frequencies humans can hear scrambled together), and had their hands covered. Living two to four days under these circumstances was enough to cause the students' brains to malfunction. Not only were their electrical brain waves abnormal, they showed bizarre hallucinations ("A tiny spaceship is firing pellets at my arm"), emotional disturbances ("The experimenter is out to get me"), and intellectual deficiencies (poor problem solving). Subjects were so starved for stimulation they would have cherished a phone book to read. Environmental conditions like these were a part of the "brainwashing" methods used on U.S. prisoners of China and North Korea during the Korean War (see the movie *The Manchurian Candidate*).

According to Fromm, the need for varied sensory input can be satisfied by two kinds of stimuli: simple or activating. **Simple stimuli** generate reflexes that call for reactions rather than actions, particularly *surface reactions* that are immediate and passive in nature. Simple stimuli are often associated with "thrills": accidents, fires, crimes, wars, arguments, sex-related movies and advertisements, and television violence. These stimuli cause knee-jerk, automatic, gut reactions. Repeated presentation of them destroys their power. **Activating stimuli** are more complicated than simple stimuli, in that they cause people to become engaged in productive activity for longer periods of time. Examples include stimulation from generating ideas, reading novels, painting landscapes, enjoying music, and being with loved ones. Activating stimuli encourage their target to be a participant in the stimulation, not a passive pawn manipulated by it (Fromm, 1973, p. 240). Rather than losing their power with repetition, truly activating stimuli continue to be potent with repeated presentation. To Fromm, activating stimuli are healthier but require greater maturity because they do not lead as quickly to excitement. Activating stimuli require great effort, patience, discipline, concentration, tolerance, and critical thinking. Rather than reacting, the person must bring these stimuli to life. Box 8.1 allows you to examine your needs.

BOX 8.1 • *Which Needs Are Most Prominent in Your Life?*

Fromm believed that all of his existential needs must be met by all people. Nevertheless, he certainly wrote or spoke nothing to contradict the possibility that some needs may be more prominent in some people than in others. In fact, part of the uniqueness of a person's individual character may be associated with paying more attention to some needs than others. An exercise will help you appreciate this point with regard to yourself in comparison to other members of your class. Below each brief statement of the several needs you will find a scale. By placing an "X" nearer one end of the scale than the other, you can indicate the degree of time and attention you devote to each need (for a given need, you can place your mark above any scale point that you deem appropriate). When you finish making the marks, you will have one more task to do before comparing your responses to those of other students.

Frame of orientation and object of devotion is a cognitive map to guide us in making sense of puzzling matters and a goal that gives meaning to our existence, respectively.

__:__:__:__:__:__:__:__

spend much time and   spend little time and
attention to this need   attention to this need

Relatedness is the necessity of uniting with other living beings, to relate to them; it is an imperative need on the fulfillment of which rests our sanity.

__:__:__:__:__:__:__:__

spend much time and   spend little time and
attention to this need   attention to this need

Rootedness is a deep craving to maintain one's natural ties and not be "separated."

__:__:__:__:__:__:__:__

spend much time and   spend little time and
attention to this need   attention to this need

Identity is the need to be aware of oneself as a separate entity, and to sense oneself as the subject of one's own actions.

__:__:__:__:__:__:__:__

spend much time and   spend little time and
attention to this need   attention to this need

Unity is a sense of oneness within one's self and with the "natural and human world outside."

__:__:__:__:__:__:__:__

spend much time and   spend little time and
attention to this need   attention to this need

Transcendence is the act of transforming one's accidental and passive role of "creature" into that of an active and purposeful "creator."

__:__:__:__:__:__:__:__

spend much time and   spend little time and
attention to this need   attention to this need

Effectiveness is the need to compensate for "being in a strange and overpowering world" by developing a sense of being able to do something that will "make a dent" in life.

__:__:__:__:__:__:__:__

spend much time and   spend little time and
attention to this need   attention to this need

Excitation and stimulation is the need for the nervous system to be "exercised," that is, to experience a certain amount of excitation.

__:__:__:__:__:__:__:__

spend much time and   spend little time and
attention to this need   attention to this need

Now, draw a line from the mark on the first scale to the one on the second scale and so forth all the way down to the mark on the last scale. You have drawn your "need profile." If all students simply hold up their books so they can see each other's profiles, all can appreciate the uniqueness of individuals' profiles. Even though the number of need scales is small, it is likely that each student's profile line will be different from that of each other student (individual differences). That observation will confirm that people and their need patterns are unique; each person is an original, unduplicated by any other person in the world.

You will come across a further consideration of "needs" later in this book. Henry Murray's theory revolves around needs to a great extent, as does that of Abraham Maslow.

183

Individual and Social Character

Individual Differences among People. Although they share common existential problems and needs, people are also different from each other. This is seen in Fromm's definition of **personality:** "the totality of inherited and acquired psychic qualities which are characteristic of one individual and which make the individual unique" (1947, p. 50). Inherited differences, and differences among people in their developmental histories, lead them to experience the same environment in different ways. People also show uniqueness "in the specific way they solve their human problem" (1947, p. 50).

Fromm actually devotes much greater attention to the concept of *character* than to personality. Character, which is based on the individual's relatedness to the world, has two forms. **Individual character** is the pattern of behavior characteristic of a given person, "the relatively permanent system of all non-instinctual strivings through which man relates himself to the human and natural world" (Fromm, 1973, p. 226). Because character involves deeply rooted habits and opinions, it serves a decision-making function. It is a semi-automatic process of action and thought that saves an individual from having to make deliberate, conscious decisions every time choices must be made. Character is analogous to reflexes in that it becomes activated as soon as appropriate stimuli are present, without the intervention of thoughtfulness. Once energy is channeled in a certain way, action takes place "true to character."

Individual Differences among Societies. Thus far, differences among people have been emphasized. A contribution unique to Fromm is his interest in identifying character differences among entire societies. **Social character** represents "the core of a character structure common to most people of a given culture . . . [and] shows the degree to which character is formed by social and cultural patterns" (1947, p. 60). Social character is clearly the product of one's society. In a sense, individual character becomes partly "lost" as it is subsumed by social character. Fromm put it this way: "the whole personality of the average individual is molded by the way people relate to each other, and it is determined by the socioeconomic and political structure of society to such an extent that . . . one can infer from the analysis of one individual the totality of the social structure in which he lives" (Fromm, 1947, p. 79).

Fromm (1947) has identified six types of social character: receptive, exploitative, hoarding, marketing, necrophilous, and productive. These types express themselves in how individuals relate to things and to people (including themselves). Fromm classifies the first five as *nonproductive,* those that yield, at best, pseudoconnection to others and, at worst, destructive relations with others. They are distorted, incomplete, or ultimately unfulfilling. In contrast, the **productive orientation** is based on love, the mutual intimacy that preserves individual integrity. Although the types are "ideals," one is likely to be dominant depending on cultural values. Also, because of the interaction between individual and culture, it is always possible for individuals to affect their society. Fromm casts each type in terms of **assimilation,** how people acquire things, and **socialization,** how people relate to others (see Table 8.1 on page 191). Also, four of the five nonproductive types were divided into two pairs. One pair was labeled *symbiotic* because people partaking of these types were involved in relations in which one member submits to the exploitation of the other. The second pair is dubbed *withdrawal,* as people of these types view other people as threats who are to be treated destructively or kept at considerable distance. A fifth nonproductive type is considered separately. Symbiosis and withdrawal are similar to Horney's moving toward and moving away from others.

People of a **receptive** orientation experience the source of all good as being outside themselves (Fromm, 1947). According to Fromm, the receptive person " . . . believes that the only way to get what he wants—be it something material, be it affection, love, knowledge, pleasure—is to receive it from [an] outside source" (p. 62). People of this type receive from others, and they show their oral nature by being fond of food and drink. Receptive people are dependent, favor saying "yes" rather than "no," listening to others rather than talking, and seeking to be loved and helped rather than giving love and help. They show "gratitude for the hand that feeds them and fear of ever losing it" (p. 62). Here Fromm obviously was influenced by Freud.

If people are religious, they want and expect everything from God and nothing from their own efforts. If they are not religious, they may wish for a "magic helper," someone who will meet their every need and solve their every problem. Should they look to many people as sources of life's benefits, they will show loyalty to many people. As a result they will stretch themselves thin and frequently get caught between conflicting loyalties and promises. More generally, they tend to be optimistic and friendly. They exude confidence in life and what it has to offer, but they show extreme anxiety when they sense that a "source of supply" may be withdrawn. In terms of assimilation, people of this type passively receive (accepting). On the socialization side, they masochistically submit (loyalty). The solution to submissiveness is not opposition to powerful others. Rather, the solution is to participate with authority figures in the implementation of power (Weiner, 2003).

The receptive orientation is found in societies that are stratified such that the lower classes depend on the upper classes. The "unfortunate members" are lead to assume that through "sacrifice, duty, and love" they will be "taken care of" by the "fortunate" (powerful) members of society (p. 108). They rationalize their masochism by arguing that it is their "lot in life" to submit to the care of others. Peasants in a feudal society may fit this model.

People of an **exploitative** orientation also experience the source of all good as outside themselves, but, rather than expecting to receive from others, they take things through force or cunning. Their orientation is to grab, steal, and manipulate, while being suspicious, cynical, jealous, and hostile. They underrate what they have, overrate what others have, and endorse the mottos "I take what I need" and "Stolen fruits are sweetest." Therefore, in the realm of love, stolen affection is a jewel, love freely offered by an unattached other is a lump of coal. Not surprisingly, they find married or otherwise attached people very attractive. Expressions of love are reserved for "marks": people who are "promising objects of exploitation" (Fromm, 1947, p. 65). Fromm's concern about exploitative people was shared by Horney.

Like the receptive type, exploitative individuals cannot do for themselves. They must take the fruits of others' labors, including their mental efforts. People of this type are intellectual bandits. Having no useful ideas of their own, they literally pick others' brains. More generally, they get no thrill from creating their own "goods," but they get a rush from taking others'. In terms of traits, exploitative types are hostile and cynical. To them there are two kinds of people, those who get in the way and must be removed, and those who are useful for some selfish purpose. Instead of the optimistic, accepting attitude of the receptive type, these individuals are suspicious of others: What are they withholding? Are they trying to do to me what I want to do to them? Instead of a friendly orientation to others, they are jealous: "Whatever others have is better than what I have." As you might guess, they are masters of the cutting remark and the subtle put-down. In terms of assimilation, people of this type are exploiting (taking). As to socialization, they relate to others in a sadistic fashion (authority). Like the receptive type, they relate to others in a symbiotic manner, but they are the takers, not the receivers.

This orientation is seen in societies dominated by dictators who exploit human and natural resources through power, ruthless competition, authoritarianism, and the "right of might." In modern times, it seems well illustrated by the Soviet Union during the Stalinist era (1920s to the 1950s). Peasants were required to give what they produced to the "state" (actually to Stalin and party members close to him). If they refused, they were "allowed" to starve; after all, they were useless. If they protested, they were "removed": sent to the infamous Soviet prisons, the gulags, or killed. Stalin was a true exploitative sadist who enjoyed sending warped communications to his victims. He would greet people warmly . . . just before having them killed (Fromm, 1973). He would assure representatives of a Soviet ethnic group that their favorite poets would not be arrested; they would be seized shortly thereafter. Box 8.2 depicts Hitler as the ultimate exploiter.

People of the **hoarding** orientation differ from the two preceding types: they believe the "goods" come from the inside not the outside, themselves not others, so security is based on an attitude of saving, of letting out as little as possible (Fromm, 1947). Rather than seeking symbiotic relations with others, they withdraw from others. They set up "a protective wall, and their main aim is to bring as much as possible into this fortified position and to let as little as possible out of it" (p. 65). Their motto is, "Mine is mine, and yours is yours" and they are misers about everything: money, material things, the past, love. They do not give love, they get it by owning the "beloved." Everything they had in the past which is now only a memory is still cherished. They would keep everything they grabbed since they were old enough to grasp, if they could. Thus, they are "sentimental": they ruminate endlessly about bygone experiences.

These people are sterile, "tight-lipped," even grim. Being prone to withdrawal, they are unpleasant to be around: they regard others as candidates for possession, not potential companions in a human relationship. Hoarding applies to information as well as everything else. They know much, but can do little with it, because they are rigid, bound by extreme orderliness. Hoarding types are compulsively clean, obsessively punctual, and irritatingly obstinate. "No!" is their favorite exclamation. To say "yes" threatens them with the possibility of giving up something. They peer through the gates of their fortresses, beckoning to those who would enter and be counted among their possessions, but never venturing forth into others' world. In terms of assimilation, they are hoarding (preserving). As to socialization, they are destructive (assertiveness).

This orientation is represented by societies adopting the Puritan ethic of hard work and success, in which middle-class stability is provided through family and possession of property. North America during the late 1600s through the early 1800s may illustrate this kind of society. The Puritan religion was thriving during a great part of that period. Self-

BOX 8.2 • *Hitler: The Ultimate Exploiter*

Adolph Hitler will forever remain something of an enigma. Was he crazy (psychotic)? Probably not: he doesn't fit the usual psychiatric categories very well. Was he psychopathic (no conscience)? Maybe, maybe not . . . he did seem to care for some people (e.g., Eva Braun, his lover), but he vowed to kill his dog Blondi if she showed any signs of cowardice. However, one of his characteristics was clearly displayed. He was an exploiter. He used the Jews to obtain the power he needed to exploit the German people.

You may say, however, that if he really hated the Jews, he was not consciously exploiting them. He was "merely" acting on his hatred. But this argument falls apart when it is realized that he had no reason to hate Jews. When young Adolph spent 1909–1913 roaming the streets of Freud's Vienna, the Jews he encountered were good to him (Shirer, 1960; Toland, 1976). For example, he was allowed to stay in Jewish hostels and a Jew gave him a coat when he had no protection against the cold. Later, he showed his appreciation to a Jewish physician who ably nursed his sick mother by sparing him when Jews were sent to concentration camps.

But his experiences in Vienna probably did help him form a strategy for gaining and keeping power. Vienna was virulently anti-Semitic during the time when Hitler inhabited its street corners trying to sell his amateurish paintings. It must have been clear to him that anti-Semitic people would rally around anyone who would tell them "how to deal with the Jews." In fact, downtrodden people in need of a cause would board any vehicle that would carry them to power. Hitler found that one could recruit willing followers by convincing them that the Jews were the reason for their unemployment and lowly status. Thus, his Vienna experiences taught him how to skillfully use anti-Semitism for the purpose of gaining power that he could then use to seduce the German people.

Germany was in chaos after it lost World War I to the Allies. The once proud German people needed a savior to lead them back to glory. Hitler's strategy was to convince them that losing the war was not their fault: they were betrayed by the Jews. In turn, so cleverly did he promise to "resolve the Jewish problem" and restore the German people to supremacy that both they and he came to believe his lies about the Jews. Willingly they grafted themselves to his pale hide. In this symbiotic state he used them to wage the European component of World War II, and he would have used them up had the war lasted a few more years. They, in turn, reveled in their masochistic attachment to their Father, their Fuehrer. Never were so many people so willing to be so thoroughly exploited.

sufficient family farms were the most basic social units of that time. Farms produced almost all that a family needed, and hard work in the family interest was necessary for survival. Insofar as people had specialized professions, such as blacksmith and candlemaker, they were even more literally defined by their jobs than we are today. The European tradition of naming people for their professions came to the "new world" with the first settlers. Thus, surnames such as "Butcher" and "Goldsmith" still exist today. Nevertheless, U.S. society of this period did not wholly fit Fromm's "hoarding" notion: the spirit of cooperation among and within family units appears to have been much greater than Fromm would have expected.

The **marketing** orientation is unique to the modern historical era in which exchanging goods for money, other goods, or services became the backbone of a "supply and demand" economy (Fromm, 1947). In this contemporary economy, supply of a commodity determined its value, not its inherent usefulness. For example, fuel is essential for running industry and automobiles and for heating homes, but its value is determined by whether it is in short supply or there is plenty of it. Thus, although the usefulness of gasoline remains constant, it is relatively inexpensive when much is available, but expensive when some world crisis decreases the supply. By analogy, people of this orientation experience themselves as saleable commodities whose "exchange value" depends on whether they are in short supply or not. They seek to package and sell themselves so that they seem unusual or rare and, thus, "in demand." While a minimum level of competence is necessary to be marketable at all, in a given profession a great many people will possess that degree of skill. Further, in almost every profession, there will be many people with much more than minimum competence. With so many people being relatively indistinguishable in terms of skills, whether a given person stands out enough "to get hired" depends on such personality traits as " 'cheerful,' 'sound,' 'aggressive,' 'reliable,' 'ambitious' . . . " (Fromm, 1947, p. 70). People battle to distinguish themselves so that they will look like "one of a kind" and thereby appear to be in short supply. Ironically, "since success depends largely on how one sells one's personality, one experiences oneself as . . . simultaneously . . . the seller and the commodity to be sold" (p. 70). Under these circumstances, people are not concerned with their lives or happiness, but with being saleable.

"One has to be in fashion on the personality market, and in order to be in fashion one has to know what kind of personality is most in demand" (p. 71). Helpfully, the media supplies the raw materials one needs to construct a marketable personality. Personality traits that have sold are depicted on TV, in the movies, and in popular magazines. "The young girl tries to emulate the facial expression, coiffure, [and] gestures of a high-priced star as the most promising way to success. The young man tries to look and be like a [role] model he sees on the screen" (p. 71). Some people do well at this game, but, in a sense, all fail in the end. One can manipulate one's traits to form a hopefully marketable commodity, but one can never be sure whether the finished product will sell. Therefore, one's self-esteem is at the mercy of the market: it is high if, on occasion, one "sells," low if one does not, and one can never predict the sales outcome for sure. Assimilation is represented here in "marketing" (exchanging) and socialization in "indifference" (fairness). Because Fromm believed that the modern capitalistic society of which you are likely a member clearly generates the marketing type, no further example is needed.

The **necrophilous character** is engrossed by death, dwells on it, and glories in it (Fromm, 1973). Contrary to the well-known clinical use of the term—a desire to have sexual relations with corpses—in Fromm's use, *necrophilous* is generalized to mean a preoccupation with death. The term dates to an incident during a speech by General Millan Astray delivered at the onset of the Spanish Civil War (1936). When one of the General's followers shouted his favorite motto from the back of the room—"Viva la muerte!" ("Long live death!")—Spanish philosopher Miguel de Unamuno arose from the audience to express his disgust: "Long live death!" is a "necrophilous and senseless cry . . . " (p. 331). This incident inspired Fromm's "death-loving" character.

The necrophilous type gains meaning and identity by transforming life into death. Fromm wrote: "Necrophilia in the characterological sense can be described as the passionate *attraction* to all that is dead, decayed, putrid, sickly; it is the passion to transform that which is *alive* into something *unalive*; to destroy for the sake of destruction; the exclusive interest in all that is purely mechanical. It is the passion 'to tear apart living structures' " (p. 332). The necrophilous person extracts a feeling of power and elation from vicariously or directly participating in the transformation of life into death. Although Fromm did not explicitly refer to assimilation and socialization for this type, it is possible to extrapolate from his writings: the assimilation term would be *necrophilous* (life to death) and the corresponding socialization concept could be "murderous" (warlike). Analogous to "symbiosis" and "withdrawal," necrophilous types are labeled "unhumanizing" because lifeless people fascinate them.

Fromm saw the necrophilous inclination emerge from dreams and the subtle actions of people. Albert Speer, Adolf Hitler's personal architect, later his armaments minister, and possibly his only friend, had a dream that symbolically illustrated the Nazi leader's necrophilous tendencies (Fromm, 1973). In it Speer finds himself in Hitler's car: "Our drive ends at a large square surrounded by government buildings. On one side is a war memorial. Hitler approaches it and lays down a wreath" (Fromm, 1973, p. 333). And Hitler lays another wreath, and another, and another. All the while he is chanting "Jesus Maria," possibly a remnant from his Catholic upbringing. By laying the wreaths on the memorials, Hitler pays homage to death, but does so in the typical mechanical, unfeeling fashion of the necrophilous person. The chant may also be seen in symbolic terms: Hitler's religion had become death.

Other dreams of death illustrate the destructive nature of the warlike, necrophilous person. One dreamer reported: "I have made a great invention, the 'superdestroyer.' It is a machine which, if one secret button is pushed that I alone know, can destroy all life in North America within the first hour, and within the next hour, all life on earth" (p. 334). Referring to another scene, the dreamer said, "I have pushed the button; I notice no more life, I am alone, I feel exuberant." This report could describe the dream of a twisted computer-game player or perhaps a deranged devotee of Dungeons and Dragons or Puppet Master. Although necrophilous gamers are rare, current electronic games in which lifelike figures are dismembered by players' "gunfire" are so realistic that use of them may have pushed Klebold and Harris into the tragedy at Columbine.

The mechanization of everything that so thrills the necrophilous person is well illustrated in another dream. The dreamer is at a party where young people are dancing, but their rhythm becomes slower and slower until everyone is immobile. At this moment two very large people enter the room carrying some equipment. One of them approaches a boy and bloodlessly cuts a hole in his back into which a box is inserted. The same is done to a girl by the other oversized person. Keys are inserted into the boxes and, when switched on, the boy and girl dance vigorously. The same "operation" is performed on all other persons present. People became machines whose aliveness can be switched on or off.

Illustrations of societies that spawn the necrophilous type are numerous and familiar. Some societies of the twentieth century include those that revolved around Hitler, Italian dictator Mussolini, and the bloodthirsty Cambodian despot Pol Pot, who slaughtered two million of his people. Unfortunately, certain leaders continue to set a necrophilous tone for their people. Witness the works of Osama bin Laden, Saddam Hussein, the Hutus of Rwanda, and certain military leaders involved in "ethnic cleansing" during the wars in Bosnia and Kosovo.

Table 8.1 summarizes Fromm's social character types, including the only positive one—**productive orientation**—an attitude of relatedness to the world and oneself that

TABLE 8.1 *Fromm's Social Character Types*

Assimilation	Socialization	
Nonproductive Orientation		
Receiving (accepting)	Masochistic (loyalty)	
		symbiosis
Exploiting (taking)	Sadistic (authority)	
Hoarding (preserving)	Destructive (assertiveness)	
		withdrawal
Marketing (exchanging)	Indifferent (fairness)	
Necrophilous	Murderous	
		unhumanize
(life into death)	(warlike)	
Productive Orientation		
Working	Loving & Reason	
		humanize
(creating)	(integrity)	

encompasses all realms of human experience: reasoning, loving, and working (Fromm, 1947). Productive people "comprehend the world, mentally and emotionally, through love and through reason" (p. 97). The productive orientation is not concerned with practical results or "success."

The human capacity for *productive reasoning* can be used to penetrate the surface of ideas, actions and emotions, get into them, and, thereby, gain understanding of their essence. The power of *productive love* can break through walls that separate people, allowing each of us genuine understanding of other people's mental and emotional cores. Productive love is characterized by care, responsibility, respect, and knowledge (note the resemblance to Erikson's "care" at the adulthood stage). *Productive work* allows people to transform materials into other forms, using reason and imagination to visualize things not yet existing. It also promotes creativity and fruitful planning. These three orientations point to the opposite of necrophilia, **biophilia,** which is love of life (Eckardt, 1992).

In essence, the productive orientation provides an answer to the basic contradictions of human existence. It suggests that a person's main task in life is to give birth to oneself, to become what one potentially is, a theme that is elaborated by the humanists covered in the next chapter. The most important product of this effort is one's own "mature and integrated" personality. This is because Fromm, like Jung, believed that every person is more than "a blank sheet of paper on which culture can write its text" (1947, p. 23). A human nature exists (Biancoli, 1992). Therefore, what is ethically good in Fromm's humanistic frame-work is the unfolding of personal powers according to the laws of human nature. This view led Fromm (1959) to propose a positive concept of mental health that is not just the absence of sickness but the presence of "well-being." To manifest well-being one must be aware, re-sponsive, independent, fully active, united with the world, and able to understand that only living creatively gives meaning to life. One must be joyful in the act of living—expressing joy throughout one's whole body—and concerned with being rather than having (Fromm, 1976). Failure to make use of one's innate human powers results in unhappiness, psycho-logical disturbance, and neurosis. It appears that Fromm saw no former or present major so-ciety able to reliably generate productive types. See how productive you are, and how much you are "into" the other orientations. Complete the scales in Box 8.3.

BOX 8.3 • *Fromm's Orientation Test*

Indicate how much each word applies to you on the following scale: 5 (very well), 4, 3, 2, 1 (not at all).

Looking left to right, you will need to sum down for the first four orientations. Sum across all of the rows that have "sum across" to the far right, then sum down and divide by two for the last orientation (far right column).

tender____	captivating____	orderly____	witty____	sum across____
gullible____	arrogant____	stubborn____	indifferent____	
optimistic____	gracious____	reserved____	curious____	sum across____
cowardly____	conceited____	suspicious____	unprincipled____	
idealistic____	assertive____	economical____	youthful____	sum across____
submissive____	exploitative____	unimaginative____	opportunistic____	
sentimental____	seducing____	obsessive____	silly____	
loyal____	self-confident____	steady____	tolerant____	sum across____
wishful____	rash____	cold____	tactless____	
sensitive____	proud____	careful____	open-minded____	sum across____
unrealistic____	aggressive____	stingy____	childish____	
devoted____	active____	practical____	purposeful____	sum across____
sum down____	sum down____	sum down____	sum down____	sum down & divide by two___
receptive	exploitative	hoarding	marketing	productive

Scores from 12 to 24 are low, 25 to 36 medium, 37 to 48 high medium, and 49 to 60 high. This scale is for educational purposes only; don't take your scores too seriously.

Reprinted with permission of scale author, Dr. C. George Boeree, Shippensburg University (http://www.ship.edu/~cgboeree).

Evaluation

Contributions

Many of Fromm's important contributions revolve around his groundbreaking social character research in an actual society and his influential books.

Social Character in Mexican Villagers: Implications for Diversity.   Fromm and Maccoby (1970) undertook a field study of social character in a Mexican village. The goal was to show that the social character common to a group could be assessed and related to socioeconomic variables. An open-ended questionnaire of about 90 items was given to 406 adult residents of a Mexican farming village. Social character among the villagers was found to be high in receptive orientation and low in exploitative orientation. Men were more receptive than women, who were more hoarding. Sociopolitically, villagers were most often submissive rather than democratic or rebellious. Fixations involving parents were almost entirely directed toward the mother. More than three-quarters of adult-male villagers who were alcoholic were receptive in character, compared with about a third of abstainers. There was also evidence for productive types.

   The hoarding orientation was most appropriate to the economic demands of peasant farming. By contrast, the receptive peasant was poorly adapted. It follows that women (hoarding) were better adapted than men (receptive). Overall, support was provided for the general hypothesis that "social character is the result of the adaptation of human nature to given socioeconomic conditions" (p. 230). But, unexpectedly, there was great diversity *within* the culture.

Interesting Books on Popular Issues.   Countless people have been influenced by Fromm's best-selling books. *Escape from Freedom* (1941) introduced the novel idea that all people at some times, and some people all the time, may desire to relinquish their freedom to "the state" or to another person. *The Sane Society* (1955) considers the insanity of many societies and offers some alternatives. *The Art of Loving* (1956) teaches people that to be in love is not merely to desire another person. It is becoming one with another but remaining oneself. *The Anatomy of Human Destructiveness* (1973) is a cogent and provocative commentary on the forces promoting life and death in contemporary culture. His 1976 book, *To Have or to Be?,* discusses humankind's critical need to control irrational social forces and proposes guidelines for a new society.

Limitations

Fromm may be regarded as more a philosopher than a scientist. His theory consists of rather isolated categories of concepts that are not systematically related to one another. For example, those under the category labels "needs" and "character types." In fact, there appears to be no conceptual glue capable of sticking these distinct categories of concepts together. They deal with different domains, in the one case the psychological realm, in the other, the social arena. At best, Fromm writes about "needs" in the context of "social character," but makes no direct conceptual link between categories.

To confirm that a person has a trait, a component of personality, one must be able to look at the person's behavior in a given situation and assume that it will generalize to many other different situations. Only then, it is widely assumed, can one say the person has a trait corresponding to the behavior. Unfortunately, personality psychologists have had major difficulties demonstrating that such a generalization is warranted (e.g., Allen, 1988a, 1988b; Allen & Potkay, 1981, 1983a; Mischel, 1968, 1977, 1984). People show a tendency to vary in their behavioral performances from one situation to the next and from one occasion to the next. If making the critical generalization at the individual level involves considerable risk, how much more cautious must we be in generalizing a social character type to many if not most members of a society? Given that people vary within themselves from occasion to occasion, as total persons they certainly must differ one from the other to a large degree. In view of the great variability within and among individuals, it is tenuous to assume that many, much less most, members of a society are "marketing types," or "receptive types," or any other type. Due to a lack of evidence it is unreasonable to believe that even a simple majority of any large society's population shares the same type. Perhaps the social character types should be recast as personality types.

As indicated in Chapter 1, collapsing across concepts is an act of theoretical parsimony. Fromm's theory could certainly benefit from conceptual consolidation. In our discussions of Fromm's personality theory, students and I have noticed several redundancies among Fromm's concepts. For example, "relatedness," the necessity of uniting with other beings, "rootedness," maintaining one's natural ties, and "unity" with the natural world, have too much in common. Students wonder, couldn't a word like "connectedness" encompass all three concepts? Even collapsing two of the concepts would simplify Fromm's theory and allow the new concept to apply to more phenomena than would be true of either concept alone. As it is, unity and rootedness each refers to very little.

While Fromm was an open person, he still had Western biases. In his theorizing, he virtually condemned melting into the collective, thereby losing oneself. From the Western *individualistic* perspective, his point is well taken. However, from the standpoint of many *collectivistic* Asian cultures, "melting into the collective" has been a tried and true survival technique for millennia.

There has been a notable lack of scientific research done to support Fromm's theory. Either Fromm's concepts are difficult to transform into concrete terms so they can be studied scientifically, or they are too alien to modern scientific thinking to be of interest to contemporary sociopsychological scientists. Even Fromm's own research on the Mexican village failed to support the existence of a single, core character that fit most villagers. A diversity of character orientations was supported instead. Only when and if Fromm's theory generates scientific data can it be legitimately called "scientific."

As a contributor to the International Fromm Page (www.erichfromm.de/english/index.html), Daniel Burston (2001) lamented modern psychology's and psychiatry's failure to understand and appreciate Fromm (www.erichfromm.de/lib_2/burston01.html). Psychoanalytic writers condemned Fromm because they incorrectly saw him as an anti-Freudian. Psychologists, blinded by dogmatic behaviorism and the need to be seen as scientists, rejected his qualitative rather than quantitative approach. Others thought his political (Marxist/socialist) inclination to be odd, especially when he applied it to psychology. Those of a more sociological bent felt that Fromm tried to "psychologize culture and society" (Weiner, 2003, p. 62). Further, his foray into "objective ethics" was alien to all those who saw ethics as a subjective, nonscientific pursuit. Burston implies that all of these slings and arrows have ensured that Fromm will have fewer followers among psychologists and psychiatrists in the future. Fromm was not listed among the top 100 psychologists of the twentieth century.

Conclusions

Maybe Fromm was more of a philosopher than a scientific theorist. Then so be it; science is not the only legitimate approach to personality. Whatever label applies, he was an original thinker and one of our most helpful commentators on modern life. Further, he was one of the first psychologists to promote optimism (Weiner, 2003). Perhaps his concepts have received relatively little attention because they are complex and, thus, difficult to study.

While his Mexican village study may not have supported his point of view very strongly, it does have important implications for diversity: even in a small village, people differ along several diversity dimensions. Another indirect contribution relating to diversity is found in the concept of basic human nature that rides roughshod over notions of racial differences (Biancoli, 1992). Diversity has many legitimate dimensions, but, as will be argued forcefully later, racial variation is not among them.

He was also a pioneer. As an early psychological humanist he did much to shape current humanistic thought, the topic of the next two chapters. His conceptions of love, optimism, and productivity, as well as union with other people and nature, were nutrients added to the fertile soil out of which psychological humanism grew. Unfortunately, the humanistic theorists whose ideas you will consider next have made little effort to remind us of Fromm's contributions. Therefore, in beginning to read the chapters on humanism, you will need to actively recall his groundbreaking ideas.

Summary Points

1. Fromm praised Freud, but took a sociopsychological stance. Fromm was born into a "neurotic" German family of Jewish descent. The suicide of a young woman following the death of her father led Fromm to Freud. He was also greatly influenced by Marxism and by existential philosophy. The massive destruction and governmental doubletalk associated with World War I shaped his humanistic and antiwar orientations.

2. Each of us has a "frame of orientation," a cognitive map of our worlds that helps us make sense of puzzling matters. We all also have "objects of devotion": goals that give meaning to our existence. Relatedness is the need to unite with other living beings that can take on two symbiotic forms: masochistic or sadistic. The positive alternative is mature love in which there is union with another, but maintenance of one's integrity.

3. In rootedness, the alternatives are destructive pursuit of substitutes for a secure, dependent state or finding new roots in the brotherhood of man. Identity is the need to be aware of oneself as a separate entity. Tragically, we tend to use nations, races, or religions as sole sources of identity. Unity is a sense of inner oneness. We can seek it through the quest for power, fame, and property. Having failed to achieve unity, we may turn to some drug or passion. The productive alternative is love and reason.

4. Transcendence is the act of transforming one's passive role of creature into that of an active creator. The alternative to creativity is destruction. Effectiveness is the need to compensate for "being in a strange and overpowering world." To be effective is to accomplish and to resist parental domination. If not effective through love, we can be effective by causing others to suffer.

5. Excitation and stimulation is the nervous system's need to be "exercised." The brain must be stimulated even during sleep. Needed sensory input is of two kinds: simple and activating. People differ among themselves, the essence of "personality." However, character was emphasized by Fromm. Individual character is a personal pattern of behavior that is deeply rooted in habits and opinions.

6. Fromm postulated six social character types. Each is cast in terms of assimilation and socialization. The nonproductive types are divided into two pairs and one isolated type. One of two symbiotic nonproductive types is receptive, oriented to experience the source of all good as being outside oneself. People of this type take from and depend on others. They show unusual loyalty to their providers and may display sacrifice, duty, and love to the powerful people who care for them.

7. The exploitive type grabs, steals, and manipulates and is cynical, suspicious, and jealous. Hitler was nothing if not exploitative. One of two "withdrawal" types, hoarding people, build a fortress, take inside what is theirs, and allow others to enter only if they will become possessions. A second withdrawal type is marketing, oriented to an exchange of goods for objects of value or services. This type submits to supply and demand economies in which they are immersed and cultivate personality traits that "sell."

8. The necrophilous type is engrossed by death. The necrophilous person extracts a feeling of power and elation from vicariously or directly participating in the transformation of life into death. Necrophilous themes show up in dreams in the form of paying homage to the dead, envisioning oneself in possession of the awesome power, and seeing people as robots whose aliveness can be turned off or on. Murderous video games are necrophilous. Societies ruled by the despots of World War II and present nations ruled by war lovers provide fertile ground for this type.

9. Productive people have an attitude of relatedness to the world, and themselves, that encompasses reasoning, loving, and working. Productive people are biophilic, lovers of life. They break down walls between people and relate to others in terms of care, responsibility, respect, and knowledge. The productive type inspired Fromm's ideas about well-being. Fromm's research in a Mexican village produced evidence of three character types. It is an example of diversity, even in a small village.

10. Fromm's books dealt with sweeping issues that were of interest to many people. However, his theory is more philosophical than scientific and lacks coherence. Fromm's social character types entail difficulties and his theory has received little scientific support. Also, he showed Western World biases. His political views, criticisms of Freud, qualitative approach, and beliefs in objective ethics alienated psychiatrists and psychologists. But he was a warm person, an original thinker, and a pioneer humanist.

Running Comparison

Theorist	Fromm in Comparison
Freud	He questioned Freud's scientific contributions, de-emphasized biological causation, but agreed that religion is an illusion.
Jung	He also was influenced by WWI, and willing to talk about value, ethics, and meaning. Identifying self with social roles was akin to Jung's Personas.
Erikson	His productive love is similar to Erikson's care of the adulthood stage. His mature love is similar to resolution at Erikson's young adult stage.
Carl Rogers	Transcendence was akin to some of Rogers's humanistic ideas (and Maslow's). He also was concerned about creativity.
Abraham Maslow and Henry A. Murray	Like these two theorists, he was concerned about needs.
Horney	They both embraced the pursuit of the real self. They both recognized the exploitative potential of humans.

Essay/Critical Thinking Questions _____

1. Was Fromm more of a sociologist than a psychologist?

2. Illustrate how one of Fromm's needs has been manifested in your own experience?

3. Can you describe a symbiotic relationship from your experience?

4. Look at your own community. What social character(s) fits it best?

5. Can you defend the application of a social character type to an entire society?

E-mail Interaction _____

Write the author at b-allen@wiu.edu. Forward one of the following or phrase your own.

1. Explain why Fromm was so popular among the public.

2. Are many societies of today slipping in a more exploitative, necrophilous direction?

3. Was Fromm really a humanist?

Every Person Is to Be Prized: Carl Rogers

Carl Rogers
www.infed.org/thinkers/
et-rogers.htm

- What happens when your experience conflicts with your Self?
- Can psychologists make world peace more likely?
- Imagine a therapist who refuses to offer patients any advice.
- Should therapists be equal partners with patients?

Psychologists often classify personality theories into categories: the psychoanalytic tradition begun by Freud, the humanistic tradition represented by Carl Rogers and Abraham Maslow, the behavioral tradition popularized by B. F. Skinner, the cognitive tradition represented by George Kelly, and the trait tradition championed by Raymond Cattell, Hans Eysenck, and Gordon Allport. Rogers is one of the leading figures in modern psychology because of the impact his humanistic principles have had on so many psychologists, professionals from other disciplines, and laypeople. His ideas have also received more systematic research, study, and validation than those of any other humanistic psychologist, and also more than some other theorists covered in this book.

Rogers, the Person

Carl Ransom Rogers was born on January 8, 1902, in Oak Park, Illinois. The fourth of six children, he was "tender and easily hurt, yet feisty and even sarcastic in his own way," necessary characteristics for survival in family give-and-take (Kirschenbaum, 1979, p. 5). His home atmosphere was marked by fundamentalist religious practices, little social mixing, and a firm belief in the virtue of hard work. Carl even recalled experiencing a slight feeling of "wickedness" while drinking his first bottle of soda pop.

Carl was a lonely, "solitary boy, who read incessantly, and went all through high school with only two dates" (Rogers, 1961, p. 6). An outstanding student, he was nicknamed

"Mr. Absent-Minded Professor" by his practical family. Like Fromm, he loved reading the Bible. He also relished popular adventure stories and creating stories of his own. During adolescence, he became fascinated with night-flying moths, which he observed and bred year-round, and he enjoyed reading advanced, scientific books on agriculture.

> There was no one to tell me that Morison's *Feeds and Feeding* was not a book for a fourteen-year-old, so I ploughed through its hundreds of pages learning how experiments were conducted—how control groups were matched with experimental groups, how conditions were held constant by randomizing procedures, so that the influence of a given food on meat production or milk production could be established. I learned how difficult it is to test a hypothesis. I acquired a knowledge of and a respect for the methods of science.... (Rogers, 1961, p. 6)

As you will see, Rogers fruitfully applied his knowledge of scientific procedure during his career. However, he used it more to show that his therapy was effective, to acknowledge the biological side of humans, and to render his concepts testable, than as a comprehensive approach to understanding people.

As an undergraduate at the University of Wisconsin, Rogers majored in agriculture and history. Later he dropped these initial majors, became quite religious, and began a curriculum aimed at the ministry. He was one of 12 U.S. students selected to travel to China for a World Student Christian Federation Conference. It proved "a most important experience" in broadening his thinking and teaching him that sincere and honest people could have very different beliefs. Much later in life he was to lose his religious zeal because of his objection to "original sin" (Thorne, 1990). He just was not able to accept that humans are inherently flawed by the mark of sin. Still later he reconsidered the Christianity preached by those who see humans as partakers of a divine nature. The trip to China was an intellectually liberating experience, but, because it was, he found himself withdrawing from family traditions. His newfound independence of thought caused his parents "great pain and stress," but "looking back on it I believe that here, more than at any other one time, I became an independent person" (Rogers, 1961, p. 7).

Rogers studied religion at the very liberal Union Theological Seminary. By chance, Teachers College, Columbia University was right across the street. Perhaps because his disaffection with religion was beginning to emerge, he enrolled at Columbia and soon drifted into child psychology, "just following the activities which interested me" (Rogers, 1961, p. 9). After receiving his Ph.D. in 1928, he worked for several years at a child-guidance center in Rochester, N.Y. During this time Rogers absorbed the views of Freud. It was at this juncture that he was influenced by Adler: "I had the privilege of meeting, listening to, and observing Dr. Alfred Adler . . . I was shocked by Dr. Adler's very direct and deceptively simple manner of relating to the child and the parent. It took me some time to realize how much I learned from him" (Rogers, quoted in Ansbacher, 1990, p. 47). Adler's example helped Rogers to reconsider the mindless testing and record keeping, as well as the dwelling on childhood traumas, that characterized the Freudian orientation at the Rochester center.

The figure having perhaps the most impact on Rogers was disaffected former Freudian, Otto Rank, who believed that the trauma of birth is the first of many "separations" people must abide during their lives (deCarvalho, 1999). Rogers invited Rank to

Rochester, where the former soaked up the views of the latter during a three-day institute. The following elements of Rank's theory had great impact on Rogers: (1) "The patient's self-acceptance and affirmation learned in the protective environment of psychotherapy" transfers to the outside world (p. 134); (2) the pre-Oedipal mother–child relationship is the prototype of the therapist–patient relationship; (3) the role of the therapist is to create positive experiences that allow patients to discover their inner personality dynamics without fear and anxiety; (4) patients should freely verbalize their thoughts and emotions with the therapist who acts only to facilitate their self-discovery; (5) the emphasis is on the patient's immediate emotional experience. As you will see, Rogers adopted all of these ideas in some form.

Rogers came to the realization that Freud's ideas were in great conflict with the rigorous, scientific aspects of his academic training. Relying on his own clinical experiences with people, he began formulating a person-centered point of view: the person seeking guidance should choose the direction of personality change. Unlike Freudians, he would not adopt the role of authoritarian doctor vis-à-vis a passive, subservient patient, because "it is the [person] who knows what hurts, what directions to go, what problems are crucial, what experiences have been deeply buried" (Rogers, 1961, pp. 11–12). This trusting of the person was shown by Jung and Rank when they shared the tasks of therapy with therapy patients. Thus, Rogers, like Rank, rejected the **medical model,** the idea that people with psychological problems are sick and need some sort of treatment, at least analogous to medication, that will make them normal again (deCarvalho, 1999; Rogers, 1987a). Consistent with this orientation, he used the term *client* instead of *patient.* He did not want to bring clients back to normal, that is, back to average. Instead he endorsed the **growth model,** helping people "remove whatever blocks to growth exist" so they could move beyond being normal or average (p. 40).

In subsequent years, Rogers held teaching, therapy, and administrative positions at Ohio State University, the University of Chicago, and the University of Wisconsin. In 1947, he served as president of the American Psychological Association. He was the first psychologist in the Association's history to receive both the Scientific Contribution Award and the Distinguished Professional Contribution Award. In the years before he died, Rogers continued to work very actively in La Jolla, California, at the Center for Studies of the Person, which he cofounded: "The days are not long enough to accomplish my purposes" (communication to Charles R. Potkay, May 9, 1985). Rosalind Cartwright, one of his former colleagues, has spoken of him as a living example of his own theory, "a man who has continued to grow, to discover himself, to test himself, to be genuine, to review his experiences, to learn from it, . . . to live honestly, fully, in the best human sense" (Kirschenbaum, 1979, p. 394).

Carl Rogers died unexpectedly on February 4, 1987, following surgery for a broken hip (Gendlin, 1988). At the time he had been particularly energetic and effective. In his last years he traveled the world, from South Africa to the Soviet Union, with a stop in Northern Ireland, in order to promote world peace and an end to conflict between warring groups (see Rogers, 1987b; Rogers & Malcolm, 1987; Rogers & Ryback, 1984; Rogers & Sanford, 1987). Fortunately, he published a number of articles during these final years, many of which are used in this chapter to help you better understand this extraordinary individual and his contributions to people everywhere. Box 9.1 examines the "real Carl Rogers."

BOX 9.1 • *The Real Rogers: Not So Emotionally Neutral, Not So "Equal," Not Really a Counselor, but a Pioneer Clinical Contributor to Understanding Diversity Issues*

Being a world-famous person, a figure larger than life, Rogers came to be regarded in stereotypic fashion. Textbook writers and some teachers have come to view him as someone (1) who never became angry, much less directed verbal aggression to someone during therapy; (2) who believed in absolute equality of therapist and client; (3) who never showed strong emotion during therapy; (4) who believed that empathy was a passive process in which the therapist merely listens to clients and simply becomes a mirror in which they could see their own emotions; and (5) who regarded himself as a counselor and was heavily identified with that area. None of these were literally true.

While conducting conflict resolution groups composed of Black and White South Africans, Rogers became enraged when a White psychologist claimed that one of the young Black revolutionaries was just trying to "get attention" (Hill-Hain & Rogers, 1988). "That was just grossly untrue . . . one white guy got up and was going to hit him and I exploded at him too" (p. 62). In the same interview Rogers said, "I draw the line when I feel that one person is hurting another person in the group" (p. 65). He also referred to this event when making the point that no one is always able to step into another person's emotional shoes, not even himself. "That's why I offered no apology for exploding at [the White psychologist]" (p. 65).

During one of his South African group sessions, Rogers was strongly affected when a key Black participant left the group (Hill-Hain & Rogers, 1988). As he sat on the floor in the middle of the group, absorbing the agony of South African Blacks, he began to cry. It was not because others were in tears. It was because he felt like "one of the group in every sense" (p. 68). This kind of reaction was rare for him: "I've been in enough groups that it takes quite a lot to really touch me personally" (p. 68).

Rogers agreed with a critic's condemnation of person-centered therapists who show absolute commitment to acting as nothing more than a sounding board, misunderstandings of empathy, and thoughtless commitment to equality between the therapist and client. "I totally agree with her . . . in deploring the inauthentic, mechanical, wooden, dogmatic, client-centered therapist. In fact, I probably feel worse about such therapists than they do, because I feel personally offended" (Rogers, 1987c). In a similar vein, Rogers wrote of empathy: "It is regarded superficially; it is regarded as passive when you just sit back and listen. To be really empathic is one of the most active experiences I know. You have to really understand what it feels like to this person in this situation. . . . To really let oneself go into the inner world of this other person is one of the most active, difficult, and demanding things that I know" (Rogers, 1987a, p. 45).

To address the issue of client–therapist equality, Rogers considered the questions he would pose for himself before each therapy session: " 'Can I be totally present to this client? Can I be with him or her?' . . . It would never occur to me to ask myself, 'Can I make this relationship an equal one?' " (p. 38). In fact, relationships in Rogerian therapy sometimes are not equal; they are tilted in the direction of the client. If Rogers and a Black person were in therapy, as was sometimes the case when he was at the University of Chicago, he would give himself over to being a student undergoing instruction in the African American experience. Only when a black client communicated that Rogers was adequately schooled would he attempt to feel as one with him or her. This procedure would be profitably adopted by all therapists who have clients of a different ethnicity than their own. Another of Rogers's diversity contributions is seen in evidence, collected over 46 years as a psychologist, that his theory was having influence on those who deal with interracial and intercultural relationships.

Rogers is often identified with counseling, a multidisciplinary pursuit sometimes practiced by professionals from nonpsychological disciplines. Even the longtime colleague who wrote

Rogers's obituary regarded Rogers as a founder of counseling as a discipline, and considered him highly identified with counseling (Gendlin, 1988). In response to Gendlin's "fine memorial," Donald E. Super (1989), who had known Rogers since 1935, pointed to the fact that Rogers's therapy section was called the Chicago Counseling Center and that his 1942 book was entitled *Counseling and Psychotherapy*. Then he wrote, "But Carl remained a psychotherapist, out of the mainstream of counseling psychology, a member of the Clinical but not of the Counseling Division [of the American Psychological Association]" (Super, 1989, p. 1161).

In view of these facts, why include "counseling" in the book title? Ray Bixler (1990) indicated that he and other students in Rogers's graduate seminar were consulted by their professor concerning an appropriate book title. Professor and students decided on *counseling* because it would recruit counselors to client centered therapy and on *psychotherapy* because the term was at the heart of their professional identities. Thus, it seems, Rogers was primarily identified as a psychotherapist, but he was open to sharing his methods with others.

Rogers's View of the Person

Rogers's point of view revolves around a subdiscipline of psychology he helped to found. **Humanistic psychology** emphasizes the present experience and essential worth of the whole person, promotes creativity, intentionalism, free choice, and spontaneity, and fosters the belief that people can solve their own psychological problems. It gained momentum during the 1950s and early 1960s with the publication of several important books (Buhler, 1962, 1965; Maslow, 1954, 1959, 1962; Rogers, 1961, 1970) and a flagship journal, the *Journal of Humanistic Psychology,* founded in 1961. Proponents of humanistic psychology proclaimed their movement a "major breakthrough," because of the primary importance it placed on understanding the entire person, "the functioning and experience of a whole human being" (Bugental, 1964, p. 25). This emphasis also characterizes points of view in which every person is understood in a comprehensive and integrative manner as being more than the simple sum of his or her parts (Kohler, 1947).

Humanistic psychology emerged from two other philosophical orientations, one of which was introduced in the last chapter. Rollo May has been the leading psychological practitioner of *existentialism* and existential psychotherapy. The term *existence* comes from the root word *ex-sistere,* which means "to stand out, to emerge" (May, 1983). To May, existentialism is an attempt to "portray the human being not as a collection of static substances or mechanisms or patterns but rather as emerging and becoming, that is to say, as existing" (p. 50). *Being* is "defined as the *individual's unique pattern of potentialities*" (May, 1969a, p. 19). He also notes that, for some existentialists, to be is *to do,* to behave in a way that has impact on self and others. In addition, he adopts Sartre's belief that we are our choices and Ephren Ramirez's assertion that the extent to which we accept responsibility for our lives determines the extent to which we become free moral agents.

May agreed with Viktor Frankl's contention that, more and more, people show up for therapy not because of the usual "neurotic" symptoms, but because they are bored and fed up with the lack of meaning in their lives. In Sullivanian fashion, May sees psychotherapy as *"two-persons-existing-in-a-world, the world at the moment being represented by the consulting room of the therapist"* (May, 1969b). To May, psychotherapy addresses six basic existential issues. First, the existing person is centered in her or his self. An attack on that center is an attack on the person's existence. What we call "neurosis" is the process by which a person attempts to preserve his or her center. Simply removing the neurosis, therefore, is not an existentially valid strategy. Instead one must address the vulnerability of the individual's center, his or her existence. Thus, neurosis is only a sign of the real problem, not itself the real problem.

The second process involves self-affirmation, which has another name, *courage,* as in Paul Tillich's (1952) "courage to be." Self-affirmation requires the will to decide, to choose. Psychotherapy must create an atmosphere in which people feel free to exercise the power to make their own choices. The third process highlights the need for all existing people to go "out from their centeredness to participate in other beings" (May, 1969b, p. 74). But venturing forth from one's centeredness poses a dilemma that must be addressed in therapy: to be, one must participate with other beings, including human beings, but to do so generates the danger that one will overidentify with others and, thereby, vacate one's own being. Fromm is present in these notions.

The fourth process is based on the principle that *"the subjective side of centeredness is awareness"* (May, 1969b, p. 77). *Awareness* in May's sense is a reflection of our biological side, which we share with other animals. We, like the seal that punctuates its sleep at ten-second intervals to look for predators, must pay attention to threats to our existence. *Vigilance* is the name for this animal-level of awareness that dictates one must attend to threats. The need to exercise it must be considered in therapy. The fifth process revolves around the uniquely human form of awareness, self-consciousness. In contrast to self-awareness, *self-consciousness* is the human capacity to know him- or herself as the person being threatened, which is to know that one is not exclusively acted on, but has a world he or she can influence. Self-consciousness changes everything. Though we share a sexual side with other animals, it becomes something different for us. It is shaped by the person who is our partner. Psychotherapy must proceed so as to acknowledge that self-consciousness raises humans above the flesh that knows only the threat of nonexistence. It carries us to a level above biology where we can see ourselves in relation to other beings and envisage our capacity to affect other beings, as well as to be affected by them.

The sixth process involves anxiety, "the state of the human being in the struggle against that which would destroy his being" (May, 1969b, p. 81). Anxiety reflects the eternal struggle of *being* in conflict with *nonbeing* and is aptly captured by Freud's Thanatos (death instinct) in its struggle with Eros, the life instinct. During psychotherapy, May would never waterdown the persons' internal experience of the struggle between being and nonbeing. Rather, he would facilitate acceptance of responsibility for making choices that may fortify the person's being, but can, if choices are poor, expose the person's being to threats. To avoid choices allows one's being to slowly erode; to make choices may preserve one's being or make it more vulnerable. It is deciding whether to hide in the darkness in the hope it will take some time for the monster to find and devour us, or deciding to run for it, whereby we elude the monster or place ourselves directly in its path.

In remarks on May's ideas, Rogers (1969a) applauded existentialism's insistence on confronting modern psychology with the "fact" that we must look inside people, not just outside, if we are to understand them. He contended that U.S. psychology is "shocked" by existentialists, who speak as if people are free and responsible and have choice at the core of their existence. He also acknowledged that, consistent with existentialistic assumptions, as a developing clinician he learned to create a therapeutic atmosphere in which clients feel comfortable in making their own decisions about the course of therapy.

Far from being "unscientific," existentialistic psychotherapy elicited a number of interesting, testable hypotheses from Rogers. Regarding May's first process, Rogers deduced the hypothesis that "The more the self of the person is threatened, the more he will exhibit defensive neurotic behavior" (p. 89). One's self is the soft underbelly of one's being. It is, at the same time, the center of the person's being and the most vulnerable part of his or her psychological anatomy. To protect it, one will resort to whatever works, even anxiety-focused methods that inflict great pain on one's own psyche. From May's second process Rogers deduced the hypothesis, "The more the self is free from threat, the more the individual will exhibit self-affirming behaviors" (p. 89). The less the threat, the less vulnerable is the self, and the more it can venture forth and flex its creative muscles in the interest of being "who one is." The third process suggested the hypothesis that the more people are free from threats to their selves, the more they can actualize the potential for participation with other beings. May's sixth process suggested the hypothesis that anxiety will recede only when one loses the fear of being the person one could be. When one accepts who one can become, she or he loses the fear of being that person. According to Rogers, all of these hypotheses are readily testable and, if confirmed, would scientifically support existentialism's underpinnings of humanism.

The second orientation contributing to humanistic psychology is a method of addressing reality that is a strong companion to existentialism. **Phenomenology** encompasses a search for essential issues, an emphasis on consciousness, the necessity of describing experience, and a desire to grasp reality as each individual uniquely perceives it. This subjective approach to knowledge and understanding is a major characteristic of humanistic and existential psychology (Heidegger, 1949; Husserl, 1961). "The only reality I can possibly know is the world as I perceive and experience it at this moment. The only reality you can possibly know is the world as YOU perceive and experience it at this moment. And the only certainty is that those perceived realities are different. There are as many 'real worlds' as there are people!" (Rogers, 1980, p. 102). May (1969a) adds that the phenomenological approach requires "the disciplined effort to clear one's mind of the presuppositions" (p. 21) that cause one to see the client only in the light of one's own theories and dogmas. Phenomenology calls for an "attitude of openness and readiness to hear" (p. 21). An experience is real for the experiencer at the time it is experienced, as seen in the qualifiers used by Rogers in his writings, such as "real for me" and "based on my experience." This is not to say that there is no objective world we can all agree on. Rather it affirms the subjective world and gives it at least equal status with the objective world.

On the one hand, it is up to each person to decide what he or she is to do or to be, based on an individualized vantage point. On the other hand, a person should leave how other persons behave and how they lead their lives up to them. Thus, people must assume responsibility for their own decisions and for no one else's. Even in the last year of his life, Rogers refused the role of expert therapist who answers clients' questions such as "What do you think I should do?" (Hill-Hain & Rogers, 1988).

Apart from questions of scientific truth, the phenomenological approach has particular implications for studying people. If we wish to understand a person, we need to get inside his or her individual world of meaning. We do so by showing **empathy,** sensing and participating in the emotions of others. Thus, humanistic psychologists focus on the meaning that each person attaches to what she or he does. As theorists and therapists, therefore, humanistic psychologists seek to avoid "the sort of scientific detachment pretended to or achieved at great cost by other orientations" such as behaviorism or neuroscience (Bugental, 1964, p. 24). Instead, they validate their discoveries through subjective experience rather than impersonal tests or experiments. This approach led to new methods for studying human experience. Like Gordon Allport, humanistic psychologists typically emphasize the *idiographic* approach: the belief that meaningful and generally applicable discoveries come from understanding one person at a time. As Rogers writes, "What is most personal is most general" (1961, p. 26).

Empathy is not just a humanistic abstraction. Growing evidence from neuroscience indicates that blood-flow increases in crucial imitation and emotional areas of the brain are coordinated with imitating or observing facial expressions associated with several emotions (e.g., happiness, anger, and fear; Bower, 2003). Imitation yielded stronger effects than observation. Even non-conscious impersonations of others' emotions simulate how others feel.

Rogers adopted an **organismic approach** in which the human organism is viewed as a total being whose physical, psychological, and spiritual aspects cannot be separated except by artificial means. In brief, it is the person who is placed first. This is why Rogers's theory of therapy is now usually called the *person-centered* approach (formerly it was *client-centered,* a phrase still used by some therapists and Rogers, even in his last articles; Rogers, 1987c; Super, 1989). The central hypothesis of the person-centered orientation is that "Individuals have within themselves vast resources for self-understanding and for altering their self-concepts, basic attitudes, and self-directed behavior" (Rogers, 1980, p. 115). Further, these resources can be tapped by providing "a definable climate of facilitative psychological attitudes" (p. 115).

Rogers differed from Freud when he assumed that the natural development of human beings is toward the "constructive fulfillment" of their inherent potentialities. Rogers aptly put it this way (quoted in Kirschenbaum, 1979, p. 250)

> I am inclined to believe that fully to be a human being is to enter into the complex process of being one of the most widely sensitive, responsive, creative, and adaptive creatures on this planet. So when a Freudian such as Karl Menninger tells me . . . that he perceives man as "innately evil" or more precisely, "innately destructive," I can only shake my head in wonderment.

In an application of the organismic approach, Rogers rejected the conception of learning he attributed to most universities. "A . . . unique element is that [my theory] is based on a learning that is experiential as well as cognitive. That is something that seems very hard for universities to accept. Most of the universities I know think that education goes on [only] from the neck up . . . That is not so! Education may be limited to that, but learning is something else" (Rogers, 1987a, p. 39). It is also an endorsement of pedagogical procedures that entail active student participation in college classroom activities. Such methods are gaining popularity among professors so rapidly they threaten to supplant the traditional 50 to 75 minutes of straight lecture (DeCarvalho, 1991). As a teacher, Rogers "distributed an optional reading list, gave a few assignments (e.g., come to class, keep a journal, write a final paper on a subject of your choice) and indicated a willingness to lecture occasionally or do a demonstration if the students requested it" (Kirschenbaum, 1991, p. 412).

Rogers recognized that his ideas had been heavily influenced by his relationships with clients in therapy. However, like Sullivan, he believed that psychotherapy relationships are only a special instance of interpersonal relationships in general, and "the same lawfulness" governs all human relationships (Rogers, 1961, p. 39). He has supported this belief in a number of popular books on such topics as freedom to learn in education (1969b), encounter groups (1970), becoming marriage partners (1972), and the revolutionary impact of personal power (1977).

Basic Concepts: Rogers

Actualization: General and Specific

The General Actualizing Tendency.   All living things display the **general actualizing tendency,** an "inherent tendency of the organism to develop all its capacities in ways which serve to maintain or enhance the organism" (Rogers, 1959, p. 196). This constructive biological tendency is the "one central source of energy in the human organism," giving rise to all other motivation (Rogers, 1980, p. 123). The actualizing tendency has four significant characteristics that express themselves through a wide range of behaviors:

1. It is *organismic*—an inborn, biological predisposition reflected in the total functioning of all living beings.
2. It is an *active* process that accounts for organisms always doing something: exploring, changing the environment, playing, creating and seeking food or sex.
3. It is *directional* rather than random; it inclines every form of life toward growth, self-regulation, fulfillment, reproduction, and independence from external control.
4. It is *selective,* meaning that not all of an organism's potentialities are necessarily developed (for example, the ability to bear pain).

Rogers illustrated the actualizing tendency by reference to the winter potatoes his family stored in their basement:

> The conditions were unfavorable, but the potatoes would begin to sprout—pale white sprouts . . . these sad, spindly sprouts would grow . . . toward the distant light of the [basement] window. They were in . . . futile growth, a sort of desperate expression of the directional tendency . . . They would . . . never mature, never fulfill their real potentiality. But under the most adverse circumstances they were striving to become. Life would not give up, even if it could not flourish (Rogers, 1979/1983, p. 228).

The organismic propensity for actualization is true of beings from potatoes, through protozoa, to rabbits, all the way to humans. If passing on one's genes is added, the organismic approach is consistent with evolutionary theory.

Self-actualization.   In addition to the general actualizing tendency, Rogers postulated a specifically human tendency, **self-actualization,** a person's lifelong process of realizing his or her potentialities to become a fully functioning person. The goal of self-actualization is "to be that self which one truly is" (Rogers, 1961, p. 166). The direction of self-actualization is toward "the good life," defined as whatever is organismically valued by the total person who is inwardly free to move in any direction.

Rogers (1961) associated the process of self-actualization with enhanced functioning in three areas. First, self-actualization involves an increased openness to **experience,** which is all the emotions, cognitions, and perceptions occurring to the organism at any given moment that potentially can be consciously considered. *Awareness* is the conscious apprehension of experience. Second, the self-actualizing person lives existentially, going with the flow of each moment in life and participating fully in it. She or he is *time competent,* experiencing life in the "here and now," without rigid preconceptions that things must be the way they have been in the past and without needing to control how things should be in the future. Third, the self-actualizing person places full trust in his or her organismic intuitions, doing what feels right after weighing all available information. She or he relies relatively little on the past or on social conventions. The self-actualizing person also is genuinely appreciative of free choice, creativity, human nature's trustworthiness, and life's richness.

The Importance of the Self

Obviously, self-actualization implies a central role for the "self" and is dear to the humanists. His interest in the self was partly inspired by clients' expressions made during therapy: "I wonder who *I am*"; "I don't want anyone to know the *real me*"; "It feels good to let myself go and just *be me.*" For Rogers (1947), the person's experience of self is a basic aspect of life. It forms and determines behavior, cognition, and feeling.

Self as Self-perceptions.   Although Rogers has never formally defined *personality,* he did define **self,** the organized, consistent, conceptual whole composed of perceptions of the characteristics of the "I" or "me," the values attached to these perceptions, and the relationships of the "I" or "me" to various aspects of life (Rogers, 1959, p. 200). The definition reflects Rogers's phenomenological approach. Its emphasis is clearly on the perceptual origins of self: a person's self is a set of perceptions that have the perceiver as its target. Further, because it is one's perceptions of one's self, the self is functionally equivalent to self-concept. It includes all of people's evaluations of their organismic functions and human relationships, which they use "to order and interpret [their] experiences" (Shlien, 1970, p. 95). Also, self-perceptions relate to other people and to perceptions provided by the senses (Evans, 1975). To illustrate, a person may have the self-perception, "I am six feet tall." She may relate this perception to other people, as in "I am taller than many people," and place a value on it, as in "I like being tall."

For Rogers, the **ideal self** is the self a person most values and desires to be. It is "the self-concept which the individual would most like to possess, upon which he places the highest value for himself" (Rogers, 1959, p. 100). Therefore, successfully pursuing the ideal self is a major precondition for feelings of worth. Rogerians often have a person describe actual and ideal selves and then ask her or him to compare the two descriptions. That is the purpose of Box 9.2.

Congruence with Experience.   Our self-concepts may be more or less in agreement with experiences related to self. When a person is in a state of **congruence,** his or her self-concept and experiences relating to self are consistent. The actualizing tendency is then relatively whole and unified, and the person shows maturity as well as psychological adjustment. In contrast, **incongruence** reflects an inconsistency between self-concept and

---

BOX 9.2 • *Adjective Descriptions of Your Actual and Ideal Self*

Instructions: On the left side of a sheet of paper, write down adjectives that best describe the self you are at the present time in your life (actual self). On the right side, write down adjectives that best describe the self you would like to be (ideal self). Work quickly, and be sure to write down single words that are found in the dictionary, not sentences, paragraphs, or words that you invent. Attempt to write down between 10 and 15 self-descriptive adjectives under each heading, but not less than five under each. Do not worry if some of your words seem contradictory; just write whatever adjectives best describe your actual and ideal self.

Your Actual Self   *Your Ideal Self*

Student subjects in research conducted by Potkay and me typically wrote down about five to ten adjectives when allowed to record as many as they want (Allen & Potkay, 1983a; Potkay & Allen, 1988). How do your words compare with those of other students in class? How are your descriptions of your self *as you are* and your self *as you would like to be* the same or different? What do you make of words present on and absent from both lists? How would you transform yourself from present self into ideal self?

Consistent with the implication that you are now a certain self (actual self) and may become another self (ideal self), Rogers believes that the self is best understood as a continuing process, not a fixed endpoint. Thus, the self, yours or anyone else's, is very likely to be undergoing change. This is why a person may organize self-views in different ways at different points in time. Our self-view of today may be contrary to your self-view of the recent past.

Other people may not see you the same way you see yourself. A student at my university was quite surprised to learn of this discrepancy while doing a self-study as a term project. She had been asked to describe her trueself with adjectives and then obtain adjective descriptions of her trueself from her mother, father, boyfriend, and best girlfriend. The words she used to describe her own self—*insecure, stubborn, impatient*—were much more negative than those used by other people in her life—*intelligent, friendly, lovable*. Her explanation was that "I failed to update my . . . self to match my trueself of today" (Allen & Potkay, 1983a).

The closer the correspondence between actual and ideal self, the greater the self-acceptance and adjustment. But remember that perceiving discrepancies between ideal and real selves may be a good sign: you are appreciating the need for positive change.

experiences relating to self. Incongruence may arise out of beliefs that are rigid, distorted, unrealistic, or overgeneralized. It may also result from the defensive tactic **denial,** which involves the inability to recognize or accept the existence of an experience that has occurred. It is reflected in the reaction "No! It can't be!" to a rumor circulating among office workers that one has failed to receive a desperately sought-after promotion. **Distortion** involves a reinterpretation of an experience so as to make it consistent with how one wants things to be, as in the reaction "You are all wrong. Yesterday the boss was very friendly to me." You can see that Rogers, like Freud and Horney, believed that people have defenses against threatening experiences.

Self-perceptions out of tune with experiences can contribute to feelings of inner confusion, tension, and to maladaptive behavior. Rogers cites the example of a boy who had been observed lifting girls' skirts. When questioned, the boy denied what he had done, stating that it "couldn't" have been he, a disclaimer that confirmed that he was in a state of incongruence. His perceptions led him to maintain a self-concept inconsistent with his actual experience. Because his self-concept did not include sexual feelings, his organismic experiences of sexual curiosity and desire were in conflict with his self-concept. He closed off his awareness to behaviors, feelings, or attitudes inconsistent with his self-concept. The boy's denial reflected *defensiveness* aimed at maintaining the current structure of the self in the face of contradictory information (Rogers, 1959). It is a typical response when one's self-concept is threatened. "His self-picture couldn't do it, and didn't do it" (Evans, 1975, p. 17).

Movement toward growth and improved adjustment in this boy would require him to revise his self-concept toward congruence. The boy would show anxiety as he became aware of the incongruence between his self-concept and his experiences because "each of us seeks to preserve the . . . picture that he has of himself and . . . a sharp change in that picture is quite threatening" (Rogers, quoted in Evans, 1975, p. 17). If the boy were able to lower his defenses, the new information about himself could be incorporated into his self-concept. Then he could consider an appropriate expression of sexual curiosity. If defensiveness continues, *maladjustment* could occur: the boy would remain unaware of internal conflicts and his growth would stagnate.

Personality Development: Some Favorable Conditions

What determines whether a person's self-concept becomes congruent or incongruent with experience? Rogers points to external circumstances, particularly of an interpersonal nature, that cause personal growth to be facilitated or blocked. His boyhood observation of his family's potatoes highlights the importance of environmental conditions as influences on the actualizing tendency of living things. The potatoes failed to realize their fullest potentials because of unfavorable conditions outside themselves.

Similarly, the interactions between people and interpersonal environments represent an important aspect of human development. The actualization tendency points all people in the direction of becoming the persons they truly are, regardless of the social environment. However, certain interpersonal conditions facilitate actualization strivings, whereas others do not. Rogers's work with clients in therapy led him to identify some necessary and sufficient conditions for positive growth and change in personality (Orlov, 1992). The conditions are receiving unconditional positive regard, developing accurate empathy, achieving congruence in personal relations, and developing positive self-regard.

Unconditional Positive Regard.   All people have needs that can be fulfilled only in human relationships. Chief among these is a universally learned need for **positive regard,** the experiencing of oneself as making a positive difference in the lives of other people and as receiving warmth, liking, respect, sympathy, acceptance, caring, and trust from others (Rogers, 1959; Standal, 1954). This need is met when other people in a person's life provide **unconditional positive regard;** they communicate, with no strings attached, that one is accepted, valued, worthwhile, and trusted, simply for being who one is. The person experiences others' acceptance without feeling that it depends on his or her doing some "right" thing or having to be the way others think the person "should" be. When we release people from Horney's "tyranny of the shoulds," we help them along the road to self-actualization. Further, no aspect of the person is judged "more or less worthy of positive regard than any other" (Rogers, 1959, p. 208). There is no generalized labeling of the person as "bad" or "good," only unconditional acceptance.

However, a person can receive positive regard under unproductive circumstances: only when he or she meets conditions of worth set up by others. Here the individual feels prized in some respects, but not in others. She or he then avoids certain experiences judged by other people to be relatively "unworthy" and seeks out certain other experiences judged by them as relatively "worthy." This occurs even if the person has been attracted to the "unworthy" experiences and repelled by the "worthy" experiences. The unproductive way is "conditional" because it involves contingencies stated in if–then terms. Significant others say, in effect, "If you say or do the things I like or want, then I will value you. If you don't, then I won't." When conditional acceptance characterizes the social environment, a child learns to behave and think mainly in ways approved by others, especially parents. The child learns, "If I do what my parents want, then I will be loved. If I don't, I won't be loved." This lesson generates incongruence between one's experience and "who one is." Under these circumstances, one's actualizing tendency is likely to become blocked. Then denials and distortions of personal experiences that are disapproved by others are likely to occur. Also, acceptance of experiences that are incongruent with "who one is" becomes probable.

A common misconception about unconditional positive regard is that people who provide it to a person must always approve of everything the person says or does. Rogers counters this error by carefully distinguishing between the individual as a person and the individual's freely chosen values and behaviors. For example, while thoughtful and caring parents always prize their child, they do so without valuing all of the child's behaviors equally. They may express pride when their child shares a candy bar with a friend, or displeasure when their child bites a friend. However, the child's specific behaviors are approved or disapproved, not the child as a person. It is the sharing that is approved and the biting that is disapproved, not the child. Although the parents undoubtedly wish the child would not bite, biting does not lead to rejection. The child continues to be prized, regardless of his or her behavior.

Accurate Empathy.   If a person is to achieve congruence of self-concept with his or her experience, therapists and other people must correctly "hear" what the individual is experiencing and refrain from judging it. Rogers believed the ability to understand another person is of "enormous" value. He found it "enriching to open channels whereby others can communicate their feelings, their private perceptual worlds, to me" (1961, p. 19). **Accurate empathy** is Rogers's term for the ability to correctly perceive the client's internal world in a nonevaluative way. Such empathic understanding goes beneath the surface of another person's words and actions, to inner feelings, attitudes, meanings, values, and motives.

Congruence in Relations with a Therapist and Others.   In order for a person to grow, significant other people, including a therapist, must naturally and openly demonstrate their willingness and ability to be themselves in relationships with that person. This state of genuineness on the part of one person toward another can be regarded as a kind of congruence: the two people feel the same level of comfort or emotional involvement with the issue they are considering. The therapist must exhibit an openness to inner experiences in such a way that it conveys congruence with the client. Even an experienced therapist might admit to the client, "I find myself frightened because you are touching on feelings I have never been able to resolve myself" (Rogers, 1959). A therapist uncomfortable with some aspect of the relationship with the client would be considered incongruent if she or he remained unaware of the discomfort, avoided dealing with it, or communicated reactions opposite to what is real for him or her. The therapist's lack of genuineness may create so much incongruence between therapist, client, and experiences occurring in therapy that the client's growth may be retarded.

Developing Positive Self-regard.   When individuals receive unconditional positive regard from others, particularly during the formative years, they will develop **positive self-regard,** a favorable attitude toward themselves. This, in turn, allows them to develop their own values in accordance with their real experiences. Although they will be aware of expectations concerning what they "should" do, they will trust their own judgments instead of being bound by those of others. Positive self-regard unlocks actualizing tendencies and allows individuals to become fully functioning humans. By contrast, when others impose conditions of worth on an individual, her or his chances of developing positive self-regard become less. In this case, people's **locus of evaluation,** the source of evidence about themselves, lies not within them but outside, in others. The judgments of others form the standard for evaluating experiences. A young woman's letter to Rogers (1980) illustrates locus of evaluation in others, rather than in oneself:

> I think that I began to lose me when I was in high school. I always wanted to go into work that would be of help to people but my family resisted, and I thought they must be right . . . about two years ago . . . I met a guy that I thought was ideal. Then nearly a year ago I took a good look at us, and realized that I was everything that he wanted me to be and nothing that I was. I have always been emotional. . . . My fiance would tell me that I was just mad or just happy and I would say okay. . . . Then when I took this good look at us I realized that I was angry because I wasn't following my true emotions.

Perhaps part of the problem with people like this is that they have confused their selves with the selves of important people in their lives (Mashek et al., 2003). They are yielding to the pressures from important others to adopt the selves of those others.

Procedures for Changing Personality:
Client-Centered Therapy

Rogers's ideas about personality development in therapy involve the assumpti   ..., ιι certain conditions exist, then a characteristic process of personality change will occur (Rogers, 1959). These conditions are positive regard, accurate empathic understanding, and congruence (Bozarth & Brodley, 1991). Also important are the client's anxiety level and motivation to change. Person-centered therapy is designed to reflect these basic premises.

The direction of change for clients in Rogerian therapy is from a personality that is fixed, separated, and tied to the past to one that is spontaneous, integrated, and flowing with experiences occurring in the present. Seven characteristic stages of this process unfold during therapy (1961). It is impossible to capture all aspects of these complex and comprehensive stages as experienced by the client, but the following observations are representative:

Stage 1. The client's communications are mostly about externals, not about self.
Stage 2. The client describes feelings but does not recognize or "own" them personally.
Stage 3. The client talks about self as an object, often in terms of past experiences.
Stage 4. The client experiences feelings in the present, but mainly just describes them, with distrust and fear, rather than expressing them directly.
Stage 5. The client experiences and expresses feelings freely in the present; feelings "bubble up" into awareness with a display of desire to experience them.
Stage 6. The client accepts his or her feelings in all their immediacy and richness.
Stage 7. The client trusts new experiences and relates to others openly and freely.

If this process occurs, then certain cognitive, emotional, and behavioral changes will occur. These changes, wrought in therapy, lead the person closer to self-actualization. They reflect increases in congruence, openness to experience, adjustment, correspondence between actual and ideal self, positive self-regard, and acceptance of self and others.

Hypothetical therapeutic sessions illustrate the course of person-centered therapy. Imagine a successful lawyer who works 60 to 70 hours a week but is dissatisfied with his life. In an early session, the client begins by talking about trivia not really related to his concerns. "I can't understand why my kids are so materialistic. They just want more junk . . . everything they see on TV. I'm just the 'horn of plenty,' satisfying their every whim." The therapist replies, "So you feel that your kids just use you to satisfy their needs." The remark reflects the client's feeling and emotions back to him so they may be affirmed, a process that makes them more available for reconsideration.

The client continues in this vein for a time and then, in a later session, he begins to express his more central emotions, but acts as if they are not his own. "It's funny, today, how people end up with careers that are unrelated to what they want to do or are capable of doing. I know this guy who is selling insurance and making a fortune, but living for a camping trip on the weekend. He's an outdoor type . . . wanted to be a forest ranger." The therapist nods, indicating that the client is understood.

On a later date the client begins really to talk about himself, for the first time. However, he talks about the past as if to analyze another person rather than his present self. "I can remember trying to copy the Mona Lisa when I was a kid. How naive can you get! Here was this little kid trying to act like a great artist. I did some pretty good drawings on my own . . . my teachers said so, but they weren't good enough to satisfy me." The therapist listens intently and utters "uh huh" to communicate that the client's feelings are appreciated.

After several sessions, the client gets around to himself in the present, but he is merely descriptive rather than analytical. "I still paint, you know. Sometimes late at night . . . sometimes on weekends. Did you know that I have an arrangement with an art gallery? I've sold some of my paintings, but didn't get much . . . can't make a living that way. They want me to come in with them . . . invest, you know, in the gallery and help manage it. Small change that would be . . . but you know I'm really happy when I'm there among those paintings . . . get a bigger kick out of selling a painting for a hundred bucks than settling a case for a hundred thousand." The therapist says, "you feel that painting is very enjoyable and that you have had some success at it." The client begins to recognize how important art is to him. In subsequent sessions, the client comes back to art more and more and talks about his current feelings to a greater and greater extent. "Well today was something else. I left work early and went to the gallery . . . I have a corner in a back room where I can paint. I'm working on something right now that really excites me. I'll have to show it to you. I know now that art is a part of me . . . heart and soul."

In the last sessions before termination of therapy, the lawyer hardly mentions law. All he can talk about is his latest work of art and his plans to slowly substitute hours at the gallery for hours at the office. Here he shows awareness of courses of action that are more in tune with his actualizing self. "I have enough money saved to help make a go of the gallery. I find that my younger colleagues take care of the law practice quite nicely. You know, I've never been happier. My kids don't seem so greedy anymore. Let them have what they want . . . I'll give them all I can. They'll eventually find themselves."

Evaluation

General Contributions

Rogers's phenomenological approach has had major influences on understanding personality. It has allowed individual human beings to speak for themselves about the nature of their own personal experiences. Rogers has guided psychological professionals in suspending views as to what a person *should be,* so they can understand who a person actually *is.* His phenomenological approach has questioned scientific psychology's so-called objective frameworks that have sought to understand people from the outside: behaviorally, mechanistically, and impersonally. Rogers has doubted the existence of an absolute way of interpreting reality, and the desirability of even seeking such a narrow "truth" (Rogers, 1980).

Rogers has also tried to enhance our understanding of people by emphasizing trust in them. Given sufficiently supportive psychological conditions, individuals can be trusted to actualize their biologically based resources and move in directions that are ultimately good for them and other people. This basic assumption is an outgrowth of Rogers's belief that all organisms have inherent, natural capacities for growth, understanding, change, purposeful direction, and the responsible use of personal freedom.

Caring about the Person in Human Relationships

Rogers has stressed the role of caring, interpersonal relationships in the process of developing, maintaining, and changing personality. In person-centered therapy, the therapist is not a detached, objective observer or "expert," but a person, "a viable human being engaged in a terribly human endeavor" (Truax & Mitchell, 1971, p. 344). Under the influence of Rogers, even behavioral therapists, often criticized for ignoring interpersonal relationships, have modified procedures "which used to seem less than human to their critics" (Gendlin & Rychlak, 1970). In the best interest of the client, Rogers laid aside traditional rules of therapy. For instance, early in his career he showed his humanitarian side by departing from child-guidance procedures and answering "Yes" to a despairing mother's question "Do you ever take adults for counseling here?" (Rogers, 1961).

Rogers's Scientific Contributions

Rogers has changed the field of psychotherapy through subjecting his clinical observations to research investigation (Rogers, 1989a). His (1942) case of Herbert Bryan was the first complete series of therapy sessions to be electronically recorded and transcribed (800 78-rpm record sides and 170 book pages). Never before had such a wealth of information been made available to psychologists, word for word, complete with "Uhm's" and pauses. Standard procedure, beginning with Freud, was for therapists to rely entirely on memory or scant notes often composed at the end of a day's therapy sessions. By exposing their practice to the scrutiny of other professionals and the public, Rogers and his students demystified psychotherapy (Wexler & Rice, 1974). They "turned the field . . . upside down" and "made possible the empirical study of highly subjective phenomena" (Rogers, 1974, p. 116).

Unlike some theorists covered so far, a number of Rogers's concepts can be translated into a form amenable to scientific testing. An outstanding example was provided by Harrington, Block, and Block (1987). They were interested in Rogers's theory about the process by which child-rearing practices determine level of creativity at adolescence. Their subject sample was composed of individuals who had been followed and periodically tested beginning at approximately age 3 and continuing to approximately age 14. They studied Rogers's writings about child rearing and creativity, then they translated his notions about that relationship into items on some instruments designed to measure child-rearing practices. One of these measures involved having parents report the practices they typically used. Some items that were judged most typical of Rogers's "creativity fostering environment" (CFE) included, "I respect my child's opinions and encourage him to express them" and "I encourage my child to be curious, to explore and question things" (p. 852). Some items judged least typical of Rogers's CFE included "I believe that children should be seen and not heard" and "I do not allow my child to question my decisions" (p. 852).

Other measures assessed parental teaching behavior during parent–child, task-completion sessions that were observed by raters. Resultant ratings were then transformed into items related to Rogers's CFE. Items judged to be most typical of CFE included, "Parent was warm and supportive" and "Child appeared to enjoy the situation." Items judged to be least typical of CFE included, "Parent tended to control the tasks" and "Parent appeared ashamed of child" (p. 852).

Creativity was assessed when subjects were teens. Items that were judged applicable to creative individuals included, "Tends to be proud of own accomplishments" and "Is curious, exploring, eager for new experiences." Items that were judged applicable to noncreative individuals included, "Is uncomfortable with uncertainty and complexities" and "Gives up and withdraws where possible in the face of adversity" (p. 853).

Harrington, Block, and Block (1987) found statistically significant, positive relationships between data from instruments with items that measured Rogers's CFE and data from instruments with items that measured creativity. They concluded that Rogers's ideas about creativity, and the circumstances that foster it, are scientifically valid. Just looking at the items they used gives one a relatively clear impression concerning what creativity is and which parental practices promote it. Box 9.3 follows Rogers the peace-keeper around the world.

The Famous Case of Gloria: A Teaching Tool

Rogers's encounter with Gloria (Shostrom, 1965) continues to be used for teaching Rogerian principles to undergraduate and graduate students. Although the therapy session was only thirty minutes long, the equivalent of many volumes has been written about it. One of the most intriguing contributions to the Rogers–Gloria literature is Wichman and Campbell's (2003a) essay on conceptual metaphors (CM) used during therapy. Three CMs were illustrated: (1) self as a container (SAAC), (2) knowing is feeling (KIF), and (3) knowing oneself is seeing oneself through others' eyes (KOISOTOE). Use of these metaphors by both clients and therapists allows the former to communicate conceptions and feelings about the self relatively easily and the latter to reflect back on understanding and appreciation of those conceptions and feelings.

Self as a Container (SAAC).   The self is a whole entity that contains much. It can be described as "deep," "full," and "whole" (Wichman & Campbell, 2003a, p. 18). Rogers helped Gloria by facilitating her attempts to accept her guilt feelings, while assuring that Gloria alone plotted the course to acceptance.

Knowing Is Feeling (KIF).   The answer to a crucial question defines KIF: how do you know whether something you've done is right? The answer is "It's right if it feels right." Gloria disclosed to Rogers an internal conversation to herself: "If you're not comfortable, Gloria, it's not right, something is wrong" (Wichman & Campbell, 2003a, p. 19). She was referring to having sex with a man who was not the father of her children (she was divorced) and the fear that her "misbehavior" would taint her in the eyes of her daughter, Pam. Roger facilitated Gloria's acceptance of her behaviors by exclaiming, "If I really feel all right about it, then I don't have any concern about what I tell Pam" (p. 19).

Knowing Oneself is Seeing One's Self through Others' Eyes (KOISOTOE).   Gloria illustrated this conceptual metaphor nicely when she declared, "I hate facing the kids; I don't like looking at myself . . . I want them to see me just as sweet as they see [their father]" (Wichman & Campbell, 2003a, p. 20). Rogers helped by paraphrasing: "You sort of feel, 'I want them to have just as nice a picture of me as they have of their dad' " (p. 20).

BOX 9.3 • *Carl Rogers: Globe-Trotting Peacemaker*

Not all of Rogers's contributions were related to "psychotherapy" and "personality theory." Rogers had great influence on individuals involved in some of the most disturbing and serious conflicts occurring in the world today. His efforts to end disastrous conflicts took him to every quarter of the globe. On a trip to Northern Ireland he attempted to induce Protestants and Catholics to regard each other as human beings rather than mortal enemies (Rogers & Ryback, 1984). Using his client-centered method adapted to a group context, Rogers brought religious rivals together in close proximity. As you might expect, initial reactions were explosive. For example, Gilda, a Protestant, whom Rogers described as young and pretty, said, "If I seen an IRA man lying on the ground . . . I would step on him, because to me he has just went out and taken the lives of innocent people" (p. 5). Yet, under Rogers's skillful guidance, individuals revealed themselves and, thereby, came to appreciate one another's humanity. After considerable interaction in the context of Rogers's group, Dennis, a Protestant, and Becky, a Catholic, spoke warmly of one another:

> *Dennis:* The general impression back in Belfast is, if [Becky] is a Catholic . . . you just put her in a wee box and that is the end of it. But you just can't do that. She has communicated to me that she is in a worse position than what I am . . . I feel that she feels the absolute despair that I would feel. I don't know how I would react if I were one of her lads. I would probably go out and get a gun . . . and end up dead.
>
> *Becky:* Words couldn't describe what I feel towards Dennis from the discussion we had at dinner time. We spoke quietly

for about ten minutes and I felt that here I have got a friend and that was it.

> *Dennis:* We sat at dinner time and had a wee bit of yarn [storytelling] quietly when you were all away for your dinner . . .
>
> *Becky:* I think he fully understands me as a person.
>
> *Dennis:* I do, there is no question about that . . .
>
> *Becky*: And for that reason I am very grateful and I think I have found a friend (p. 5).

These same techniques were used in the encounter between Black and White South Africans that reduced Rogers to tears (Hill-Hain & Rogers, 1988) and in the former Soviet Union (Rogers, 1987b). This last adventure in group interaction, played out in Moscow and Tbilisi, was responsive to Rogers's larger concerns. He had in mind more than just settlement of local conflicts. For the last several years of his life, Rogers wrote passionately about the need to eliminate nuclear weapons, a concern that I share with him (Allen, 1985). He believed that social scientists could contribute much toward the end of the nuclear threat (Rogers & Malcolm, 1987). In fact, it was his fervent wish that his group interaction methods, used so successfully to alleviate local tensions, might be applied to international conflicts that have the potential to produce nuclear holocaust (Rogers, 1987c, 1989b; Rogers and Ryback, 1984). I can picture a group composed of the U.S. and Russian presidents and their underlings interacting under Rogers's guidance. Because he is gone, the best we can do is to apply his wisdom and sensitivity, and we had better hurry.

Wichman and Campbell (2003b) use many of the same quotes from the Rogers–Gloria film to illustrate the three main therapeutic tools used by Rogers to facilitate a client's efforts to change: empathy, genuineness, and unconditional positive regard. Rogers "displayed empathy for Gloria's struggle" by offering, "Life is risky. To take the responsibility for being the person you would like to be with [Pam] is a hell of a responsibility"

(p. 180). Rogers displayed genuineness by laying out for Gloria his nonexpert role in her pursuit of positive change. Regarding helping her get rid of her guilt feelings, Rogers told Gloria, "this is [a] . . . very private thing that I couldn't possibly answer for you. But I sure as anything will try to help you work toward your own answer" (p. 180). Rogers also displayed unconditional positive regard through this same statement, by assuring Gloria that he believed in her ability to solve her own problems.

Limitations

Although emphasis on subjective experience is a major contribution, it creates limitations in regard to the scientific status of Rogers's personality theory and therapy. The major weaknesses thus generated are: (1) difficulty in translating some concepts into testable form; (2) problems involved in accepting self-reports; and (3) the effectiveness of nondirective therapy for some individuals. Also discussed are concerns about Rogers's basic assumptions, some allegations that Rogers's "genuineness" in therapy was limited and that, before he died, he repudiated, if not his entire point of view, at least his views on humanistic education.

Acceptance of Conscious, Self-reported Experience.   In his classic text on personality, Gordon Allport (1937) alluded to the inclination of behaviorists and psychoanalysts "to distrust the evidence of immediate experience" and dismiss the self, ego, or "person" in psychology. While scientific evidence has shown that "self-concept" is amenable to measurement, these critics of self notions make some telling points. First, self-perceptions may be incomplete or inaccurate representations of the self because of people's limited ability to see themselves realistically. Second, accurate self-perceptions may not be reflected in self-statements if the individual is unwilling to communicate them. Third, both self-perceptions and self-statements may not correspond to what the person is doing, thinking, and feeling. While difficulty in measuring concepts does not make them useless, it does render them scientifically suspect.

The Nondirective Approach.   Unlike most other psychotherapists, Rogers has accumulated considerable evidence supporting the effectiveness of his therapeutic procedures (see Kirschenbaum & Henderson, 1989). Nevertheless, these methods are apparently not for everyone. In the filmed psychotherapy session mentioned earlier, the client, Gloria, was rather obviously frustrated with Rogers's unwillingness to offer expert advice. Despite her continued contact with Rogers later, at the time of the session some viewers thought that Gloria preferred the other two therapists to Rogers. Not long ago I overheard some counselors expressing similar frustration. They were describing an observation of a Rogerian session in which the client was seeking advice and not getting any. It seemed obvious to them not only that the client needed advice but what advice he needed. Despite their observations, the therapist persisted in merely nodding and saying "Uh huh." Perhaps Rogers's predominantly intelligent and not-so-severely disturbed clients were better off left to their own devices. However, other clients, who may be more disturbed and less well equipped, may need some suggestions as to how they might deal with their problems. In addition, there are indications that Rogers became discouraged with two-person interactive therapy (Lakin, 1996). During his time as a professor and therapist in Wisconsin, he used

the nondirective method with a wide variety of clients, ranging from the u
verbal people to profoundly disturbed individuals. Apparently the results of this ...
were disappointing, because thereafter Rogers virtually abandoned two-person interactions
in favor of group methods. However, currently some of his followers believe that his point
of view can be useful to severely disturbed people, including those with *post-traumatic
stress disorder* (PTSD, Joseph, 2004).

Some Problems with Basic Assumptions. Stating Rogers's basic assumptions is difficult because he did not define *personality*. One can approximate specification of his underlying assumptions only indirectly, by reading between the lines of his statements about
"self." One of Rogers's most basic assumptions is that people are inherently "good." As
classroom discussions on the topic always show, just as it is philosophically difficult to declare that humans are essentially "bad" (unworthy) it is hard to defend the blanket judgment that people are basically "good" (worthy). One can more easily argue that people are
neither "good" nor "bad." Rather, they are exceedingly complex and fully capable of both
goodness and badness. An alternative perspective is seen in the question, "How do we maximize the goodness and minimize the badness?"

Allegations Regarding Rogers's Genuineness and Repudiation of His Views. No
matter who a theorist might be, no matter how benevolent, reasonable, and honest he or she
may seem, no matter how solid her or his point of view may appear, it will be criticized,
given only that fame finds the theorist. This fact is important to keep in mind when one considers any criticisms and allegations against anyone. Two charges have been lodged against
Rogers. Quinn (1993) alleges that recordings of Rogers in therapy, including the Gloria
case, show that Rogers's genuineness is limited, because he adamantly refused to be con-
frontational. Supposedly, to be truly genuine, all that the therapist encounters, feels, and
thinks must be fair game for placement on the therapeutic table, including feelings that the
client has behaved in ways that the therapist wishes to confront. Graf (1994) countered by
arguing that (1) all the recordings Quinn refers to are of short-term therapy demonstrations,
too preliminary to include most of Rogers's typical reactions, and (2) including confronta-
tion when the therapist may feel the need of it is something other than genuineness: namely
it is likely to be a case of giving the therapist's issues priority over the client's. Graf con-
cludes that viewing Rogers in more extended sessions confirms his complete genuineness.

The second allegation is that, before he died, Rogers repudiated his humanistic educational philosophy and even his entire point of view. This astounding charge was leveled
by William Coulson, who, according to Kirschenbaum (1991), made the allegation in other
than professional journals (for example, on the radio). Coulson claimed to have co-
developed humanistic education with Rogers and Maslow, then, along with them, abandoned it in the light of research results that failed to support it. Kirschenbaum makes it clear,
by use of numerous quotes from Rogers, that Rogers never abandoned humanistic education, much less the general humanistic, person-centered point of view. In fact, Kirschenbaum shows that Rogers became an even more radical humanistic educator as time went on.
Further, Coulson was never able to point out any published statements by Rogers that clearly
renounce humanistic education. While Rogers was, as always, flexible and backed away
from some elements of humanistic instruction, he consistently supported it. In fact, once he
developed a point of view or practice he usually stuck with it (Bozarth, 1990).

Conclusions

Carl Rogers was many things to many people, but disliked was hardly ever one of them. He was a person who practiced what he preached. As a result, Rogers was the warm, accepting kind of person that he hoped we would all become. In reading the various interviews with Rogers and tributes to him offered by his many disciples, it is evident that his followers were not just interested in his point of view. They were sincerely devoted to Rogers. These loving colleagues and friends comforted, protected, and nourished him, just as he did them. To them, he exemplified the best of the human spirit. He could truly meld into another person so that he became one with her or him. In so doing, he surrendered himself in the interest of someone else, perhaps the most noble act a human can perform. Rogers was 5th on the list of text citations, number 9.5 in the survey, and 6th overall, but did not make the journal citation list.

Summary Points

1. Rogers learned principles of science and growth from an agricultural book. He cut his teeth on Freud, but later abandoned psychoanalysis and the medical model in favor of the growth model. He was mentored by Adler and, especially, Rank. As an adult, Rogers became a warm person who backed away from religion temporarily, but was somewhat different from his image.

2. He could become angry and agitated, he thought equality in therapy was not an issue, he was sometimes overcome with emotion during therapy, he deplored the rigid use of the client-centered method, and he was not heavily identified with counseling. At the same time, he contributed to understanding diversity as it applies to interracial relations and therapist–client ethnic mismatches.

3. Humanistic psychology emphasizes the present experience of the whole person. Rollo May offered six processes that link existential psychology to the humanistic movement. The phenomenological approach, central to Rogers's view, assumes that the reality that one knows is subjective and personal. However, we can participate in the private world of others through empathy, a process that is embedded in the brain. He applied these notions to create humanistic education.

4. People are viewed in a positive light and are seen as capable of solving their own problems. Relationships with people in therapy are only instances of those that occur everyday. People have an inherent "general actualizing tendency" that is organismic, active, directional, and selective. Self-actualization is a lifelong process of realizing one's potentialities that involves openness to experience, awareness, living existentially, and trust in one's organismic functions.

5. The existence of the self is verified by statements like "Who am I?" and "This is what I like." The self is functionally equivalent to "self-concept." It can be related to an "ideal self." Congruence occurs when our self-concepts are in agreement with what we actually experience. Incongruence is the opposite. It entails denial and distortion.

6. Some necessary conditions for growth are (1) unconditional positive regard, (2) accurate empathy, and (3) congruence. Unconditional positive regard concerns being regarded with acceptance and trust just for who one is no matter what, but not necessarily acceptance of one's behavior. Accurate empathy means correctly perceiving the client's world in a nonevaluative way. Congruence is applicable to therapist–client relationships.

7. Unconditional positive regard can lead to positive self-regard, but not if the locus of evaluation is in other people. Personality change flows from fixed, separated, and tied-to-the-past to spontaneous, integrated, and "in-the-present." Progress in therapy proceeds from talk about externals, to disowned descriptions of feelings, to self in the past, to feelings in the present that are merely described, to feelings freely expressed in the present, to full acceptance of feelings, to relating to others openly and freely, and trusting in new experiences.

8. Rogers's contributions include allowing people to speak for themselves with regard to the nature of their feelings. His methods led to questioning the attempt to understand people from the outside. He promoted trusting people, attributed positive motivations to them, and honored their natural actualizing tendencies, while recognizing that they do not always behave well. The case of Gloria illustrates the use of conceptual metaphors and implementation of the three conditions for growth (see point 6).

9. Rogers, while humanizing other approaches, adopted the motto "do whatever is necessary to enhance the person." As a scientist he has demystified psychotherapy and revised mechanized approaches to it. Some of his concepts have been translated into measurable form as evidenced by Harrington, Block, and Block's verification of his proposed relationship between child-rearing practices and creativity. Rogers attempted to do something about serious world conflicts and nuclear war.

10. Limitations of Rogers's point of view include problems of translation of some concepts, problems with the self-report method he used, and inadequacy of the nondirective therapy method for some people. There are also problematic issues of basic assumptions. Allegations of lack of genuineness and abandonment of humanistic education have been lodged against him. Despite these shortcomings, Rogers exemplifies human warmth and concern for the well being of each person.

Running Comparison

Theorists	Rogers in Comparison
Freud	Rogers was optimistic and positive, and rejected Freud's probing into the past, but shared his belief in defenses.
Jung	He shared Jung's mutual participant orientation to therapy, individuation (self-actualization), interest in the self, and belief in wholeness and uniqueness of each person.
Adler	He learned to be direct and straightforward from Adler.
Abraham Maslow	He shared ideas with Maslow, especially self-actualization.

Gordon Allport	He shared Allport's idiographic approach, humanism, and concern for the self-concept.
Harry S. Sullivan	He shared Sullivan's interest in two-person interactions.
Karen Horney	Her real self was like self-actualization. Both pointed to the clash of actual and ideal selves.

Essay/Critical Thinking Questions

1. How is existentialism related to humanism?

2. Picture yourself as a self-actualized person. How would you describe yourself?

3. Indicate the ways your self-concept is incongruent with your actual experience of yourself.

4. Reconcile "original sin" with "humans are inherently good."

5. What does it take to be truly genuine? Must one express whatever one feels?

E-mail Interaction

Write the author at b-allen@wiu.edu. Forward one of the following, or phrase your own.

1. Was Rogers an atheist?

2. Was Dr. Rogers much like Mr. Rogers of TV children's show fame?

3. Tell me what central notion was at the heart and soul of Rogers's theory.

CHAPTER 10

Becoming All That One Can Be: Abraham Maslow

- Can a psychologist who despised his mother turn out right?
- Must we meet our basic physiological needs before we can address other kinds?
- What is the highest level of personality development?

Abraham Maslow
www.ship.edu/
~cgboeree/maslow.html

The two brightest stars in the humanistic firmament are certainly Carl Rogers and Abraham Maslow. Not surprisingly, they share much in common. Both are more concerned with the here and now rather than with the past. Both flirted with the ideas of Sigmund Freud briefly, and both were influenced by Alfred Adler. Both also emphasized the importance of self-actualization in personality functioning and development, but here the similarities fade. For Rogers, self-actualization was one of several central concepts. By contrast, Maslow emphasized it above all other concepts. According to Rogers, self-actualization was within the grasp of most people, but to Maslow it was reserved for a special few.

As people they were quite different. Rogers came from a traditional family. Maslow considered himself an abused and neglected child and a victim of prejudice. Rogers was totally warm and accepting and assumed the basic goodness of humans. Maslow could show the same traits, but in his youth he seethed with suppressed anger and was more than willing to acknowledge the sinister side of human nature. Yet, in their own separate ways, both humanists sought to help people lay aside others' expectations and become what they were destined to be.

Maslow, the Person

When Samuel Maslow arrived in the United States from the Ukrainian city of Kiev, he brought little with him, except the ability to speak Russian and Yiddish, a language common among European Jews (Hoffman, 1988). Soon he moved in with relatives residing in New York City. There he met and married his first cousin Rose, a woman who would prove more devoted to religion than to her family. Abraham, the first of their seven children, was born April Fool's Day 1908. Fate played a trick on him, giving him parents who were part of a master plan to ensure his eternal torment.

Maslow claimed that his mother was cold, vicious, superstitiously religious, and dedicated to making him miserable (Hoffman, 1988). Even the most trivial of his youthful transgressions inspired her to declare that God would strike him down. Continual threats of divine retribution affected Maslow profoundly. For one thing, it nurtured the scientist in him: "I tested . . . that if you do such and such, God will strike you down. If I climbed through the window, [I was told that] I wouldn't grow. Well, I climbed through the window and then checked my growth" (p. 2). As he was not stunted, Maslow concluded that religion was a virulent form of superstition, a position to which he clung tenaciously.

The experiments saved his sanity, but they did not deliver him from continued religious harassment at the hands of his mother. While undergoing the religious instruction she forced on him, he was required to proclaim his love for mother Rose. When he choked on the words, dropped materials from which he was reading, and fled in tears, his ever "insightful" mother exclaimed, "You see! He loves me so much he can't even express the words!" (p. 11).

His mother's alleged cruelties were numerous and varied. She would see to it that he received less food than his siblings, an affront to his status as eldest son, and a not-too-subtle message: insofar as food means "love," he was unloved (Hoffman, 1988). One day young Maslow brought home some prized 78-rpm recordings, laid them and the rest of his collection on the living room floor for inspection, and absent-mindedly left the room without honoring her command to "pick up your mess." When he returned she was screaming, "What did I tell you?" and grinding her heels into his treasured recordings (p. 8). On another occasion he brought home two kittens and spirited them away to the basement, but Rose heard the meowing and confronted him. He had dared to bring stray cats into her house and feed them from her dishes. While Maslow watched in horror, she picked up each kitten in turn and smashed its head against the brick basement wall until it was dead. To the dismay of his siblings, Maslow publicly expressed his antagonism toward mother Rose several times during his life. When she died, he refused even to attend her funeral.

In contrast to mother Rose's cruelty, Maslow's father Samuel was merely absent. Probably owing to the sad state of his marriage, he left early in the morning for the long trek to his job and made a point of staying late at work to chat with his cronies. When he finally arrived at home, his children were often already in bed. During childhood, Maslow basically had no relationship with Samuel. When Maslow grew to young adulthood, however, the elder Maslow's business failed, a victim of the Depression, and the father became a ward of the son. They lived together and became friends. Thus, like Adler, and unlike Freud or Sullivan, Maslow was something of a father's son, not a mother's boy.

Like Julian Rotter, whose ideas will be covered in this text, Maslow's fledgling intellect was nourished by the Brooklyn libraries. But life in Brooklyn for Jewish boys was harsh, and access to the libraries difficult. He learned to stay on Jewish turf lest he fall prey to ethnic youth gangs that controlled surrounding areas. When he ventured forth to visit the local library, he had to use special paths, ones with handy escape routes. In self-defense, Maslow tried to join a Jewish gang, but they wanted him to kill cats and throw stones at girls, acts that were against his nature. Instead, he skillfully sneaked from home to the library with such high frequency that he soon finished the children's books and was awarded an adult's card.

At school, anti-Semitism was also an everyday problem. Once, when he won the class spelling bee, his bigoted teacher refused to accept the outcome. The "horrible bitch" pitched words at Abraham until he fumbled one: *parallel* (p. 4). Then she announced to the class that she knew all along he was just a fake. Still, Maslow did well at school, so well he was dubbed "that smart Jew." Added to these miseries was the problem of Maslow's appearance. Like Horney, he felt unattractive. Gangly and afflicted with a prominent nose, he was subjected to ridicule. His own father asked the whole family, "Isn't he the ugliest kid you've ever seen?" (p. 6). Occasions like these gave Maslow a serious inferiority complex and led him to describe his childhood as "miserably unhappy" (p. 6).

After attending a select boy's high school, where he performed reasonably well in all but a few key courses, Maslow began a career as an itinerant college student. He wanted to attend revered Cornell at Ithaca, NY, one of the few universities in the Eastern United States that did not have strict quotas limiting the number of Jews admitted. His best friend, cousin Will, was accepted there, but Maslow lacked the confidence to apply. Having given up on Cornell, Maslow enrolled at the City College of New York in the winter of 1925. There he found some joys and some sorrows. Trigonometry proved to be a major source of grief. He hated it so much he missed class often. Thus, he failed, despite having passed the tests. Unlike most of us, he could not grind through life's drudgeries. If Maslow could not bear to do something, he refused to do it, even if doing it was a practical necessity.

During this period he worked briefly as a busboy, but he felt mistreated and walked off the job. Following a semester on academic probation, Maslow decided to attend law school. Soon after enrolling in a less than prestigious school, he became bored. True to character, he quit, disappointing his father at whose behest he had tried law. While he sampled academic pursuits, Maslow flirted with socialism, but never became the activist that Adler and Fromm had been. Perhaps he was preoccupied with other matters, most especially his attraction to first cousin Bertha. His fear of approaching Bertha, "who I couldn't get close to . . . anyhow" and his desire to join Will led to Maslow's transfer to Cornell in 1927 (p. 24).

Just as had been the case for Sullivan, Cornell was mainly a bad experience for Maslow. Despite its relative lack of exclusionary policies regarding Jews, anti-Semitism was alive and well in Ithaca and on university grounds as well. Accordingly, Maslow located in Collegetown, a community that contained housing for "lesser-status . . . Bohemians and those neither interested in nor acceptable to the [fraternities]" (p. 25). Besides fraternities, many Ithaca landlords banned Jews and the *Cornell Sun,* a university-sanctioned student newspaper, barred Jews from its staff.

Cornell also provided Maslow with his first exposure to psychology. As was true for George Kelly, the beginning psychology class made the discipline seem less than inviting. Maslow had the bad luck to enroll in a class assigned to a pretentious dinosaur among professors by the name of Edward B. Titchener. A disciple of Wilhelm Wundt, psychology's founder, Titchener had come to Cornell in 1892 as the chief U.S. proponent of Wundt's "structuralism." Some 35 years later Maslow witnessed the spectacle of Titchener, adorned in academic robes, parading to the lectern followed obediently by an entourage of his graduate students. There he espoused a theory considered long dead by nearly everyone but himself. Such lame academic fare was one of two important reasons why Maslow transferred back to City College after only one semester.

The other reason was Bertha. But, when they met, inherent shyness prevented him from expressing his tender feelings for her. One day he was sitting beside his sweetheart, longing to touch her, when Bertha's assertive sister Anna witnessed his reticence. Growing impatient with Maslow's timidity and Bertha's passivity, Anna pushed the reluctant lovers together and exclaimed, "For the love of Pete, kiss her will ya!" Then "life began" (p. 29).

By the spring of 1928, Maslow was restless again. He had learned of the liberal atmosphere at the University of Wisconsin and of the school's psychology department, which included Kurt Koffka, one of the original Gestalt psychologists. So, once again, he transferred. The summer before moving to Wisconsin, he visited a former City College professor who recommended *The Psychologies of 1925,* a book containing an essay by John B. Watson, the leading behaviorist of the time. Maslow later wrote, "The thing that really turned me on was Watson's chapter. . . . In the highest excitement, I suddenly saw unrolling before me . . . the possibility of a *science of psychology* . . . " (p. 33). How ironic it was that a future humanist would be beckoned to his academic destiny by a psychologist devoted to simple stimulus–response relationships. But Maslow was stuck on psychology, despite the discovery that Koffka was actually only a visiting professor. While his career had been launched, his personal life was still on the beach. Bertha was in his every thought. Finally, he could stand it no more. He proposed via telegram and she accepted. On the last day of 1928, they were married.

Wisconsin's small and not-yet-esteemed psychology department contained faculty and students who would eventually become famous. Professors were also congenial: students were treated more like colleagues than underlings. By 1930, when he had finished his B.A. degree, he had already taken many graduate courses. During his subsequent graduate school years, he was exposed to the likes of Clark Hull, soon to become the foremost learning theorist of the 1930s. However, he eventually migrated to the laboratory of Harry Harlow, whose influential research with monkeys was considered in the Sullivan chapter.

As time passed and Maslow achieved fame, anger left over from childhood mistreatment and resentment toward anti-Semites faded. He began to develop the warmth and trust that early experiences had disallowed. However, there was still an undercurrent of bitterness that seemed to obstruct his best efforts on occasion. Alderfer (1989) noted that unlike Rogers, Maslow had trouble leading *sensitivity training groups*—an assemblage of people who come together to reveal their inner feelings and to achieve intimacy with others. "The man whose intellectual work played such an important role in the then rapidly growing humanistic psychology movement was unable to act in ways . . . consistent with his own theory" (p. 359). When the protest era of the 1960s emerged, Maslow was a natural for the role of guru, the wise leader of soul-searching youth. However, Alderfer suggests that Maslow was uncomfortable with young people's propensity for questioning authority. Maslow courageously overcame a tragic childhood, but it left its indelible mark on him.

Maslow continued working at Wisconsin while leisurely finishing his dissertation—completed in 1934—then he took a temporary position at Teachers College, Columbia University, Rogers's doorway to academe. Finally Maslow landed a permanent position on the faculty of the brand new Brooklyn College (1937–1951). The rest of his academic career was spent at Brandeis University (1951–1969), where he chaired the psychology department for ten years. In 1968, he served as president of the American Psychological Association. After several bouts with poor health dating to early midlife, Maslow died of a heart attack in 1970.

Maslow's View of the Person

The Evolution of a Theorist

Maslow's love of music and his attraction to freethinking politicians and academicians rested uneasily with his initial devotion to the study of neurologically programmed behaviors in animals (Hoffman, 1988). Yet success is a magnet that has pulled many researchers along, even against their wills. After early publications with Harlow, Maslow gained his own fame by showing that what looked like sexual behavior in monkeys—the constant mounting of one monkey by another—was actually dominance behavior. "The higher a monkey's dominance position, the more likely it is to mount its subordinates; the lower its position, the more likely it is to be mounted by others" (p. 61). Although he helped to establish interest in primate "dominance hierarchies," Maslow eventually abandoned the study of mechanistic animal behavior.

During the interval between getting his Ph.D. and finding a permanent position, Maslow searched desperately for a stable means of livelihood. Because the Depression was ongoing, he opted for future security and entered medical school. But, as always when he did something for reasons other than intrinsic interest, he became bored and dropped out. Earlier attempts to work at the famous Yerkes primate facilities also fell through. Facing a poor job market and an "old gentile boy" network—he had already been denied a research grant because of anti-Semitism—Maslow was ready to take anything. Much to his joy, famed learning psychologist Edward L. Thorndike became interested in his work. Thorndike, of Columbia University Teachers College, had been the author of the "law of effect," a basic principle of learning. By this time, however, he had become a generalist. Instead of watching cats learn to escape from boxes, he had grand plans for applying psychology and was awarded the unheard of amount of $100,000 to carry them out. Maslow could return to New York City, continue his research, and make a living in the process.

While still immersed in his animal studies at Wisconsin, Maslow had become interested in the Freud–Adler quarrel. Now he found himself in the middle of the most exciting place at the most fascinating time during the early history of personality psychology.

New York City was sparkling with the brilliance of Horney, Fromm, Adler, and others, including Gestalt psychologist Koffka. Among these luminaries, Adler was singled out by Maslow as having special impact on him. When Maslow showed up for a series of lectures by the renegade ex-Freudian, he was pleasantly surprised to find a nearly empty classroom. Having few competitors for Adler's attention, he learned much. Undoubtedly, Adler's social interest, law of movement (directed free choice), striving for superiority, and the pre-humanistic idea "creative power of the individual" heavily influenced Maslow.

The Gestalt Influence

However, it was the Gestalt psychologists who probably contributed the most to Maslow's intellectual evolution. The New School for Social Research in New York City had become the "University in Exile" for European scholars fleeing Hitler. Among them was the founder of Gestalt psychology, Max Wertheimer, an inspiring teacher, but not a prolific writer. Thus, it was left to Koffka to lay some important planks in the flooring of Maslow's theory.

Gestalt psychology—initially concerned only with perception—held that simple perceptions were "wholes" made up of integrated parts (Matlin & Foley, 1997). One could consider the parts or the whole, but not both at once. Thus, a mosaic, the tiny tiles that form faces and figures in works of art (and in institutional flooring), could be appreciated as a whole, or its parts could be considered. More importantly, once the whole is formed, the parts and the whole are not separable, but are inextricably tied up together: a whole is an integration of parts. Gestalt theory was largely composed of "laws of organization" that explained how parts are formed into wholes. Among these are: (1) grouping similar objects together to form a whole; (2) grouping proximal (near) objects; and (3) the law of closure, incomplete objects such as a circle with a section out are completed by "the mind's eye." Another is the familiar *figure ground* rule: scenes are divided into a *figure* in the foreground displayed against a *background*. This principle is illustrated by the "vase and the face" reversing picture that has portions alternating as figure or background. True to Gestalt theory, one sees a white vase on a black background, or black faces on a white background, not both at once.

The idea of wholeness and of parts that are inextricably tied to the whole became fundamental to Maslow's thinking: "Our first proposition states that the individual is an integrated, organized whole" (1954, p. 63). To elucidate this point, Maslow drew an analogy to the study of the stomach. The top end of the intestines can be investigated by extracting a specimen from a cadaver and examining it as if it normally functioned independently of the body from which it was taken. Alternatively, the stomach can be studied in living, breathing organisms. To Maslow, the latter is much preferred, because the stomach cannot be fully understood apart from the living body into which it is integrated. It is not the stomach that "is hungry," it is the individual. "Furthermore, satisfaction of hunger comes to the whole individual, not just to a part of him" (p. 63).

The Existential Influence

While Maslow (1969b) declared that he was not an existentialist, he acknowledged enough coincidences between his view and that of the existentialists to confirm that he was affected by the "meaning of being" movement. In response to comments by Rollo May, Maslow pointed out important issues that existentialism brought to his mind. He noted that, due to the collapse of values outside individuals, they have no choice but to look inward to the self as a source of values. He credited existentialism for emphasizing the "human predicament presented by the gap between human aspirations and human limitations (between what the human being *is,* what he would *like* to be, and what he *could* be)" (p. 51). Maslow also indicated that existentialism brings to mind a provocative contention: as one ascends toward self-actualization, he transcends his culture and becomes "a little more a member of his species and a little less a member of his local group" (p. 52).

Maslow also credited existentialism for posing the crucial question: what is so essential to humans that without it they would no longer be defined as humans? The existentialists, according to Maslow, also correctly pointed out that psychologists have been ducking consideration of the links between the issues of responsibility, courage, and will in the making of personalities. We cannot have "free will" if we do not have the courage to take responsibility for our own development. Finally, he indicated that the existentialistic focus on the future is vitally important, as self-actualization is meaningless without reference to the future. He did, however, scold existentialists for seeing the self as emerging from the choices people make. This view was deemed too narrow because it ignores the physiological and genetic inputs into personality.

Motivation

Motivation comes from the root word *motion* and refers to the process by which organisms are propelled toward goals. To Maslow, motivational factors underlie personality. However, *drive,* a simple tension that demands to be satisfied—hunger is an example—is not an entirely satisfactory motivational concept. While it is a psychological tradition and seems easily understood, Maslow (1954) considered drive to be inherently ambiguous. Looking at behavior that appears associated with a certain drive may mislead us. People apparently behaving at the behest of the hunger drive may find food and eat it. However, their ultimate goal may be security, not reduction of the hunger drive. Likewise, people engaging in sexual behavior may actually be seeking increased self-esteem. It is these end-goals—security and self-esteem in the examples—that hold the key to understanding people. Such goals transcend the particular life circumstances of the given person. Goal-seeking can be cast as **needs** for certain satisfactions that are sought by all humans, regardless of their culture, environment, or generation.

Maslow, like Henry Murray, took the unique point of view, overlooked by most theorists, that a given behavior, thought, or feeling may occur at the behest of multiple motivations (Maslow, 1954). We are in the habit of attempting to find *the* reason for every significant action displayed by either ourselves or others. Actually, human behavior is extraordinarily complex. Anything a person does is likely to be traced to many motivations, not just one. A person "suffering" from paralysis of the arm for which no physical basis can be found may experience many motivational benefits: pity, love, and attention, to name a few. Only the rarest of thoughts, behaviors, or feelings stem from just one motivational source. To learn more, see Box 10.1.

BOX 10.1 • *Why Do We Do What We Do? Let Us Count the Reasons . . .*

Psychological professionals and nonprofessionals alike can sometimes be quite simple-minded about human thought, behavior, and feeling. Even obviously complex actions like proposing marriage, committing suicide, and changing careers may be discussed as if only one motive is involved. "He proposed because he is in love"; "People commit suicide because they hate themselves"; "She changed careers for more money." Rarely are single motives able to explain such complex actions.

Below are several ordinary decisions, activities, or psychological conditions. Contemplate each and for each imagine that you are the person involved. Then write down as many reasons why you "did what you did" as you can conjure up. An example precedes the exercise items.

I spent the afternoon cleaning out my cabinets and closets. I wanted to get organized. I couldn't find anything. I wanted to be neat like my sister. I felt the need to expend some energy. I wanted to take something apart and put it back together again. I was depressed and needed a distraction. I was bored and needed to fill some time.

"I went shopping all afternoon and didn't find a thing."

"I ate everything I could find in the house."

"I wrote my Mom a nasty letter."

"I told my best friend, 'I care for you more than anyone else.' "

"I took the afternoon off, started a novel, and read until 3 A.M."

According to Maslow, while the needs a person experiences are universal, the methods used to satisfy them may be specific to the individual's culture. Everyone has a need to bolster and maintain self-esteem, which can be boosted by being a good hunter, a superb athlete, an outstanding pottery maker, or a feared "witch doctor," depending on the culture. Likewise, environment may determine the particular form of need satisfaction, but Maslow was quick to point out that the role of environment is often overemphasized. Exactly how the urge to eat is satisfied will depend in some degree on whether we find ourselves in L.A., Chicago, New York, or Houston. It may also depend on whether we are on a camping trip, in a shopping mall, or stuck at Aunt Sue's house. However, an environmental circumstance does not force certain satisfactions on us. Rather our perceptions of that circumstance and operations on it shape need fulfillment. By making reference to "environmental barriers," Maslow explained that environments are what we make of them: "a child who is trying to attain a certain object . . . , but who is restrained by a barrier of some sort, determines not only that the object has value, but that the barrier is a barrier. Psychologically there is no such thing as a barrier; there is only a barrier for a particular person who is trying to get something that he wants" (p. 74).

Finally, a motivation cannot be considered in isolation from other motivations. Like Murray, Maslow believed that the satisfaction of a given need may depend on the prior, simultaneous, or subsequent satisfactions of other needs. We can hardly be creative if we have chronically empty stomachs. During the process of supporting and comforting other people, we can expect to receive self-esteem bolstering comments from them. Only after we have secured a safe apartment in a big city can we expect to enjoy interactions with family at home. Motivations relate to other motivations in a multidimensional matrix of almost infinite complexity.

Chipin

Basic Concepts: Maslow

Five Basic Needs (Place Satisfactions Before Love, Esteem, and Self-Actualization)

Maslow (1954, 1970) offers two answers to the question "Do people live by bread alone?" When people have no bread, the answer is "yes." But, when bread is plentiful, the answer is "no." Consider the example of desperately hungry people who constantly think about food, dream about food, and have recollections only about food. All other interests are unimportant. Life itself is defined in terms of eating. To them, Utopia is a place where there is plenty of food. As ex-POWs and concentration camp inmates can testify, once a person has been severely deprived of food, food becomes all that matters.

However, the picture is quite different when bread is available and a person's belly is continuously filled. Gratification of hunger frees people to pursue higher-order needs. When these additional needs emerge, they begin to dominate the individual, taking the place of hunger. After this second level of needs is satisfied, still higher-order needs emerge. Maslow's needs form a hierarchy ranging from basic biologically based needs to abstract, uniquely human needs.

Physiological needs encompass specific biological requirements for water, oxygen, proteins, vitamins, proper body temperature, sleep, sex, exercise, and so on (Maslow, 1954). When food is scarce, seeking food is not a means to some other end; it is an end in itself. **Safety needs** include security, protection, stability, structure, law and order, and freedom from fear and chaos. These needs are readily inferred from negative reactions of children to sudden disruption and unpredictability in their lives. In fact, if children or adults are observed to be endangered and threatened, their condition has been activated by some current, potent stimulus. Veterans home from Vietnam had plenty in their stomachs. However, many spontaneously recoiled when a car backfired nearby or when the peculiar whirring, whipping sound of a helicopter occurred within hearing range.

Belongingness and love needs orient the person toward affectionate relations with people, and a sense of place in family and groups. Maslow viewed the increasing popularity of sensitivity groups during the 1960s as a reflection of a widespread hunger for interpersonal contact, intimacy, and togetherness. He saw the "thwarting of love needs" as a fundamental cause of human maladjustment (Maslow, 1970). The growing number of children in foster homes and the numerous children of divorce often operate from this level.

Esteem needs are of two kinds: (1) there are personal desires for adequacy, mastery, competence, achievement, confidence, independence, and freedom; and (2) there are desires for respect from other people, including attention, recognition, appreciation, status, prestige, fame, dominance, and dignity (Maslow, 1954). Satisfaction of esteem needs results in feelings of worthiness, psychological strength, and a sense of being useful and necessary. "But thwarting of these needs produces feelings of inferiority, of weakness, and of helplessness" (p. 91). Academically, athletically, and interpersonally successful children have high esteem. Those who are denied opportunities to succeed do not.

The quintessential longing is the **need for self-actualization,** "the desire for self-fulfillment . . . the tendency for [one] to become actualized in what [one] is potentially"

(Maslow, 1954, pp. 91–92). What a person *can* be, that person feels compelled *to become,* whether athlete, parent, or community leader. Musicians experience a powerful need to make better music, artists to paint more meaningfully, poets to write more potent lines. Each person hears a voice from within that whispers "Be true to your nature." It is in the manifestations of self-actualization that people differ the most. Because each person is different from other people, that which each person feels the need to become is unique. "At this level, individual differences are greatest" (Maslow, 1970, p. 46). Figure 10.1 presents the Hierarchy of Needs.

Maslow characterized the first four basic needs as **deficiency needs** or **D-needs,** the satisfaction of which allow the person to avoid physical sickness and psychological maladjustment (Goble, 1970; Maslow, 1968). Citing evidence from research, Maslow concluded that an individual's food preferences are a fairly clear indication of actual physiological needs or deficiencies of the body (Young, 1941, 1948). If the body is lacking a particular biochemical substance, the individual will attempt to satisfy the deficiency by developing a hunger for the missing nutritional element. D-needs meet the following criteria: (1) people yearn to gratify D-needs; (2) deprivation sickens or stunts people; (3) gratification cures deficiency illnesses; (4) steady supplies prevent illnesses; and (5) healthy people do not show deficiencies. Impoverished people tend to experience D-needs continually.

Although self-actualization emergence awaits the prior satisfaction of lower-order needs, meeting these needs only sets the stage for self-actualization. Self-actualizing people enjoy sufficient gratification of their basic needs, and they show freedom from illness. More importantly, they show positive use of their capacities and display motivations linked to personal values. Further, self-actualization is different from lower-order needs. It is a *growth need,* not a D-need.

Needs lower in the hierarchy are *prepotent,* more urgently demanding than higher-order needs. They occur earlier in the developmental process and require gratification prior to higher-order needs. Safety is a "stronger, more pressing, earlier appearing, more vital need" than belongingness, and the need for food is prepotent to both (Maslow, 1959,

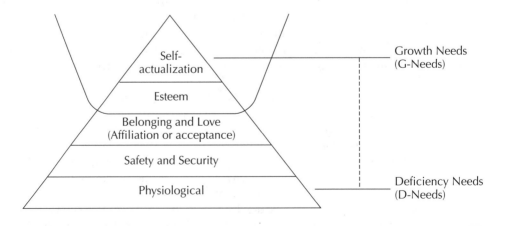

FIGURE 10.1 *Maslow's Hierarchy of Needs*

p. 123). However, complete fulfillment of lower needs is not a prerequisite for addressing higher needs. Well before complete satisfaction of a lower need, people begin to pursue the next highest need on the hierarchy. New needs emerge gradually as lower needs are satisfied. If belongingness/love needs are poorly satisfied, esteem needs may not be visible at all. However, with moderate love satisfaction, the esteem need may arise to some degree.

There are, of course, apparent contradictions to the order of needs appearing in the hierarchy. India's Mohandas Gandhi was willing to deny his own safety and physiological needs for self-actualization and higher-order values, including personal dignity, social equality, and political freedom. However, just as people do not realize complete satisfaction of lower-order needs and then *suddenly* experience the next highest need in full bloom, they cannot *suddenly* deny lower-order needs while continuing to pursue high-order needs. Gandhi was able to gradually deny lower order needs as he focused on higher-order needs. Had he been abruptly placed in a Nazi concentration camp and *suddenly* reduced to an animalistic level via torture, starvation, and exhaustion, he might have been scratching for food and clinging to survival like other inmates (Allen, 2001). Abruptly take away the satisfaction of basic physiological needs and most people would slide down Maslow's hierarchy. The comfortable and secure can choose not to eat, sleep, or even breathe. People precipitously reduced to a basic survival level are usually compelled to eat if they can.

In the most typical reversal of needs, the relatively higher-order need self-esteem is pursued before belongingness and love. People who tread this path develop a vacuous sense of esteem based on the misguided belief that powerful, respected, and feared people will be loved. It is also possible to experience permanent loss of a need, as in the case of an antisocial (psychopathic) individual whose cravings for love during infancy were never met (Allen, 2001). By adulthood, the desire and ability to give and receive affection have been lost. A sensitive period in this person's development was probably bypassed, similar to animals who lose their sucking or pecking reflexes when these are not exercised soon after birth. Circumstances may cause some people to not progress beyond the first two levels. For example, someone who has experienced chronic poverty or unemployment may continue to seek only minimal satisfactions in life, such as obtaining just adequate food or shelter. Because homeless people may not get beyond the first two levels, they may not experience the motivation to form relations with others (belongingness) and to "take pride in themselves" (esteem).

Human Nature Is Born, Not Made

Although environmental factors such as culture, family, and parents may function as sun, food, and water to human actualization, they are not its seed. For Maslow (1970), human nature is inborn, not made. It has an essential, built-in structure comprised of potentialities and values that are intrinsic to all members of the species. Maslow considers all human needs and values *instinctoid,* or instinct-like, because of their biological, genetic, and universal characteristics. Thus, all basic and higher-order needs are, "in the strictest sense," biological needs (Maslow, 1969a, p. 734). Maslow used the term *instinctoid* because the term *instinct* is fraught with problems. Instinct, when applied to humans, has traditionally placed them on the same plane with lower animals. Although his career was launched by animal research and he sometimes drew analogies to animal-study results, Maslow rejected the assumed strict continuity of humans and other creatures. In Maslow's thinking, *sexual,* when applied to human beings, was analogous to but not the same thing as *sexual* in other beings. Further, the idea of instincts seems to imply that we are born only with lower-order needs. From this perspective, higher-order needs, such as love, are developed after birth by associative learning. For example, while the infant is being fed, the mother "expresses love." Thus, according to the associative account, love gains its power and, in fact, its very existence as a motivating force, through its association with feeding. Maslow rejected this account, asserting instead that the prior satisfaction of physiological, safety, and belongingness/love before esteem and self-actualization is a precondition for the emergence of higher needs, not evidence that they depend on lower-order needs.

Self-Actualizing Persons: "Superior Personalities"

Maslow did not believe that all choices or choosers are equal. Consider an analogy to animal choosers. Chickens allowed to select their own diet showed great individual differences in ability to choose beneficial foods (Young, 1941, 1948). Some were "good choosers" and some were "bad choosers." Good choosers became stronger, larger, and more dominant than bad choosers, allowing them to get the best of everything. Later, when diets selected by good choosers were forced on bad choosers, the latter did get stronger, bigger, healthier, and more dominant, although they never reached the level of good choosers. Thus, organisms who were good choosers could select what was good for the bad choosers better than the bad choosers actually chose for themselves.

Maslow believed that human choosers operate similarly. He attempted to understand the values embedded in human nature by observing the cream of the human crop. "Only the choices and tastes and judgments of healthy human beings will tell us much about what is good for the [entire] human species in the long run" (Maslow, 1959, p. 121). Maslow studied the "best" of human personalities, defined as those he viewed as being the most psychologically healthy, mature, highly evolved, and fully human. He designated a few of these superior persons *self-actualizers,* people who fulfill themselves by making complete use of their potentialities, capacities, and talents, who do the best they are capable of doing, and who develop themselves to the most complete stature possible for them. Self-actualizers live Nietzsche's exhortation, "Become what thou art!"

A list of likely self-actualizers would include Abraham Lincoln, Thomas Jefferson, Sojourner Truth, Albert Einstein, Eleanor Roosevelt, Harriet Tubman, Cesar Chavez, Albert Schweitzer, Jane Addams, Frederick Douglass, Kahlil Gibran, Paul Robeson, Sitting Bull, Susan B. Anthony, Adlai Stevenson, Mildred "Babe" Didrikson, Martin Luther King, Jr., Malcolm X, Gandhi, and Mother Teresa. Reflecting his belief that self-actualizers are as rare as these famous figures, Maslow's (1970) initial screening of 3,000 students yielded only one actualizer, partly because typical students are too young to have had the experiences necessary for a good approximation to self-actualization. Some common characteristics of self-actualizers are summarized in Table 10.1.

Superior psychological health, a step in the direction of self-actualization, applied to less than 1 percent of college students, those Maslow saw as "growing well." Thus, full-

TABLE 10.1 *Characteristics of Self-Actualizing Persons*

Clear, efficient perceptions of reality and comfortable relations with it

Acceptance of self, others, and nature

Spontaneity, simplicity, and naturalness

Problem centering (having something outside themselves they "must" do as a mission)

Detachment and need for privacy

A forceful will and relative independence from environment

Continued freshness of appreciation

Mystic experience, peak experience

Gemeinschaftsgefuhl, feeling of kinship and identification with the human race (the same German word used by Adler and later translated as *social interest*)

Personal relations with others (deep but limited in number)

Democratic character structure

Ethical discrimination between means and ends, between good and evil

Philosophical, unhostile sense of humor

Creativeness

Transcendence of any particular culture, resisting cultural molding

Imperfections: sometimes thoughtless, socially impolite, cold, boring, irritating, stubborn, ruthless, forgetful, humorless, silly, angered, superficially prideful, naively kind, anxious, guilty, and conflicted (without maladjustment)

blown self-actualizers are extremely rare. Maslow declared that only a tiny fraction of the general population met his criteria for self-actualization. Further, being self-actualized is not all good. Self-actualizers tend to be self-centered, self-absorbed people (bottom of Table 10.1). Box 10.2 highlights a self-actualized person.

BOX 10.2 • *A Self-Actualized Person I Have Known*

That he is an older person may partly explain his status as "self-actualized." People tend to broaden and increase in depth as they grow older. Because he has fully appreciated his meaningful experiences, he is steeped in wisdom. He cares about the substantive, not the trivial. While he is courteous, he is not terribly concerned about what other people think of him. Instead, he cares about what he thinks of himself. Not surprisingly, he speaks with passion about issues dear to him, whether his audience is ordinary citizens or powerful people.

Though he possesses and cherishes an ethnic identity, he is not bound by his culture. He identifies himself with humans everywhere. Literally, he is a citizen of the world. He has lived all over the United States and in several other countries. Each of his days begins by communing with nature. A new natural scene leaves him awestruck. He is one with whatever shares his space, be it a garden or other people. His presence calms, warms, instructs, and lingers after he is gone. He has become who he is.

Needs and Values beyond the Pale, and Experiences from the Mountain Top

Accompanying self-actualization are certain special needs. These include **cognitive needs,** motivations to know, to understand, to explain, and to satisfy curiosity, and a variety of **aesthetic needs** related to beauty, structure, and symmetry. Such needs have been identified collectively by Maslow (1967) as **meta-needs** or **growth needs (G-needs),** terms used "to describe the motivations of self-actualizing people" (Maslow, 1970, p. 134). All of these meta-needs are closely enmeshed with the overriding need for self-actualization and are not, in the strictest sense, "motivated" but meta or beyond motivation. **B-values,** ultimate or end-goals of meta-need fulfillment, are more likely to be possessed by self-actualizers than by others (Maslow, 1967). They include truth, goodness, beauty, unity, wholeness, transcendence, aliveness, uniqueness, justice, order, simplicity, richness, effortlessness, playfulness, self-sufficiency, and meaningfulness.

Maslow also believed that self-actualizers are more likely than others to have **peak experiences,** intense, mystical experiences associated with simultaneous feelings of limitless horizons, powerfulness, and helplessness, a lost sense of time and place, and great ecstasy, wonder, and awe (Maslow, 1970). These experiences are highly personally important and strengthen or transform people. They come from love and sex, bursts of creativity, moments of insight and discovery, and times of fusion with nature. Peak experiences are natural phenomena, not supernatural, and were described by William James long ago (1958).

Evaluation

Contributions

Maslow's contributions are many and diverse. The emphasis here is on his beliefs that human values and needs are inherent and that humans are self-directing, his insightful criticisms of psychological science, his speculations about a psychological Utopia, and his contributions to diverse fields and disciplines.

Humans Have Inherent Needs and Values and Are Self-Directing.   Maslow (1959, 1967, 1969) insisted that needs are as much a part of the human constitution as voice boxes and symbolic thought. He placed emphasis on (1) the existence of universal human needs and values, and (2) their biological origin. Like Rogers, Maslow believed that "the organism is more trustworthy, more self-protecting, self-directing, and self-governing than it is usually given credit for" (1970, p. 78). Also like Rogers, he believed strongly in a universal, inborn *organismic valuing process,* or "bodily wisdom": recall the chicken study. He also observed psychologists' increased confidence in "the internal wisdom of our babies" (Maslow, 1959, pp. 120–121). Infants can make good choices with regard to diet, time of weaning, amount of sleep, time of toilet training, need for activity, and so on. This point of view contrasts with that of B. F. Skinner, who emphasized environmental control over infant behavior.

Insightful Criticisms of Psychological Science.   While one can draw useful analogies between humans and animals, their essential natures differ. Clinicians rely too heavily on samples of maladjusted people, thereby offering a warped view of human nature based on observations of disturbed and miserable lives. Others ignore individual differences by adopting a statistical-averaging procedure in which findings from all subjects/clients are thrown into a single hopper. This technique mixes information from healthy and sick people equally, resulting in a concoction that is neither vintage champagne nor cheap wine.

Psychological Utopia: Eupsychia.   Maslow (1970) firmly believed that self-actualization could be promoted by the presence of good people who would be part of a good environment. It would (1) offer the individual all necessary raw materials needed for creative and spiritual endeavors, as well as basic need fulfillment; (2) allow the individual to pursue her or his own wishes, demands, and choices; (3) accept delays and abandonment of choices; (4) respect the wishes, demands, and choices of individuals; and (5) "get out of the way" whenever appropriate.

To make the criteria for the ideal environment more concrete, Maslow speculated about a future **Eupsychia** (yew-sigh-key-ah), a utopian society characterized by psychological health among all its members. Its philosophical base would be anarchistic, meaning there would be no governmental imposition on individual liberty. Basic and meta-needs would be respected, much more than usual. There would be more free choice as well as less control, violence, and contempt. It also would be Taoistic in its philosophy, valuing what is simple, loving, and unselfish. Overall, the good environment would stress spiritual and psychological forces as well as material and economic ones. Eupsychia would not work for all, however. "When we speak of free *choice* in human beings, we refer to sound adults or children who are not yet twisted and distorted" (Maslow, 1970, p. 278). You may find it interesting to compare Maslow's conceptions of the Utopian society with those of B. F. Skinner.

Contributions to Many Fields and Concerns.   Maslow's hierarchy has been especially useful to people concerned with personnel management, marketing, and organizational operations (Alderfer, 1989; Buttle, 1989). In organizational settings, relations among employees within and between management levels will not be smooth and efficient unless each employee recognizes the need satisfactions being sought by other employees. Only with such understanding will employees be able to facilitate one another's need satisfactions and integrate the pursuit of satisfactions with company goals. Creativity will be locked out of the executive boardroom unless high-level management personnel are encouraged and aided in attempts to approximate self-actualization. Finally, the marketing of products will be less than optimally effective if the needs that products address are not considered when decisions about product "packaging" are made. Maslow's book, *Eupsychian Management* (1965), is in large part devoted to these issues. Maslow's hierarchy also has been useful in speech-language pathologist training (Houle, 1990). Prior to a conference between a pathologist and his or her advisor, one of Maslow's needs was selected to be a conference focus.

Blind and sighted athletes were compared on responses to Shostrom's Personality Orientation Inventory (POI) measure of self-actualization (Sherrill et al., 1990; Shostrom,

1966). An example similar to a POI item is "select one: (a) I enjoy my life" or "(b) I do not enjoy my life." Blind and sighted athletes were identical in self-actualization profiles, except that blind athletes scored lower on Existentiality and Self-acceptance. Athletes as a group scored lower than the general population on two major POI scales: Time Competency and Inner-Directedness. However, they were average or strong in Self-Actualizing Value, Feeling Reactivity, Spontaneity, Self-Regard, and Acceptance of Aggression.

Supporting Evidence

Self-Actualization.   Maslow credits a follower of Gestalt tradition, Kurt Goldstein (1939), with originating the concept "self-actualization." Goldstein saw "the drive of self-actualization" as the only uniquely human motive (Maslow, 1954). Although Maslow's position was broader than Goldstein's, they both believed that organisms strive toward growth and utilization of available resources.

Shostrom (1966) cited a study on POI self-actualization scores of clients who received 27 months of therapy. The therapy group was significantly higher on self-actualization than a beginning-therapy control group. More recently, Kasser and Ryan (1996) found an inverse relationship between self-actualization and the need for social prestige: the lower the importance of aspirations for financial success, an appealing appearance, and social recognition, the higher was self-actualization.

Hierarchy of Needs.   Graham and Balloun (1973) first had participants freely describe the most important aspects of their lives and, second, rate their present *degree of satisfaction* at the physiological, security, social (acceptance by others), and self-actualization levels. Graduate students rated the descriptions as to *desire expressed for satisfaction* of the four needs. Results supported the hypothesis that there would be greater satisfaction of lower-order needs than higher-order needs. Analysis of the relationship between the first and second measures confirmed the hypothesis that the *degree of satisfaction* of any given need would be negatively correlated with *desire for satisfaction* of that need: the less the satisfaction, the more the desire for satisfaction.

Williams and Page (1989) developed measures relevant to the safety, belonging, and esteem levels of the hierarchy. For each of these levels they assessed: (1) need gratification (perceptions of the degree to which a need is being gratified); (2) need importance; (3) need salience (the degree to which a need is "on one's mind and demands one's attention"); and (4) self-concept (as related to a given need level; for example, one could have a positive or negative self-concept regarding how much others are seen as caring for oneself). Generally, the student subjects were functioning at the esteem level. Evidence supporting this conclusion included: (1) "importance" scores were highest for esteem needs and self-concept was most in tune with that level; (2) the needs at the two lower levels were rated as important, but not particularly "on the mind" (salient); and (3) need gratification was high for all levels, but, of the three under investigation, it was lowest for esteem. One of the other confirmed predictions was that the higher the safety-need gratification, the lower the safety self-concept, because, having met safety needs, the individual would be pursuing needs at higher levels. Fourteen of 16 total predictions were confirmed.

As you will see, a number of psychologists have failed to support Maslow's hierarchy of needs. To address some of these negative outcomes, Wicker, Brown, Wiehe, Hagan, and Reed (1993) examined failures to support the hierarchy and found that non-supporting research often measured "importance" of need satisfaction. These studies frequently found that lower-order needs were not less important than higher-order needs being currently addressed, an apparent contradiction of hierarchy assumptions. But Wicker and colleagues suspected that "importance" was ambiguous. For example, imagine a person who finds creative gardening very "important." On a hot and humid day, while working in her garden, a point of discomfort is reached at which she stops gardening and flees to her air-conditioned house. Gardening still reigns supreme in "importance," but another need has become more pressing. "Importance" may be a poor measure, because it confounds the value of a need with its pressing nature. Wicker and colleagues felt "intention" ("I intend to get out of this heat") would provide a better measure of needs' pressing nature. In fact, when they used both an "importance" and an "intention" measure, only the intention measure confirmed hierarchy assumptions: the more subjects felt they had attained satisfaction of a need, the less they intended to address the need. Another study by Wicker, Wiehe, Hagan, and Brown (1994) found more support for the hierarchy using "intention" and another measure rather than "importance." Wicker and Wiehe (1999) had one group of college students write an essay about successfully being close to another person and had another group write about lack of success at the same pursuit. Consistent with Maslow's theory, only the first group reported strong attainment of esteem goals. They felt they had satisfied belongingness and love needs and could successfully pursue esteem.

The hierarchy of needs continues to be useful. For example, it has been used to help children of the world who have suffered calamities (e.g., natural disasters, violence, and abuse) to get in touch with their basic needs (Harper, Harper, & Still, 2003).

Peak Experiences.   Research findings have contributed some support to Maslow's concept of "peak experience." Ravizza (1977) interviewed 20 athletes in 12 different sports who reported expanded views of themselves as fully functioning individuals. Their "greatest moment" in sports showed many similarities to Maslow's description of the peak experience: loss of fear (100 percent of sample), full attention or immersion (95 percent), perfect experience (95 percent), god-like feeling of control (95 percent), self-validation (95 percent), universe as integrated and unified (90 percent), and effortlessness (90 percent). Nevertheless, some aspects of Maslow's description were not met: the athletes' experiences were more narrow in focus than broad, more oriented to the body than to cognitive or spiritual reflection, and more germane to immediate circumstances than to bringing about major changes in their lives. Thus, athletes' "greatest moments" were only partially equivalent to Maslow's peak experiences.

After Mathes, Zevon, Roter, and Joerger (1982) reviewed the research literature on peak experiences, they developed a 70-item scale to measure peak experience tendencies, the Peak Scale. An "empirical picture" of individuals reporting peak experiences that was consistent with Maslow's theorizing emerged after five studies using the scale. Individuals who scored high on the Peak Scale evidenced cognitive experiences of a transcendent and mystical nature, as well as feelings of intense happiness. High scorers reported living in terms of B-values such as truth, beauty, and justice. Women, but not men, tended to show slightly higher self-actualization scores on the POI compared with people who did not report peak experiences.

Some Proposed Changes in the Hierarchy.   Rowan (1999) suggested that deficiency motivation could occur at any level of the hierarchy, even at the self-actualization level. Further, the opposite of deficiency motivation, abundance motivation, could occur at any level, even at the physiological level. For example, a deficiency motive at the self-actualization level would be "searching for peak experiences out of boredom" and an abundance motive at the physiological level would be "eating for aesthetic pleasure" (p. 131). While this is an interesting point of view, it deviates too much from Maslow's theory: to Maslow, deficiency motivation is, by definition, confined to the lower levels of the hierarchy. Also, abundance motives seem out of place at the lower levels.

A proposal by Kiel (1999) is also intriguing. I have often wondered why the broadest, most complex motivation is represented by the tiny apex of the triangle. Kiel has similar concerns. She suggests that the triangle might be recast as a pedestal with a bowl at the top encompassing esteem and self-actualization (see the previously unexplained bowl in Figure 10.1). "In this new 'open triangle' model, the boundlessness of self-actualization is evident" (p. 168). Alternatively, one could turn the triangle upside down, balanced on its apex with the top-to-bottom order of needs the same as before ("physiological" needs are at the apex). Either way, the endless process of developing higher needs would be better depicted.

Limitations

Criticisms of Maslow's work are most frequently lodged against self-actualization, followed by the hierarchy of needs and "peak experiences." Maslow has been charged with arbitrariness, dismissal of culture, and failure to consider alternatives. In addition, research relating to his ideas has generated contradictions.

Self-actualization.   When Maslow supported self-actualization by observing "superpersonalities," he used a small arbitrarily-selected sample that was neither objectively observed nor systematically assessed. "Self-actualizers" were selected by Maslow himself based on reviews of a variety of materials never made public. Selectees reflected obvious bias toward Western culture. While he recognized some of these shortcomings (1959), other commentators have emphasized the shaky nature of his methods for identifying self-actualizers and the traits they supposedly possess.

Phillips, Watkins, and Noll (1974) compared a measure of Maslow's "self-actualization" with a measure of existentialist Viktor Frankl's "self-realization": the POI (self-actualization; Shostrom, 1966) and the Purpose in Life Test (PIL) (self-realization; Crumbaugh & Maholick, 1969). Although the "self-actualization" and "self-realization" measures should have been closely and uniformly related, which would have validated both, they were related in some ways and not in others. Tosi and Hoffman (1972) could only validate the POI as an index of the specific concept "healthy personality," not of the general concept "self-actualization."

Mittelman (1991) reviewed several articles that criticized Maslow's theory and its hallmark concept "self-actualization." He concluded that "self-actualization" can be rescued only if it is reduced to "openness," defined as being open to information, including that provided by the environment and by other people. The remainder of self-actualization he deemed difficult to defend. Heylighen (1992) found "self-actualization" inherently ambiguous. In his opinion, Maslow was not consistent in his treatment of the concept. For example, the self-actualization expressed in Maslow's theory is not the same as that manifested by his super-personalities. Consistent with this observation, the theory does not predict that self-actualizers would turn out to be somewhat self-centered. To save the day for Maslow, Heylighen redefined *self-actualization* as "perceived competence to satisfy basic needs in due time." Heylighen and Mittelman show that self-actualization is a rather nebulous concept that must be clarified if it is to be useful.

More than any other criticism of Maslow's central concept, the most damning has to be the charge that his conception of "self-actualization" is neither universal nor the "best" rendition of "human fulfillment." Ajit K. Das (1989), in a paper entitled "Beyond Self-Actualization," suggested that other notions of "fulfillment" exist in non-Western societies and may, in some respects, be more attractive than "self-actualization." In contrast to self-actualization, Das offers "self-realization," extracted primarily from Buddhism. Compared to self-actualization, self-realization is a more active process. It does not just happen after lower needs are satisfied, with the only given being that one is free to develop potentialities; one must actively work at self-realization. Further, the self-absorption that characterizes self-actualization is relatively de-emphasized in the case of self-realization in favor of concern for others. Box 10.3 contains some information about self-realization that, when compared with Table 10.1, will allow you to see the difference between it and self-actualization. Then you can draw your own conclusions about which is "best."

Buddha

Transcending Culture.   Maslow apparently believed that being more identified with people everywhere—a citizen of the world—is a good thing, and, indeed, it can be. But if rising above one's culture means abandoning it in favor of a broader identity, he made a serious mistake. A great part of "who one is" is the culture in which one was reared. People abandon their cultures at their own peril. If one is reared African American, for example, she or he will be seen as African American by others, some of whom may be less than fair and impartial. Not identifying with one's culture means not being prepared for this kind of reception, which can be disastrous. So, when some White-looking African Americans passed as White they alienated themselves from their families and, in a real sense, lost their souls (Davis, 1991). *Passing* was rather common only from the end of the Civil War until the end of World War II. It faded because the personal costs were too much and because of the Black Pride movement led by Marcus Garvey during the 1920s. To deny one's culture is to deny oneself.

BOX 10.3 • *Diversity: An Asian Religion's Alternative to Self-Actualization*

In Buddhism, the way to Nirvana, the ultimate state characterized by obliviousness to care, pain, and external reality, is to first grasp the Four Noble Truths and then follow the Eightfold Path (see Das, 1989).

The Four Noble Truths

1. Dissatisfaction and suffering are inherent in the lives of humans.
2. Dissatisfaction and disappointment arise from people's desires and cravings. Most people are not able to accept life as it is. Instead they deny that craving creates tension and attempt to prolong pleasant experiences even as they try to shorten unpleasant experiences.
3. Suffering is abolished only by eliminating cravings. One need not deny all desires, but only the most demanding desires that dominate one's life.
4. The way to eliminate craving and dissatisfaction is to follow the Noble Eightfold Path.

The Eightfold Path
(broken down into three categories of behaviors)

1. Adhere to moral conduct—right speech, right action, right livelihood—which requires that no act harmful to self or others be committed and that one actively help others. The mind must also be kept free of evil thoughts.
2. Maintain mental discipline—right effort, right alertness, and right concentrations—which requires control of one's mind. After a rigorous period of training, one will be able to control one's thoughts and feelings and also empty one's mind of all contents so that perfect tranquility can be achieved.
3. Develop intuitive wisdom—right understanding and right purpose—which requires correct understanding of the Four Noble Truths, and the tendency to abide by them.

Peak Experiences.   Many of Maslow's concepts are difficult or impossible to translate. "Truth," "joy," and "beauty" are examples. "Peak experiences" provide another illustration. Different researchers and theorists have used the phrase differently, lending a flavor of arbitrariness to it (Mathes, Zevon, Roter, & Joerger, 1982). Also, there are contradictions regarding it. Peak experiences are assumed to be the province of high "self-actualizers" who are supposedly very rare people. Yet, while Sherrill and colleagues (1990) found that athletes tended to be relatively low on self-actualization, Ravizza (1977) found that athletes are prone to having peak experiences, albeit limited ones. Further, peak experiences may not be so unique and natural. Rather, anyone may obtain them through artificial means such as the drug LSD (Leiby, 1997). After a late-in-life, near-fatal heart attack, Maslow developed a new version of peak experiences (Heitzmann, 2003). A *plateau experience* is perceiving the extraordinary in the ordinary. It is more voluntary and durable than a peak experience, but less dramatic. Thus, Maslow himself felt that "peak experience" needed qualification.

The Hierarchy.   Alderfer (1989) saw enough deficiencies in the hierarchy that are relevant to business and industry to warrant replacing it with his own. With obvious disapproval, Buttle (1989) indicated that Maslow's hierarchy "is reified, if not deified, in the marketing literature" (p. 201). He went on to declare that "Maslow never explained why he selected the five basic needs, why they were ranked as they were, or why others were not included" (p. 202). Buttle concluded his criticism of the hierarchy by suggesting alternative conceptions of needs for use in marketing.

Neher (1991) goes a step farther, criticizing the hierarchy in general, not just its specific applications. Among his complaints is that Maslow stubbornly downplayed influences of culture, which he saw as only creating some variation in the *methods* by which needs are fulfilled. Maslow even saw culture as opposing organismic need fulfillment. How could a culture survive if it opposed the fulfillment of physiologically based needs? Neher goes on to imply that the hierarchy itself, rather than just the methods of need satisfaction, would have to be different for different cultures. For example, cultural norms peculiar to a society, such as those governing child rearing, would have to exert strong influence on which needs have priority.

Neher also notes that Maslow viewed self-actualization as somehow different from the other needs in that only lower-order needs are quelled by satisfactions. How can self-actualization be a "need" if it acts differently from the other needs in being the only one not quelled by satisfactions? Neher points out, that, in fact, *any* need may be stimulated rather than quelled by satisfactions (a boost in self-esteem whets the appetite for more inflation of self-esteem; the more security you have the more you want).

Unlike Maslow, some students in my personality classes do not see placing esteem before belongingness and love as an aberration. They find it hard to understand how a person can obtain love and acceptance from others if she or he does not first develop self-love and self-acceptance. "Others will not like you until you like yourself." Further, some students wonder whether belongingness and love aren't separate needs. Aren't the feelings that come with belonging to a peer group different from the emotions that accompany "being in love"?

Conclusions

Many of the criticisms lodged against Maslow's work seem less telling in view of research evidence produced relatively recently. Witness the validating work by Wicker and colleagues (1993, 1994) and Williams and Page (1989). The allegation that he relied on arbitrarily obtained "simple observations and descriptions" in conceiving of self-actualization will grow irrelevant if scientific evidence increasingly supports his assumptions about the concept. The growth in the application of his hierarchy to various professional areas may some day obliterate the charge that the needs are not universal and are misapplied to some areas.

Maslow considered his most important educational experiences to be those that taught him what kind of a person he was: psychoanalysis, his marriage to Bertha, and the "thunderclap" of having a child. World War II also had a dramatic impact on him, making him want "to prove that human beings are capable of something grander than war and prejudice and hatred" (quoted in Hall, 1968, p. 54). He advised his two daughters, "Learn to hate meanness." Thus, Maslow became a caring and wise person, if not the warm and relatively untroubled individual that was Carl Rogers.

Maslow's unique approach to understanding human experience was to find "the best" humankind has to offer—that fraction of the population who display genuine self-actualization, peak experiences, understanding, and creativity. Having discovered "the best," he used them to show us how to become better than we are. Although these superior personalities tell us much, none can better inform us about how to be than the example set by Maslow himself.

Maslow was not listed on the journal citation list, but was number 14 on the text citation list, number 19 in the survey, and number 10 overall (Haggbloom et al., 2002).

Summary Points

1. Abraham Maslow was the first of seven children born in 1908 to a neglectful father and a cruel mother. During childhood, Maslow's first love were the books of the Brooklyn Library, access to which was perilous due to neighboring anti-Semitic gangs. After undistinguished performance in high school, Maslow enrolled in City College, law school, Cornell, and finally the University of Wisconsin. There he became a "monkey psychologist."

2. Maslow used a research position under Edward L. Thorndike as a return ticket to New York City where he fell under the influence of Adler, existentialism, and the Gestalt psychologists. Armed with Gestalt holism, Maslow turned his attention to motivation, the process by which people are propelled toward goals. These goals can be cast as "needs" for certain satisfactions that are sought by all humans, regardless of culture, environment, or generation.

3. While needs are universal, methods of satisfying them can be culturally or environmentally determined. Maslow believed that needs are formed into a hierarchy, with more primitive, lower-order needs demanding satisfaction before more complex and uniquely human needs are addressed. Physiological (D) needs demand satisfaction first; second, safety needs; third, belongingness and love needs; and fourth, esteem needs.

4. "Self-actualization" is "the tendency for [one] to become actualized in what [one] is potentially." D-needs are prepotent: stronger and demanding prior satisfaction before other needs can be addressed. Needs are not met in all-or-none fashion, but higher-order needs cannot be met until lower-order needs are largely satisfied. In exceptional cases, people may deny lower-order needs and still pursue higher-order needs, as Gandhi did.

5. Human nature is inborn, not made. Thus, even self-actualization needs are instinctoid, because of their biological, genetic, and universal characteristics. The rare self-actualizers show the rest of us what is good for us. They are people who fulfill themselves by making complete use of their potentialities. Although self-actualizers possess such positive traits as spontaneity, autonomy, ethicality, and creativity, they may also be thoughtless, prideful, and socially impolite.

6. Self-actualizers have their own sources of motivation, B-values. They also have peak experiences: intense, mystical feelings of powerfulness and helplessness. Maslow believed that humans have universal, positive needs and values and are self-directing. In fact, organisms, if left to their own devices, can do well choosing what is best for them. His optimistic view of people led him to propose Eupsychia. This proposal assumes that environments can be contrived that will foster the satisfaction of higher-order needs.

7. Maslow's ideas have been applied to business and speech pathology. Researchers have found that blind athletes, and athletes in general, show a unique pattern of responses to the POI. Shostrom confirmed that people who would be expected to make a better approximation to self-actualization scored higher on POI dimensions than others. Kasser and Ryan found self-actualization negatively related to need for social prestige. Graham and Balloun reported that individuals display greater satisfaction of lower- than of higher-order needs.

8. Williams and Page demonstrated that self-concept is most in tune with the level of the hierarchy at which a person is currently operating. Wicker and colleagues showed that failures to support the hierarchy are reversed if intention rather than importance is investigated, and that people primed by essay writing to "belong" turned to esteem needs. While there is some evidence for peak experiences, they may be realized only partially, and people not expected to have such experiences report them.

9. Rowan argued that deficiency and abundance motivations occur at all levels of the hierarchy. Kiel supports a broadening of the top of the hierarchy. The needs hierarchy has been replaced in some fields and Maslow's failure to explain its origins has been noted. Self-actualization deficiencies include Maslow's arbitrary selection of self-actualizers to study, their selfishness, the nonuniversality of self-actualization, and the rival notion, self-realization. Transcending culture can mean abandoning one's culture, a perilous act.

10. Mittelman and Heylighen have redefined self-actualization. Neher claims that the hierarchy is different for different cultures and self-actualization is too different from other needs. Students have suggested that esteem belongs before belongingness and love. They also wonder whether belongingness and love are separate needs. Nevertheless, research may erase many of the criticisms of self-actualization and the hierarchy. Maslow was an exemplary human being, despite a troubled upbringing.

Running Comparison

Theorists	*Maslow in Comparison*
Adler	He also was a father's boy. Adler's concepts of social interest, striving for superiority, and creative power of the individual probably influenced him.
Horney	He also felt unattractive. Her "basic anxiety" is like his safety needs.
George Kelly	His first experience with psychology also was not positive.
Henry A. Murray	He also believed behavior is a function of many needs and the satisfaction of any need may be tied to the satisfaction of others.
Sullivan	He also believed needs may be satisfied through interpersonal relations.

Essay/Critical Thinking Questions _____

1. How about a hierarchy of feelings, of rewards? Construct your own psychological hierarchy.

2. Does Maslow have the needs in the right order? Write a brief argument for another order.

3. Argue that lower-order needs are as worthy.

4. Show how two products appeal to a different hierarchical need.

5. Can you describe peak experiences you have had?

E-mail Interaction _____

Write the author at b-allen@wiu.edu. Forward one of the following or phrase your own.

1. Do you really believe Maslow was an abused child, or was he just paranoid?

2. Which is better, a self-actualizer or a self-realizer?

3. Tell me how I can raise my self-esteem to a high level and keep it there.

Marching to a Different Drummer: George Kelly

George Kelly
http://ship.edu/%7Ecgboeree/
kelly.html

- Are the principles of science applicable to life's problems?
- Can you imagine you are a child again, relating to your mother?
- Who is the happiest person in your life?

One of the issues running through most previous (and subsequent) chapters has been whether the "inside" or the "outside" of people is stressed by theorists. As you will see, the behaviorists generally look only outside. As you already know, the psychoanalysts are rather exclusively concerned with the inside. Other theorists, covered in later chapters, consider both perspectives. This chapter focuses on a theory of personality that emphasizes an internal aspect, cognition. It introduces an important figure in yet another break with Freud, a break as profound as the rift created by the humanists. George Kelly was in the vanguard of the "cognitive" revolution.

Kelly, the Person

George Kelly, born in a small Kansas town (1905), was the maverick son of a preacher. A rugged individualist, quite literally of pioneer stock, he was skeptical concerning psychological principles from day one of his first psychology class. Sitting in the back row of the introductory psychology classroom, Kelly tilted his chair against the wall and waited for something interesting (Kelly, 1969). After two to three weeks he had only one clear impression, his professor seemed nice. Then one day he was inspired to sit up and take notice. A capital "S" and a capital "R" were prominently displayed on the blackboard, connected by an arrow pointing from the former to the latter. Here, thought Kelly, is the meat of the matter. Unfortunately, further lectures only disappointed him. Many years later he wrote of the experience (1969, p. 47):

> Although I listened intently for several sessions, after that the most I could make of it was that the 'S' was what you had to have in order to account for the 'R' and the 'R' was put there so the 'S' would have something to account for. I never did find out what that arrow stood for—not to this day—and I have pretty well given up trying to figure it out.

And he pretty well gave up on psychology for the time being, choosing instead to pursue a career in engineering. Three years later he was out of engineering and back in school, forced by the Great Depression to learn something more practical. Being interested in sociology and labor relations, he thought it high time to have a look at Freud. "I don't remember which one of Freud's books I was trying to read," wrote Kelly (1969, p. 47), "but I do remember the mounting feeling of incredulity that anyone could write such nonsense, much less publish it." Skepticism, ironically, may explain why he eventually became a psychologist. Kelly needed to practice his superb gift for healthy skepticism and psychology provided the perfect forum: it appears all psychological principles can be questioned.

Skepticism was sometimes accompanied by sarcasm. When prompted to consider Russian physiologist I. P. Pavlov's famous conditioning research (dogs salivating to a bell), he spoke with tongue not so deeply buried in cheek: "Salivation . . . takes place in a manner that suggests the anticipation of food, or perhaps hunger—I am not sure which. . . . Whatever it indicates, Pavlov seems to have demonstrated it and there is no reason we should not be grateful even though we are not quite sure what it was he demonstrated" (Kelly, 1980, p. 29). When inspired to cite examples of people who fail to benefit from experience, he recalled a naval officer with "a vast and versatile ignorance," and a school administrator who "had one year of experience—repeated thirteen times" (Kelly, 1963, p. 171). He even took a verbal swing at all of his colleagues. In observing that his fundamental assumptions apply to everyone, he wrote, "The same goes for psychologists, who are known to have human characteristics too" (p. 25).

Sometimes, however, he was more motivated to generate laughter than to engage in mild ridicule. In making the point that people orient to the future, not the past, he described a peculiar approach to driving: "A friend of mine, . . . driving her car, . . . customarily closes her eyes when she gets caught in a tight spot. This is an anticipatory act; she suspects something may happen that she would prefer not to see. So far, it hasn't happened, though it is hard to understand why" (Kelly, 1980, p. 26).

If sarcasm was a characteristic of Kelly, it certainly was overridden by a more central feature of his personality, warmth. He practiced therapy to help people and to learn from them. In 30 years as a psychotherapist, he never collected a penny for his services.

In the summer of 1965, Kelly's associates at Ohio State gathered to salute their colleague and friend who had just been granted an endowed chair at Brandeis University. Papers were read by three of Kelly's former doctoral students and by a visiting professor from England, who had spread Kelly's ideas through several of Britain's universities. At the end of these presentations, Kelly rose to invite the entire assembly to his house for dinner. Nearly 100 accepted the gracious offer.

Above all, Kelly was open-minded. Perhaps this aspect of his personality stemmed from his extreme versatility, which is clearly reflected in his own words (Kelly, 1969, p. 48):

> I had taught soap-box oratory in a labor college for labor organizers, government in an . . . institute for prospective citizens, public speaking for the American Bankers Association, and dramatics in a junior college . . . I had taken a Master's degree with a study of workers' use of leisure time, and an advanced professional degree in education at the University of Edinburgh, and . . . I had dabbled . . . in education, sociology, economics, labor relations, biometrics, speech pathology, and cultural anthropology, and had majored in psychology . . . for a grand total of nine months.

Kelly's training in psychology yielded a Ph.D. from Iowa State University in 1931. While his early career was spent at Fort Hays State College in Kansas, Ohio State University claimed him for more years than any other academic institution. His extraordinary versatility led Kelly to a dozen or so universities, each for an appreciable period of time, and around the globe for the purpose of applying his theory to the problems of the world. Little wonder that he embraced the assumption, adopted by many philosophers of science and dismissed out of hand by few, that in the realm of science there are no truths (Hempel and Oppenheim, 1960). In psychology, as in other sciences, there are theories that are supported by evidence to varying degrees, but no truth. For a personality theorist, this was an unusual assumption, but then Kelly was an unusual theorist.

Unfortunately, Kelly died in his early 60s (1967), having produced relatively few writings. Fortunately, he has had such a strong impact on his students that his writings, as well as numerous speeches, lectures, and conversations, have been thoroughly mined. The psychological "gold" from several posthumous articles edited or written by his students contributed greatly to this chapter.

Kelly's View of the Person

As you recall, Freud thought of humans as helpless particles blown about by the hidden winds of hedonic impulse. Jung viewed humans from a broader perspective, but one might argue that he regarded them as captives of their ancestral past. Adler, Sullivan, Fromm, and Horney saw people as the products of their social environments. By contrast, Rogers and Maslow assumed that humans are capable of determining their own fates. True to character, Kelly did not even approximate the orientation of any other theorists. Rather, he declared that people are governed by an internal process: the way they construe events in their worlds. While internal, this process results from consequences of an external factor—social relations (Kelly, 1955). Kelly also thought that people had free will, in that they could choose from many alternative ways to conceive of people, most of which emerged from their relations with others. Further, Kelly's conception of time was different from that of theorists covered so far, except possibly Adler. While he did not neglect the distant past, the recent past, or the present, he declared humans to be basically future-oriented, determined largely by their predictions of future events (Kelly, 1980).

It is interesting to speculate about how Kelly came to adopt such an intellectual, pragmatic, and "hard-nosed" point of view. He was an engineer and a person made practical by the Great Depression. It was natural for him to orient to thinking rather than other psychological modes such as feelings and behavior. As a victim of the Depression, little wonder that he looked more to the future than to the dismal present. As one who kept changing not only location, but also himself, he paid little attention to the past.

Perhaps Kelly's most important departure from the precepts of traditional psychologists was that he saw himself as no different from those he studied and attempted to help in therapy (Kelly, 1969; for more about the inconsistency between researchers' views of themselves and of the people they study, see Allen, 1973, and Allen & Smith, 1980). Most psychologists, he charged, viewed themselves as objective, rational scientists who ascertain the causes of people's actions and suggest corrections for maladaptive behavior. On the other hand, their clients in therapy and their research subjects are seen as incapable of objective observation, unable to sort out the causes of their behavior, and inept at developing a systematic program for positive behavioral change. By contrast, Kelly saw himself as a scientist in his roles as research psychologist, psychotherapist, and just plain person. Further, he viewed clients, research subjects, and people in general as scientists. Thus, he saw no difference between himself and others. To understand how all of us operate daily like scientists, consider Kelly's recollection of how he discovered "people as scientists" (Kelly, 1969, pp. 60–61):

> A typical afternoon might find me talking to a graduate student at one o'clock, doing all those familiar things that thesis directors have to do: encouraging the student to pinpoint the issues, to observe, to become intimate with the problem, to form hypotheses . . . to make some preliminary test runs, to relate his data to his predictions, to control his experiments so that he will know what led to what, to generalize cautiously, and to revise his thinking in the light of experience. At two o'clock I might have an appointment with a client. During this interview I would . . . be . . . helping the distressed person work out some solutions to his life's problems. So what would I do? Why, I would try to get him to pinpoint the issues, to observe, to become intimate with the problem, to form hypotheses, to make test runs, to relate outcomes to anticipations, to control his ventures so that he will know what led to what, to generalize cautiously, and to revise his dogma in the light of experience. At three o'clock I would see [the] student again. Likely as not he was either dragging his feet, hoping to design some world-shaking experiment before looking at his first subject to see firsthand what he was dealing with, or plunging into some massive ill-considered data-chasing expedition. So I would try to get him to . . . [do] . . . all the things that I had [tried to get him] to do at one o'clock. At four o'clock another client! Guess what! He would be dragging his feet, hoping to design a completely new personality before venturing his first change in behavior, or plunging into some ill-considered acting-out escapade, etc., etc.

Students doing research, their advisors, clients in psychotherapy, their psychotherapists, and "people on the street" behave like scientists daily. Sometimes they do well at it and sometimes badly, but they do it everyday (Hermans, Kempen, & van Loon, 1992).

Basic Concepts: Kelly

Personality as a System of Constructs

Underlying all of Kelly's thinking are the cognitive structures known as **constructs,** ways of construing events or "seeing the world" so that the future is anticipated (Fransella, 2003; Kelly, 1980). Thus, his theory was called "Personal Construct Theory" (PCT). The individual's **personality** consists of an organized system of constructs that may be ranked as to importance. "Construct" became the foundation on which Kelly built his most basic theoretical framework or *postulate,* a basic assumption that is the starting point for a theory. It is a broad statement that is just accepted; it cannot be directly tested. Kelly's **fundamental postulate** is the assumption that a person's psychological processes are routed through various channels, or pathways, by the ways in which she or he anticipates events (Kelly, 2003; Kelly, 1963). In a sense, ways of "seeing the world" form the channels that are directed toward the future. The person is *pulled* along through life by predictions, as opposed to being *pushed* by unconscious impulses and drives or pricked into action by stimuli in the environment.

To set the stage for Kelly's other theoretical concepts, it is helpful to build on the notion of constructs by looking at how two individuals, Jim and Joan, go about an afternoon in their lives. As you read, pay special attention to the words in italics.

Jim's Problem. "What's wrong now?" Joan inquired as she approached a figure who was slumped against the wall outside a classroom. Jim's reply was inaudible, partly because his hands covered his face and partly because he was too depressed to speak up. Undeterred by the lack of a response, Joan continued, "Let me guess . . . It's Professor Martinson again."

Jim's head sprang upright. Though his hair cascaded over his eyes, it failed to hide the fierce look distorting his face. "Damn it," he was nearly screaming. "I've tried everything. I give up."

Joan looked around self-consciously, hoping that, somehow, students passing them in the hall had not noticed the outburst. Then she eased down next to her friend and softly entreated, "Tell me about it."

"It's the same thing . . . same old thing," he muttered.

Joan leaned back against the wall and exclaimed with a sigh, "Ok then, tell me about your latest clash with Martinson."

"He hates me, I'm sure of it. The jerk said we could turn our papers in late, if we had a good excuse. Well, I had a good excuse . . . it was spring break . . . I was stuck in Florida . . . we were in somebody else's car. I mean, how could I get home?"

Joan's chin drew back and down. A familiar frown curled her lips. Martinson had looked much the same when Jim had first related the "stuck in Florida" story. It was that incredulous look.

Jim's Constructs. "See there, see there," rasped Jim. "You're no different. I thought I could expect some sympathy from you . . . you're supposed to be a *good friend,* someone with a little *intelligence.* Go away . . . just get lost."

Joan moved closer and slipped her arm around Jim's shoulders, but he elbowed her away. "Jim, you know you can *trust* me . . . I am your *good friend,* but gimme a break. I know you believe that your excuse is OK . . . let me just put it this way . . . try it on some other people; I'll bet you that you'll get the same reaction."

There was silence for a minute, then Joan continued. "Look, let me make a suggestion. Why don't you . . . "

"That's not all," Jim broke in. This time he was shouting. Joan was looking for a place to hide. "He laughed at me! . . . said he was just kidding about the excuse. 'I don't take excuses. The other students know that . . . it was just my way of making a joke' . . . Does he ever think I'm *stupid*! He probably thinks he couldn't *trust* me farther than he could throw me. And I thought *educated* people were my kind of people. Well, you live and learn."

Joan's Suggestions for Change. "That's what you said the last time you had it out with him." Joan could sense the taste of foot-in-the mouth the minute she uttered the words. Jim climbed to his feet. He'd had enough of her, but before he could get away, Joan grabbed his shirt sleeve and dragged him back down. "Look, I'm sorry," she pleaded, "but it's just that sometimes it seems like you don't learn anything from *experience.* I mean you just stick with an old idea, no matter what. Why is it so important that Martinson like you? I don't care whether he likes me or not."

After a time Jim settled down and he began to chatter amiably with his friend, which was usual for them. They talked about Jim's relationship with Martinson. "OK, you win," asserted Joan. "So you have some kind of fixation for Martinson—father figure is what my psych teacher would say—OK, I accept that. Now let me give you a suggestion . . . try this out. I mean you have had plenty of time to *evaluate* him. You think he's one of the '*good guys,*' right?" Jim shook his head in a vigorous "no" sign, but Joan ignored him. "What you have to do is let him know you think he belongs in select company. I mean, as I see it, you expect him to think you're a '*good guy,*' but you won't put him in that same category. I know how you are. Surely you can understand that people like those who like them—it's sort of a law—but they can't read your mind. You have to communicate your feelings to people. If I know you, you've been very stiff and formal with Martinson. Am I right?"

Jim's head was hanging down, "Yeah," he mumbled, "you do know me."

"Actually, what it amounts to," Joan was talking rapidly now, "you think he's a '*good guy,*' you *admire* him and you want him to *admire* you. I know, because, if I like someone, I want that somebody to throw a little *admiration* my way."

"*Admire?*" Jim was puzzled. "*Trust* maybe, but *admire?* I don't resort to hero worship."

"Well you had better consider *admiration.* If you like someone, *admiration* is a way to communicate it without saying it . . . I mean, without using words . . . the sound of your voice will do."

"All right," said Jim, almost in a whisper, "I'll try it."

Joan's Constructs. Now Jim hopped up and offered Joan a hand. They left the building and strolled along leisurely toward their dorms. Silence prevailed for a while, then Jim casually remarked, "You know, sometimes I wonder who I am. Who am I anyway?" he was smiling as he posed the question.

"Good ole Jim, that's who you are," came the reply. "A little weird, but fun to be around."

He hugged her playfully. "OK, who are you, smarty?"

"Is that a serious question?"

"Yeah?" he queried. "Who are you?"

"Well, I don't stay up at night thinking about it, but I guess I'd answer in terms of who I'm *like* . . . you know, similar to."

"And who is that?" said Jim in a sober voice adopted to match her own suddenly serious tone.

"I guess I'm an *athlete* at heart," mused Joan, a member of the varsity track team. "Serena Williams, that's who I'm like . . . or uh . . . who I'd like to be."

"Tough break," kidded Jim. "You don't have her killer instinct."

Joan went along with the teasing and added, "Nor do I have the ability . . . but who knows, maybe I'll get better and maybe track will be as big as tennis some day."

They reached the crossing that split the paths to their dorms and paused for a moment. "Big bash at the Gin Mill this Saturday, need a ride?"

"No thanks," responded Joan as she backed down the path to her dorm. "I'm going home . . . back to God's country . . . down on the farm . . . with the good *neighbors* and the wide open spaces . . . "

"And the horse manure," interjected Jim in a loud voice, as they were now many yards apart.

She lobbed a rock at him. "You can have your stinking old city, full of dopers and muggers. You love it . . . I'm going back where everything is small and people are concerned . . . "

Jim's and Joan's Personalities.   It is instructive to analyze Jim's and Joan's conversation from Kelly's point of view. A look at Figure 11.1 will allow you to examine some concrete examples of constructs (Kelly disliked the concrete, but could not avoid it). The left part of the figure displays Jim's **construction system:** an organization of many constructs with the more important, and often more abstract, at the top and the less important constructs at the bottom. The constructs at the top are called **superordinate** while the ones at the bottom are called **subordinate.** Joan's system is on the right.

The Construction System Is the Individual's Personality.   Jim's most superordinate construct is represented by "trust–distrust," while Joan's most superordinate construct is "evaluative–descriptive." To evaluate is to pass judgment on, to describe is to label someone or something. A construct can be thought of as a special kind of concept (Kelly, 1963). Constructs have two opposite poles, like an automobile battery. The **emergent pole** is the primary and principle end, like *good* in good–bad and *intelligent* in intelligent–stupid (Kelly, 1955). The **implicit pole** is the contrasting end, like *uneducated* in educated–uneducated and *not admired* in admired–not admired. Normally, the emergent pole is formed first, but, as soon as it develops, the implicit pole usually comes into

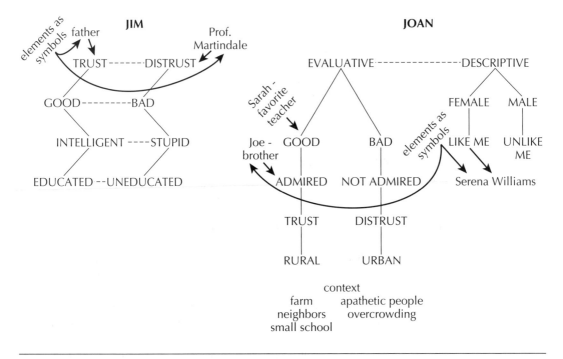

FIGURE 11.1 *Joan's and Jim's Construction Systems*

existence. Like Jung, Kelly believed people see the world in terms of opposites. These contrasts exist even if a person adopts a construct such as tolerant–intolerant and is unaware of the implicit pole or it has not been expressed. Adopting *tolerant* usually brings *intolerant* with it.

Scrutinizing Jim's construction system reveals that he is highly dependent on the construct "trust–distrust," his most superordinate construct. Like other constructs, it has what Kelly called a **range of convenience,** the extent and breadth of the event-category to which a construct applies. For example, trust–distrust is applicable to events involving people, such as the episodes of Jim's conflict with Professor Martinson. Because it is reasonable to assume that Jim experiences many events involving many different people, trust–distrust may be said to have a wide range of convenience. Nevertheless, it has its limits. Trust–distrust is scarcely applicable to solving mathematical problems or to viewing architecture. A superordinate construct's range of convenience may be thought of as including its subordinate constructs. By contrast, a construct's **range of focus** refers to the events to which it is most readily applied. Trust–distrust is most applicable to relations with friends and family, rather than to relations with casual acquaintances.

Jim's construct, trust–distrust, also can be characterized as relatively **impermeable,** a reference to certain constructs that tend not to change in terms of range of convenience or place in the construction system. In fact, Joan noted that Jim's constructs are impermeable in general. Trust–distrust is also part of Joan's system, but it is much more subordinate. Thus, the construction systems of Jim and Joan display **commonality,** a reference to the sharing of constructs by two or more people whose experiences are similar (Kelly, 2003). Jim and Joan are both students, thus, as you might expect, Figure 11.1 reveals that they do share constructs.

In contrast, **individuality** refers to differences among construction systems both in terms of the constructs comprising the system and in terms of how the constructs are organized. Such differences are due to differences in experiences. Joan is an athlete, Jim is not. Jim's problem, as Joan pointed out, is that he, unlike her, has failed to profit from **experience,** what one learns from the events of the past. Jim continues to try the same old strategies with Professor Martinson, and they are not getting him what he wants, mutual trust. Thus, Joan suggests a change in Jim's construction system. She thinks that Jim should embrace a new construct, "admire–not admire," and reorganize his construction system to be more like hers, with "trust–distrust" subordinated to "admire–not admire." Joan is trying to save Jim from **anxiety,** what a person experiences when his or her construction system does not apply to critical events, as Jim's fails to apply to events in his relationship with Professor Martinson. Joan should be cautious. In suggesting a new construct, she may subject her friend to **fear,** the experience one has when a new construct appears to be entering the system, and may become dominant. On the other hand, she need not worry too much about subjecting Jim to **threat,** the realization of the possibility that one's entire construction system will be overhauled. Joan is suggesting a new construct and some reorganization, not a major upheaval.

Joan as Scientific Psychotherapist. Joan the psychotherapist acts like a scientist in attempting to make a better scientist of Jim. She pleads with him to make his constructs more permeable. More importantly, she suggests a hypothesis for Jim to test. She feels that expressing admiration will allow Jim to obtain the mutual trust that he wants to exist in his relationship with Professor Martinson. To test the hypothesis, Jim is told to try admiration out on Martinson. He then can observe to see how it works. If admiration has the intended effect, he should **replicate,** repeat a test in the hope the results will be the same as before. Replication provides the basis for anticipating future events. If one can repeat an observation of the successful application of a construct, one can be confident that the construct will apply again in the future, under similar circumstances. The greater the number of replications, the greater the confidence. In fact, replication is the best evidence science can provide.

If Jim carries out Joan's suggestions, he would confirm one of Kelly's most basic principles, **constructive alternativism,** the assumption that a person's present interpretations of her or his life situation are subject to revision and replacement (Kelly, 1963). It is assumed that a construction system cannot remain the same, but must change with changes in the person's life.

Relations among Constructs

Figure 11.1 reveals that Jim's and Joan's construction systems are organized differently. Jim's system is organized by **extension of the cleavage line,** a reference to the observation that the poles of Jim's subordinate constructs fall directly under the corresponding emergent and implicit poles of his superordinate constructs. Thus, "good" falls under "trust," "bad" under "distrust" (Kelly, 1963). However, Joan's system begins at the top by **abstracting across the cleavage line**—whole constructs fall under superordinate emergent and under superordinate implicit poles. In Joan's case, all of her constructs fall under her most superordinate construct, "evaluative–descriptive." The whole construct "good–bad" falls under the emergent pole, "evaluative," while the whole construct, "female–male" falls under the implicit pole, "descriptive." This feature of Joan's system makes it more complex and flexible than Jim's. She can approach her life situations from an evaluative stance (there are good people and bad people) or from a purely descriptive stance (there are North Americans and Africans).

Elements are objects, beings, or events. The **context** of a construct is composed of all those elements to which the construct applies. The context of Joan's construct, "urban–rural," includes the elements farm, neighbors, apathetic people, and overcrowding. Whereas "range of convenience" and "focus of convenience" refer to rather gross and abstract event categories such as "relations with authority figures" and "leisure activities," context and elements refer to the actual, concrete people or objects that exist in a person's life.

A **symbol** is one of the elements to which a construct applies that illustrates the construct. Figure 11.1 indicates that, for Jim, "father" symbolizes the trust–distrust construct. For Joan, "Serena Williams" symbolizes the construct, like me–unlike me. Of course, the picture of Jim and Joan as indicated in their conversation and in Figure 11.1 is oversimplified. Kelly probably would argue that no one's personality could be neatly represented in a figure. For one thing, the figure would have to be as large as a house, and, for another, many constructs are too abstract to be represented as concretely as in Figure 11.1. Also, people normally do not blurt out their constructs as cooperatively as did Joan and Jim. As you will see, more sophisticated methods for getting at constructs are needed. Kelly's views are contrasted to those of other theorists in Box 11.1.

Personality Development

How did Jim and Joan acquire their construction systems (develop their personalities)? Kelly's comments about the transition from childhood to adulthood supplemented his theory nicely.

Predictability

Because "anticipation of future events" is a cornerstone of Kelly's PCT, it is not surprising that "forecasting the future" has a prominent place in his discussion of construct development in children. **Predictability** refers to the ability to predict the future. A construct is as useful as the degree of predictability it provides (Hermans et al., 1992). Thus, parents, the major components of every child's environment, are well advised to provide predictability. If they fail to do so, their child's need for anticipation of the future may be reflected in some rather extreme behavior (Kelly, 1955). For example, if "predictability" is a scarce commodity in certain children's lives, they may cling to instances of it, even if their resultant behavior has negative consequences. As an illustration, assume that a child,

BOX 11.1 • *Similarities of Kelly's Ideas to Those of Other Theorists*

Kelly's theory in relation to other theories warrants special attention because it did not closely resemble any of them, but shares assumptions with some of them. While Kelly chastised the behaviorists for their alleged obsession with minutia, such as "Ss and Rs," he did share a broad assumption with B. F. Skinner, who advocated the arrangement of environments to maximize rewards. Analogously, Kelly held that constructs could be changed by human intervention.

Similar to Albert Bandura and other social learning theorists, Kelly was future oriented: "...everything [people do] follows lines laid down in [their] effort[s] to anticipate what will happen.... [People] never wait to see what will happen; [they] look to see what will happen (Kelly, 1980, pp. 26–27).

Kelly wrote, "The phenomenological psychologists, of whom I certainly am not one, usually take the view that it is only the experience of the passing instant that is...essential..." (Kelly, 1980, p. 22). But he shared some assumptions with the humanists and phenomenologists (Benesch & Page, 1989). In fact, his position has been viewed as essentially phenomenological (Tyler, 1994).

Like Rogers (and Jung), Kelly did not believe that one and only one set of procedures is effective in therapy: "Unlike most personality theories, the psychology of personal constructs does not limit itself to any pet psychotherapeutic technique" (Kelly, 1980, p. 35). Like Rogers (and Jung), Kelly also held that therapy is an *experience* in which both therapist and client participate and contribute as partners: "Psychotherapy [is] an experience.... Psychotherapy takes place when one person makes constructive use of another.... The professional skills of the therapist, as well as much of his repertory as an experienced human being, are brought into the transaction" (p. 21). Further, like Rogers, Kelly thought of therapy as an opportunity to become one's own self, relatively free of the constraints imposed by society and other people: "Psychotherap[y's goal], ... is not to conform to oneself ... or to society ... [The] objective is for man continually to determine for himself what is worth the price he is going to end up paying ... to keep moving toward what he is not ... (Kelly, 1980, p. 20).

As with Skinner and Rogers, creativity was one of Kelly's concerns: "The creativity cycle we envision is one that employs both loosening and tightening in a coordinated fashion. The cycle starts with a loosened phase in which construction is vague, elastic, and wavering. Out of this fertile chaos shapes begin to emerge and one seeks patiently to give them definite form until they are tight enough to talk about and to test" (Kelly, 1980, p. 34).

Johnny, has parents who treat him in a consistent manner only with regard to a few issues, all involving punishment. Johnny cleans his room; sometimes it is noticed, sometimes not. Johnny helps fold clothes and sometimes he is praised. However, Johnny has noticed that, should he stop up the bathroom sink while playing "laundry," the consequent overflow brings a highly reliable reaction from his parents. They apply the palm of a hand to his bottom. So, a naive behaviorist might assert that Johnny will avoid stopping up the sink. Not so, according to Kelly. Stopping up the sink is the best way to acquire the precious predictability that Johnny so badly needs.

Dalton and Dunnett (1992) considered Kelly's construct types that relate to predictability. **Tight constructs** yield unvarying predictability while **loose constructs** yield varying predictability (Kelly, 1955). Dunnett and Dalton indicate that tight construers are "organized rigidly, full of regular habits, and fast held views of the world" (p. 56). In contrast, loose construers "seem to make different predictions at the drop of a hat. Other people find them difficult to predict . . . because their constructs do lead to varying predictions" (p. 56).

Dependency Constructs

Even given a reasonable amount of predictability in a child's social environment, early construction systems will still be characterized by impermeability of the few simple constructs that compose them. Children are small, weak, and vulnerable. They must depend on others for survival. Thus, the bulk of a child's early construction system is constituted by **dependency constructs,** special constructs that revolve around the child's survival needs. A "mother" construct would be an example. For a young child, the "mother" construct might have a context containing elements such as warmth, nourishment, and safety from frightening sounds. (Notice the similarity to Jung's mother archetype and mother complex and to Sullivan's conception of mother–child relations.)

At first the child might see the world in terms of "like mother–not like mother." The construct is very global and mother is seen in a very limited manner. The university classes she teaches and the Chamber of Commerce committees she chairs play no role in the child's conception of her. She is warmth, comfort, and food. However, with growth and development, the construct will become more permeable and she will be more than warmth and kindred elements. In time, the entire construct will likely disappear altogether and "mother" will become a symbol for some other construct or an element of several constructs. The general disposition to impermeability of constructs dissolves in the tide of ever increasing maturation.

Role Playing

The extent to which one can appreciate the construction system of another person is the extent to which one can adopt a role in a relationship with that other person (Kelly, 1963; Kelly, 2003). A **role** involves behaving in ways that meet the expectations of important other people in one's life.

In turn, such behavior provides the predictability that one requires. Thus, a six-year-old may assume that her role relative to her parents is that of the passive, compliant "seen but not heard" child. If she behaves in a passive, compliant, quiet manner, she predicts that she will be fed, cuddled, provided with toys, and so forth. At least during childhood, the hypothetical child's assumed role might work out fine, provided she correctly perceives that her predictions are confirmed.

However, assume that all does not go so well. Assume that her observations are faulty and she is seeing confirmation of her predictions that, in fact, does not exist. Eventually, she will have to stop deluding herself. Sooner or later she will have to face up to the fact that her parents do not really want a passive, compliant, quiet child. Perhaps in "reality" they expect her to play the role of the assertive, active, independent child. The outcome of such a revelation would be **guilt,** the result of the person's perception that he or she is being dislodged from some critical role, one that was thought to be very important in relating to important people (Kelly, 2003). In more common terms, guilt in this case comes from not measuring up, not being one's parents' child, not fitting the mold that important others have sculpted for oneself.

Choices: The C-P-C Cycle

Whenever individuals face significant or dramatic change in their life situations, whether it is a short-term variation or a long-term upheaval, they must search their systems of constructs for dimensions that will best accommodate the change. They must make an **elaborative choice,** a selection of an "alternative, aligned to one . . . construct dimension, which appears to provide the greater opportunity for the further elaboration of [one's] . . . system" (Kelly, 1980, p. 32). "At a certain stage in one's development it may be more promising to choose to do something that will help . . . define [one's] position more clearly and thus consolidate . . . gains. . . . But at other times one will choose to extend his [or her] system so it will embrace more of the unknown and bring more of the future within [one's] grasp" (p. 32).

No matter which of the two directions we take in confronting life changes, the process is the same. We go through the C-P-C choice cycle. First we construe. "To do this we go through a **circumspection phase,** a period of 'trying on for size' the various constructs available in our personal repertory" (Kelly, 1980, p. 32). To illustrate the process, suppose a person receives a promotion on short notice. Now, for the first time, she is boss to several employees and must decide how to relate to them. If she does not have many relevant constructs, this phase will not take long and she may look like "a person of action." If circumstances are changing too rapidly for her to keep up, she may race through this phase of the cycle and appear to be impulsive. Of course, she may take her time. In any case, she next moves to the **preemption phase,** a period during which "one construct is allowed to preempt the situation and define the pair of alternatives between which the person must make his [or her] choice" (Kelly, 1980, p. 33). Henceforth, unless she backtracks, she will stick with the construct that has surfaced. Suppose that construct is "authoritarian–egalitarian." Finally, commitment occurs, the principle of elaborative choice takes over, and she makes a **choice,** a decision between the alternatives provided by the construct that has preempted the situation (Kelly, 2003). She chooses to be authoritarian in her relations with her new subordinates. Thus, she completes the C-P-C cycle: circumspection, preemption, and choice.

Evaluation

Contributions: Supporting Evidence and Practical Applications

Poles.   A critical, testable aspect of Kelly's theory is the assumption that people cast their worlds in terms of opposites: each construct has two poles (Kelly, 2003). If that supposition proved false, the structure might tumble. Predictions of the future would fail if a construct, for example, was represented by "all people are good," rather than "some people are good" and "some people are bad." In fact, if each construct had only one pole, there would be nothing to predict: all people would be treated in an equally positive (or negative) manner. Life would be one certainty after another.

Accordingly, Kelly (1963) made special reference to some work by William H. Lyle, a former student. Lyle first selected numerous words that appeared to belong to four bipolar categories "cheerful–sad," "broad-minded–narrow-minded," "refined–vulgar," and "sincere–insincere" (eight class labels). A pilot sample of subjects then arranged the words into the eight different classes. In a main study subjects were given the same words and told to place them into the eight classes. Results revealed classifications exactly matching the four categories "cheerful–sad," "sincere–insincere," and so forth. Subjects tended to lump together "cheerful" with "sad" words and "sincere" with "insincere" words. In short, they classed or organized the words into sets of opposites, just as Kelly believed constructs are organized.

Extension of Kelly's Theory.   Benesch and Page (1989) investigated the circumstances under which individuals are able to appreciate the important constructs of other people. Subjects were recruited in triads, each consisting of three people who were close acquaintances. One triad member was designated the "target." The other two members, called "peers," reacted to the target in various ways that amounted to attempting to specify the target's constructs. Targets also indicated their own constructs. Results revealed good correspondence between targets' and peers' perceptions of targets' constructs. Peers tended to accurately perceive targets' constructs—they matched targets' self-perceived constructs—when those constructs reflected high meaningfulness and high stability (consistent use of constructs). Commonality among the contents of these friends' construction systems may have helped them appreciate each other's critical constructs. Results extend Kelly's theory by indicating the conditions under which individuals are able to "read" others' constructs.

Kelly's PCT was originally used as a way to conceptualize personality and as a basis for helping people in therapy, but is now employed to account for specific circumstances faced by a restricted category of people, for example, elderly people who have lost a spouse. Viney, Benjamin, and Preston (1989) found that elderly people who had suffered the loss of a spouse displayed *guilt:* they felt dislodged from important roles. As an illustration, a woman whose husband had died felt dislodged from roles that involved core constructs, wife and homemaker. Viney and colleagues suggested that elderly people who have lost spouses lack the means of validating their core constructs and need help in locating new sources of validation.

Cognitive Complexity.   One of Kelly's basic beliefs was that an effective construct system is well differentiated (Tyler, 1994). Probably inspired by this belief, former Kelly student James Bieri (1955) defined a new dimension, cognitive complexity–cognitive simplicity. A **cognitively complex** person has a construction system containing constructs that are clearly differentiated, that is, sharply distinguished one from the other. Complex people cast other people into many categories and thus see much variety in people. On the other hand, a **cognitively simple** person has a construction system for which distinctions among constructs are blurred—a poorly differentiated system. They cast other people into a few categories. Hypothetically, an extremely cognitively simple person would use mainly one construct such as good–bad, lumping half of humanity into the "good" class and the other into the "bad" class. Bieri showed that cognitively simple people have difficulty differentiating themselves from others (they tend to assume that others are like themselves). In contrast, complex people draw sharp distinctions between themselves and others.

Kelly (1955) believed that the more constructs one uses the better she or he will be at predicting future events, including the behavior of others. Bieri confirmed this assumption: complex subjects were better at predicting the behavior of others. If people use mainly one construct, say "good–bad," they are likely to put themselves in the "good" class. Given little information about other people—which was the case in Bieri's experiment—they predict that others are good, like themselves. Complex people use many constructs, some for application to themselves and some for application to the many other people in their lives. Table 11.1 summarizes the characteristics of cognitively complex and simple people.

In early studies, Signell (1966) reported that children tend to increase in cognitive complexity during the period 9 to 16 years of age, and Sechrest and Jackson (1961) found that social intelligence—an index of social effectiveness—was strongly related to cognitive complexity. In a more recent study Linville (1982) reported that: (1) students who were more simple in their representations of older males were extreme in their evaluation of older males; (2) individuals who were induced to adopt a simple orientation toward food used in a study of taste gave more extreme evaluations than did those induced to adopt a more complex orientation; (3) young males gave older males more extreme evaluations than they gave to members of their own age group; and (4) these young college students had more constructs available for use for describing their own age group than an older age group.

Complexity/simplicity sheds some light on nonverbal communication processes. Uhlemann, Lee, and Hasse (1989) developed a measure of subjects' sensitivity to nonverbal cues that were systematically displayed by a counselor performing on videotape. Subjects were categorized into four levels of cognitive complexity based on a test of complexity. They were also subjected to one of three levels of arousals: (1) low—they were alone while viewing the video; (2) moderate—others were present; and (3) high—the others present were supposedly "observers" who would evaluate the subjects. Because of higher social intelligence and greater sensitivity to the behaviors of other people, a complex person

TABLE 11.1   *Comparison of Cognitively Complex and Simple People*

Cognitively Complex Person	*Cognitively Simple Person*
Maintains a clear distinction among constructs	Distinction among constructs blurred
Casts others into many categories	Casts others into few categories
Can easily see differences between self and others	Has difficulty in seeing differences between self and others
Skilled at predicting behaviors of others	Inept at predicting behaviors of others

should be more able to decode nonverbal cues in ways that allow discrimination among people. Results showed the expected effects, but were qualified by level of arousal. When arousal was moderate or high, high-complex subjects were more discriminating among nonverbal behaviors than low-complex subjects, an advantage which would allow them to discriminate among people more effectively.

Interest in the observation that people are more complex in their construal of the "in-group" (their own group) than they are of the "out-group" (another group) has been growing. Bernadette Park and her colleagues, Carey Ryan and Charles Judd (1992), reported that subjects produced more constructs in describing the in-group compared to the out-group. Subjects also saw more subgroups within the in-group compared to the out-group.

Tetlock and his colleagues have shown, contrary to original assumptions, that it is not necessarily "better" to be complex than simple. Examining historical records of pre-Civil War politicians, Tetlock, Armor, and Peterson (1994) found that a category of politicians who showed partial tolerance for slavery were more complex than either extreme slavery supporters or abolitionists. Given that slavery is morally indefensible, even partial support of it by complex people is contrary to arguments for their moral superiority.

In a study with a similar theme, Tetlock, Peterson, and Berry (1993) looked at the personality profiles of business-administration master's degree candidates. Their results draw a complicated picture that does not readily fit the "complex is better" original portrait. Complex candidates' self-reports reflected high openness and creativity, but they were low on the valued trait "conscientious" and also low on the sometimes valued trait "social compliance." They were high on initiative and self-objectivity, but were also high on narcissism, antagonism, and power motivation. These results show that cognitive complexity is, well, complex.

Gruenfeld and Preston (2000) found support for two hypotheses in the research literature: (1) majority members of a group, because they control outcomes, are open-minded about alternatives, especially if they face a vocal minority; (2) cognitive complexity is especially strongly manifested in defense of the status quo, because change threatens to reduce complexity in complex people. They found that U.S. Supreme Court Justices showed greater complexity in defense of legal precedents (status quo) than when they overturned precedents by their opinions. However, this effect was strongest for authors of majority rather than minority opinions. These results seem to have strong generality. For example, imagine that an experimenter asks a group of subjects to devise a procedure for solving each of a series of problems that are all of the same kind (e.g., how to advertise several similar products). After a procedure has been devised, the experimenter asks the subjects to individually either come up with a better procedure or defend the original procedure. Subjects who choose to defend the old procedure should show greater cognitive complexity. Alternatively, subjects *assigned* to defend the old procedure may show more complexity than those *assigned* to devise a new procedure. Examples of cognitively complex and simplex people are presented in Box 11.2.

The REP Test. Among Kelly's most enduring contributions is the **Role Construct Repertory (REP) Test,** an assessment device designed to reveal an individual's construct system (personality). It also has been a helpful tool for use during therapy. As you will see,

BOX 11.2 • *An Interview with a Cognitively Simple and a Cognitively Complex Person*

An interviewer (iv) asks a cognitively simple (cg) and a cognitively complex person (cc), "What do you think about the people you work with?"

cg: "Oh, they all are pretty much the same."

cc: "They are quite varied; I like that."

iv: "Do you mean that they are different from you?"

cg: "Actually no, they seem pretty much like me."

cc: "Yeah, each is different from me."

iv: "So could you describe them for me?"

cg: " I guess so. They seem fairly nice."

cc: "You mean each one? That would take a while."

iv: "Just pick one to describe."

cg: "Sally is nice. So are Sue and Joe."

cc: "Well, unlike me, Joe talks a lot. He's the most friendly."

iv: "So in what other ways can you describe them?"

cg: "Hmmmm, that's hard. Let's see . . . they seem pretty considerate."

cc: "Some are thoughtful, some inconsiderate, some trustworthy, some not. . . . I could go on."

iv: "So, 'thoughtful' is different from 'considerate'?"

cg: "I'm not sure."

cc: "Definitely."

iv: "Can you describe them in other ways?"

cg: "Ah, . . . I don't think so. I've pretty much covered it."

cc: "Yeah, but do you have several hours?"

iv: "What do you think your coworkers are like when they are at home?"

cg: "Well I don't know . . . I guess they'd be about the same at home as at work."

cc: "Pardon me, but that is a dumb question. They could be anything at home."

iv: "Would you be surprised to learn that one of them writes computer games and another is an award-winning gardener?"

cg: "Wow, that is surprising. I don't do things like that. I can't believe they do those things."

cc: "No surprise to me. Like I said, they could be doing anything at home."

it is being even more broadly applied at present and promises to be applicable to an expanding variety of problems in the future.

The Rep Test and PCT in Business and Industry. In the place of Kelly's traditional titles, self, mother, father, etc., applied researchers have inserted a variety of labels that are relevant to various situations in business and industry (Jankowicz, 1987). For example, through the use of products' names in place of the usual role titles, researchers discovered the constructs applied by home testers to cosmetics and perfumes. They could then use the dimensions represented by the constructs, for example, poignant–bland, to rate the products. This method allowed the researchers to get at the heart of consumers' conception of the products, an achievement that might have eluded them had they tried to use dimensions *they* thought were relevant. In an analogous fashion, researchers discovered the beliefs, values, and items of knowledge used by senior managers so that this information could be used by new managerial employees to smooth the way into their novel positions of authority. Jankowicz, who works in the banking industry, has concentrated on identifying the "constructs the effective loan agent used and to examine whether they are different in kind and extent from the constructs used by less effective loan agents, effectiveness being defined objectively in terms of the relative size of loan defaults" (p. 485). Dalton and Dunnett (1992) outlined other business/industry REP applications.

The REP grid (see Figure 11.2) has often been used with people displaying a variety of psychological problems. Examples include response to psychotherapy by people who suffer from nervous tics (O'Connor, Gareau, & Bowers, 1993); differentiation between successful and unsuccessful psychotherapy clients (Catina & Tschuschke, 1993); assessment of "quality of life" among medication-therapy, anxiety disordered patients (Thunedborg, Allerup, Bech, & Joyce, 1993); detecting increases in construed similarity of self and others following psychotherapy (Winter, 1992); and identification of the disordered thinking that is characteristic of schizophrenia (Pierce, Sewell, & Cromwell, 1992). Other REP grid uses include measurement of construct change as a result of a teacher education workshop (Fischl & Hoz, 1993); indexing educational psychologists' competencies (McClatchey, 1994); and assessment of cognitive and social representations of body parts and by-products among potential organ donors (Oliviero, 1993). Complete your REP test profile using Box 11.3.

Fixed-Role Therapy. Though Kelly was not tied to a particular kind of therapy, he did develop a unique therapeutic method. In **fixed-role therapy** a client plays the role of an imaginary character who possesses certain constructs that are in contrast to his or her actual constructs (Kelly, 1955). The therapist uses the client's actual constructs as a basis for creating the construct(s) of the imaginary character. The process goes something like this: (1) the client describes himself in terms of central and troublesome constructs; (2) the therapist, in the simplest case, writes a fixed role for the imaginary character, requiring the client to assume a construct that demands very different behavior than is usual for him (his verbally aggressive tendencies to cut in when others are talking and to talk over them are replaced with an orientation to "biting the tongue" and "letting others speak their piece"); (3) the client tries the role, then he and the therapist discuss reactions of others to the new character; and (4) the client does not necessarily adopt the new role, but gains some insight into what it is like to be on the other side of the role he normally plays.

PCT and Diversity. Because of PCT's one-person-at-a-time, open-ended, flexible, and content-free nature, including its REP Test and fixed-role therapy, it has great potential for use in many and varied cultures and subcultures. Because it is a way of viewing the world, rather than an internal entity with specific content like "extrovert" (content: out-going, talkative, social), a construct is not restricted to any culture. People partaking of any culture can state their constructs. Contrast this open-ended, content-free essence with the nature of typical trait theories. A trait such as "assertiveness" may have no meaning in some non-Western cultures because there are minimal individual differences on it (in some cultures,

BOX 11.3 • *Your Own Construction System*

List A contains 15 role definitions. Read each carefully. In each blank, write the first name of the person who best fits that role in your life. It is essential to use the role definitions as given in List A. If you cannot remember the name of the person, put down a word or brief phrase that will bring the person to mind. Do not repeat any names; if some person has already been listed, simply make a second choice. Thus, next to the word *Self* write your own name. Then next to the word *Mother* put your mother's name (or the person who has played the part of a mother in your life), and so on, until all 15 roles have been designated with a specific individual.

List A: Definition of Roles for the Demonstration

1. *Self:* Yourself _____.
2. *Mother:* Your mother or the person who has played the part of a mother in your life. _____.
3. *Father:* Your father or the person who has played the part of a father in your life. _____.
4. *Brother:* Your brother who is nearest your own age, or, if you do not have a brother, a boy near your own age who has been most like a brother to you. _____.
5. *Sister:* Your sister who is nearest your own age, or, if you do not have a sister, a girl near your own age who has been most like a sister to you. _____.
6. *Spouse:* Your wife (or husband), or, if you are not married, your closest present girl (boy) friend. _____.
7. *Pal:* Your closest present friend of the same sex as yourself._____.
8. *Ex-Pal:* A person of the same sex as yourself whom you once thought was a close friend of yours but in whom you were badly disappointed later. _____.
9. *Rejecting Person:* A person with whom you have been associated, who, for some unexplained reason, appears to dislike you. _____.
10. *Pitied Person:* A person whom you would most like to help or for whom you feel most sorry. _____.
11. *Threatening Person:* The person who threatens you the most or the person who makes you feel the most uncomfortable. _____.
12. *Attractive Person:* A person who you have recently met who you would like to know better. _____.
13. *Accepted Teacher:* The teacher who influenced you most. _____.
14. *Rejected Teacher:* The teacher whose point of view you have found most objectionable. _____.
15. *Happy Person:* The happiest person who you know personally. _____.

Now look at the first row of the matrix in Figure 11.2 (on p. 264). Note that there are circles in the squares under Columns 9, 10, and 12. These circles designate the three people whom you are to consider in sort number 1. (Rejecting Person, Pitied Person, and Attractive Person). Think about these three people. In particular, how are *two of them alike* in some way that *differentiates them from the third person?* When you have decided the most important way that two of them are alike, but different from the third person, put an X in the two circles that correspond to the two persons who are alike. Do not write anything in the third circle; leave it blank. Next, write a word or short phrase in the column marked "Emergent Pole" that tells how the two people are alike. Then, in the column marked "Implicit Pole," write a word or short phrase that explains the way the third person is different from the other two. Finally, consider the remaining 12 persons and think about which of these, in addition to the ones you have already marked with an X, also have the characteristics you have designated under "Emergent Pole." Place an X in the square corresponding to the name of each of the other persons who has this characteristic. When you have finished this procedure for the first row, go to the second row (sort number 2). The process

(continued)

BOX 11.3 Continued

Sort Number	Self (1)	Mother (2)	Father (3)	Brother (4)	Sister (5)	Spouse (6)	Pal (7)	Ex-Pal (8)	Rejecting Person (9)	Pitied Person (10)	Threatening Person (11)	Attractive Person (12)	Accepted Teacher (13)	Rejected Teacher (14)	Happy Person (15)	EMERGENT POLE	IMPLICIT POLE
1								○	○		○						
2		○	○	○													
3				○									○	○			
4		○				○							○				
5	○								○		○						
6				○			○						○				
7			○				○				○						
8					○						○			○			
9							○	○				○					
10	○			○	○												
11		○	○								○						
12							○	○			○						
13	○						○	○									
14	○	○	○														
15				○					○				○				

FIGURE 11.2 *Your Construction System*

should be repeated until the procedure has been carried out for each of the rows. In summary, the steps to be followed for each row (sort) are:

1. Consider the three people who are designated by circles under their names. Decide how two of them are *alike* in some important way, and *different* from the third.
2. Put an X in the circles corresponding to the two people who are *alike;* leave the remaining circle blank.
3. In the "Emergent Pole" column, write a brief description of the way the two people are *alike.*

4. In the "Implicit Pole" column, write a brief description of the way the third person is *different* from the two who are alike.
5. In the same row, consider the remaining 12 persons, and place Xs in the squares corresponding to all those (if any) who can also be characterized by the description in the "Emergent Pole" column.
6. Repeat steps 1 through 5 for each row of the matrix. Now sit back and look at what you have done: you have written out your construction system.

most people are nonassertive; in other cultures, most are highly assertive). Likewise the REP test can be easily recast to fit any culture. For example, role-persons who have mostly Western relevance (attractive person) can be replaced by culturally relevant role-persons (pious person). In a similar fashion, the fixed-role therapy method can be adapted to different cultures. A fixed role written for the imaginary character could be peculiar to any culture. The only requirement is that a construct is assigned that demands very different behavior than what is usual for the assignee. Applications of PCT to many cultures would highlight both differences and similarities among cultures. It could, thereby, increase intercultural understanding.

Limitations

The Notion of Opposites.
Kelly's theory is based on the notion of opposites as manifested in constructs. The most obvious attack on this central idea is that some candidates for "construct" do not involve opposites. Either the opposite is missing altogether, or it is not a true opposite. For some candidates the only specifiable opposite to the emergent pole is the negation of that pole. For example, "admire–not admire" was purposely used in the Jim and Joan illustration. "Admire–not admire" would certainly qualify as a construct (so would just about any set of two words that are apparent opposites). However, the implicit pole is the negation of the emergent pole; it is not something, but the absence of something. One can admire a person, but not to admire a person is rather ambiguous. It implies no definite relationship or action. Similarly, scrutiny of a list of words that were all generated during the process of self-description (disclosure of constructs) reveals a large number of emergent poles the opposites of which are negations (Allen & Potkay, 1983a). For example, "awful" and "bizarre" seem to have no opposites except "not awful" and "not bizarre."

While, in some cases, implicit poles are merely negations of emergent poles, in others, they may be absent entirely. Kelly himself acknowledged that his clients sometimes could not articulate an implicit pole for a construct. He assumed that, in such cases, clients possessed a **submerged pole,** one that has either never been put into word form, perhaps because the construct is new, or is being suppressed (a client insists "all people are good" in order to escape the perception that people are bad and out to get him; Kelly, 1963). Maybe some people do submerge some implicit poles, or it may be that in some cases they did not express an implicit pole because none exists for them.

But what about Lyle's research support of Kelly's notion of opposites? Examination of the word list mentioned previously reveals that all of the eight labels for the eight classes of words used in Lyle's study have extreme favorability values. For each of the four sets of words, one member of the pair refers to a characteristic that is highly valued and desired by people in our society, while the other word refers to a highly undesirable characteristic (see Table 11.2). Also, all eight emergent poles have rather obvious opposites that are not just negations. One might wonder, do the emergent poles of real people's constructs all have such clear opposites? Do the constructs of real people have poles that are so extremely different in favorability? It seems intuitively obvious that some real people would have some constructs with no opposites to emergent poles and constructs with poles that are not extremely different in favorability.

TABLE 11.2 *Lyle's Word Categories and Associated Favorability Values**

Cheerful	475	Sad	213
Broad-minded	425	Narrow-minded	142
Refined	342	Vulgar	77
Sincere	504	Insincere	107
Average (mean)	437		135

*From Allen and Potkay (1983a); 600 is maximum favorable; zero is minimum favorable.

The Idiographic Approach and the Vagueness of Some Concepts.   One reason for some problems with Kelly's PCT is that each person's construct system is different from that of each other person. Researchers must resolve the paradox inherent in studying single individuals in order to make *generalizations* about construct systems that are *different* for different people. Also, like those of several other theorists, some of Kelly's concepts are too vague to verify empirically. Among these are some of Kelly's attempts to include emotionality in his theorizing: (1) threat that the system of constructs may be overhauled; (2) anxiety that the system does not apply to critical events; and (3) fear that new constructs may be dominating. Unfortunately, Beck (1988) investigated these concepts and found some results opposite of predictions. Further, the applications of the words "threat," "anxiety," and "fear" seem odd. Shouldn't "fear" be applied to the most damaging circumstance, which would appear to be that "the system of constructs may be overhauled"? One could just as well argue that "anxiety" might be best applied to "new constructs may be dominating" and "threat" might more profitably pertain to "the system does not apply to critical events." In short, the assignment of labels to concepts seems arbitrary.

Finally, "range of convenience" and "range of focus" are subject to confusion with "elements" and "context." When the latter were considered earlier, it seemed necessary to cast them as "concrete" and the former as "gross and "abstract." In fact, I contrived the concrete–abstract distinction because the two sets of concepts are difficult to tell apart. Kelly apparently did not regard the two sets of concepts as confusable and, thus, provided no method by which they can be clearly differentiated.

Shortcomings of the REP.   One of the REP test's virtues is also a major limitation. It involves an idiographic approach, one person at a time. Each REP outcome is unique to the person who produced it. A given person's constructs, as revealed by her or his REP responses, may not be meaningfully compared with those of other persons, much less generalized to all other people. Such is the case even in industry and business applications. The REP outcomes produced by successful loan officers cannot be readily generalized to other loan officers, whether successful or not. Just as a radiologist's method for reading an X-ray is unique to her or him, one's REP outcome is specific to oneself. In fact, the REP reflects the highly idiographic PCT from which it is drawn. Thus, it is alien to the most popular orientation in the United States: nomothetic—identifying universal characteristics and broad principles that can be generalized across all humans. Parity in popularity with other major theories will have to await a change in the major U.S. orientation. Kelly was not listed among the top 100 psychologists of the twentieth century (Haggbloom et al., 2002).

Conclusions

George Kelly is certainly one of psychology's most original thinkers. In fact, research support for his theory may not be optimally great, because it is so original researchers may not know how to approach it. Although some of his ideas resembled those of some other theorists, Kelly did not directly borrow from anybody. His theory is composed mainly of fresh, new ideas. Nothing resembling ids, archetypes, or needs exists in the theory. Little wonder that some U.S. psychologists have had trouble relating to PCT. In Britain it is a different story: his popularity is great. A new handbook on his theory should continue that popularity (Fransella, 2003).

Kelly is to be congratulated for emphasizing what others have ignored. He, more than any other psychologist, has made cognition the primary basis for the study of personality. Also, Kelly's "one subject or client at a time" approach is not lacking in merit just because it is not often embraced in the United States. My colleague, Charles Potkay, and I personally favor the idiographic approach (see Allen & Potkay, 1983a; Potkay & Allen, 1988). Humans are just too complicated and each is too unique to readily generalize from what one displays to most others (also see Allen, 1988a, 1988b). Finally, because Kelly has provided a cognitive basis for understanding personality at a time when the cognitive approach is burgeoning, many of his ideas are here to stay. Constructs, complexity–simplicity, the REP test, and many other contributions will likely guarantee Kelly a place in the psychological literature well into the next century.

Summary Points

1. George Kelly's background ranged from engineering to labor relations. He made a point of rejecting "stimulus–response" and Freudian psychology. He was a warm friend and mentor to colleagues and students. Thought processes were the key to understanding people and that people, as well as therapists and researchers, act like scientists in their daily pursuits.

2. Constructs are ways of construing events. Jim's and Joan's conversation illustrates two different construction systems, each having superordinate and subordinate constructs that have emergent and implicit poles. A construct's range of convenience is the extent of the event-category to which it applies and its range of focus is the events to which it most readily applies.

3. Some constructs are impermeable, while some are characterized by commonality and others by individuality. Anxiety occurs when a construction system does not apply to critical events, fear when a new construct enters a system and may be dominant, and threat when a system appears to be facing overhaul.

4. Joan recommended that Jim adopt "admired–not admired," try it out, and then try it again (replicate). Kelly believed in people's ability to change what controls them (Skinner), was future-oriented (Bandura), and was in agreement with the humanists on some issues. He was not an advocate of a particular therapy (Rogers and Jung), and he was interested in creativity (Skinner and Rogers).

5. Jim's construction system was organized by extension of the cleavage line. Joan's system reflected abstracting across the cleavage line. A construct's context is all the elements, objects, or events to which it applies. A symbol is an element to which a construct applies that serves as its name.

6. Children will do whatever is required to achieve predictability. Tight and loose constructs vary on the predictability they yield. Dependency constructs tend to dominate early systems, but eventually they give way to more permeable constructs. However, misreading others' expectations, leading to becoming dislodged from important roles, results in guilt. The C-P-C cycle is circumspection (trying on for size), preemption (a construct defines alternatives), and choice (decision between alternatives).

7. Friends are able to appreciate each others' critical constructs. PCT sheds light on the plight of elderly people who have lost a spouse. Only cognitively complex people have constructs that are clearly differentiated. Complexity increases with age and simple college males described older males in less complex terms and gave them more extreme evaluations. Complex subjects were more discriminating of nonverbal behavior when moderately or highly aroused.

8. People apply more constructs to the in-group and see more subgroups among in-group members. Being cognitively complex is not necessarily "good." U.S. Supreme Court Justices were more complex if their opinions defended the status quo. This result may have strong generality. In Kelly's popular REP test, individuals indicate the important people in their lives and pick two who are alike in some way and different from the third.

9. The REP procedure is useful in business and industry. Its grid has many applications beyond assessment of people's psychological problems. In fixed-role therapy, a client adopts the role of an imaginary person having a construct(s) that contrasts with the client's. Kelly's PCT is ripe for use in investigating similarities and differences among cultures.

10. Limitations of PCT include that some constructs have no real opposites to their emergent poles. Lyle's work in support of PCT suffers for nonrepresentativeness of the words he used. Some of Kelly's concepts have not been clearly verified by research. Some concepts may be inappropriately applied. Other concepts are confusable. Finally, the REP test suffers from being too "idiographic." Yet Kelly's novel ideas and idiographic approach are catching on, especially in Britain.

Running Comparison

Theorist	Kelly in Comparison
B. F. Skinner	Both believed that people could be changed, and both were interested in creativity.
Rogers	Kelly also held that individuals have choices and agreed that therapists should not limit themselves to traditional methods. Both were concerned with creativity and for both, clients were more like partners.

Maslow	"Becoming oneself" was a major goal in therapy for both.
Jung	They both cast psychological reality in terms of opposites.
Sullivan	Kelly's view of mother–child relations was similar to Sullivan's.

Essay/Critical Thinking Questions

1. Based on your completion of the REP test, draw your construction system (see Figure 11.1).
2. Indicate the constructs of a close friend or romantic partner.
3. Imagine that you suffered "threat" as Kelly defines it. How would you cope with it?
4. What dependency constructs characterized your childhood construction system?
5. What evidence can you provide to support the argument that you are a complex individual?

E-mail Interaction

Write the author at b-allen@wiu.edu. Forward one of the following or phrase your own.

1. How would I benefit from taking the REP test?
2. Tell me what is good about being cognitively simple.
3. Do you really support studying one person at a time?

12

The Social-Cognitive Approach to Personality: Walter Mischel and Julian Rotter

- Do people tend to size up a situation before deciding how to behave in it?
- Do your abilities have anything to do with your personality?
- Does our personality operate apart from our environments?
- What determines our outcomes: traits and efforts, or fate and chance?

Walter Mischel
www.fmarion.edu/
~personality/exper/Mischel.html

George Kelly's cognitive approach laid good groundwork for this chapter. The theorists covered here, Walter Mischel and Julian Rotter, emphasize our cognitions about the *social situations* that we encounter. Their theories are relatively closely connected; Mischel was a student of Rotter. That personality cannot be considered apart from the social situations in which it unfolds is a basic tenet of both theories. Skepticism about the basic assumption underlying *traits*—behavior is quite stable across social situations—was initiated by Rotter and made a major issue by Mischel. Consequently, neither apply the label "trait" to any of their basic features of personality. However, Mischel's theory goes well beyond his mentor's and, as a result, it has inspired more scientifically sound research recently. Thus, his view will be emphasized. Nevertheless, their general orientations are similar enough that they may be placed in the same theoretical category, **social learning,** acquiring useful information through interacting (relating) to people and other elements of the environment (Phares, 1976).

Mischel: A Challenge to Traits

Walter Mischel may some day come to be regarded as the founder of modern personality theory. Mischel expanded on mentor Julian Rotter's social learning ideas in two important ways. First, he went far beyond Rotter in questioning *traits,* permanent, invariable, internal entities that determine stable behavior across most social situations (Mischel & Shoda, 1994; Mischel, Shoda, & Mendoza-Denton, 2002). Beginning with his famous 1968 book, Mischel started a revolution that caused psychologists to rethink their assumptions about traits. Although the "firebombing" of basic assumptions about traits has subsided, some of those assumptions lie smoldering in the ruins. Trait psychology will never be quite the same.

Second, in place of *traits* Mischel inserted cognitive and affective (feeling) processes as the major determinant of behavior (Mischel & Shoda, 1998; Shoda, Tierman, & Mischel, 2002). In so doing he originated some productive thinking about personality and, at the same time, opened up whole new research vistas. Mischel's work is living proof that personality may be conceptualized without reference to "traits" in the traditional sense.

Social learning theory emphasizes how people learn from other people. It addresses personality and, in some of its forms, amounts to an **interaction point of view,** the interplay between *internal entities* or personal factors and *social situations* is emphasized, rather than either in isolation from the other (Ayduk, Mischel, & Downey, 2002; Mischel & Shoda, 1995, 1998; Shoda & Mischel, 1993). For Mischel, certain personal cognitive/affective factors interact with situations to produce behavior. However, this point of view, called **social–cognitive learning theory,** proposes that important factors are cognitive and affective processes rather than traits. Specifically, Mischel's **personal factors** are memories of previous experiences from the past history of an individual that determine what the person employs for producing behavior at the present time. In interaction terms, Mischel's theory predicts that the history of rewards and punishments experienced in a given situation, and skills, strategies, and affects developed in that situation will determine present behaviors.

Mischel, the Person

Like Adler and Freud, Walter Mischel is Austrian (*American Psychologist* (*AP*), 1983). He was born February 22, 1930, in Vienna, near Freud's home, a site he paid "a great homage visit" during 1996 (personal communication, August, 1997). Also, like Adler and Freud, Mischel and his family fled Vienna when the Nazis overran Austria in 1938. Following two years as refugees, Mischel's family settled in Brooklyn, the childhood home of Maslow and Rotter. Mischel attended primary and secondary school there and was the recipient of a college scholarship. Unfortunately, his father's illness required that he temporarily forgo postsecondary education in favor of employment. Later, while working as a stock boy, elevator operator, and assistant in a garment factory, young Mischel attended New York University, where he pursued interests in painting, sculpture, and psychology. His passion for art was fueled in part by exposure to life in Greenwich Village, where a youthful B. F. Skinner also spent some time.

Just as Kelly had been turned off by S-R psychology studies in rat laboratories, so was Mischel. He much preferred reading Freud, the existentialists, and poetry. By 1951, Mischel had made a professional choice in favor of clinical psychology and entered the master's of arts program at the City College of New York. There he studied with Gestalt-oriented Kurt Goldstein, who had been one of Maslow's mentors. During this period he became a social worker, helping impoverished teens and elderly people. It was these real-life experiences that soured him on the usefulness of Freudian notions and projective testing as avenues to understanding people. Thus, he resolved to pursue a more research-oriented clinical program, leading to the pursuit of a doctorate at Ohio State during the Rotter–Kelly era. From 1953 to 1956, Mischel soaked up the wisdom of Rotter and Kelly. Although Mischel may be considered a Rotter student, he also relies considerably on Kelly's thinking (Mischel & Shoda, 1995; Shoda & Mischel, 1993). Kelly's cognitive "constructs" and his belief that research subjects and clinical clients can be "scientists" had much impact on Mischel.

Armed with a solid cognitive background, Mischel spent 1956–1958 in a Trinidad village studying religious cult groups that practiced spirit possession. He assessed cult members' fantasies, cognitions, and actions both during possession and while in a normal state. Out of this work grew his interests in "choice preferences for delayed, more-valued outcomes versus immediate, but less-valued outcomes" (*AP*, 1983, p. 10). These experiences led to his studies of delay of gratification and his determination to investigate people in their natural environments, not the laboratory.

Following two years at the University of Colorado, Mischel became an assistant professor at Harvard, where he came under the influence of Gordon Allport and Henry A. Murray, among others. In 1962 he moved to Stanford, where he chaired the department from 1977 to 1978 and again beginning in 1982. He is currently at Columbia University in New York City, where he bears the title of Robert Johnston Niven Professor of Humane Letters in Psychology (personal communication, August, 1997). In 1991 he was elected to the American Academy of Arts and Sciences. In June of 1997 he received an Honorary Doctor of Science degree from his alma mater, Ohio State University. Finally, Mischel was awarded membership in the United States's most respected scientific organization, the National Academy of Sciences (June 2004). He has been working on a project to enhance self-control on the part of high-risk New York City children, "painting more than before," and "immensely enjoying life in the Big Apple."

Mischel's View of the Person

Mischel's 1960s work in developing methods for identifying potentially successful Peace Corps volunteers led directly to the foundation of what is, perhaps, his most important thesis: "under appropriate conditions people may be able to predict their own behavior as well as the best available [technical] methods" (*AP*, 1983, p. 10; also see Shrauger, Ram, Greninger, & Mariano, 1996). That is, he came to believe that people know themselves better than psychologists can come to know them by use of their best personality assessment techniques (1973). Mischel's almost phenomenological attitude, "if you want to know about people, ask them about themselves," greatly influenced Charles Potkay and me in our own investigations of people's self-descriptions (Allen & Potkay, 1983a; Potkay & Allen, 1988). In a recent study, compared to judgments of targets by others who knew them well, targets were more accurate in judging their own emotions and more accurate about their level of extraversion (Spain, Eaton, & Funder, 2000).

Mischel stated this position even more clearly in his classic book, *Personality and Assessment* (1968), in which he challenged the basic assumption underlying notions of "traits": cross-situational consistency. He declared that objective observations indicate that people tend to discriminate between one situation and the next, leading to change in behavior from situation to situation. Such cross-situational inconsistency would predict that measures of traits would be poor predictors of corresponding behaviors. Indeed, Mischel showed that the correlations between measures of behaviors in various situations and measures of traits hover around .30, thus accounting for only about 9 percent of behavioral variation. When trait testers responded with attempts to improve their measures, Mischel suggested that they had missed the point: " . . . much of the personality assessment practiced at that time stereotyped individuals into categories that grossly oversimplified their complexity and that had limited predictive value for the individual case" (*AP,* 1983, p. 10). Even now trait assessors are missing the point when they attempt to measure personality (Cervone, Shadel, & Jencius, 2001).

These proclamations left Mischel with a dilemma: people perceive cross-situational consistency in their own and other people's behavior, but scientific observations offer little confirmation of those perceptions. Mischel and his colleagues offer a means to account for the discrepancy between perceived and actual consistency. They showed that certain *prototypical behavior*—behavior that exemplifies a behavioral category, such as "verbal aggression"— does have *temporal stability:* the same behavior is performed in the same situation, on successive exposures to the situations. However, this temporal stability is often mistaken for cross-situational consistency. For example, a prototype of verbal aggressiveness is objecting to, arguing with, disputing, and "putting down" other people. A student may see displays of this prototypical behavior by a classmate as stable, because the classmate may show it in the *same situation* (class) across many points in time (during most class sessions). The student's temporally stable aggressiveness may be mistaken for cross-situational consistency, because the observer fails to recognize that the aggressive behavior is occurring repeatedly in the *same* situation across time, not across *different* situations.

You may wonder how we would ever expect accurate reports from people about their own behavior when they mistake temporal consistency for cross-situational consistency. In fact, we should not expect accuracy unless we ask people the right questions. If one asks people, in effect, "are you consistent" or "is your friend consistent," they will say "yes, of course." In our society we value being consistent, which often means "reliable" (Cialdini, 1985). However, instead of this or other leading questions, one can ask people to describe themselves behaving in a social context. In effect, they are asked to describe how they behaved in a given situation. For example, "*If* you are at a residence hall meeting, *then* would you be verbally aggressive?" With this kind of questioning, people reveal that they vary from situation to situation (Allen & Potkay, 1983a; Potkay & Allen, 1988). In a similar vein, if we ask a person what some other person "is like," the response may be some global trait label (Shoda & Mischel, 1993, p. 579). But, instead, if we ask that person to under-stand, empathize with, or remember something about another person, the response will be richer and include situational information. Box 12.1 explores personal stereotypes.

Instead of offering yet another definition of *personality,* Mischel refers to a **Cognitive Affective Personality System** (CAPS) which "is characterized by . . . available cognitive and affective [or feeling] units" such that "when certain configurations of situation features are experienced by the individual a . . . subset of cognitions and affects become activated" (Mischel & Shoda, 1995, p. 254). A situation, by its unique nature, activates cognitive/affective units appropriate to that nature and these units then determine behavior (Shoda & Mischel, 2000). The process begins with detection of features of a situation. A **feature of a situation** is some part of the total situation, such as one of its physical characteristics, or, more importantly, a factor associated with people who are present when the situation is unfolding. Feature detectors stimulate cognitive–affective processing units that influence the strength of behavioral units, which determine behavioral outcomes. In effect, situations provide the grist for the CAPS mill that produces behavior. For example, Marie detects a menacing person, a bully, who she knows is likely to push and shove her, which gives her a frightened feeling. This process elicits a behavioral tendency to hide. Marie slips into a nearby closet and closes the door behind her.

Since its introduction, CAPS has grown in sophistication as data supporting it accumulates (Mischel, Shoda, & Mendoza-Denton, 2002; Zayas, Shoda, & Ayduk, 2002). In one of two computer simulations, "A hypothetical personality was simulated [by a] . . . network of five situation feature detection input units, 10 cognitive-affective units and 5 behavior output units" (Shoda, Leetierman, & Mischel, 2002, p. 319). Forty such "personalities" were each exposed to 100 "situations." In the case of one example "personal-

BOX 12.1 • *Trait Labels Are Personal Stereotypes*

Have you ever found it burdensome for others to slap a trait label on you? A stereotype of a group (trait label applied to the whole group)—for example, "lazy"—implies that most group members show the behavior corresponding to the label: they act "lazy." By analogy, if you are labeled "irresponsible," it is implied that, regardless of the situation you are in, you can't be counted on. You may resent this label, because (1) you think that overly responsible people are conformists, and (2) though you are not always "responsible," in situations you think are important you can be counted on. So, maybe we could start a revolution of sorts. Let's object when someone tags us with some label, such as "kind" (it is burdensome to have to be kind regardless of situations), "clownish" (it is too much to expect that a person will provide the comic relief at every gathering), or "irritable" (it is unfair to say that one is "always irritable"; one may be irritable only when especially annoying people are around). Further, recognizing that it is unfair and a handicap for others to hang a personal stereotype on you may help you empathize with members of a group who, for example, are stereotyped as "violent," meaning most of them are expected to commit violent acts. Just as you are seen in a monolithic, one-dimensional, unfair way when you are, for example, stereotyped as "irresponsible," members of certain ethnic and racial groups are viewed similarly when they are stereotyped as "violent." Some few members of the group may be violent in a few situations, but, for a large group, most members will not be violent in most situations.

ity," repeated cycling of the 100 situations led *not* to 100 output states, but instead led to four clusters of stable end states. Each stable end state, called an **attractor,** represents a "state of mind," such as a set of beliefs, or a set of affective states (e.g., states of security and resentment). Across the 40 personalities an average of 2.18 attractors were extracted. Thus, relatively few stable cognitive–affective end states are activated by many situations. In turn, these few end states produce the output of behavior initiated by reactions to the many situations. To put it another way, in response to many different situations, the CAPS system settles into different attractor states in such a way that a few such states accommodate many different situations. Consistency of personality, therefore, derives *not* from behavioral consistency across many different situations. Rather, it arises from stable cognitive–affective states that accumulate in the "mind" as a result of repeated exposure to many situations. Through additional computer simulations, Shoda and colleagues went on to show that the behavior produced by one "personality" represents a situation presented to another "personality." In this way, the two personalities settle into attractor states that allow each to react appropriately to the behavior of the other.

Basic Concepts: Mischel

Competency.   Chief among cognitive faculties that are activated by certain situations are abilities that allow effective performance in those situations. **Competency** embraces both the cognitive ability to size up a situation so that one understands how to operate effectively in it and the ability to perform behaviors that will lead to success in the situation. It involves "knowing what to do" in a situation and being able to do it. Some people may not know that the ability to engage in "small talk" is critical to success at parties. Others may know the importance of small talk, but just cannot do it. Still others recognize the significance of small talk and do it well. Only this last set of people would have the competencies leading to success at parties. Of course, people vary in how many competencies they possess. Some people have a large "bag full of tricks" they can use in a wide variety of situations. Others, unfortunately, have rather few competencies and can operate efficiently in a relatively small number of situations. Shoda, Mischel, and Wright (1993) have shown that different situations demand different competencies of those who operate in them. Further, individuals who have much competence can vary their behaviors appropriately across situations to meet the varying situational demands for competency.

Characterizing Events.   "Sizing up" a situation is a more intricate and demanding process than it may appear to be, because each situation tends to be complex: constituted by many features. Features generate *events,* occurrences that are produced by features of a situation. "Stuffiness" is an example of an event produced by a feature of a possible college class situation, a small poorly ventilated room. More potent events are the behaviors that are performed by people who operate in a situation.

   Characterizing events associated with a situation is placing them into meaningful categories. It is an early and critical step in sizing up a situation. A person may characterize events associated with an entire situation, or with individual features of it. For example, a student may place verbal events associated with the college class situation into the "silence is golden" category, one signifying that speaking out is inappropriate. Another student may decide that the college class is the appropriate place for voicing any opinion that is relevant to the topic at hand. Obviously, these two people will behave quite differently in class. Which person is most successful will depend on who "reads" the dominant feature of the situation—the professor—most accurately. Does the professor prefer "silence is golden" to "free expression of opinions?"

In addition to such global characterization, or instead of it, a person may place specific events associated with a situation into several separate categories. These specific events are often behaviors of critical persons who are found in the situation. For example, a student may characterize instances of rapid and enthusiastic professorial speech as attempts to "impart important information," the stuff tests are made of. Such a characterization could lead to some frantic notetaking. The same student may interpret a dramatic pause following the presentation of a "main point" as a signal that it is time for students wishing to express their vital interest in the professor's lecture to pose questions. Shoda and Mischel (1993) have concocted a similar example to show that individuals with different goals categorize situations differently, such that the same situation may call forth different behaviors from the individuals: one person sees the approach of a homeless individual as an opportunity to promote a justice goal through an offer of money, while another person who does not share that goal sees the approach as an irritation.

Special note should be taken of the observation, made from the point of view of a given individual, that others' actions are not the only important behavioral events in a situation (Mischel, 1973; Mischel et al., 2002). A particular person who is trying to size up a situation is also one of its features. That person's own behaviors are important events associated with the situation. One of the most valuable cognitive competencies that a person can possess is the realization that there are certain behaviors he or she can perform that will change a situation, making it one in which he or she can operate more effectively (Mischel & Shoda, 1995). People do not just passively respond to situations, they actively shape them (Shoda & Mischel, 2000; Zayas, Shoda, & Ayduk, 2002). For example, suppose hypothetical person Sue finds herself at a business meeting during which the participants are all talking loudly and all at once. In this setting, she is not able to "do her thing," which is to calmly apply precise logic to practical problems. Being somewhat soft-spoken, Sue feels the need to change the situation to better suit her capabilities. Thus, she makes her way to the front row, waves her hand so that the presiding official cannot miss it, and raises a "point of information." This action causes the official to pound her gavel until there is silence in the room and then to turn the floor over to Sue. Now Sue has transformed the situation into one in which she has a long past history of effective operation.

Expectancies.   An extensive past history in a situation is likely to give a person a good grasp of what to expect when certain stimuli are present and when certain behaviors are performed. For Mischel, a **stimulus** is a very definite, well-defined feature or event associated with a situation and can be either physical or behavioral (Mischel & Shoda, 1995). Anybody who has spent years as a lawyer will likely believe that certain stimuli lead to predictable outcomes in the courtroom. When the person dressed in black robes emerges from an adjoining room and steps behind the bench, lawyers have the expectancy that everyone will rise. For Mischel, an **expectancy** is a belief based on past experience that provides a prediction of future outcomes (Mischel & Shoda, 1995). In our courtroom example, the stimulus can be a feature of the situation—the judge—or a behavior—the bailiff's verbalization "all rise." In either case, the stimulus gives rise to the expectancy of certain outcomes, often behaviors. People have beliefs with regard to what will occur should they or others behave in a certain way in a given situation. That is, people have expectancies concerning the outcome of particular behavioral performances. Knowing the rules of the court, lawyers can easily predict what will happen if they continually interrupt the proceedings by shouting at each other. In sum, knowing a situation is, in part, knowing what will result from the performance of a given behavior in the situation. It is also knowing what will happen when a certain stimulus is present.

Values of Outcomes.   In sizing up a situation so that successful behaviors can be performed, it is not enough to know what to do and to be capable of doing it. If one fails to accurately characterize the situation, its features, and its events, one will not know *when* to do whatever will lead to success. Further, one also must know what to expect when specific stimuli emerge from the situation and when specific behaviors are performed in the situation. Additionally, success in the situation may depend on **values of outcomes,** how much one prizes results of behavioral or stimulus occurrences in the ongoing situation. In fact, **success** itself may be defined as effectively performing the behaviors that yield the outcomes that are valued by the performer. Attaining some *goal* is typically a valued outcome.

   Psychotherapy can provide valued outcomes. People familiar with a particular form of psychotherapy will know that clients who make favorable references to themselves experience a definite outcome, approval from the therapist (Mischel, 1973). Among those people are some who, when acting as clients, will greatly value the approval that results from favorable self-reference. Other clients, however, will not value approval or will value it less. It is a good bet that the frequency of favorable self-reference will be very different for the two groups of knowledgeable clients. The value of an outcome, be it a behavioral outcome or the outcome of some stimulus, is a powerful part of "sizing up" a situation. Knowing the outcomes that are typical of a situation, a person will adopt strategies yielding behaviors that will increase the likelihood of valued outcomes.

Self-regulatory Plans.   A final aspect of sizing up a situation is one's own **self-regulatory plans,** rules established in advance of opportunity for behavioral performance that act as guides for determining what behavior would be appropriate under particular conditions. Self-regulatory plans involve more than rules covering a kind of situation, such as being at a party (Mischel & Shoda, 1995). People are aware that situations do not stay the same from one point in time to the next. A given situation will tend to vary even on a single occasion during which it is in effect. Have you attended a party where everyone engaged in the same activities throughout the entire duration of the affair? Probably not. Parties often start with "feeling each other out," figuratively speaking, until people are acquainted or reacquainted with one another, and, thus, feel comfortable with one another. Then the merrymakers loosen up, and the fun really begins. Although one may have plans for parties in general, such as how to dress, whether to approach others or wait for them to approach oneself, and so forth, one must also have plans concerning what to do at different phases of the party. For example, what to do if somebody has too much to drink and what to do when "things are dragging a little." People generally have answers to these and other questions worked out in advance, in the form of plans.

Supporting Evidence

Delay of Gratification (DOG).   Self-regulatory plans tend to be different for different people, because each person has a unique past history of experiences in situations. Furthermore, plans are flexible. They may change permanently due to experience or may be altered temporarily due to the demands of the situation (Mischel & Shoda, 1995). Much of Mischel's and colleagues' research efforts have gone into determining how children accomplish the self-regulatory task of **delaying gratification,** postponing some pleasure so that it can be enjoyed to the maximum degree or in its most optimal form. In a review of their work, Mischel, Shoda, and Rodriguez (1989) report that enduring individual differences in this variety of self-control have been found as early as the preschool years.

Shoda, Mischel, and Peake (1990) described the procedures they have used in several studies to demonstrate that preschool DOG-ability is positively related to adolescent competence. Their basic method has a long history (Miller, Riessman, & Seagull, 1968). In these studies, an experimenter first asked children to identify which of several objects they found most desirable (for example, marshmallows or pretzels). Then they were placed in a room stripped of distracters and asked whether they would prefer a little or much of the desired object (for example, one versus two marshmallows). Then the experimenter announced she must leave and indicated, "if you wait until I come back . . . then you can have this one [points to two marshmallows]. If you don't want to wait you can ring the bell and bring me back any time you want to. But if you ring the bell then you can't have this one [points to two marshmallows], but you can have that one [points to one marshmallow]" (p. 980). If you ring the bell then you can't have this one [points to two marshmallows], but you can have that one [points to one marshmallow]" (p. 980).

Children use different strategies to accomplish DOG: (1) covering up the preference (for example, M&Ms) or leaving them in the open; (2) thinking of the preference abstractly or concretely (M&Ms are "round buttons" rather than "yummy and chewy"); and (3) thinking of the task or the enjoyability of the preference ("I'm waiting for the M&Ms" or "The M&Ms taste yummy and chewy"; p. 360). Overall, Shoda, Mischel, and Peake (1990) found positive correlations between preschool seconds-of-delay-time and adolescent cognitive/academic competence as well as the ability to cope with stress/frustration. They also found that particular coping strategies used in preschool (e.g., covering preferred items such as M&Ms) were related to certain adolescent personality factors such as the degree to which the child is sidetracked by minor setbacks, yields to temptation, is distractible, has self-control, and copes with important problems.

Ayduk, Mendoza-Denton, Mischel, Downey, Peake, and Rodriguez (2000) followed up studies done between 1968 and 1974 in order to explore the relationship between impulse control among rejection sensitive people and DOG. People who are rejection sensitive (RS) tend to be "hot responders." They "fly off the handle," lash out at, and retaliate against those who are accused of rejecting them. People who as nursery school children were able to delay gratification and who were high RS as adults were able to inhibit antisocial responses to perceived rejection (e.g., aggression) and reactions that diminish well-being (e.g., drug use). DOG buffered high RS people against interpersonal difficulties and personal problems.

But what would happen if people contemplating a rejection were able to do so under conditions that generate "cool" rather than "hot" reactions? Ayduk, Mischel, and Downey (2002) devised those conditions by having participants think about a past rejection under "hot" instructions ("Think about your experience in terms of the feelings and the emotions involved. How did your heart beat?" p. 445) or under "cool" instructions ("Think about the event in terms of its objects and the spatial relations between them. Where were you standing with respect to the people and the objects around you?" p. 445). Then participants worked on a "lexical decision task": they hit a "word" key if they saw an actual word (e.g., aggressive) on a computer screen or a "nonword" key if they saw a nonword (e.g., akmow). Words for which the "word" key was hit very quickly were assumed to be more accessible (come to mind more easily) than words for which the "word" key was hit after an appreciable lapse of time. Results showed that hostile words were more accessible for "hot" instructions participants than for "cool" instructions participants. Hostile reactions in the form of words like "anger" and "hate" came more readily to mind under "hot" than "cool" conditions.

People Are Interactionists, Not Trait Theorists.   A number of years ago, Gene Smith and I showed that, contrary to a popular belief among many psychologists, when asked the "right" questions, ordinary people reveal themselves to be interactionists, not trait theorists (Allen & Smith, 1980). In relevant research, people usually are asked to "observe" someone's behavior and then to indicate whether that person's behavior was caused by her or his "traits" or the situation he or she was operating in. If, instead, people are asked to choose the most plausible explanation of behavior from definitions of several such explanations, including a definition of *trait,* a definition of a *situation,* and one of *interaction,* they choose *interaction.* Mischel and his colleagues have gone beyond this beginning effort by showing that specifying the situation in which a behavior occurs or qualifying a trait explanation of behavior improves people's predictions of behavior. Shoda, Mischel, and Wright (1989) investigated adults' impressions of children's aggressive behavior. When situations were specified ("child hits when provoked"), rather than unspecified ("child hits"), impressions (for example, "is an odd child") were more accurate in predicting differences among children in overall, actual aggression. Other work by Wright and Mischel (1988) took a closer look at the "trait" statements children and adults used to explain behavior. This more careful observation revealed the use of qualifiers (the target person *sometimes* is aggressive) and conditional statements (the target person is aggressive *when* teased by others). These outcomes indicate that ordinary people recognize that behavior is not altogether cross-situationally consistent (*sometimes*) and its performance often depends on the existence of certain situations (*when*).

More recently Mischel and his colleagues have come to use *if . . . then* language to describe the behavior–situation relations that are peculiar to particular individuals (Mischel & Shoda, 1995, 1998; Mischel et al., 2002; Shoda & Mischel, 1993). For example, if Kwanda, a school teacher, is confronted with an aggressive child, she will implement calming procedures. On the other hand, Marty, another teacher, will respond with his own aggressiveness.

Further, people who associate with Marty and Kwanda, and thus must understand them, are capable of appreciating the *if . . . then* relations peculiar to each of them (Shoda & Mischel, 1993; Zayas et al., 2002). These people may sometimes be heard to make utterances such as "Marty is very aggressive," but they often preface such sweeping, trait-like attributions with qualifications or probability statements like "Marty only gets aggressive *when* somebody gets in his face" or "If someone gets in Marty's face, *then* he is aggressive."

On Individual Differences, Trait Theory, and If . . . Then Relations.   For trait theorists, two people can both be labeled "irritable" if, when the behaviors they display are averaged across the situations in which they operate, their irritability scores come out to be the same. The trait orientation is then embarrassed when both individuals show inconsistency in "irritability": they vary some from one situation to the next in their irritable behaviors. In fact, even though they share the same overall or average level of irritability, they are not identically "irritable" people who should be expected to be consistent in irritability. Mischel and Shoda (1998; Mischel et al., 2002) point out that two persons, 1 and 2, may both be "irritable" but the two may show irritability in different situations. For example, situation A is one in which personal interactions are rarely initiated (e.g., a business meeting) and situation B is one in which such interactions are frequent (parties). *If* person 1 becomes irritated when ignored, *then* she will be irritated in situation A, but not B. *If* person 2 is irritated when others attempt personal interaction with him (he is happier left alone), *then* he will be irritated only in situation B.

Just as there are individual differences in *if . . . then* relations, there are individual differences in an important, broad disposition (Mischel & Shoda, 1998; Mischel et al., 2002). People differ in **discriminative facility,** a sensitivity to the subtle cues in a situation that influence behavior, which amounts to a kind of social intelligence. Those who possess sensitivity to cues that influence behavior in situations will be socially intelligent: their behaviors in situations will often gain the approval and support of others. Those lacking in sensitivity will not be successful. People who are sensitive in this way are good at *if . . . then* relations. Thus, as long as the trait orientation—emphasis on general or overall dispositions—takes into account *if . . . then* relations, it can usefully cast people into different dispositional categories. "Rejection sensitivity" is another example of a general disposition that is useful as long as *if . . . then* relations are taken into account. Different people can be equally sensitive to rejection overall, but each is rejection-sensitive in a different set of situations than the others. Box 12.2 compares Mischel's position with that of trait theorists.

Mischel Summed Up: Consistency of Cross-Situation Behavioral Patterns

Mischel and his colleagues published a study of 84 children in a summer camp that graphically depicts Mischel's point of view (Shoda, Mischel, & Wright, 1993). These children's behavior was recorded and scored on verbal aggression (teased, provoked, or threatened), as well as physical aggression, compliant behavior, and prosocial behavior. The recordings were made in different *nominal* situations, such as woodworking and cabin meetings,

BOX 12.2 • *Comparing Trait Theory with Social–Cognitive Theory (SCT)*

Cervone, Shadel, and Jencius (2001) and Cervone and Shoda (1999) contrasted SCT with the Big Five position, the major, modern trait point of view (e.g., Goldberg, 1993). Big Five advocates believe that personality can be cast in terms of just five dimensions: conscientiousness, agreeableness, neuroticism (emotional stability), openness to experience, and extraversion (CANOE). A central problem with this position, not shared with SCT, is that *trait* is defined in circular fashion: *trait* is used to "explain" overt behavior and behavior is used to confirm the existence of internal traits. An "explanation" that depends on what it "explains" is just a description, not a true explanation. The Big Five position and other trait points of view are, therefore, merely descriptive, not explanatory.

By contrast, SCT refers to dynamic cognitive and affective processes that respond in sync to situational stimulation so that behavior relevant to a particular situation is generated. Thus, SCT explains behavior by reference to continuous processes beginning with situational feature detection and extending through cognitive–affective processing units to behavioral units, and, finally, to behavior. For example, Germane detects a helpful person, called a teacher's aide, and *knows* that she will help him with his writing, which gives him a warm *feeling*. This process elicits a behavioral tendency to approach her, which he does.

From the Big Five perspective, traits are all one needs to consider in attempts to "explain" behavior. Traits are activated by unknown forces and then "cause" behavior. Extraverted people act extraverted "no matter what." By contrast, SCT recognizes the importance of the context (situation) in which behavior is produced. Nevertheless, it is not the situation as a whole that influences behavior through CAPS. Rather, it is specific features of situations that are influential. Also, unlike the Big

Five position, SCT posits that people's capabilities, beliefs, strategies, plans (e.g., self-regulatory), and goals (including satisfying values) all feed into the production of behavior. SCT does recognize that there are extraverted behavioral tendencies, but a person's beliefs may dictate that she is talkative with a male friend encountered at a party, but shy around a boss who approaches her at the same party. She does not deem it appropriate to be extraverted "no matter what." Further, unlike the Big Five position, SCT recognizes that a term such as *conscientious* not only does not necessarily mean the same thing to different people, it does not mean the same thing to the same person when she or he operates in different situations (Cervone, 2004; Shoda et al., 2002). Each person has embraced her or his own connotations of *conscientious* and may not assume the same connotation for each situation.

SCT is more idiographic than the Big Five position (Mischel et al., 2002). SCT follows each person across situations and time with the expectation that he or she will show a unique pattern of behavior and, thus, will tend to behave somewhat differently in different situations. By contrast, it follows from the Big Five orientation that each person has a relatively static position on each Big Five dimension, so that she or he will show much the same behavior in each different situation. Big Five advocates consider an entire population of people, each with her or his place on each of the five dimensions. In comparison, SCT tends to study each individual separately and conceives of each person dynamically, never assuming that he or she is plugged into static positions on any dimensions. In sum, SCT acknowledges the complexity of each person and his or her life circumstances, while the Big Five orientation regards all people as relatively simple.

where the children were confronted with five different *interpersonal* situations: when a peer initiated positive contact; when a peer teased, provoked, or threatened; when praised by an adult; when warned by an adult; and when punished by an adult. Indexing behavioral variation across these five interpersonal situations was the goal of the research.

The results are well illustrated by Figure 12.1. As you can see, child number 17 showed low cross-situation consistency in verbal aggression: the child's behavior is below the norm (zero line) for "peer approaches," but well above the norm for "adult punishes." Notice, however, there are two lines: the solid line represents responses to the interpersonal situations at time 1, while the dotted line is the verbal aggression behavioral profile at time 2. While cross-situational consistency is low at both times, the cross-situational *behavioral profiles* are highly consistent across times 1 and 2: when confronted with the set of situations a second time, the child shows very much the same pattern of behaviors across the situations as she or he displayed upon the first encounter with the situations. While subjects as a group showed low cross-situational behavioral consistency, as a group they tended to display much the same patterns of behaviors at the two different times (solid and dotted lines much alike). These results nicely illustrate Mischel's theory. Although people do not show cross-situational consistency, each can be characterized by a unique behavioral pattern or profile across situations which she or he displays repeatedly and which is different from other people's patterns. These real-life results define interactionism in new, more meaningful terms: each person shows a temporally consistent, unique relationship between his or her particular personal cognitive/affective processing units and a set of situations.

An interesting question left open by the summer camp study is how people make sense of others' behavior that changes from situation to situation. Plaks, Shafer, and Shoda (2003) argued that by appreciating another person's goal, observers of that person can see coherence in her cross-situationally variable behavior. To make their point, Plaks and col-

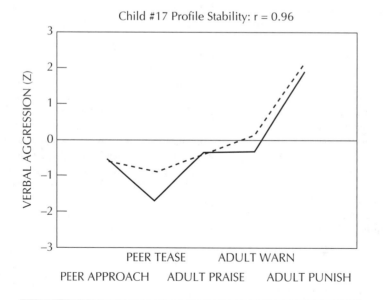

FIGURE 12.1 *A Child's Behavior-Situation Profile at a Time 1 and at a Time 2*

leagues contrived Joanne 1, whose goal was "good grades." It was arranged that she showed conscientiousness in situations that involved making "good grades." To accommodate this goal, she seeks help from a teaching assistant and asks many questions in class. On the other hand, she wastes money and her exercise program is disorganized. Her systematic cross-situationally variable conscientiousness behavior reflects her goal. Her pattern of behavior was then compared to Joanne 2, whose behavior across situations was random with regard to conscientiousness. Joannes 3 and 4 were unvariable: moderately or extremely conscientious, regardless of situations. For these last three Joannes, goals were not decipherable. Observer participants who were exposed to the differently variable behavior of the four Joannes rated Joanne 1's behavior significantly more coherent than that of the other three Joannes. Since her pattern of behavior revealed her goal, her variable behavior in the service of her goal made sense to observers.

An analogous pattern of results was also produced by observer participants who were exposed to the cross-situationally variable behavior of a fraternity's members compared to that of an Introductory Psychology class members. Because the class was likely to be seen as a random assembly of people, it was expected that a decipherable "good physical fitness" goal would be attributed only to the fraternity group. Results for the Intro Psych group revealed no differences in coherence ratings among the following conditions: a condition for which cross-situational variability was systematic, a cross-situationally unvarying condition, and a randomly varying condition. In contrast, for the fraternity group, observer participants saw the systematically cross-situationally variable behavior as more coherent than the behavior shown in the other two conditions. The varying behavior of a group is likely to be seen as coherent if the group is expected to have a goal and if the goal is decipherable.

Evaluation

Mischel's Contributions

Walter Mischel started an intellectual revolution in personality psychology. He opened up minds with his declaration that the notion of trait, and the assumption of behavioral stability that lies behind it, is of limited utility for understanding and predicting behavior. Personologists who had previously just accepted "trait" were forced to dredge up the assumptions underlying the concept and support them. The result was more incisive thinking and greater caution in using *trait*. Trait theorists sharpened their definitions and honed their research techniques.

Further, the intuitively reasonable position, "interactionism," which earlier was unsuccessfully championed by Julian Rotter, suddenly became the "position of choice." Faced with undeniable evidence that behavior varies considerably across situations, rather than remaining stable, most trait theorists found it expedient to call themselves "interactionists." Unfortunately, many of them continued to operate as if behavior is rigidly stable across situations. The net result was mainly lip service to the observation that certain behaviors occur mostly in particular situations that elicit them from particular people, not in all situations. The fact that "lip service" very often is followed by real change virtually ensures that interactionism will actually catch on in the future. Then the perspective of personologists will be more in tune with that of the people they study (Allen & Smith, 1980). A big boost for this needed change comes from the Mischel team's recent demonstrations of the *if . . . then* principle.

In addition, Mischel's work on delay of gratification has numerous important implications (Mischel et al., 1989; Ayduk et al., 2000; Ayduk et al., 2002). Early ability to delay gratification has been solidly related to later academic achievement, emotional stability, and impulse control. It follows that techniques useful in enhancing delay should be developed and taught to children. Examination of the procedures used by Mischel and colleagues and the results they have obtained indicates that such techniques could be readily developed. These methods for enhancing delay may be especially beneficial to "children at risk," a growing constituency of our public schools.

Limitations

The complaint, made in a previous edition, that Mischel's view mentions *affect* but does little with it has very limited validity today. Articles by Cervone and colleagues (1999; 2001) and Mischel and colleagues (Ayduk et al., 2002; Mischel et al., 2002; Shoda et al., 2002; Zayas, 2002) take a giant step in the right direction toward defining the role of affect.

Conclusions

The alleged "neglect of affect" in Mischel's theory is fast becoming irrelevant. "Rejection sensitivity" is an example of an important affective process now being considered (Ayduk et al., 2000; Ayduk et al., 2002). Mischel's position is becoming more appreciated, because others are beginning to heed his call for consideration of the context (situations) in which behavior relating to dispositions is expressed (Cervone et al., 2001; Cervone & Shoda, 1999).

Mischel's challenge to "traits" is one of the most important events in the modern history of personality research. However, a contribution of possibly greater importance has been largely ignored. Personologists should take another look at his theory with an eye to what it tells them about alternatives to understanding personality. For too long it has been assumed that personality cannot exist without the behavioral consistency assumed by trait theorists (Allen, 1988a; 1988b). To the contrary, Mischel's work has shown that there are other ways to cast personality that are not burdened by trait assumptions. In fact, quietly Mischel has quietly demonstrated that personality can be constructed in nontrait terms. His cognitive approach eschews "trait" accounts for personality development and functioning without making tenuous and limiting assumptions about cross-situational behavioral consistency. Instead, there is consistency in the pattern of behaviors a person displays across situations. Much the same pattern is shown across a set of situations each time the set is encountered. If Walter Mischel has taught us nothing more than to consider alternative conceptions of personality free from trait assumptions, we have learned a profound lesson indeed. Mischel was ranked 24.5 on the text citation list and 25th overall, but was not listed on the journal citation list or the survey (Haggbloom et al., 2002).

BOX 12.3 • *Mischel Actively Takes Diversity into Account*

Mischel's position vis-à-vis diversity is similar to Kelly's. Neither embraces content-laden traits, thereby avoiding the embarrassment of theoretically important traits failing to have meaning in cultures and subcultures different from that of European-Americans. But Mischel's position also avoids the problem posed by cultures whose participants often fail to use trait labels when describing themselves or others. Shoda and Mischel (1993) cite evidence that when East Asians (Japanese) are asked to describe themselves they tend to refer to social roles ("I am a college student"). By contrast, Westerners (Americans) resort to trait labels ("I am honest"). When asked to explain others' behaviors, Indian Hindus mention the context of others' behavior ("It was dark") while, again, Westerners (Americans) tend to apply trait labels ("He's a coward"). Morris and Peng (1994) and Lee, Hallahan, and Herzog (1996) report similar evidence in a comparison of Americans and Chinese. Menon, Morris, Chiu, and Hong (1999) compared East Asians and North Americans on attributions of causality to dispositions of individuals or to dispositions of groups. Japanese and Chinese were more likely than North Americans to attribute the cause of a calamity to a group than to an individual who was involved in the mishap. To illustrate, a violation of stock market rules was attributed to the company that committed it, not to the employee who was most involved with it.

As you learned earlier, Richard Nisbett (2003) has shown that East Asians (e.g., Chinese) think differently than North Americans and Europeans (Westerners). Sanchez-Burks, Lee, Choi, Nisbett, and Zhao (2003) investigated the degree to which these different modes of thinking influence communications at work and in nonwork settings. In general, East Asians tend to be more indirect than Westerners in what they say to others, because they are more concerned about maintaining harmonious social relations than are Westerners. An example of indirectness is "Your paper is interesting." "Reading between the lines" of what was said, the paper's author might con-

clude that the paper is of questionable worth. Further, Westerners tend to find concern for social relations less appropriate in a work setting than in a nonwork setting. East Asians tend to reverse this bias. These researchers' data bore out their expectations: Westerners were less indirect overall than East Asians, but, more importantly, they were less indirect at work than in a nonwork context while East Asians were more indirect at work.

East and West differ in another sense of communication. Ross, Xun, and Wilson (2002) showed that when Canadian students born in China spoke in Chinese, relative to when they or others spoke in English, they made more collective ("we") than individualistic ("me") statements. They also showed lower self-esteem and more agreement with Chinese cultural views. Finally, they made similar numbers of favorable and unfavorable self-statements and positive and negative mood statements. The English-speaking groups reported more favorable than unfavorable self-statements and more positive than negative mood statements. Language evokes culture and Eastern culture places greater emphasis on smooth social relations and self-effacing orientation compared to Western culture.

As Nisbett (2003) noted, East Asians are more flexible in their thinking and find no contradiction in being inconsistent across different situations or having inconsistent views of themselves. Consistent with this view, Suh (2002) argued that it is more a Western belief that consistency in views of the self across different situations is a prerequisite for psychological well-being. If so, only for Westerners would consistency be associated with high positive subjective well-being (SWB; happiness). Results of Suh's work showed that North Americans who viewed themselves as consistent across situations also had higher SWB, lower negative affect, and higher positive affect. In a second study, maintaining a consistent view of the self across different situations was less strongly related to SWB, positive affect, and negative affect for Koreans than for Americans. Finally, while Americans evaluated people who

(continued)

BOX 12.3   Continued

showed cross-situational consistency in self-views more favorable than inconsistent people, Koreans showed no preference for people with consistent and inconsistent self-views.

As these results show, the East Asian worldview is more open-ended, flexible, and variable than the Western worldview. East Asians take social and physical context more into account than do Westerners. Kitayama, Duffy, Kawamura, and Larsen (2003) presented American and Japanese participants with a line drawn vertically from the middle of the top edge of a square. Their task was to draw a line in some new variable-size boxes that represented the original vertical line. There were two sets of instructions. The absolute instruction was to draw the line to be the same length as the original line. The relative instruction was to draw the line so that its length was in the same proportion to the new boxes' sides as the original line was to the sides of the original box. As expected, the Japanese made fewer errors when acting under the relative instruction while the Americans made fewer errors when acting under the absolute instruction. East Asians find it easier to take the context in which they are working (the new boxes) into account than do Westerners.

As you have seen, culture is embedded in language and language can shape cognitive processes (Shoda & Mischel, 1993). Thus, characterizations of situations can vary across cultures and subcultures, because, even where the language is the same for two or more cultures or subcultures, usage can differ by culture or subculture.

Take, for example, the White culture and Black subculture. The Black subculture is an amalgamation of African and American traditions. To illustrate the impact of this fact, consider an old African adage: "If you throw a stone into a pack of dogs, the one that yelps is the one that was hit." Now suppose a Black person tells a group of Whites that "Whites are racists!" Whites, because of their unique cognitive devices, are likely to see the remark as an attribution to all Whites and be offended. But the Black person, having at least slightly different cognitive devices, may have intended something quite different. The Black person may have been casting a stone into a crowd of Whites to see who yelps. The one(s) who yelps when the "racist" stone lands may be viewed as racist(s), not "all whites."

Rotter: Internal versus External Control of Our Behavior

Rotter, the Person

Like Maslow, Julian B. Rotter traces his roots to Brooklyn, New York, where he was born to Jewish parents in 1916. Noting the obligation to acknowledge the "teacher who most contributed to my intellect," Rotter (1982, p. 343) takes a page out of Maslow's book by citing the Avenue J Library in Brooklyn. As a high school student, he spent so much time with his "teacher" that he soon exhausted its wisdom, at least in the category of fictional works. Thus, he searched the stacks for something new and stumbled onto books by Adler and Freud. By his senior year in high school, he was interpreting other people's dreams. His senior thesis was entitled, "Why We Make Mistakes."

Rotter pursued psychology while an undergraduate at Brooklyn College, but not as a major. Like George Kelly, the background of the Great Depression caused Rotter to

Julian Rotter
http://psych.fullerton.edu/
jmearns.htm

choose a practical major, chemistry. Nevertheless, he took more psychology than chemistry. This combination of a hard science and a psychology emphasis paid big dividends when Rotter later entered graduate school in psychology.

While pursuing his studies, Rotter was inspired by the lectures of social psychologist Solomon Asch, a student of Gestalt psychology who is famous for his conformity research. In turn, Asch got Rotter interested in the ideas of Kurt Lewin, a pioneer in the study of group dynamics who was strongly influenced by the Gestalt movement. These more socially oriented individuals must have had a great impact on Rotter, because he emphasized the importance of social situations over traits. Rotter, like Rogers and Maslow, acknowledged Adler's importance to his intellectual development. During Rotter's college years, Adler resided in Brooklyn. His almost evangelistic lectures further convinced young Julian that psychology was his destiny.

After Brooklyn College, Rotter arrived at the University of Iowa with empty pockets. Thanks to the the psychology department's chair, Lee Travis, he was able to earn enough to survive and pursue a master's degree. Years later he reciprocated by helping my colleague-to-be, broke Ohio State graduate student, James Joyce. Soon he was enrolled in one of Kurt Lewin's seminars where he became convinced that interactions between people and the social situations in which they find themselves are of central importance.

Determined to be among the first clinical psychologists, he pursued a Ph.D. at Indiana University. Having finished his work by the early 1940s, Rotter looked at job prospects with some trepidation, fearing that academic doors would be closed to Jewish people. Fortunately, he was able to land a clinical position in a state hospital where he taught for the first time. Unfortunately, World War II intervened and Rotter joined the Army, serving as a psychologist. There, among other contributions, he devised a method for reducing the incidence of "absence without leave." It was in the Army that Rotter began work on his social learning theory.

Having his choice of universities, he selected Ohio State, where George Kelly was among his colleagues. After Kelly gave up the clinical directorship in 1951, Rotter took it over. While he was happy and productive at Ohio State, the fascist spirit of Communist-baiting Senator Joe McCarthy was all too alive and well in the Midwest. Accordingly, in 1963, Rotter moved east to the University of Connecticut, where he is currently Professor Emeritus. There his thinking on social learning fully crystalized.

Rotter's View of the Person

Rotter (1966) believes that people gripped by the forces of a powerful situation show a general trend in behavior. However, within such situations, people still exhibit individual differences in behavior. To make his point, he referred to several studies in which some subjects were exposed to a *chance* or *skill* condition. In the chance condition, subjects were told that luck would determine how well they would do, but in the skill situation their own abilities would determine their performance (Phares, 1962, is an example study).

Although there were individual differences within both conditions, skill condition participants outperformed chance condition participants. Further, regardless of whether they had been in the chance or skill condition, some subjects tended to show the **Gambler's Fallacy,** the expectation that a failure on one attempt means that success on a subsequent attempt becomes more likely. People who are prone to the gambler's fallacy think that a string of losses means they will surely soon be winners. They "reason" that luck determines their outcomes and luck is supposed to change. Other individuals show the opposite of the Gambler's Fallacy. They believe that skills determine outcomes. A string of successes means that they have mastered the situation and will continue to experience success.

Basic Concepts: Rotter

Reinforcement Value, Psychological Situations, and Expectancy

Rotter's social learning theory is based on five main concepts (Rotter, 1975, 1982, 1990). **Reinforcement** refers to anything that has an influence on the occurrence, direction, or kind of behavior (Phares, 1976). **Reinforcement value** is the degree of preference for any reinforcement to occur if the possibilities of many different reinforcements are all equal (Rotter, 1954). The value of a reinforcement depends on how much it is preferred by an individual, compared to other reinforcements that are equally available. Imagine a woman named Martha who sometimes dates a man named Fred. For Martha, going out with Fred has low reinforcement value, because, given a choice among several other dates, Fred would be just about the last selected.

A **psychological situation** is characterized in a way peculiar to a person, allowing the person to categorize it with certain other situations, as well as differentiate it from still others (Phares, 1976). Situations are in the "eye of the beholder." If a given situation is seen in a certain way by a particular individual, that is the way it is for that person, no matter how strange the categorization might seem to others. For some individuals, an exhibition of classical music is "entertainment," for others it is "a scholarly endeavor," and for still others it is a waste of time. Further, a given person will see classical music as belonging in the same category as other forms of entertainment, such as baseball and movies. Others would place it in the same category as reading or researching library files, forms of scholarly pursuits. In terms of our dating example, Martha plans to attend a rock concert, which she considers to be a social gathering. She believes one should take a companion to a concert, but it should be a person one would not be afraid to ignore when opportunities to mingle with others arise.

Expectancy is "the probability held by the individual that a particular reinforcement will occur as a function of a specific behavior on his part in a specific situation or situations" (Rotter, 1954, p. 107). Our hypothetical Martha has every reason to expect that, should she pick up the phone and dial Fred's number, he will be right over. Fred is madly in love with her, a feeling she does not reciprocate. That is, Martha has the specific expectancy that calling Fred will be reinforced by his presence with her at the concert, an outcome of high likelihood and, in and of itself, of low reinforcement value. But she also expects opportunities to mingle with her friends at the concert, an outcome of high reinforcement value.

In addition, Martha has a relevant **generalized expectancy,** an expectancy that holds for a number of situations that are similar to one another to some degree (Rotter, 1966, 1992). The operation of generalized expectancies becomes more probable when individuals are faced with new or ambiguous situations that they characterize as bearing some resemblance to known situations (Rotter, 1966). Martha has been to relatively few rock concerts, but she expects that these will be like other social occasions. Her generalized expectancy is that whether she impresses her friends will depend on chance rather than her social skills (whether her friends are "in a good mood," the concert goes well, and so forth). On the basis of these assumptions about Martha, we can predict that she will call Fred, who will escort her to the concert where she will encounter friends whom she will impress or not, depending on "what fate has in store."

Locus of Control: Internals and Externals

Rotter (1966, 1967) identified a generalized expectancy that is associated with as famous a personality measure as exists in psychology. **Locus of control** refers to "the degree to which persons expect that . . . reinforcement [and other outcomes] of their behavior is [dependent on their] behavior or personal characteristics versus the degree to which [they believe it is due to] chance, luck, or fate, . . . powerful others, or is simply unpredictable" (Rotter, 1990, p. 489). That is, the control of outcomes can be perceived as located in one's own behaviors and skills, or as residing in luck and chance. According to Rotter, locus of control is " . . . one of the most studied variables in psychology and the other social sciences" (1990, p. 489). People who believe in **external locus of control** perceive that reinforcement of their behaviors is due more to luck, chance, fate, powerful others, or complex and unpredictable environmental forces, rather than determined by their own behaviors, efforts, or characteristics (Rotter, 1966). Individuals believing in **internal locus of control** perceive that reinforcement is dependent on their own behavior or characteristics—not fate, luck, or chance. People who believe in internal locus of control are often called *internals,* while those who believe in external control are called *externals.*

Beliefs in external control or in internal control are certainly individual difference factors. However, Rotter (1975) is extremely careful to point out that calling a person an "external" or an "internal" is not a reference to a "trait" or a "type" (Rotter, 1990). In fact, he has chastened researchers who apply factor analysis to his measure of locus of control and conclude that the method has little generality across circumstances (Rotter, 1990). He never indicated that external or internal loci of control would generalize strongly across situations. As illustrated in the Gambler's Fallacy study, situations can determine locus of control, just as people's beliefs about control can determine their behavior in a situation. Being a generalized expectancy, locus of control may determine outcomes if a situation is ambiguous. But, if a situation by its nature is associated with chance outcomes or outcomes dependent on personal skills, the situation, not the locus of control, will determine outcomes. Complete the I-E scale in Box 12.4.

BOX 12.4 • *An I-E Scale*

Instructions

For each item, select the alternative that you more strongly believe to be true. You must select one and only one alternative for each item. Be sure that the alternative you select for a given item is the one you actually believe to be most clearly true, not the one you think that you should choose or the one you wish were true. Remember that this is a measure of your personal beliefs. There are no correct or incorrect answers and no high or low, good or bad scores.

Spend little time on each item, but *do make a choice* for each item. You will sometimes find that you believe both statements or neither one. Please make a decision anyway.

1. a. I often find myself saying something to the effect of "What will be will be."
   b. I believe that what happens to me is my own doing.
2. a. I deserve credit for most of my accomplishments.
   b. I've been fortunate to have done well on a number of occasions.
3. a. When your time comes, you pass away; that's just the way it is.
   b. I plan to live a long time, and I wouldn't be surprised if I made it to 100.
4. a. I'm a pretty confident person. I can make things happen.
   b. Sometimes I'm amazed at how things seem to happen to me all by themselves.
5. a. I feel like a Ping-Pong ball. Life just bounces me back and forth between happy and sad.
   b. If I want to be happy, I just choose a fun thing to do and go to it.
6. a. You get what you deserve and deserve what you get.
   b. I don't feel guilty about the good things that happen to me or moan about the bad things. It could just as well have happened to someone else.
7. a. I wish the world wasn't full of so many bullies.

b. If people start to coerce me, I just stand up and look them in the eye.
8. a. People are good to me because I treat them right.
   b. I don't know when to expect that people are going to be nasty to me or nice.
9. a. I plan things, and they turn out as I expect.
   b. "Come what may," that's my motto. I'm a tumbleweed, caught in the wind.
10. a. I live my life one day at a time.
    b. I plan my day, my week, my month, and my year. I look ahead.
11. a. I'm not afraid to risk life and limb. What the heck, you could fall in the shower and break your back.
    b. I'm pretty careful at driving, sports, and so forth. I expect to keep this body a long, long time.
12. a. I feel pretty helpless when I'm with friends. I usually end up doing what they want.
    b. My friends and I are democratic about deciding what we'll do together, but my voice is always heard.
13. a. My voice is heard above the crowd.
    b. People just seem to drown me out.
14. a. When it comes to making love, if my partner wants to, fine; if not, that's OK too.
    b. I tend to decide when, where, and what my partner and I do in the love category.
15. a. I enter many lotteries, drawings, and things like that. I keep hoping I'll strike it rich.
    b. I steer clear of everything from bingo to poker. The odds are too long.
16. a. I'm always rooting for the underdog.
    b. Me, I stick with the winners.
17. a. In this country, anyone with some talent and some sweat is going to make it.
    b. If you're lucky, you're rich; if not, join the crowd.
18. a. Minorities are doing better because they are getting more education and working harder.

b. Minorities are doing better because they are finally getting a few breaks.

19. a. Some people wander around under a black cloud, while the sun shines on others.

 b. Let's face it, some people have ability and use it; some have it and waste it; and some just don't have it.

20. a. Life is a great glob of complexity. It would take an Einstein to win at it.

 b. It's really quite simple: if you're good and work hard, you succeed.

21. a. I like to compete because if I win it's great, and if I lose I can say "the gods frowned on me."

 b. I like to compete because if I win, I can say "I did it."

22. a. I think we should help each other, because misfortune could strike any of us.

 b. I think people should help themselves. If something bad happens to them, they caused it, and they can fix it.

23. a. Sometimes I feel powerful, able to do whatever I want.

 b. Sometimes I feel powerless, the victim of mysterious forces.

24. a. Things happen that puzzle me. I just can't make sense of them.

 b. Give me enough time and enough information, and I can usually make sense of anything.

25. a. We are likely to be swept up in the ebb and flow of events.

 b. If we can get to the moon, we can change the course of mighty rivers and make the weather do our bidding.

Give yourself a point if you chose each of the following alternatives: 1.a.; 2.b.; 3.a.; 4.b.; 5.a.; 6.b.; 7.a; 8.b.; 9.b.; 10.a.; 11.a.; 12.a.; 13.b.; 14.a.; 15.a.; 16.a.; 17.b.; 18.b.; 19.a.; 20.a.; 21.a.; 22.a.; 23.b.; 24.a.; 25.a. The higher the score, the more external you are. If you scored 20 to 25 on the I-E scale, you are in the *high external* range. A score of 0–5 makes you *high internal*. Most people fall between those extremes.

Characteristics of Internals and Externals

Conformity and Maladjustment.   Because externals believe that they are hapless victims of their environments, one would expect that they would be more conformist. Indeed, Phares (1976) reports that externals are more likely to conform in the standard conformity experiment. More generally, they tend to be more compliant (Blau, 1993). By the same token, internals react against attempts to influence them, even sometimes moving in a direction opposite of the influence attempt.

Rotter (1966) originally hypothesized that there would be a curvilinear relationship between locus of control and psychological adjustment, with both extreme internals and extreme externals being maladjusted. However, more recently, he has conceded that such is probably not the case (Rotter, 1975). It seems that externals are considerably more likely to be maladjusted, relative to internals. Other research finds externals to be more "worn out" and "uptight" (Ferguson, 1993).

Phares (1976) reported that externals are higher in anxiety and lower in self-esteem than internals. In terms of more serious maladjustment, externality may be associated with schizophrenia. More recent work supports the possibility that psychological problems are related to externality (Hermann, Whitman, Wyler, Anton, & Vanderzwagg, 1990; Ormel & Schaufeli, 1991).

Substance Abuse.   Perhaps surprisingly, Phares (1976) reported that internals may be more likely to abuse substances such as alcohol. It may be that high internality scores among substance abusers can be explained by the fact that research subjects are often recovering abusers who are continually told "your cure is up to you." Alcoholics may, therefore, be using their I-E responses to reflect what they think is expected of them. If so, they may not be real internals. Alternatively, they may be internals who "self-medicate" to avoid externally imposed medications. Further, a recent study found no relationship between parental alcoholism and children's locus of control, a result contrary to the intuition that children of alcoholics would be relatively external (Churchill, Broida, & Nicholson, 1990).

Learning Disabilities (LD) and Externality.   In may seem intuitively compelling that LD students would tend toward externality. After all, they "should" feel that they have little control over their academic and career destinies. However, though this belief has been strong, even among professionals who work with LD people, Mamlin, Harris, and Case (2001) reviewed the literature and found serious fault with all the sources of evidence supposedly supporting the belief. Apparently, that LD people are externals is more stereotype than fact. Box 12.5 provides a profile of an external.

Divorce and Marital Adjustment.   Although a person may be generally characterized by internality or externality, a study of divorce illustrates how internality–externality changes with the ebb and flow of life's fortunes. Doherty (1983) reported that women increased in externality following divorce, and then dropped back toward internality with the passage of time. Nevertheless, more recent work shows that externals and internals react to divorce differently. Barnet (1990) asked 107 divorced men and women about how long it took them to decide on a divorce, their locus of control, stress due to divorce, and adjustment to divorce. Internals showed more predivorce decision distress and less postdecision distress than externals. They were also less distressed overall than externals. Because internals believe that they have control, they tend to display more distress-inducing lengthy deliberation over whether to divorce, relative to externals. For the same reason, they adjust better to divorce once a decision is made. Contrary to previous results, men were more external and experienced more postdivorce maladjustment.

Other work suggests that internals may be less likely to experience a divorce, because they are better at resolution of marital conflicts. Miller, Lefcourt, Holmes, Ware, and Saleh (1986) had married couples complete a special Marital Locus of Control (MLC) questionnaire and then resolve some conflicts. In an example of conflict resolution, husbands and wives were instructed in private. One was told to assume "you are resigned to visit in-laws" while the other was to assume "you have reservations about visiting [your] in-laws and plans are not finalized." Then they got together in front of a video camera and resolved this and two other conflicts. Analyses of the MLC responses and the videotapes revealed that individuals who were internal for marital satisfaction were more active and direct in problem solving than externals. Also, internals were more effective in communicating and achieving their desired goals and showed higher levels of marital satisfaction than externals. Regard-

BOX 12.5 • *Profile of an External*

Ned is a very superstitious person. He has been known to walk a block out of his way to avoid the possibility that a black cat seen in the neighborhood might cross in front of him. If he spills salt at the table, he sprinkles a bit in his right palm and tosses it over his left shoulder. These practices are supposed to ward off bad luck. He wears the same old sweat-stained cap to every summer softball game. While driving in the country, every time he sees a white horse he licks the middle fingers of his right hand, stamps them on the palm of his left hand, and then pounds the palm with the right fist. These peculiar practices are supposed to bring good luck and he thinks he has had his share. Because he believes that recipients of "good luck" are special, he often exclaims, "It's better to be lucky than good." And, of course, he buys several lottery tickets every week. Friends estimate that, over the years, the cost of his tickets is around $5,000. Occasionally he wins $5 or $20, and once he even won $200, but the total is, at best, a few hundred dollars. His losses just make him more certain that the next ticket purchase will win him millions.

Ned's favorite sayings are "That's life," "What will be will be," and "Come what may." He thinks that his destiny was laid out when he was conceived so there is no use in trying to shape his own future. If everything is predetermined, why plan? This attitude makes him appear "spontaneous" to some friends. Indeed, he is always ready to drop whatever he is doing and join friends in whatever they want him to do. Other friends see him as irresponsible. Though he is married with two kids, he has no life insurance and no retirement plan. He thinks taking these two steps would be a waste of time and money because his children and wife, Lula, have their own destinies that cannot be altered by his or anyone else's intervention.

Though he is bright enough to make more money at another job, he won't go looking. He believes that, if there is something better out there, it will come to him. The only time he did change jobs was when he found a newspaper on a park bench, and opened it to the want ads with a job offer circled in pencil. "Fate" he thought, so he responded to the ad and landed the job. The same kind of thing led him to Lula. A year after graduating from high school, he was calling one of his old girlfriends but misdialed and got Lula instead. Before he discovered his mistake, he asked her out and, thinking he was another boy named Ned she once dated, she accepted. When further conversation revealed the errors, they laughed at themselves, but decided the date was meant to be, so they went out. It was love at first sight; they were married that June (both are Geminis). You may wonder, how does she put up with his "just let things happen" attitude? She would be puzzled by the question, because, you see, she thinks like him.

ing marriage in general, Johnson and colleagues (1992) reported tentative results suggesting that married people are more internal than either single or divorced people.

Locus of Control: Getting More Complex. A couple of recent studies illustrate the complexity of Locus of Control's relationship to other variables. Potosky and Bobko (2000) report that internals are more likely to have positive attitudes toward computers, a not so surprising outcome: computer mastery appears to require a belief in one's computer skills. However, surprisingly, Locus of Control played no role in the positive relationship between attitudes toward computers and experience with them.

Johansson and colleagues (2001) investigated the relationship of health control beliefs to health issues in a genetic study involving elderly twins. They found that a factor that combined genetic and environmental influences related significantly to scores on the Powerful Others scale. Counterintuitively, this same factor was unrelated to scores on an Internal scale.

Mental and Physical Health; Fiscal and Work Orientations.   People who lack normal emotions, called *alexithymics,* display three sets of symptoms: (1) "difficulty identifying feelings and distinguishing them from bodily sensations of emotions," (2) "difficulty describing feelings," and (3) "externally oriented thinking" (Hexel, 2003, p. 1264). Austrian psychologist Martina Hexel found that her internally oriented participants reported fewer symptoms measured by all three alexithymia scales than did externally oriented participants. Further, compared to high external participants, high internal participants scored higher on secure attachment style (confidence) and lower on two variations of insecure attachment style (need for approval and preoccupation with relationships are variations of the anxious/ambivalent style).

People with bowel problems—such as Irritable Bowel Syndrome (IBS), Chronic Idiopathic Constipation (CIC), and Crohn's Disease (CD)—may be different from others in terms of locus of control. Hobbis, Turpin, and Read (2003) found that people with CD were higher on the "controlled by powerful others" scale than people with the other two disease types and non-patients. Also, non-patients were higher on internal locus of control than people having all three types of diseases.

Lim, Thompson, Teo, and Loo (2003) related locus of control to the fiscal attitudes of Singaporean Chinese. They found that internals were prone to budgeting their money while externals viewed money as a source of power and positive evaluation. Externals also tended not to be generous with their money.

Strauser, Ketz, and Keim (2002) related locus of control to the four subscales comprising a measure of Work Personality (WP), the capacity "to deal successfully with the work environment" (p. 24): acceptance of work role, ability to profit from instruction or correction, work persistence, and work tolerance, all measured on a 4-point scale (1 = problem area, 4 = definite strength). Locus of control was represented by a measure of Work Locus of Control (WLC): external item: "Getting the job you want is largely a matter of luck"; internal item: "People who perform their jobs well generally get rewarded for it" (p. 24). The WP scale, "work persistence," significantly predicted WLC: the stronger the "work persistence," the higher the work internality. Further, there was a significant correlation between WLC and WP indicating that the stronger the work personality the higher the work internality.

Evaluation

Contributions to Controlling Our Lives

There seems to be little question that locus of control is here to stay. If anything, interest in it is increasing (Rotter, 1990, 1992). As long ago as 1975, Rotter was able to count at least 600 studies dealing with the I-E measure. Inspection of journals during the late 1980s and 1990s indicates that the number has greatly increased. A computer search of the psychology literature produced during the late twentieth century and early twenty-first century revealed that hundreds of locus of control articles were published.

Rotter (1954, 1966, 1990) was a pioneer in recognizing that one can account for human behavior only by considering multiple determinants, including situational effects. He has always maintained that mindless use of only a personality measure is a fruitless approach to understanding people. Further, internality–externality resembles a trait dimension only in that people can be distributed along the continuum. However, rather than being discrete, positions on the internality–externality dimension blend one into the other, more so than is alleged in the case of traits. Also, a person will vary her or his position at different points in time and under differing circumstances. This "sliding scale perspective" suggests that the meaning of internality–externality must be considered in the context of many other factors. This more complex orientation to personality guarantees Rotter a place in the future of psychology.

Limitations

Locus of control is the centerpiece of Rotter's point of view. Evidence for and against this crucial notion in large part determines the validity of his theory. Rotter himself has noted some problems with "locus of control." In 1966 he presented evidence that it overlaps with **social desirability,** the need to please others by displaying the characteristics that are valued in our society (for example, goodness, honesty, sincerity, and so forth). The implication of this association is obvious. In completing the I-E Scale, subjects and clients may be trying to favorably impress researchers or psychotherapists, rather than accurately reporting their actual characteristics. One could argue that the extent to which social desirability is manifested in I-E responses is the extent to which locus of control scores reflect response distortion rather than being an index of an actual personality factor. Davis and Cowles (1989) showed that social desirability continues to be a problem for Locus of Control measures.

Conclusions

The key to being a personality theorist with lasting impact is to have a few continually useful concepts associated with one's name. Freud has his "psychosexual stages," Jung his "archetypes," Adler his "style of life," Rogers his "unconditional positive regard," and Maslow his "hierarchy of needs." Rotter has his "internals and externals." A hundred years from now, when some theorists covered in this book are forgotten, Rotter probably will still be a name known to most psychologists. Aside from locus of control, Rotter should also be remembered for two other reasons: (1) his recognition that stability of personal attributes across social situations is limited, and (2) his belief that considering the interplay between personal and environment factors is essential to understanding people. Rotter was 18th on the journal citation list and 64th overall, but was unlisted on the text citation list and on the survey (Haggbloom et al., 2002).

Summary Points

1. Born in Austria, Mischel was reared in Brooklyn. As an undergraduate he studied art and psychology. Turned off by S-R theory, he embraced clinical psychology and eventually earned a clinical Ph.D. at Ohio State University. There he was influenced by Rotter and Kelly. His studies in Trinidad launched his interest in delay of gratification.

2. Mischel found little relationship between measures of traits and behavior. This position created a dilemma: people perceive stronger cross-situational consistency than exists. The Cognitive Affective Personality System (CAPS) is constituted by available cognitive and affective units that are activated by features of situations. Attractors are "states of mind" that represent stable end states that arise from repeated exposures to situations. Situations provide the grist for the CAPS mill that produces behavior.

3. Competency is the cognitive ability to size up a situation and to perform behaviors that will lead to success. Situations have features that include people and physical aspects. Characterizing events associated with a situation is placing them into meaningful categories. People with different goals characterize situations differently.

4. From the person's point of view, one of the most important features of a situation is her- or himself. An expectancy is a belief based on past experience that provides a prediction of future outcomes. Sizing up situations also involves establishing values for outcomes. Success is effectively performing behaviors yielding outcomes valued by the performer.

5. In DOG experiments, children used various methods for delaying, such as covering the preferred object. Recent research showed that DOG ability helped rejection-sensitive people cope. Cool instructions can help people avoid hot reactions to rejection. People prove to be interactionists when they are asked the "right" questions. Mischel showed that adults more accurately predict children's aggression if the context is specified. Prediction is better with use of "qualifiers" and "conditional statements." A comparison of Cognitive Social Theory (CST) with the Big Five position reveals that only CST regards people as complex, dynamic, and flexible.

6. Each person displays her or his own repertoire of *if . . . then* situation–behavior relations. The Mischel group showed that children's cross-situational behavior patterns are repeated each time they encounter the same set of situations. Mischel has addressed diversity by noting that not all cultures have participants who use trait labels to describe themselves or others. If we know a person's goal we can make sense of her or his variable behavior across situations. East Asians attribute cause to collectives rather than individuals.

7. East Asians tend to be more indirect in communication with others, especially at work. Chinese in Canada tend to be more collectivistic, self-effacing, and mixed in mood when speaking Chinese. Only Westerners, not East Asians, tend to be consistently highly positive in SWB. Rotter was born in Brooklyn and was nurtured by the Brooklyn Library. As a high school student he read Freud and Adler. When he entered Brooklyn College, he chose chemistry as a major. After training at the University of Iowa, he completed a clinical Ph.D. at Indiana University. Following service in World War II, he accepted a position at Ohio State.

8. Subjects in a "skill" condition performed better than subjects in a "chance" condition, but there were individual differences within the chance and skill conditions. Reinforcement influences the occurrence, direction, or kind of behavior. Reinforcement value is the degree of preference for any reinforcement to occur. An expectancy is the probability held by the individual that a particular reinforcement will occur.

9. Rotter's generalized expectancy led to the development of the internal–external dichotomy and the I-E Scale. Research has shown that externals are more conformist and more maladjusted, but less prone to substance abuse than internals. There is apparently no truth to the stereotype that learning disabled people are highly external. Internality–externality may change during the divorce process. Also, married people may be more internal.

10. Locus of control has been related to alexithymia, bowel problems, fiscal attitudes, and work personality. Unfortunately, social desirability contaminates the I-E dimension.

Running Comparison

Theorist	Mischel in Comparison
Kelly	He endorsed Kelly's cognitive constructs and "people can be scientists."
Bandura	Mischel also emphasized expectancies and cognitive control of behavior.
Allport	He also believed that dispositions must be considered in relation to the situations in which they are expressed.

Theorist	Rotter in Comparison
Kelly	He used some of Kelly's language.
Albert Bandura	He also believed that people are pulled by the future.
B. F. Skinner	They both talked about *reinforcement,* but Rotter had a broader definition.

Essay/Critical Thinking Questions

1. How good were you at delaying gratification (DOG) as a child?

2. Do the *if . . . then* analysis on your own behavior.

3. Pick a set of situations. How would you behave across them on "verbal aggression"?

4. Come up with a scenario in which someone is "guilty" of the Gambler's Fallacy.

5. What we call "reinforcing" or "rewarding" is somewhat in the eye of the beholder. Can you provide three examples of outcomes that are reinforcing to you, but not to one of your friends?

6. Are you an internal or an external? Give examples illustrating your choice.

E-mail Interaction _____

Contact the author at b-allen@wiu.edu. Forward one of the following or phrase your own.

1. You "sound" Mischelian. Are you?

2. Tell me how it could be good to be an external.

3. What else besides traits and behavior–situation relations may play a role in personality?

13

Thinking Ahead and Learning Mastery of One's Circumstances: Albert Bandura

- Do people learn much from imitating others?
- Are we pushed by our past histories or pulled by our anticipation of future rewards?
- Does biology *or* cognition or other internal events *or* the environment drive behavior?

Albert Bandura
www.emory.edu/EDUCATION/
mfp/bandurabio.html

Albert Bandura's account of how we acquire new behaviors, thoughts, and feelings is in the "social learning" category, but it is broader than the theories of Mischel and especially Rotter. In fact, you are are about to consider what is possibly the most comprehensive theory covered in this book, and a point of view that may well be more applicable to the full range of human functioning than any other. Bandura's ideas help explain how we acquire everything from motor behaviors—how to swing a tennis racket properly—to how we overcome irrational emotions, such as fear of snakes. He and his colleagues have studied and elucidated human functions ranging from prosocial orientation toward others to the cognitive processes that allow humans to oppress other humans. More generally, his theory helps to explain how we gain mastery over our life circumstances. Here is an opportunity for you to acquire knowledge that will be truly useful to you in your life.

Bandura, the Person

Albert Bandura, possibly the most generally admired of living psychologists, was born to a Polish father and a Ukranian mother on December 4, 1925, in the Canadian village

Mundare, Alberta (*American Psychologist,* 1981). Though his parents were not formally educated, they valued learning. His father taught himself to read in Polish, Russian, and German (see Web site on p. 299).

"My town" is his answer to the common question "Where do cold fronts come from?" Bandura attended a typical small town school of the day, which contained elementary through high school in one facility ((*American Psychologist,* 1981). It was, however, not devoid of virtues. Due to a shortage of teachers and resources, pupils were forced to learn on their own initiative. Sometimes that included group initiative. Because only two high school teachers were responsible for the entire curriculum, and were not competent in some areas, Bandura and his peers formed study groups to educate themselves (*Monitor on Psychology,* 1992). Perhaps his school days were at least partly the source of Bandura's faith in the power of self-directiveness.

Bandura, like Skinner, could be a bit of a prankster. Once he and fellow students stole their trig teacher's only trigonometry book. Later in graduate school, Bandura and other students pinned a dead rat to the psychology bulletin board with a note exclaiming that the rat was done in by their famous professor Kenneth Spence because it was running mazes in accord to rival theorist Tolman's point of view (see Web site on p. 299).

The path to a more hospitable environment, and a college degree, lay through the forbidding Yukon. Young Bandura took a job patching the Alaskan Highway, which was slowly sinking into its muskeg foundation. There he encountered a variety of individuals, ranging from parole violators and debtors to divorced men avoiding alimony payments. While his coworkers were less than model citizens, they were enterprising. Running a concoction of potatoes and sugar through a home-made still produced an ample supply of raw vodka, enough for an entire month (Stokes, 1986a). Unfortunately, this source of periodic bliss was interrupted one month when the grizzly bears that inhabited the area beat the men to the still. For some time thereafter Bandura witnessed considerable human misery and some very frisky bears. These observations may well have contributed to his interest in innovation and the psychological problems of everyday life.

Chance has always intrigued Bandura (Bandura, 2001a). While an undergraduate at the University of British Columbia, Bandura first experienced the enormous impact of chance. In order to share transportation with a group of engineers and pre-med students, he had to arrive at school early. As chance would have it, the only early class available was introductory psychology. He took it, loved it, and the rest is history (Stokes, 1986b).

After obtaining an undergraduate degree, he enrolled at the University of Iowa, where Spence had the psychology department under his spell. Because of Spence's prominence, and Iowa's ties to Yale and Neal Miller, the furor over learning theories that raged at the time consumed Bandura and his classmates.

While at Iowa, chance struck Bandura again, this time delivering a gentle blow to the heart. During a golf outing with a male friend, his eyes fell on one of two women playing one green ahead (Stokes, 1986a). The twosome became a foursome and, a few months later, Bandura was wed to Virginia Varns, a teacher in the College of Nursing. Her career brought another chance encounter of significance. "The Great Imposter," Ferdinand Waldo Demara, showed up as a resident in obstetrics at her hospital, once again posing as a physician. Demara was known to have performed successful operations, though he had no medical training. It is amazing what people can do if they believe they can do it.

Once, during one of his convention lectures about chance, a book editor arrived late and, because of the overflow audience, was forced to take a chair near the lecture-hall entrance. The chair happened to be next to a stranger . . . the woman he would eventually marry (Bandura, 1998a). Even though he has many such examples in his collection of real-life chance occurrences, he is quick to point out that chance is only one factor in people's lives. In fact, that we are almost always able to control our lives is reflected in one of Bandura's favorite aphorisms: "Chance favors only the prepared mind" (Pasteur, quoted in Bandura, 1998a).

On receiving his doctorate in 1952, and finishing an internship in clinical psychology at the Wichita Guidance Center, Bandura was appointed instructor at Stanford University. Working his way up through the ranks, he became a full professor in 1964 and occupied an endowed chair in 1974. Because he loves the area, in particular San Francisco's fine restaurants and Napa Valley's quaint wineries, it seems that he is unlikely to leave.

In 1980 he received the American Psychological Association's (APA) award for Distinguished Scientific Contributions. He was cited "For masterful modeling as researcher, teacher, and theoretician" and for "innovative experiments on a host of topics including moral development, observational learning, fear acquisition, treatment strategies, self-control . . . and cognitive regulation of behavior. . . . His . . . warmth, and humane example have inspired his many students . . ." (*American Psychologist,* 1981). Since the 1980 award, his awards and contributions include membership in the ultimate scientific organization, the National Academy of Sciences, 14 honorary degrees, and in 2003, he received one of the APA's more prestigious awards, the James McKeen Cattell Award. If not already, before he is finished he will become the most decorated psychologist ever.

Bandura's positive qualities, rivaling those of Rogers, are clearly seen in students' responses to him. On his 65th birthday he was surprised by a gathering of friends and students, like that afforded Kelly. On his seventieth birthday, students at St. Edwards University, who had been studying his theory, sent him a birthday card filled with gentle sentiments and signed by each class member. Students at another college wrote a rap song in tribute to him and his theory. Bandura receives many letters from college students, probably because they sense that he has genuine concern for them as well as a willingness to answer their questions and to supply them with needed information. He, like Freud before him, devotes considerable time to answering letters. Just as Freud was sensitive to the implications of his theory on the lives of real people, so is Bandura. Bandura is currently continuing his work and offering his expertise to U.S. government agencies and Congress. However, his most cherished moments are playing with Timmy and Andy, twin children of one of his two daughters.

Bandura's View of the Person

Inside/Outside and Reciprocal Causation

A major issue in the area of personality has been whether forces inside or outside of individuals control their behavior. Bandura's theory relates behavioral consistency to the inside/outside question. Advocates of determination by factors outside of individuals emphasize the variability of behavior, due to action of the environment. Those who believe that control of behavior comes from within assert that stable processes from inside individuals give rise to stable behavior. By contrast, Bandura is concerned with the interplay of inside and outside factors and, thus, his theory focuses on both the variability and consistency of behavior (Bandura, 1977, 1989a, 1998b). "[P]eople . . . function as contributors to their own motivation, behavior, and development within a network of reciprocally interacting influences" (Bandura, 1989a, p. 6; emphasis added). To Bandura, *personal factors*—such as cognition, biological variables, and other internal events—*behavior,* and the *external environment* have reciprocal influences on one another: each influences the other and is influenced by the other. Figure 13.1 displays these reciprocal relationships.

Personal Factors, Behavior, and the External Environment

Behavior Can Affect Cognition, Feelings, and Even Neurobiology.   Figure 13.1 implies some rather remarkable and even surprising assumptions. It is not so amazing that behavior could affect certain personal factors, such as those in the cognitive category. If you do a thing well the first time you attempt it, you may change your thinking about your ability to do it. Should a child attempt to approach a porpoise while visiting a marina and succeed in touching it on the first try, he might come to view "making friends with seagoing mammals" as a thing "I can do." Likewise, success on a first attempt may change certain internal events, such as feelings about the circumstances involved with the success. Individuals may develop positive feelings about being in the water with our ocean-dwelling relatives. However, that such behavior might affect their neurobiological functions may come as a surprise (Bandura, 2001a; Bower, 2003). If, over several years, they repeatedly read, talk about, and write about seagoing mammals, they will develop a "neurological network" for processing information about them. In turn, learning about whales and porpoises will be easier in the future.

Environments and Beliefs May Affect Neurobiological Functioning.   A woman who takes up residence in a dorm suite occupied by several women adopts a new envi-

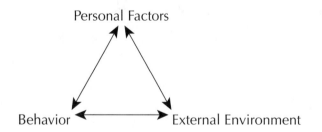

FIGURE 13.1 *Reciprocity in the Relationship between Personal Factors, Behavior, and the External Environment*

ronment that may affect hormonal cycling. In time, the onset and ending of her menstrual cycle may come to match that of her suite-mates (Matlin & Foley, 1997). Cognitions, such as beliefs and expectations, can also impact on hormonal cycling and its accompaniments. If the woman, because of religious indoctrination, believes that "the curse" will strike her every 28 days, she will more regularly experience depression and physical discomfort premenstrually than other women (Paige, 1973). Regardless of her religious beliefs, if she comes to expect that she is about to start her "period," whether or not she really is, she may experience certain physiological changes, such as increased water retention (Ruble, 1977).

Behavior Affects Environment and Vice Versa.   It is obvious that humans' behaviors can affect their physical environment: witness the tragic increase in pollution due to thoughtless human behavior in the service of immediate gratification (Bandura, 1995). Influence in the other direction is equally obvious: because of pollution-driven ozone depletion, some people may have to avoid sunny beaches in the future.

Cognition and Feeling Influence Behavior and Environments.   According to Bandura's model (Figure 13.1), cognitions and internal events, such as feelings, influence both behavior and environments (Bandura, 1989a). If certain people believe that their behavior will not succeed in a given setting, the odds are great that it will fail (Bandura, 1995). If they feel frightened when entering a given situation, they will avoid it. If their feelings and beliefs about forested lands are indifferent or negative—"turn them into commercial properties"—they will allow the forests to vanish.

Free Will, Personal Agency, and the Power of Forethought

In recent years, Bandura has turned his attention to what people can contribute to their own fruitful motivation and effective action (Bandura, 1995, 1998b). Unlike B. F. Skinner, who admonishes us to abandon the "false" assumption of free will, Bandura (1989b) believes that people can, through their own cognitive mechanisms, gain a significant measure of control over their environments (Bandura, 2001a). People can develop a sense of **personal agency,** a condition in which they come to believe that they can make things happen that will be of benefit to themselves and to others.

Recently, Bandura (1999a, 2000a) has alluded to *proxy agency,* enlisting others to help control circumstances affecting one's life. Relying on a family member is an example. However, this form of control has its downside. People may surrender control to a despot (Hitler) who does not have their best interest in mind. More generally beneficial is *collective agency,* the power to exercise control over life circumstances that is embedded in people's shared belief in their collective ability to produce desired outcomes (Bandura, 1998b, 1999a, 2000a). Collective agency does not come from a "group mind" that swirls like a fog above the heads of group members. Rather, it is the product of individual group members' contribution to their group's impact on life circumstances. Personal agency and collective agency are involved in a reciprocally influential relationship (Bandura, 2000a). Amnesty International aids political prisoners via the efforts of individual members who share beliefs about human rights.

Consistent with the contention that people have "free will" to a meaningful degree, Bandura believes that people not only select the situations in which they will operate, they create many of those situations. One may feel forced to go to class or work, but one may choose to attend a concert or drop in on a friend. People may insert themselves into ready-made situations, or they may create their own: "throw a party" or start a debate. They may also transform situations forced on them into circumstances that are more amenable to their efforts at control. Finally, they may non-consciously evoke actions and strategies in others: competitive people elicit competitive behaviors in others (Zayas et al., 2002).

Learning

In contrast to some others who theorize about learning, Bandura believes that learning occurs because people are thoughtful about the consequences of their responses. In support of these assumptions, Bandura (1977) reports considerable evidence that learning is difficult for humans if there is little or no awareness of the link between behavior and consequences. Further, it is nearly certain that learning is facilitated by awareness. Being aware makes people capable of **forethought,** anticipation of "likely consequences of . . . [future] actions" (Bandura, 1989a, p. 27, 1994a, 2001a). Forethought frees people from the tyranny of past rewards or reinforcements and the drudgery of trial-and-error learning (Bandura, 1999a). People behave in anticipation of future consequences; they do not behave exclusively in the present time because present circumstances resemble those associated with reinforcement in the past. "Eye to the future," as opposed to "eyes in the back of the head," is a philosophical position that Bandura shares with Kelly.

Behaviorists prefer animal research subjects; Bandura prefers humans. Animals do not have symbolic thought; people do. People can record consequences of actions as language structures or sets of symbols and, thereby, form hypotheses concerning what will happen in the future (Bandura, 1995, 1999a). If one observes that smiling at waiters yields efficient and prompt service, she or he will store that observation in words and construct the hypothesis that smiling works with waiters. This hypothesis operates as a motivator for smiling behavior in the presence of waiters and will, therefore, increase the likelihood of smiling at waiters on subsequent occasions.

Basic Concepts: Bandura

Observational Learning

On his arrival at Stanford, Bandura fell under the benevolent influence of Robert Sears, who was studying familial antecedents of social behavior and identification learning. Branching off from this work, Bandura and his first doctoral student, Richard Walters, launched a series of studies on aggression in children that are still being cited today (for example, the famous Bobo doll studies). Their investigations into **observational learning,** learning by observing models as they perform useful behavior, demonstrated that "Modeling is not merely a process of behavioral mimicry" (Bandura, 1989a, p. 18). People who observe a model learn the value of a behavioral performance in terms of what it will achieve. Because of its importance to human functioning, it is not surprising that observational learning's representation in the brain has been sought and located (Iacoboni et al., 1999). However, recent work shows that monkeys, who do not have cognition in the same sense as do humans, nevertheless react neurologically when performing a grasping action *or* when they observe a human do it (Bower, 2003). Even our primate cousins do not merely mimic. Other work shows that non-primates, such as birds, do show mimicry, though it is uncertain that their ability to match responses of other members of their species constitutes "observational learning" (Zentall, 2003).

Social *and* Cognitive *in Bandura's Version of* Social–Cognitive Theory of Observational Learning

Another principle underlying Bandura's social–cognitive theory is tied up in the term *social*. People learn as much vicariously, through observing the behavior of others, as they learn through direct experience. Further, the terms *cognition* and *social* are close associates, because cognition is the vehicle by which people learn from other people. If an individual watches another person receive a reward as a consequence of a behavioral performance, the observer will likely think (cognition), "If I behave in the same way, I'll receive the same reward." Observing another person model some behavior that results in reward is enough for learning to occur; rewards need not be directly received. In fact, individuals may learn even if their observations in no way include rewards. In some cultures, the word *teach* is the same as the word *show* (Bandura, 1999a). Box 13.1 compares mimicry with observational learning.

BOX 13.1 • *Monkey See, Monkey Do?*

Evan is twenty-two months old and bright. She already speaks in complete sentences. It seems she picks up everything her parents do. Whenever her father gets an "ouchee" (injury to a body part), he rubs it vigorously. Evan does the same thing. Whenever her mother makes a mistake, she exclaims, "Oh hell!" Should something go awry for Evan (she knocks a dish off the table), she utters "Oh hell!" in the same emphatic tone as her mother. Is this mere mimicry as in one animal observing another and doing as the other has done? Rather than mere mimicry, learning from watching others involves awareness of what the model has done and thoughtfulness about the implications of the model's behavior. Evan's "Oh hell!" acknowledges that she made a mistake and that it is a serious matter to be avoided in the future. Probably even monkeys are aware of what they see other monkeys do, and, in some sense, its implications (recall Rollo May's discussion of awareness in non-primates found in Chapter 9). Research indicates that only the simplest form of learning occurs without awareness (Clark & Squire, 1998). Recently I was discussing with other adults a child who referred to her father by use of a "dirty word." We used the word during our conversation. Our granddaughter, seated in an adjoining room, seemed not to overhear us. However, later she used the same curse word in the same way with reference to her grandmother! The first mentioned child was six years old and the second was four years old. Little pitchers have big ears.

Learning by Other People's Example

Models and Modeling.   There are two fundamental concepts associated with observational learning. A **model** is a person who performs some behavior for an audience, showing how it is done and what benefits accrue from it. **Modeling** refers to the act of performing a behavior before one or more observers. When people learn from observing others, they do not simply soak up whatever models have to offer. They begin observations of others with certain predispositions that determine what they learn from what they see. People want to master aspects of their own particular environments. Thus, they look for those behaviors, among the many displayed by available models, that will allow mastery.

Symbolic Representation.   People do not passively adopt a model's behavior (Bandura, 1989a). They "turn it over" in their minds, relating it to information they already have, rehearsing it, criticizing it, and thereby remembering it if it is useful. In addition, people may transform information learned from a model into symbolic form so that it can be quickly and easily turned into action in the future. For example, one may ask, "Which way to the psychology building?" and hear, in reply, "Follow me." If the questioner is a psychology major, and, thus, will frequently use the directions, the model's movements might at first be visualized as a series of right and left turns, then as "right (r), left (l), r, l, l, r." In this way information provided by the model is represented symbolically, after it was initially accepted in more concrete form.

      Symbolic modeling involves verbal and pictorial means to convey information necessary for adoption of behaviors associated with rewards. In symbolic modeling, people transcend the bounds of their environments by learning without direct experience (Bandura, 2001b). Observers learn from TV and movie actors who operate in environments that the observers have not and probably could not experience. However, models need not be actual people (Bandura, 1994a). TV presentations, especially advertisements, provide good examples of symbolic modeling. A well-set table containing food items for sale may create anticipations of future rewards just as does behavior modeled by a person.

      The pervasiveness of the media in the future, especially the Web, will enhance the role of symbolic modeling (Bandura, 1999a). A single model can, through a single Web site, affect thousands of observers, one at a time. For example, a Web site conveying "how to make a bomb" not only symbolically communicates information transformable into bomb-making behavior, it also communicates that bomb-making is an acceptable, even laudable, thing to do, which, of course, it is not.

Turning Observations into Behavior.   Of course, people do not stop with accepting models' behavior and transforming it into symbolic form. They will attempt to turn their observations into behaviors. The extent to which they are successful will depend in part on whether they have the skills to execute the modeled behaviors. Success will also depend on whether people have gleaned all the relevant elements of the modeled behavior from observations before they try to behave. Given these conditions are met, observers create an *internal representation* of the behavior and then hone and refine it, along with the behavior itself, to suit their particular needs (Bandura, 2000b, 2001a). This "polishing" is accomplished by an interplay between behavioral performances and the internal representation. For example, a ball player who has watched an expert hitter will have a mental representation of the hitter's swing. When she practices the swing, she will compare her attempt to her mental image and change the swing to coincide with the image. At the same time, as the swing evolves so that it becomes successful, the mental representation will change to accommodate peculiarities of the newly effective swing.

Attractive Models. Characteristics of models and observers are also important in determining what is learned, or even whether anything is learned. People do not observe whoever happens to be present. We are drawn to models whose attractiveness stems partly from certain of their characteristics we find interesting (e.g., appearance, style, and confidence) and partly from their success in general and on specific tasks. On the other hand, what people learn from models or other sources is, in part, determined by their own capabilities that existed prior to observations (Zimmerman, Bandura, & Martinez-Pons, 1992). If observers are unschooled in chemistry, they are unlikely to benefit from a laboratory demonstration in that field, no matter how effective the model.

Incentives. Reinforcements or rewards for the performance of behaviors enter the learning sequence in three different ways. First, a person may observe a model being rewarded for performing a behavior. Such an observation would produce an **incentive,** any circumstance, concrete or abstract, that creates an anticipation of positive outcome following the performance of a behavior (Bandura, 1989a). For example, a child observes another child receive lavish praise for preventing an altercation between some younger children. In the future the development of another conflict situation between younger children will act as an incentive for the observer to intervene in anticipation of praise. Second, the model, for example, a parent trying to teach an observing child to pronounce a word, may reward the child's efforts to reproduce the verbal behaviors being modeled. Third, and perhaps most important, the observer may reward him- or herself for a good approximation to correct performance of a response (Bandura, 1994b). So if some children are trying to learn the utterance *arithmetic,* they may "pat themselves on the back" when they come close to the proper pronunciation. Thus, an opportunity to pronounce a word involves incentives.

Goals and Self-Regulation

Goals are anticipated achievements that are in line with current personal standards. Goals in and of themselves are immensely important determinants of performance (Bandura, 1999a, 2001a). Bandura (1991a) shows that the more challenging the goals people set the more effort they put into task performance. A goal, however, is pursued vigorously only if the goal-setter receives feedback indicating progress toward the goal. Thus, Bandura (1991a) reported that experimental subjects who set goals and received feedback regarding progress-to-goals exhibited highly effortful performance. Their effort was high in an absolute sense and also in comparison to subjects who (1) only set goals, (2) only got feedback, or (3) neither set goals nor got feedback. Subjects in the last three conditions showed equally low effort. To be effective motivators, goals should be specific rather than general and capable of being broken down into sub-goals that can be ordered in terms of priorities:

foundation goals are attained first to provide building blocks for final goals (Bandura, 2000b, 2001a).

Even with effort, goal attainment remains uncertain without the institution of **self-regulatory processes,** internal, cognitive–affective functions that guide and govern efforts toward goal attainment (Bandura, 1991a). These processes include self-persuasion, self-monitoring, self-praise (and criticism), appraisal of personal standards, readjustment of standards, acceptance of challenges, and reactions to performances (Bandura, 1990a, 1991a, 1994b, 1999a, 2000b; Caprara, Steca, Cervone, & Artistico, 2003; Caprara et al., 2000). All of these may be regarded as attempts at self-influence. Bandura (1990a) indicated that, the greater the number of self-influence factors brought to bear on a task, the greater the increase in performance motivation.

Flexibility is part of the art of self-regulation during attempts to attain goals. People who can abandon unattainable goals and redirect their efforts to alternative goals show high subjective well being (happiness (SWB); Wrosch, Scheier, Miller, Schulz, & Carver, 2003).

Self-Efficacy

One of the most powerful self-regulatory processes is **self-efficacy,** a belief concerning one's ability to perform behaviors yielding an expected outcome that is desirable (Artistico, Cervone, & Pezzuti, 2003; Bandura, 1989a, 1989b, 1994b, 2000b; Caprara, Steca, Cervone, & Artistico, 2003; Caprara et al., 2000). When self-efficacy is high, one has confidence that she or he can perform behaviors allowing control of a difficult circumstance. Self-efficacy may be thought of as a specific form of confidence. While no one can be confident about everything he or she does, every person can develop beliefs in abilities to perform certain specific behaviors, each of which will yield a desirable outcome in a particular context.

As an illustration of the relationship between self-efficacy level and outcome expectancy, consider a contrast between Sarah and Sam on the matter of public speaking. Both individuals expect that making an effective public speech will be met with applause and other positive social outcomes. However, Sarah has strong feelings of self-efficacy with regard to critical behaviors involved in public speaking. She feels that she can obtain the relevant information that will go into her speech, organize it properly, memorize it, and present it in a clear and articulate manner. On the other hand, Sam has a different conviction with respect to self-efficacy. He feels that he can adequately perform only a few of the behaviors that will lead to the desired outcome.

Self-efficacy influences not only whether a person will attempt a behavior, but also determines the quality of performance once an attempt is made. High efficacy, entailing expectations of success, will generate persistence in the face of obstacles and frustrations. Persistence eventually leading to success will yield further bolstering of self-efficacy. Low efficacy will lower effort, thereby increasing the probability of failure and the likelihood of further decreases in efficacy (Bandura, 1991a).

The single most efficient method for boosting self-efficacy is *performance accomplishment* (Bandura, 1999a). Doing is believing. If a person with low self-efficacy can somehow be induced to perform a feared or repugnant behavior, self-efficacy may be dramatically bolstered. However, vicarious experience can also be effective, especially if people with low self-efficacy can view persons who share their fears perform the inhibited behaviors (Bandura, 1994b). **Participant modeling,** in which the person with low self-efficacy imitates a model's efficacious behavior, can be very beneficial, even when persuasion and other influence attempts have failed. Because, when faced with a threatening situation, people read their state of efficacy by reference to their level of emotional arousal, any methods that will lower arousal will increase feelings of efficacy (1994b). Successful actual performance or positive vicarious experience are methods of lowering arousal.

Other Things We Learn from Models, besides Behavior

Expectancies.   Behavior is not all that is learned from models. In **vicarious expectancy learning,** people adopt other peoples' expectancies concerning future events, especially expectancies of those with whom they share relevant experiences (Bandura, 1977, 1989a, 1994a). For example, people who have lived through a hurricane, but suffered little from its devastating winds, still have witnessed the suffering of people like themselves who were victims. Accordingly, they adopt the victims' expectations. Thus, their vicarious expectancy of disaster may be almost as strong as that of actual victims as reflected in their willingness to join with others in preparing for future storms. In general, vicarious expectancy learning is most likely to be transmitted to people from models with whom they share many experiences (Bandura, 2000b).

Creativity, Facilitation, and Innovation.   An individual first accepts the behaviors of a model and then may creatively branch out from there. Thus, Beethoven adopted the forms of Haydn and Mozart, later going well beyond those artistic styles into his own greater emotional expressiveness (Bandura, 1977). By contrast, in **response facilitation** nothing new is learned, but some old responses may be disinhibited as a result of watching a model's performance (Bandura, 1977, 1989a). In this case, the model's behavior acts as a social prompt, communicating that it is OK to perform the behavior that was inhibited. For example, a person who is fearful of dancing, because religious training made the practice seem "evil," may experience disinhibition of dancing by watching a "good" person dance with no ill effects. As Box 13.2 illustrates, great historical figures have maintained their creativity through their resilience.

Diffusion of innovation occurs when models try something new and, thereby, display its benefits and advantages to others (Bandura, 2001b). Once people have accepted an innovative behavior, its longevity will be partially determined by the permanence of the incentives associated with its adoption. The more permanent the incentives for adopting something new, the longer the innovation will stay around. Fads are short-lived, because adoption results only in fleeting social recognition. Hula hoops are an example. By comparison, the automobile illustrates a novelty that has become permanent. People who drive desirable cars are afforded continuous social recognition and also needed transportation.

There are some definite restraints on the adoption of novelties, however. These include lack of the skills needed to perform behaviors associated with the novelty (Bandura, 1993). Soccer is finally catching on in this country, thanks to the super model, Pele, but

BOX 13.2 • *Self-efficacy Maintained in the Face of Defeat: Resilience*

If people did not have ways to maintain self-efficacy in the face of defeat and humiliation, the world of science, literature, and art would be impoverished. Have you ever heard of James Clerk Maxwell? Probably not. Even the people of his day, the nineteenth century, were pretty much ignorant of him as well (Sagan, 1995). Yet his discoveries regarding the electromagnetic spectrum showed that light is related to electricity and led to the discovery of radio and TV. But he was "odd." As a young man he was called "daffy," which to his British peers meant "not quite right in the head" (p. 10).

Psychologist Hadley Cantril once showed Albert Einstein some visual illusions constructed by fellow psychologist Adelbert Ames (Cantril, 1960). When Cantril complained that the fascinating implications of Ames's illusions were being dismissed by other visual perception psychologists, Einstein replied that he had "learned many years ago never to waste time trying to convince my colleagues" (p. vii).

Robert Goddard, considered by many the "father" of the modern rocket, "was bitterly rejected by his scientific peers on the grounds that rocket propulsion would not work in the rarefied atmosphere of outer space" (Bandura, 1994b, p. 76). Still, he never lost faith in his innovative ideas about rockets. His persistence should have been better remembered on that fateful day in 1969 when " . . . one step for mankind . . . " was heard around the world.

Successful authors typically suffer many rejections before finally being blessed with a best seller. William Saroyan received literally thousands of rejection letters before he finally got published. James Joyce's classic *Dubliners* was rejected by 22 publishers. It took Gertrude Stein 20 years of frustration before she finally got published. When one of e. e. cummings's works finally was published, his dedication read "With no thanks . . . " to the 16 publishers who had previously rejected his work (Bandura, 1990a, p. 145). In the world of art, Van Gogh sold only one painting during his life and died a pauper. But he left hundreds of paintings now worth many millions. Auguste Rodin could not get his art into the best museums and Frank Lloyd Wright's unique architectural works were initially shunned.

How did they manage to persist in the face of multiple rejections and humiliations? They showed unbelievably effective and hardy self-regulatory processes. Apparently e. e. cummings maintained his self-efficacy as a writer by anticipating the time when he could chastise his detractors. Maxwell persisted with little attention from others because his ability to satisfy his own curiosity kept his scientific self-efficacy high. Ames's and Cantril's persistence in the face of rejection paid off in eventual fame as visual perception theorists (Ittleson & Kilpatrick, 1951). Van Gogh and Frank Lloyd Wright may have persisted because their art was its own reward. Goddard enjoyed solving problems so much that a problem in need of solution was a stronger incentive than others' lack of faith was a disincentive. All of them undoubtedly called on friends to bolster their self-efficacy when it was flagging, praised themselves for meeting their own standards, and looked on defeat as a challenge. Whatever their particular reactions to defeat and frustration, each one of them showed remarkable **resilience,** the ability to absorb the slings and arrows of outrageous fortune and still believe that one can accomplish what one desires to do (Bandura, 2000b, 2001c). Self-efficacy that can take the hard knocks will survive to be justified by success. No matter what one might think of Bill Clinton, he certainly has admirable resilience. Whenever you witness the success of a Black person (Colin Powell) or Latino(a) (Anthony Quinn) or American Indian (Senator Ben Lighthorse Campbell), you are seeing resilience. It is the stuff that overcomes adversity. Contrary to earlier assumptions, new evidence suggests that resilience is not rare, not the same as recovery from trauma, and not limited to post-trauma periods (Bonanno, 2004). People can remain resilient even throughout extended periods of trauma. Because they are resilient, even abused children and children of substance abusers can grow up to be strong and effective adults. How do they deal with adversity? They may employ positive emotions to rebound from stressful events (Tugade & Fredrickson, 2004).

adoption has been limited to those with adequate athletic skills. Likewise, computers now pervade most of life's spheres, but at least minimum "computer literacy" is needed to "surf the Net" or create a Web page. Given at least minimal skills, self-efficacy regarding performance of a to-be-adopted innovation is critical (Bandura, 1994a). Anything that models of innovations can do to boost self-efficacy will increase the likelihood of adoption (Bandura, 2001b).

Rewards

While behavior is often acquired vicariously, it is primarily maintained by rewards. There has been much debate concerning the relative importance of **extrinsic rewards,** rewards originating outside the individual, for example, money, and **intrinsic rewards,** rewards from within the individual, for example, self-satisfaction (Bandura, 1977). Extrinsically rewarded behaviors appear to be done for tangible payoffs. In contrast, intrinsically rewarded behaviors seem to be "done for their own sake." From Bandura's vantage point, both are necessary for a full account of human action. External rewards are needed to direct a person's attention to a behavior and to institute initial performance. Nevertheless, long-term maintenance of the behavior depends largely on development of intrinsic rewards. For instance, in order to begin the task of teaching a child to write, tangible rewards—privileges or even money—will likely be needed to generate beginning attempts. Such rewards may have to be presented even on a sentence-by-sentence basis. The child may then progress to performing for less tangible rewards, such as praise from parents for a job well done, though the payoff is still external. Finally, if writing behavior is to be maintained, the child must learn what constitutes good writing behavior so that she can praise herself "under her breath" for writing a grammatically correct sentence. If she does so, intrinsic rewards have come into play.

Intrinsic motivation refers to the desire for intrinsic rewards, leading to the pursuit of the same. One of the problems with the notion of intrinsic motivation is that its presence is often inferred from the persistence of a behavior in the absence of any obvious external rewards. As Bandura (1977) notes, such an inference is unwarranted: if a person watches TV for many hours a day, one would be hard-pressed to invoke "intrinsic motivation." More than likely, the lack of behavioral alternatives explains persistently gazing at the tube. To be sure that intrinsic motivation is at work, one must observe the persistence of behavior in the absence of appropriate external rewards, but in the presence of other behavioral alternatives.

Problems with support for the operation of intrinsic motivation can be avoided by recording observations focused on a kind of self-regulation, **self-evaluation,** a process that involves assessing one's performance at various points along the way to task completion and issuing a vocal or "under-the-breath" judgment of its value (Bandura, 2001a). Thus, a clarinetist who repeatedly sounds a note, sometimes pausing to frown and shake her head, is engaging in self-evaluation. When a smile follows an attempt at the note, observers can conclude that the clarinetist has positively rewarded herself. Most forms of "practice" are intrinsically motivated, and, therefore, under the control of intrinsic reward.

Intrinsic reward is not the only way that one's behavior may be maintained in the absence of immediate, external rewards. **Vicarious reinforcement** occurs when one observes another person being rewarded for performing a behavior (Bandura, 2001b). An observation that helping others settle a dispute is followed by many warm "thank yous" is likely to transform cases of interpersonal conflict into cooperative circumstances. According to Bandura, vicarious reinforcement can induce people to try an undesired food, give up a valued object, and disclose personal matters, any of which could be beneficial (Bandura, 1977). In addition, vicarious punishment can be efficient. Bandura (1977) cites a study in which observers of models who were punished for performance of a prohibited behavior later were just as unlikely to perform the behavior as were the models.

External rewards, of course, do not have any inherent absolute value (Bandura, 2001b). Value of rewards is relative, established by the process of **social comparison,** determining how well one is doing in life by comparing oneself to those who share one's life situation (Festinger, 1954). A factory worker does not determine how well he is doing in life by comparing himself with the plant manager. Instead he compares himself to people doing the same job. If, for example, he is earning as much, or a little more, than people who share the same job, he can conclude that he is doing fine. "X" number of dollars earned per month is valued or not valued, depending on its standing, relative to what comparable others are earning. According to Suls, Martin, and Wheeler (2002), the choice of a person with whom to compare depends on the potential comparison person's relevant expertise, similarity to the chooser, and previous agreement with the chooser. Further, there are circumstances for which a person may compare with another person who is superior or inferior with regard to relevant issues involved in the comparison. One may compare with an inferior person when one desires to bolster one's current status and with a superior person when one aspires to rise in status.

Defensive Behaviors

Defensive behaviors are adopted in order to cope with unpleasant events that are anticipated on future occasions (Bandura, 1977). Anxiety is an associate of early defensive behavior, not the cause of it (Leventhal, 1970). Initially, the unpleasant event is accompanied by both anxiety and defensive behavior. An anxious child takes a big stuffed bear to bed "to scare the wolves away." But after the defensive behavior is seen as a way to avoid the unpleasant event, it is performed in the absence of anxiety. Because defensive behavior is due to anticipating the avoidance of unpleasant events in the future, rather than for the purpose of coping with present anxiety, it is very difficult to eliminate. The absence of the unpleasant event is "proof" to the performer that his or her defensive behavior is "working." Therefore, if a child is asked, "Why do you take that huge stuffed bear to bed?" the now calm child replies, "Because it keeps the wolves away." When the response is, "But there are no wolves around here," the retort is, "See how well it works." "The way out" may be through modeling. If a trusted model can be observed operating in the context of the unpleasant event without performing the defensive behavior, and the unpleasant event fails to occur, the defensive behavior may be discarded. "See me in bed? No bear, but no wolves ever get me."

But modeling is not the only way to deal with anxiety-provoking circumstances. Those with low self-efficacy for dealing with threat will be highly anxious, worry, dwell on their deficiencies, and view their environments as especially threatening. In contrast, people with high self-efficacy for dealing with threat take action to make their environments less "dangerous." They are able to control their thoughts, eliminating continuous rumination about disaster, so that their emotions are self-regulated. Controlling thoughts is difficult and always only approximated, but it is possible, as is reflected in one of Bandura's adages: "You cannot prevent the birds of worry and care from flying over your head. But you can stop them from building a nest in your hair" (Bandura, 1998b, p. 39).

Evaluation

Supporting Evidence

Self-efficacy.   Self-efficacy has been one of the hottest research topics of the 1980s, 1990s, and earlier 2000s. In view of the enormous number of studies on this self-regulatory mechanism—many more than could be reviewed here—a few research projects have been selected for consideration because they aptly demonstrate the power of self-efficacy.

Bandura, Reese, and Adams (1982) recruited spider phobics through newspaper ads. A *phobia* is an intense, irrational fear of an object that is not particularly dangerous. Subjects, ranging in age from 16 to 61 years, showed extreme fear of spiders. At the mere sight of or even a picture of a spider, one subject would experience shivers, pounding of the heart, shortness of breath, and sometimes vomiting for hours.

Subjects first were administered a behavioral avoidance test, consisting of 18 items, each progressively more threatening than its predecessor (see Table 13.1). At the beginning of the experiment, the best a subject believed she could do was to view a wolf spider at a considerable and safe distance, a near-zero score. Self-efficacy judgments were made by presenting subjects with the 18 performances listed on the behavioral test, and for each, asking them to indicate on a 100-point scale the degree of efficacy that they felt with regard to performing the behavior. Next, subjects were randomly assigned to low or medium efficacy-treatment conditions.

First, an experimenter placed the spider in a plastic bowl and poked it with her finger. Next she removed the spider from the container and handled the creature as it crawled

TABLE 13.1   *Example Items for the Behavioral Avoidance Test*

Approach plastic bowl containing spider

Look down at the spider

Place bare hands in the bowl

Let spider crawl freely in a chair placed in front of [yourself]

Let spider crawl over gloved hands

Let spider crawl over bare forearm

Handle spider with bare hands

Allow spider to crawl on lap

all over her. Then she herded the spider all over a chair. At regular intervals during the treatment, each subject took the efficacy test, which was repeated until each subject reached the level of efficacy corresponding to her assigned treatment condition (low or medium efficacy). Low behavioral efficacy was defined as being able to allow the spider to roam over a chair placed near the subject and being able to place a hand in the bowl containing the spider. Subjects in the medium efficacy condition continued in treatment until they reached maximum efficacy: holding the spider in a gloved or a bare hand. The efficacy test and the behavioral test, performed earlier, were repeated at attainment of medium efficacy and repeated again at maximum efficacy. Low-efficacy subjects were also given both tests after attaining low, medium, and maximum efficacy.

There was a direct, straight-line relationship between subjects' assigned level of self-efficacy and their behavioral performance after the treatment. Subjects assigned to the low-efficacy condition achieved low performance on the behavioral test after treatment, while those in the medium-efficacy condition achieved medium behavioral performance after treatment. Also low-efficacy subjects' behavioral performance was measured when they were at low efficacy and when their efficacy was raised to a medium level. There was again a direct relationship between efficacy level and performance. If a subject indicated that she could, at most, place her hands on the inverted bowl with the spider inside, that was all she could do. Self-efficacy predicted performance almost perfectly. In about two hours, life-long spider phobics were able to touch a creature that had previously terrorized them. Self-efficacy is so powerful in a practical sense, it can transform lives.

In a similar study, Wiedenfeld, O'Leary, Bandura, Brown, Levine, and Raska (1990) used snake phobics. In addition they measured effects on the immune system during self-efficacy acquisition and the relationship of those effects to certain physiological responses and endocrine (hormone) secretions. A behavior avoidance test was used again but a harmless corn snake was substituted for the spider. In contrast to Bandura and colleagues (1982), all subjects went through all phases of self-efficacy enhancement, from a pretest/baseline phase, through an efficacy-growth phase, finishing with a maximal efficacy phase. During the pretest/baseline phase, subjects' self-efficacy was measured (it was uniformly very low), and indexes of endocrine, physiological, and immunological functioning were obtained. During the efficacy-growth phase, subjects were exposed to the corn snake. An experimenter modeled progressively more threatening interactions with the snake and invited subjects to emulate her behavior. This two-hour session was later followed by an additional two-hour treatment during which subjects were brought up to and maintained at maximal self-efficacy and performance attainment.

Self-efficacy showed the same course of development reported by Bandura et al. (1982): it stayed at rock-bottom levels during pretest assessments, rose dramatically during efficacy-growth phase assessments, and stayed near the maximal strength "100" level during maximal-efficacy phase assessments. Levels of immune-system components, such as blood lymphocytes, helper T cells, and suppressor T cells, were assessed during the three phases. Indexes of these components showed dramatic changes from the baseline in the direction of immune-system enhancement during the efficacy-growth.

Cortisol elevations are often associated with the immune-system suppression and heart rate acceleration that typically accompanies stress. The slower was acquisition of self-efficacy during the study, the greater were cortisol levels and heart rate accelerations and the more sluggish was immune-system functioning. In contrast, rapid acquisition of self-efficacy was associated with relatively high immunological status. Not only was self-efficacy enhanced, but, for most subjects, immune-system functioning was enhanced. These results suggest the exciting possibility that social–cognitive theory will yield methods for eliminating the multiple suppressions of phobics' immune systems that may accompany periodic thoughts of, and real-life exposures to, feared objects.

Self-efficacy for Dealing with Social and Health Problems. Bandura's social–cognitive theory takes a proactive rather than a reactive approach to substance abuse (Bandura, 1999b). Rather than promoting the view of addicts as powerless drug abusers, they are taught to use delay tactics when the urge to use threatens them and to develop the ability to visualize the negative consequences of substance use and the positive consequences of sobriety. They learn that cognitive processes, not physical dependency, determine relapse. Long-term abstinence eliminates physical dependency and also causes cognitive devices to weaken. For example, self-efficacy to delay satisfaction of an urge to drink by avoiding places where alcohol is served may fade during recovery, if it is not strengthened through periodic rehearsal. Consistent with this position, Bandura cites a study that showed it was self-efficacy to remain abstinent, not frequency of cravings, that predicted actual abstinence. He also reported that permanent abstainers have higher initial self-efficacy than either nonabstainers or relapsers. Self-efficacy at the end of treatment predicted who would relapse, and high self-efficacy people regarded a relapse as a temporary setback and redoubled their efforts.

Epel, Bandura, and Zimbardo (1999) studied 82 homeless people in the Northern California Bay area. Their self-efficacy for finding housing and a job was assessed along with their time perspective. Coauthor Philip Zimbardo had previously shown that, compared to those oriented to the present, future-oriented people are more self-efficacious in many different arenas. As predicted, those high in self-efficacy searched more for housing and employment and stayed in temporary housing for a shorter time than those with low self-efficacy. Those high in future orientation were homeless for a shorter time, were more likely to enroll in school, and reported more positive benefits from their homeless condition than did present-oriented people.

Schwarzer (2001) developed a model for changing health-related behaviors that included perceived health self-efficacy, outcome expectancy, and risk-perception as input variables. Mediating factors included intention and planning. Behavior-determining factors included initiative, health maintenance, and recovery from setbacks. Schwarzer showed that self-efficacy is the only input variable that is crucial to all components of the mediating and behavioral levels of the model. That is, health-behavior change attempts fail if self-efficacy wanes at any level of the model.

Optimism about dealing with one's health problems is a form of self-efficacy. Shelley Taylor is assessing the effects of AIDS victims' optimism about controlling their disease on their medical progress (Weaver, 2003). She finds that the more optimistic victims are about controlling their disease the longer they live. Optimism apparently works by lowering stress and its physiological effects. Being over-optimistic, even to the point of appearing naive, may be a cure for many of life's ills (Allen, 2001). A whole book devoted to positive psychology, including optimism, attests to the beneficial impact of an affirmative orientation on all of our lives (Lopez & Snyder, 2003).

Applications of Bandura's social cognitive theory (SCT) are helping people deal with health and social problems in such places as Mexico, China, and Tanzania, Africa (Bandura, 2002; Smith, 2002). In Tanzania, for example, television dramas involving positive models who practice safe sex, family planning, and who show respect for women are increasing salutary behaviors in these categories. In Mexico, television drama models displayed the benefits of literacy. The day after a broadcast, 25,000 people showed up to a literacy-booklet distribution center mentioned during the telecast. In another Mexican example, contraceptive use skyrocketed during a drama series promoting reduction in fertility rates. In China, a television series promoting small family ideals, female empowerment, and valuing female babies won major Chinese television awards. The behavior of negative role models also has considerable impact. In a Tanzania television series, Mkwaju is a long-distance truck driver whose wife tolerates his unfaithful and alcoholic behavior at first, but eventually leaves him and starts her own successful business. In the meantime, Mkwaju develops AIDS. The number of lives saved and lives improved is not yet known, but it must number in the many thousands. The mark of a really great theory is its practical usefulness.

Self-efficacy at Work, at a Party, and Beyond the Park Bench. Strauser, Ketz, and Keim (2002) related Job Readiness Self-efficacy (JRSE; example item: "I am confident in my ability to get along with my supervisor," p. 24) to Work Personality (WP; "Learn[s] new assignments quickly," p. 24) and to the Work Locus of Control Scale (WLCS; "Getting the job you want is mostly a matter of luck," p. 24). JRSE was positively and highly significantly related to WP and was negatively and highly significantly related to external locus of control. That is, high JRSE corresponds to a strong work personality and to high internal job-related locus of control.

As everybody knows, those who tend to be shy are inclined to avoid the party scene. Thus, promoting personality factors that mitigate against shyness is of considerable importance to the social well-being of shy people. To isolate these factors, Caprara, Steca, Cervone, and Artistico (2003) had 364 Italian teens respond to a shyness scale ("I am often uncomfortable at parties and other social functions," p. 956) on a first occasion (Time 1) and on a second occasion two years later (Time 2). Several personality variables, measured at Time 1, were related to each other and to shyness on the two occasions: Perceived Self-efficacy to Manage Negative Affect (SEMNA; "I can calm myself in stressful situations," p. 594), Perceived Self-efficacy to Manage Positive Affect (SEMPA; "I can show liking for a person toward whom I am attracted," p. 954); Perceived Social Self-efficacy (SSE: "I can express my opinions when other classmates disagree with me," p. 954); Perceived Filial Self-efficacy (FSE; "I can talk to my parents about my feelings toward them," p. 595); and Emotional Stability (ES; emotional control, "If I feel anxious I can find ways to cope with it," and impulse control, "If someone irritates me, I can prevent myself from being mean to that person"; both examples contrived by the author).

These researchers found that strong abilities to manage positive affect (SEMPA) and negative affect (SEMNA) were associated with high levels of social (SSE) and filial (FSE) self-efficacy. SEMNA and FSE were strongly, positively related to emotional stability (ES). Social Self-efficacy (SSE) was strongly and negatively related to shyness at both Time 1 and Time 2. However, ES was negatively related to shyness only at Time 1. Also reflecting the power of SSE to moderate shyness was the finding that high SSE at Time 1 predicted reduced shyness two years later. Therefore, results showed that high self-efficacy to manage both positive (SEMPA) and negative (SEMNA) affect promoted high Social Self-efficacy (SSE) which had direct negative impact on shyness at both Times 1 and 2. In addition, the ability to manage negative affect (SEMNA) and relating well to one's parents (FSE) predicted Emotional Stability (ES). In sum, findings suggest that teens displaying strong social self-efficacy are insulated against shyness and teens who can manage negative affect and get along with their parents are emotionally stable.

Paul Simon and Art Garfunkle recently traveled around the United States singing their great hits, including "Old Friends," about old friends past seventy who spend their time sitting on park benches (Paul and Art are in their early sixties). It is implied that elderly people can do little more than sit comfortably and watch life pass them by. Artistico, Cervone, and Pezzuti (2003) reported that, according to past research, elderly people recorded lower self-efficacy to perform various tasks and actually performed less well on the tasks than young people. But they go on to argue that such results were found in the past partly because there was little attention to how relevant the tasks were (Cervone, 2004) from the perspectives of the young and elderly research participants. To prove their point, they recruited 20 young (20–29 years old) and 20 elderly (65–75 years old) Italian participants. These people were then exposed to problems previously selected to be relevant to young people ("Dealing with a computer crash"), to elderly people ("Wanting to be visited by relatives more frequently"), and a difficult cognitive problem not relevant to either group. Compared to elderly people, young people reported higher self-efficacy beliefs and the strongest performance on both the cognitive problem and the problems relevant to young people. In contrast, compared to young people, elderly people reported higher self-efficacy beliefs and the strongest performance on the problems relevant to them. Elderly people need not be viewed as sitting around on park benches for want of tasks they believe they can do well and that they can, in fact, do well. Give them a task that is relevant to them (Cervone, 2004) and they will show stronger self-efficacy to do the task and will do it better than will young people.

Self-Efficacy and Academic Achievement.   Why do children do poorly in school? Of course, there are many reasons, but some of them are amenable to control: they can be manipulated to improve performance. To study a few of these controllable factors, Bandura, Barbaranelli, Caprara, and Pastorelli (1996a) enlisted the help of 279 Italian children ranging in age from 11 to 14 years. Among the variables they investigated were socioeconomic status (of children's families), parental academic efficacy (parents' beliefs they can positively affect their children's academic achievement), the children's academic efficacy, parental academic aspirations (for their children), children's academic aspirations, children's self-regulatory efficacy (children's perceptions that they are able to resist peer pressure to engage in high-risk activities), prosocialness (kind and cooperative inclination toward peers), children's social efficacy, peer preference (children's popularity with peers), problem behavior, and depression.

Some results were surprising. For example, contrary to popular beliefs, *socioeconomic status* had no *direct* effect on academic achievement. It operated through *prosocialness* and *parental academic aspirations.* The higher the socioeconomic status the higher the *prosocialness* and the lower the problem behavior, a condition associated with increased achievement. The higher the status, the higher were *parental aspirations* and, in turn, children's achievement. Thus, low socioeconomic status was important only because it was associated with low parental academic efficacy and academic aspirations. It follows that parents of any socioeconomic level could develop their academic efficacy and aspirations, thereby greatly benefiting their children.

Parental academic efficacy was positively related to *parental academic aspirations,* which was positively associated with children's academic achievement. *Parents' academic efficacy* was also positively associated with *children's academic efficacy,* which, in turn, was both directly and indirectly positively related to children's academic achievement.

Children's high academic efficacy was associated with strong *prosocialness,* which was associated with high popularity, a condition relating to low problem behavior and high achievement. Also, *children's social efficacy* and *academic efficacy* were negatively related to depression, which was negatively related to achievement.

Thus, parents did have strong impact on their children's academic achievement, but more indirectly. "Parental sense of efficacy that they can influence what teachers expect of their children, how much time [teachers] devote to them, and how much [teachers] help them academically is . . . more likely to yield a direct path of influence than parental efficacy to increase their children's interest and involvement in scholastic activities" (e.g., encourage children to do homework; p. 1217). Parents with high academic efficacy and high academic aspirations had children with high academic achievement. Children who had high academic efficacy, high social efficacy, and high academic aspirations showed high prosocialness, high popularity with peers, low depression, and low problem behavior, all of which contributed to high academic achievement.

The same research group (Bandura et al., 2001) used the same Italian subject population and essentially the same procedures to investigate the relationship between the same set of variables and children's career trajectories. On completing middle school these children chose a professional school to begin preparing for some of the following careers: science/technology, medicine, education, art, social service, management, police/military, or agriculture. First, socioeconomic status had important influence only on parents' academic efficacy and academic aspirations and only the latter began the path to careers. Parental academic aspirations began a path through children's social efficacy, academic aspirations, literary/art efficacy to professor/writer/designer careers (relationships between all pairs of points were positive; e.g., children's social efficacy related to their academic aspirations +.22). Another path was the same through academic aspirations but was routed through educational/medical efficacy to doctor/nurse/pharmacist careers. Parental inputs were filtered through children's perceived efficacies and aspirations to career efficacies. The latter led to career choices. Perhaps surprisingly, children's perceived efficacies, not academic achievement, determined career efficacy.

The Pervasive Effects of Prosocialness.   The same team plus Philip Zimbardo (Caprara et al., 2000) investigated the impact of prosocialness on academic achievement, aggression, and popularity. Self, peer, and teacher reports comprised both aggression and prosocialness scores. Peers rated subjects on whether they were desirable as play and study mates. Aggression had no effects on measures of academic achievement and popularity, but prosocialness had direct positive impact on both academic achievement and popularity. A second analysis looked at earlier prosocialness, aggression, and achievement. It showed early aggression and academic achievement were unrelated to later academic achievement and popularity. By contrast, early prosocialness was positively related to later academic achievement and later popularity.

A study similar to the others by Bandura and his Italian colleagues (1996b) focused on *moral disengagement,* the tendency to employ cognitive devices to excuse immoral acts. Moral disengagement was related to two variables: delinquent behavior and aggressive behavior. Prosocialness, aggression proneness (peer-nominated), and guilt and restitution (self-regulatory sanctions against one's self for committing transgressions) were considered as possible links along the path from moral disengagement to both delinquency and aggressive behavior.

Moral disengagement was higher in males than females. The source of this result was males' greater use of moral justifications, euphemistic language, minimizing injurious effects, dehumanization, and blaming victims. Moral disengagement bore a direct, positive relationship to delinquency. It also was indirectly related to delinquency: high disengagement was associated with low prosocialness and guilt/restitution as well as high aggressive proneness, all of which was associated with increased delinquency. Those who morally disengage tend to be low in prosocialness, have few thoughts of guilt/restitution, and high proneness to aggressiveness. All three conditions relate to delinquency.

Surprisingly, moral disengagement did not relate *directly* to aggressive behavior. However, it did take an indirect route to aggressive behavior through the other three variables. Moral disengagement was associated with lowered prosocialness and guilt/restitution as well as high aggression proneness, conditions that were related to increased aggressive behavior. Children who morally disengage are low in prosocialness (uncooperative/unkind), tend not to feel guilty after transgressing, and are seen by peers as prone to aggression, all of which are associated with aggressive behavior. Previous studies had found moral disengagement unrelated to race or socioeconomic status. The Italian results indicated disengagement was not related to socioeconomic status.

Bandura and the Italian team plus Camillo Regalia (2001) studied the relationship of transgressive behavior (lying, cheating, stealing, aggressing, and being destructive) to children's academic efficacy, social efficacy (belief in control over social activities), self-regulatory efficacy (belief in ability to resist peer pressure), moral disengagement, rumination (thinking about sources of anger), irascibility (spoiling for a fight), and prosocialness. Transgressive behavior was measured at two points in time. Both academic efficacy and self-regulatory efficacy were directly and negatively related to transgressive behavior at both times. The effects of academic efficacy and social efficacy were funneled through prosocialness via rumination to transgressions at time one. Both academic efficacy and self-regulatory efficacy were negatively related to moral disengagement, which was positively related to transgressive behavior at time two. Thus, the higher the academic and self-regulatory efficacy the lower was transgressive behavior. Academic efficacy and social efficacy also related negatively to transgressive behavior through prosocialness.

Prosocial behavior may stem, in part, from the effects of having one's behavior copied by others. Unintentionally, we mimic the behaviors of others (van Baaren, Holland, Kawakami, & Knippenberg, 2004). In so doing we generate prosocial behavior in them that is not directed only to us. Even if we are strangers to those we mimic, when we copy people's behaviors we induce prosocial behavior in them that benefits ourselves as well as third parties.

In sum, prosocialness was positively related to academic achievement and popularity, negatively related to moral disengagement and aggression, and, indirectly, negatively related to delinquency. It was the pathway through which academic efficacy and social efficacy bore negative relationships to transgressive behavior. Prosocialness appears to promote academic achievement and popularity while helping to lower the likelihood of transgressive behavior, delinquency, and aggression. But what lays the early foundation for prosocialness? It may partially be a mutually responsive orientation (MRO) between mother and child in which there is shared positive affect and mutual responsiveness to each other's emotional states and needs (Kochanska, 2002; see Box 6.2 on p. 136). MRO leads to strong conscience development in children, which may be an important precursor to prosocialness.

Implications of Social–Cognitive Theory for Moral Functioning

Crime.   Social–cognitive theory has implications for the well-being and prosperity of humans in the future. For example, it has important implications for something we are all concerned about, crime.

Why do people steal and commit other crimes despite the threat of arrest and imprisonment? A look inside the prisons suggests an answer. Poor people and people of color are greatly over represented in our penal institutions. People will survive, and, in so doing, they will choose methods of survival from whatever is available to them. Two factors govern selection of criminal behavior as a means of survival. First, it is one of the few behavioral alternatives open to those relegated to the bottom of the social ladder. Second, compared to other available alternatives, the incentives are great relative to the likelihood of negative future outcomes (that is, being caught and imprisoned). One could work at a dead-end job, for low pay—"flipping burgers at Mickey D's"—and suffer certain humiliation and failure to prosper, or one could resort to crime. Perhaps you will be able to imagine that making thousands weekly selling crack cocaine is more alluring than working for minimum wage at a fast-food outlet if these are among the few alternatives available to you. In the case of many crimes, effort is minimal, the likelihood of being caught and imprisoned minimal, and the outcome highly positive, relative to investment. It follows from these conjectures that public pronouncements to the effect "people are imprisoned for criminal behavior" will fail to deter crime.

The middle class and above have more numerous and better behavioral alternatives available, compared to the poor and victims of social discrimination. The solution to many social ills, most especially crime, lies in making the full range of behavioral alternatives available to all the people, not just the relatively privileged.

Doing Evil and Avoiding the Cognitive and Emotional Consequences (3-D GAMBLE).
Bandura's social–cognitive theory has implications for the understanding of other troubling behaviors (Bandura, 1989a, 1990b, 1991b, 1995). As Bandura observes, "Over the years, much cruelty has been perpetrated by decent, moral people in the name of religious principles, righteous ideology, and social order" (1977, p. 156). Yet, "character flaws" do not adequately explain humans' inhumanity to humans. Instead, the culprit is an intricate game of mental gymnastics. "People do not ordinarily engage in reprehensible conduct until they have justified to themselves the morality of their actions" (Bandura, 1999c, p. 194).

Social–cognitive theory helps to explain how individuals engage in inhumane behaviors without suffering severe psychological consequences. **Self-exonerative processes** is the general name given to cognitive activities that allow people to dissociate themselves from the consequences of their actions. Moral disengagement employs these devises (Bandura, 1999c). Religion, ideology, and "order," all noble in concept, are abused in practice when they are invoked to justify doing evil. "Noble causes" can be invoked to break the connection between behaviors and their consequences. Actual outcomes of behaviors that would otherwise be considered immoral and unforgivable are covered up, shoved aside, and, thereby, effectually replaced by acceptable outcomes. For example, Klansmen adopt a religious facade, including the cross symbol, to cloak their vicious behavior in an aura of righteousness (see *Klanwatch,* a publication of Southern Poverty Law, 1001 South Hull St., Montgomery, Alabama 36101).

However, Klan behavior is sometimes so savage it is difficult to justify, even "with God on our side." In order to engage in torture and murder Klansmen must first mentally obliterate their victims' humanity. **Dehumanization** is a cognitive process that involves lowering the status of certain people from "human being" to "lesser being" (first of three Ds). In Bandura, Underwood, and Fromson (1975), an experimenter was overheard calling would-be victims of electric shock "animalistic" and "rotten." They received more shock than subjects called "perceptive" and "understanding" (unbeknownst to subjects, no shock was actually delivered). It is difficult to perform, much less justify, torturing and killing of human beings, but it can be done to beings judged "not human" (Bandura, 1990b). Thus, labeling people "gooks," "hymies," "spicks," "spooks," or "injuns" makes them fair targets for ultimate cruelty.

Advantageous comparison is a cognitive mechanism by which " . . . deplored acts can be made to appear righteous by contrasting them with flagrant inhumanities" ("a" in gamble; Bandura, 1990b, p. 171). When confronted with accusations that the Nazis mistreated the Jews, Hitler was in the habit of citing the subjugation of American Indians by the U.S. Army and the oppression of Indians by the British (Speer, 1970). The British of yesteryear and other colonialists were in the habit of dismissing the harm they did to conquered "natives" by pointing out all the "good" they did in the process of colonialization: Western religion and "civilization" were brought to the "savages."

Euphemistic labeling is the cognitive process of assigning a name to deplorable behavior that makes it seem innocuous or even laudable ("e" in *gamble;* Bandura, 1990b, 1991b, 1995, 1999c). The "Vietnam experience" included many such labels. Destroying crops and jungle habitats was called "defoliation." Disenfranchising and physically relocating whole villages of people was called "pacification." Killing as many as possible and collecting their bodies like trophies was called "body count." These labels, produced by the military hierarchy, were partly responsible for the atrocities in Vietnam, not the soldiers to whom they were supplied. If one could replace the entire set of soldiers who served in Vietnam with another group, the result would be the same (Allen, 1978). The Nazis, of course, were masters of euphemistic labeling. "Euthanasia Program" was the fancy name given to gassing mentally and physically handicapped people (Dawidowicz, 1975). "The Final Solution of the Jewish Question" was the official title of the human tragedy now known as the Holocaust (Shirer, 1960).

Blaming victims for their own fate is all too common a cognitive exercise ("b" in *gamble;* Bandura, 1990b, 1991b, 1995, 1999c). Rapists often blame their victims: "She was dressed sexy"; "She was flirtatious"; "She shouldn't have been out that late."

Displacement involves placing the blame for one's deplorable acts onto others (second of the three Ds; Bandura, 1999c). Soldiers who murder civilians and say "I was only obeying orders" are transferring the blame to their superiors. **Diffusion of responsibility** is spreading the responsibility for reprehensible behavior to others who are present (the third D; Bandura, 1999c). It allows one to walk right by a person who is suffering a calamity and hardly notice, so long as there are many others present to whom one may spread the responsibility for helping (Latane and Darley, 1970).

In **moral justification,** inhumane behavior is made "acceptable" because perpetrators claim it serves socially worthy or moral purposes ("m" in *gamble;* Bandura, 1990b, 1991b, 1999c). Hitler constructed a peculiar moral code to which he referred whenever his savage acts seemed to require justification: the "destiny of the German people" justified any and every act performed in its own interest (Shirer, 1960). Famed World War I marksman, Sergeant Alvin C. York, never could have performed his many heroic deeds had he not been able to reconcile his behavior with his religious beliefs. He registered as a conscientious objector, but that status was denied. Unconvinced by his battalion commander's Biblical citations of conditions under which Christians are permitted to kill, York retired to a mountainside for a marathon of prayers. He emerged dedicated to killing "the enemy." Moral codes have often been used to justify all manner of cruelties, including those committed in the name of religion. In fact, none of the world's great religions condones maiming, torturing, or killing human beings. Another of Bandura's favorite aphorisms fits here: "Those who can make you believe absurdities can make you commit atrocities" (Voltaire, quoted in Bandura, 1999c, p. 195). Hitler persuaded many thousands of Germans to accept his absurd beliefs about human "races" and, in so doing, induced them to slaughter many millions considered members of inferior "races."

Gradualistic moral disengagement, a process during which people slowly slip unaware into what was normally unacceptable behavior, has made monsters of everyday people ("g" in *gamble;* Bandura, 1999c). Terrorists are trained in a step-by-step process that takes many months. With each step, a mental wave swells and pounds against the belief that taking human life is wrong. By the end of training, abhorrence of killing is fully eroded. "Development of the capability to kill usually evolves through a process in which recruits may not fully recognize the transformation they are undergoing" (Bandura, 1990, p. 186). In the famous "obedience to authority" studies by Stanley Milgram (1974), subjects were gradually sucked into ostensibly harming another human by the graduated procedure of escalating electric-shock punishments with each error on a learning task.

Self-Evaluation and Self-Sacrifice/Altruism. While certain immoral behaviors can be predicted and explained by social–cognitive theory, so can some forms of self-sacrifice and altruism. *Self-evaluation* can be so dominant that it becomes more important than external rewards and punishments. Mother Teresa, winner of the 1979 Nobel Peace Prize, had such strong convictions concerning the elimination of human suffering that she worked for years in obscurity and deprivation to bring comfort to the poor, ill, and lame of Calcutta, India. During the early 1980s, a young man rushed to the aid of a woman who was being raped on a public street. His actions showed his disdain for the dangers associated with intervening when a man attacks a woman, dangers that explain the inaction of other bystanders. Similarly, Lenny Skutnik stood among several people as he watched a woman flounder in the Potomac following the crash of her plane. Seeing the helpless victim slowly disappear into the icy water, Skutnik dove in and hauled her to shore. His efforts received national acclaim, including introduction to the Congress by the President of the United States (*Life,* January 1983). During the early 1980s, a crowd formed beneath a ninth floor window where a man was poised to jump (Mann, 1981). It happened in Los Angeles, city of notables, one of whom was on the scene. Muhammad Ali talked the man from his perch. The crowd cheered. Altruism well modeled is well appreciated.

Other models of noble behavior include Martin Luther King, Jr. and Susan B. Anthony, a pioneer warrior in the battle for women's rights. King had "a dream," the fulfillment of which was more important to him than life itself. Assassination haunted him wherever he went, but he refused to be silent or to cease his travels. Dr. King faithfully continued his mission until the end. Anthony was a respected educator whose life could be described as very comfortable and secure. She readily jeopardized these advantages because she could not abide the absurdity and insensitivity of beliefs and practices to which

Martin Luther King, Jr.

Susan B. Anthony

BOX 13.3 • *Diversity: The "Battle of the Sexes" Is a War with Millions of Women Victims*

Men beating the women in their lives, sometimes seriously injuring or even killing them, is a tragic but familiar facet of life around the world. Abusers use the full range of self-exonerative processes: "I know men who would kill their wives for less" (advantageous comparison); "It was a shoving match. I just pushed her around a little" (euphemistic labeling); "I only do it for her own good. She needs it; she behaves better after it happens" (moral justification); "The bitch got what she deserves" (dehumanization). And, of course, abusers blame their victims: "She made me do it because she just wouldn't keep the house clean"; "She drove me to it because of her constant complaints every time I come home late"; or "I had no choice. She wouldn't stop looking at other men." Until this web of cognitive delusions is no longer spun in the heads of some men, women will suffer and the perpetrators will experience an erosion of their own humanity. Sadly there is evidence that abusive males and their victims may seek out each other. Zayas and colleagues (2002) describe results of a dating study in which abused females selected the personal ads of potentially abusive males. Males selected ads describing females with a self-depreciating attachment style that had been shown to be associated with involvement in abusive relationships. Zayas and colleages (2002) also described work in which females displaying an anxious ambivalent attachment style unconsciously produced behaviors that attracted abusive males. In this case, instead of actively seeking abusive males, they set up a situation that attracted abusers.

the women of her day were subjected. Nor could she tolerate slavery. The humane exploits of these and many other individuals remind us that people are capable of compassion and kindness, attributes that will more strongly dominate cruelty and indifference when more is known about social learning processes. Box 13.3 covers a dark side of human behavior.

Limitations

While most theories have shortcomings, including Bandura's, the criticisms lodged against social–cognitive theory in the previous edition of this book seem, generally speaking, no longer applicable. "Explaining" outcomes after the fact, while true of social–cognitive theory, is not peculiar to it; any theory can be misused in this way. Further, every theory faces the problem of establishing boundaries: specifying what it can and can not explain. Again, this problem is real for social–cognitive theory, but not unique to it. Also, it is just no longer true that there is insufficient support for Bandura's notions about self-exonerative processes. The Italian studies on prosocialness relating to moral disengagement, transgressions, and aggression alone wipes out that allegation. If Bandura's social–cognitive theory has a unique fault at this point in time, it is that practical implications of its research results have been growing faster than the ability to implement them.

Conclusions

Bandura's social–cognitive theory makes powerful predictions and generates useful applications in a large number of arenas for human behavior. You have seen how the theory suggested techniques that, in a matter of hours, eliminated phobias that had plagued individuals for years. You have also seen how the theory provides hope that education can be made more effective through manipulation of parental and children's academic efficacy and how self-exonerative processes can be understood sufficiently to decrease the likelihood of their use. In view of these accomplishments, it is reasonable to argue that Bandura's theory has greater practical applicability than most, or possibly all, of the other theories covered in this book. Further, social–cognitive theory is on the cutting edge of the cognitive movement in psychology. As such, it represents an orientation that will guarantee continued growth in psychology's scientific prominence. Decades from now, when the contributions of cognitive psychology are reviewed, the name Albert Bandura will often be heard and seen in print.

Albert Bandura is a fine person with a keen sense of humor and a genuine concern for others. That fact is richly displayed in a videotaped interview of him (Evans, 1988). Also, he writes with uncommon clarity, just as did Karen Horney. Easy access to the interesting thoughts expressed in Bandura's writings is only one reason you should consider reading *Self-efficacy* (Bandura, 1997). It may well improve your life.

Bandura is number five on the journal citation list, number three on the text book citation list, number five in the survey, and number four overall (Haggbloom et al., 2002). These are the highest ranks accorded a living psychologist; the few rated ahead of Bandura are all deceased.

Summary Points

1. Bandura, Canadian-born and bred, was educated in the best tradition of the country school. After graduation, he worked in the Yukon, where he encountered workers so unusual as to stimulate an interest in psychology. After completing his doctorate, he was hired at Stanford, where his unique contributions began with his and Walters's work on observational learning showing that "modeling is not merely a process of behavioral mimicry."

2. His cognitive–social theory holds that personal factors—including biological ones—behavior, and the external environment reciprocally influence one another. To Bandura, learning is difficult without awareness. Observational learning is learning by watching. People are active when they learn vicariously from a model. They take information from models, "turn it over" in their minds, and put it into symbolic form. Then they hone and sharpen what they have learned, translate it into behavior, and compare their performance with an internal representation.

3. Rewards play a role in defining incentives. Self-reward is a very important factor. Even very young children do not merely mimic though non-primates do. Goals are vitally important to productive human behavior. Ability to abandon unattainable goals in favor of alternatives promotes happiness. Resilient people rely on them in the face of rejection. Defensive behaviors are adopted in order to cope with anticipated unpleasant events. Self-efficacy is a specific form of confidence that influences not only whether a person will attempt a behavior, but also the quality of performance. Managing to perform a feared or repugnant behavior will likely boost self-efficacy.

4. In participant modeling, a person performs behavior in imitation of an efficacious model. In vicarious expectancy learning, other peoples' expectancies concerning future events are adopted. In response facilitation, old responses may be disinhibited. Diffusion of innovation occurs when prestigious models try something new and thereby display its benefits. Extrinsic rewards originate outside the person and intrinsic rewards inside. Intrinsic motivation involves self-evaluation. Vicarious reinforcement occurs when one person observes another being rewarded. Reward value is established by social comparison, which may depend on expertise of the comparison person and his/her similarity to and past agreement with the chooser.

5. In a spider phobic study, subjects' efficacy exactly matched their performance. Snake phobics' self-efficacy was enhanced through modeling, resulting in close contact with a snake and enhancement of the immune system. Self-efficacy of alcoholics has a powerful impact on the course and success of recovery. Future oriented homeless people with high self-efficacy successfully found a residence and a job. In a model of health maintenance, health self-efficacy has important impact at every stage of the model, and optimism is vitally important in dealing with disease.

6. Self-efficacy is also crucial among the elderly, people with bowel disorders, and workers. Parental academic efficacy and parents' academic aspirations for their children are related to children's academic performance. The relation of these factors to the academic achievement passes through children's social efficacy, their prosocialness, their popularity with peers, and their problem behaviors. Children's eventual career choices began with parental academic aspirations and passed through children's social efficacy and academic aspirations.

7. Prosocialness was positively related to academic achievement and popularity but negatively related to transgressive behavior. Moral disengagement was directly related to delinquent behavior, but it was also indirectly related to delinquency through prosocialness, aggression proneness, and guilt and restitution. The path to aggressive behavior was indirect through the same three variables. Crime is generated, in part, by limited behavioral alternatives available to the poor and oppressed.

8. Most people cannot do evil to other humans unless they engage in self-exonerative processes. Dehumanization is one of the mechanisms they can use. Others include advantageous comparison and euphemistic labeling. Blaming victims for their own fate, displacement, and diffusion of responsibility are self-exonerative processes. Moral justification involves making inhumane behavior "acceptable" by claiming that it serves social or moral purposes.

9. In gradualistic moral disengagement, people slowly slip unaware into what was normally unacceptable behavior. Through the process of self-evaluation, people like Mother Teresa, Martin Luther King, Jr., and Susan B. Anthony risked life and security for the sake of human rights. Unfortunately self-exonerative processes are being used to justify violence against women. Men who assault women resort to advantageous comparison, euphemistic labeling, moral justification, dehumanization, and blaming the victim. Sadly, abusive males and victimized women may be drawn to each other.

10. Bandura's theory was previously faulted for having no clearly defined boundaries, but this allegation fits many theories. Neglect of moral functioning was also alleged, but new research eclipses this allegation. The breadth of the theory is real. Further, it is reasonable to argue that his social–cognitive theory has the greatest practical applicability of any theory.

Running Comparison

Theorist	Bandura in Comparison
Mischel	Both deal with self-regulatory mechanisms, but reject traits.
Rotter	He also is concerned with expectancies.
B. F. Skinner	He emphasizes anticipation of reward, not Skinner's past history of reward.

Essay/Critical Thinking Questions

1. How might environmental conditions affect your neurobiology?

2. What does social comparison say about friendship and rivalry?

3. What examples of resilience can you cite from your own experience with people?

4. Name a practical implication of Bandura's theory not found in the text.

5. Is the text too easy on social–cognitive theory? Come up with some unique criticisms of it.

E-mail Interaction

Write the author at b-allen@wiu.edu. Forward one of the following or phrase your own.

1. Why do men beat women?

2. What can parents do to promote their children's education?

3. Can one be too optimistic?

It's All a Matter of Consequences: B. F. Skinner

- Are the principles used to train animals relevant to understanding personality?
- Does environment determine behavior? Language? Creativity?
- Would you be willing to rear a baby in a box?

B. F. Skinner
www.ship.edu/~cgboeree/
skinner.html

The theories reviewed so far all have been concerned with "what is inside," or a combination of "what is inside" and "what is outside." By contrast, **behaviorism** is a school of psychology for which the basic subject matter is "outside"; it is overt (observable) behavior. Consistent with the view of other scientists, behaviorists believe that the science of psychology should deal only with phenomena that can be verified by the senses. They eschew entities buried away in the "mind," such as private thoughts, feelings, expectations, or motivations (Baars, 2003; Baum & Heath, 1992).

Two types of behaviorists differ from B. F. Skinner: they are the pre-Skinnerian classic behaviorists and the methodological behaviorists (those who use behaviorists' methods but may depart from their assumptions). These two kinds of behaviorists have confined themselves to events that are currently observable—they focus on the here and now. Skinner developed a broader point of view, called **radical behaviorism,** which considers currently observable events and also potential future events that can be observed and measured (Rutherford, 2003; Salzinger, 1990). Therefore, Skinner contemplated future environments that could be arranged so that desirable behaviors are promoted. He believed that we can design environments that select behaviors—pick some behaviors to be strengthened rather than others—that are likely to be good for the people who behave, as well as for others. This point of view may sound utopian. In fact, it is. Skinner designed a utopian society when he wrote *Walden Two* (1948), a book about a community in which punishment is shunned and rewards guide people in the full exploitation of all their natural abilities and characteristics. Skinner wished to make this a better world.

Skinner, the Person

Burrhus Frederic Skinner, born in 1904, spent his early years in Susquehanna, Pennsylvania, but spent his formative years in Scranton (Skinner, 1976a). Late in life, he remembers not being close to his parents and not being interested in pursuing the Protestant traditions of his family (Liptzin, 1994). He also remembers becoming intrigued with psychology at a very early age. As with most people, his first interest was in the more mystical psychological phenomena. While a third grader, he had an "extrasensory experience": he excitedly raised his hand to report that he had read a word just at the same moment his teacher spoke it. As an older child, he was fascinated by performing pigeons at a country fair, and, during his college years, he wrote a play on "glands that change personality" and a term paper analyzing Hamlet's madness. As a young man, Skinner recalls thinking about thinking while paddling a canoe.

After having received his undergraduate degree in English from a small New York school, Hamilton College (1926), Skinner drifted for a while (Skinner, 1976a). He very much wanted to be a writer, even receiving encouragement from Robert Frost. During his "Dark Year" Skinner suffered at home in Scranton as his father, a lawyer recently discharged from his employer, waited for young Skinner to "do something" (Baars, 2003). Instead of being productive, Skinner failed as a novelist. Baars (2003) claims that lack of success as a writer led Skinner to renounce the mental life. Then, as if he had stumbled onto the "truth," he discovered behaviorism from books by H. G. Wells and Bertrand Russell, a begrudging fan of early behaviorist John B. Watson. Wells pondered what to do with a single life jacket if he were standing alone on a pier, with George Bernard Shaw floundering in the water on one side and Pavlov slowly disappearing from sight on the other (the reference was to I. P. Pavlov [1927], the famous Russian who taught dogs to salivate at the sound of a bell). The jacket was awarded to Pavlov—by implication, behaviorism—and so were Skinner's intellectual loyalties.

Soon thereafter, Skinner enrolled in the psychology graduate program at Harvard. During this period he spent some time in Greenwich Village, sampling the Bohemian lifestyle. There, in a nightclub, he noticed an attractive young woman, and, as was often the case when he found a woman interesting, he boldly introduced himself. When she discovered that he was to be a psychology student, she professed a desire to be hypnotized and he accommodated her. It was an important experience for two reasons. It cemented his identity as a psychologist, and it was the beginning of an affair. Skinner took up residence with the woman and, thereby, revealed a willingness to defy danger: the woman was married and often received visits from her husband, who was away on military duty. This unsettling arrangement eventually led Skinner to decide that the lifestyle of Greenwich Village was not for him.

Other aspects of Skinner's personality are revealed in *Walden Two* (1948). It is no accident that a main character and obvious alter ego, "Professor Burris," is a straightforward, typical academic who resorts to his intellect rather than his emotions when trying to make sense of life. He has "little personality." However, paradoxically, Skinner was capable of being frivolous and, on occasion, could even be a prankster. At his graduation ceremony, he delivered an oration in Latin that was designed to satirize the school administration. When a school official loudly queried "Why don't they bow when they're given a diploma?" Skinner made a point of bowing grandly on receiving his diploma. The "cheap joke," as he put it, inspired laughter from the audience.

If one takes seriously what Skinner (1976b) says about himself, he has a personality that is difficult to pin down (Skinner, 1983a). Skinner himself has offered little help. In preparation for an earlier personality text by Charles Potkay and me, Potkay asked Skinner to complete a personality questionnaire. Skinner replied that he hated to be "crotchety," but he did not believe in such measures.

Still, Skinner did not show a well-defined personality. That is, for every trait that can be inferred from his self-reports of behavior, he has also indicated behavior associated with the opposite trait. As a young man, Skinner was shy but outgoing, cautious but adventurous, intellectual, yet sometimes quite silly. His personal life was rather conservative, but he occasionally violated sexual conventions. Perhaps it is all by design. It would not do for a person to have a clearly evident personality if he wishes to deny the existence of personality (Skinner, 1989). Despite these disclaimers, one can read a great deal about personality between the lines of Skinner's writings. Consulting both his autobiography and his early writings, one can see the "objectivity," concreteness, and emotional detachment that characterized him (Demorest & Siegel, 1996). But did he have a mental life: consciousness (Baars, 2003)? Of course he did. It is true that he stripped consciousness of causal properties (it was the result, not the cause, of behavior; Vargas, 2003); however, he could, like all of us, lay his profession aside when he was not at work and give himself over to his mental life (Kihlstrom, 2003). In any case, Skinner has proved that a person can be interesting, even if he does not clearly manifest a large number of consistent traits and an all-encompassing mental life.

Skinner often played the iconoclast (Dinsmoor, 1992). He seized every opportunity to tweak the nose of the psychological establishment. For example, he was often accused by humanitarian and libertarian critics of devising fascist methods for the coercive regulation of human behavior. Noticing that his critics blanched at the mention of the word *control,* he used it often. This tactic also served to bait his adversaries. By going out of his way to seem to represent what they hated most, he "goaded" them into "ill-considered responses" to his sometimes inflammatory writings (Dinsmoor, 1992, p. 1458).

At the same time, Skinner could be the breathlessly naive "discoverer" of nature's truths, similar to one of the child characters in a Steven Spielberg movie. Recounting his first observation of "extinction" (the disappearance of a learned response), Skinner (1979; see Iversen, 1992) described how he, like other great scientists, made his momentous "discovery" by accident (for example Marie and her husband Pierre Curie discovered nuclear radiation by accident). Once, he left his lab after placing an animal in an apparatus that automatically delivered food when the animal pressed a lever. On his return, he found that an equipment failure had prevented food delivery. This fortunate mishap provided him with "the first" extinction graph. Gripped by scientific fervor, Skinner gushed, "All that weekend I crossed streets with particular care and avoided all unnecessary risks to protect my discovery from loss through my death" (Skinner, 1979, p. 95; also see Iversen, 1992).

Skinner was perhaps the most decorated psychologist of his time. He was elected to the scientists' "hall of fame," the National Academy of Sciences. He also received the Warren Medal from the Society of Experimental Psychologists (1942), the Gold Medal for Distinguished Scientific Contributions from the American Psychological Association (1958), and the National Medal of Science. In 1990 he received both the American Psychological Society's William James Fellow Award and the American Psychological Association's Presidential Citation for Lifetime Contributions to Psychology (Salzinger, 1990). After a long bout with leukemia, Skinner died on August 18, 1990, eight days after speaking at the presentation of his last award (Vargas, 2003; Skinner's daughter, Julie). Unruffled even by his deadly disease, near the end Skinner joked with his family that he would recommend leukemia as a way to go, because it was relatively painless and left him with his wits.

Skinner's View of the Person

Environmentalism: The Importance of Consequences

After abandoning Watsonian and Pavlovian psychology early in his career (Vargas, 2003), Skinner (1972g) denied the repeated accusation that he is an "S-R," or stimulus-response, psychologist (Iversen, 1992; Salzinger, 1990). According to the S-R conception, a stimulus in the environment, such as "the door within the door" that constitutes the dog's entrance into the house, absolutely demands a response from the dog, namely, entering the house. Not so, says Skinner. The dog's door sets the occasion for the response "enter," but it does so with some probability, not absolutely (Moxley, 1992). Further, to understand behavior, a dog's or a person's, one needs a concept that is missing from the S-R account (Vargas, 2003). A **consequence** is an event that occurs after a response has been performed and changes the probability that the response will occur again. For the dog, gaining entrance to the house is the consequence that will increase the likelihood that it will poke its nose through its door in the future. "Consequences" are so central to Skinner's point of view that it is in the title of one autobiographical volume (Skinner, 1983b).

While not an S-R psychologist, Skinner stands "guilty" of the charge of being an environmentalist (Skinner, 1983a). For him (1971), the environment controls everything, but, as you will see, is itself subject to control. He often referred to parallels between the environment–behavior relationship and "natural selection," the process developed by Charles Darwin to explain how humans and other animals evolved to their present state (Salzinger, 1990; see Flynn, 2003, for a related point of view).

Natural selection can be illustrated by an example. In Costa Rica, on a mountaintop near the Poas volcano, there exists a certain flower with a curved stem and a deep recess formed at the base of its petals and extending into its stem. When a species of hummingbird took up residence on the mountaintop, only a few mutants among them had beaks that were sufficiently long and curved to dip into the flowers' stems far enough to reach their valuable contents. These oddities were the birds that survived, propagated, and prospered on the mountaintop. The environment, specifically the flower type, selected for survival those birds with the ideally shaped beaks that allow them to successfully perform the flower-stem insertion response.

Likewise, humans, over thousands of generations, have become able to effectively perform certain behaviors. The environment has selected certain human physical characteristics, such as agile fingers and hands, because these traits permit the performance of critical behaviors that have survival value (permit adaptation to the environment). Certain European people have among them men with very stout thighs and calves. These characteristics may have been selected for pushing a primitive plow in early agricultural times. Thus, the environment selects physical traits that permit behaviors having survival-promoting consequences, such as the provision of food. Survival, in turn, allows reproduction and, thereby, propagation of the genes controlling the traits.

Further, Skinner points to individual differences in the kinds of consequences that are likely to generate behavior (Skinner, 1948). Only some people are genetically disposed to effectively build novel objects from available materials. These people are likely to emit many responses that involve construction. Because typical environments provide numerous important consequences of such responses (provision of a house for escaping the weather), chances are that "building" behavior will often be selected and will increase in likelihood.

However, Skinner emphasizes that genetic input, determined by the environment through natural selection, predisposes individuals to certain behaviors rather than others, but it only defines the potential for behavioral development (Rutherford, 2003). The particular environment into which each of us is born determines our own peculiar repertoire of behaviors. An individual born with artistic potential will show artistic behaviors only if the opportunities relating to artistic acts are available in her or his particular environment (Skinner, 1972c). An environment cannot select artistic behaviors if it does not provide important consequences for such behavior. In sum, the actual behaviors a person develops depend on the characteristics of his or her environment.

"Beyond Freedom and Dignity"

If a stimulus has some probability of giving rise to a response, if our genetic dispositions define our inclinations toward behavioral development, and if our particular environments determine the actual behaviors we will develop, we are all slaves to our environments. That is, we lack freedom (Dinsmoor, 1992; Skinner, 1948, 1971, 1983a). This alarming proclamation, and others found in *Beyond Freedom and Dignity* (Skinner, 1971), shot Skinner's most successful book to the top of the *New York Times* best-seller list (Rutherford, 2003). According to Skinner, **freedom** refers to our belief that we can choose from various behaviors rather than having our actions controlled by the environment (Skinner, 1972f). Obviously, Skinner does not accept the belief that he attributes to us. To him, it is a fact that we are controlled by the environment (1983a, 1983b, 1989). To deny environmental control is to risk being controlled by subtle and malignant circumstances and by malicious people (Dinsmoor, 1992). Governments and malevolent people sometimes control human beings for the benefit of the controller (Skinner, 1987a). Often, we do not detect the harm done to us by this control, because there may be immediate positive consequences, while negative consequences are deferred until a later time. For example, we may stand aside while our government is lax in regulating the level of pollutants that are allowed to escape into our waterways and air. We fail to react because "jobs are preserved" and "the economy is stimulated," immediate, positive benefits for us all. However, we should realize that lax regulation of pollutants has negative consequences in the long run (Skinner, 1983a).

Skinner (1971) asked, "Why shouldn't *we* decide the course of environmental control over our behaviors?" The alternative is to leave the control of behavior up to chance, or, worse, leave it up to people who would control us for their own gains. Radical behaviorism is well illustrated by the belief that we can create control of our behavior by manipulating our environments to increase the likelihood of beneficial consequences (Salzinger, 1990). We are not autonomous, but we can gain a measure of autonomy by changing aspects of our environments that relate to desired consequences. When we demand freedom, what we really mean is freedom from negative or aversive consequences and access to positive consequences (Dinsmoor, 1992). We can have that freedom only by arranging our own consequences, not by assuming we can control our behavior directly or by leaving consequences to "government" or "fate." Thus, Skinner does concede that we have freedom, but in a highly qualified sense. We can arrange our environment so that the consequences we desire become likely, but, having done so, we are under the control of our creation (Skinner, 1983 a, b).

This conception of "freedom" and the qualifications of it make critics of radical behaviorism wrong when they charge that Skinner wanted to impose coercive control over human behavior (Dinsmoor, 1992; Rutherford, 2003). Skinner wished to eliminate the aversive techniques of control favored by despots. In the place of these totalitarian methods he would substitute control by positive consequences that may be arranged by those desiring benevolent control.

While some measure of freedom can be achieved, dignity is unobtainable. "We recognize a person's **dignity** or worth when we give him *credit* for what he has done" (emphasis added; Skinner, 1971, p. 58). When, in our everyday lives, we cannot readily identify the consequences that control an individual's behavior, we attribute the behavior to the individual rather than to the environment. Thus, when a person makes an anonymous donation to a worthy cause, we assume it was done because of something inside the person called altruism. In so doing, we ignore the consequences in the person's early environment that have determined his or her behavior. For example, the person may have been exposed to a cultural environment that "honors" (consequence) selfless giving. To credit people when they "do good" is to ignore the consequences that gave rise to "doing good" (Skinner, 1983a). Skinner (1971) suggests that we should identify those consequences and bring them under control so that more people can "do good" more often. To accept his suggestion is to give up taking credit for what we do, to give up "dignity." In return, he assures us that crediting the environment instead of ourselves will lead us to seek out some benevolent consequences for controlling behavior. The result of that search will be a behavioral technology that will ensure that "doing good" is a frequent occurrence and "doing bad" a rarity.

Attributing the "personality trait" "altruism" to another person when she or he behaves generously, while we ignore environmental determinants, is called the "fundamental attribution error" (Hineline, 1992). But we do not tend to make this error when attributing a cause to our own behavior. Typically, we say our own behavior is "caused" by something in the environment. When we do, we show that we are capable of appreciating environmental determinism (Allen, 2001).

Skinner practices what he preaches. In *Walden Two* (1948), his main character, Frazier, who designed the utopia described in the book, repeatedly denies that people are to be credited with what they do. Skinner himself once ended a speech with the following (Skinner, 1972g):

> And now my labor is over. I have had my lecture. I have no sense of fatherhood. If my genetic and personal histories had been different, I should have come into possession of a different lecture. If I deserve any credit at all, it is simply for having served as a place in which certain processes could take place. I shall interpret your polite applause in that light.

Box 14.1 covers how words referring to behavior were converted to mentalistic words.

BOX 14.1 • *Descriptive Words Once Referred to Behavior, but No More*

Among the threats to his position that have bedeviled Skinner throughout his career is **mentalism,** the belief that thoughts and feelings determine behavior, not external consequences (Baars, 2003; Baum & Heath, 1992; Skinner, 1983b). He has lamented the birth and development of the "cognitive revolution," a movement that stresses the importance of thinking processes in determining behavior (Skinner, 1989).

Many of the words that we use seem to support the cognitive orientation in that they refer to internal conditions, thoughts, or states of mind: *experience, attitude, comprehension, need, will, worry,* and *intention.* Nevertheless, Skinner (1989) believed that these terms originally referred to behavior, not internal conditions. In earlier times, people were more behavioristic, but something happened between then and now to change that orientation. Partly because people like to take credit for what they do, and partly because people are unable to see the often subtle consequences of their behaviors, the meanings of words changed. One of the mechanisms by which these terms became converted into mentalistic words relates to the observation that feelings and thoughts occur after or at about the same time as behaviors. However, rather than cause behaviors, these clearly evident thoughts and feelings are mistaken for causes because of their close proximity to behavior. The real "causes" of behaviors are their consequences, which are less often evident or proximal.

"*Experience* is a good example [of a word that involved mentalism] . . . the word was not used to refer to anything felt or introspectively observed until the 19th century. Before that time, it meant, quite literally, something a person had 'gone through' (from the Latin *expiriri*) . . . " (Skinner, 1989, p. 13). Skinner provides many other examples. *Intention* came from the Latin word *tendere* and originally meant 'to physically stretch or extend,' a reference to behavior. *Image,* which we now take to mean 'an internal copy of something,' originally meant 'a colored sculpture of a head and shoulders,' from the Latin word *imago.* Later it meant 'ghost,' but in neither case was it something inside the head. The words *anxious* and *worry* originally meant 'choke' as in "the dog worries the rat that it caught" (p. 15). *Aware* once meant 'to be cautious,' to *comprehend* meant 'to seize or to grasp' and to *solve* used to mean 'to dissolve,' as sugar is dissolved in water.

Consistent with his beliefs, the terms he used when he wrote or spoke in public referred to behavior. Even when caught "off stage" Skinner could be the behaviorist he recommended that everyone should be. When my wife and I encountered him at a psychological convention, we could not resist introducing ourselves. Skinner responded simply, "I'm waiting for friends." He made reference to what he was doing, not to anything he might have been thinking or feeling.

Basic Concepts: Skinner

Skinner claims not to have a theory (Skinner, 1983a), and is viewed by some people as antitheory (Kendler, 1988; Rockwell, 1994). Others felt he was only opposed to some theories, particularly those proposing mental entities (Schlinger, 1992) and that he actually looked forward to the emergence of a behavior theory based on careful observation (Chiesa, 1992). In any case, Skinner's point of view has all the trappings of a theory, including numerous concepts.

Operant Conditioning

Skinner's approach to psychology focuses on what many psychologists call "instrumental" conditioning (see Kimble, 1961). Skinner's term is **operant conditioning,** a process by which an organism operates on its environment with consequences that influence the likelihood that the operation, or behavior, will be repeated. The behavior that constitutes the operation on the environment is often called an *operant* (Lee, 1992). "Respondent conditioning," Skinner's equivalent to the kind of conditioning done by Pavlov, is not covered here because it explains little of what we do compared to operant conditioning (Vargas, 2003).

 Contingent is a close second to *consequence* as the key word in Skinnerian terminology. If event B is **contingent** on event A, the occurrence of B depends on the prior occurrence of A (Holland & Skinner, 1961; Lee, 1992). If the singing of birds is contingent on the rising of the sun, the occurrence of singing depends on the prior appearance of the sun. In *operant conditioning,* consequences are contingent on the prior performance of some response, often a very discrete and concrete behavior, such as the "handshake" of a trained dog. Three kinds of consequences can be involved in operant conditioning: positive reinforcement, negative reinforcement, and punishment.

Positive Reinforcement and Extinction

Reinforcement occurs when some *event* is contingent on the prior performance of some response and the response changes in likelihood of occurrence on future occasions. *Reinforcer* is a term often used in reference to *a stimulus that is presented* (event) as a consequence of a response. **Positive reinforcement** is a *process* whereby some event, usually a stimulus, *increases the likelihood* of a response on which the presentation of the event is contingent. Food is a primary positive reinforcer. When a baby's crying responses produce its parent with food in hand, crying becomes more likely in the future. It is easy to see why the word *reinforcement* was chosen. *Reinforce* generally means 'strengthen,' and the occurrence of an event that "*positively* reinforces a response" strengthens it, in the sense of increasing its likelihood of being repeated.

 Skinner (1983a) often placed a pigeon in a cage that bears the technical name *free-operant chamber,* but has become popularly known as the *Skinner box.* As Figure 14.1 reveals, it looks like any other cage for housing animals, except that it has a panel that the pigeon can peck (A). Pecking the panel activates a food magazine (B) that releases grain down a tube (C) into a cup (D) inside the cage (rats press a lever). In the simplest

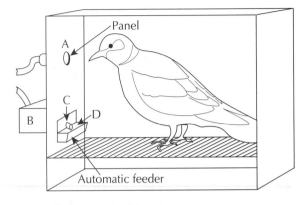

FIGURE 14.1 *Skinner Box: Pigeon pecks A, which activates food magazine at B, causing food to be delivered through tube C to cup D*

case, every peck of the panel (response) is followed by the presentation of some grain (reinforcer).

Notice the kind of response that occurs in operant conditioning. Responses that occur are initiated by the animal, rather than occurring automatically. The pigeon can peck many times, or none at all. It can peck forcefully or softly. Also, it is the pigeon that gets things going. Nothing happens until the pigeon starts pecking, and it must perform responses itself.

Operant conditioning often begins when an animal starts responding more or less at random. A pigeon pecks quite a lot, for no apparent reason. Placed in a Skinner box, it will peck all around, eventually peck the panel, and grain will come down the tube into the cup. The pigeon will eat the grain and then wander around some more. Sooner or later, it will peck the panel again, with the same result as before. If one watches closely, it is evident that the time between pecks becomes less and less, until the pigeon is pecking at a fairly high rate. When the **rate of responding** becomes stable, conditioning is said to have been completed and a new response acquired. Rate of responding is also an index of *strength of conditioning.* In general, the higher the rate, the stronger the conditioning. **Extinction** occurs when a previously reinforced response is no longer followed by the same reinforcer and the response eventually decreases in frequency (Iversen, 1992).

Operantly conditioning more complex responses requires special procedures. Suppose one wishes to teach a dog to turn in a circle. One would use **shaping,** a process by which natural variability in behavior is exploited so that a new behavior is acquired by reinforcing *successive approximations* to it (Epstein, 1991; Iversen, 1992). A hungry dog will often turn right and left in seemingly random fashion as it anxiously waits to be fed (note that animals are primed for operant conditioning if they have been deprived of a reinforcer). When it makes a pronounced turn to the right (or left), give it a bit of food (primary positive reinforcement). Wait for an even more pronounced turn in the same direction—a closer approximation—before providing more food. By reinforcing more and more complete turns—successive approximation—a full turn will soon be shaped. In shaping turning, it is usually best to allow the dog to initiate turns. However, some dogs may need *prompting:* they may have to be coaxed into performing at least an approximation of the desired response (Skinner, 1983b).

Positive reinforcement occurs every day in the life of every person, including a typical college student. Events occur during a student's day that include behaviors that have been reinforced many times in the past. At noon, the student makes his way to the cafeteria in his dorm, where he presents his student ID, picks up a tray, and fills it with food. These behaviors are positively reinforced by the provision of food. The student proceeds to class, where his "class attendance" behavior is reinforced, as usual, by his outstanding professor's stimulating lecture. Next, the student retires to the library for an afternoon of study, the reinforcement for which will be partially delayed until test day. For now, studying is followed by a rather abstract reinforcement, "the joy of learning." Next, the student reports to work, where it happens to be payday. His work behavior on that day, and several preceding it, is reinforced with a paycheck.

Negative Reinforcement and Punishment

Positive reinforcement, post-response stimulation that is pleasant in some sense, is not the only means by which behaviors are learned. *Aversive stimulation* is unpleasant, painful, or harmful. **Negative reinforcement** is a process whereby the likelihood of a response *increases* when it is followed by the *termination, reduction,* or *absence* of an aversive stimulus (Holland & Skinner, 1961). Such stimuli are called *negative reinforcers.* Behaviors that lead to success in escaping (terminating) or avoiding (ensuring the absence of) negative reinforcers will increase in probability of occurrence in the future. In fact, cases of avoidance (or escape) are cases of negative reinforcement.

Escape and avoidance behaviors are illustrated by use of a shuttle box, as depicted in Figure 14.2. The box, actually a cage, has an electric-grid floor and a partition down the middle. The animal is placed in the box on one side of the partition, and uncomfortable but not harmful electricity is activated on that side only. The animal *escapes* by simply jumping to the side without shock. The jump is reinforced by the termination of the shock. Examples of escape condition all involve *ongoing aversive stimulation* that is terminated by some behavior. A relatively trivial example is placing a hand on a hot stove: withdrawal of the hand is reinforced by termination of the unpleasant burning sensation. Escape conditioning can be used to terminate smoking or drinking behavior. A person who wishes to quit smoking (or drinking) is wired for mild electric shock. Whenever he takes a drag on a cigarette (raises a glass of alcohol to his lips), he is shocked. He can escape the shock by snuffing out the cigarette (pouring out the alcohol).

Avoidance learning becomes possible when a light is placed at each end of the box (see Figure 14.2). First, the animal learns to escape. Then, the light on the side containing the animal is illuminated a short time before the shock is activated. At first, the light seems to have no influence on behavior. However, after a number of presentations of the light

Grid floor (top view): electrified tubing

Partition

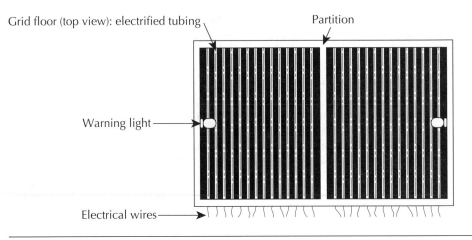

Warning light

Electrical wires

FIGURE 14.2   *A Top View of the Shuttle Box*

followed by the shock, the animal will begin to jump when the light is illuminated, before the shock is delivered, thereby *avoiding* it. Real-life examples of avoidance behavior are plentiful. Anytime a child regularly faces some kind of aversive stimulation, such as having to baby-sit a younger sibling after school, he will develop an avoidance response, such as taking up a sport after school. Washing dirty dishes may be avoided by mowing the lawn. Cleaning the disaster area that is one's room may be avoided by washing the car. Thus, sports participation, lawn mowing, and car washing *increase* in likelihood because they allow *avoidance* of "aversive stimulation." Many neurotic or phobic reactions are avoidance behaviors. Consider a person who becomes very anxious in social situations (parties or meetings), because she is prone to committing some humiliating faux pas or other social error. Her avoidance of social gatherings is reinforced by the absence of anxiety. Consider a person who is afraid of flying in airplanes. Taking a train, or bus, or car is reinforced by the absence of fear.

    Punishment is a process whereby the likelihood of a response *decreases* when it is followed by *presentation* of an aversive stimulus (Skinner, 1971). (This process is technically known as *positive punishment. Negative punishment* is the withdrawal of positive stimulation: "All right, no TV for you tonight!") The two kinds of reinforcement that involve aversive stimulation are exact opposites. Whereas negative reinforcement involves an *increase* in responses followed by the *termination, reduction,* or *absence* of aversive stimulation, punishment involves a *decrease* in responses followed by the *presentation* of aversive stimulation. If a child's hand is spanked for getting into the cookie jar, punishment decreases the likelihood of cookie pilfering. When a child is "grounded" for hitting another child, the likelihood of assaulting other children will go down.

    Skinner long maintained that the aversive control technique "punishment" is not an efficient way to control behavior (Skinner, 1948; and see Benjamin & Nielson-Gammon, 1999). He (1971) argued that punishment may lead to only temporary suppression of a behavior that is not desired by the punishing agent (parent). An organism may inhibit an undesirable behavior until the punishing agent is no longer present. Then the behavior may be performed at a high rate, making up for responses that were suppressed when the

BOX 14.2 • *Deterring Aggressive Behavior: What Won't Work*

Eight-year-old Rudolph, or Rudy, as his parents call him, has the nasty habit of hitting people who irritate him, including Aliza, his mother. Aliza reacts by hitting him back . . . hard. She thinks it works, because, for the time being, he stops hitting her. She doesn't seem to notice that, after some lapse of time, Rudy hits her again. In contrast to striking back when Rudy attacks her, Aliza resorts to threats of physical punishment should Rudy hit his sister Alice, age 4. When Rudy attacks his sister, Aliza exclaims loudly, "Wait 'til your father gets home!"

Unfortunately Aliza leaves the children alone often and for relatively long periods (she works in the financial market, using her home computer, and closes the door of her office when she is working). When she is on her computer, Rudy has his way with Alice. He beats her up and takes her toys and "special candy" (M&Ms). And he doesn't worry about getting caught, because he tells Alice he will break her treasured bicycle if she tells on him. Nevertheless, on a few occasions, he has failed to hear his mother leave her office and he has been caught in the act of hitting Alice.

Hours after the aggressive transgression, Rudy's father, Hermann, comes home and ceremoniously "spanks" Rudy. Actually, Hermann has little stomach for whippings, so he relies on theatrics: he drapes Rudy over his knees and swats his behind several times with his big, soft hand. Rudy dutifully responds with howling and tears, though objective observers would judge that he has suffered mild discomfort, but no pain. Aliza is taken in by this farce. Later, when Rudy became aggressive at school, she expressed surprise. "I've done all I can," she lamented. "I spank him regularly and see that his father does also."

First, consider the actual punishment Aliza metes out. Rudy hits her, she hits him back even harder. There are three reasons why her behavior is worse than ineffective; it promotes aggressiveness. What is our first impulse when someone hits us? For many of us, it is to hit back (though most of us don't act on that impulse). Thus, his attack provokes her and her retaliation provokes him, though he may take it out on a safer target, like Alice (Baron, 1977). Aggression begets aggression: the

odds that Rudy will aggress in the future increase. Second, true to Bandura's research, she is an excellent model for aggressiveness, and, obviously, he is a quick learner (Gershoff, 2002). Third, he learns a more subtle lesson: one can get away with aggression, if one is big and strong enough.

How about threat of punishment as a means to deter future aggression (Allen, 2001; Baron, 1977). First, Skinner knew that aversive stimulation can work extremely well to control behavior under certain conditions (Solomon & Wynne, 1953). Chief among these conditions is that the punishment be very severe (for example, painful electric shock is used). History offers many examples of severe punishment's ability to absolutely control behavior; witness the success of the Nazi SS concentration-camp guards' ability to control inmates' behavior. Also, a number of other conditions promote the effectiveness of threatened punishment for deterring aggression, besides its severity (1). These are (2) the threatened punishment must be highly likely to occur; (3) it must occur immediately after the aggressive behavior; (4) the aggressor must not be very angry; and (5) the aggressor must have relatively little to gain from aggressing (Baron, 1977).

It should be clear that these five conditions do not hold when Rudy is threatened with physical punishment for attacking his sister. First, he can count on his father to make the punishment a great deal less than severe. Second, the odds of punishment ever happening are low, because Rudy only hits Alice when he is reasonably sure no one will know (when Aliza is at work on her computer). Third, the time lapse between the aggression and Hermann's administration of punishment is hours, not immediately, after the aggressive act. Fourth, Rudy is always very angry (it's his nature). Thus, he is unlikely to be terribly concerned about the consequences of acting on his anger. He aggresses in the thoughtless "heat of passion." Fifth, he has much to gain: Alice's toys, M&Ms, and submission. Little wonder he gets worse and worse.

By the way, do the conditions that promote the effectiveness of punishment hold when our criminal justice system attempts to deter assault with threats of punishment (prison or worse)?

(continued)

BOX 14.2 Continued

When one person is about to attack another, does the would-be assailant count on (1) severe, (2) highly likely, and (3) immediate punishment? Is it probable that (4) he is not very angry and (5) has little to gain by aggression? Unless the answer is "yes" in all five cases, threats of punishment through our criminal justice system are unlikely to be effective. However, should the threatened punishment be severe, highly likely, and immediate, the implications for our democratic society would be dire indeed. Lining up assailants caught in the act and immediately shooting them probably works to deter assault. It also works to trample human rights and keep vicious dictators in power.

Like Aliza and our criminal justice system, we give lip service to the belief that punishment deters aggression and other forms of antisocial behavior. But do we really believe it? One criterion of really believing in punishment as a deterrent of aggressive/antisocial behavior is whether we act according to the belief. Carlsmith, Darley, and Robinson (2002) provide evidence that lip service to deterrence gives way to endorsement of a "just deserts" perspective when people must punish wrongdoing ("just deserts" means that punishment is appropriate to the harm done). The switch occurred when participants meted out punishment after reading vignettes about intentionally committed harm (e.g., embezzlement to maintain a lavish life style). These researchers showed that severity of punishment was poorly predicted by factors related to deterrence (hard to detect harmful acts require more punishment if deterrence is to work and the greater the publicity about the harmful act the greater the likelihood that deterrence will work). At the same time, factors related to "just deserts" (absence of mitigating circumstances, seriousness of the offense, and moral outrage) strongly predicted severity of punishment. Apparently deterrence is a philosophy we endorse verbally but do not back up with our behavior. Maybe we should reconsider our beliefs about deterrence.

Other evidence in support of Skinner's view that punishment is counterproductive comes from recent work on physical punishment of children. Physical or corporal punishment (e.g., such as spanking or other forms of hitting) has become controversial since the publication of a massive study finding that it is associated with many negative outcomes for children (Gershoff, 2002). Outcomes occurring during childhood were elevated aggression, low internalization of morality, poor parent–child relationships, subnormal mental health, delinquency, and antisocial behavior. Outcomes occurring after physically punished children reach adulthood were increased tendency to be a perpetrator of abuse of child or spouse, aggression, and poor mental health.

Kazdin and Benjet (2003) reviewed this study, reactions to it, and other related research. First, they noted that corporal punishment is popular in the United States. Fully 74 percent of parents having children younger than 17 years of age used physical punishment and the figure climbed to 94 percent for parents of three- and four-year-old children. Second, they noted that related research shows an association between harsh corporal punishment and increased morbidity and mortality due to illnesses such as heart disease, cancer, and lung disease (and when it is very harsh—as in child abuse—deleterious brain changes). Third, they indicated that the deleterious effects of corporal punishment appear to be a function of how severe it is and how frequently it is used. Fourth, they acknowledge a point consistent with criticisms of Gershoff's study: occasional mild corporal punishment may complement other forms of child behavior management, such as time out and reasoning with the child. However, Kazdin and Benjet also note that, so far, research has failed to reveal any possible deleterious or beneficial effects of mild corporal punishment. Thus, though research results do not yet allow the conclusion that physical punishment of children should never be used, results clearly do not support the frequent use of harsh corporal punishment. More broadly, Skinner's belief that punishment is counterproductive has, by and large, been confirmed.

TABLE 14.1 *Varieties of Reinforcement*

Reinforcement occurs when some event is contingent on the prior performance of some response and the response changes in likelihood of occurrence on future occasions.

Positive reinforcement is a process whereby some event, usually a stimulus, *increases the likelihood* of a response on which the presentation of the event is contingent.

Extinction occurs when a previously reinforced response is no longer followed by the same reinforcer and the response eventually decreases in frequency.

Negative reinforcement is a process whereby the likelihood of a response *increases* when it is followed by the *termination, reduction,* or *absence* of a stimulus.

Punishment is a process whereby the likelihood of a response *decreases* when it is followed by *presentation* of an aversive stimulus.

punishing agent was present. Cookie stealing and assaultive behavior will go to higher than usual rates to make up for opportunities missed while punishing agents were present. Also, punishment may be accompanied by such unfortunate side effects as fear, anxiety, aggression, failure to perform beneficial responses, and, in humans, loss of self-esteem, confidence, and initiative.

Table 14.1 will allow you to compare the various kinds of reinforcement at a glance.

The Development of Humans: Language, Personality, and Child Rearing

Although Skinner rejects the notion, "personality," his beliefs about how behavior is acquired relate well to the concept. In this section, Skinner's ideas for the design and construction of critical human activities relating to personality are examined.

Development of Speech. A central part of child rearing and child development is the role the family plays in language learning. Skinner (1957, 1972e) contends that learning to use words orally is a relatively simple matter. When a child of age two is confronted with the stimulus "red light" and utters the word *red,* he is reinforced by the "verbal community" (Mom, Dad, and siblings). When the child puts two words together, for example, "That red," his verbal behavior is again reinforced. Correct insertion of a verb ("That is red") is reinforced similarly, leading to the use of complete, grammatically-correct sentences. More technically, oral language use is learned by the formation of contingencies between verbal responses and reinforcements delivered by the verbal community. So-called *rules of language* are learned by a similar process. If the child says, "I am five years old," instead of "I are five years old," praise by Mom and Dad will follow (Skinner, 1976a). Thus, language acquisition is explained by operant conditioning.

As soon as Skinner's book on language learning appeared (Skinner, 1957), major objections were raised by linguist Noam Chomsky (1959). Chomsky asserted that an innate, genetically-programmed "language faculty" (LF) is needed to account for the explosive rate at which young children learn language (Palmer & Donahoe, 1992). He reasoned that children's abrupt and rapid verbal learning cannot be explained by plodding, step-by-step operant conditioning. Children are pre-set at birth to appreciate grammatical rules that allow them to acquire language in leaps and bounds. Support for this view comes from the exceedingly rapid language acquisition rate, and also from observations of children's speech errors. Suppose a child errs in saying "Look, the deer*s* are running across the road." Her comment indicates both knowledge of the rule for forming the plural and, in view of the error, that she could not have acquired the rule through reinforcement (parents do not usually reinforce incorrect speech).

While initially Skinnerians seemed unable to handle Chomsky's challenge, modern radical behaviorists are fighting back, partly by finding flaws in the LF. They have suggested that the LF is like the little person (homunculus) in an individual's brain who interprets all sensory inputs (and in that little person is another who interprets for the first, etc.). Further, Palmer and Donahoe (1992) argue that language units have to "already be segmented into phrases, words and parts of speech" for the LF to make its interpretations (p. 1351). So what good is it? Other questions about the LF include: "If it is inherited, who can trace the evolutionary history of its development?" and "If it is inherited, who can locate the relevant genes on human chromosomes?" These questions seem more damning than Chomsky's questions about behaviorism.

Building a Personality.   Skinner wastes no opportunity to dismiss personality from the realm of science. In Chapter 1 of *Beyond Freedom and Dignity* (1971), he mocks the notion of "disturbed personality" (pp. 8 and 16) and flatly states: "We do not need to try to discover what personalities, states of mind, feelings, traits of character . . . or the other perquisites of autonomous man really are in order to get on with scientific analysis of behavior" (p. 15). Yet, in that book, and in *Walden Two* (1948), he subtly, and perhaps unwittingly, indicates that people do have personalities, at least in the sense of showing individual differences in behaviors that are relatively constant across time and situations. Sometimes he even referred to personality in a way that assumed its existence (Benjamin & Nielsen-Gammon, 1999, p. 162).

In *Walden Two,* the person one might think would be given even less personality than Prof. Burris is "blessed" with a rich and full repertoire of behaviors that distinguish him from others. Frazier, the founder and leader of Walden Two, is an impulsive individual whose temper flares on many occasions. He shows a great deal of self-confidence, but seems rather vulnerable underneath all the bravado. At one point, Frazier bursts forth:

> You think I'm conceited, aggressive, tactless, selfish. You're convinced that I'm completely insensitive to my effect upon others . . . You can't see in me any of the personal warmth or the straightforward natural strength which are responsible for the success of Walden Two. My motives are ulterior and devious, my emotions warped (pp. 236–237).

It seems that the author who condemns personality provides excellent examples of "lots of" personality (Frazier) and "little" personality (Burris) in his only novel. In *Beyond Freedom and Dignity* (1971), not only is it implied that people have personality, but Skinner alludes to the possibility of developing and changing personality by design.

In commemoration of the year 1984, Skinner wrote a new episode in which a resurrected George Orwell, who wrote the futuristic book *1984,* seeks admittance to Walden Two

BOX 14.3 • *Baby in a Box*

Skinner has been controversial at least since his wartime attempts to use pigeons to guide missiles (Skinner, 1972d). However, nothing he has done has caused more comment than rearing his infant daughter, Deborah, in a box. Skinner (1972a; Rutherford, 2003; Vargas, 2003; and see Benjamin & Nielsen-Gammon, 1999) described the apparatus used to house the child, along with the behaviorist's rationale for the unusual procedure. He writes that his wife, Eve, decided it was time to apply science to the nursery, in the interest of saving labor, presumably her own. The first consideration, quite properly, was the physical and psychological well-being of the child. Deborah's "box" was spacious, providing ample room for the child and her toys. The open area in front was normally covered by a removable pane of safety glass. The floor of the compartment was covered with a sheet that could be replaced instantly by means of a roller device. Also, the child wore only a diaper, but was kept quite comfortable with no clothes, as her box featured temperature (heat) and humidity control.

Unconfined by clothes, Deborah was free to move her limbs in any way she wished. Compared to some babies who are restrained by clothes, she joyously exercised with all her might. The result was the development of strong back, leg, and abdominal muscles. By-products of the exercise were unusual agility of the feet and excellent hand–foot coordination. Deborah often played for hours with toys suspended from the ceiling of the box. Manipulating a music maker with her feet, the baby was able to compose her own tunes, much to the amusement of the family.

Feeding and changing the child took only about one and a half hours a day, but this was only a small portion of the time devoted to her. The "box" was actually a bed; she had a play pen just like any other child and was taken out of both when she wanted to interact with family members (Vargas, 2003). Far from being neglected, Deborah was the center of attention. Neighborhood children were continually parading past the box for a chance to see and play with the "baby in the box." Instead of receiving less affection than other children Deb-

orah may have received more affection of higher quality. Freed from much of the drudgery of caregiving, her parents had more time for affection and a stronger inclination to display it.

Some of Skinner's techniques and "suggestions for a better society" were viewed by critics as mechanical and even tyrannical (Benjamin & Nielsen-Gammon, 1999; Haney, 1990). Skinner himself was seen by some as a cold, unfeeling scientist (Baars, 2003; Rutherford, 2003). Putting his baby in apparent isolation only confirmed these perceptions of the famous behaviorist. Rumors persisting to this day include: Deborah had a psychotic breakdown, she committed suicide, and she brought a lawsuit against her father, nonsense that she found amusing, but disturbed her mother (Benjamin & Nielsen-Gammon, 1999).

In fact, Skinner was a warm and responsive father to Deborah and to his other daughter, Julie (Vargas, 2003). They often exchanged poems and touching notes. It was Skinner's self-selected duty to read the girls stories before bedtime (Vargas, 2003). He also quickly laid his work aside when the girls visited his home office. There are many examples of tenderness and concern for his daughters in the last volume of his autobiography (Skinner, 1983b). For example, when Debs, as he called Deborah, broke a leg on a ski trip to the Deux Alps, Skinner dropped professional obligations and flew to Geneva. Then he drove to Grenoble under dangerous winter conditions so he could care for her. When she arrived home, being confined to crutches, she was understandably cranky. A day after being somewhat unpleasant, Deborah wrote her father the following note: "Dear Pop, How are things? This is just a note to tell you I love you. Love, Debs. P.S. & that I apologize for my poor behavior of yesterday . . . " (Skinner, 1983b, p. 234). A later note to Debs contains an astounding passage for a radical behaviorist to write: "I'm not embarrassed by any supposed shortcomings of yours or afraid you will prove to the world that I am a bad psychologist. Live your own life, not mine, Be yourself. I like your Self" (p. 235). "Self" theorists of the Rogers mold take note. By the way, Debs became an

(continued)

BOX 14.3 Continued

accomplished and successful artist. Julie is a professor.

The "aircrib," mistakenly called a "box" in the *Ladies Home Journal* article that introduced it to the public and a "Skinner box" by detractors, got off to a shaky start in the commercial market (Benjamin & Nielsen-Gammon, 1999). Especially in 1945 when the article was published, *box* meant 'coffin,' as all too many people experienced seeing relatives returning home from the war in a "box." "Skinner box" meant that Debs had been crammed into something like Figure 14.1 and treated like a pigeon or a rat. Because of these incorrect attribu-

tions, some members of the public were irate. One Los Angeles resident even wrote Indiana University, where Skinner was psychology department chair at the time, and demanded that they launch a lawsuit against their "crackpot scientist" (p. 159). Nevertheless, the aircrib was marketed and was an initial success according to owners. It died eventually, probably because of people's suspicions regarding psychotechnology—they believed it would lower sensibility to the child's needs and lessen parent–child contact—not because it wasn't a good idea.

(Skinner, 1987a). Burris and Frazier appear to be their same old selves, despite the passage of considerable time. Thus, Skinner provides testimony to the stability of personality.

Whether or not one finds Skinner's attempt to dismiss internal entities (traits) convincing, it still must be granted that his notions implicitly include individual differences in behaviors that are somewhat constant across time and situations, the popular assumption underlying personality. If the relatively constant behaviors that signify personality can be changed through environmental intervention, it should also be possible to develop a personality by design. In fact, Skinner wrote "Creating the Creative Artist" (1972c) in which he implies that the disposition for creating art may be inborn, but will not be manifested without the development of contingencies between artistic endeavor and reinforcement.

But what exactly is reinforcing in a work of art, such as a painting? It has been argued that the content of a painting is somehow rewarding in and of itself, "intrinsically rewarding." However, if one examines popular subjects for paintings, Skinner asserts, those objects with survival value predominate (Skinner, 1983a), "extrinsically rewarding" objects. For example, the human hand, a form of great strength and capability, is a frequent subject. Pictures of food are also common in paintings. More abstract are portraits depicting family and loved ones, themes that have been associated with survival throughout the evolutionary history of humans. Paintings are reinforcing because of their content, but it is not some intrinsic value of a picture as such. Rather, the content, food and the human form, has value because of the evolutionary history of human beings and factors from the history of the particular artist. This orientation is somewhat Jungian.

During the lifetime of each artist, there are themes embedded in his or her works that especially appeal to people in the artist's community. When depicted on canvas, these themes result in a form of reinforcement that is familiar to us all, praise. Needless to say, the artist in question will represent in her or his works those themes that are repeatedly followed by reinforcement. Thus, the artist's own history of reinforcement, as well as the history of human beings, shapes her or his behavior when confronting the canvas.

However, creativity, in the sense of an idea that no one has ever had before, is an illusion (Skinner, 1972c). True, a successful artist does not merely copy the works of other artists, but does "copy" from her or his own experience. The resultant work of art may be unique in that no one has ever expressed the experience exactly as has our hypothetical artist. However, the work is not wholly original in that it represents an experience common to many people. Again, Skinner sounds somewhat like Jung. Further, once an artist has arrived at a form of expression that is at least an unusual rendition of some experience, and therefore is reinforced, he or she is likely to repeat that expression throughout his or her career. To support this contention, Skinner points to Picasso. Supposedly, only the first of Picasso's paintings was not derivative. All the works that followed stemmed from the first effort. Consistent with this view, many of our "original ideas" may not be our own. In fact, some possibly large percentage of them were non-consciously plagiarized from other people (Carpenter, 2002).

Skinner was a highly credible expert on creativity because he was a highly creative person. Not only did he program pigeons to pilot missiles, he also programmed his home office to facilitate professional productivity and smooth transitions to his role as father (Vargas & Chance, 2002). For example, he rigged a reading light to a clock so that one switch turned on both. This provided him with a signal to start working (light) and a way to time how long he had worked (clock). When Julie or Debbie came for some fatherly attention, he clicked off the switch, wheeled around in his swivel chair and, with a big smile, exclaimed, "Hello. What can I do for you?" (p. 55). After the interaction was over and the girls left, he clicked the switch on and went back to work, warmed by the time with his girls and secure in the knowledge that his work period would be accurately timed.

These were not his only inventions. He was the creator of the "teaching machine" (Rutherford, 2003). This device would, with the turn of a crank, present a student with a question such as "Who discovered America?" and allow her to choose an answer, then display the correct answer ("American Indians." Not the answer you were expecting?). With this method, the student's behavior—indicating the correct answer—could be reinforced (or not; if not, the student had other chances). These machines once sold well and were used in educational settings. The original variety is rare today, but the influence of the teaching machine lingers on, even if we fail to recognize Skinner's influence. For example, he had impact on me, though I didn't know it until recently. When personal computers were new and there was little software available (late 1970s and early 1980s) I used Basic to write a program that would teach my son the multiplication tables. It presented the multiplication problems randomly. When he got one right, it never appeared again. After each correct answer, a reinforcer appeared on the screen, such as "slam dunk" or "you did it." If he responded incorrectly, nothing happened (non-reinforcement). He went from knowing few of the multiplication problems to getting them all correct in just three minutes (up to 10×10).

Skinner and others have shown that the sooner a reinforcer is delivered following a correct response, the stronger is the learning. Following this lead, I (and many colleagues) provided students with immediate feedback concerning the correctness of answers to multiple-choice questions. In one example, I used a scoring machine in class that would make an occasional "rat-tat" sound when a student got most questions correct, but sounded like a machine gun when a student got many incorrect (that, admittedly, was a problem).

Nowadays Internet courses in many disciplines—psychology and others—use the same principle: students provide an answer on a Web page and then are immediately given the correct answer so they may be reinforced (or not). When I teach an online course, I can give my students very quick feedback, even to essay answers.

Few people valued Skinner's early attempts at training animals to do tasks that would be too dangerous or impossible for humans. But maybe he started something that could be highly useful today. Although Skinner's Harvard lab, started in 1948, was finally closed in 1998, researchers are still using Skinnerian principles for training animals to do what humans and tiny robots cannot do or not do as well as animals (Azar, 2002). For example, rats with a backpack attached to electrodes implanted into their brains can be guided and monitored from a kilometer away as they crawl through tiny cracks and crevices using their noses to find target objects. One such target could be a person trapped under some rubble. Rats could also be trained to locate explosives. Some day small robots may be able to operate similarly, but it will be a very long time before any robot possesses an ability to smell as sensitive as that of rats. In another example, pigeons were trained to detect objects floating at sea which could turn out to be men overboard. While the pigeons were accurate 93 percent of the time, human flight crews showed only 38 percent accuracy. This level of accuracy, duplicated by pigeons locating defective pills on a drug-factory conveyer belt, may distinguish animals from humans and robots.

If a person, Skinner, could inspire so much creativity in the realm of education and applied science, could a community find ways to encourage the pursuit of creativity in the form of art? A simple answer is mass exposure to art. Widespread display of art would help to develop artists in two ways. First, there would be an increase in the number of people who would appreciate art, and thus be able to reinforce artists with praise and attention to their works. Second, large-scale exposure to art would uncover most of those people who are genetically disposed to create works of art. Similarly, great athletes cannot be produced in a society in which sports are not played. If the opportunity to reinforce athletic prowess is not available, athletes will not develop, even though the genetic potential is present in members of the society. Proportional to population, the former East Germany won far more Olympic medals than any other country (in absolute numbers they were often second only to the former USSR). Skinner would explain this phenomenal success by reference to the interplay of genetics and reinforcement. Rather than simply working with the same material available in other countries and doing a better job with it, East Germany thoroughly exploited excellent material by making athletic opportunities readily available and by constructing contingencies between athletic performance and reinforcement.

What kind of society would promote such development by design? It might seem to be a society in which "talent scouts" go on frequent quests for those characteristics that are needed by the society. To the contrary, in *Walden Two* the greatest number and variety of pursuits and accompanying reinforcements imaginable are made available to all members of the community. People receive credits for the jobs they perform daily, and, with some flexibility, they have to earn a certain number of credits per week in order to continue in the community. In contrast to real societies, *Walden Two* offers the most credits for tasks that are tiresome, difficult, and uninteresting (for example, collecting garbage) and the fewest credits for tasks that are enjoyable and interesting (for example, giving a lecture on a favorite topic). Under this system, *Walden Two*'s physicians might receive fewer credits per unit time than laborers. Therefore, physicians would have to work longer hours than laborers to earn the same number of credits.

The net result of the *Walden Two* credit system is that most people try a wide variety of pursuits, but eventually migrate to those that they are genetically disposed to perform well. "Planners," such as Frazier, presumably because of their inherited disposition to "leadership," spend much of their time planning life in the imaginary society, but sometimes they tend the garden or chop wood. Other members of the community may work at mending fences, repairing the barns, and feeding the animals on many more occasions than they are employed at teaching or serving on committees. *Walden Two* describes an efficient society because experiences rich in number and variety are arranged, creating an environment that selects behaviors the performers are best equipped to enact. It is not necessary to search for talent. Because the society offers the opportunity for performance and reinforcement of almost any behavior, talent simply emerges. By the way, *Walden Two* is not entirely hypothetical. Some young people built a replica of Skinner's utopia near Richmond, Virginia (Kinkade, 1973). This wasn't the only attempt to replicate *Walden Two* (Rutherford, 2003). It was successful, but might have benefited from changes that Skinner would have made in *Walden Two,* if he could have done it over (Skinner, 1983a). Box 14.4 covers Skinner on diversity and equality at *Walden Two.*

Evaluation

Contributions

Studies in the Skinnerian tradition number in the thousands. The *Journal of the Experimental Analysis of Behavior* has been, since its founding in 1958, devoted entirely to research inspired by Skinner. For this reason, and because you have already had a glimpse of Skinnerian research methods in the section on operant learning, this section is issue oriented.

The Interrelationship of Genetic Disposition and Reinforcement.   Gromly (1982) reports an attempt to investigate the interrelationship between the genetic disposition of individuals and the history of reinforcement during their lives. He states:

> Although learning theory and biological viewpoints are sometimes presented as competing explanations for behavior, they are more likely complementary. This appears to be so in the development of personality traits. One direction this complementary process might take is that, within the limits of their particular environment, people tend to select experiences that suit their biological dispositions. In this way, the selection of preferred experiences by individuals acts as an amplifier of differences that already exist (p. 255).

Skinner would likely agree with Gromly's statement, with one exception: people do not select experiences from their environment, the environment selects individuals' behaviors and, thus, it selects the experiences that accompany the behavior. People who are genetically disposed to be articulate may end up on the debating team, where their ability to

BOX 14.4 • *Skinner on Diversity and Equality of Opportunity*

Skinner showed concern for culture and cultural change (Pennypacker, 1992). Not surprisingly, he thought cultures develop according to operant principles. People find themselves in a physical environment that selects certain behaviors rather than others. For example, the behaviors—planting, cultivating, and harvesting papaya—may be selected in the case of certain people living in a particular environment where papaya grow. Out of these behaviors come others: by-products of papaya are used for decoration and rituals develop relating to farming papaya.

Cultural change can also be accounted for by behaviorism. Africans brought to the United States as slaves carried rich cultural traditions with them. These included food preferences and all that goes with them as well as methods of communication. Obviously, some of these behaviors relating to food no longer were reinforced: the foods were not present in the United States so rituals regarding these foods disappeared. Other cultural traditions, however, were associated with behaviors that were selected by the new U.S. environment, which provided reinforcement for them. Some Africans, while still in Africa, communicated with drums, using a sort of Morse code (long before Morse made his code). This communication method proved highly useful to Africans isolated on different plantations. Use of the drum code was reinforced by news of relatives and friends. Thus, change and maintenance of culture can be explained by operant principles.

If there is substance to the charges that Skinner promoted fascist control of human behavior, one would expect that equal opportunity for a variety of people would not exist in a Skinnerian world: certain people would rule (e.g., males) and certain groups of people (e.g., women and poor, uneducated people) would be excluded from power (Rutherford, 2003). According to Dinsmoor (1992) nothing could be further from the truth about life in a community run on Skinnerian principles. In *Walden Two*, half of the Board of Governors were women. No groups were ever consigned solely to menial tasks. True, people migrated to the jobs that fit their skills and reinforcement histories best, but everybody continued to do everything: leaders, professors, and physicians performed manual labor at least occasionally. Finally, would George Orwell, who loathed his literary creation "Big Brother," be welcomed at *Walden Two* if Skinnerianism did not reject fascist control? The answer is as obvious as Skinner's disgust with malevolent control of behavior.

Equality of intellectual potential is also Skinnerian. Lying behind programs to raise the intellectual performance of disadvantaged children is the assumption that poor performance can be improved because it is due to impoverished environments, not innate intellectual deficiencies (Greenwood et al., 1992; Johnson & Layng, 1992). Thus, children who might otherwise be written off can experience an academic boost through manipulations of environmental contingencies.

---

speak well will be amplified, provided that a team is available to them (being on such a team would multiply genetic effects, according to Flynn, 2003).

To illustrate the possible link between genetic disposition and experiences, Gromly had university fraternity men keep a log of their experiences. Essentially, "logging experiences" amounted to recording the situations encountered and the corresponding behaviors performed. A sample log entry would be "played basketball today." They also rated themselves on scales designed to assess the possibly genetic dispositions "energetic–physically active" and "sociable–extraverted, socially outgoing." Results showed a close relationship between what the men reported doing and scores on "energetic" and "sociable." Thus, measures of the genetic disposition, "energetic" and "sociable," were closely related to behaviors and accompanying experiences consistent with those dispositions. In Skinner's terms, the *environment selected* energetic and social behaviors for those people who were genetically inclined to be essentially extraverted. It is important to note that the behaviors of such people in one environment are not likely to be the same as those of the same people acting in another environment. A given environment does not simply extend and refine a genetic disposition. It leads to specific and concrete behaviors that go far beyond the global and abstract genetic disposition (Skinner, 1972e).

Behavior Therapy.   The phrase, **behavior therapy,** psychological therapy employing behavioral techniques, first appeared in print in an article by Skinner and a colleague that described their use of the then-new methods (Skinner, 1983b). Almost all of the vast number of techniques that fall under "behavior therapy" were directly suggested by behavioristic research or have been validated by that research (Skinner, 1972j). These methods include positive reinforcement, negative reinforcement, and punishment. Behavior therapy has been successfully used for everything from treatment of obesity, heavy smoking, and alcoholism to treatment of children who do not talk or relate to adults (autistic children) and treatment of psychotic adults (people who have withdrawn from reality; see Ullmann & Krasner, 1965).

It is beyond the scope of this book to consider even a small sample from the massive psychotherapeutic tool chest of behavior therapy. However, to get a flavor of behavior therapy and to see how it relates to Skinner's ideas, consider a hypothetical example suggested by Skinner (1972). Consider a child of five who is not psychotic or autistic, but who is so shy and withdrawn that he almost never talks or relates in any way to adult strangers. Imagine that the child is placed in a room on one of two chairs positioned side by side in front of a vending machine. Candy is known to be a good reinforcer for the child, and the machine is capable of vending the child's favorite confection. The machine is operated by an observer who is hidden behind a one-way mirror (the observer can see the child, but the child sees only his reflection). After a few minutes, an adult stranger enters the room and takes a seat next to the child. Nothing happens for a long while, and the adult leaves, returning shortly. Each entry is a trial. Several trials occur before the child finally utters a word to the stranger. Immediately, the vending machine operator presses a button, and out of the machine comes the child's favorite treat. More trials may occur before the child speaks again, but each episode of speech is reinforced by candy. Soon the child is talking regularly to the stranger and to other strangers who replace the original adult in order to spread the response to adults in general.

Whenever the child speaks to the stranger, the stranger replies. The replies occur at the same time as the candy reinforcement is being delivered. Thus, the stranger's replies become **secondary reinforcers,** stimuli that come to have all the properties of primary reinforcers (such as candy) through association with primary reinforcers (Kimble, 1961). Thereafter, replies can reinforce the child's utterances. Now the child can go out into the real world and talk to people, with each string of utterances being reinforced by people's replies. This feature makes it likely that the conquest of the child's shyness will generalize beyond the laboratory.

Limitations

Perhaps Skinner has been most severely criticized for discounting thought, feeling, consciousness, and other phenomena that exist "in the head" and, thus, cannot be directly observed (Baars, 2003; Kihlstrom, 2003). He admitted that individuals, including himself, do have thoughts and feelings, but he argued that there is no need to consider these internal entities in order to understand people (Skinner, 1983a; Vargas, 2003). He believed that feelings or emotions are by-products of behavior, not its determinants (Skinner, 1971). According to this point of view, one flees (behavior), *then* is afraid (emotion). Assuming this sequence of events, emotions cannot be determinants of behavior. His easy adoption of the behavior–emotion sequence and rejection of its opposite (people are afraid and then flee) seems unwarranted. According to J. Jung (1978), the position that Skinner endorsed is not amenable to testing by experimental procedures and has been subjected to severe criticism.

Emotions and thoughts can be important even when divorced from behavior. A few years before his death, famed British actor Sir Laurence Olivier was interviewed on TV (*60 Minutes,* January 2, 1983). He recounted that, at one point in his career, he had developed severe stage fright. While portraying Shakespeare's Othello, Olivier was so overcome with fear and thoughts of inadequacy that he had difficulty catching his breath and wondered if he could continue. Yet, somehow he finished. When his portrayal of the troubled Moor was shown on *60 Minutes,* nothing in his performance revealed even a trace of his internal agony. The critics had also noticed nothing unusual; as always, they had praised Olivier's performance. There were no external consequences to his stage fright. However, the solely internal terror suffered by the actor was recalled as one of the most notable experiences of his life. Emotions and accompanying thoughts can be extremely important in the lives of people, even when unaccompanied by any external manifestations, behavioral or otherwise.

Many of us have solved a never-before-encountered mathematical or other complex problem in private. By a reasoning process, we have come up with an answer that had never occurred to us before, and, thus, could not have been the object of reinforcement in the past. Neither is it currently subject to reinforcement by the verbal community. This common experience, and others like it, is evidence that thoughts unrelated to behavior are important to everyday functioning (Hayes, 1978).

By his own admission, Skinner's behaviorism (as presented in 1989) cannot account for the process by which we take in information through our senses and give meaning to it. Skinner and his works are virtually absent from the pages of books on sensation and perception (see Matlin & Foley, 1997). But this observation highlights an important point regarding post-Skinner Skinnerianism: radical behaviorism must change if it is to survive. Examples of this needed change abound. Just a little leaning in the mentalistic direction can allow behaviorism to reasonably account for phenomena that have been beyond its reach. For example, just allowing for the social learning theorists' "expectations" of future reinforcements would improve behaviorism's explanatory power. It could then account for humans' ability to anticipate the development of reinforcing circumstances not yet in existence.

In fact, a move in this direction is under way. Kimble (2000) asserts that "cognition" and "affect" must become a part of behaviorists' account of human action. He would also add "potential," which implies future orientation, as well as "adaptation" and "coping," which imply "free will." DeGrandpre (2000) has suggested that Skinner's response-consequences sequence is teleological or purposive: the organism responds for the purpose of receiving consequences. Obviously, this interpretation contradicts Skinner's basic, anti-mentalistic orientation. This "problem" would be corrected by an R—C → [S—R] conception in which the response (R) is followed by a consequence (C), which reinforces the *relationship* between the stimulus setting the occasion for the response (S) and the response (R). Thus, a stimulus, sight of a dog's "master" (S), gives rise to a sitting-up response (R) by the dog that is followed by the consequence, food (C), which strengthens the relationship between the sight-of-master stimulus (S) and the sitting-up response (R). Skinner's basic formulation is already being rewritten to include the S—R process he rejected.

With regard to the Skinner–Chomsky debate, the weight of current evidence favors neither side (Seidenberg, 1997). Children are neither born with a "language facility" (LF) nor do they learn language through reinforcers provided by the "verbal community." Rather, they are able to "naturally and automatically encode statistical aspects of caregiver speech without overt guidance or reward" (p. 1601). That is, children's brains are (probably) innately able to figure the probability that a given speech form is interpretable in a given way, considering the context in which it is used. Imagine a mother who, in reference to friends, says "They are real dear." Her child "calculates," based on past encounters with the sound of *dear,* that the odds are poor its mother means 'four-legged creatures with antlers.' Instead, the child bets its mother means that the friends are dear to her.

Conclusions

Skinner's ideas have certainly inspired numerous researchers and theorists to discover many new ways to predict and control behavior. His concepts have directed attention to specific aspects of human behavior and have stimulated a formidable amount of research, commentary, and criticism. When he died, newspapers and popular magazines were filled with acknowledgments of his contributions. Psychologist Eric Ward, who worked with Skinner, characterized Skinner's impact as so great that it has profoundly affected school teachers and parents, not just other psychologists (Hopkins, 1990). As an example, he mentioned "time out," a method now known to most teachers and parents. Originally, "time out" meant an interruption in the delivery of reinforcers while a pigeon pecked a panel other than the one connected to the food cup (that is, pecks went unreinforced). "Time out," when applied to children, "involves briefly interrupting the rewards inadvertently stemming from bad behavior" (p. A9) by ignoring misbehavior (not following it with reinforcers) or placing the children where their "bad behavior" cannot be reinforced.

As proof that Skinner has continued to have great impact right up to the present time, just prior to his death articles written in praise of his position appeared in several publications, even in some that are apparently alien to behaviorism. For example, a month before his death, an article extolling his position was published in the *Humanist* (Bennett, 1990). Earlier he had received a prestigious humanist award (Rutherford, 2003). Soon after his death, he was said to have had much in common with existentialists (Fallon, 1992).

Even if the criticisms noted above are valid to some degree, it is still probably true that Skinner's point of view is one of the most general in all of psychology. It is difficult to find an introductory psychology book that does not consider Skinner in several different chapters. Likewise, social psychology, developmental psychology, personality, and psychotherapy texts typically devote considerable space to Skinnerianism. More importantly, through his contributions to child rearing and behavior therapy, he has had an important and positive influence on literally thousands and thousands of lives.

In an earlier edition, I confidently predicted that Skinner would someday pass Freud as psychology's most revered contributor. In Haggbloom and colleagues (2002) Skinner was eighth in journal citations, second in text citations, first in the survey of psychologists, and first overall (Freud was third). While Kihlstrom (2003) is correct to reject Baars's (2003) claim that Skinner was the most famous scientist of his time—Einstein clearly held that title—he is incorrect in asserting that Skinner was not the most revered, famous, and influential psychologist of his time. Some fifteen years after his death, he is the number-one psychologist in the history of psychology. All of his competitors, including the earliest psychologists, are listed behind him (Haggbloom et al., 2002).

Summary Points

1. Skinner's Ph.D. was from Harvard, where he spent most of his career. As a youngster, Skinner flirted with mentalism. However, after college, a failed attempt to be a writer, and a sojourn in Greenwich Village, he was converted to behaviorism. As a young man Skinner was naive about his scientific contributions; as an older person he was iconoclastic. Skinner showed a variety of behaviors and his personality was hard to pin down.

2. Skinner emphasized environmental consequences of responses and the process of environmental selection of behavior. In *Beyond Freedom and Dignity,* he asserted that freedom is possible in a limited sense, but dignity is an illusion. We regularly acknowledge environmental control when we attribute the cause of our own behavior to our environments. He showed that many mentalistic words originally referred to behavior.

3. In operant conditioning, the organism operates on its environment with consequences that increase the likelihood of the operation. In positive reinforcement, a stimulus increases the likelihood of a response on which its presentation is contingent. Shaping is done by successive approximation. In negative reinforcement the likelihood of a response *increases* when it is followed by the absence of an aversive stimulus. In punishment the likelihood of a response *decreases* when it is followed by the presentation of an aversive stimulus.

4. Punishment works to deter aggression only under limited conditions. Skinner's opposition to physical punishment is confirmed in the "just deserts" and "spanking" research. Skinner believed that language develops via reinforcement by the verbal community. Chomsky offered an innate "language faculty" as a substitute for the behavioristic account. This position has at least as many flaws as the behavioristic view.

5. Skinner reared his daughter, Deborah, in a "box" with the following advantages: freedom from child-care drudgery, more time for affection, and more opportunities for creative child play. False rumors had Deborah attempting suicide and suffering a psychotic

breakdown. A citizen even complained to Skinner's university. Deborah and Julie turned out well and had a warm and close relationship with their father, who would always drop his work to interact with them and read them bedtime stories.

   6. Skinner explicitly rejects the notion "personality," but he often supported ideas that are consistent with popular conceptions of personality. Skinner has striven to show how society can promote the development of traits such as "creativity" and "leadership" by providing opportunities for reinforcement of "creative" and "leader" behaviors. Skinner's often unacknowledged applied contributions include organizing one's work space, "teaching machines," and other techniques to facilitate education.

   7. A culture develops through the environment's selection of the behaviors of the people inhabiting it. Culture changes with shifts in environments. Maintenance is seen when new environments also select certain cultural behaviors. In *Walden Two,* Skinner supported gender equality and he relegated no group to menial tasks. Skinnerian methods to boost academic performance assume the intellectual equality of all children.

   8. Gromly's work with fraternity men who kept logs that recorded extraversion-related behaviors supports the interplay of genetic disposition and reinforcement. Men presumably disposed to these traits tended to show behaviors and accompanying experiences corresponding to the traits. Skinner was a pioneer in the area of behavior therapy.

   9. Skinner's belief that emotions accompany or follow behavior has been criticized as scientifically untestable. His ideas have been rejected by some critics because reinforcement cannot account for solutions to problems that have never before been used by the problem solver, and emotions/thoughts that remain entirely internal. Skinner's behaviorism will survive only if it becomes flexible by adding a social–cognitive flavor and if it becomes more future oriented.

   10. Revision of Skinner's response–consequence sequence has been suggested. Research supports a probabilistic theory of language learning rather than Skinner's or Chomsky's. Skinner has inspired many fruitful theoretical and practical approaches to understanding and controlling behavior. His death was followed with an outpouring of testimonials to his many contributions, some from unexpected sources. Skinner's work has influenced virtually every branch of psychology and has even touched rank-and-file citizens. As the text author predicted, Skinner is now the most revered psychologist in psychology's history, supplanting Freud.

Running Comparison

Theorist	Skinner in Comparison
Freud	Unlike Freud, Skinner believed in external causation and condemned "mentalism."
Rogers	He acknowledged a self not unlike that of Rogers who also was concerned with creativity.
Jung	Like Jung, he alluded to symbolism in art that reflects humans' evolutionary past.

Essay/Critical Thinking Questions _____

1. Paint a picture (profile) of Skinner's personality (as in Chapter 1).

2. Could punishment be used to eliminate the self-mutilative behavior of an autistic child?

3. In the context of a Walden Three create a personality that is characterized by leadership.

4. How would you extinguish the attention-getting behavior of a child?

5. Defend "spanking" of children.

E-mail Interaction _____

Write the author at b-allen@wiu.edu. Forward one of the following, or phrase your own.

1. What will be Skinner's status in the future?

2. How could I teach my dog to walk on its hind legs?

3. Is spanking ever justified as a child-behavior-management technique?

Human Needs and Environmental Press: Henry A. Murray

- Can forbidden love be more important than professional success?
- What happens when more than one need arises at the same time?
- Can dreams predict real-life outcomes?

Henry A. Murray
http://mhhe.com/mayfieldpub/
psychtesting/profiles/murray.htm

You have now come round the full circle, almost. Unconscious processes, emphasized by Freud, have been considered, as well as reactions to Freudian thought. The interpersonal approach of Sullivan and the sociopsychological orientation of Fromm have been covered. Rogers and Maslow have proposed their humanistic concepts of empathy and self-actualization. You have contemplated the cognitive constructs of Kelly and the interplay of the social environment with cognitive processes offered by Mischel, Rotter, and Bandura. Finally, the radical behaviorism of Skinner provided you with a stark contrast to the others. In this chapter, the thinking of Henry A. Murray establishes the cables and pillars for the required bridge from these several basic points of view to the orientation that has dominated modern personality research, personality traits.

In one way or another, Murray's thinking resembles that of most theorists covered so far, but, at the same time, it remains unique. Jung stimulated Murray's interest in psychology. Murray acknowledged a debt to Freud, but, like Horney, used Freudian thought as a point of departure from which he launched his own theory. Murray, like Sullivan, clearly was interpersonally oriented: relations among people are critical in his theory. In some little-known research, Murray devoted considerable time to the dyad: relations within a group of two (Robinson, 1992). He was also sociopsychological: though he neglected Fromm, he borrowed heavily from social psychologist Kurt Lewin. Murray was definitely also cognitive and the interplay between internal needs and the external environment was prominent in his thinking. Despite his disdain for experimental psychology, he even showed some affinity for the ideas of his contemporary, B. F. Skinner. Murray states, "We may see . . . that certain effects are more fundamental to life and occur more regularly than any observed action patterns. This agrees with Skinner's conclusions" (Murray, 1981a, p. 140). Like Skinner, Murray believed it is the end effect of an action that is unique and relatively important. The action itself could be any number of behaviors, each equivalent in terms of its effects. Also similar to Skinner, but unlike the social learning theorists, Murray believed that behavior is more "pushed from the rear" than "pulled from the future" (Murray, 1981a). Murray had an intellect for all seasons. The trek across his broad mind is a journey from the first part of this book to the last.

Murray, the Person

Henry A. Murray was born in 1893 to well-to-do parents who occupied a brownstone house on the present site of Rockefeller Center, New York City (Anderson, 1988). He described himself as "an average, privileged American boy" who may have been embarrassed that his family's Long Island, N.Y. second home was so grand it shamed some of his rich friends' primary homes (Anderson, 1990, p. 305). Unlike most other theorists, he never developed a meaningful relationship with his mother. He once dreamed that she was a helpless invalid held like an infant in his arms. It was as if he longed to offer her the nurturance she denied him (Robinson, 1992). Although he did not reject his mother as did Maslow, like Maslow he felt that his mother favored his siblings. She was an emotionally bland, prim and proper socialite who rarely showed affection or concern for her middle child. Once he said to her, "You make my feelings hurt me" (Anderson, 1988, p. 141). On and off throughout his life, Murray attempted, sometimes lamely, to establish a relationship with her. He once even tried to administer his Thematic Apperception Test to her. Finally, he gave up and declared them "dead to each other" (p. 141). Although, as a child, his overt reactions to maternal rejection were mild, later, as an adult, he must have been seething inside. Even in his late sixties, Murray still spoke of the "marrow of misery and melancholy" that plagued him through the years (p. 141). In addition, he stuttered most of his life, an affliction that was more "psychological" than physiological: it diminished to a mild stammer by the 1930s and largely disappeared later in his life, when time lessened the hurt. It never prevented Murray from receiving prestigious appointments. During World War II, he served with the Office of Strategic Services (OSS) predecessor to the CIA (Morgan, 2003). By the post-World War II period, when Murray was called as an expert witness in the trial of accused traitor, Alger Hiss, he faced cross-examination by the F. Lee Bailey of his day without once stammering (Robinson, 1992).

Murray described his father as "a nice guy" (Anderson, 1988, p. 142), a euphemism for 'amiable dolt.' Anyone he found mediocre was described similarly. The elder Murray was a disappointment for a number of reasons: he was not bright (he could not follow conversations between his physician sons); he was not self-sufficient (he married the boss's daughter); he lacked ambition; he was predictable (a conservative banker by profession); and his values and way of life were commonplace and unimaginative. In fact, Murray came to see himself as the opposite of his father. Still, as he matured, the scintilla of respect Murray had granted his father increased somewhat (Robinson, 1992).

One might wonder what sort of father would have gained Murray's respect and affection. Murray had trouble sustaining admiration for anyone. He wrote James Anderson (1988) during 1981, "I'd admire someone for a while, and then it would fade, and it would be someone else. These were all tentative things" (p. 143). According to Anderson, Murray was imbued with a certain "specialness." Perhaps it was a fault, but it may have also been a virtue. Believing that his ideas had truth value, and that he was the natural leader of any group to which he belonged, drove Murray to conceive of original ideas and to inspire creative thinking in others (Robinson, 1992). He was narcissistic by his own declaration, and sometimes joked about it. Erik Erikson, Murray's former research associate, "imagined what Murray's fantasy would be: to put a statue of himself in place of Napoleon's on the column in the Place Vendome in Paris" (p. 169). The leader of the team producing the timeless *Explorations in Personality* (1938) might be cast as the benevolent dictator.

While this sense of specialness may not be equivalent to arrogance, it did give him a feeling of privilege. Like many "great people," one intimate romantic relationship was not enough. His wife, the former Josephine L. Rantoul, whom he married in 1916, was a traditional woman—a "good wife and mother"—but was insufficiently intellectual to fully satisfy Murray. Perhaps to fill the void, he became involved with Christiana Morgan, a research collaborator, confidante, friend, and lover. But, in his day, maintaining two romantic relationships was very difficult, yet he could not give up either woman. When he became enthralled with Jungian thought, partly because of Morgan's enthusiasm for the Swiss psychiatrist, he acceded to her insistence that he visit Zurich to speak with Jung. There he found a solution to his dilemma. Jung, it turned out, had a similar problem, and adopted the usual solution: he arranged for his lover, Toni Wolff, to occupy a house near his own. Despite Jung's attempts to discourage him—it was risky—Murray emulated his new Swiss colleague. Though not provided a nearby house, Morgan was usually not far away.

Christiana was much more than a mere paramour; she was the center of his universe throughout most of his adult life. So intense was their passion that they built a tower as a monument to their love (skeptics please see the picture in Robinson, 1992, facing p. 178). In full view of his wife, Jo, and Morgan's husband, Will, Christiana and he carried on a stormy romance beginning from soon after they met until the day she died. Despite protests to the contrary, because of Christiana's influence Murray never escaped the grip of Jungian thought. He and Christiana became characters out of Jungian mythology. As living reflections of anima and animus, they exchanged gender identities on occasion, but more often reveled in his "masculine" dominance and her "feminine" submission.

But Robinson (1992) contends that their attraction was more intellectual than sexual. She was the light in the background, illuminating many of Murray's most important works.

She was also a source of his torment. Deep and troubled, her brooding poetry seemed to characterize the gloomy side of their romance. As they jointly tried to moderate the misery of Jo and Will—Murray was fond of Will and grieved at his death—Christiana knew she would never fully possess Murray. Her hunger for him was so great that she starved emotionally for lack of him, wasting away from drink and despair. Shortly after calling her "disgusting," he found her alcohol-infused, lifeless body face down in the surf off a Caribbean island where they were vacationing (Robinson, 1992, p. 357). It had not been long since Jo had succumbed to a heart attack. Murray later announced that he and Christiana were to be married only weeks hence. He had lost a part of his soul and he knew it.

Anderson (1988), through numerous communications over several years, made an in-depth analysis of Murray's personality. Besides the sense of specialness, and the narcissism that went with it, Murray had a clear recognition of his intellectual gifts. He also had a powerful need for achievement and a sense of independence that was forced on him by the lack of parental connections. While his desire for intimacy was strong, he was wary of closeness. Nevertheless, he achieved intimacy, especially with women. With men it was different. Murray searched for weaknesses in his male associates and used his findings to assert his superiority. At the same time, he had a need for heroes, but quickly found all candidates for that role to have clay feet.

Despite his sometimes bubbly enthusiasm, his inner core of melancholy persisted. Depression enveloped him at several points in his life. His gloominess even affected his literary preferences: Murray's interest in the doleful classic *Moby Dick* was so intense that he became a leading authority on it. In a conversation with Murray, Freud was impressed with Murray's expertise on "my favorite American novel!" (Roazen, 2003, p. 4). Herman Melville, its despondent and perplexing author, became Murray's alter ego (Robinson, 1992). Yet, his belief in himself was undying and his intellect was towering. Henry A. Murray was destined to make major contributions.

Murray's academic credentials were as illustrious as they were unusual. After graduating from one of the most exclusive Eastern boy's schools, Groton, he enrolled at Harvard during 1911. There he did all the "right things": Murray was captain of the crew team (rowing)—equivalent in stature to football captain—and a social butterfly who was into drinking and carousing. Attaining something close to a gentleman's "C" average, he was granted an undergraduate degree in 1915 (Robinson, 1992). Following medical training at Columbia University, leading to the M.D. degree, Murray completed a 20-month internship in surgery (Smith & Anderson, 1989). During this period he helped care for future president Franklin D. Roosevelt, who was beginning his struggle against polio, and he launched a successful career as a medical researcher (Smith & Anderson, 1989). It was in this time frame that he also experienced his first meaningful relationship with a woman, a frail prostitute dying of syphilis over whom he hovered with genuine compassion (Robinson, 1992). For four years Murray studied the development of the chicken embryo at the Rockefeller Institute. Twenty-one articles reporting his research appeared in the leading medical and biochemical journals (Anderson, 1988). His interest in biochemistry was so strong that Murray went to study at Cambridge University in England, where he received a Ph.D. in the field during 1927. By this date, he had become a respected pioneer in the fledgling field of biochemistry, but he was not satisfied with himself.

Murray was an enigma, a tantalizing mystery. He fell for people with a "schoolboy crush," only to seemingly reject them a short time thereafter. Still, his loyalty to people who supported him was undying. He was inconsolable when wife Jo died. His brother's death during World War I was never fully accepted. Even his affection for Christiana's husband, Will, never ceased. Likewise, the deaths of close colleagues were devastating. He was insensitive and arrogant, yet soft and vulnerable; he was a confidant to presidents, though he was a hated rival to major academic figures; he knew limitless joy and bottomless despair. Hollywood take note: Henry A. "Harry" Murray was a remarkable person who led an extraordinary life, bordering on the incredible.

Murray's View of the Person

Early Exposure to Psychology

Like Kelly and Maslow, Murray found his first encounter with psychology while an undergraduate anything but inspiring. He said of his German-trained professor of experimental psychology, "A bud of interest in psychology . . . was nipped by the chill of Professor Munsterberg's approach" (quoted in Anderson, 1988, p. 146). Later, he wrote to Anderson of his dismay with Munsterberg's denial that "psychology had anything to do with people" (p. 146). Thus began a lifelong quarrel with experimental psychologists.

Even during his training as a medical researcher and biochemist, Murray was undergoing a "profound affectional upheaval" (Anderson, 1988, p. 146). "He suddenly and unexpectedly found himself 'in a blaze, . . . which would go on for three years and eventually pressure him to embrace . . . psychology' " (pp. 146–147). But, just as his exposure to experimental psychology brought him no comfort, neither did his first inquiries into Freudian thought. Having overheard some students talking about Freud, Murray consulted W. Courtney, a medical school neurologist and the revered father of a classmate. Courtney compared Freud's ideas to vomit. In an attempt at Freudian humor, he punned, "I regard [Freud's ideas] . . . as the greatest phallusy of the age" (quoted in Anderson, 1988, p. 146). Despite this rude introduction, Murray eventually gained some respect for Freud and his notions. However, Courtney's response was of little help at a time when Murray needed to embrace some psychological point of view.

It was in 1923 that Murray stumbled onto Jung's just translated *Psychological Types* (reprinted in 1961). The experience was a revelation to him and may have been a case of predestination, because he met the Jung enthusiast Morgan about the same time. It was in 1925 that Murray succumbed to Christiana's persistent urging and traveled to Zurich for three intense weeks with Jung (Smith & Anderson, 1989). Murray wrote of the experience (1981b, pp. 80–81):

> Dr. Jung was the first full-blooded, all-encompassing, spherical human being I had ever met . . . He [opened] . . . 'the great flood-gates of the wonder-world . . .' and I experienced the unconscious in [a] way that cannot be drawn out of books. . . . All this and more I owe to Dr. Jung.

Consistent with his personality, Murray's admiration for Jung faded—"he wasn't good with his concepts . . . he'd believed anything I told him that was along the lines that he liked . . . but he would overlook what did not fit his theories" (Anderson, 1988, p. 155). Elsewhere he mused that Jung was "so very imaginative," perhaps "too imaginative" (Roazen, 2003, p. 19). Nevertheless, his relationship with Christiana ensured that he would never abandon Jung. He continued to cite Jung and his theory reflected Jung's propensity for polarities.

In 1927, Morton Prince, recently commissioned to establish the Psychology Clinic at Harvard, wanted to hire an assistant. It was to be a psychology faculty appointment that included lecturing and clinic duties. Because Murray was absent from the United States, a friend and professor of physiology interceded on his behalf, declaring to Prince, "Here's this brilliant chemist in England. You want a scientist, don't you?" (p. 149). Despite "being entirely inadequate," Murray was offered the job and accepted. Within two years Prince was dead and Murray was clinic director. Needless to say, his education in psychology was even more abbreviated than that of Kelly, his companion in skepticism about experimental psychology. Murray was the featured lecturer in the first psychology courses he regularly attended.

Why Did Murray Become a Psychologist?

Jung was part of the answer. Murray's disaffection with his medical and biochemical work, which he found to be rote and lifeless, was another (Anderson, 1988). His work with medical patients did give him some intimate contact with other human beings, but he described it as "necessarily brief and superficial" (p. 149). More importantly, work in medical science allowed Murray no contact "with the deeper wellsprings of his personality . . . with his own inner life" (p. 149). In the end, it was the "marrow of misery and melancholy" that became the strongest magnet drawing him to psychology. Murray fit the stereotype of the maladjusted individual who becomes a psychologist to solve personal problems. In fact, he applied the stereotype to the preppie students who he believed had enrolled in his abnormal psychology class to address their problems (Anderson, 1990). But it worked. As Murray developed his own point of view, he grew stronger until he could be described as a well-adjusted person.

Developing a Unique Approach to Understanding People

Murray at first flirted with orthodox psychoanalysis. As a leader of the Boston Psychoanalytic Society, he was instrumental in recruiting Franz Alexander, a favorite of Freud's among graduates of the Berlin Psychoanalytic Institute. In the early 1930s, Alexander became Boston's resident psychoanalyst and engaged Murray in training analysis which lasted nine months, the last three in Chicago.

It is safe to say that Murray was not terribly impressed with psychoanalysis, at least not favorably (Anderson, 1988). In effect, he laughed his way through analysis, never being serious about it—"I was too busy, otherwise-attached" (p. 158). Though he liked Alexander, they were never really in sync. Among the few comments Anderson got from Murray about his analysis was in regard to Alexander's wife, a blond, flamboyant, race-car driver who seemed incompatible with the stout, unemotional, former student of Freud. Murray imagined that she was attracted to him.

Murray was to regard the analysis episode as time not especially well spent. Learning about the contents of his unconscious did not cure his stuttering, nor did Freudianism help him understand his relationship with his parents. Because he thought of his father as a "nice guy," he was certain that the Oedipal situation did not apply to him. In the end, he dismissed Alexander as another "nice guy" and declared himself disillusioned with psychoanalysis, a statement he later contradicted (Robinson, 1992).

There were some subtle signs that Murray was affected by the nine months with Alexander. First, there were covert signs that an underlying current of hostility flowing deep within Murray was whipped into waves. Not only was Alexander described as fat and bland, his office was said to be "very depressing, the color of feces" (Anderson, 1988, p. 159). Second, Murray must have been influenced, because thereafter he felt obligated to address Freud's notions in his own writings (Murray, 1981a). He also practiced psychoanalysis, though sparingly (Anderson, 1988).

Freud's influence on Murray was evident in other ways. Prominent among these was the belief that complex internal processes cannot be illuminated by scientific experiments. Experiments treat people like machines, cut from the same mold, with components that can be considered apart from the whole. Murray, like Maslow, came to believe that humans are dynamic wholes, not meaningfully divisible into parts and pieces.

Needless to say, Murray's Harvard colleagues did not care for his complaint that dividing psychology into the subdisciplines they held dear fragmented the person and, thus, was a serious error. He fought with them "like dragonflies" (Anderson, 1988, p. 157). Department Chair E. G. Boring warned Murray that he would be ostracized from the American Psychological Association for life if he published a paper containing comments such as "[John] Watson's proposal [is] naive, juvenile perversity." Robinson (1992) claimed that Boring literally quaked with the fear that Murray was about to puncture psychology's soft underbelly, precipitating its demise. Further, Murray persisted in opposing what he called the "scientism" of academic psychology. To him psychologists were playing at real science—of which biochemistry was an example—for the purpose of basking in the reflected glory of physical scientists. In so doing, they were failing to understand that psychology not only could not but *should not* be like the other sciences. It should be designed to study whole people and whole people cannot be fitted into test tubes or under microscopes.

The only colleague who was clearly sympathetic to Murray was Gordon Allport, a social psychologist and personality theorist. In preference to his colleagues' concern with "sensory elements" and "conditioned responses," Allport's ideas should have appealed to Murray. But, when Allport made friendly overtures to Murray, Murray reacted as usual. Allport was initially dismissed with "He thought of consciousness as large . . . and the unconscious as a little bit of a thing" (Anderson, 1988, p. 154). Still, he dedicated a book to Allport, team-taught classes with him, and, at times, referred to him as a friend (Robinson, 1992). Murray emerged from his years at Harvard with the perception of himself as a lone hero fighting for the truth. With the dry wit that characterized him, he commented, "at departmental meetings there were five votes in favor of psychophysics and one vote in favor of" psychoanalytic theory (p. 153). Through all of this, however, Murray showed his tendency to rebound from rejection.

Basic Concepts: Murray

Propositions

Murray offered several basic "propositions" on which his theory was founded (Murray, 1981a). Among the most crucial was that the object of study should be individual organisms, not aggregations of them. This premise is consistent with an even more fundamental principle: holism, studying the whole organism, not pieces of it. He stressed that people are not just inert bodies passively responding to external stimulation. He also believed a human being could not be understood by studying even a rather extended episode in her or his existence. One must study the **long unit** of the organism, its life cycle. "The history of the organism is the organism" (p. 127).

Murray contended that "an organism is within an environment which largely determines its behavior" (p. 127). In fact, much of what is now inside the organism was once outside: a present need for security may have originated in past threats arising in the environment. Because the internal and the external are so intimately connected, it is necessary to view the organism as a product of "creature–environment" interactions that may be considered the "short unit" of psychological inquiry. Thus, the long unit, an individual life, may be thought of as a succession of related short units, or episodes.

The organism usually responds to patterns of meaningful wholes, not discrete "sense impressions." "In turn the reactions of the organism to its environment usually exhibit a **unitary trend,** activity that is organized and directional in nature, not willy-nilly, trial-and-error" (p. 128). An activity itself can be cast as an **actone,** a pattern of bodily movements in and of itself, divorced from its effect. Therefore, a certain condition of the organism, hunger, can be followed by several different actones, picking fruit, or buying a meal, each of which yields the same end effect, food in the stomach. Although Murray acknowledged *temporal consistencies,* he also endorsed behavioral variability is a fact of the organism's life.

A *neurologically-based process* occurring early in the chain of events ends in an effect. "Since, by definition, it is a process which follows a stimulus and precedes an actonal response, it must be located in the brain" (p. 131). **Regnant** is the name given to "dominant configurations in the brain" that correspond to internal representations. An image of a food object is the regnant response to the hunger need aroused by smells from the environment. Murray proposed this concept to acknowledge the fact that everything we call "psychological" ultimately arises out of brain action. However, Murray made it clear that, while "activities of nerve cells and muscle cells are necessary conditions of the whole action . . . they are not in any full sense its cause" (p. 131). Brain action enables the chain of events leading to some effect; it is not the sequence's final cause. "Cause" lies in a complex of interrelated external and internal events that is too intricate and vast to be encompassed by a simple statement. In fact, "cause can go the other way." Personality is not the slave of the brain; it is somewhat the other way round.

Brain processes correspond to what we call "consciousness": humans are able to reflect on themselves as a result of regnant processes. The conscious images we experience arise from regnant processes. There are also unconscious regnant processes: "An unconscious process . . . must be conceptualized as regnant even though the [person] is unable to report its occurrence" (p. 132). Murray legitimized unconsciousness by linking it to brain processes.

Definition of Needs

Like Maslow, Murray's most central concept is **need,** "a [physiochemical] force . . . in the brain . . . , [that] organizes perception, . . . intellection, . . . and action in such a way as to transform . . . an . . . unsatisfying situation [into a more satisfying one]" (Murray, 1981a, p. 189). Murray characterized a need as equivalent to a drive (he often used them interchangeably) that moves the concept in a biological direction. Here Murray differed greatly from Maslow, who took great pains to distinguish between "drives," which he thought to be of secondary importance, and "needs," which he emphasized. Murray also alluded to another equation relevant to the organization of this text. His ideas provide a bridge to the later discussion of "traits" because a need can sometimes be thought of as "a more or less consistent trait of personality" (p. 142). He hastened to add that it can, at times, be considered a "temporary happening" (a state).

Varieties of Needs

Murray (1981a) divides needs into two basic categories. **Psychogenic needs** are secondary to biological needs and are derived from them, but, being one step away from the biological side of the organism, are psychological in nature. These needs, like those of the other category, fall under levels of a higher-order factor represented by *vectors,* forces with directional properties. **Adience** refers to the positive-need-promoting vectors that describe movement toward objects and people. Several examples of adient psychogenic needs are well-known, even to the public. **n Achievement** indicates the drive to "overcome obstacles, to exercise power, to strive to do something difficult as well as [and as] quickly as possible" (Murray, 1981a, p. 157). **n Affiliation** refers to the desire for friendships and associations: "To greet, join, and live with others. To co-operate and converse sociably with others. To love. To join groups" (p. 159). **n Succorance** is the dependent attitude of seeking aid, protection, and sympathy by crying for mercy and help from affectionate, nurturant caretakers. This need has the flavor of unresolved Basic Anxiety, Horney's central notion. **n Order** involves arranging, organizing, and putting away objects; to be tidy, clean, and scrupulously precise. **n Dominance** is the drive to influence, control, persuade, prohibit, dictate, lead, direct, restrain others, and to organize the behavior of a group. **n Exhibition** is desiring to attract attention to one's person by exciting, amusing, stirring, shocking, or thrilling others. **n Aggression** refers to an assaultive or injurious orientation to others, including to belittle, harm, blame, accuse, ridicule, punish severely, react sadistically toward, or even murder. **n Abasement** involves surrendering, complying, accepting punishment, apologizing, confessing, atoning, and generally being masochistic. This need brings to mind Horney's portrayal of people with the masochistic need for submission to a lover (Clare).

   Abience is the name given to the negative-need-promoting vectors that describe movements away from objects and people. There are fewer clear examples of abient psychogenic needs, but some of them will be familiar. **n Autonomy** is the drive to resist influence or coercion, to defy authority, seek freedom, and strive for independence. **n Inviolacy** is an attitude of attempting to prevent depreciation of self-respect, to preserve one's good name, to avoid criticism, and to maintain psychological distance. **n Blamavoidance** refers to avoiding blame, punishment, and ostracism by inhibiting asocial (or even unconventional) impulses and being a well-behaved, law-abiding citizen. **n Infavoidance** is an orientation to avoiding failure, shame, humiliation, or ridicule by concealing disfigurement and refraining from attempts at anything seen as beyond one's powers. **n Contrarience** is the drive to act differently from others, to be unique, to take the opposite side, and to hold unconventional views.

The **viscerogenic needs** involve basic biological drives, and, though they form the foundation for the psychogenic needs, are relatively straightforward. This is the companion to the psychogenic needs category. *Adience* viscerogenic needs—characterized by an approach orientation to objects—include n Inspiration (need to inhale oxygen), n Water, n Food, n Sentience (need to experience sensory gratification, for example, sucking and bodily contact with another person), n Sex, and n Lactation. *Abience* viscerogenic needs, characterized by an avoidant (or expellant) orientation to objects, are n Expiration (need to exhale carbon dioxide), n Urination, n Defecation, n Noxavoidance (need to get rid of noxious stimulation), n Heatavoidance, n Coldavoidance, and n Harmavoidance. See Table 15.1 for several of Murray's most central needs. Box 15.1 provides an exercise relating to the table.

TABLE 15.1 *Summary of Murray's Needs ("Cesa Bach sa 'I Do!' In a flash, I wed u." Each letter begins a need label.)*

Adience Vectors (positive needs)	*Abience Vectors* (negative needs)
PSYCHOGENIC	
n Achievement	n Autonomy
n Affiliation	n Inviolacy
n Succorance	n Blamavoidance
n Order	n Infavoidance
n Dominance	n Contrarience
n Exhibition	
n Aggression	
n Abasement	
VISCEROGENIC	
n Inspiration	n Expiration
n Water	n Urination
n Food	n Defecation
n Sentience	*n Noxavoidance*
n Sex	n Heatavoidance
n Lactation	n Coldavoidance
	n Harmavoidance

BOX 15.1 • *Are You Avoidant/Withdrawn or Approaching/Attached?*

Murray's needs are cast into two broad factors: *avoidant/withdrawn (abience),* avoiding objects and people or withdrawing from them, and *approaching/attached (adience),* approaching objects and people or submissively/controllingly attaching oneself to them. Examine all of the psychogenic needs and viscerogenic needs (in italics) in Table 15.1: there are nine Adience and seven Abience needs. Honestly decide which are prominent among the needs that typically drive you. Check off all of the ones you choose. Where does the balance lie? If 70 percent or more of your choices fit in the Adience category you may score yourself as approaching/attaching. For example, if you checked ten needs, and seven of them were

in the Adience category, you may be regarded as "approaching/attached." On the other hand, if 55 percent or more of your choices fall in the Abience category, you are better characterized as avoidant/withdrawn (for example, if you made eleven choices and six were in the Abience category). If you fail to meet either percentage criterion, you fit in neither the approaching/attached nor the avoidant/withdrawing categories. Of course, this is an exercise. Attach no special meaning to being in either category; neither is necessarily good or bad. However, if you are at one extreme or the other, perhaps you will examine your behavior in the future and decide that a better balance would be better for you.

Strength of Needs and Interactions among Them

Strength.　The **strength** of a need is measured in terms of its frequency, intensity, and duration (Murray, 1981a). A need is strong if it occurs under given conditions with high frequency. It is also strong if it occurs occasionally with great intensity. Finally, a need is strong if, once aroused, it continues to endure for a long time in the absence of satisfaction.

Interrelation of Needs.　During everyday life, an individual may experience the arousal of several needs, either all at once or in succession. Consequently, it is common to observe a person take a particular course of action designed to satisfy several needs. Like Maslow, Murray believed that people are complicated; they rarely do anything for only one reason.

Fusion of needs is Murray's name for a single "action pattern that satisfies two or more needs at the same time" (p. 161). An example would be an individual who gets paid to sing a solo in public (F n AcqExh; F = fusion). The person is satisfying n Acquisition—making money—while also taking care of n Exhibition—getting attention from others.

Subsidiation of needs occurs "When one or more needs are activated in the service of [one or more other needs]" (p. 161). In the following sequence, each need is subsidiary to the succeeding need, with the last-mentioned need (n Achievement) being the most prominent: the one served by all the rest.

A politician removes a spot from his suit (n Noxavoidance) because he does not wish to make a bad impression (n Infavoidance), and thus diminish his chances of winning the approval and friendship of Mr. X (n Affiliation), from whom he hopes to obtain some slanderous facts (n Cognizance) relating to the private life of his political rival, Mr. Y, information which he plans to publish (n Exposition) in order to damage the reputation of

Mr. Y (n Aggression) and thus assure his own election to office (n Achievement): (the need preceding the "S" is subsidiary to the one following it; n Nox S n Inf S n Aff S n Cog S n Exp S n Agg S n Ach) (Murray, 1981a, p. 162).

Contrafactions. **Contrafactions of needs** are cases in which needs are related to their opposites in alternating phases. For example, "A phase of Dominance is succeeded by a phase of Deference. A wave of Aggression is followed by a wave of Nurturance . . . Abstinence follows indulgence . . . etc." (p. 163). A person who is a Napoleon at work is a grovelling serf at home. Similar to contrafactions are Jung's "equivalence" and his belief that dream content contradicts waking orientations.

Conflict. **Conflicts of needs** occur when needs oppose each other "within the personality, giving rise when prolonged to harassing spiritual dilemmas" (p. 163). "A woman hesitates to satisfy her passion because of the disapproval of her family ("C" = "conflict"; n Sex-C-n Blamavoidance) . . . A man hesitates to satisfy his desire to fly an airplane because of fear (n Achievement-C-n Harmavoidance)" (p. 163). These oppositions balance needs so that neither gets out of hand.

Need Integrates (Complexes)

Needs may form the core of structures that, in turn, are central components of the personality. A critical predecessor to the formation of these core structures is **cathexis,** a process by which an object evokes a need. The object may be "cathected" by the need or the person with the need. This Freudian term originally meant the investment of psychic energy in some object, as an infant may cathect its mother. If the object is present, the need is likely to be aroused. "Objects" can be either inanimate entities or people. Common cathexes, with objects listed first and the cathected (c) needs second, are: garbage (c Noxavoidance); lighting (c Harmavoidance); doctor (c Succorance), infant (c Nurturance); hero (c Deference); autocrat (c Autonomy).

A **need integrate or complex** is formed when images "of cathected objects . . . become integrated in the mind with the needs and emotions which they customarily excite" (p. 179). Integrates are much more abstract than needs, and, thus, harder to put into words. They are recurrent phenomena that fill our dreams, hallucinations, illusions, and delusions. A complex may come to consciousness (or unconsciousness) because of an encounter with a real-world object that resembles the image that excites the need integrated with it. For example, a bird floating effortlessly in the air may be cathected by the need to be free (n autonomy). If so, the person with the complex would be expected to dream of birds flying and to see them as illusions when they are not actually present (in wallpaper; in leaves; in sidewalk cracks). Complexes *make us do* something, such as pursue independence from others.

Need integrates or complexes manifest themselves in many forms, not just in dreams. For example, complexes show up in artistic expression, drama, ritual, religion, fantasies, desires and temptations, fiction, fairytales, plays and movies, art objects, and even child (or adult) play. At a more global rather than individual level, cultures can be sources of complexes. One may see complexes manifested in the art objects, stories, and religious practices that are part and parcel of a culture. The "cross" in Christian cultures would be an example. Notice that need integrates appear to be more like the archetypes of Jung than Freud's "complexes." Dreams are analyzed in Box 15.2.

Environmental Press

Murray devoted considerable space to the environment in which the person is embedded. Environmental elements that influence the person are called **press,** which designates a directional tendency in an object or situation (*press* is also plural). The cathexis of an object

---

BOX 15.2 • *Are Dreams Clairvoyant?*

If complexes are at all like archetypes, they may relate to themes repeated over and over in human history. This repetition suggests that "history repeats itself." Should such be the case, manifestations of complexes, as may occur in dreams, might predict future events. Hence, past events of a certain nature that are reflected in complexes and manifested in dreams may foretell future events of the same nature. A case in point may be instances of kidnapping/murders. Because kidnapping/murders have occurred many times in human history, they are a part of human lore. Thus, they may form the basis for complexes shared by people. Given this reasoning, people's dreams may be clairvoyant: able to predict the details of an actual kidnapping/murder. Murray (1981c) capitalized on a much-publicized event in order to ascertain whether dreams can predict future events. A few days after the baby of famous aviator Charles Lindbergh was kidnapped, but before any details of the crime were known to the public, Murray placed an ad in a newspaper to solicit descriptions of dreams relating to the crime. Some 1,300 people responded.

The facts of the case were that the baby had *died* instantly after suffering blows to the head resulting in *three fractures of the skull.* Its *naked body* was found in a *shallow grave* in some *woods* near a *road* several miles from the Lindbergh home. An ex-convict of German extraction was later convicted of the crime (his relatives are still denying his guilt).

Of the 1,300 dreams, many did contain references to "foreigners" or "foreign accents." This outcome was probably due to suspicion of "aliens" that was rampant in the United States then (1932) and now. However, in only about 5 percent of the dreams did the baby appear dead. Further, only ten dreams were at all accurate in predicting the details of the crime when those became known. Seven dreams referred to the baby as deceased, and two others implied as much. Five of the ten dreams made definite references to the wooded locale where the body was found. Five referred to a grave, two of them indicating that it was shallow. Three dreams referred to a road near where the baby was found, and another implied that a road was nearby. One dream indicated explicitly that the baby was naked, another implied nakedness, and, in a third, that the baby was clothed only in a diaper. Of the ten dreamers, three claimed they had their dreams before the kidnapping had even occurred. Two of the three included mention of the Lindberghs, one also referred to "woods," and the one without mention of the Lindberghs did refer to a "roadside" and "diaper only." Only three of the ten dreams included death, a grave, and a wooded locale.

The very fact that the dreams were collected argues that Murray endorsed the *possibility* that dreams are clairvoyant. Therefore, it is a tribute to his objectivity that he drew negative conclusions regarding the ability of dreams to predict the future. He correctly interpreted results as due to happenstance: by chance one would expect ten (or more) of 1,300 dreams to contain some accurate information relating to the facts of the crime as revealed later.

involved with complexes *makes the individual do something or other.* In contrast, the "press of an object is what it can *do to the subject* [person] or *for the subject*—the power that it has to affect the well-being of the subject in one way or another" (Murray, 1981a, p. 187). "Everything that can supposedly harm or benefit the well-being of an organism may be considered *pressive,* everything else is inert" (p. 185). A dominant person in an individual's life is a press that restricts and restrains the individual.

A press may be a sign of things to come. Individuals often actually perceive the pressive object. But they infrequently think of the object in the present tense, as expressed in "the object is now doing this or that to me." Instead, the individual anticipates: "The object may do this or that to me (if I remain passive) or I may use the object in this or that way (if I become active)" (p. 185). However, Murray is quick to point out that press are not entirely anticipatory. Very often, aspects of the present situation excite images of past pressive situations. These images allow the individual to operate smoothly and effectively relative to present press because the person has past experience to act as a guide. Table 15.2 contains examples of press.

Thema

Needs and press are internal and external entities, respectively. In view of Murray's holistic position and his inclination to see all factors relating to the individual as integrated, one would expect that he would see a way to merge needs and press. Indeed he did. A **thema** is a combination of a particular need and a particular press or pressive object. In the case of thema, some object is present that holds promise to do something to the person or for the person, thereby generating a need consistent with it. Examples include: a friendly sociable companion is present, resulting in the activation of n Affiliation (p Affiliation > n Affiliation); a combative, belittling person is present evoking n Aggression (p Aggression > n Aggression); a restraining, prohibiting person is present giving rise to n Dominance (p Dominance > n Dominance). Often a press leads to the activation of a need that reciprocates it, opposes it, or compensates for it: a rejecting person may inspire the rise of n Rejection resulting in reciprocity of rejection; a dominating person may initiate n Autonomy; a belittling person may initiate n Achievement.

TABLE 15.2   *Press*

---

p Affiliation object is a friendly, sociable companion

p Nurturance object is a protective, sympathetic ally

p Aggression object is a combative person, one who censures, or one who belittles

p Rival (recognition of) object is a competitor

p Lack (economic) object is the condition of poverty

p Dominance object is a restraining, prohibiting, or imprisoning person

---

TAT collage

Evaluation

Contributions

Needs.   One of Murray's two lasting contributions to the field of personality is definitely his conceptualization of needs. A description of how Murray's needs are used by numerous researchers would fill an entire, separate book. Here coverage is limited to a critical, practical application of Murray's needs: personality tests.

Douglas N. Jackson's Personality Research Form (PRF) is a personality-trait measure based on 20 of Murray's needs translated rather directly into 20 trait scales (Jackson, 1984). After three revisions of the PRF manual, Jackson's measure ranks "as the fourth most frequently cited personality test in the psychological research literature" (Paunonen, Jackson, & Keinonen, 1990). These same researchers devised a nonverbal stick-figure version of their test that should be useful for eliminating language as a factor in comparing personality test responses across cultures.

Work by Jefferson Singer (1990) reconceived 16 of Murray's needs as "life goals." For example, one goal statement was, "I would like to be a leader and sway others to my opinion" (based on n Dominance; p. 541). Another was, "I would like to have as sensual and erotic a life as possible" (based on n Sentience and n Sex combined; p. 541).

The Thematic Apperception Test.   Murray's most timeless contribution was development of a much-used projective test, the **Thematic Apperception Test (TAT),** an instrument for assessing a person's self-reflective perceptions (apperceptions) revealing thema
that are evoked by some ambiguous pictures (Murray, 1981d). With use of the TAT, research subjects or clinical clients are told that they are participating in a "test of creative
imagination" (p. 391). Then, one at a time, they are shown each of 20 (or more) pictures
mounted on cards, such as a boy with a violin, a woman holding a man, and a girl with a
doll. Subjects or clients are asked to "make up a plot or story" about each picture (p. 391).
To assist them, they are asked some questions: "What is the relation of the individuals in
the picture? What has happened to them? What are their present thoughts and feelings?
What will be the outcome?" (p. 391). The TAT was, and is still, used to reveal Murray's
needs and for other purposes (e.g., to reveal personality orientations and traits that go well
beyond Murray's needs).

An advantage of the TAT is that the subject/client can interpret the pictures in innu-
merable ways because they are inherently ambiguous. Thus, whatever the subject/client
says about the pictures comes from his or her own unique unconscious mind. Advantages
include subject/client responses that are spontaneous and relatively uncontaminated by any
cues provided by researcher or clinician. Such responses are rich with information, can be
mined to great depths, and may provide a glimpse of the unconscious that cannot be
achieved otherwise.

The narratives provided by subjects/clients have been scored in various ways. In early
uses, these stories were analyzed informally and subjectively by the test administrator (Murray, 1981d). Analysis of a card usually involved the card as a whole, rather than each individual human figure on the card. Beginning around 1949, researchers obtained data that
allowed more concrete, less subjective means of analyzing narratives inspired by pictures.
The most frequent responses were catalogued so that future users of the TAT could check
to determine whether a client or subject was providing a typical or atypical response to a
given card. Cards were rated using various scaling methods to determine the degree to which
they suggested achievement, aggression, sex, and so forth (see Hibbard, 2003).

While these efforts helped to objectify TAT analysis, scoring was still somewhat hap-
hazard and unsystematic. To begin improvement, Charles R. Potkay listed some problems:
(1) total cards are typically considered despite the fact that a given card may contain two
figures that contribute to stories in different, even opposite, ways; (2) when objective methods are used to aid analysis, scales are employed that may limit subjects' or clients' responses or suggest to them how they should respond; and (3) when more objective methods
are used, they usually involve only a few concepts (for example, achievement and aggression) rather than the many concepts subjects/clients may have had in mind while making
responses (Allen & Potkay, 1983a).

To remedy these shortcomings and expand the applicability of the TAT, Potkay and
his colleagues had subjects generate any words that came to their minds when they looked
at single figures on each card rather than the whole card (see Potkay, Merrens, & Allen,
1979, in Allen & Potkay, 1983a). This method is the Adjective Generation Technique or
AGT. The instruction is simply "write down [some number of] adjectives" (Allen &
Potkay, 1983a; Potkay & Allen, 1988). With use of the AGT, (1) single figures are consid-

ered, (2) problems with scaling techniques are avoided, and (3) subjects can use any concepts contained in their vast repertoires of words.

Sixty male and sixty female subjects viewed seventeen male and seventeen female figures featured on twenty-two cards and then described each with three adjectives. Table 15.3 contains a sampling of the figures investigated, and, for each, the three words used most frequently. The entries in Table 15.3 will give you a good idea of the kinds of pictures contained in the TAT and their nature as defined by the most frequently used descriptive words. Because gender of subjects made no difference, percentages are for all 120 subjects.

Considering that subjects could choose any words from the many hundreds available to each of them, the fact that many chose exactly the same word to describe a given figure reflects remarkable agreement. See especially the high frequencies of word use in figures 1, 3, 5, 7, 10, 14, 15, and 16 in Table 15.3. There were certain themes running through the figures. They tended to be old and sad, but, if they were male, they were angry and lonely, and, if females, loving. The adjectives that subjects generated were also scored on FAVorability, ANXiety, and FEMininity. "Man embracing woman" came out on top in terms of

TABLE 15.3 *Descriptions of Figures and the Words Most Frequently Used to Describe Them (% of subjects using word in brackets)*

TAT Figure	Three Most Used Adjectives
1. Boy with violin	bored [42], tired [32], sleepy [25]
2. Woman with books	pretty [18], young [18], intelligent [11]
3. Man working in fields	strong [43], hardworking [30], muscular [28]
4. Woman downcast	sad [25], upset [17], depressed [14]
5. Man holding woman	angry [34], mad [12], determined [10]
6. Woman holding man	loving [26], pleading [14], concerned [8]
7. Woman with back turned	old [31], sad [16], hurt [11]
8. Man looking down	worried [20], young [16], sad [11]
9. Man with pipe	angry [12], mean [8], domineering [8]
10. Man with gray hair	old [38], wise [22], understanding [13]
11. Girl with doll	young [28], bored [25], uninterested [9]
12. Woman daydreaming	thoughtful [19], thinking [10], wondering [10]
13. Woman on beach	scared [18], hurried [17], frightened [12]
14. Man embracing woman	loving [45], happy [14], old [10]
15. Boy sitting	lonely [45], young [21], poor [18]
16. Woman nude	dead [37], tired [13], exhausted [12]
17. Man silhouetted	lonely [15], searching [14], alone [13]
18. Man at lamp post	lonely [25], alone [18], old [10]

FAV. The figure reflecting the highest ANX was "woman on beach." "Woman holding man" was most FEM.

It is interesting to note that female figures were higher on FAV than males. Also, the emotional tone emerging from the figures is intriguing: they are melancholy, sad and depressed, reflective, and lonely, just as was Murray. Box 15.3 describes an actual clinical use of the TAT cards.

The TAT Today.   The TAT continues to be one of the most used projective tests. Several studies illustrate its many applications and its flexibility. In comparison to the TAT responses of nondemented psychiatric patients, Alzheimer's patients used fewer words to describe pictures and tended to drift away from adherence to instructions (Johnson, 1994). Compared to a nonsexually abused group, sexually abused children and teen females showed more primitive and simple characterizations of people, inability to invest in people except for need gratification, and a tendency toward extreme and immature functioning (Ornduff, Freedenfeld, Kelsey, & Critelli, 1994). In another sexual abuse study, compared to a group with no abuse history, abused girls showed sexual preoccupation and, secondarily, guilt (Pistole & Ornduff, 1994). Other findings include the identification in TAT picture-descriptions of causal explanations for "bad events" (Peterson & Ulrey, 1994), evidence for the validity of the TAT (Alvardo, 1994; Rosenberg, Blatt, Oxman, McHugo, & Ford, 1994), and a demonstration of the TAT Problem-Solving Assessment protocol's ability to show that training in problem solving works (Ronan, Date, & Weisbrod, 1995).

BOX 15.3 • *Clinical Analysis Using the TAT*

Murray (1981d) and Christiana Morgan interpreted TAT narratives produced by a Harvard undergraduate called "B." B was a deferential and submissive music major who constantly squinted his eyes, as if in response to a photographer's flashbulb. It gave him the appearance of puzzled anxiety. Overall, he was an "unobtrusive, banal" individual (p. 402). B came to the clinic because unsettling images were intruding on his reading, preventing him from retaining the meaning of what he read, but not the impressions of the printed page. Thus, he lost the sense of what he was reading, but unfailingly recalled the printed pages, allowing him to get high marks on exams.

These images seemed, at first glance, to be as bland as the individual they tormented. He saw scenes from both his distant past—pastures and brooks, buildings, and woods—and from his recent past—Harvard Square and the Boston State

House. Nothing from B's autobiography or intake interview suggested an explanation of his symptoms. He had been brought up in a proper, Southern, Methodist family by parents he regarded with equal favor. However, he was more like his morally "right" father in general disposition if not in emotional intensity: the father's temper was explosive. His mother nagged him often, but showed him lavish affection. He frequently quarreled with his younger sister. As a child he was timid and was fearful of water, animals, and automobile accidents. Periodically he dreamed of being chased by a bull.

B's self-description revealed sensitivity, reticence, avoidance of athletics, and feelings of inferiority. The disclosure of frequent doll-play sessions with his sister, unusual neatness, and extreme sensitivity to smells seemed an unconscious effort to portray an effeminate nature. Thoughts of death often plagued him, particularly after seeing a man killed in a fall from a hayrick. These fears were reinforced when he was comforted at his grandmother's funeral when he broke into tears. Sex was alien to him: he did not masturbate until age 18, had still not experienced intercourse, and was appalled on contemplating that his parents had done what farm animals do to produce offspring. According to Murray, "He held a theory of anal intercourse [and] several experiences of fellatio occurr[ed] at about the age of 10, but" none occurred since (p. 403). As a child he slept with his father while his mother slept with his sister, all on the same porch.

In response to the card, "The nude figure of a man clinging to a pole," B called the figure a "sailor" who scaled his ship's mast in an escape attempt made after having been chased from his cabin because of "some morbid . . . homosexual crime" (p. 403). He is shot down by a fellow sailor. Four months later, after psychoanalysis, he altered the story by indicating that the sailor climbed the mast in an insane effort to escape the horror of his unsuccessful attempt at homosexual relations. His face "distorted and carnal," he hurled himself into the sea (p. 403). The card "man clinging to a rope" inspired fears of being trapped on a high perch. Murray noted the "obvious" homosexual themes of the first two stories, and manifestations of B's admitted fear of heights in all three.

In response to the "boy with violin," B told a tale of musical triumph at a recital, but spoiled the achievement by declaring that the boy subsequently lost "hands or fingers" and had to abandon music (p Injury > n Achievement [failure]). After psychoanalysis, B gave a more neutral description of "boy with violin." B said the "boy huddled against a couch" had flown into a rage and shot a horse or dog, thus his current state of remorse. He related that, as a child, he had directly participated in beatings of animals and vicariously participated in a decapitation. After psychoanalysis, the emphasis in his story was less on brutality and more on the figure being remorseful and having learned a lesson. Murray saw themes of self-punishment, castration anxiety, sadism, and bestiality in B's narrative.

B said that the "girl standing alone" is "about to be attacked by a demented person. She has gone on a picnic with him. A coming storm increases the carnal instincts of the boy. He attacks the girl" (p. 404). To "malicious-looking man grasping the arm of a young girl [who recoils in terror]," B offered, "When the time comes he takes her to attack her." (p. 404). These stories of girls being attacked hinted at a sadistic heterosexual orientation. Based on the last story, as well as a memory of a movie in which a scientist fills a woman's veins with ossifying material and of a movie hero's wife dying in childbirth, Murray saw B as prone to fantasies of women being killed during intercourse or childbirth.

B was also given some of the Rorschach inkblots. In one, he saw a man looking at a medical book in which there is an illustration of a dissected male or female. In another, a man is seen engaging in a sexual act in which the object addressed sexually is an embryo or a part of a miscarriage. Murray inferred necrophilia.

Murray concluded that B felt guilt over, and fear of, homosexuality. He also showed evidence of anal sadism, masochism, and a castration complex. His castration anxiety may have stemmed from having had his first nocturnal emission while sleeping in contact with his enormous, temperamental father, possibly the bull of his dreams. He also showed womb fantasies, sadistic trends, and necrophilia. B fantasied about pregnancy and tried to picture himself in his mother's womb. Once he dreamed of opening a woman up and filling her womb with straw. Another time he fantasied that he was pregnant. To build in masochism, just after the pregnancy fantasy, he became constipated and lay doubled up on the floor groaning with abdominal pain. The necrophilic and anal themes were manifested in his "most exciting fantasy" during which he opened one grave after another performing anal intercourse with each corpse in turn (p. 407). It seemed to Murray that birth, death, and sexual intercourse were closely linked in B's mind.

Hibbard and colleagues (2000) found that Whites and Asians scored relatively similarly in terms of proneness to use of defense mechanisms, as revealed by TAT responses. Also, the defense mechanism scoring procedure was, in general, valid for the two groups. From a diversity perspective, it is interesting that Whites scored higher on "denial," though the groups did not differ on other mechanisms. Ackerman and colleagues (1999) investigated the validity of a method (SCORS) for scoring the nature and quality of personal relationships, as reflected in responses to TAT pictures. As predicted, of four categories of personality disordered subjects, borderline personality disordered subjects (see the Horney chapter) had the lowest scores on "affect tone": they showed a more negative emotional tone than the others. They also scored lower on identity, which is consistent with their diffuse and vague sense of identity. Lilienfeld, Wood, and Garb (2000) critiqued projective techniques and reported that the TAT faired relatively well compared to other projective tests, including the Rorschach. In rebuttal, Hibbard (2003) found numerous errors of commission and omission in the Lilienfeld and colleagues' analysis. The TAT, which fared better than the Rorschach in Lilienfeld and colleagues' critique, remains viable after Hibbard's defense of it.

Porcerelli, Abramsky, Hibbard, and Kamoo (2001) used the defense mechanism and SCORS scales to score the TAT responses of a serial rapist-murderer. His scores were deemed pathological on several dimensions. For example, his "affect tone" was malevolent, dysphoric, and sadistic, and he projected hostile feelings and intentions onto TAT figures.

Wesley Morgan (1995; not related to Christiana Morgan) traced the history of each TAT picture's development. Among several interesting disclosures were indications that Christiana Morgan was a major figure in early TAT research and the senior author of early TAT articles, but was absent from later publications. Health problems, alcoholism, and her desire to withdraw from the responsibilities of academic life apparently account for her absence (personal communication from Wesley Morgan, June 7, 2001). TAT pictures were adapted almost exclusively from contemporary paintings and magazine art (see Morgan, 1999, 2000, 2002, and 2003 for descriptions and histories of the TAT pictures). Christiana, whose ability to produce original art of good quality was limited, was good at redrawing others' works and did early redrawings that eventually became TAT pictures. Apparently, she originated only a couple of TAT pictures, one of which was redrawn by Samuel Thal, a professional artist who took over the redrawing tasks from Christiana. Thal contributed no original drawings to the TAT pictures (personal communication from Wesley Morgan, June 7, 2001). Eleanor Clement Jones, a short story writer, also contributed from 1930–1933 by searching illustrated magazines for possible TAT pictures (Morgan, 2002).

Limitations

Deficits of Murray's theory and methods fall into three categories: (1) he failed to differentiate his concepts from other similar notions; (2) he tried to explain everything; and (3) his methods, especially those associated with the TAT, were loose and intuitive rather than scientific.

At some points in his writings, Murray seems almost confused about the nature of his ideas. Are needs actually drives? Are they really traits of personality? If Murray could

BOX 15.4 • *Diversity: Murray and the Social Class Wars*

Social class is a neglected source of diversity and classism is an often ignored variety of oppression. Murray's authoritarianism may have, in part, come from assuming the upper-class license to lead, an elitist norm of his era (Robinson, 1992). Many of the young, middle-class Ph.D.s who worked with him complained about his arrogance and aloofness. Some felt almost like sharecroppers on his plantation. During the 1960s, Murray took a dim view of the war in Vietnam, but he rejected hippie/protesters' defiance of authority (Robinson, 1992). While he shared their reverence for sexual freedom, especially for women, he disdained their other unconventional behaviors. His social class gave him a "sense of propriety" and an understanding that illicit sex as well as illegal substance use was a private matter, not for public display.

While Murray's sense of privilege was overt, most of us are too subtle about our class as-

sumptions to be conscious of them. Many of us lack the sense of concern for working people that characterized our grandparents during the post-Depression period. As a result, poor, working-class Americans suffer in silence, their identity obscure. While people of color are disproportionately represented among the U.S. poor, many people do not realize that the majority of the poor are White (Blauner, 1992). Among them is a group who can call no government program their own: young White males who are poor. If their numbers begin to swell and their discontent expands proportionately, we will all pay for their dismal condition. They are a major target of Klan, neo-Nazi, and militia recruitment campaigns. These examples remind us of two diversity "principles": (1) diversity includes everyone, and (2) no group has exclusive claim to being oppressed.

not decide, he was not alone. Indecision may have also characterized researchers who used his needs. As indicated earlier, Jackson (1984) thinks of needs as "traits," and Singer (1990) conceives of them as "goals." Concepts are scientifically useful only insofar as they are clearly distinct from other concepts (Allen & Potkay, 1981, 1983b). Consistent with this lack of clear differentiation among concepts, some of his ideas do not fit well into appropriate categories. For example, n Play, to amuse oneself and seek diversion, was not in Table 15.1 (p. 364). It does not fit under Adience or Abience.

Murray felt obligated to explain everything and reconcile his point of view with everyone else's position (1981a). He mentioned many of the popular concepts of his day, either rejecting them and asserting that his ideas were better or squaring them with his own. Thus, he attempted to reconcile some of his ideas with those of Skinner, but he rejected Watson's position out of hand. Theories that try to explain everything explain nothing very precisely.

So thorough was his rejection of experimental psychologists and "scientism" that one wonders whether the former biochemist abandoned science altogether. The TAT is a good case in point. Murray guided his colleagues in more or less arbitrarily selecting TAT pictures. What he finally decided on were hardly the ambiguous figures appropriate to a projective test. Potkay and colleagues have shown them to be gender-biased, females favored over males, and invested with definite meaning that is shared by subjects (see Allen & Potkay, 1983a; Potkay & Allen, 1988). Further, for many years, scoring of the TAT was unsystematic to the point that the quantitative methods so dear to science could not be used. Murray himself (1981d) tended to ramble in analyzing TAT narratives, revealing no particular system and often drawing unclear conclusions. Sources of the TAT are considered in Box 15.5.

While Lilienfeld and colleagues (2000) were kinder to the TAT than to the Rorschach, they found fault with the TAT. To begin with, most TAT users rely on their clinical intuition to "score" TAT responses. Only 3 percent use any scientifically derived scoring method. Some TAT researchers argue that there is reason to expect that TAT scores would be *uncorrelated* with self-report measures, such as personality tests. Others argue the opposite. There are results supporting both of these contradictory positions. TAT research has produced results that contradict the validity of TAT scoring methods. For example, one study found that depressed people had more positive "affect tone" scores than normal people, though the difference was not statistically significant. Lilienfeld and colleagues did acknowledge some results supporting the SCORS method (see the discussion of Ackerman et al., 1999, covered in an earlier section). However, they found some serious contradictions in the same data. For example, the antisocial personality disordered group—a type known for their immorality—did not differ from the other personality disordered groups in terms of TAT moral standards scores. I would add that scores derived

BOX 15.5 • *What (or Who) Suggested the TAT to Murray?*

Was the TAT solely Murray's original idea or did some preexisting test, or some other person, suggest his famous projective test to him? Anderson (1990) notes that an early 1930s student of Murray's, Cecilia Roberts, described to him how she showed a picture to her son and had him tell a story about it. According to Gieser and Morgan (1999), Murray may have gotten the idea for the TAT from Thomas Wolfe's novel, *Look Homeward Angel,* which he used in several lectures to his 1930 personality class. In this book, the main character, Eugene Grant, "is asked along with other children to write about a picture they had been shown" (p. 57). A third possibility is that Christiana Morgan and Murray knew about psychiatrist Louis Schwartz's use of stories about pictures during the early 1930s.

So, which is it? Wesley Morgan " . . . happens to like the *Look Homeward Angel* . . . " explanation, but he has "no particular reason to doubt Murray's report that the idea came from Cecilia Roberts" (personal communication from Morgan, June 8, 2001). Morgan (2002) later indicated that Roberts's daughter claimed Cecilia and her second husband Crane Brinton cynically remarked that Murray did not publicly credit her mother until Cecilia returned to the Harvard community by marrying Professor Brinton. Morgan does not believe that Christiana Morgan and Murray knew of Schwartz's work until well after Roberts told Murray of her demonstration using her son. Neglected in these speculations are Christiana Morgan's contributions to the TAT that go beyond her original paintings and drawings of others' pictures of people. From the summer of 1926 until the spring of 1928, Christiana used Jung's active imagination to produce more than 100 visions, many of which she rendered as paintings (Morgan, 2002). These paintings were the basis of Jung's vision seminars (Heuer, 2001). As Murray would have known about these paintings and their influence on Jung, they may have been part of the series of inspirations leading to the TAT.

by the TAT SCORS method were, at best, moderately able to predict the American Psychiatric Association's (APA) criteria for personality-disorder diagnoses (the APA's *Diagnostic and Statistical Manual, DSM IV,* was used). That is, the criteria that psychologists and psychiatrists use to diagnose personality disorders were not strongly related to SCORS. It was equally unimpressive in predicting personality-disorder scale-scores of the highly respected Minnesota Multi-Phasic Personality Inventory-2 (MMPI-2). Finally, the previously mentioned report of a study comparing Whites and Asians on TAT scores (Hibbard et al., 2000) was not all good news for the TAT. Paradoxically, the defense-mechanism scores, derived with the use of a method developed in research involving mostly White subjects, was more valid for Asians. Further, " . . . the overall validity co-efficients were low" (p. 363). Murray's name was omitted from the four lists of outstanding twentieth century psychologists (Haggbloom et al., 2002).

Conclusions

Despite his much celebrated narcissism—and it probably was real—Murray could be a warm and kind person who inspired the love and admiration of countless psychologists. As a measure of his impact, tributes to him began *before* he died. It is obvious from reading them that he touched the professional and personal lives of many colleagues. True, many of his ideas may not have been well differentiated from other concepts. However, the measure of a theorist's contribution is often more in how much he or she inspires others to new professional heights than whether the theorist's ideas, as originally proposed, were without flaws. While Murray's name is not often mentioned in the current psychological literature, his needs and the TAT received hundreds of mentions. As for the TAT, no one can deny its historical significance: it is one of the most cited and used tests ever. Rather than a fault, some would consider it a virtue that TAT output might be understood mainly by intuition. Clinical intuition may be a better tool for helping real people than scientific methodology.

Summary Points

1. Henry A. Murray was the child of wealthy parents. He fought stammering and a "marrow of misery and melancholy" most of his life. His private and professional lives were heavily influenced by his colleague and mistress, Christiana Morgan. Examination of their relationship reveals his great complexity. As an adult he developed a sense of "specialness" and a distinct narcissistic orientation. These inclinations led him to distrust male colleagues and dismiss others' points of view.

2. After graduating with an M.D. and a Ph.D. in biochemistry, and spending several weeks with Jung, he worked in the Harvard Psychological Clinic and immediately ran afoul of his "scientistic" colleagues. Drawn to psychology because of his personal problems, he pursued his own brand of "psychoanalysis." He underwent psychotherapy, but got little from it except support for his belief in the unconscious.

3. Murray believed that internal representations are regnant, related to "dominant configuration in the brain." To him, a need is a force in the brain that transforms an unsatisfying situation into a more satisfying one. *Need* was nearly synonymous with *drive* and also overlapped with *trait*. Needs are segmented into positive (the adience vector) psychogenic—for example, n Achievement—and negative (the abience vector) psychogenic—for example, n Autonomy.

4. Needs can be specified in terms of strength. In *fusion* of needs there is an "action pattern that satisfies two or more needs at the same time." Subsidiation of needs occurs "when one or more needs are activated in the service of another need," and contrafactions of needs are cases for which needs alternate with their opposites. But in conflicts of needs, needs oppose each other.

5. A need integrate or complex is formed when images of cathected objects become mentally integrated with the needs and emotions that they typically excite. Complexes are recurrent phenomena that fill our dreams, hallucinations, illusions, and delusions and are also found in artistic expressions. Murray found no evidence for clairvoyance of dreams.

6. Press "do to" or "for" people and often are referred to in the future tense. A thema is a combination of a particular need and a particular press or pressive object. Jackson's much-used Personality Research Form (PRF) is a trait measure based on Murray's needs. Murray's needs have also been profitably translated into "life goals." The Thematic Appreciation Test (TAT) consists of one or more human figures mounted on cards. Murray's student Cecilia Roberts received belated credit for suggesting the TAT.

7. Potkay and colleagues used the AGT and showed that TAT figures had definite, shared meaning: females were more favorably depicted, and the tone of the figures was melancholy. Recent research showed that the TAT was valid for both Asians and Whites and that the SCORS scales make some accurate predictions about personality disorders. A history of its cards reveals Christiana Morgan's role in card development and the origin of card-pictures. Her active imaginative visions influenced Jung and possibly Murray.

8. Using the TAT, Murray and Morgan analyzed B, a student ruled by his large, temperamental father. As a child B was plagued by thoughts of death, portrayed himself as effeminate and fearful, and reported what were regarded as homosexual experiences. Themes in B's narratives evoked by TAT cards included homosexuality, anality, heterosexual sadism, masochism, and necrophilia. Murray's evident classism was a source of pain for his colleagues.

9. Limitations of Murray's point of view included his failure to differentiate his concepts from similar notions. Faults with the TAT scoring methods include contradictory outcome expectations and research results, as well as moderate predictive validity of the SCORS method. While serious shortcomings of the TAT were uncovered by Lilienfeld and colleagues (2000), Hibbard's (2003) defense of the TAT renders it viable.

10. Despite these shortcomings, Murray, the subject of several tributes even before his death, inspired many psychologists to develop his concepts in meaningful ways. His needs and the TAT continue to be heavily cited, even if he is rarely given credit, and stand as monuments to his genius.

Running Comparison

Theorist	Murray in Comparison
Freud	He defended Freud, psychoanalysis, and the unconscious.
Skinner	He also emphasized the "push from the rear" and the importance of the effect of an action.
Horney	n Succorance resembles her basic anxiety and n Abasement resembles her masochistic submission.
Sullivan	They both were interpersonally oriented.
Maslow	He also believed humans are dynamic wholes who rarely respond to one need at a time.
Jung	Need integrates were like Jung's Archetypes. He borrowed Jung's polarities and "contrafactions of needs" (equivalence).
Gordon Allport	He also studied individuals, not groups, and ignored the sensory side and conditioned responses in favor of personality traits.

Essay/Critical Thinking Questions

1. What would Murray have been like without Christiana Morgan?

2. Can you argue that one can solve personal problems by becoming a psychologist?

3. Give examples of thema that often are seen in your social interactions.

4. What are some other TAT deficits besides those discussed by critics?

5. Had Murray been middle class, would he have been a different person and theorist?

E-mail Interaction

Write the author at b-allen@wiu.edu. Forward one of the following or phrase your own.

1. Murray seems to occupy the extremes of many dimensions. Tell me what he was really like.

2. What was the most important need in Murray's long list?

3. For what will Murray be remembered?

16

The Trait Approach to Personality: Raymond Cattell and Hans Eysenck

- How many kinds of intelligence are there? Is intelligence the same the world over?
- Do your genes determine your personality and your intelligence?
- Can personality be reduced to just three dimensions?

As you have seen, Murray's needs were used as if they were traits. He was, however, not nearly as dedicated a trait theorist as the two covered in this chapter. Raymond Cattell and Hans Eysenck conceived of personality rather exclusively in terms of traits or trait-like entities. Cattell was an empiricist. He believed in isolating and reducing the raw material of personality to a manageable data pool, collecting massive amounts of data from the pool, and using intricate statistical methods to tease facts about personality from the data. Thus, he proceeded in a manner opposite to that of all the theorists considered so far, except for Skinner. Eysenck shared many interests with Cattell. They both used the statistical technique, factor analysis, to discover a few central traits. Nevertheless, only Eysenck embraced experimental psychology. He believed that researchers should take the principles developed in the psychology laboratory and relate them to personality by using experimental procedures. Because of their differences, it is not surprising that the two personality psychologists arrived at different sets of traits to characterize personality.

Cattell, the Person

Raymond B. Cattell was born (1905) near Birmingham, England, the son of Mary Field and Alfred Ernest Cattell (Horn, 2001). "Design engineer" was the grand title Cattell gave

Raymond B. Cattell
www.fmarion.edu/~personality/
corr/cattell/cattell.htm

to his father's position in his grandfather's manufacturing business (Cattell, 1974a). Raymond's father was congenial and inclined to deliver dinnertime lectures on history and current topics. The son has little more to say about the father, except to show veiled disappointment at the discovery, following the administration of IQ tests, that the "design engineer" was the intellectual inferior of his mother. She is also only briefly mentioned, but he implies a warm relationship with her and hints that the high intelligence he attributes to himself came mostly from her. This judgment, made soon after he became a psychologist, is interesting because it shows an early belief that intelligence is mostly inherited.

Cattell describes his childhood as basically happy, but he is quick to add that it was "not easy" (Cattell, 1974b, p. 88). He described his parents and teachers as "exacting." One gets the feeling that the symptoms of stress Cattell showed later in his life were born of the strong drive to achieve instilled in him by the circumstances of his family's middle-class standing and the pressure exerted on him by his parents (Cattell, 1974a). British middle-class is closer to U.S. professional class than to U.S. middle class. Still, the claim to happiness appears to be genuine.

Three years before World War I started, the Cattells moved to the magnificent coast of Devonshire. There, he and his brothers and friends "sailed, swam, fought group battles, explored caves, landed on rocky islands . . . " and generally enjoyed an idyllic childhood (p. 62). In 1937, he wrote a book about the area (Horn, 2001). Even the war, when it arrived, became something of a plaything. Cattell was appointed a "sea scout" and charged with watching the coast for enemy ships. Like Fromm, Adler, and Jung, he was impressed with the destructiveness of modern warfare. "I enjoyed [the scouting] though [I was] awestricken to see the holes as big as a house that torpedos and mines could blow in steel plates. And then came the long trainloads of wounded from the Flanders . . . still in their bloodstained bandages" (p. 63). Young Cattell helped care for these stricken soldiers.

Schooling at the "selective secondary school" where Cattell was on scholarship continued despite the sacrifice of the best teachers to the war effort (Cattell, 1974a, p. 63; Horn, 2001). However, the school's headmaster kept his position throughout the war. This "very intelligent and hard-driving man, a cousin of [Rudyard] Kipling [author of the *Jungle Book*]" provided Cattell with a first scholastic role model (p. 63). The intellect and motivation of the man were not all that impressed Cattell: "He divided his time between giving me personal sessions in science and mathematics, and thrashing me for various original deviations from school regulations" (p. 63).

"At fifteen, I passed the Cambridge University entrance examination (. . . in which I was granted first-class honors), but since my scientific interest indicated London University, and my parents were loath to leave me on my own in London at that age, I did not go until sixteen" (p. 64). This proclamation is interesting in that Cambridge, much more than London University, is world famous and especially known for its excellence in science. It seems that every institute with which Cattell was associated was a haven for intellectual giants. Perhaps it was his way of saying that he was quite brilliant. In his writings he sometimes drew analogies between his own work and that of famous scientists.

While he may be a bit of a braggart with regard to his intellectual powers, his beliefs about himself are hardly delusions. After distinguishing himself in secondary school, Cattell graduated *magna cum laude* in chemistry at the ripe old age of nineteen, but almost immediately he decided to apply his intellectual acumen to the pursuit of psychology. Just before he received his degree, he was mesmerized by IQ researcher Sir Cyril Burt's speech on the mental testing work of Sir Francis Galton. Immediately he was fascinated with psychological assessment. Despite protests from friends that he would go unemployed—there were only a handful of psychology chairs in all of England—he, like Murray and Rotter, deserted his test tubes in favor of working with some of the most notable figures in the world of psychological measurement, including Burt and famed statistician, R. A. Fisher (Horn, 2001). In 1929 he received his Ph.D. in psychology and entered the field.

Early "fringe jobs in psychology" included Director of the Leicester Child Guidance Center and psychological advisor at an experimental school (Cattell, 1974b, p. 90; Horn, 2001). During this period, there was time for research planning, but little research (Cattell, 1974a). Having time to contemplate, he became convinced that intelligence is mostly inherited. In 1936 he wrote an article for the *Eugenics Review* in which he answered "yes" to the question "Is our national intelligence declining?" (Loehlin, 1984). The argument began with the assumption that the higher the social class the higher the intelligence. It proceeded with the observations that lower social classes were having more children. The conclusion was that more children among the less intelligent lower classes was driving the average national intelligence down. Out of these efforts came Cattell's book *The Fight for Our National Intelligence* (1937), which contained the bold prediction that England's intelligence was in for a fall.

But, alas, it did not happen. Fifteen years later, there was actually a slight increase in national intelligence (Loehlin, 1984). IQ continues to rise in England and elsewhere in the world (Dickens & Flynn, 2001; Flynn, 1999, 2000). This disappointment did not deter Cattell from continuing his membership in the controversial Eugenics Society (Cattell, 1974a). **Eugenics** is the application of genetics to the improvement of human biological and psychological characteristics. It, of course, has animal applications. In its most benevolent form, it was dedicated to exhort people to choose spouses and carefully monitor the number of children with an eye to promoting positive traits and discouraging negative traits. In its more malevolent form, it advocates "species improvement by controlled breeding" (McGuire & Hirsch, 1977, p. 61), even to the point of calling for government programs to control human breeding.

This period between graduation with the Ph.D. and his first secure job in a real academic setting was a time of frustration and stress. Probably owing to long hours and laborious administrative duties, Cattell developed a "functional stomach disorder" from which "I have ever since suffered" (Cattell, 1974a, p. 68). The hard work, the stress, the stomach problem, and the low pay also took a toll on his marriage. Finally, his wife, who was accustomed to better, could stand the meager annual salary and the "dark damp basement flat" no more (p. 68). She left, and he yearned for a fresh start. Frustrated with his job and his life, he looked for positions in the United States.

At about this time, Edward L. Thorndike, who was the salvation of Maslow, came to Cattell's rescue (Cattell, 1974a). The author of the "law of effect" (principle of reinforcement) had read *The Fight for Our National Intelligence* (1937) and was so impressed that he offered Cattell a position at Columbia University Teachers College in New York City. From there he moved to the G. Stanley Hall Professorship at Clark University and then to a lectureship at Harvard. After a time at Duke University, he accepted a Research Professorship at the University of Illinois, where he remained from 1945 to 1973. During his life he married three times and fathered five children (Horn, 2001). He retired to Oahu, where he was associated with the University of Hawaii. Retirement to some is a perpetual vacation, but, like Fromm, Cattell saw it as an opportunity to produce a torrent of papers and books that inflated his already impressive résumé: he is credited with a total of 43 books and about 575 articles (Horn, 2001). Cattell died on February 2, 1998.

Cattell's View of the Person

Cattell's Approach to Understanding the Person

One of the great virtues of Cattell's position is that he makes a refreshingly different basic, philosophical assumption. Unlike some other theorists, Cattell did not begin with "ideas off the top of the head," based on nothing more than simple intuition or subjective clinical observation. As an empiricist he believed that one collects data first, then filters and sifts them through various statistical techniques until the facts emerge. These facts then generate hypotheses that can be tested. Thus, the proper mode of reasoning is first *inductive,* reasoning from particular observations to a more general statement of position. Next it becomes *deductive,* reasoning from a general statement to particular observations. The cycle then is repeated. He operates along the **inductive-hypothetico-deductive spiral,** "the detecting of regularities in observational data leads to a hypothesis from which experimental consequences are deduced, [leading] to further data from which new regularities are induced, and so on in an ever-expanding spiral" (Wiggins, 1984, p. 189). The empirical approach is the method of astronomy, and, often, physics and chemistry, but too rarely personality psychology.

Personality Defined

In straightforward fashion Cattell defined **personality** "as that which tells what a [person] will do when placed in a particular situation" (Cattell, 1966, p. 25). It is expressed in a simple formula: $R = f(S.P)$, where R stands for the "nature and magnitude of a person's behavioural response, . . . what he [or she] says, thinks, or does," which is some function (f) of S, the "stimulus situation in which [the person] is placed," and P, the nature of her or his personality (p. 25). While these conceptions seem delightfully simple, in fact getting from P to R is a complicated matter.

Nature and Nurture

Cattell is noted for coming down on the nature side of the nature/nurture debate (Hirsch, 1975). Based on his and others' research, he argued that a number of human characteristics, most especially intelligence, are controlled to a great extent by the genes (Loehlin,

1984). Therefore, Cattell believed that people are shaped by genetic influences. The relative emphasis on genetic influences should not be taken to mean that Cattell totally neglects the environment (Cattell, 1979, Vol. 1). The "S" in R = f(S.P) is consistent with attention to the environment(s).

Factor Analysis

One of the ways one can isolate and verify traits is by seeking quantitative support for them in patterns of statistical correlations. To uncover these patterns, Cattell uses *factor analysis,* a statistical procedure for determining the number and nature of factors underlying larger numbers of measures (Kerlinger, 1973). The basic assumption is that certain simple responses intercorrelate, or vary together, and, thus, may be grouped together to define a separate psychological dimension or factor. By determining "what goes with what," factor analysis reduces large amounts of data from a complex to a simpler form (Spearman, 1927).

To grasp the concept "factor analysis," imagine that a psychological test made up of many questions is administered to a group of a few hundred people, including you. Suppose that you and a few dozen other subjects answer "Yes" to a certain test item (e.g., "Yes, the item statement ['I am anxious.'] applies to me") and you all also answer "Yes" to several other items. That set of items would be intercorrelated. Now assume that a different group of subjects, not including you, endorses a different set of items. This second set of items would be intercorrelated. These two sets of items would form two different clusters, each with a different common denominator. Factor analysis identifies sets of items, such that item-members of each set share some common denominator. This process is the "analysis" in factor analysis. The **factor** in factor analysis refers to a label that is applied to a data cluster (set of items) and suggests what it is measuring. Once a factor has been identified, based on the researcher's best judgment about the psychological dimension that the cluster of items seems to measure, a label is assigned. Judgments are guided by the content of items making the greatest contribution to a cluster identified as a factor. "Consciousness" is an example of a label assigned to a factor. In turn, contributions of items to a factor are determined by statistical **loadings,** correlations of particular items with a given factor.

Factors resulting from factor analysis are not all of the same order of comprehensiveness or generality. Some are **primary factors,** which are relatively pure and narrow in scope. It can be arranged statistically that primary factors are independent (Cattell, 1966; Eysenck, 1984). Others are **secondary factors,** which encompass several primary factors and are called "superfactors" or "second-order factors" (Cattell, 1966; Eysenck, 1984). Cattell (1966) and others believe that extraversion–introversion is a secondary factor that subsumes certain primary factors.

Basic Concepts: Cattell

Traits

Trait Subsidiation.   A **trait** is a permanent entity that does not fade in and out like a state; it is inborn or develops during the life course and regularly directs behavior. Cattell has developed quite an elaborate method for classifying traits. It springs from **subsidiation,** the idea, possibly borrowed from Murray, that some psychological entities are subsumed under others. Thus, traits are arranged in a hierarchy, from the most general and fewest in number, to the most specific and greatest in number. The **common trait** is " . . . a trait which can be measured for all people by the same battery [of tests] and on which [the people] differ in degree rather than in form" (Cattell, 1966, p. 368). Almost everyone can be given a position on a common trait dimension, varying, for example, from "extraverted" to "introverted." In contrast the **unique trait** is "so specific to an individual that no one else could be scored on [its dimension]" (p. 28). An example would be the tendency to raise one's voice at the end of each sentence. Cattell paid very little attention to unique traits.

Second-Order Traits.   At the top of the hierarchy are the most all-embracing or **second-order traits,** "superfactors" that subsume the other traits ("secondary factors" define second-order traits; look between the top two horizontal lines in Figure 16.1). That is, other traits fall under secondary traits: each secondary trait may be thought of as composed of lower-order traits that all relate to the secondary trait's label. Cattell mainly dealt with two of these higher-order factors. One is *exvia–invia,* "A factorially established broad dimension within the area of behaviour popularly referred to as extraversion-introversion" (p. 369). The other second-order trait is *anxiety,* feelings of tension and upset, the source of which is difficult to identify. Two of six others that he considered appear often in factor-analytic studies: an intelligence measure and an index of "good upbringing" (having "good manners"; Cattell, 1994).

Source Traits.   Figure 16.1 depicts Cattell's hierarchy of trait varieties and their relationships to factor types. The **source trait** is "a [primary] factor-dimension, stressing the proposition that variations in value along it are determined by a single unitary influence or source" (Cattell, 1966, p. 374). Each relates to a set of behaviors that resemble each other. For example, *emotionality* is a trait that refers to behaviors such as calmness, jitteriness, "cool-headness," and "excitability."

Source traits are further broken down into three categories. An **ability trait** is reflected in the kind of "response to the complexity of a situation, [that is selected after] the individual is clear on what goals he wants to achieve in that situation" (p. 28; leftmost entry in Figure 16.1 under "Source (Primary Factor)"). Most of Cattell's efforts in the "ability" category have been concentrated on "general intelligence," as measured by the IQ test to which I will return later. The second category is the **temperament trait,** "a general personality trait [that] is usually stylistic, in the sense that it deals with tempo, persistence, [and so forth] covering a large variety of specific responses" (p. 28). "Emotional versus stable" ("emotionality"; Wiggins, 1984) is a good example.

Compared to the other two categories of source traits, Cattell devotes relatively more attention to the **dynamic trait,** which refers to motivations and interests (Cattell, 1966; middle three entries in Figure 16.1 under "dynamic"). This subcategory may receive more attention because it is complex, composed of three interrelated subordinate categories. Like Maslow's needs, dynamic traits are goal-directed. The most basic is the **erg,** "an innate source of reactivity, such as is often described as a drive [or instinct], directed to a certain goal . . . " (p. 369; rightmost of the three entries in Figure 16.1 under "dynamic"). The term comes from the Greek *ergon* for 'work' or 'energy.' Although there are many examples of ergs, a couple of representative cases will suffice to illustrate the concept. The operation of the *sex erg* is signified by expressions such as "I want to satisfy my sexual need" (p. 190). An illustration of the *fear erg* is seen in "I want us to attack and destroy any formidable military power that actively threatens us" (p. 189).

The second dynamic trait category relates to the first. An erg is manifested in an **attitude,** an expression of an ergic goal that is generally subsidiated to an erg(s). In Figure 16.1, "attitude" is the leftmost of the three entries under "dynamic" and is illustrated by the two quoted expressions at the end of the preceding paragraph. The third dynamic trait category is **sentiment,** " . . . a *set* of attitudes the strength of which has become correlated through their being all learnt by contact with a particular social institution [such as] sentiment to school, to home, to country" (emphasis added, p. 374; middle of the three entries under "dynamic" in Figure 16.1). Thus, sentiments organize and coordinate attitudes in the service of ergs. Illustrative sentiments are: (1) *sentiment to religion:* "I want to see the standards of organized religion maintained or increased throughout our lives"; (2) *sentiment to career:* "I want to make my career in the Air Force" (pp. 191–192). (Note the reference to society's institutions in both expressions.)

The relationship among attitudes, sentiments, and ergs is reflected in the **dynamic lattice,** " . . . the tracing of the subsidiation of attitudes . . . ending in the satisfaction of a number of primary ergic goals" (p. 369). A partial illustration of the dynamic lattice shows relationships among attitudes, sentiments, and ergs (Figure 16.2). Note that, for the protection erg, the sentiment is "country" and the related attitude set includes "Armed Forces" and "President of the United States." For sex at the ergic level, the attitudes address husband's appearance and husband's physical condition. For the self-submission erg, attitudes address Catholic Church and Knights of Columbus. Figures 16.1 and 16.2 succinctly sum up Cattell's theory.

Surface Traits.   **Surface traits** are "a set of personality characteristics which are correlated but do not form a factor, hence are believed to be determined by more than one influence or source" (p. 375). They are the most subordinate traits: responses to the individual test items with which the researcher begins factor analysis. Surface traits are gut-level feelings, thoughts, and actions, the atoms of the personality molecule (the quarks may be neurological events, as Murray believed). Examples are "I enjoy scuba diving" and "I practice yoga." These surface traits would fall under the source trait conservative–experiencing (to the experiencing end; see Figure 16.3).

Intelligence

Cattell endorsed the conception of intelligence fostered by Charles Spearman, an early mental tester. Spearman promoted "g," which supposedly subsumes the so-called primary mental abilities and forms a common core of general intelligence (McGuire & Hirsch, 1977; Schonemann, 1989, 1992). Cattell assumes that this general factor of intelligence is largely due to the genes (Cattell, 1966). In a paper Cattell said he read at the American Psy-

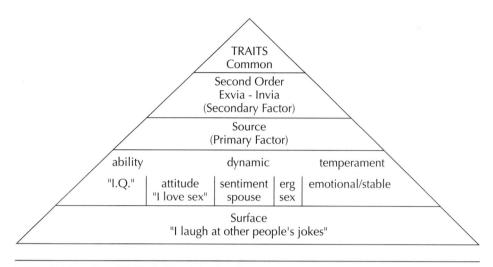

FIGURE 16.1 *Cattell's Trait Classification System*

chological Association convention in 1940, he argued that "g" fell into two categories (Cattell, 1984b; Cattell claimed that D. O. Hebb offered the same classification at the same time). Fluid general ability (g_f) is " . . . that form of general intelligence which is largely innate and which adapts itself to all kinds of material, regardless of previous experience with it" (Cattell, 1966, p. 369). Whereas he reports that early evidence indicated "g" was 80 percent inherited, he claims that g_f is nearly 100 percent inherited. Only prebirth accidents and postbirth trauma, such as head injury, prevent g_f from being fully inherited. In contrast, crystallized general ability (g_c) is "a general factor, largely . . . abilities learned at school, representing . . . applications of [g_f], and amount and intensity of schooling; it

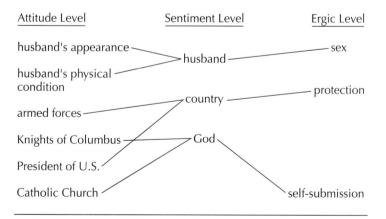

FIGURE 16.2 *The Dynamic Lattice*

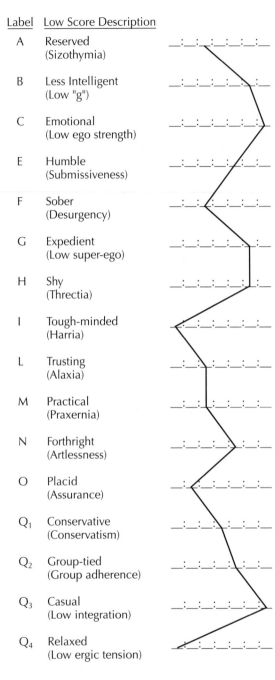

Label	Low Score Description		High Score Description
A	Reserved (Sizothymia)		Outgoing (Affectothymia)
B	Less Intelligent (Low "g")		More Intelligent (High "g")
C	Emotional (Low ego strength)		Stable (High ego strength)
E	Humble (Submissiveness)		Assertive (Dominance)
F	Sober (Desurgency)		Happy-go-lucky (Surgency)
G	Expedient (Low super-ego)		Conscientious (High super-ego)
H	Shy (Threctia)		Venturesome (Parmia)
I	Tough-minded (Harria)		Tender-minded (Premesia)
L	Trusting (Alaxia)		Suspicious (Protension)
M	Practical (Praxernia)		Imaginative (Autia)
N	Forthright (Artlessness)		Shrewd (Shrewdness)
O	Placid (Assurance)		Apprehensive (Guilt-proneness)
Q_1	Conservative (Conservatism)		Experiencing (Radicalism)
Q_2	Group-tied (Group adherence)		Self-sufficient (Self-sufficiency)
Q_3	Casual (Low integration)		Controlled (High self-concept)
Q_4	Relaxed (Low ergic tension)		Tense (Ergic tension)

FIGURE 16.3 *Technical (in parentheses) and Popular Labels for the 16 PF Factors a to Q_4*

appears in vocabulary and numerical ability [tests]" (p. 369). g_c is acquired intelligence that is largely determined by quality of schooling and is little affected by the genes.

Evaluation

Contributions

Cattell's work has been programmatic, undertaken systematically rather than piecemeal. He believed that each person has his or her own "permanent" position on each trait dimension.

Assessing Personality with the 16 PF. True to his empiricist nature, Cattell began with the most basic, elemental reflections of personality, trait descriptive words (Wiggins, 1984). He reduced 4,500 trait words from the comprehensive list produced by Allport and Odbert (1936) to 160 synonym groups. These groups were eventually reduced to 171 terms by eliminating synonyms. The 171 *trait elements* were intercorrelated and 36 clusters of correlations were isolated. Each cluster was a *surface trait*. Ten more were later added to make a total of 46 surface traits. This set was the grist for Cattell's factor-analytic mill. Eventually 16 primary factors were isolated. The resultant 16 scales were given to 10,000 subjects. The final outcome was the 16 Personality Factors test or **16 PF,** a test of adult personality measured in terms of 16 source traits (Cattell, Eber, & Tatsuoka, 1970).

In business and industry, the 16 PF has served as an aid to decisions about employee selection, efficiency, turnover, and promotion. In education, it has aided the planning of individualized programs for students and the prediction of school achievement. The 16 PF's handbook contains 125 profiles depicting ideal trait levels for various jobs, including airline pilots, mechanics, teachers, nurses, and electricians (Cattell, Eber, & Tatsuoka, 1970). In clinical settings, the 16 PF has been used to diagnose behavior problems, anxiety, neurosis, alcoholism, drug addiction, and delinquency.

BOX 16.1 • *Your Own 16 PF Profile*

You can create your own 16 PF profile by placing an "X" in the scale interval that you think represents your level on each factor and then drawing a line through the "Xs." Be honest with yourself; ignore the line for "John Skyman" while you are creating your own profile. After you have completed your profile, then you can compare it to "Skyman." In any case, you should recognize that your perceptions of your positions on the scales would not necessarily coincide with your actual positions if you took the 16 PF. In the actual test, for each factor there are several items over which a score is computed to represent the final factor score. You would not know your positions on the factors with confidence until you responded to all of the items.

Figure 16.3 depicts the 16 PF scales. The zigzag line through the middle of the scales is the personality profile of a hypothetical pilot, "John Skyman," derived from the profiles of 360 real pilots. Follow the line and see how "John" scored on each scale. To get a feel for the scales, do the exercise in Box 16.1.

Limitations

Because he relied on it so heavily, Cattell's theoretical structural and research interpretations rest on the validity and meaningfulness of factor analysis. Unfortunately, it is commonly said of factor analysis that researchers never get anything out of it they did not put there in the first place. This is because the results of factor analysis are extremely dependent on several biasing influences.

The Choice of Factor-Analytic Method Is Arbitrary.   Eysenck (1984) points out that one of the methods used in conjunction with factor analysis can force factors to be independent of one another. Another method can force factors to agree with theory. Cattell's 16 PF work involved a third method that allows factors to be correlated with one another. This procedure makes the factors "impure," according to Eysenck. In view of this impurity, he asked, "Why not use the second order factors as they are fewer in number and more inclusive?" Regarding who is correct, Cronbach (1970) wrote, "There is no one 'right' way to do a factor analysis any more than there is a 'right' way to photograph Waikiki Beach" (p. 315).

Subjective Judgments Remain.   Arbitrariness and subjectivity on the part of researchers enter into the picture at four points. First, certain factor-analytic solutions are promoted rather than others, not only by preselecting data likely to be "relevant" to researchers' biases, but also by their later estimates of how many factors are likely to be present in the data. Cattell (1973) and the Eysencks (1969) refer to this as "the number of factors problem." Different decisions on the number of constructs needed to account for personality partly explains why different numbers of trait factors have been proposed. Goldberg (1981) observes, "The number of primary personality factors in Cattell's system is in the 20-to-30 range, . . . the 16 most famous [are the] 16 PF. When his data were made available to others, however, virtually everyone . . . found only 5" (pp. 156–159). Second, items entered into factor analysis may be chosen solely on the basis of the factor analyst's biases rather than on previous research. Third, once factors have been identified, cutoff values are required to establish whether an item makes a meaningful contribution to a factor. Loadings of .40 to .60 on a factor are likely to be judged quite acceptable by most factor analysts. But what about .35 to .10? Any decision is arbitrary.

The fourth and the most serious limitation is that the factor analyst interprets and labels all factors. By looking at the items encompassed by a factor, the analyst must subjectively decide what to call it. Labels that are consistent with the analyst's theory are typically assigned. Other analysts might label the factors differently, according to their own biases. This helps explain why one researcher's "neuroticism" and "extraversion" (Eysenck) are another's "anxiety" and "exvia" (Cattell).

Nature–nurture: Heritability. Cattell cast almost everything he studied according to how much of its variability is determined by the genes and how much by the environment. As you recall, nearly 100 percent of the variation (individual differences) in fluid intelligence is supposedly accounted for by the genes, but the figure is much smaller for crystallized intelligence (Cattell, 1966). Among 16 PF factors, some are thought to be controlled more by the genes than by the environment and some are thought to be more environmentally controlled (Cattell, Schuerger, & Klein, 1982).

Heritability popularly refers to the proportion of the variability in a trait that is accounted for by the genes. (See McGuire & Hirsch, 1977, for a discussion of the different indexes of heritability.) Heritability has been estimated in various ways, sometimes rather directly by use of correlations between the IQs of identical twins reared apart (they are correctly assumed to be genetically identical, and incorrectly assumed to be reared in entirely different environments). To his credit, Cattell has used a new method to go beyond the limited twins method. This method considers not only identical and fraternal twins but also brothers and sisters and unrelated people.

In an example study using the new method, heritability was estimated for the 16 PF factors ego-strength, super-ego strength, and self-sentiment (self-concept maintenance; Cattell, Rao, & Schuerger, 1985). Results indicated that self-sentiment is more genetically determined and super-ego strength more environmentally determined, with ego-strength falling between the two. However, heritability estimates varied markedly depending on the method of estimation used. Also, results were not entirely in line with those of a highly similar study reported by Cattell, Schuerger, and Klein (1982). Further, Cattell's attempts at applying genetic interpretations to some of his calculations have come under fire for mathematical shortcomings. Although attempts to specify the genetic underpinnings of personality traits has a long history, such efforts may have a short future (Azar, 2002b). Because the genes that might contribute to the development of a particular personality trait may number in the dozens, many researchers are abandoning the search for "personality trait genes." The use of statistical techniques to make statements about genetic determination of personality traits has all the problems outlined in this section.

Again, to his credit, Cattell acknowledged the variations in estimations with variation in technique, but he attempted to strongly interpret results anyway. This double-think about heritability results highlights a fact that is often ignored by Cattell and others: heritability estimates are good only for the population used, at the the time it is used (Hirsch, 1975; McGuire & Hirsch, 1977; Weizmann, Wiener, Wiesenthal, & Ziegler, 1990). They do not generalize to other populations or to another sample taken from the same population at another time. Further, these measures . . . provide no information about how a given *individual* might have developed under . . . [different] conditions . . . " (Hirsch, 1975). Just as a specimen of a tree species develops differently on the top of a mountain than down in a valley, a given individual might have turned out differently if reared under different conditions than those that actually existed for her or him. It is important to note that, because heritability is a population statistic, it is interpretable for the single population contributing data to the estimate. For example, heritability estimates made using Whites are meaningless when applied to Blacks. Issues related to these considerations are covered in Box 16.2.

BOX 16.2 • *Intellectual Diversity: Variety and Relativity*

That intelligence is one thing, "g," probably constitutes a consensus among psychologists interested in mental ability. Cattell has broken it down further. However, he seems only to be saying that the one thing, "g," can be conceived of as one part that is inherited (g$_f$) and another part that is mostly not inherited (g$_c$) but is dependent on the other part. While there may be a consensus, there is also a growing minority of dissenters who believe that intelligence is extremely complex, not just one thing but many things.

Prominent among them is Robert Sternberg (1988), who believes that there are three broad categories of intelligences, not just one called "g." One kind is essentially "g": it is the ability to collect information and analyze it. A second kind is basically *creativity:* it is putting pieces of information together into something entirely new. The third kind may be thought of as *"street smarts"*: it is solving everyday practical problems and adapting to one's changing environment. The last two are not really measured on IQ tests, but do *contribute to people's survival and prosperity*—a broad conception of intelligence. Sternberg (2003) reports that the Rainbow Test (including his three components) improves prediction of college success and increases diversity on campuses where it is used, compared with campuses using only traditional tests (IQ-related achievement and entrance tests).

Another dissenter is Howard Gardner (1983), who believes there are seven intelligences rather than only "g." Among his intelligences are some that amount to "g," but there also is musical ability and bodily-kinesthetic ability, which is, roughly speaking, the "right stuff" for athletics. There are two others that may be interpreted as the ability to know oneself and the ability to know others. Most of Gardner's intelligences are not measured on intelligence tests that are designed to assess only "g." Obviously, if IQ tests did include Sternberg's and Gardner's intelligences, some people's scores would go up (those individuals possessing the "new" intelligences) and some

people's scores would go down (those without the "new" intelligences).

Peter Salovey and Jack Mayer introduced the notion of "emotional intelligence," or EQ in 1990. Between then and Salovey's new book with David Sluyter (1997), Daniel Goleman (1995) published a book that has made EQ world famous. EQ involves the ability to monitor and control one's emotions so that they facilitate, rather than hinder, whatever one wishes to do or accomplish. People with high IQ, but little ability to monitor and control their emotions, are not likely to be successful in all domains of their lives. For example, Goleman discusses a physician who is very intelligent, IQ-wise, but is emotionally bland, rendering him unable to appreciate the feelings of others. This unfortunate condition ruined his relationship with the woman in his life, and, obviously, would be of no help to his career.

Peter Salovey and John Mayer, co-conceivers of "Emotional Intelligence," along with David Caruso, have developed a new *ability* test of Emotional Intelligence, the Mayer-Salovey-Caruso Emotional Intelligence Test (MS-CEIT; Dittman, 2003). Brackett and Mayer (2003) found the MSCEIT to be more independent of often-studied personality and well-being measures than are *self-report* tests of emotional intelligence (e.g., a measure of the Big 5 *personality* traits and a Diener-measure of subjective *well-being;* see the discussion of these measures in the Eysenck section). The following is an example of a self-report measure: people endorse (or do not endorse) items relating to emotional intelligence: Your long-term partner has ended your relationship and you are upset because you wanted the relationship to continue. Your response (choose one): (1) You stay home every night and cry about the breakup; (2) You decide to make the best of it and find healthy outlets for your feelings; (3) You get involved with someone you don't care about just to be with someone; (4) You immerse yourself in many projects—maybe you won't think about it (endorsing choice

2 raises one's emotional intelligence score). In contrast to self-report measures, "The MSCEIT [ability instrument] measures perception of emotion by having people rate how much of a particular emotion is being expressed in pictures of faces or designs and landscapes that express a basic emotion or blends of emotions" (Brackett & Mayer, 2003, p. 1148). Caruso, Mayer, and Salovey (2002) found essentially the same result using an earlier "emotional intelligence ability test" (eiat): the eiat was largely independent of well-studied personality measures (e.g., the 16PF). These results show that ability-based measures of emotional intelligence, that are valid in the sense of being independent of personality and other relevant measures, are being developed at an encouraging rate.

Goleman suggests that there are five qualities of EQ. First is *self-awareness,* the ability to recognize a feeling as it happens. Only a person who is fully aware of his or her feelings can control them. People who explode periodically do not become aware of their emotions quickly enough to harness them. Second is *mood control,* the ability to do or think something to change a bad mood into a better one. No one can stop having bad moods, but high EQ people can do something to stop a bad mood from getting worse and, maybe, change it into a good mood. If a motorist cuts off a high EQ person in traffic, he or she may avoid negative emotions by thinking "perhaps the motorist is experiencing an emergency." The third is *self-motivation,* the ability to get oneself going toward goals important to oneself. Great athletes are self-motivators. They practice endlessly and will not be deterred from the pursuit of "winning." One of their methods is incurable optimism. They do not think of losing; if something goes wrong, they do not blame it on themselves. If they should lose, they bounce back (Bandura's resilience). Fourth is *impulse control,* which is the kind of self-regulation that includes what Mischel called "delay of gratification." You may recall that children who could delay gratification (eating two marshmallows later, instead of one now) grew up

to be high achieving teens. Fifth is *people skills,* possession of a level of empathy sufficient to appreciate and respond appropriately to others' feelings. Almost all jobs involve working with people. Obviously, high IQ, but low EQ, is not a prescription for success on most jobs. You cannot be a good "team member" if you cannot appreciate and respond empathetically to other members' feelings. Measures of EQ are being developed and will be embraced by business executives.

Most psychologists who are interested in intelligence apparently think that it is absolute: the same thing the world over. It is assumed that, to test the intelligence of the Australian Aborigines (native Australians) or the people of Tibet, the most one needs is someone to translate the U.S. IQ test into another language. But suppose intelligence is relative: it is related to the specific sociophysical environment of a people. In one environment abilities A, B, C . . . are critically important to survival and prosperity. In that environment, people who have A, B, C . . . are intelligent and those who do not are not intelligent. But, in another environment, abilities X, Y, Z . . . are critically important, because, compared to the first environment, different skills are needed for survival and prosperity. Actually, because of the barren, hilly, amorphous environment their ancestors had to master, Australian Aborigines' children have stronger spatial–visual ability than Australian children of European descent (Kearins, 1981, 1986). The original Australians, for most of their history, needed this kind of intelligence to find their way in their vast and irregular surround. They had to be able to look at this misshapen hill or that undulating terrain and remember it or they would get lost and, possibly, die. Aborigines' children remembered the position of each of several irregular objects (e.g., rocks) placed in squares drawn on a surface better than European-Australian children (Kearins, 1981). If the spatial–visual ability measured on this test were more heavily weighted on IQ tests, Aborigines' children's scores would go up and European children's scores would go down.

The notion of heritability itself is suspect when used as Cattell and others have employed it. It was originally developed to estimate how successful animal breeders would be in their efforts to promote certain desirable traits through breeding (McGuire & Hirsch, 1977; Weizmann, Wiener, Wiesenthal, & Ziegler, 1990). It was never intended to be used as a means to partition the variance in a trait into that accounted for by the genes and that accounted for by the environment. In fact, the very act of dividing up variation in a trait, whether intelligence or personality is considered, is suspect from a genetic point of view. Consider an analogy. The question "In computing the area of a rectangle, which is more important, its length or its height?" makes no sense. Likewise, asking "Which is more important, heredity or environment?" may be meaningless (Hirsch, 1975). Every genetic disposition is expressed in an environment and different environments may be associated with different expressions. Likewise, no environmental influence exerts itself apart from potential genetic input. Separating the genetic contribution to a trait from that of the environment in which it is expressed may make no sense. That environmental effects explain everything psychological is just as wrong-headed as the belief that the genes explain everything. Thus, it seems clear that Cattell's heritability work is, at best, controversial and should be viewed with considerable caution.

That genes' expressions are influenced by the environments in which expressions occur has important implications. One such implication is that genes and environments may interact such that, for certain psychological factors, genetic effects are strong under some environmental circumstances, but environments dominate under other circumstances. In an especially clear demonstration of gene–environment interaction, Avshalom Caspi and colleagues (2002) investigated the effects of the monoamine oxidase A gene (MAOA) on violent behavior. MAOA breaks down biochemical substances that allow communication between nerve cells. Previous research had shown that when a null (inoperative) version of this gene is on the X chromosome (male), antisocial behavior increases in likelihood. The Caspi group hypothesized that when MAOA activity is low (null gene present) violent antisocial behavior will be high, but only if participants' childhood environment was characterized by maltreatment. They found that for Conduct Disorder, Convicted for Violent Offense, Disposition Toward Violence, and Antisocial Personality, when MAOA activity was low, all four of these orientations were high, but only if the participants had been maltreated during childhood. In the absence of maltreatment, there was no difference between low and high MAOA activity participant groups. For participants with high MAOA activity (effective gene present), maltreatment had nil effects. The presence of the null version of the MAOA gene in people results in violent or antisocial orientation only when maltreatment characterized their childhood environment.

Eric Turkheimer and colleagues Haley, Waldron, D'Onofrio, and Gottesman (2003) used new sophisticated statistical techniques in an attempt to sort out when genetic effects on intelligence (IQ) are strong and when environmental effects are strong. Based on previous research, they hypothesized that genetic effects would relatively strongly influence IQ when middle class and higher socioeconomic (mid-to-hi-soe) people are tested on IQ, but that environmental effects would relatively strongly influence IQ when low socioeconomic (lo-soe) people are tested. This hypothesis had not been tested before because only mid-to-hi-soe people had been used in almost all of the previous studies, almost all of which had shown strong genetic and weak environmental effects (for this type of research, if genetic effects are strong, environmental effects are weak and vice versa). The data for the Turkheimer and colleagues study was drawn from a sample of nearly 50,000 mothers and nearly 60,000 of their children (identical and fraternal twins were included, but all types of familial relationships were considered). Results showed that for the full IQ scale and for performance IQ (perhaps including elements of g_f) the lower the socioeconomic status the stronger the environmental effects—and the weaker the genetic effects. This interaction, however, was weak for verbal IQ, though it was visibly present in graphs of the data. Thus, genetic variation may largely determine who is intelligent (in the IQ-sense) among mid-to-hi-soe people, but environmental variation appears to differentiate between intelligent and not so intelligent lo-soe people.

Genetic determinism, the belief that the genes absolutely shape crucial traits such as intelligence, took a big hit when James Flynn (1999, 2000, 2003) showed that scores on the most popular measure of intelligence, IQ, have been increasing rapidly worldwide. Rapid change in a trait cannot be "genetically determined" because genetic change takes many, many generations (Cavalli-Sforza, 2000). Thus, environmental factors must account for the rapid increase in IQ. To add insult to injury, the part of "g" that Cattell and others declare to be almost entirely "inherited," g_f, is changing more rapidly than g_c, which is not supposed to be "inherited."

Recent work by Tamara Daley and colleagues Whaley, Sigman, Espinosa, and Neumann (2003) shows how powerful the Flynn effect can be in raising g_c and especially g_f over a short period. These researchers also produced evidence to suggest that environmental enrichment may be behind these increases. Participants were children tested in 1984 and their families compared with children tested in 1998 and their families, both from the Embu tribe of Kenya, Africa. Over the 14-year period, scores on the Raven Colored Progressive Matrices, a measure of g_f, increased 26.3 IQ points on one index and 11.2 IQ points on another index. These were greater gains than found for industrialized nations. There was also a small but significant increase in Verbal Meaning scores (g_c) over the 14 years. Factors that changed over the 14-year period for the Embu participants that might explain the increase in intelligence included improved nutrition, increased environmental complexity (e.g., availability of TV and print material), decreased family size (more money for each child), increased education and literacy of mothers, and increased pre-school attendance. Evidence indicated that health status and birth order played no role in the increases. Apparently environmental enrichment—fueled by a shift in values toward emphasis on schooling, education, and literacy—accounted for gains. Once again, the gains were mostly in terms of g_f which Cattell and others who promote "g" thought would be most resistant to change, because it is "inherited."

Genetic determinists, such as Cattell, cannot use their point of view to explain either the rapid change in IQ or the rapid change in g_f, because of the short-term nature of the change. Further, these facts do not fit well with the claim that Whites' alleged advantage over Blacks in average IQ is "inherited." Genetic determinism cannot explain the observation that Blacks' IQ is increasing somewhat more rapidly than Whites' (Flynn, 1999, 2000) or that the Black–White IQ gap is closing (Neisser et al., 1996).

Is the 16 PF a Significant Legacy?   The 16 PF is certainly a useful personality assessment instrument, but how much is it revered by users of personality assessment tools?

According to Watkins, Campbell, Nieberding, and Hallmark (1995), of available personality tests, the 16 PF was ranked 25th out of 38 instruments in frequency of use by clinicians. But perhaps the 16 PF is primarily a research instrument. If so, it should be frequently cited in the research literature. Yearbooks produced by the Buros Institute of Mental Measurement (*Mental Measurement* and *Tests in Print*) indicate that, from 1985 (Mitchell, 1985) to 1995, the 16 PF was ranked no higher than thirteenth (Conoley & Impara, 1995) and as low as the twentieth most cited among 50 tests (Murphy, Close, & Impara, 1994). It was not mentioned in Impara and Plake (1998). Apparently, the 16 PF is not in the top tier of most used and cited tests.

The Disaster at the End of Cattell's Life: The American Psychological Association's (APA) "Life Achievement Award" Given to Cattell, Then Taken Away.   During early August, 1997, the APA announced in the pages of its flagship journal, the prestigious *American Psychologist,* that a "Gold Medal for Life Achievement in Psychological Science" award would be bestowed on Cattell. The Medal was to be presented at the APA's mid-August annual convention in Chicago. I was there when the award was withdrawn. At the onset of the convention an article was published in the *New York Times* citing accusations by historian Barry Mehler that Cattell harbored racist views (Hilts, 1997). The APA quickly suspended the award presentation and appointed an investigative panel. In January of 1998, Cattell withdrew from further consideration for the award. The panel never acted.

Two of Mehler's quotes from Cattell's writings were particularly inflammatory. One, from a 1994 newsletter, *Beyondist,* created for Cattell's "Beyondism" movement, suggested that Cattell thought Hitler to be not so bad after all: "Hitler actually shared many values of the average American. He admired . . . family values . . . " (quoted in Hilts, 1997, p. A10 y). The quote goes on to suggest that Hitler's attempts at eugenics, though misguided in practice, were sound in principle. "It [eugenics] favors preventing the birth of those who would inevitably be miserable and incapable of living a normal, happy life. It encourages the birth of those who look after themselves and others, who invent and enrich the culture, . . . " Another quote by Hilts was from Cattell's 1972 book, *A New Morality from Science: Beyondism:* "At what point voluntary euthanasia or *genthanasia* by groups becomes appropriate is a difficult question. [ ] Scrupulous consideration is indicated before allowing a breed of humans—however maladapted—to become extinct" (Hilts, 1997, p. A10 y, emphasis added; see Cattell, 1972, p. 220 for the bracketed portion omitted from the *Times* article). And what is *genthanasia?* As opposed to "*genocide* . . . [which is] reserved for literal killing off of all living members of a people . . . *genthanasia* [is reserved for] what has above been called 'phasing out,' in which a moribund culture is ended, by educational and birth control measures, without a single member dying before his time" (Hilts, 1997 p. A10 y; see Cattell, 1972, p. 221). The implications of the two quotes are clear and chilling: certain groups are to be eliminated because they are unworthy of taking up precious space on earth.

William H. Tucker (1994) mined Cattell's early works to find alarmingly racist statements. For example, in his 1933 book, he assailed *race mixing* resulting in "hybrids" that suffer from "seriously defective . . . intellectual and moral development . . . " (Tucker, 1994, p. 240). Even then Cattell shied away from suggesting that "undesirables" be killed off, opting instead for birth control, regulation by sterilization, "and by life in adapted reserves and asylums, [where] the races which have served their turn [can] be brought to euthanasia" (Tucker, 1994, p. 242). In his *Fight for Our National Intelligence,* Cattell (1937) adds that no motorists "would hesitate to run over . . . a feeble minded [child] in preference to a healthy, bright child" (Tucker, 1994, p. 243). Tucker goes on to indicate, using quotations from early Cattell books, that Cattell was anti-Semitic, which, not surprisingly, made him sympathetic to the Nazis' race policies (Tucker, 1994).

Perhaps Tucker was referring to the "old Cattell," not the reformed Cattell of the last two decades (see Hilts, 1997, for Cattell's claim to have changed). To find out, I went to the more recent edition of Cattell's *Beyondism: Religion from Science* (1987). Indeed it is a "cleaned up" version of the 1972 book, containing fewer blatantly genocidal and racist statements. However, on pages 189 and 190, he lists and discusses six categories of people, and strongly implies that we can do without three of them, the "mentally deficient," "mentally handicapped," and the "dull normal." One suspects that the latter would contain people of color. As he had earlier done, in 1987, he condemns race mixing: "In the U.S.A., praises are traditionally sung to the Melting Pot, but the first requirement in successful plant hybridization is a rejection of perhaps 90% of the hybrids as unsuccessful" (p. 202). "The same holds for hybrids of racial groups." Elsewhere he opined: "The . . . worship . . . of [hypocritical humanitarian efforts] . . . [that] prolong the duration of genetic and cultural failure and block a seemly appropriate extinction of chronically misfitting types is contrary to all Beyondist principles" (p. 138). Also, he offered " 'A' is a classics professor—famous for his researches . . . 'B' is an ordinary person who does some gardening for me. He has been in jail . . . ; he can barely read the newspaper. Yet in democracy as now practiced, the wishes of B in public affairs can completely cancel A's . . . contribution . . . if [society] . . . gives equal voting powers to individuals so disparate" (p. 223). In the *Beyondism* of 1987, how would eugenics be carried out? " . . . adjusting income tax . . . [and providing] child allowances, . . . would encourage those to have children who have a higher probability of more gifted children" (p. 215). It follows that people expected to "have a [lower] probability of more gifted children" would be paid not to have any.

Mehler (1997) documented Cattell's continual surreptitious association with elements of the radical right. Cattell is constantly and currently quoted in neo-Nazi publications. However, not all elements of the right would embrace Cattell. His disdain for Christianity would make him an enemy of the "religious right."

One may ask, how could the APA's Gold Medal awards panel have missed two books with the intriguing partial title *Beyondism?* How could they have missed Congresswoman Cardis Collins's (D-IL) protest that Beyondists were providing input into decisions regarding athletic scholarships. Further, Hunt (1998) reported that the panel must have known about Cattell's racist beliefs, because at least two of those who recommended him for the award condemned those beliefs in their letters to panel members. Information on *Beyondism* was out there for the APA panel, in plain sight, but perhaps they were not primed to see it. Maybe the attitude that "one should consider only scientists' scientific contributions" when deciding who gets awards pervades psychology. Certainly this attitude is held by some psychologists (see the comment attributed to several APA Award winners on p. 9 of *The National Psychologist,* Jan./Feb., 1998). This attitude implies that an organization should be unconcerned about how an award candidate's views and actions reflect on their group. To condemn this attitude as succinctly as possible, I offer one trivial, but clear, analogy and one that is closer to home. If only professional contributions are relevant when deciding on who gets a group's awards, Pete Rose would be in the Baseball Hall of Fame, despite having bet on baseball games. Also, German psychologist E. R. Jaensch would get a medal for his seminal work on eidetic imagery (picture memory), despite the fact that he was supporting the Nazis during their era.

For years, Cattell's colleague Jerry Hirsch (1997) has tried to show that Cattell's points of view that have racist implications should be ignored because there is no scientific support for them. Hirsch (1997) alleged that Cattell habitually avoided peer review by self-publishing (in his books) and by publishing in unreviewed write-ups of conference presentations. I will add that Cattell, unlike other famous personologists, rarely published in the most esteemed journals with the most demanding editorial reviews, such as the *Journal of Personality, Personality and Social Psychology Bulletin,* and the *Journal of Personality and Social Psychology.*

It should also be noted that a search of the July issues of the 1940–1942 *Psychological Bulletin,* which contain the complete programs of the American Psychological Association (APA) conventions for those years, reveals no presentation title or abstract supporting Cattell's claim to have introduced fluid and crystallized intelligence at an APA convention during this period. However, D. O. Hebb did present a paper on two kinds of intelligences at the 1940 convention.

But why fret about eugenics? Has it been done in this hemisphere during the twentieth century? Yes, in Canada, between 1927 and 1972 (*Peoria Journal Star,* March 12, 1998, and in 1998 in other U.S. and Canadian papers; also see Tucker, 1994). Recently, there was a public outcry among Canadian citizens when the Alberta government abandoned a plan to compensate involuntarily sterilized mental patients. It is time to lay *eugenics applied to entire groups* in a grave too deep for future efforts at exhumation. Box 16.2 challenges Cattell's view of intelligence.

Conclusions

Because youthful Cattell became so obsessed with eugenics that mature Cattell could not free his mind of it, the memory of both will always be tainted. However, even if one ignores his eugenics and heritability work, one can still point to genuine Catellion contributions. Cattell's empiricist stance is in stark contrast to the "off the top of the head" theorizing of many personologists covered in this book. Perhaps personality psychologists should be more like astronomers than chemists. Because what psychologists study is complex and difficult to "get the hands on," or even "the eyeballs," they should be cautious in forming hypotheses until after many observations are made. As mentioned several times before, the worth of a scientific contributor is often determined as much by whether the contributor inspires others to think new and useful thoughts as by his or her own ideas. Cattell has literally trained dozens of personality psychologists. Some of them, such as Jerry Wiggins, have gone on to prominence. If one had to point to a measure that taps personality more completely and meaningfully than all the others, one could well vote for the 16 PF. It is perhaps the most carefully developed by use of the most sophisticated methods. It was not "done in a day," like some measures, but evolved over many years of careful research. Finally, the model of scientific contribution is not to "make your mark" with a few publications based on a few studies, each done in a short time, early in a career. Cattell was active in psychology into his nineties. He was seventh on the journal citation list, not listed on the textbook citation list or the survey citation list, but number sixteen overall (Haggbloom et al., 2002).

Eysenck: 16 = 3—Conceiving of Personality in Three Dimensions

Hans Jurgen Eysenck
www.ship.edu/~cgboeree/
eysenck.html

Eysenck and Cattell are often linked, perhaps because they both are pioneer factor analysts and both were trained in Britain. Both are associated with heavy use of complicated statistical methods. Both believe that personality and intelligence are strongly determined by the genes. Both have spent a professional lifetime trying to reduce personality to only a few dimensions. They even had the same mentor, Sir Cyril Burt, who became infamous for faking data on the inheritance of IQ. But there were differences. In fact, they carried on quite a debate on how many dimensions one must consider in order to account for personality, 16 or 3. Eysenck's argument for only three occupies most of the remaining pages of this chapter.

Eysenck, the Person

Hans Jurgen Eysenck was born in Germany on March 4, 1916, to a moderately known actor, Eduard Eysenck, and an aspiring actress, Ruth Werner (Gibson, 1981). He came of age during the deprivations of the period following World War I. After his parents' marriage was dissolved, Eysenck lived with his maternal grandmother, who raised him in a permissive atmosphere. As a result (or maybe it was his genes), he was a strong-willed boy, accustomed to having his own way. For example, at eight, he bit the finger of a teacher who was trying to punish him for his adamant refusal to sing. Later, in high school, he proved a teacher wrong in his claim that Jews were lacking in military valor. Interestingly, he did it with statistics: Jewish soldiers received a disproportionate number of German medals for valor during World War I. Also, he refused to attend the lectures of a teacher who failed to give him the highest essay grade. Such behavior inspired Gibson (1981) to write: "Eysenck appears to have . . . a very good opinion of his own abilities" and "of himself" (p. 18).

In 1933, the year of the Nazi takeover, Eysenck would leave Germany, because his stepfather, Max Glass, a movie producer–director, was Jewish. Thus, in the summer of 1934, Hans, Max, and Ruth departed for France, where Max successfully resumed his career. There Eysenck briefly pursued an advanced education, until a visit to Exeter, England, led to a love affair with Britain. At eighteen, in the autumn of 1934, the affinity for England was still so strong that it lured him to London. There he entered University College with the intention of pursuing a "hard" science curriculum. Unfortunately, he had a deficiency in science that would have required time and money to correct. Accordingly, he enrolled in psychology, which was just beginning to be recognized as a "science."

As fate would have it, Eysenck entered what then was the most scientific psychology department in England. It was a site of intense activity in psychometrics, psychology's measurement movement. Even as an undergraduate, he did research with Sir Cyril Burt, who helped him collect the data that went into his first publication. Eysenck took only three years to finish his psychology doctorate with honors.

In the same year, 1940, Britain declared war on Germany and Eysenck was labeled an enemy alien. Barred from the armed forces, he did research at the Mill Emergency Hospital, which was associated with the Maudsley Hospital, later his lifelong research center. During this period, and later, Eysenck was accused of being a "fascist," probably because he was a German who seemed to espouse "heredity is everything," and, thus, personality traits and intelligence cannot be changed. Given this view it seemed to follow that, if you have low intelligence, you were born with it and there is no hope for you. This position was in defiance of social programs that assumed "environment is everything" and that traits and intelligence can be changed. Despite these handicaps, Eysenck moved up the academic ladder. In 1950 he was granted the position of reader at the University of London. In 1955 he became a professor even as he maintained his dominant position at Maudsley. From these positions of power he defied the psychological establishment and began a long campaign for acceptance of his "Big 3." Like Cattell, Eysenck was actively pursuing psychology right up to the day he died, September 4, 1997.

Eysenck's View of the Person

Eysenck was apparently not a warm and accepting person like Carl Rogers (Gibson, 1981). His condemnation of psychotherapy (Eysenck, 1952a), for which he narrowly escaped physical assault, may have emerged from his inability to muster empathy for neurotic clients. Like Cattell, he believed a continuous program of research conducted over many years is the proper approach to understanding people, but he advocated a different research program (Eysenck, 1984, p. 335; emphasis added).

> Thus, Cattell starts from the generation of hypotheses about the major factors involved, [and] stays [with] factor analysis . . . I follow exactly the opposite line. Starting out with a theoretical model . . . *I use factor analysis to test theories rather than to originate them.* I . . . use [theory] from . . . psychology and physiology to link the factors . . . with causal hypotheses which led outside factor analysis altogether.

Eysenck added, "Cattell has been opposed to current theories emerging from experimental laboratories, and has openly criticized 'brass-instruments' psychology" (p. 329). By contrast, Eysenck did real experiments and relied on evidence and hypotheses from experimental psychology. Also, he alternated between experimental procedures and factor analysis until he felt that he had honed and refined the concepts with which he was working.

Central to the difference between Eysenck and Cattell, and critical to Eysenck's uniqueness relative to other personality theorists, is the question, "at what level does one find the traits that are necessary and sufficient in number and nature to account for personality?" Contrary to Cattell and his 16 factors, Eysenck believed personality can be parsimoniously understood, with no loss of thoroughness or depth, by reference to only three second-order factors. But neither has given an inch, as is evident in Cattell's (1986) response to Eysenck (also see Eysenck, 1997).

Basic Concepts and Contributions: Eysenck

Traits and Types in Eysenck's Theory

As with Cattell, the essence of Eysenck's theory is that personality can be described in terms of **traits** represented as statistical primary factors and defined as "theoretical constructs based on observed intercorrelations between a number of different habitual responses" (Eysenck & Eysenck, 1969, p. 41). Examples of traits relevant to Eysenck's theory include physical activity, impulsiveness, risk-taking, responsibility, worrisomeness, carefreeness, and sociability, all originating with the ancient Greeks. Traits, in turn, are often grouped in categories called **types,** second-order dimensions made up of statistically intercorrelated primary traits. Eysenck prefers "second-order" to "superfactors" (1984). He has identified three such factors, reporting that they "or others remarkably similar to them" have been found repeatedly in different studies (1981, p. 6). Eysenck's three second-order factors or types are: E, Extraversion–introversion; N, Neuroticism–stability; P, Psychoticism–super-ego functioning. These types are essentially the same as Cattell's second-order factors exvia–invia and anxiety and his primary factor "super-ego strength" respectively (Eysenck, 1984). Eysenck did not believe that each person is either E or not E, 100 percent N or not at all, totally P or totally not P. Thus, most of us are **ambiverts,** people who show medium degrees of extraversion and introversion.

Biological Determinism

Among psychologists, it would be difficult to find a more radical advocate of biological and genetic determinism than Eysenck. He always maintained that there is a "substantial" hereditary basis to personality (Eysenck, 1990). Over the years he has also contended that intelligence is genetically determined (Eysenck, 1971, 1974). He complained that psychology's avowed purpose is to study the behavior of organisms, but psychologists have failed to appreciate the degree to which organisms respond differently to the same environmental stimuli, independent of learning. "Personality is determined to a large extent by . . . genes; . . . while environment['s] influence is severely limited. [For] personality [and] intelligence . . . genetic influence is overwhelmingly strong, and the role of environment . . . is . . . slight (Eysenck, 1976, p. 20).

Eysenck (1990) estimated that, across all trait dimensions, including E, N, and P, about 60 percent of individual differences in personality is determined by the genes. He also indicated that E, N, and P are closely tied to physiology (Eysenck, 1967; Eysenck & Eysenck, 1969, 1976). To illustrate, extraversion (E) has been linked with the brain's **ascending reticular activating system** (ARAS), which acts as an arousal mechanism. The core of the system is the reticular formation of the brain's stem. When stimulated by sensory input, this formation sends messages through ascending nerve fibers to arouse the cerebral cortex, the brain's upper crust that coordinates the activities of lower brain areas. In turn, the entire organism is activated. Only if the sensory input originates in environmental events having survival value does the cortex send messages back down to the reticular formation telling it to continue promoting arousal. This feedback loop determines whether we *continue to attend to* given environmental events or not. Extraverts' nervous systems are held in check by their ARASs. They need and, thus, seek arousal. By contrast, introverts' ARASs promote excitation of their nervous systems. They do not need and, thus, avoid arousal. Eysenck linked neuroticism (N) to the limbic system, the brain's emotional center that regulates such functions as sex, fear, and aggression. Psychoticism (P) has been linked with the endocrine glands, specifically the ones that secrete sex hormones.

One source of support for Eysenck's (1990) genetic position is research involving genetically identical twins and fraternal twins who bear no more genetic similarity to one another than any two siblings. Because they are genetically identical any differences between identical twins is due to the environment. By the same token, any similarities are assumed to be due to the genes. In contrast, differences between fraternal twins may be due to either the genes or to the environment (Eysenck, 1967). Eysenck (1967, 1990) points to empirical findings that show identical twins to be much more alike in personality than fraternal twins, even when identical twins have been separated early in childhood and raised in separate environments. This sameness of identical twins' personalities is thought to be due to their genetic sameness. Also, he contended that identical twins are more alike in criminal and neurotic behavior than fraternal twins. Further, he asserted adopted children are more similar to their biological parents than to their adoptive parents on a number of trait dimensions.

Toward a Scientific Model of Personality

Eysenck's (1981) **scientific model for studying personality** involves two interlocking components: (1) *description,* which seeks to answer questions about "what" personality is, for example, what are the identifiable individual differences in traits and types?; and (2) *explanation,* which seeks to answer questions about "why" personality is the way it is, "What are the causes of those individual differences?" In Eysenck's model, concepts are sought that will help reduce human behavior to a few variables that are tied together by laws that should enable psychologists to explain past events and to predict future events.

Measuring and Describing E, N, and P

Reducing Observable Events to a Few Variables.   Like Cattell, Eysenck adheres to *subsidiation,* Murray's concept. Imagine a pyramid that has four levels representing the personality traits and responses falling under "extraversion." At the base of the pyramid are **specific responses (SR),** everyday behaviors or experiences that may or may not be characteristic of an individual, such as saying "Hi" to a neighbor. At the next level up are **habitual responses (HR),** specific responses (Cattell's surface traits) that recur under similar circumstances, such as *regularly* saying "Hi" to a neighbor. At the third level, habitual responses are organized into *primary factors,* or traits. For our extraversion example, these are sociability, impulsiveness, activity, liveliness, and excitability. Extraversion is at the top of the pyramid, the level of *secondary factors* or types. Thus, the four primary traits " . . . would form a constellation of traits intercorrelating amongst themselves and giving rise to a higher order construct, the type" (H. Eysenck & S. Eysenck, 1969, p. 41). Obviously, Cattell and Eysenck are very close on what is subsidiated to what, but Cattell emphasized primary factors and Eysenck second-order factors (see the pyramid in Figure 16.1, p. 387).

The MMQ, MPI, and EPQ.   The Maudsley Medical Questionnaire (MMQ) introduced the concept of neuroticism (N), the Maudsley Personality Inventory (MPI) added extraversion–introversion (E), and the Eysenck Personality Questionnaire (EPQ) added psychoticism (P) (Eysenck, 1952b, 1959; S. Eysenck & H. Eysenck, 1968, 1976). Using the MMQ, Eysenck found that 1,000 neurotic soldiers scored twice as high on N as 1,000 normal soldiers. N scores tend to decrease with age, to be higher for women than for men, and for persons in lower socioeconomic classes. High Ns are emotionally overresponsive and unstable, anxious, worrisome, moody, restless, touchy, often complain of bodily symptoms, and are prone to breakdown under stress. People with low N are emotionally stable, calm, carefree, even-tempered, and reliable.

The MPI included E as well as N items. In general, E scores tend to be higher for men than for women, to decrease with age, and to be unrelated to socioeconomic class. Persons with high E scores tend to be sociable, popular, talkative, craving excitement, taking chances, impulsive, practical jokers, easygoing, optimistic, on the move, short-tempered, poor at emotional control, and unreliable. Low E scorers (introverts) are retiring, fond of books, distant except to close friends, introspective, quiet, cautious, unimpulsive, serious, organized, reserved, pessimistic, ethical, imperturbable, controlling of feelings, and reliable. Box 16.3 contains a measure of N and E.

The EPQ added P items to those assessing N and E. Clinically "psychotic" people, especially schizophrenics, showed the highest P scores. Also high were criminals and others showing antisocial behavior. P scores tend to be higher for men, to be lower for middle-class people, and to decrease with age. People with high P scores are solitary, troublesome, uncooperative, hostile, cruel, unempathetic, sensation-seekers, like odd things, like films of war and horror, undervalue people, are socially withdrawn, sexually impersonal, deficient in thought and memory, distractible, devalue education, are suspicious, have mood disturbances, show motor disturbances, are suicidal, have psychotic relatives, are delusional, hallucinatory, and creative. The flavor of P is seen in Eysenck's (1970) description of a high P man, aged 21. When asked to explain his endorsement of the EPQ "liking parties" item, he answered, "Well, at parties you get free grub, free likker and a chance to screw some bird, don't you?" Then, with an angelic smile, he added, "And sometimes you can break up the place, too" (p. 427). The EPQ has recently been revised to fit

BOX 16.3 • *The Maudsley Personality Inventory (MPI), Short Form*

Instructions: The following questions pertain to the way people behave, feel, and act. Decide whether the items represent your *usual* way of acting or feeling, and circle either a "Yes" or "No" answer for each item. If you find it absolutely impossible to decide, circle the "?," but use this answer sparingly.

1. Do you prefer action to planning for action? YES ? NO
2. Do you sometimes feel happy, sometimes depressed, without any apparent reason? YES ? NO
3. Are you happiest when you get involved in some project that calls for rapid action? YES ? NO
4. Do you usually take the initiative in making new friends? YES ? NO
5. Are you inclined to be moody? YES ? NO
6. Would you rate yourself as a lively individual? YES ? NO
7. Are you frequently "lost in thought" even when supposed to be taking part in a conversation? YES ? NO
8. Do you have frequent ups and downs in mood, either with or without apparent cause? YES ? NO
9. Are you sometimes bubbling over with energy and sometimes very sluggish? YES ? NO

10. Are you inclined to be quick and sure in your actions? YES ? NO
11. Does your mind often wander while you are trying to concentrate? YES ? NO
12. Would you be very unhappy if you were prevented from making numerous social contacts? YES ? NO

(Adapted from H. Eysenck & S. Eysenck, 1969; used with permission of Hans Eysenck.)

Now try to group the items into two categories: put together the six items that seem to go together, then look at the other six items to see if they go together. If not, then categorize again until you come up with two sets of six items each that seem to measure two different types. When you finish, you have performed a crude factor analysis. Categorize now before going on.

If you grouped items 2, 5, 7, 8, 9, and 11 together and labeled them as N and items 1, 3, 4, 6, 10, and 12 as E, you have done well. Obviously, if you said "yes" to most N items, especially numbers 2 and 8, which are loaded .75 and .74 on neuroticism, you are "high on neuroticism" (but do not take it too seriously; a six-item test result is not to be trusted without further evidence). Just as obviously, if you indicated "yes" to E items, especially numbers 6 and 12, which are loaded .68 and .64 on extraversion, you are extraverted.

research result-data better (Petrides, Jackson, Furnham, & Levine, 2003). With this new version, the genders do not differ on E and N, but men score higher on P.

Before going on, take the MPI (Box 16.3).

Supporting Evidence

The Lemon Juice Test for Extraversion–introversion.   Eysenck contended that the more people's scores show them to be introverts (Is hereafter), the more strongly they should salivate to lemon juice, because Is have a higher level of cortical arousal through the ARAS than extraverts (Es hereafter; Corcoran, 1964; S. Eysenck & H. Eysenck, 1967).

Thus, "under conditions of equal stimulation, [the reaction of nerves in the muscles and glands] would be greater for introverts" (p. 1047). In fact, Is do salivate more than Es when pure lemon juice is placed on their tongues. They are hypersensitive to external stimulation, which they try to avoid because their ARASs are overactive.

Loud Commercials Are More Appealing to Es.   As everybody knows, commercials on TV and radio are played at a louder volume than the programs surrounding them. This strategy is assumed to overwhelm resistance to persuasion, thereby increasing the likelihood that listeners will purchase the advertised products. Cetola and Prinkey (1986) found that only Es favored commercials played at a louder volume than the preceding program. They actively seek the stimulation they lack due to their underactive ARASs. Louder volume did not matter for Is.

Drugs, Liquor, Coffee, and Tobacco.   Eysenck believed that depressant drugs, such as alcohol, will have a more detrimental effect on Es, because their ARASs already limit their arousal (1962). On the other hand, stimulants, such as coffee and cigarettes, will be more detrimental to Is, because their ARASs already allow them too much arousal. In partial support of the hypothesis, Jones (1974) reported that, although the detrimental effect of alcohol applied to Is and Es alike, it was significantly worse for Es. Gupta and Kaur (1978) showed that a stimulant, dextroamphetamine, improved the efficiency of Es but interfered with Is' performance on a perceptual judgment task.

Explaining Real-life Behavior: Mass Hysteria.   In 1965 a polio epidemic dominated press coverage of a town where a British secondary school was located, causing outsiders to avoid the "polio town." Later that year, an outbreak of physical symptoms occurred among girls attending the school (Moss & McEvedy, 1966). On day 1, students attended a lengthy church ceremony, during which 20 girls fainted. The next day, new fainting began to occur during school assemblies. Fainters rested on the floor, where the sight of them generated excitement and fear, resulting in overbreathing, dizziness, headache, feeling cold or hot, shivering, nausea, and faintness. Soon the behavior resumed spontaneously at school assemblies. Medical lab findings were negative. All 25 girls who fainted on day 1 and went to school on day 2 were affected, while none of the girls absent on day 1 were affected on day 2. Also, those still suffering on later days had been among those affected on early days. Consistent with the "mass hysteria" label, the number of new occurrences was higher during school assemblies than classroom sessions. The EPQ was given to 535 of the students and results showed that affected students were high on both E and N.

Extraversion: King of the Personality Concepts.   Extraversion (vs. introversion) may well be the most investigated and substantiated personality concept ever and Hans Eysenck is in large part responsible for its popularity and usefulness. Some recent example studies illustrate the importance of Eysenck's central concept.

The research literature links extraversion to psychological factors that have implications for people's well-being. Amirkhan, Risinger, and Swickert (1995) found extraversion to be positively related to "seeking social support" and optimism, two concepts known to be important in coping with stress. Magnus, Diener, Fujita, and Pavot (1993) found that extraversion predisposed research participants to experience positive life events. Robinson, Solberg, Vargas, and Tamir (2003) noted that extraversion predicts subjective well-being (SWB; happiness) but does so more strongly among people who take longer to distinguish between neutral and positive events (they confuse neutral for positive events, perceiving them as the same). Zelenski and Larsen (2002) found that extraversion and neuroticism measured by the EPQ were loaded on the same factor as "reward expectancy" and a scale measuring reward responsiveness, fun seeking, and drive. John Gabriel and Turhan Canli used functional magnetic resonance imaging of the brain to show that those high in extraversion react more strongly to positive relative to negative stimuli than those low in extraversion (Carpenter, 2001). In another personality-neuroscience study using the same imaging technique, Canli, Sivers, Whitfield, Gotlib, and Gabrieli (2002) found that activation of the emotional center *amygdala* in response to a face with a happy expression was more highly correlated with extraversion than all of the other Big 5 traits (see following discussion), was uncorrelated with neuroticism, and the relationship did not hold for angry, fearful, and sad expressions. David, Green, Martin, and Suls (1997) showed that introversion was negatively related to positive mood and positively related to negative mood, while extraversion was only positively related to positive mood. Lucus and Fujita (2000) correlated several measures of pleasant emotions with several measures of extraversion, including the EPQ, and found that the more extraverted were subjects the more highly pleasant were the emotions they displayed. Fleeson, Malanos, and Achille (2002) showed that participants were happier (SWB) when acting extraverted than when acting introverted.

Region of residence matters both in terms of differences among regions and average trends across regions. Knight (2003) reported that research supports stereotypes about U.S. regions: Midwesterners are more *agreeable, conscientious,* and *extroverted* than people in other regions. To round out the Big 5 (see the following discussion), Northeasterners are the most *neurotic* and Westerners and Northeasterners are the most *open to experience.* Lucus, Diener, and colleagues (2000) performed several studies involving subjects from many countries and found that, across studies and countries, extraversion was positively correlated with pleasant emotions. They argued that the core of extraversion is the tendency to approach rewarding stimuli. Thus, the tendency for extraversion to be associated with many forms of "positivity," including positive emotions, stems from extraverts' attraction to positively valenced stimuli (reward).

In a study related to Lucus, Diener, and colleagues, and for which SWB was measured at the national level, Steel and Ones (2002) found that neuroticism correlated significantly negatively with national SWB while extraversion correlated significantly positively with national SWB. Consistent with Lucus, Diener, and colleagues, and evolutionary theory, Campbell, Simpson, Stewart, and Manning (2003) found that extraverted men, who are known to be reward-sensitive, emerged as leaders of a group, but only if they were evaluated on leadership by a woman. They may have been showing off their leadership ability to the woman evaluator.

Ed Diener is probably the strongest contributor to the study of SWB. Martin E. P. Seligman is the guru of the "positive psychology" and optimism movements. Together they (2002) investigated the factors that contribute to SWB. Basically they compared very happy people with very unhappy people (there was a middle group that tended to be between the two extremes on most measures). Compared to very unhappy people, very happy people were higher on extraversion and on agreeableness as well as lower on neuroticism and other psychopathology measures. Very happy people also had more positive close relationships (friends, family, romantic) and experienced more positive feelings (but not at the ecstatic level). However, they did report occasional negative moods.

But extraversion's association with positivity and SWB are not its only advantages. Lieberman and Rosenthal (2001) hypothesized that extraverts are better than introverts at pursuing multiple goals simultaneously, which they called "multi-tasking." The more multi-tasking demands increased, the more extraversion was positively correlated with reaction times. Thus, the greater the multi-tasking demands, the more the following was true: the greater subjects' extraversion scores, the faster were their reactions. The researchers deemed their results to be in tune with Eysenck's ARAS theory of extraversion.

Eysenck's Last Word

In his final article, Eysenck laments the observation that, when research results produced by different studies disagree, researchers throw up their hands and go on to something else. If they looked further, they might discover that the different results were found because the studies probably involved different uncontrolled, extraneous variables (e.g., in one study subjects were made to be anxious; in a second study, they were induced to relax). New experiments controlling for the extraneous variables (e.g., subjects' anxiety level) would resolve the conflict between results and save the hypotheses. He also pleaded for a more theoretical orientation in which theory guides early experiments, then factor analysis is used to refine the early results. Next, do more experiments. Merely classifying traits and leaving it at that, as is done with factor analysis, will never allow personologists to support the claim that traits cause behavior.

Eysenck was number three on the journal citation list, unlisted on the textbook citation list, number 24 on the survey of psychologists, and number 13 on the overall list (Haggbloom et al., 2002).

Limitations

Arousal and the E-I

While there seems to be general agreement that Is are, on average, more sensitive to stimulation and react more negatively to it, this difference is being laid at the door of newly specified brain mechanisms, not the ARAS (Stelmack, 1990). Despite this development, some researchers continue to support Eysenck's ARAS theory (Bullock & Gilliland, 1993). Further, work by Gerald Matthews and his colleagues shows that the effect of extraversion on task performance is a complex function of several factors, including, surprisingly, the time of day at which a task is completed (Matthews, Davies, & Lees, 1990; Matthews,

Jones, & Chamberlain, 1989). Level of arousal (high or low) affects both Es and Is in the A.M., but in the P.M. only Is are affected by arousal level.

Lieberman and Rosenthal (2001) mention J. A. Gray's alternative to Eysenck's theory, which emphasizes emotional rather than sensory reactivity and virtually equates extraversion to impulsivity. They suggest that Gray's point of view—and those of other extraversion theorists—may have more explanatory power for some purposes than Eysenck's.

Genes and Controversy

Eysenck's work in behavior genetics is as suspect as Cattell's. Like Cattell, he has been scalded by some critics for applying heritability to differences between groups, such as "blacks" and "whites" (Hirsch, 1975). Furthermore, Eysenck's suggestion that personality factors are largely genetically determined is sometimes given no support or only qualified support by other researchers. For example, Loehlin, Horn, and Willerman (1990) found that the primary source of change in some personality factors, including extraversion, was *individual experience,* not the genes. However, consistent with the genetic hypothesis, they did find that with increased age children tended to change in the direction of their real parents' personalities.

It should be noted that Eysenck and Cattell are not being criticized for studying the genetics of behavior, personality, and intelligence. It would be absurd to suggest that the genes have nothing to do with these psychological entities (Hirsch, 1981). Undoubtedly, directly or indirectly, the genes play a role in all things psychological. The problem is that the heritability method used by psychologists artificially partitions the variation in a psychological trait into a portion accounted for by the genes and a portion accounted for by environment. Genes, and the environments in which they are expressed, are inextricably connected, so that their contributions to a trait cannot be completely separated. Psychologists need to become real geneticists, trained in biological laboratories, so they can do genetics as it traditionally has been done, with populations, not behaviors or cognitions (Azar, 2002, p. 45; Hirsch, 1964). Properly trained psychologists could directly assess the genetic underpinnings of psychological traits rather than relying solely on statistical approximations. In fact, such work is being done (Brunner, Nelen, & Breakefield, 1993; VandeWoude, Richt, Zink, Rott, Narayan, & Clements, 1990).

The Bell Curve: Race and Environment

Richard Herrnstein's and Charles Murray's *The Bell Curve* (1994) continues to cause waves on the academic pond. Critics from a variety of disciplines condemn its claim that intelligence is mostly due to the genes. Given that the claim is correct, Herrnstein and Murray assert that the intellectual elite will literally inherit the technological society of tomorrow. Herrnstein and Murray also point to an IQ gap favoring European Americans over African Americans and imply that it might be "inherited." As a prologue to their race/IQ discussion, they pledged to eschew use of *race,* because the term has uncertain status at best. But they continued to use *race* throughout their discussion anyway, thereby opening themselves up to some serious criticisms.

Problems with comparing "whites" and "blacks" on IQ begin with those racial designations (Allen, 2002, 2003; Allen & Adams, 1992; Katz, 1995; Montague, 1997; Weizmann et al., 1990; Yee, Fairchild, Weizmann, & Wyatt, 1993). One can hardly meaningfully compare two groups on anything if experts cannot agree on the criteria for separating people into the two groups. Even if there were a consensus on criteria for dividing people into racial groups, how would one show that a racial gap on IQ was "inherited"? The heritability index could not be used, because it is applicable to a single population, not comparisons of two populations. In short, "Is a 'black'–'white' IQ gap inherited?" is a bogus question. Further, that "races" exist at the most basic level, genetic differences among racial groups, has not been established (Allen, 2002, 2003; Cavali-Sforza, 2000; Cavali-Sforza et al., 1994). To put it another way, there is no scientific support for "races."

There is a way to finesse the debate on whether intelligence—which is probably much more than IQ—is "genetically determined." That environmental interventions can change the expression of genetically "determined" traits is as certain as the observation that medical science can prevent the occurrence of genetically "determined" diseases, genetically determined deformities can be reversed with plastic surgery, and genetically scrawny people can become strong via weight lifting. Even if intelligence were totally "genetic," genetic input may be eclipsed by early exposure to enriched environments. It has long been known that animals bred to be "bright" and other animals bred to be "dull" turn out equally highly intelligent when reared from birth in an enriched environment (e.g., a sort of animal Disney World: a very complex environment; see, for example, Cooper & Zubek, 1958). In recent years, William T. Greenough and his colleagues have shown that enrichment actually increases the complexity of nerve cells' branches, thus providing an explanation of the enrichment effect on animal intelligence (e.g., Greenough, Black, & Wallace, 1987). What about humans? In recent years, Craig T. Ramey and his colleagues exposed children, for whom the genetic prediction would be low intelligence, to environmental enrichment beginning in infancy. In one study, exposed children showed dramatically higher intelligence test scores relative to comparable children provided no early enrichment (Campbell & Ramey, 1994). Further, they maintained their advantage to age 12, when the research ended. Current research is revealing environmental effects on intelligence that range from prenatal experience (Devlin, Daniels, & Roeder, 1997) to school experience (Neisser et al., 1996). Devlin and colleagues found that, when the prenatal womb environment is factored in, heritability estimates drop dramatically. Genetic "anatomy" is not necessarily intellectual destiny. To his credit, late in his life Eysenck acknowledged the validity of this observation (*Monitor,* 1993).

Big 5 or Big 3 (or Big 16)?

Finally, Eysenck, in effect, has shrunk personality to just three dimensions, which are "second order" but match other's primary dimensions, and thus may not be genuine types. While many trait theorists have reduced personality to just five dimensions, virtually no one agrees with Eysenck's smaller number (see the *American Psychologist,* Comments,

Dec., 1993). The five are Conscientiousness, Agreeableness, Neuroticism (Emotional Stability), Openness to Experience, and Extraversion (CANOE; Guastello, 1993; Kroger &
Wood, 1993). But are five enough or are sixteen really required? Eysenck (1993) sees conscientiousness and agreeableness as collapsible into Psychoticism. Thus, it is three after
all. But Big 5 advocates (e.g., Goldberg, 1993) could just as easily argue that Psychoticism is merely a confounding of conscientiousness and agreeableness. So we are back to
five. On the other hand, Cattell has matched the Big 5 to five of his eight second-order
factors (Cattell, 1993; Guastello, 1993). However, we have already seen that Cattell
(1994) believes that his sixteen primaries have more predictive power.

The Big 5 has all the problems outlined in Box 12.2 (p. 281): it can only be used to
describe observations after they occur, and, therefore, is not a genuine theory. But don't
count it out yet. Srivastava, John, Goslin, and Potter (2003) have shown that the Big 5
might be made more flexible, which would give it some predictive power. They have shown
that rather than people's positions on the Big 5 dimensions being written in stone, people
change on C, A, and N throughout most of adulthood. All participants increased in C and
A to varying degrees during early and middle adulthood. Women declined in N during
adulthood. These changes were thought to be due to a variety of developmental influences.
So where does all this leave us? Perhaps we should entertain the possibility that personality is much too complex to be characterized by three, five, or even sixteen factors
(Shadel & Cervone, 1993).

Conclusions

Hans Eysenck should be a model for other trait psychologists in that he is one of the few
who uses the experimental method consistently, and the only major theorist to do so. It is
almost as if others are afraid to use experimentation lest they find that their "stable" traits
do not remain stable when subjected to experimental manipulations. While Eysenck's work
with extraversion has been qualified, it has made the concept one of the most important in
the personality field. Jung conceived of extraversion, but Eysenck showed that it intrudes
on many aspects of human functioning. Eysenck was number three on the journal list, omitted from the text list, number 24 in the survey, and number 13 overall (Haggbloom et al.,
2002).

Summary Points

1. Cattell was English-born, the son of middle-class parents. After graduating with
honors from London University, he chose psychology over chemistry. Following some
"fringe jobs," he finally ended up with E. L. Thorndike in the United States. From there
he went to several prestigious jobs. He was involved with the eugenics movement. Cattell follows the inductive-hypothetico-deductive spiral. $R = f(S.P)$ expresses his belief that
both personality and environment contribute to responses. Factor analysis, his technique

of choice, extracts primary and secondary factors and specifies loadings of items on these factors.

2. Cattell emphasizes common traits. Traits are subsidiated under one another as follows: second-order traits; source or primary traits (ability, temperament, and dynamic: attitudes, sentiments, ergs); and surface traits. He believes that his 16 primaries are better predictors than second-order traits. He believed that intelligence is largely inherited and is subdivided into fluid and crystallized forms. Cattell's lifelong project, the 16 PF, includes 16 trait dimensions. Its uses range from personnel selection, through academic achievement to clinical diagnosis. Cattell has produced tests for many purposes.

3. Factor analysis involves often arbitrary choices between several different procedures. Data sources are subjectively selected and so are criteria for deciding magnitude of loadings and factor labeling. Heritability is applicable to a single population, not to other populations or to group differences. Heritability inappropriately separates genetic and environmental input. Researchers are abandoning the search for genes underlying personality because too many genes are involved. The same criticisms of statistical methods to specify the genetic contribution to g apply to the same pursuits regarding personality traits. Research on the null version of the MAOA gene and violence proneness shows that environment (presence or absence of maltreatment) determines the gene's expression.

4. Rapid, worldwide IQ increases cannot be explained by genetic determinism and is a problem for fluid g. The 16 PF has had limited success. Research shows that when socioeconomic status is low, environment replaces genetics as the determinate of intelligence. The Flynn Effect in Kenya generated a 26-point increase in g_f in only 14 years. Intelligence may be more than "g" (Sternberg and Gardner list three and seven intelligences, respectively). EQ may be yet another form of intelligence. New research shows that EQ can be measured reliably and is distinct from other psychological factors. Contrary to Cattell, intelligence may be regarded as relative to sociophysical environment. Finally, Cattell's involvement with eugenics through his Beyondism movement and its racist orientation caused the loss of a prestigious award late in his life. Eugenics involving groups is indefensible.

5. Eysenck, born in Germany, was a strong-willed child. After fleeing the Nazis, he earned a Ph.D. in London. He believed that personality is more than adequately encapsulated by three second-order factors and that factor analysis should be used to confirm theory, not generate it.

6. He did real experiments and used concepts from experimental psychology and physiology. His "Big 3" are extraversion–introversion (E), neuroticism–stability (N), and psychoticism–superego functioning (P). Extraversion is linked to the ARAS. His scientific model for studying personality has two components: description and explanation.

7. His basic methods are sophisticated statistical techniques and objective questionnaires. He subsidiates specific responses and habitual responses to primary and secondary factors. People who score high on E are impulsive, optimistic, sociable, and rather unreliable. High Is are the opposite. High Ns are unstable, anxious, worrisome, and moody. High Ps are solitary, troublesome, hostile, cruel, drawn to oddities, sexually impersonal, and distractible.

8. Is react to stimulation more readily than Es. Is salivate more to lemon juice, are deterred by stimulants, and react less strongly to alcohol. Mass hysteria may be explained by high E and N scores. Modern work ties extraversion to "positivity" such as positive emotions and stronger amygdaloid reactions to happy faces among extraverted people. Extraversion has now been directly related to happiness. Es excel at multi-tasking.

9. Attraction to rewarding stimuli may be at its core. Extraversion has been related to nation's happiness, and along with other Big 5 traits, to U.S. regions. In his last article Eysenck argued that theory and experimentation must be emphasized over correlational methods (factor analysis) and be integrated with them. Eysenck's postulations about heredity have been, at best, partially supported, and his assumptions about the ARAS have not been fully supported: the relation of E-I to arousal may be complicated and indirect.

10. Rival theories, such as Gray's, may have as much explanatory power. *The Bell Curve* agrees with Eysenck: IQ is mostly inherited. But it errs in phrasing the question, "Is a 'Black'–'White' IQ gap inherited?" The whole notion of race has been questioned. In addition, it ignores strong evidence that early enrichment may overwhelm genetic input. The argument over three or five personality dimensions may miss the point: even 16 does not do justice to the complexity of personality. The rival to Eysenck's 3 factors and Cattell's 16 is the Big 5. It has all the problems outlined in Box 12.2 and is not a real theory. However, attempts to make it more flexible may save it. Eysenck's extraversion work is a major contribution.

Running Comparison

Theorists	Cattell in Comparison
Freud	He used many Freudian concepts.
Skinner	Like Skinner he began with raw observations, the empirical approach.
Murray	He borrowed Murray's subsidiation.
Maslow	Dynamic traits are like Maslow's goal direction.

Theorist	Eysenck in Comparison
Cattell	Both were concerned about the number of traits accounting for personality.
Skinner	Both did lab research.
Jung	He revised Jung's extraversion.
Murray	He borrowed Murray's subsidiation.

Essay/Critical Thinking Questions _____

1. Can you defend eugenics?

2. Argue in support of Pete Rose's admittance to baseball's Hall of Fame.

3. How many intelligences are there? Can you name some not mentioned in the text?

4. Categorize the 16 PF traits into temperament, ability, and dynamic classes.

5. Look at the list of traits attributed to high E, N, and P individuals. Can you see any overlap?

E-mail Interaction _____

Write the author at b-allen@wiu.edu. Forward one of the following or phrase your own.

1. Was Cattell a member of the radical right?

2. Give me a shortcut to understanding Cattell's theory.

3. How many trait dimensions are there: three, five, or sixteen?

Personality Development and Prejudice: Gordon Allport

- Which is most admirable, confidence bordering on arrogance or true humility?
- Why do we value a good sense of humor?
- Are being "prejudiced," being a "racist," and harboring "racism" the same?

Gordon Allport
http://inside.salve.edu/
walsh/allport_3.html

Gordon Allport is at least the equal of trait theorists Cattell and Eysenck, but he was a different person with a different style. As a person, Allport preached and practiced humility (Allport, 1967). As a theorist, his point of view was broad and open, encompassing the ideas of other theorists and including room for change. Further, Allport, like Kelly, took the hard road to understanding personality. Rather than assume that all people can be fitted to a small number of trait dimensions, he believed that each person is unique, distinguished from others by her or his own peculiar traits. Finally, the breadth of Allport's theoretical interests exceeds that of most personality theorists. His concern for social problems led him to study diverse topics ranging from people's senses of humor to prejudice. By careful consideration of his groundbreaking work, you will be able to gain significant insight into personality development, maturity, and prejudiced thinking.

Allport, the Person

Gordon Willard Allport was born November 11, 1897 in Montezuma, Indiana, the last of three sons (Allport, 1967). While Allport's father, a physician, was "pure English," his mother, a school teacher, was a mixture of German and Scottish (p. 4). Allport's versatile father was in business before becoming a doctor and eventually combined medicine with business.

Like the atmosphere in which Rogers was reared, Allport's home life was character-ized by warmth as well as "Protestant piety and hard work" (p. 4). His father's motto was, "If every person worked very hard and took only the minimum financial return required by family needs, there would be just enough wealth to go around." This "broad humanitarian outlook" dictated a philanthropic orientation that was adopted by the entire family. Because his father lacked adequate hospital facilities, the Allport house became a hospital and fam-ily members its staff. Gordon recalled tending to office work, washing bottles, and inter-acting with patients. Just as his family's interactions were virtually free of strife, Allport's relations with others were unburdened by conflict. He was able to work successfully with a wide variety of people, including students who relished the friendly exchange of ideas that occurred in his graduate seminars. Just as he refused to engage in verbal combat with Murray he sought common ground when interacting with others.

As a young adult, Allport tried to replace his more fundamental religious beliefs with a broader humanitarian religion. In the midst of trying on one religious garb or another, and failing to find a good fit, he remarked on the essentials of any global view that he might adopt: "Humility . . . [was] indispensable for me" (p. 7). Being the baby of the family con-tributed to his sense of humility. His older brothers were largely successful, especially Floyd, a Harvard-educated experimental psychologist in whose footsteps Gordon was destined to tread. Throughout his life, humility was manifested in frequent self-effacing re-marks. Regarding being second in his high school class of 100, he commented, "Apparently I was a good routine student, but definitely uninspired" (p. 5). When he first had the op-portunity to perform volunteer social service, he found it "deeply satisfying, partly because it gave me a feeling of competence (to offset a generalized inferiority feeling)" (pp. 6–7). Just before his death in 1967, as he was ruminating about his possible contributions, he ex-pressed surprise at the numerous honors he received. Only his favorite was deemed worthy of mention: his former students gave him two volumes of their own writings inscribed, "From his students—in appreciation of his respect for their individuality" (p. 24).

After Gordon graduated from high school in 1915, he considered Harvard. With characteristic modesty, Gordon remembered "squeezing through the entrance tests" (p. 5). Despite initial experiences that were no better than Murray's, Kelly's, and Maslow's, he was attracted to psychology. Like Murray, his first psychology teacher was Munsterberg, whose appearance reminded Allport of Wotan, the god of war to whom Jung had alluded. He got no more out of the beginning class than the other three, but he was not discouraged. Neither did he falter when hostilely confronted by the professor who nearly turned Maslow away from psychology, E. B. Titchener. This relic from psychology's early years demanded that Allport describe his dissertation project then glared at him as he complied. Later, Titch-ener groused to one of Allport's advisors, "Why did you let him work on [a personality] problem?" (p. 9). During this period, a mischievous young Allport danced, drank "hootch," and made fun of stodgy people like Titchener and mental tester Charles Spearman (Baren-baum, 2003).

Allport took courses from many of the famous psychologists of the day, but soci-ology and social ethics also fascinated him. After a brief hitch in the Students' Army

Training Corps during World War I, he returned to college full-time. Initially, he pursued social ethics by volunteering to work in various social service capacities (e.g., the Humane Society). In his junior year, he wrote a magazine piece on the legend of former Harvard student John B. G. Rinehart (Winter, 1996, 1997). Allport addressed some doubts about Rinehart. Was he a manipulator? Allegedly, he yelled his own name from below his dorm room and then ran back to his room to answer, making it appear that he was a known person. Whatever Rinehart's real character, Allport reinterpreted the admittedly ambiguous facts about the Rinehart case, projecting his own benevolence onto Rinehart. But the most famous of Allport's two life history cases (see Barenbaum, 1997) was "Jenny," the mother of his college roommate, "Ross" (Allport, 1965). It seems that Jenny virtually adopted young Gordon and his wife Ada in preference to her own son, whom she condemned as a "contemptible cur" (Winter, 1997, p. 727). Allport came to regard Jenny and her family as an exception to the rule that most families function well.

After finishing his undergraduate studies in 1919, Allport took a one-year job teaching English and sociology at Robert College in ancient Constantinople, Turkey. Near the end of his stay, he received notice of his acceptance into Harvard's psychology graduate program. Perhaps to celebrate his new status, on the way home he stopped off in Vienna to visit Freud. With youthful audacity that later would embarrass him, Allport announced to Freud "that I was in Vienna and implied that no doubt he would be glad to make my acquaintance" (p. 7).

Freud sent a reply "in his own handwriting inviting me to come to his office at a certain time" (p. 7). Entering Freud's office, Allport looked in wonder at the "red burlap room with pictures of dreams on the wall" (pp. 7–8). But, to Allport's dismay, the "master" stood by mute while his young visitor gawked at the famous artifacts. Finding the silence awkward, Allport began to comment on the apparent dirt phobia of a boy he encountered on the tram he rode to Freud's address. The child repeatedly complained to his mother about the "dirty man" beside whom he was forced to sit. The stern and dominant demeanor of the mother provided Allport with a ready explanation for the boy's problem. True to form, "Freud fixed his kindly therapeutic eyes" on young Allport and queried, "And was that little boy you?" (p. 8). Allport was "flabbergasted" but, at the same time, was "guilty" and "amused" that Freud had "misunderstood" his reasons for telling the story. He believed the therapist in Freud was probing for defenses to overcome and completely missed the "rude curiosity and youthful ambition" that were the actual motivations behind the dirt-phobia story (p. 8).

Allport did very well in Harvard's psychology graduate program and found it rather easy, but, as usual, he lamented his imagined academic shortcomings. After only two years of course work, he received his doctorate in 1922 at the age of 24. His dissertation, *An Experimental Study of the Traits of Personality: With Special Reference to the Problem of Social Diagnosis* was probably the first major thesis on personality done in the United States.

After a fellowship in Europe, including exposure to the Gestalt view, he took a temporary lectureship in social ethics at Harvard (1924) where he taught the first college course on personality (Nicholson, 1997). When offered a permanent position in social psychology, he quickly accepted. By the end of the 1930s, Allport completed his first book on personality (1937) and was elected President of the American Psychological Association (1939). During World War II he advised the government on morale and on "rumors." He also offered advice on the causes of war and methods for maintaining a lasting peace. In

The actual couch used by Freud in the psychoanalysis of many notables

1954, he published his famous book on prejudice. A year and a half before his death in 1967, Allport was awarded an endowed chair in social ethics.

With typical modesty, Allport devoted considerable space to detailing his many efforts in the interest of charities and social welfare. A self-proclaimed "social reformer," he never missed an opportunity to condemn oppression and to praise social consciousness. He was the epitome of the Renaissance man. No other theorist covered in this book was on the cutting edge of so many new movements or involved in such a diversity of academic pursuits.

Allport's View of the Person

Humanism?

Allport's warmth and social consciousness suggest a humanistic orientation. He occasionally referred to himself as a humanist, authored a 1955 book partially entitled *Becoming,* and has been credited with coining the phrase "humanistic psychology" (DeCarvalho, 1991). Consequently, it is clear that he was a humanist at the personal level, but not on a professional level. Humanism is not even entered in *Becoming*'s index. He was concerned about the self, but not other humanistic concepts. Thus, his point of view was not mainstream humanism. Box 17.1 contains his views on existentialism, a major pillar of humanism.

BOX 17.1 • *Allport on Existentialism, Humanism, Phenomenology, and Death*

In the same book by Rollo May (1969) containing comments on *Existential Psychology* by Rogers and Maslow, Allport provided some of his own observations (Allport, 1969). He, like Rogers, took a dim view of the dark and dismal outlook of some European existentialists. Resignation and acceptance of anxiety, despair, and death were not seen as healthy points of view. Instead, Allport praised the more optimistic client-centered, growth, and self-actualized orientations of humanism. He even chastised May for partially adopting the gloomy Freudian perspective. As an alternative he offered a more cognitive inclination that looks at patients, such as May's Mrs. Hutchens, as victims of distorted thinking that could be corrected. But he praised existential therapists' tendency to emphasize the client's phenomenology at the beginning of therapy and suggested that it might be extended to all of therapy. Phenomenology offers a way to discover distorted thinking and opportunities for revising it.

Despite several reservations, Allport had many kind words for existentialism. He agreed with Maslow that "Existentialism deepens the concepts that define the human condition" (p. 94). This broad focus contrasts with psychology's piecemeal approach that fails to construct a unified picture of the person. Existentialism can help psychologists paint a picture of a whole person.

While existentialism may dwell too much on death, psychology has too little to say about it. Though he condemned Freud's Thanatos, which implies that we actively seek death, he acknowledged that existentialism has legitimized the consideration of death. But he goes on to suggest that existentialism, as well as psychology, would profit by viewing death through the prism of religion. For reasons that you will soon appreciate, he predicted that people who embrace religion because it is useful to them will be more afraid of death than those who genuinely adopt the principles of their religion.

Emphasis on Unique Traits and Behavioral Variability

Allport was a pioneer in the study of personality traits, but he was a maverick among trait theorists (Allport, 1966; Zuroff, 1986). Whereas Cattell and Eysenck emphasized common traits at the expense of unique traits, Allport did the opposite (Allport, 1966, 1967). Like Kelly, he preferred to look at people one at a time and found that a given person's traits were generally not applicable to other people. This orientation was in sharp contrast to that of Cattell and Eysenck, who were **nomothetic theorists,** inclined to derive general laws concerning how a few traits apply to all people. By contrast, Allport was an **Idiographic theorist,** inclined to study each individual's unique traits without attempting to find a place for each along a small number of trait dimensions. The idiographic approach, although still a minority orientation, is gaining advocates. For example, Pelham (1993) argued that the idiographic strategy provides greater predictive power. Ironically, it also allows for insights into universal patterns of human behavior (an example is, "all humans have anxiety that each expresses uniquely").

Cross-situational behavioral consistency, so dear to the hearts of typical trait theorists, was a matter of less concern to Allport (Allport, 1966; Zuroff, 1986). He would have agreed with Aldous Huxley, "The only completely consistent people are dead," with Ralph Waldo Emerson that " . . . consistency is the hobgoblin of little minds," with Oliver Wendell Holmes

Sr., "Don't be 'consistent,' but be simply 'true,' " and with American artist John Sloan, "Consistency is the quality of a stagnant mind." He believed that "behavior in different situations was often inconsistent, even contradictory, because different traits are aroused to different degrees in different situations" (Zuroff, 1986, p. 993). Allport was an early interactionist who wrote that variability of behavior across situations is meaningful, not error, and that a given trait is activated only in a certain situation or class of situations (Zuroff, 1986).

De-emphasizing the Freudian Unconscious

The visit with Freud convinced Allport that "depth psychology . . . may plunge too deep" (Allport, 1967, p. 8). Much to the irritation of Murray, he felt that psychologists would do well to look for overt motivations, rather than immediately probe the dark depths of the unconscious. Allport was often critical of psychoanalysis, even parting company with his own brother when one of Floyd's books was deemed "too psychoanalytic for my taste" (p. 8).

Basic Concepts: Allport

Personality Defined

According to Allport, **personality** "is the *dynamic organization* within the individual of those *psychophysical* systems that *determine his characteristic behavior and thought*" (1961, p. 29). *Dynamic organization* referred to the interplay of forces within an integrated system with tightly connected components. Activation of one component of the system activates others in an orderly fashion. A personality springs into integrated activity much like an orchestra: the conductor waves her baton signaling the violinists to play; when they sound a certain note, the drums begin to roll and so forth until all the components of the orchestra are active. The term *psychophysical* simply "reminds us that personality is neither exclusively mental nor . . . neural (physical)." The word *determine* refers to the fact that the "personality is something that does something" (p. 29). In *his characteristic behavior and thought,* use of the singular pronoun and the word *characteristic* in reference to "behavior and thought" reminds us that action and cognition are unique to a particular person.

Traits

Definition of Traits.   In Allport's view, a **trait** "is a neuropsychic structure having the capacity to render many stimuli functionally equivalent, and to initiate and guide equivalent . . . forms of adaptive and expressive behavior" (p. 347). In more straightforward terms, a trait "guides" a person to respond to similar (but not identical) elements of the environment (stimuli) in much the same way. "Hostile person" is a stimulus belonging to a category of stimuli that has members that may take on different forms—different people are hostile in different ways. But, whatever the forms, similar responses are called for

BOX 17.2 • *The Adjective Generation Technique: A Method Inspired by Allport*

In several of this book's exercises you were asked to produce words to describe someone. This Adjective Generation Technique (AGT), first used in 1969, was developed by Charles Potkay and me (Allen & Potkay, 1983a; Potkay & Allen, 1988). The original idea for the AGT came from an Allport (1961) classroom demonstration. A stranger walked into his classroom, gave a short ambiguous speech and left. Allport then asked students to describe the stranger, "Allport . . . just look[ed] at the words to get a general qualitative idea of the kind of impression the visitor had made on class members" (Allen & Potkay, 1983a, p. 3). He did not score the words in any way. Students generated the words, rather than checking words on a list or points on a dimension, either of which might be more a reflection of the assessor's orientation than the students'. They could use any descriptive words in their vocabularies. Further, they were unlikely to paint an ingratiating picture of themselves, because they performed anonymously and had no idea whether their words would be scored in any way.

Unlike Allport, Potkay and I have often scored the words. Words could simply be counted to see how many are produced when people generate as many as they desire. This method tells assessors how prominent the target of descriptions was in the minds of describers: the more words, the more prominent. Words also might be categorized and their frequency in each category compiled. In one study, words most used to describe "good teachers" versus "poor teachers" were compared: good teachers were *intelligent, clear,* and *humorous,* while poor teachers were *boring, dull,* but *knowledgeable* (see M. Ward in Allen & Potkay, 1983a). In addition, each of nearly 2,200

words has been assigned a value indicating degree of FAVorability (the desirability of a word attributed to someone), ANXiety (the amount of anxiety connoted by a word attributed to someone), and FEMininity (the femininity vs. masculinity of a word attributed to someone). When people describe themselves, one can assess how FAVorable their descriptions are, how much ANXiety descriptions reflect, and how FEMinine are the describers.

Daily Log Sheet

Date: _____

Write down five (5) words to describe yourself. Use only single words that can be found in the dictionary, no sentences or phrases.

_____

_____

_____

_____

_____

Briefly write down what happened to you that you regard as significant.

_____

The AGT can be used to get to know yourself better. Make 30 copies of the "Daily Log Sheet" and describe yourself for thirty days as well as what happened to you each day. Do it at the end of each day. It takes only a few minutes. Just looking at the words will show you how you are evolving over days and how "what happens to you" affects your view of yourself.

within a given *environmental context.* If the context is a formal party and the hostile person is a guest, the appropriate response would be to calm the person. On the other hand, Allport asserted that a different context would call forth a different response to functionally equivalent stimuli: in a nursery school context, regardless of which child is hostile to other children, physical restraint may be called for.

Allport proposed eight characteristics of traits. First, he believed that traits *do exist* in people. Second, traits are *more generalized than habits.* Third, traits *may determine behavior.* Fourth, traits' existence may be established by *systematic observation.* Fifth, traits are only *relatively independent of each other.* Sixth, traits are *not matters of moral functioning* (they are not to be confused with "character"). Seventh, *inconsistencies are real,* but do not mean traits are nonexistent. Behavior related to "kindness" may be inconsistent across situations because only some situations call forth "kindness." Inconsistency may also be apparent because different behaviors may reflect "kindness" under different circumstances, even within the same context (sometimes you have to be cruel to be kind).

Eighth, traits may be considered *in relation to the rest of the population* or *in relation to the rest of the possessor's personality.* **Common traits** "are . . . those aspects of personality in respect to which most people within a given culture can be profitably compared" (Allport, 1961, p. 340). Obviously, Cattell and Allport agreed on the meaning of *common trait.* But Allport's de-emphasis of common traits is apparent in the reference he made to them while derogating "dimensionalism": he condemned distributing everyone along each of a few common trait dimensions. To Allport, a **personal disposition (p.d.)** is a trait that is unique to a particular individual. P.d. means approximately the same thing as Cattell's "unique trait." In his 1961 book, Allport is careful to use "common traits" in reference to traits that all people have, but possess in varying degrees, and p.d. when referring to traits that are unique to particular persons. *Conscientiousness* has universal meaning when used in reference to a trait possessed by many, but has specific meaning when used in reference to a trait possessed by a particular person (John's conscientiousness applies to his job as a mail carrier and to his role as father of seven children). Oddly, by the time he wrote his seminal 1966 paper, Allport had lapsed into using *trait* to refer to both.

Using *trait* in reference to both "common traits" and "p.d." raises a perplexing question: how can *trait* refer to two things at once? The puzzle becomes an enigma when Allport acknowledges that the same labels may be used for both common traits and p.d.s. A person can somehow be uniquely "conscientious," yet, all people can be placed on the "conscientiousness" dimension. Allport attempted to resolve this paradox by indicating that a trait label has a different *flavor* when referring to a particular person than when the reference is to people generally. For example, most people can be cast as reflecting some degree of *anxiousness:* "Little Susan has a peculiar anxious helpfulness all her own" (Allport, 1961, p. 359). Notice that more words are needed to describe "Susan's" trait than the single word *anxious,* which suffices to describe what most people display to some degree. "Anxiousness" must be qualified when applied to a particular person. Not surprisingly, Allport believed that trait labels fit common traits more readily than p.d.s.

Cardinal, Central, and Secondary p.d.s

P.d.s can vary in terms of how close they are to the core of an individual's personality. A **cardinal p.d.** is pervasive and outstanding in the life of a person. A word referring to a cardinal p.d. is often our choice as an overall description of a person. Names of historical or fictional characters are often used in reference to cardinal traits: quixotic, narcissistic, sadistic, Emersonian, Falstaffian, or Faustian. More common terms may also refer to cardinal p.d.s: flaky, saintly, sober, realistic, immoral, and obnoxious. A **central p.d.** is one of the entries on the relatively large list of traits we use to summarize an individual's personality. We list central p.d.s when we write a person a letter of recommendation. So-and-so is meticulous, thoughtful, even-tempered, and generous but shy and moody. Even farther removed from the core of personality are **secondary p.d.s,** dispositions that are "less conspicuous, less generalized, less consistent, . . . less often called into play . . . [and] more peripheral" (Allport, 1961, p. 365). Therefore, a person may be sporadically helpful, intermittently humorous, and occasionally melodramatic, thereby displaying secondary p.d.s. Unfortunately, any term might be used in reference to any of the three types of p.d.s and there is no distinct dividing line between one kind of p.d. and the next.

Personality Development

The Proprium and the Seven Stages of the Developing Self

Allport (1961) devotes a chapter to what he calls "sense of self," formally labelled the **proprium,** "me as felt and known . . . the self as 'object' of knowledge and feeling" (p. 127). But "Why not simply [use] the term *self* . . ." as usually defined (p. 127)? He answered: "This chapter has been devoted to the sense of selfhood, not the nature of selfhood. Our discussion . . . is primarily psychological, not philosophical . . . it is much easier to feel the self than to define [it]" (p. 137).

Early Infancy.   **Early infancy,** the first stage, involves no sense of self. Infants initially are unable to separate themselves from their environment. They are conscious, but not self-conscious. If an infant picks up an object, the fingers and the object are one and the same. If she hurts her own foot she has no idea that it is *she* who inflicted the pain. She melts into Mother and they become fused. Later, as motor skills help the infant work out of this early phase, she crawls about and bumps into objects. In this way, she learns about "other world" objects that are apart from her body, but she does not yet know she is apart from that other world.

Bodily Self.   The most primitive predecessor of selfhood emerges during the second part of the first year. Infants display signs of **bodily self,** sensations that emanate from the muscles, joints, tendons, eyes, ears, and so on. Children experience frustrations relating to the body, such as a stubbed toe or hunger. These also contribute to appreciation of the bodily self, which becomes the foundation of selfhood and remains with us forever. However, it is noticed only under unusual conditions. To appreciate how all your bodily parts and elements are "you," contrast swallowing your own saliva with spitting it into a cup and drinking it. Your saliva is a part of you that you take for granted until it becomes physically separated from your body, then it is alien.

Self-Identity.   Emerging at age two, Allport's third stage is **self-identity,** the continuity of self over past, present, and future that results from the operation of memory. "Today I remember some of my thoughts of yesterday, and tomorrow I shall remember some of my thoughts of both yesterday and today; and I am certain that they are the thoughts of the same person—of myself" (p. 114). Because we all are changing over time, even as adults, this feeling of continuity is essential to a sense of self. The learning of language underlies appreciation of continuity. Words are what one remembers that assure him he is the same person today as yesterday. Most important is the child's name, a word that serves as an anchor to which the ship of self-identity is tied. Each time "Johnny" hears his name—as in "Good Johnny!"—his feeling of self-identity is strengthened.

Self-esteem. Bodily self is the cornerstone of selfhood, and self-identity its framework. **Self-esteem** is pride in one's pursuits and accomplishments. It is the walls and the roof of the self. During the third year, Allport's fourth stage, one of the child's favorite exclamations is "Let me!" "Me" has evolved beyond being only a body and a sense of continuity to a feeling of instrumentality, the ability to successfully manipulate the environment. "I can do it" implies "I am what I am able to do; don't diminish me by doing for me." This prideful insistence on doing for oneself is matched by shame at having others do for one. Born with self-esteem is its fraternal twin, negativism. Allport writes of a child whose first words on arriving at his grandmother's were "Grandmother, I won't." "Reverse psychology" may well have been inspired originally by this negativism: Mother exclaims, "I don't want you to eat your broccoli, it's bad for you."

Extension of Self. Senses of body, of continuity, and of pride are a great part of our self-structure, but do not include the most important elements of the environment, other people. During Allport's fifth stage (4 to 6 years), the child develops a fourth aspect of selfhood, an egocentric component. Children think that Santa Claus and even God are there to serve them. However, this self-focus contains an advancement. "He" becomes not merely himself, but is extended to include all that he "possesses." It is "his dog, his house, his sister." This **extension of self** is expanding oneself to include all those significant aspects of one's environment, including people. Now, family and self are one. They are like an external conscience that may turn on the child should he fail.

Self-image. Associated with this fledgling relationship to others is a fugitive fifth aspect of self that also emerges during the fifth stage. The **self-image** is composed of the hopes and aspirations that develop from the perceptions and expectations that others have of oneself. Parents say the child is "good" or "naughty." Peers say that she is "smart" or "fat." She must do this, do that, be this, be that—whatever others expect. To discover whether she is living up to her developing self-image, she will compare others' expectations of how she should behave with her actual behavior.

Rational Coper. During the sixth stage (6 to 12 years), the self-image continues to develop, and a new aspect emerges: **rational coper,** the sense of selfhood that is not merely able to solve problems, but also can reason them through "in the head" and come up with logical solutions. The rational coper is much like Freud's "ego." It tries to efficiently satisfy the demands of the body (id), society (superego), and the external environment. As the rational coper develops, children become able to think about thinking.

Propriate Striving.   During the seventh stage, adolescence, the individual continues to develop the self-image and experiences a renewed search for self-identity. Now self-identity
focuses on tying together the teenager and the would-be adult. A teen may ask, "How can I
be an adult and still be me?" Continuity must be maintained in the face of a major transition from one phase of life to the next. Society does little to solve teenagers' dilemma. They
can join the army, but cannot legally drink. So teens experiment by rebelling. They stay out
late, drink, and are sexually active—all the while hoping that their parents' restrictions on
these activities will help define them. They want to become adults, but simultaneously to be
faithful to themselves as they were. When thoughts turn to adult pursuits, another component of selfhood comes into play: **propriate striving** is planning for the future by setting
long-range goals. During adolescence, people come to realize that success in life will depend on planning ahead. To involve effective propriate striving, goals must be reasonably,
narrowly focused and in tune with people's abilities. Earlier, there may have been thoughts
of being a movie star or a famous athlete. Now, to be mature, goals must be realistic and
embodied in a step-by-step plan for attainment.

By adolescence, individuals are experiencing Erikson's "identity crisis." They are
trying to find their own identities apart from their parents. Adolescents try to cast off the
conscience that parents, peers, and society have forced on them and build their own. At this
point, conscience shifts from outside the self to within. Now, self-esteem is bolstered by
doing what is "right." The self-image includes aspiring to do what ought to be done, and
propriate striving encompasses plans to be a fair, kind, and otherwise worthwhile person.
As adolescence passes into adulthood, people no longer perform good deeds to avoid a
vengeful conscience, but to strive actively for worthy goals that will support a mature self-
image. Table 17.1 summarizes Allport's theory of personality development.

TABLE 17.1   *Allport's Evolving Sense of Self*

Proprium (the self as felt and known)		
Stage	*Aspect of Selfhood*	*Definition*
1	Early infancy	No sense of self
2	Bodily self	Awareness of bodily sensations
3	Self-identity	Continuity of self
4	Self-esteem	Pride in one's pursuits
5	Extension of self	Self includes significant aspects of environment
	Self-image	Hopes and aspirations based on others' expectations
6	Rational coper	Reasoning and solving problems "in the head"
7	Propriate striving	Planning for the future

The Mature Personality

As individuals continue to evolve, progress toward a *mature personality* is measured in terms of how well adults meet six criteria.

Extension of the Sense of Self.   Extension of self is not fully formed even after the first ten years of life. At adolescence, it reaches out like the tentacles of a confused octopus. It does not know what experiences and roles to grasp for the self, and which to cast aside. With the advent of "puppy love," however, "The boundaries of self are rapidly extended" (1961, p. 283). The welfare of someone else becomes important to one's own welfare, in fact, may be identical to one's own. As maturity advances, "loneliness" is reflected in "new ambitions, new memberships, new ideas, new friends, . . . new hobbies, and above all one's vocation" (p. 283). All of these new pursuits become incorporated into the self. This transition from teen to adult involves cognitive development that allows cleaner differentiation of self from others (Labouvie-Vief, 2003).

Not only does the self take on the new, it also transforms the old. One may continue to do what one did, but the original reasons for doing those things fade. Old pursuits may become detached from original motivations. Allport's name for this transformation is **functional autonomy,** a process by which a new system of motivation evolves from an older one, but stems from tensions different from those of the original.

This transformation is illustrated by Kahlil, the son of a politician who initially goes into politics so that he can "follow in his father's footsteps." Later, he becomes fascinated by and enmeshed in the political process. He pursues politics for love of the process and for the power and glory of it, rather than to be like his father. Allport argued that much of what we do that is important to the self has become functionally autonomous from the original motivations. The new motivations are more abstract than the old. They include "aesthetics," "intrinsic interest," and "human well-being."

One problem of maturity is to extend oneself into the spheres of one's life. For example, Yin works in a factory, knows many people, pays union dues, drinks at the local tavern, and finds movies to be significant diversions. However, he is constantly *task-involved* and rarely *ego-involved.* "He has not extended his sense of self into any of the significant areas of his life . . . the economic, educational, recreational, political, domestic and religious." (p. 284). To be mature one must detach oneself from the "clamorous immediacy of the body" and find self-related reasons for doing whatever one does (p. 285). Yin could become involved in his union for reasons of "fair and equitable treatment of workers," or local politics in the interest of "cleaning up the neighborhood."

Warm Relating of Self to Others.   By extending the self, a person of warmth is capable of great *intimacy.* Warm relationships reflect a genuine capacity for love involving family, friends, and lovers. But mature warmth also entails *compassion,* a form of detachment. Gossip and possessiveness are avoided. Others are allowed to lead their own lives free of intrusions. "Both intimacy and compassion require that one not be a burden or nuisance to others, nor impede their freedom in finding their own identity" (p. 285).

Emotional Security (Self-acceptance).   To Allport, "self-acceptance" includes avoidance of overreaction to "drives" or gut issue needs. Mature people are neither constantly seeking sexual gratification nor prudish and repressed about sex. They accept sexual urges as a part of themselves. Mature people do have fears and well they should, there are real dangers "out there." But, they do not recoil in terror at the thought of roaming a large city or at the prospect of confronting hostile protesters. Self-acceptance assures mature people that the exercise of reasonable prudence will allow them to successfully cope with dangers.

Self-accepting people have high **frustration tolerance;** when things go wrong, they do not pitch a tantrum, blame others, or wallow in self-pity. Instead they accept some of the blame and find a way around the obstacle, or, failing that, resign themselves to some unpleasantness and bide their time until things get better. Part of self-acceptance is to know one is fallible, but to believe one is capable of compensating for faults as well.

Realistic Perceptions and Skills. "Maturity does not bend reality to fit one's needs and fantasies" (p. 289). The mature person seems to "see things" more clearly than others and, thus, has more wisdom than others. But does this mean that one has to have high intelligence to be mature? Allport answers that intelligence helps in the achievement of maturity, but does not guarantee it. Mature people are also problem solvers. "Although we often find skillful people who are immature, we never find mature people without problem-pointed skills" (pp. 289–290). Not only are they capable of solving task-related problems, they are capable of losing themselves in a task. They are problem-centered.

Self-objectification: Insight and Humor. Imagine someone who announces, "I'm a master of the English language and a person who knows himself well." Immediately, this person apologetically adds, "I don't mean to infer that I'm more smarter than others." Allport believed that most of us are like this individual in that we believe we have *insight* into ourselves, but we really do not. Can we obtain what we falsely claim? We can, at least by approximation. However, even if we assume there is a single, stable "true person"— thereby ignoring the possibility that a person is always in a state of flux—we still could never know that "true person." No one is privy to all the complexities and subtleties that constitute a person, not even the person. Thus, the best we can do is to look at the discrepancy between what a person believes about herself and what other people believe about her. The less the discrepancy, the greater the insight.

In a study wherein subjects rated each other, the correlation between ratings of insight and sense of humor was .88. What makes a sense of humor such a close associate of insight? A **genuine sense of humor,** as opposed to an appreciation of sexual and aggressive jokes, is being able "to laugh at the things one loves (including, of course, oneself and all that pertains to oneself), and still to love them" (p. 292). Insightful people communicate that they know and accept their own limitations and deficiencies by laughing at their shortcomings. Being insightful, such people are good judges of others and are accepted by them. Perhaps the key to the close correlation between insight and humor is that a person with a good "sense of humor" communicates a match between perceptions of self by self and by others. Friends know a person's faults and find evidence for insight in the match between their knowledge of the person's deficiencies and the person's acknowledgment of those shortcomings.

The Unifying Philosophy of Life and Religion. One primary element in a unifying philosophy of life is **directedness,** having a goal or goals in life toward which one strives.

BOX 17.3 • *A Mature Person I Have Known*

As an eighteen-year-old he was flying World War II raids over Europe in obsolete Royal Air Force bombers. They were falling out of the sky like rain in the tropics. He calculated the odds of continued survival and realized that he could expect to live through only a few more missions. So his hand flew up fast when an officer asked for volunteers to fly missions in North Africa. It would be dangerous too, but he figured that at least he had a chance in Africa.

He figured right, as he usually does. After the war, he immigrated to the United States and served for a time in the Air Force. Seeking to better himself, as he always has, he entered college, despite not having a high school education. Several years later he had a Ph.D.

As he grew older, like anyone who has lived many years, he had some troubles, none more serious than his heart attack. But he said it changed him. He began to more thoroughly appreciate the small things, like a crisp fall morning.

As he grew older still, his wife passed away and he retired from his university professorship. He faced both with the courage and grace that characterizes him. He is now doing what he has always done, educating himself. Though he is the most widely read person I have ever known, he doesn't think he knows enough. Each day he spends hours reading to learn more.

My friend had to mature fast. Had he not, he would never have made it beyond his teens. But the thing about him that amazes me is that he continues to mature. How does he do it? By acting on his realization that there is always more to learn.

The goals may change as one's life circumstances change, but they must be in place if one is to claim a mature personality. For example, goals may change after a series of "bad luck" incidents. Goals also evolve with maturity and become more realistic. As a postadolescent may have to admit, some earlier goals (e.g., becoming a corporate executive) are unlikely to be achieved. Allport points especially to the late twenties as a time of goal-shattering disillusionment accompanying the early phases of marriage and career.

Allport believed that a coherent *religious sentiment* is central to the unifying philosophy that enables maturity of personality. He was not heavily invested in organized religion, but he seemed fascinated with the possibility of a higher power that is the center of human experience. He saw religious orientation as the most comprehensive and integrative of the six value orientations.

Religious sentiment can be immature: a deity is adopted who favors the person's immediate interests much as Santa Claus did during childhood. Another form of immature sentiment is the tribal type: "God favors my people to your people" (p. 300). In both cases the motivation is **extrinsic,** utilitarian, and in the service of self-esteem maintenance. Extrinsic people (Es) *use* their religion (Allport & Ross, 1967). In contrast, the motivation behind a mature religious sentiment is **intrinsic:** religion is an end-in-itself, something that one surrenders to, not something to use. Intrinsics (Is) *live* their religions (Allport & Ross, 1967). Their religious faith is all-engrossing and all-encompassing. Religious sentiment, like humor, transports life's troubles from the routine context to a perspective that is more universal and generally meaningful. Like humor, religious sentiment allows one to avoid taking things too seriously: whatever is currently happening in life is trivial relative to the universal scheme of things.

BOX 17.4 • *Type of Religiousness: Prejudice, Self-Deception, Psychological Adjustment, Optimism, and Health*

Allport and Ross (1967) showed that extrinsic and intrinsic orientations have implications well beyond religion per se. They found that extrinsic orientation was moderately related to prejudice toward various groups (r = [approximately] .30). Across various religious groups, Is were less prejudiced than Es who, in turn, were less prejudiced than indiscriminately proreligious people.

Donohue (1985) did an extensive review of the literature on extrinsic/intrinsic religiousness. Allport originally thought that E and I orientations were at opposite ends of the same continuum (E–I is bipolar). Consistent with the bipolar assumption, many studies found E and I to be mildly negatively correlated (r = [approximately] –.20). However, relations of E and I to other psychological measures implied that the two orientations were better viewed as independent. For example, I tended to be unrelated to prejudice, but E was clearly related to prejudice (r = [approximately] .30), as Allport and Ross had found. Also, I tended to be unrelated to fear of death, but E was positively related to that fear.

Burris (1994) found that, for people scoring above the I mean (average I score), the E–I relationship was indeed negative, but it was not for those scoring below the I mean. Thus, high I orientation is the opposite of E. Deeply and genuinely religious people are very different from those who pursue religion for external, utilitarian, self-interested reasons. But all is not well with Is. They show evidence of self-deception and a tendency to manipulate the impressions they make on others. Es have deficiencies too. High Es showed more depression than low Es, and E orientation was associated with maladjustment.

Ryckman, Thornton, and Gold (1999) found that hypercompetitive people (see Horney chapter) scored relatively low on an I scale and relatively high on an E scale. True to Allport's original conception of Is and Es, hypercompetitives tended to be prejudiced.

Insofar as Is, at least high Is, are "fundamentalists," it would be expected that they would be more optimistic relative to less devout religious people. Fundamentalists get their optimism from their religious reading materials (Sethi & Seligman, 1993). Thus, deeply religious people are healthfully optimistic, compared to maladjusted, depressed high Es. They are also self-deceptive, impression managers. But, as Bandura (1994b) suggests, painting a more highly positive picture of oneself than the facts warrant may be good strategy. It is what high Is may do and it is associated with optimism, a factor that is positively correlated with physical health and negatively correlated with depression.

It has long been suspected that religion plays a role in health. After all, if deeply religious people are more optimistic than others, they should enjoy better health. Powell, Shahabi, and Thoresen (2003) point out that rigorous research on the relationship between religion and health is in its infancy. However, they were able to find a sufficient number of acceptable studies to draw some conclusions. For healthy people, regular church attendees, compared to infrequent attendees, show a 25 percent lower death rate. They also report that *religion* or *spirituality* protects against cardiovascular disease (they do not separate these two factors). This advantage is apparently explained by the healthier lifestyle that is promoted by religious involvement or spirituality. There was also some admittedly subjective evidence that "being prayed for" improves recovery from acute illness. However, they found that the kind of "depth of religiousness" implied by "intrinsic religious motivation" failed to promote health. Finally, there was no evidence that religion or spirituality improves recovery from cancer or recovery from acute illness. Other evidence suggests that the moderate use of religious coping (e.g., seeking comfort from church members) lowered depression among people whose partners had been diagnosed with cancer (Dittman, 2003b). Although the status of religion as a positive force in generating good health is still uncertain, religion–spirituality is increasingly an issue during therapy (Kersting, 2003). Similar to Jung's policy, some therapists are beginning to use clients' religious beliefs to help them deal with their psychological problems.

Generic conscience is central to the development of personality and is a unifying force in personality: it lays down comprehensive guidelines for nearly all of a person's conduct. Ultimately, it is the source of accepting responsibility for oneself and the wellspring of one's responsibilities to others. Allport distinguishes maturity's generic conscience from the child's "must sayer" conscience that metes out guilt for failure to honor any of its demands. The mature, generic conscience is not troubled by a knee-jerk need to avoid any transgression. Minor slips and sins are not the mature person's concern. Only adherence to personally selected moral standards is relevant to the self of the mature person. These standards include some of society's moral strictures, but are not limited to them.

Personality and Prejudice

Personality development can take unexpected turns. Witness the relationship between religion and prejudice. But just what facets of personality development—childhood (and adulthood) experiences—shape prejudice? Before seeking an answer, it is necessary to consider "prejudice" and related concepts from Allport's view and that of others he has influenced.

There are three reasons why Allport's book, *The Nature of Prejudice* (1954), published in the year of the U.S. Supreme Court's school-desegregation decision, is the single most important work ever done on the subject. First, it was the earliest comprehensive discussion of prejudice that was based on a significant body of scientific research. Second, it was extremely influential in shaping social scientists' thinking concerning prejudice. Third, because Allport has had so much influence on prejudice research done since 1954, it is relatively easy to fit some of today's findings regarding prejudice into his theoretical framework.

> *Everyone's a little bit racist, sometimes.*
> *Doesn't mean we go around committing hate crimes.*
> *Look around and you will find,*
> *No one's really color-blind.*
> *Maybe it's a fact we all should face.*
> *Everyone makes judgments based on race.*
> *You're a little bit racist. Alright! . . .*
> *If we could just admit*
> *That we are racist (a little bit)*
> *Even though we all know that it's wrong*
> *Maybe it would help us get along.*
>
> (From *Avenue Q,* a Broadway play)

Prejudice Defined

According to Allport (1954), **prejudice** is felt or expressed antipathy based on a faulty and inflexible generalization and may be directed toward a group as a whole, or toward an individual because of membership in the group. Thus, prejudice is negative feelings regarding members of some group that are sometimes only felt internally and sometimes expressed openly. It is based on the faulty generalization that most, or all, members of some group, such as Native Americans, possess certain negative traits, such as drunkenness. Such a generalization is always erroneous in the sense that no trait will apply to most, much less all, members of a large group (even skin color varies greatly among people who are "black").

Discrimination usually has meant directing more negative behaviors toward a particular group, compared to others, but may include having more negative thoughts and feelings about some group relative to others. People can be discriminatory in regard to their feelings and thinking, just as they are in terms of their behavior ("I *hate* them [feelings] because they are *trash* [thinking]"). Many measures of prejudice amount to asking people—usually via questionnaire—how much they discriminate so their level of prejudice can be inferred. For this reason, it is possible to offer a more empirical definition of prejudice that is consistent with Allport's theoretical definition. Prejudice measures typically ask about *self-perceptions* of discrimination. Therefore, *prejudice* may be seen as the degree to which *people believe that they discriminate against members of some group* in terms of directing relatively more negative behaviors, as well as thoughts and feelings, toward group members. As prejudice is most often assessed with the use of questionnaires completed anonymously, people's pronouncements about their level of prejudice probably represent what they really believe.

Social Distance

Given this empirical definition, it is immediately obvious that what people believe about their level of discrimination may not be accurate. Because nobody has total insight, some people who honestly claim not to discriminate against others may do so anyway. To explore this logical conclusion, it is necessary to consider **Social Distance (SD),** a measure of discrimination that requires individuals to indicate how close to themselves they would allow members of some group to come. Allport (1954, p. 39) listed the items of the SD scale as follows:

> I would admit (members of some group)
> 1. To close kin by marriage
> 2. To my club as personal chums
> 3. To my street as neighbors
> 4. To employment in my occupation
> 5. To citizenship in my country
> 6. As visitors only to my country
> 7. Would exclude from my country

Notice that the social relations to which the members of some group can be admitted vary from those involving a great deal of *intimacy* with group members, *commitment* to them, and *permanency* of relationships involving them (top of list) to those involving no intimacy, commitment, and permanency (bottom of list).

Not only do people who strongly claim not to discriminate against some often-disparaged group really believe themselves, these self-proclaimed "unprejudiced" people probably do not discriminate under most circumstances. Nevertheless, would they discriminate when asked to accept the same group's members for social relations that entail high intimacy, commitment, and permanency? To answer the question, I gave some White college students a test to determine the degree to which they were prejudiced against Blacks (Allen, 1975). Based on their scores, some students were classified as "unprejudiced," some as "prejudiced," and some as "ambivalent" (gave mixed signals about their level of discrimination). All of these subjects were then asked to indicate the degree of closeness they would allow Blacks by use of an SD scale composed of items 1 and 3 (Triandis, Loh, & Levine, 1966). Results showed that all categories of these White subjects, even those who claimed they did not discriminate according to race, in fact did so. When it comes to relations involving intimacy, commitment, and permanency, even "unprejudiced" subjects show racial discrimination.

Although unprejudiced White subjects did discriminate on the SD scale, when it came to indicating whom they admire, another part of the same study showed that they actually expressed more admiration for Blacks than for Whites. (This so-called reverse discrimination effect reverted to no discrimination when subjects thought they were hooked up to a lie detector machine.)

But why do all categories of Whites, even self-proclaimed non-discriminators, in fact discriminate when it comes to choices for intimate, committed, permanent social relations? Whites show great individual differences in prejudice, but they do not display great individual differences in discrimination for intimate, committed, permanent relations. Perhaps there is some underlying dimension for which individual differences are not great that explains why most such people sometimes discriminate by race.

In the case of discrimination against Blacks, such a dimension appears to exist. **Racism** is widespread negative sentiment directed toward people of color (Allen, 1975, 2001). Recently, Sears and Henry (2003) suggested that racism may also involve high individualism—the belief that people are solely responsible for their successes as well as failures and should not expect nor accept help from anyone—accompanied by the belief that Blacks violate individualistic values. It has been argued that racism is a part of the mainstream culture in this country (Gaines & Reed, 1995). When people incorporate their culture, largely through the process of identification, they swallow it whole. They ingest not only the good aspects of their culture, of which there are many, they also consume the bad—racism. Because most people fully adopt their culture, most Whites would incorporate racism within themselves. This may be the reason that even unprejudiced Whites show discrimination in some areas: racism rears its ugly head when it comes to making choices of others for intimate, committed, permanent relations, although it fails to show up in other realms (deciding whom to admire). It also may show up in subtle ways that are covered in the next section. In contrast, racism is often reflected in a wide spectrum of prejudiced people's expressions and behaviors. The top of Figure 17.1 shows the degree to which racism is *incorporated* by Whites who range across the prejudice spectrum. You can see that racism is rather universally incorporated, even by the "unprejudiced." The bottom of Figure 17.1 shows the degree to which racism shows up in the *social choices and reactions* of Whites who range across the prejudice spectrum. You can see that racism clearly, openly, and regularly shows up only in the social choices and reactions of high prejudiced people (bottom). Note that, with this schema, only high prejudiced people are considered "racist." Thus, unprejudiced Whites are indeed nondiscriminatory in terms of most of their social choices and reactions (bottom, right-most part of Figure 17.1). But they, like others, show

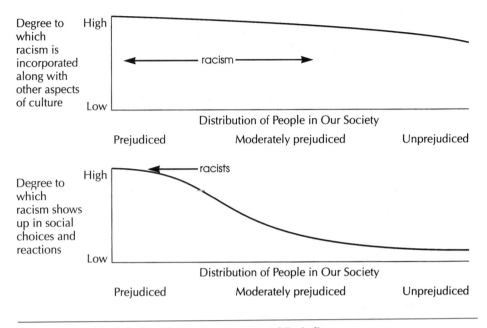

FIGURE 17.1   *The Relationship between Racism and Prejudice*

racial discrimination in terms of relatively rare choices for intimate, permanent, committed social relations. We will see that unprejudiced Whites also show racial discrimination on subtle measures that reveal the non-conscious effects of racism.

Subtle Manifestations of Racism

Anti-Black sentiment would not be a matter for such great concern if it showed up only in the relatively rare reactions that entail intimacy, commitment, and permanency. On the other hand, if it could be demonstrated that racism's effects are present in ways that are beyond our conscious control, we might begin to believe that it is a more widespread problem. Subtle reactions that are beyond conscious awareness could occur in a wide range of circumstances and result in just as much or perhaps more harm to targets than obvious and open reactions.

Gaertner (1973) was one of the first to investigate subtle reactions. Liberal and conservative White subjects were given an opportunity to aid a Black or a White person who issued a plea for help over the telephone. Subtlety was reflected in "premature hangups": cutting off the call after learning of the caller's race, but before the help request was made. Younger liberals more frequently hung up on Black than White callers. There was also an overall tendency for all subjects to claim that they would not discriminate by race, but to do so when actually called.

Evidence of discrimination in help-needed situations is hard to detect with the untrained eye. Actual discrimination against Blacks may escape witnesses because it may appear that Whites' nonhelpfulness is due to something other than the race of the victim, such as the presence of other potential helpers. Nonhelpful Whites may also not be aware of their own racial discrimination for the same reason.

Frey and Gaertner (1986) reasoned that if Whites' failure to help Blacks could be attributed to some nonracial characteristics of the Blacks, they would help Blacks less than Whites. When failure to help Blacks could be attributed to their race, Whites would show no discrimination lest they reveal their bigotry to themselves and any onlookers. As expected, Frey and Gaertner found that when a Black person who had shown little effort on an easy task asked for help, she received less help than a White who also showed low effort on the easy task. Thus, when Whites could say to themselves that their failure to help was due to the lazy, ineffectual behavior of the help requester rather than to race, they discriminated against Blacks. When their nonhelpfulness would be attributed to the race of the requester because she worked hard on a difficult task, Whites showed no discrimination. Failure to help Blacks can be disguised as nondiscriminatory as long as it can be attributed to characteristics other than race.

It follows from Frey's and Gaertner's results that racial bias may be shown by White jurors if motivations for verdicts and sentencing cannot be readily attributed to race of the accused. In one of their experimental conditions, Sommers and Ellsworth (2001) ensured that race was not an issue in a mock jury trial study by not bringing up race in a trial summary given to White mock jurors. However, race of the assailant–defendant and victim was disclosed in an initial description of the two. In a second experimental condition, race was made an issue by indicating that the defendant was a minority on his basketball team and had been subjected to racial remarks and unfair criticism. Only when race *was an issue* and, thus, racism could be readily attributed to the White mock jurors, was there no discrimination in conviction rate and sentencing. When race *was not an issue,* the Black defendant was more likely to be convicted than the White defendant and to receive a harsher sentence.

Shirley Weitz (1972) had White unprejudiced subjects practice instructing Black fellow subjects via audiotape in preparation for a later experiment in which they supposedly would actually do the instructions. White subjects also selected what type of interaction they preferred to have with the Black subjects during a subsequent experiment. Further, they indicated whether they wanted to wait with the Blacks while the experiment was being prepared. None of these responses are readily controlled by conscious processes. Finally, the White subjects indicated their attitudes toward Blacks. The more positive were attitudes toward Blacks, the more negative was the tape-recorded tone of voice during the instruction preparation. Also, the more positive the attitudes, the less willing were White subjects to select a relatively intimate interaction with the Black participants and the less willing Whites were to wait with Blacks for the experiment to begin. Once again people whose verbalizations indicated fair-mindedness showed discrimination against Blacks, but this time they did so by means so subtle that their bias probably escaped their own notice as well as that of onlookers.

Since these efforts to confirm that even low prejudiced subjects show signs of racism when subtle methods are used, powerful and sophisticated measures have been developed. These new methods have produced results supporting the contention, presented in the first part of this chapter: even participants who score very low on standard prejudice tests show signs of racism.

The new methods "prime" participants for the subsequent presentation of stereotypes by first presenting them with a very brief presentation of a race-related word, such as *Black* or *White*. The priming word may even be presented so quickly that subjects do not consciously recognize its presence. For example, a priming word such as *black* is presented first on a computer screen followed by a stereotypical word such as *lazy*, and subjects are asked to respond as quickly as possible to the stereotypical word by pressing a key. The time lapse between when the word comes on the screen and when the key is pressed is typically the measure of racism's influence. Wittenbrink, Judd, and Park (1997) showed that all kinds of White subjects, even those low in prejudice, responded faster to negative stereotypes of Blacks following the prime *black* than to positive stereotypes of them. When the prime word was *white*, results were the opposite: reaction times were faster to positive stereotypes than negative stereotypes.

John Dovidio and Samuel Gaertner have developed a theory of differences between subtle or implicit prejudice and explicit or overt prejudice. They and their colleague Kelly Kawakami (2002) used a technique developed earlier that was similar to that of Wittenbrink and colleagues (1997), but involved Black and White faces as primes followed by positive (e.g., good, kind, trustworthy) and negative (bad, cruel, untrustworthy) words. The faces were presented at just 22.5 milliseconds, too fast to be consciously recognized but slow enough to influence participants' subsequent responses (later debriefing showed that participants were unaware of the faces). A mask projected on the place where the words were seen took the form of either an oval with a "P" in it or a rectangle with an "H" in it. The "P" stood for "person" and the "H" stood for "house." White female participants were to hit a key representing "P" if they thought the word on the screen applied to people or hit a key representing "H" for house if the word applied to a house (e.g., drafty, furnished, roomy). A participant's implicit prejudice (subtle display of racism) score was calculated in the following way: the degree to which she responded faster to the negative words following the Black prime compared to the White prime versus the degree to which she responded faster to positive words following the White prime compared to the Black prime. The higher the score on this reaction time measure the more the implicit-subtle racial bias. Similar to Wittenbrink and colleagues (1997), Dovidio, Gaertner, and colleagues had earlier reported that White participants responded faster to negative words following the Black prime compared to the White prime and faster to positive words following the White prime compared to the Black prime.

Next participants were given over to another experimenter who told them that they would interact sequentially with two other students. For some participants, if the first "other student" was Black, the second one was White. The order was the opposite for other participants. Unbeknownst to participants, both were confederates of the experimenter. They discussed "dating in the current era. . . ." Sessions were audio and video taped. Then the confederate was taken to another room and she or he and the participant rated their own impressions of how they behaved and how the other person behaved (gender of confederates did not affect results). "Perceived friendliness" was the crucial measure. Both discussants rated the applicability to themselves of words like "cruel," "friendly," and "cold." Using videotape without sound, coders rated the nonverbal behaviors on the "friendliness" scale. Verbal "friendliness" was rated using the audio tape. Friendliness bias was the extent to which friendliness was greater toward the White than to the Black confederate. Earlier in the semester all participants had taken a measure of explicit-overt prejudice.

One type of measure was "explicit-overt" (highly controllable): explicit prejudice measure, verbal friendliness, and self-perceptions of friendliness. The other kind was "implicit-subtle reactions" reflecting racism: reaction time measure, nonverbal friendliness, confederate perceptions of friendliness, and electronic tape observers' friendliness ratings. Results indicated that the implicit-subtle measures tended to be positively and significantly related to each other, but unrelated to the explicit-overt measures. By contrast, the explicit-overt measures tended to be positively and significantly related to each other, but they tended to be unrelated to the implicit-subtle measures. Although our overt-explicit reactions may show no taint of racism, these easily controllable reactions *fail to predict* our difficulty to consciously control subtle-implicit reactions. The latter are tainted by racism. While most Whites are highly aware of their positive overt-explicit reactions, they tend to be oblivious of their implicit-subtly biased reactions. This dual consciousness causes them to be puzzled and frustrated when interacting with Blacks who see both kinds of reactions and respond with negativity. Making matters worse, Blacks may see Whites' subtle-implicit negative reactions as intentional and their explicit-overt positive reactions as attempts to deceive. Relations between Blacks and Whites will improve when Whites come to recognize that they display racism in their subtle-implicit reactions and Blacks learn that those reactions on the part of Whites are not consciously intended.

Nail, Harton, and Decker (2003) tested hypotheses drawn from Dovidio and Gaertner's theory. One hypothesis was that only politically liberal Whites, not political moderates and conservatives, would favor a Black police officer caught on video tape beating up a White motorist over a White officer caught on video tape beating up a Black motorist. The favorability was in terms of an overt-explicit *double jeopardy* rating: whether an officer, after being acquitted in a state court, was unfairly subjected to a civil suit in a federal court. The more an officer was judged to have been subjected to double jeopardy, the greater the favorability toward the officer. Results showed that political liberals did favor the Black officer, while moderates showed no bias, and the conservatives favored the White officer. A second hypothesis from the Dovidio–Gaertner theory was that liberals, because of a conflict between conscious favorability to Blacks and unconscious negativity toward them, would worry that they might reveal prejudice against Blacks. This concern on the part of liberals should be translated into high physiological reactivity in the presence of Blacks. To measure physiological reactivity, participants were hooked up to a skin electrical-conductance measuring device and to a heart rate–recording device. Specifically, liberals should be the only group who, when touched by a Black experimenter, would show greater physiological reactivity than when touched by a White experimenter. Indeed, on both measures liberals showed higher reactivity to the touch of a Black experimenter than to the touch of a White experimenter. The other two groups showed about the same reactivity levels on both measures when touched by the Black and the White experimenters. White people who view themselves as untainted by racism, and act accordingly in most cases, will nevertheless show hyper-reactivity in the presence of Blacks, because they non-consciously sense that they harbor underlying negativity toward Blacks.

In case you wondered, the reverse discrimination effect is still around. You may have observed that open, blatant displays of racism are getting more and more rare as time goes by. It's just not cool to express prejudice. Dovidio and Gaertner (2000) did a comparison across time—1988–1989 compared to 1998–1999—and found that, while blatant displays of prejudice declined over the period, subtle forms of prejudice remained constant.

Though it was not the goal of their research, Jason Mitchell, Brian Nosek, and Mahzarin Banaji (2003) produced results that address the issue of "reverse discrimination": people can say that they and others are not prejudiced because they can point to situations where reactions to Blacks are actually more favorable than reactions to Whites. Participants first each rated Black athletes and White politicians so that three liked Black athletes and three disliked White politicians were selected for presentation to each. The Greenwald version of the subtle reaction format was used (this method is described in Box 17.5). For an *occupation classification* part of the experiment, a name appeared on a computer screen and the words "politician" or "athlete" appeared to the left or right. For the *race classification* part of the experiment, the words "Black" or "White" were to the left or the right. A correct response was, for example, pressing the "A" key if the name was of a politician and the label "politician" was to the left and the "number 5" on the numeric keyboard if the name was of an athlete and the word "athlete" was to the right. The procedure was the same for race classification, but the category labels on the screen were "Black" and "White." Participants' reactions were measured in milliseconds. Preference was shown, for example, by faster reactions to "athletes' " names than to "politicians' " names or to "Whites' " names than to "Blacks' " names. For the occupation task, liked Black athletes were preferred to disliked White politicians, a result that is consistent with White participants' conscious liking of Black athletes and disliking of White politicians. However, when classification was by race, disliked White politicians were preferred to liked Black athletes. This result is in line with the non-conscious favoring of Whites over Blacks, because "Black is bad" and "White is good" are consistent with what is in the backs of most of our minds.

These results are very convincing in showing that subtle reactions reveal prejudice against outgroups such as people of color. However, it appears that these biased reactions emitted by even low prejudiced people may be more about prejudice in favor of one's own group than rejection of an outgroup (Dovidio and Gaertner, 2000). Is it possible to find a realm in which a stereotype specific to an outgroup promotes subtle reactions toward that outgroup? The answer appears to be "yes" in the case of the "violent Black man" stereotype. This stereotype is so pervasive and so non-conscious that it is literally dangerous to Black men. Evidence is seen in several cases of police opening fire on Black men and killing them, even though they were unarmed. Perhaps the most famous case illustrating this danger is that of Amadou Diallo, who was shot at 41 times and hit 19 times by New York City police when he reached for a wallet in his pocket (he was unarmed; Correll, Park, Judd, & Wittenbrink, 2002). In this and all such cases of which I'm aware, there was not enough time for the mostly White police to think "There's a Black man . . . he's got a gun . . . better shoot him!" It happened quickly and automatically, because it was enabled by the "violent Black man" stereotype that is in almost all of our heads.

Keith Payne (2001) used a subtle reaction measure involving the speed with which participants responded by hitting a "tool" (e.g., vice grip pliers) key or a "gun" key after being primed by a Black male face or a White male face. Participants were faster—measured in milliseconds—in identifying the gun by hitting the "gun" key if they had been primed with a Black as compared to a White face. More importantly, they falsely identified a tool as a gun more often if primed by a Black face rather than a White face. These results reveal a strong unconscious association in the minds of these White subjects between possession of violent weapons and being a Black man. In case you are wondering, gender of participants appears not to be an important factor in the "violent Black man" stereotype studies.

Payne, along with Alan Lambert and Larry Jacoby (2002), repeated Payne's (2001) study using basically the same procedure as before, but with a new wrinkle: associations *congruent* with the "violent Black man" stereotype—Black man with a gun, White man with a tool—and associations *incongruent* with the stereotype—Black man with a tool, White man with a gun—were compared under three different conditions. One was essentially the same as in the 2001 study, while a second condition involved informing participants of results of previous studies and telling them to *avoid using race* as they responded. In a third condition subjects were informed about previous results and told *to use race* during their responding. As in the previous study, tools were more often misidentified as guns by the White participants when primed by a Black face and guns were more often misidentified as tools when primed by a White face. As the time available to respond became shorter and shorter, participants in all three conditions were more likely to make identification mistakes of the congruent type—Black man with a tool mistakenly seen holding a gun, White man with a gun mistakenly seen holding a tool—than of the incongruent type—Black man with a gun mistakenly seen holding a tool, White man with a tool mistakenly seen holding a gun. Amazingly, this effect was stronger in the two conditions where participants' attention was drawn to race (conditions 2 and 3) than in the condition in which race was not mentioned (condition 1). Attention to race only made subtle reactions more reflective of prejudice when participants have to respond very fast.

The Park, Judd, and Wittenbrink team, this time led by Joshua Correll (2002), did a similar study, but used more of a video game format. Pictures of White and Black men shown against various backgrounds depicted a gun or other objects in hand (silver can, black cell phone, or a black wallet). This time the keys were labeled "shoot" or "don't shoot." Obviously shooting at an unarmed man was an error, as was not shooting at an armed man. Several results emerged across four studies: unarmed Black men were more likely to be "shot" than unarmed White men, the "don't shoot" key was used more often for the armed White man than for the armed Black man, participants "shot" more quickly at an armed Black man than at an armed White man, participants used the "don't shoot" button more quickly for an unarmed White man than for an unarmed Black man, and results consistent with all of the above were found for both White and Black participants in one study. The "violent Black man" stereotype is even in the heads of Black people, as the Reverend Jesse Jackson once acknowledged.

Anthony Greenwald, one of the pioneers in studying subtle reactions revealing prejudice, and his colleagues Mark Oakes and Hunter Hoffman (2003) took the quick reaction

BOX 17.5 • *External and Internal Influences on Attempts to Avoid Displays of Racism*

The Implicit Association Test (IAT), developed by Anthony Greenwald and colleagues, is perhaps the most used measure of subtle reactions revealing underlying racism. In studies of subtle racial bias, participants are frequently presented with Black names (e.g., Malik) and White names (e.g., Josh) and pleasant (e.g., lucky) or unpleasant (e.g., agony) words. As quickly as they can, participants respond with a key press when presented with Black names paired with unpleasant words and by pressing a different key when presented with White names paired with pleasant words (congruent with bias against Blacks). They also respond to Black names paired with pleasant words and White names paired with unpleasant words (incongruent with bias against Blacks). Participants show IAT race bias to the extent that they respond faster to the congruent pairings than to the incongruent pairings. After harvesting data from thousands of internet participants using the IAT, they estimate that 75 percent of whites show significant subtle bias (A. Greenwald, personal communication, February 16, 2004; Nosek, 2004; Nosek, Banaji, & Greenwald, 2002). Of course, this figure means that 25 percent of Whites do not show evidence of racism, even on measures of subtle reactions to Blacks. Understanding these relatively rare people could help to explain how some White people have avoided the taint of racism. Knowing their characteristics might allow the development of methods for eliminating racism that could be taught to other people.

Patricia Devine and her colleagues have devised ingenious methods for isolating and studying some of those individuals who show not even subtle displays of racism. E. Ashby Plant and Devine (1998) developed and validated a scale that reveals two kinds of motivations to avoid displays of prejudice: External Motivation to Respond Without Prejudice (EMS) and Internal Motivation to Respond Without Prejudice (IMS). People who score high on the EMS factor endorse items such as "I try to hide any negative thoughts about Black people in order to avoid negative reactions from others" (p. 830). High IMS people

endorse items such as "Because of my personal values, I believe that using stereotypes about Black people is wrong" (p. 830).

In the first of several experiments, Devine, Plant, Amodio, Harmon-Jones, and Vance (2002) used a subtle-implicit reaction assessment method similar to that of Dovidio and colleagues and Fazio and colleagues. Black and White faces were primes that were followed by positive (e.g., "pleasant") or negative (e.g., "awful") words. As quickly as possible, participants hit a "good" key for a positive word or a "bad" key for a negative word. Reaction times were translated into a "facilitation" or f-score: the higher the f-score the more a face-type (Black or White) facilitated quick responding to subsequent "good" or "bad" words. They found what others reported: Black face primes facilitated reactions to negative words more than White faces. More importantly, High IMS–Low EMS participants were the only group for whom Black face primes *did not* facilitate reactions to negative words (in fact they scored below the baseline or zero point). All other groups scored significantly above the zero point: High IMS–High EMS, Low IMS–Low EMS, Low IMS–High EMS. For all of these groups, Black faces significantly facilitated reactions to negative words at a level significantly above the baseline or zero point.

In a second study, the IAT (Black and White names were primes) was used. Again the High IMS–Low EMS group had the lowest IAT race bias scores compared to other groups, but all groups scored significantly above zero. In a third study, Black and White faces were again used, but with the IAT procedure. Results were the same as in study one that also used faces and basically the same as in study two: High IMS–Low EMS participants showed the lowest IAT race-bias scores and their group score was not significantly different from zero. A "business manipulation"—some participants had to listen to an audiotape while doing the reaction time task—had no effect on responses. This result implies that High IMS–Low EMS participants were not just good at intentionally controlling their responses, because attending to the tape would have prevented controlling responses.

Amodio, Harmon-Jones, and Devine (2003) used another subtle-implicit reaction measure to assess differences between High IMS–Low EMS participants and the other groups. The eyeblink startle response to a blast of white noise (containing all of the auditory frequencies that humans can hear) occurs automatically and apparently cannot be controlled. As predicted, according to one eyeblink startle response index, High IMS–Low EMS participants showed lower emotional reactions to Black faces than either High IMS–High EMS or Low IMS participants. Further, according to a negative emotional reaction index calculated using the eyeblink startle response, High IMS–Low EMS participants were the only group that showed no difference in negative reactions to Black and White faces. The other two groups showed significantly more negative reactions to Black than to White faces. Finally, another study that included Asian faces *failed* to reveal the bias involving these faces that is shown for Black faces. This outcome means that reactions to Black faces were not simply responses to an outgroup; these reactions were unique to Black faces.

Amodio, Harmon-Jones, Devine, Curtin, Hartley, and Covert (2004) successfully replicated the results of the Black–White face primes/gun–tool studies. Participants were quicker in identifying guns that followed Black faces compared to White faces and were slower in identifying tools that followed Black faces compared to White faces. Tools were more often mistaken for guns when they followed Black faces compared to White faces, but guns were more often mistaken as tools when they followed White faces compared to Black faces. More importantly, a measure of brain-wave–response to conflict created by errors was "significantly larger when tools were erroneously classified as 'guns' following Black [faces] . . . than when tools were erroneously classified as 'guns' following White faces" (p. 91). The pattern of results replicating earlier Black face–White face/gun–tool study re-

sults was found in the context of larger brain reactions to race-biased errors. This association of replicated results and brain reactions suggest that racism reflected in the errors is non-conscious in nature.

Recently Devine and colleagues attempted to discover the mechanism used by High IMS–Low EMS people to avoid displays of racism even on subtle-implicit measures of racial bias. Neuroscience work focusing on areas of the brain that may be involved in detection of errors and subsequent error control may have uncovered the relevant mechanism. This work indicates that the Anterior Cingulate Cortex (ACC)—a body below the frontal cerebral cortex—detects conflict-born errors and signals the Lateral Prefrontal [cerebral] Cortex (LPFC) to guard against repeating the errors (Kerns, Cohen, MacDonald, Cho, Stenger, & Carter, 2004). The ACC can be called the *error detector* and the LPFC the *regulator* that protects against further errors. For example, when research participants are presented with the word "yellow" printed in red ink and are asked to report the ink color, the conflict born of word–color incongruence generates high ACC activity, which alerts the LPFC. If after one incongruent word–color presentation ("yellow" printed in red ink), another follows immediately ("blue" printed in green ink), the LPFC regulator lowers the response time for correctly responding "green" compared to responding "red" the first time. Functional magnetic resonance imagery (fMRI) recordings in the ACC on the first presentation predicted fMRI recordings in the LPFC on the second presentation. This outcome indicates that the LPFC is gaining control over the erroneous tendency to speak the word rather than correctly report the color. Amodio, Devine, and Harmon-Jones (2004) developed a brain wave index of control over errors involving the ACC detector/LPFC regulator mechanism. Using participants classified as High IMS–Low EMS (hypothesized to be good regulators based on past research), High IMS–High EMS (poor regulators), and Low IMS (nonregulators), they repeated the Payne gun–tool experiment. In terms of reaction time measures and error measures, results were almost

(continued)

BOX 17.5   Continued

identical to those of Payne and colleagues and Devine and colleagues. More importantly, Amodio and colleagues (2004) found that *only* for "good regulators" was their brain wave index of control at the preconscious level higher when the crucial Black face–tool combination was presented (tool could be mistaken for a gun) than when the Black face–gun combination was presented. Also, compared with either poor regulators or nonregulators, on Black face–tool presentations good regulators showed higher brain wave amplitudes indicating control of responses. Thus, good regulators "are, overall, more sensitive to the possibility of making prejudiced-related errors (e.g., responding gun on Black-tool [presentations])" . . . "and may be more efficient in engaging control mechanisms preconsciously in efforts to prevent such errors" (personal communication from Patricia Devine, 2/23/04 and 2/22/04).

Some neuroscience research has directly tapped reactions of the *amygdala,* perhaps the most important emotional center below the cerebral cortex. Phelps and colleagues (2000) obtained IAT reactions, eyeblink startle responses (both measures of subtle reactions reflecting racism), and Modern Racism Scores (a measure of explicit or conscious prejudice). These three indexes of racial bias were related to fMRI recordings in the amygdala. For the two subtle measures and amygdala recordings, White and Black faces were primes or stimuli. They found that amygdala recordings were positively correlated with IAT re-

actions and eyeblink startle responses, but were uncorrelated with Modern Racism Scores. Implicit subtle reactions reflecting racism are at least partially mediated by one of the brain's most important emotional centers, the amygdala. At the same time, conscious-overt expressions of prejudice are unrelated to the amygdala's activity.

Both Fazio and colleagues' and Devine and colleagues' work suggests that part of the reason some White people are able to avoid displays of racism, even when subtle-implicit reactions are measured, is that they have a history of positive contact with Black people. Plant and Devine (2003) supported this possibility by assessing White participants' reactions to interactions with Black people as a function of their reports of the quality of their previous interactions with Blacks. Their results showed that the more positive the previous contact with Black people, the less the need to avoid interactions with Blacks, the less the hostility regarding such interactions, the less the anxiety concerning interactions with Black people, and the more positive the outcome expectancies regarding avoidance of prejudicial displays during such interactions. Positive previous contact with Black people may indeed be a key to explaining the existence of White people who apparently are untainted by racism, at least in the sense of being able to control the effects of the negative racial stereotypes that are in all our heads. Studying such people could help in the development of methods to reduce racism.

procedure one step further. They used a video game format in which a Black or White police officer holding a gun, Black or White criminals holding a gun, and citizens holding harmless objects appeared from behind one of two garbage dumpsters. Feedback through headphones informed participants as to whether their responses were correct (e.g., a loud scream was heard whenever a police officer was shot). Reactions had to be made in less than one second. White participants were to take the perspective of a fellow police officer and click a mouse button to shoot at the criminal, press the space bar as a safety signal to the "fellow" police officer, and to take no action in the case of unarmed civilians. There were two basic results: participants were more likely to confuse guns and harmless objects if these were held by Black men; Black citizens were more likely to be "shot" than their White counterparts. Obviously this study is directly relevant to real-life cases.

"Race" Differences

Allport (1954) traces continued interest in alleged racial differences to arguments that sub-categories of humans exist and can be arranged in a hierarchy from best to worst. It makes thinking and life itself simpler to believe that there are big differences between one "race" and the next, and few difference among people of a given racial designation. It was also gratifying: one could declare one's own race "best" and view the members of other races as uniformly inferior.

Allport asserted that gender mirrors how we react to the races. "Only a small part of our human nature is differentiated by sex. . . . [T]he vast proportion of human physical, physiological, psychological traits are not sex linked" (p. 109). Yet, despite the evidence of no difference on critical traits such as IQ, "women are regarded as inferior, kept in the home . . . [and] denied many of the rights and privileges of men. The special roles assigned to them are far in excess of what sexual genetic difference would justify. So it is with race" (p. 109). That we may habitually exaggerate gender differences is the focus of much research (Allen, 1995; but see Eagly, 1987).

Allport, a pioneer in questioning "race," makes two important points about the concept. First, most of the world's people are of "mixed stock"; thus, most do not fit any racial category. Second, "Most human characteristics ascribed to race are . . . [actually] ethnic, not racial" (p. 113). Today, the validity of "race" is again being challenged (Allen, 2002, 2003; Cavalli-Sforza, Menozzi, & Piazza, 1994; Katz, 1995; Weizmann et al., 1990; Yee et al., 1993; Zuckerman, 1990). Cavalli-Sforza (2000), a highly respected geneticist, has explored much of the world in search of genetic evidence for "races" and found none. Geneticist J. Craig Venter, head of Clera Genomics—the private group that was first to specify the human genome—extracted the genome from a Black, an Asian, a Latina, and some Whites to make the point that, genetically speaking, "races" don't exist (Recer, 2000). Also, it now appears that three conditions must be met before "race" is applicable to humans: (1) consensually accepted criteria for differentiation among races must be developed and shown to actually erect clear boundaries between one "race" and the next (e.g., hair texture and facial bone structure); (2) variability within "races" must be adequately reconciled with assumptions of intraracial uniformity (e.g., variability in IQ within races far exceeds differences between races in average IQ); (3) overlap among races must be reconciled with the assumption that "races" are meaningfully distinct (the distributions of scores for any two races on any psychological factor will greatly overlap; Allen & Adams, 1992). None of these conditions have, in fact, been met. Maddox and Gray (2002) may be the first researchers to show that "race" and skin color have lives of their own, though we tend to confound them. Using ingenious computer techniques they varied "race" and skin color independently of each other. Three Whites and three Blacks discussed some issues (race condition). Three light-skinned Blacks and three dark-skinned Blacks also discussed the issues (skin color condition). Analogous to the observation that members of the "other group" all look alike, White and Black observers of the discussions confused who said what if the speakers were members of the *same* racial *or* skin color group. By contrast, they had relatively little trouble identifying who said what if the speakers were members of *different* skin color *or* racial groups. We tend to lump together people of the same "race" *and* we also tend to lump together people of the same skin color, which is a reason why we confuse them in various ways.

Stereotypes

According to Allport, prejudice affects our thinking as well as well as our feelings. It is associated with the development of beliefs concerning the traits supposedly possessed by all or most members of a group. A belief of this sort is called a **stereotype,** an exaggerated belief that members of a group possess a certain trait; "Its function is to justify (rationalize) our conduct in relation to that [group]" (p. 191). Such beliefs may have a "kernel of truth" to them. In centuries past, Jews were "money handlers" in Europe, simply because they were allowed few alternatives for making a living. The problem is that this veridical observation evolved to become "most [or all] Jews are obsessed with making money." Though there may be a "kernel of truth" to a stereotype, it is almost always false to assume that most of any large group possess any trait one can conjure up (excepting those characteristics that define the group; e.g., all Catholics are Catholic).

Allport lists the following stereotypes of Blacks that were held by Whites at the time he was writing his 1954 book: unintelligent, morally primitive, emotionally unstable, overassertive, lazy, boisterous, fanatically religious, gamblers, flashy dressers, criminal, violent, reproductively prolific, occupationally unstable, superstitious, happy-go-lucky, ignorant, musical. To find out how these stereotypes might have changed, each of 81 White undergraduate students was asked to write down five words to describe Blacks (Allen, 1996). Sixty-three Black students were given the same instruction. Next the words most frequently used to describe Blacks were tallied.

Whites' stereotypes of Blacks are still negative. Though some content remains the same—"musical" and "loud" (boisterous)—there have been some changes. Blacks are now seen as "humorous" and "athletic." Blacks agreed with Whites on "independent," but mention "athletic" much less often and include "intelligent," omitted by Whites.

Unlike the vast majority of other stereotype studies, this one involved asking Blacks to indicate stereotypes of Whites. (Usually Blacks are not asked, or stereotypes of various White ethnic groups are assessed, not Whites in general.) Results indicated that Blacks and Whites show limited agreement. Blacks are more negative about Whites than Whites are about themselves. Both agree that Whites are "greedy" and "smart," though Whites are more extreme in this perception. In a switch over time, Whites now see themselves as "lazy," but no longer see Blacks that way (Blacks rarely used the word "lazy"). They also see themselves as "intelligent," but Blacks do not. These results were produced by procedures with certain advantages. One plus is that subjects produced the words from their own vocabularies, rather than being forced to choose from some limited, possibly biased, list. This fact probably accounts for results not predicted on the basis of previous research, such as Whites being seen as "corrupt," "prejudiced," and "greedy" and Blacks as "friendly," "funny," and "humorous."

Painting the Picture of the Prejudiced Personality

The traits that highly prejudiced people share can be summarized in the phrase *threat oriented,* partly because they view the world as a threatening place (Lambert, Burroughs, & Nguyen, 1999). However, some of the threat comes from within. The prejudiced person "seems fearful of himself, of his own instincts, of his own consciousness, of change, and of his social environment" (p. 396). To put it another way, very prejudiced people suffer from "crippled egos." By promoting oppression of other groups, they can ensure that their own status in society is not threatened.

Covered next are some specific traits that Allport believed prejudiced people tend to have in common. This consideration is relevant to the question, "If most Whites incorporate racism when they swallow their culture whole, why do only a relative few turn out to be *racists?*" (highly prejudiced). The answer may partially lie in the practices used to rear them and in their childhood experiences. These practices and experiences may act on racism, dragging it from the fringe to the core of some people's personalities, thereby pushing them into the "racist" category.

In support of this contention, Towles-Schwen and Fazio (2001) found that, of two motivations to control displays of prejudice, one—*restraint* in showing prejudice to avoid disputes—was positively related to viewing parents as prejudiced and having infrequent and negative contact with Blacks during secondary school years (people with this motivation tended to endorse, "If I were participating in a class discussion and a Black student expressed an opinion with which I disagreed, I would be hesitant to express my own viewpoint," p. 163). In contrast, subjects whose motivation was born of *concern* about acting prejudiced had positive interactions with Blacks and saw their parents as unprejudiced (they tended to endorse, "I get angry with myself when I have a thought or feeling that might be considered prejudiced," p. 163). It may be that early experience of parental prejudice and of infrequent, negative contact with Blacks may be among the building blocks of a racist orientation. The opposite experiences may help prevent development of a racist orientation. However, true to the contention that racism is pervasive, Towles-Schwen's and Fazio's White participants showed uniformly negative reactions toward Blacks on a subtle reaction-time measure similar to that used by Dovidio, Gaertner, and colleagues. Further, their scores on the measure were unrelated to either kind of motivation to avoid showing prejudice. However, in a more recent study these same researchers (2003) investigated *concern* versus *restraint* with regard to rated willingness to interact with and anticipated comfort during interactions with various people including Blacks. For these White participants, the greater the concern, the greater the willingness/comfort anticipated while interacting with Blacks. Though results failed to reach conventional levels of statistical significance, they also reported a trend toward *low* scores on *restraint* being associated with *high* willingness/comfort. Also, consistent with Allen (1975), regardless of *concern* and *restraint* White participants anticipated low willingness/comfort when interacting with a Black partner if the interaction involved no clear script concerning how to behave and the interaction required intimacy.

Ambivalence about Parents.   As one kind of "ism" tends to resemble other kinds, Allport (1954) often used anti-Semitism as a model for the "isms." Research showed that anti-Semitic women students are ambivalent toward their parents. While they overtly praised their parents, on projective tests these women covertly showed hostility toward parents. Tolerant subjects were the opposite: they were overtly critical of their parents, but the projective tests revealed no underlying hostility toward them. Prejudiced students' hostility toward their parents may stem from child-rearing themes of obedience, punishment, and actual or threatened rejection.

Moralism.   Allport reported that very prejudiced people tend to be highly moralistic as reflected in high attention to cleanliness and good manners. When the anti-Semitic students were asked what would embarrass them the most, they "responded in terms of violations of mores and conventions in public. Whereas [the] non-prejudiced spoke more often of inadequacy in personal relations" (p. 398). Again, child-rearing practices are implicated. The prejudiced had parents who punished them severely for any show of interest in their genitals and for aggression against the parents. The result is children who are guilt-ridden and full of self-hatred due to repeatedly being reminded of their wickedness. As adults, their suppressed hostility explodes onto members of other groups and their rigid morality is the source of a rationale for rejecting those group members.

Dichotomization.   Highly prejudiced people literally see in Black and White. There is good and there is bad; there is right and there is wrong. This orientation was forced on them by parents who dished out approval and disapproval categorically: everything the child did was either right or it was wrong, there was no middle ground. Little wonder that, as adults, they see only two classes of people: those who are acceptable and those who are not.

Need for Definiteness.   Allport believed that very prejudiced people are distinguished by their unique cognitive processes. Consistent with their tendency to classify everything into two categories, they show another critical characteristic. They have little **tolerance for ambiguity,** their cognitive orientation requires that everything be clearly distinguished from everything else, questions have definite answers, and problems have simple solutions. In short, prejudiced people want everything to be clear-cut, no gray areas. Consistent with this orientation, Peterson and Lane (2001) found that *right wing authoritarians* (RWAs), a type who tend to be prejudiced, had low grade-point averages if they majored in the liberal arts. They suggest that the ambiguous nature of the subject matter in liberal arts courses may account for RWAs poor performance. Inspired by Allport's belief that prejudiced people have a strong need for definiteness, Schaller, Boyd, Yohannes, and O'Brien (1995) found that forming erroneous stereotypes, a tendency of prejudiced people, was positively related to high Personal Need for Structure.

Externalization.   Allport saw very prejudiced people as lacking in self-insight. They do not see their own faults; they project them onto other people. Further, "things seem to happen 'out there' " (p. 404). In Horney's terms, they externalize. Rather than believing that they control what happens to them by use of their own resources, they believe that fate controls them. Rotter would class these people as externals. Allport explained: "It is better and safer for a person in inner conflict to avoid self-reference. It is better to think of things happening to him rather than as caused by him" (p. 404). Also, prejudiced people externalize punishment: "it is not *I* who hates and injures others; it is *they* who hate and injure me" (p. 404).

Institutionalization.   Allport believed the highly prejudiced person prefers order, especially social order. He finds safety and definiteness in his institutional memberships. "Lodges, schools, churches, the nation, may serve as a defense against disquiet in his per-

sonal life. To lean on them saves him from leaning on himself" (p. 404). Also, the prejudiced are more devoted to institutions than the unprejudiced. The anti-Semitic college
women were more wrapped up in their sororities and more patriotic. While patriotic people are not necessarily prejudiced, Allport referred to evidence that very prejudiced people
are almost always super-patriots. He cites an investigation in which club members completed a lengthy belief questionnaire in return for a monetary contribution to their clubs.
The large number of variables examined were reduced to only one trait held in common:
nationalism, an orientation condemned by Adler, Fromm, and Erikson. Allport is quick to
point out that "the nation" to these people is not what it is to most. When most people think
of "the nation," what comes to mind is the people, the principles of the Constitution, and
the lands. Instead, prejudiced people view "the nation" as something that will protect them
from people seen as unlike themselves and that will preserve the *status quo.*

Authoritarianism.   Allport believed that very prejudiced people are uncomfortable with
democracy. "The consequences of personal freedom they find unpredictable" (p. 406). It
is easier to live in a power hierarchy where everyone has a place and the top spot is occupied by an all-powerful person. In a word, prejudiced people are **authoritarian,** they show
high deference for authority figures, submission to the power of authority, and a need to
command those seen as lower in the power heirarchy than themselves. Allport cites a study
in which prejudiced people listed dictators such as Napoleon when asked whom they admired most, while unprejudiced people listed figures such as Lincoln. Authoritarianism is
seen in prejudiced people's mistrust of others. Authority embedded in a strong nation can
save oneself from suspected others. "To the prejudiced person the best way to control these
suspicions is have an orderly, authoritative, powerful society. Strong nationalism is a good
thing. Hitler [wasn't] so wrong . . . America needs . . . a strong leader" (p. 407).

It seems that authoritarianism has been construed as a right-wing or conservative
phenomenon. In fact, it is more complex. Krauss (2003) studied authoritarianism in Ro-
mania, a former communist state affiliated with the former Soviet Union. Although
authoritarianism was related to support for Soviet-style communist principles, it was unrelated to support for the socialist left, positively related to support for the radical right,
and negatively related to support for middle-of-the-road pro-Western parties.

Whitely (1999) compared authoritarian orientation with social dominance orientation (SDO), "the extent to which one desires that one's in-group dominate and be superior
to out-groups" (p. 126). While SDO was related to most forms of prejudice toward Blacks
and homosexuals, high authoritarians tended to stereotype homosexuals and have negative
feelings about them. Saucier (2000) confirmed what Allport implied: authoritarianism is
related to conservatism.

SDO continues to be mentioned in the same breath as authoritarianism and, in fact,
may seem to be a rival to authoritarianism. However, Duckitt, Wagner, Du Plessis, and
Birum (2002) present evidence that the two notions may be more complements than rivals,
with each referring to different, though related, personality dimensions. Working with
American and White Afrikaners (South Africans) college student participants, they found
that "social conformity" and "belief in a dangerous world" most influenced authoritarian
orientation, while "toughmindedness" and belief in a "competitive jungle world" most

influenced SDO. The finding with regard to "belief in a dangerous world" fit Allport's attribution to authoritarians: mistrust of others and need for the protection of a strong nation. However, the two concepts were significantly positively related and both were highly positively related to both nationalism and prejudice.

A team of French researchers, Guimond, Dambrun, Michinov, and Duarte (2003), revealed the path through which SDO plays a role in prejudice. They found that, for their French student participants, occupying a *position of high status and power* operated through SDO to generate prejudice. That is, occupying a high status/power position in a society was strongly and positively related to SDO, which, in turn, was strongly and positively related to prejudice. At the same time, "occupying a position of high status and power" was unrelated to prejudice when the effects of SDO were filtered out. Thus, a situational variable, "position of high status and power," interacting with a personal variable, SDO, predicted prejudice. Interestingly, they found that SDO was higher among students in the upper levels of law training than those in the lower levels, while it was the reverse for psychology students. It may be that psychology training mitigates against SDO, while law training promotes SDO (at least in France). By the way, there is no reason to believe that French students are meaningfully different from American students.

Evaluation

Contributions

Allport's more general ideas seem to have had greater impact than his specific concepts or his theory as a whole. His idiographic approach is periodically mentioned to remind us that seeking general principles applicable to all people may not be the best way to understand humans (Pelham, 1993).

Allport is considered the voice of moderation with regard to the matter of behavioral consistency (Zuroff, 1986). While Allport did not see evidence for a high level of cross-situational behavioral consistency, he was quick to argue that there is sufficient repetition of behavior to support the existence of p.d.s. The idea of p.d.s itself is important because it suggests that each person is even more unique than is generally recognized. Allport appreciated that understanding humans is very difficult, because each is so different from the others and each is extremely complex. Further, Allport's notions about personality development have been highly influential.

The publication of *Nature of Prejudice* was the most important event in the history of studying prejudice up to that time. Despite its age, the book continues to be cited and to inspire research. Allport's belief that prejudice can be reduced by positive, equal status, interracial contact supported by organizational officials and occurring in an atmosphere of cooperation is still accepted today (Dovidio, Gaertner, & Validzic, 1998; Scarberry, Ratcliff, Lord, Lanicek, & Desforges, 1997).

While not many of Allport's specific terms are often on the lips of personologists, there are exceptions. "Cardinal, central, and secondary dispositions" have been given more than lip service because they point to a crucial consideration: the centrality of dispositions (traits) to the life of the individual. "Functional autonomy" is influential because it suggests how temporary dispositions that may be of no special importance to a person can evolve into long-standing dispositions that characterize her or him.

Limitations

Allport's "theory" may be regarded as several mini-theories that are, at best, loosely tied together. In a sense, he seems to have jumped on his horse and ridden off in all directions at once. He does have a theory of traits and a personality development theory, but the connection between the two was not made explicit. As he was both a personologist and a social psychologist, he wrote on diverse topics such as the self and prejudice. Little wonder he did not tie things together very well.

Allport's emphasis on unique rather than common traits has put him out of the mainstream. The primary thrust of personality theory has been to state general principles that apply to all people and to specify traits possessed by most people to some degree (Big 5). Allport's insistence that each person is extremely unique makes the task of understanding humans look very daunting.

The boundaries between some of Allport's concepts are so indistinct as to be exceedingly hazy. The outstanding example is "cardinal, central, and secondary" p.d.s. Within a single person, there seems to be no concrete basis for deciding why one p.d. is "cardinal," another "central," and still another "secondary." Also troublesome is that a given trait can be both a common trait and a p.d. It does not help much to indicate that a trait such as "kind" has a different "flavor" when found in one person as opposed to another. How is it that the same trait is different when possessed by different people? In a sense Allport argues for a lack of continuity between people. Each person is an island unto herself or himself and must be understood using principles unique to him or her. Such conceptions make the study of people very costly. Other possible limitations of Allport's views are covered in Box 17.6.

Conclusions

Some people find fault with Allport's idiographic approach. Others, including myself, believe that he has correctly understood the complexity of people and the extraordinary uniqueness of each person. These insights make it appropriate to regard any statements of general principles applicable to all humans as exceedingly difficult to support. Many personologists have acted as if understanding people is easier than understanding chemistry or physics. In fact, people are the most complicated entities on this Earth. Facing up to the difficulty of explaining them is the first step in the grueling task of sorting out all that complexity.

While Allport may be criticized for creating a series of mini-theories, does writing a grand all-encompassing theory make sense? After all, even Einstein failed when he tried to compose a theory unifying the major physical forces. In view of human complexity, it may be naive to attempt a theory, such as Freud's, that explains most things psychological. Even theories restricted to explaining everything about personality may be too ambitious. Given the present "state-of-the-art" methods we have in personality, mini-theories may be the best we can do.

A few of the theorists covered in this book are notable for the individuals they were. Like Kelly, Allport received a warm, genuine tribute from his students. Like Rogers, he

BOX 17.6 • *Allport and DuBois on the Black Experience and the Nature of Prejudice and Stereotyping*

African American social psychologist Stanley Gaines and Edward Reed are among Allport's many admirers (Gaines & Reed, 1994, 1995). Nevertheless, they feel that Allport's writings contain some serious shortcomings. They (1995) contrast Allport's view, that "Black" experience is simply a variant of "White" experience, with the position of W. E. B. DuBois, a famous Black historian and student of American psychology's founder, William James. DuBois believed that a certain duality, resulting from their unique experience, characterized the self-conceptions of Blacks. African Americans see themselves as American and not American, as citizens and not citizens, and as participants in the American dream but excluded from that dream. Blacks are caused to think of themselves as "White" as well as "Black": they are often enticed to "be White" by the media and by White acquaintances, but are constantly reminded that they are "Black" and, thus, can never be accepted in the "White" world. The conflicting poles of this duality are seen in the condemnation by Blacks of Blacks who "act White." An African American is supposed to "act Black." To put this predicament into perspective, consider the question, "Wouldn't it be odd if 'Whites' were supposed to 'act White'?" Speaking of oddities, weird is the way wannabes are regarded: "White" people who "act Black."

Another DuBoisian duality is collectivism, which is natural to people of African descent, and

individualism, which (mostly male) Whites hold up to Blacks as the means to "making it" in America. Blacks must figure out how to fit both of these extremes. Gaines and Reed (1995) also point out that Allport had his own duality: extropunitive—blaming others—and intropunitive—blaming oneself. Allport saw some Blacks as extropunitive and some as intropunitive. Gaines and Reed viewed Booker T. Washington, known for his attempts to appease Whites, as intropunitive and DuBois, founder of the National Association for the Advancement of Colored People (NAACP), as extropunitive. But they also feel that the dichotomy is false. Because of the oppressive circumstances of Blacks, each would reflect some mixture of extropunitive and intropunitive orientation.

Gaines and Reed also rejected the notion attributed to Allport that prejudice and stereotyping naturally flow from normal cognitive processes. To the contrary, prejudice/stereotyping stem from slavery and its legacy of oppression, as well as attempts to justify both that cruel institution and its horrific aftermath. Racism came to America with the culture that Whites brought from Europe. Slavery and oppression flowed directly from the arrival of that culture (see Allen, 1978, for a historical perspective consistent with this view). In turn, prejudice/stereotyping stems from slavery and oppression.

seemed undistracted by the pursuit of fame; his concern was for the well-being of people. Allport's life is a reminder that truly meaningful psychological theorizing provides many benefits for human beings. Allport's name was not on the journal citation list, but was 18th on the text list, 14.5 in the survey, and 11th overall (Haggbloom et al., 2002).

Summary Points

1. Allport was born into a warm and philanthropic home. Always humble, he dismissed his academic feats in high school and later. The baby of the family, he followed older brother Floyd to Harvard. There, his first experience with psychology was less than positive. Still, he adopted the discipline and received a doctorate from Harvard. While Allport's theory was not humanistic, he was positively inclined to existentialism, a building block of humanism.

2. Unlike others, he was idiographic, inclined to study each person's unique traits. The idiographic view is currently gaining strength. He was also a forerunner of the interactionists. The Freudian unconscious was, to Allport, just as overemphasized as behavioral consistency. The Adjective Generation Technique came from Allport's tendency to abandon typical methods in favor of what works to understand people. Personality is the dynamic organization of psychophysical systems that determine characteristic behavior and thought.

3. A trait has the capacity to render many stimuli equivalent and to guide adaptive behavior. Traits are not habits or character, but can be common or p.d.s. Traits have a different flavor when attributed to a particular person rather than to people in general. Cardinal, central, and secondary p.d.s refer to the centrality of traits within the personality. Allport's stage theory of personality development is founded on the proprium, "me as felt and known." The "bodily self" refers to sensations of the body. Self-identity is continuity of the self over time.

4. Self-esteem is pride in one's pursuits and accomplishments. In extension of self, the self expands to include important elements of the environment. Self-image is composed of hopes developing from others' expectations. The rational coper can solve problems in the head. Propriate striving involves laying plans for the future. Extension of the self in the mature personality is based on functional autonomy. Warm relating to others in maturity is founded on intimacy and compassion.

5. Self-acceptance entails reasonable handling of urges and high frustration tolerance. Realistic perceptions of useful skills, insight, and humor are essential for maturity. Laughing at ourselves tells others that we have insight. A unifying philosophy of life involves directedness. Mature, intrinsically motivated, religious sentiment is essential to maturity. Extrinsics tend to be prejudiced and hypercompetitive, but high intrinsics have traits related to good psychological and physical health, though they are self-deceptive and impression managers.

6. Involvement in religion has recently been directly related to good physical health. Generic conscience is concerned with self-selected principles, not with sins. According to Allport, prejudice is felt antipathy based on faulty generalizations. Empirically speaking, prejudice is what people say about their discrimination. Even "Whites" who claim not to discriminate by race do so when making choices that entail high intimacy, commitment, and permanency.

7. Underlying racism may be the reason why almost all majority people discriminate in some ways. Subtle measures—such as voice tone, juror decisions when race is not an issue, and "priming"—show that even "low-prejudiced" Whites discriminate by race.

Dovidio and Gaertner found that subtle measures relate to each other but are unrelated to overt-explicit measures. Overt-explicit measures tend to be interrelated, but unrelated to subtle-explicit measures. Nail and Decker found that only political liberals show strong physiological reactions to being touched by a Black person.

8. Race differences may be reduced to ethnic differences because "race" is a questionable concept condemned by some respected geneticists. Three conditions necessary for differentiating groups into races have not been met. A stereotype, the belief that most members of a group possess a certain trait, may contain a kernel of truth, but is false when applied to almost all members of a large group. Stereotypes of Blacks are still negative, but have changed in content.

9. A study of Black's attributions to Whites reveals several negative stereotypes. The prejudiced personality is "threat-oriented." There is evidence that perceptions of parents' prejudice level and amount and quality of contact with Blacks may contribute to becoming racist or not. Towles-Schwen and Fazio found concern for displaying prejudice positively related to willingness/comfort in relating to Blacks. Prejudiced people have underlying feelings of hostility toward their parents and are highly moralistic. Several "gun–tool" studies showed that tools are mistaken for guns when in the hands of Blacks. More specifically, in "video games," compared to White men, unarmed Black men were more likely to be "shot," armed Black men were "shot" more quickly, a "don't shoot" button was hit more slowly for unarmed Black men, guns were more likely to be confused with harmless objects if held by a Black man, and Black citizens were more likely to be "shot" than White citizens. Prejudiced people dichotomize everything, show a high need for definiteness, and do poorly in college if their major lacks it, tend to externalize their own hostility, and are devoted to their institutions, most especially "the nation." Authoritarianism is associated with conservatism and shows a different pattern of prejudice and discrimination than SDO. Americans and White South Africans were likely to show "toughmindedness" and "competitiveness" if high on SDO while high authoritarians showed social conformity and believed in a dangerous world.

10. When classifying by "race," Whites preferred disliked White politicians to liked Black athletes. Devine's group found that high internal–low external Whites were the only group not to react negatively to Blacks on the subtle-implicit IAT. This same group was also the exception to the negative reaction to Blacks with eye blink and brain wave responses. Also, they found that this same group's non-conscious brain reactions indicated that they quickly gained control over prejudiced subtle responses. DuBois casts the uniqueness of Blacks' experience in terms of dualities: being a part of America and being excluded; collectivism and individuality. He also contended that prejudice and stereotyping result from slavery and its legacy of oppression. Allport voiced moderation on "behavioral consistency" and his "personality development" is influential. *The Nature of Prejudice* was a landmark contribution. Certain of his specific concepts have been useful, but his theory is really several mini-theories. His emphasis on p.d.s puts him out of the mainstream and the borders between the three kinds of p.d.s are murky. Still, his emphasis on the uniqueness and complexity of people may be realistic. His warmth and concern set him apart.

Running Comparison

Theorist	Allport in Comparison
Freud	He thought that Freud dug too deep but used some of his terms.
Fromm	His economic orientation and Fromm's marketing type are similar.
Murray	He disagrees with Murray on the importance of the unconscious.
Maslow	They both alluded to multiple motivations.
Kelly	Like Kelly, he adopted the "one person at a time" approach.
Cattell and Eysenck	He disagreed with them on emphasizing common traits.
Rotter	His prejudiced people were like Rotter's externals.
Horney	Prejudiced people show her "externalizing."

Essay/Critical Thinking Questions

1. How was Allport like his parents?

2. Could laughing at oneself be carried too far?

3. Can you describe some subtle indexes of racism that are not covered in your text?

4. How is the need for "definiteness" in prejudiced people linked to their prejudice?

E-mail Interaction

Write the author at b-allen@wiu.edu. Forward one of the following or phrase your own.

1. Tell me how unique I am. Is there anyone out there quite like me?

2. It seems that Allport was trying to promote religion. Tell me whether he was.

3. If racism is a thing that is wrong with White culture, what is right about it?

Where Is Personality Theory Going?

- If the notion "trait" were abandoned, what should take its place?
- What are the methodological problems confronting the study of personality?
- What is known about personality that can be confidently stated?

Underlying Assumptions

Underlying assumptions, whether made explicit or not, are the legs on which each theory stands. Personality theories can be differentiated on the basis of their assumptions. Laying out assumptions reveals the strengths and weaknesses of theories and exposes an assumptive pattern that is unique to each theory.

Temporal Orientation: Past, Present, and Future

Different theorists have different orientations regarding time. Some believe that what we do, think, and feel depends on what has happened to us in the past, sometimes the distant past. Others believe that what is happening right now, in the present, is all that one needs to know in order to understand people. Still others believe that people's attempts to anticipate the future determine their present and future thoughts, feelings, and behaviors.

Freud, of course, referred almost exclusively to the past. To a lesser degree, so did Skinner. The difference was that Skinner considered only what could be appreciated with the senses while Freud focused on mental entities that cannot be appreciated sensorially. Others, such as Jung, Horney, Sullivan, Murray, and, perhaps, Erikson, followed Freud in homing in on past influences that may have had some overt manifestations initially, but have come to be unobservable. Cattell and Eysenck were oriented to the past in that they believed that traits, with which we are born or that we develop early in life, determine our present and future.

The present was more of a concern for the humanists and kindred souls, such as the existentialists. Orientation to the future is relatively new and has its origins in cognitive psychology. George Kelly was a leader of the cognitive revolution and was among the first to emphasize the future. He believed that what people do, think, and feel is in the service of anticipating the future. At the same time, he rejected the phenomenologists' near-obsession with "the passing instant." Adler was ahead of his time in emphasizing "future goals." Rotter, Mischel, and Bandura joined him in assuming that people's expectations about the future drive their present thoughts, behaviors, and feelings.

Free Will?

Freud, of course, thought that we are driven by forces we cannot comprehend. Our ids and urges cause us to do what we do. Jung agreed, but he believed that our ancestral past, not our sexualized unconscious, make us who we are. To some extent, Murray agreed with them, though he leaned more toward Freudian unconscious factors. The humanists were at the other extreme. They, and the existentialists, believed that humans not only can, but must, take charge of their lives. All cognitive personologists promote the idea that people can, through cognitive processes they manipulate themselves, determine to a significant degree what happens to them in the future. Bandura explicitly endorses free will when he writes about "personal agency." Some think that Skinner assumed the ultimate deterministic position. To the contrary, he thought that we can arrange our environment so that the consequences we desire become likely. But, if we do, we are then under the control of our creation.

Consciousness and Unconsciousness

Explicitly or implicitly, personality theorists emphasize consciousness or unconsciousness. Freud was very explicit: as indicated by his iceberg analogy, the unconscious is most of the mental space, or psyche. It is what makes us behave, think, and feel. Jung, Horney, Sullivan, and Murray also assigned a significant role to the unconscious. In contrast, Skinner scoffed at all mentalistic notions. He acknowledged "consciousness" but believed that it need not be considered to understand the only psychological factor that mattered to him, behavior. Whether there was an unconscious was a question not worth addressing.

The humanists, including the existentialists, emphasize consciousness. What is "on the mind" *now* is of paramount importance to them. Allport did not totally reject the unconscious, but he cautioned against "digging too deep" during efforts to understand people. In the process of mining the psyche, one could dig right past what is really important. Social–cognitive psychologists Rotter, Mischel, and Bandura endorse consciousness implicitly by emphasizing people's thought processes. They have little to say about unconsciousness. Cattell and Erikson gave lip service to some of Freud's notions that imply unconsciousness, but place their emphasis elsewhere. Only notions linked to the biological side of individuals were of interest to Eysenck. Finally, Fromm transcended the whole debate by theorizing on a cultural rather than an individual level.

Developmental Stages

Freud's use of "stages" set a trend for personologists. Jung followed suit, as did Sullivan, but Erikson made an art form of it. Except for Freud, no psychologist's developmental stages have received more attention than Erikson's critically important life-span stages. He convinced most psychologists that personality is a whole-life process. Allport extended the development stages of personality by factoring in the evolution of the self.

Humans: "Good" or "Bad"?

Freudians have a reputation for depicting "humans" as "bad" in that they are seen as self-centered, pleasure-seeking bundles of impulses. People are thought to have little control over their lives and little concern about anything except themselves. While Jung had a somewhat more benign view of humans, Horney, Sullivan, and Murray have been attributed with an equally pessimistic perception of people. Fromm was also rather down on humans, though he confined his nihilism to their social side. Cattell and Eysenck also derogated humans in that they argued for the genetic position—people are shaped mostly by their genes—which meant that only a relatively few are intelligent and, therefore, worthy. It was the humanists—especially Rogers—who unequivocally cast humans in a positive light: they are "worthy," "valued," and capable of determining the courses of their own lives. Maslow agreed, but did so covertly. Social–cognitive theorists have been optimistic about people, as was Allport. Despite his reputation to the contrary, Skinner was also rather upbeat about people. He thought that humans could arrange their environments so that tragedies such as violence, exploitation, war, and poverty could be eliminated.

Internal or External Causation?

Of course, Freud thought that internal factors determine what people do, think, and feel. The same can be said for Jung, Horney, Sullivan, and Murray, who were all fans of unconsciousness, anxiety, or neurosis. Though he favored internal entities called "traits," not unconscious forces, Cattell belonged to the "internal" camp. Fellow trait theorist Eysenck can also be considered biased toward internal causation, but his biological bent is mostly responsible for his turn inward. Adler's social orientation moved him more in the direction of external causation. Fromm made basically the same assumption for much the same reason. Kelly and Mischel leaned toward internal causation because they are cognitive personologists, though both considered "situations." In contrast, Rotter and Skinner both relied heavily on the external event, "reinforcement," though they conceived of it differently. Allport, the social psychologist but also the trait theorist, went both ways. However, Bandura was unique in building an explicit rationale for a simultaneously external/internal orientation.

Bipolarity: Opposites Repel

Jung was perhaps the leader of many psychologists who believed that each psychological characteristic falls along a dimension with the pole at one end being the opposite of the pole at the other end (e.g., extraversion–introversion). Trait theorists such as Cattell, Murray, Eysenck, and Allport endorsed this point of view. The poles of Erikson's crises fit the bipolarity mold, as do Kelly's constructs. Others assumed bipolarity for at least a few of their concepts: Adler (inferiority–superiority), Rotter (internals–externals), and Skinner (acquisition [of a response]–extinction [of a response]).

Philosophical or Empirical?

Some personality theories are more philosophies than sets of formal propositions based on empirical evidence (data obtained through unbiased observation). Fromm's point of view may be the clearest example. He was trained in philosophy and sociology rather than empirical science. Karl Marx was at least as important to Fromm as was Freud. The humanists can also be fitted into the philosophical pigeonhole if one assumes that existential philosophy was at the core of their positions. Carl Rogers, however, was a pioneer in collecting observations of clients during therapy, and Maslow had strong scientific training. However, neither did much research. Horney and Sullivan were more philosophical than scientific in their theorizing. At best they and Murray could claim *only* observations of patients to support their positions.

Obviously, Freud had only observations of patients to back up his concepts and his observations cannot be called "unbiased." The same can be said about Jung. On the other side of the coin, no one was more the empiricist than Skinner. Cattell also belongs in the empiricist category. In some sense he was as strictly an empiricist as was Skinner. His theory emerged from observation without the benefit of any preexisting theory. Bandura, Mischel, and Eysenck are the best examples of theorists who start with theory from which they derived hypotheses to guide their observations.

Holism versus Fragmentation

The classic personality theories, Freud's and those that were extensions of or reactions to psychoanalysis (Jung's, Horney's, Sullivan's, and Murray's), tended to fragment humans. Ids, egos, and superegos, or neurotic needs and real versus ideal selves, or self-systems and modes of experiences, or psychogenic needs, actones, and complexes characterize these theories. In all fairness, Murray called for the consideration of the person as a whole. The whole person was to include neurobiological and psychological aspects welded into one unit, but his neurological notions about humans were shallow and couched in nebulous terminology. Thus, we are left with his psychological ideas, which hardly unified the person. It was really the humanists, principally Rogers and Maslow, who, more than others, discussed humans in holistic terms and who treated each of them as a whole, integrated being. They also, at least implicitly, delved into the spiritual aspect of humans. Yet, even their recognition of the "organismic" side of the person failed to consider biological issues in any explicit sense. Cattell and Eysenck did give lip service to biology when they applied their naive "genetics" to personality traits. In contrast, Skinner was overt in his concern for the genetic foundation of behavior. His understanding of genetics at the conceptual level was unique. But Bandura is the leader in emphasizing personal factors—including those of a biological nature—along with external environmental phenomena that are shaped by and also shape people's behavior. Only Allport was highly explicit in his efforts to call attention to the spiritual side of humans as he considered their social and personal (trait) facets.

Genetic versus Environmental Causation

From a genetic perspective, it is not reasonable to discuss genes apart from the environments in which they are expressed. Nor is it reasonable to consider environments apart from the genes that, in some degree, construct and alter them. Thus, dogmatic environmental determinists are just as wrongheaded as myopic genetic determinists. Separating genetic influences and other biological factors from the impact of the external environments may someday become passé. Still, there can be no doubt that the genes play a role in fashioning psychological characteristics, a fact that personologists must take into account more fully in the future. To do so, more of them must be trained by biological geneticists so they can search for actual genes contributing to the expression of personality characteristics. Their tasks will be daunting because personality entities are each very complex and are thus likely to be influenced by many genes. However, more sophisticated future techniques will eventually allow genuine psychologist-geneticists to specify the interplay of environment and genes in the expression of personality characteristics.

If this view is correct, then the older personality theories are out of sync with the growing trend toward connecting personality functioning to *correctly interpreted* biological evidence. Freud, Jung, Adler, Horney, and Murray fashioned their theories during an era that arrived and departed before sophisticated methods were developed to allow a clear look at the biology of thinking, feeling, and behaving. Now it is possible to do better. Such new observational techniques as MRIs (Magnetic Resonance Imaging), PET (Positron Emission Tomography), and CT (Computerized Tomography) scans are allowing psychologists, often in partnership with biologists, to look directly at the links between biology and behavior, thought, and feeling. In the future these methods may permit the more complicated concepts of Mischel and Bandura to be cast in more biological terms. Already, biology—principally genetics—is supporting Allport's claim that there are no human "races."

Idiographic versus Nomothetic Theory

Nomothetic refers to theory that involves general "laws" that apply a relatively few attributes to all people. *Idiographic,* in contrast, refers to theory that promotes the study of each person's unique attributes and does not attempt to characterize his or her personality in terms of a small number of dimensions. At first blush, there appears to be only one idiographic theorist, Allport. He was also the individual who popularized the two contrasting approaches to theorizing as they apply to traits. Ironically, Allport's emphasis on unique traits generates a paradox: he used the same trait labels employed by nomothetic theorists but asserts that, somehow, each label implies at least a somewhat different trait when it is applied to different people. Thus, one may ask, "Are there no living idiographic theorists?" There may be at least one. Mischel's most recent work fits the idiographic mold so well that it stands as a prime example of that orientation. In his research, each participant is observed behaving in the same set of social situations. Almost invariably, each participant displays a pattern of behavior across the situations that distinguishes her or him from every other participant. This is a complicated way to cast personality, but it rings true to what real people observe about other people and themselves. Intuitively, we know that our ability to function successfully in a variety of different situations depends on adopting behaviors that are fitted to our past experiences in those varied situations. Because each of us has a unique history in each of any set of situations, we will each show a somewhat different behavioral pattern across the situations. That we would behave much the same in different situations would seem counterintuitive to most of us.

It seems reasonable to add that Kelly may be regarded as an idiographic theorist, at least at the level of methodology. His REP test takes one person at a time and each displays at least a somewhat different set of constructs.

Conceptualizations

Categories of basic concepts differ across the various personality theories. Some center on "traits" ("states" are implied) while others concentrate on behavioral dispositions and social situations. Still others emphasize cognitions and a few consider temperaments.

Traits

I've gone on record pointing out a basic fault with the notion of traits, a conceptualization that has dominated modern personality theories (such as those of Cattell, Eysenck, Allport, and, some say, Murray). No discrete line of demarcation can be drawn between traits and their conceptual opposite, states. Such is the case because no one can answer the question, "How frequently must a behavior be displayed before one can infer a 'trait,' as opposed to inferring a supposedly infrequent 'state'?"

Another problem with traits, to which Bandura has alluded, is that they are supposed to be internally represented. Unfortunately, no one has been able to convincingly say how they are represented inside people except possibly in the activation of uniquely functioning bodies such as the brain's amygdala (emotions). The closest to an internal, biological representation of traits that researchers have claimed to find is that some few of them are "genetically determined." While it is a near certainty that someday genetic links to personality functioning will be found, so far the purely statistically and highly suspect heritability method has produced the only results that seem to support this position. Traits continue to be invented by researchers—for example, "thrill seeking"—and are declared to be "genetically determined" though even the heritability method allots only a small percentage of their variability to the genes.

Behavioral Dispositions

Alternatives to traits include "behavioral dispositions," a notion burdened with few of the problems that plague traits. A "disposition" is just an inclination toward something or other. Thus, one need not assume that a behavior to which people are disposed will be expressed with great consistency across many different situations. "Internal representation" is not a problem because the motor (behavioral) areas of the brain are relatively well understood. Also, the state–trait problem is avoided because a high frequency of behavioral performances need not be assumed before the existence of a disposition can be inferred. The problem with this position is that there are other aspects of personality—emotions, for example—that cannot be directly represented by behavior (emotions may have external, behavioral manifestations, but they are internal, physiological processes by their very nature). The role of cognition must also be factored in.

Cognitions

Cognitions represent another alternative to traits. Mischel's "competencies," Rotter's "expectancies," and Bandura's "self-regulatory processes" are cognitively based conceptions that avoid the problems associated with traits. The cognitive entities of these theorists are skills (competencies), anticipatory responses (expectancies), or rules to govern future behavior (self-regulatory processes). None of them require counting the frequency of behaviors or assuming cross-situational behavioral consistency. Thus, according to the cognitive view, people's uniqueness—personality—is expressed in the distinctiveness of their cognitive processes, not in the different positions they occupy on the different trait dimensions.

Temperament

Another conceptualization that offers advantages over traits is "temperament," which is mentioned by Cattell but then dismissed. Because temperaments are very broad dispositions—for example, being hyperactive versus being placid and inactive—referring to them brings with it no requirement that each be related to specific behaviors. Immediately the problems associated with the frequency counting/behavioral consistency disappear. In addition, broad dispositions seem, intuitively, more likely to have discoverable genetic underpinnings. There are an indefinite number of traits, with more likely to be "discovered" in the future. If the number of traits is indefinitely large, so is the number that are "inherited." This assumption strains the capacity of the genetic system (the human genome would have to be indefinitely large in size). In contrast, temperaments, by their very nature, are relatively few in number (psychological entities that are very broad must be relatively small in number). It seems entirely reasonable that some of them would be significantly influenced by the genes.

Constructs

"Construct," a notion popularized by Kelly, has been used differently by other psychologists. As it is more usually employed, a construct is a concept that is based on observations of relations among empirically verifiable events (events that we can record with our senses). To Kelly, a construct is a way of construing events or "seeing the world" so that the future is anticipated. In practice (using the REP test) constructs are bipolar and, thus, seem trait-like. However, when one remembers that the REP test is an idiographic device, a given construct (e.g., educated versus uneducated) can be regarded as different when possessed by different people. This observation frees constructs from the burdens of traits, but leaves them in an idiographic quandary: if everyone's set of constructs is different from that of everyone else, how can general principles emerge from studying construct systems?

Situations

It is absurd for radical trait theorists to claim that behavior corresponding to traits be almost entirely consistent across many situations. By the same token, it is absurd for "situationalists" to claim that each situation demands the same behavior from everyone in it. While one cannot be sure just who these situationalists are, most must belong to the group called "social psychologists." As one who is well informed about social psychologists, I think most, if not all, of them would agree with a straightforward proposition: there are only a small number of situations that are so powerful that they force the same behavior from each person performing in them. An example would be the famous "obedience to authority" situation created by social psychologist Stanley Milgram. Even in that prime case, not everyone behaved the same at the behest of authority. Most obeyed but some defied authority. The situations we find ourselves in no more absolutely dictate what we do than the traits attributed to us.

Methodologies

Reliance on Case Histories, Anecdotes, and Unsubstantiated Notions

There is no need to reiterate the shortcomings of case histories here (e.g., observations of single cases do not extrapolate to people in general). That is done in Chapter 1, where I also cover their virtues (e.g., they can illustrate and elucidate important points). While modern theorists have not depended on case histories to support their theories, classic theories are largely based on case histories. Examples include the theories of Freud, Jung, Horney, and Murray. Personologists should consider backing away from reliance on ancient ideas that were based on arbitrary and subjective interpretations of case histories. Freud's interpretations of his client's ruminations during therapy provide exemplary illustrations of case histories' shortcomings.

Some of the support Freud claimed for his theory came from what amounted to anecdotes. The "case history" of Little Hans is an example. Freud only met briefly with Hans on one occasion. Freud received almost all the information he had about Hans from the child's father, an enthusiastic fan of psychoanalysis. Jung may have made even greater use of anecdotes. Jung's own personal experiences constituted some of the stories that he took seriously. When he and Freud heard a noise emanating from a bookcase, Jung "predicted" that it would occur again. It did, but almost certainly by coincidence. His apocalyptic vision of floodwaters that contained floating bodies and the "rubble of civilization" was regarded as an accurate prediction of World War I. Anecdotes may also illustrate important points, but they should not be mistaken for scientific evidence.

Further, Freud and Jung also provide examples of how unsubstantiated notions can become accepted as important truths. It appears psychoanalysis's most basis assumption—

for patients to be cured it is necessary to dig up horrors submerged in their pasts—came from a patient of Freud's mentor, Josef Breuer. Anna O apparently conveyed this notion to Freud through Breuer. Where did it come from? Probably it originated in mythology. No hard evidence to support it was ever provided. Similarly, Jung's most basic idea, the collective unconscious, apparently came from nowhere (except possibly his imagination). There is no support for his claim that it came from the hallucinations of a patient.

Correlation Is Still Not Causation

Most personality research is correlational. That is, variables are just examined "as is": no manipulations of them occur (there is no attempt to purposely set the values of any variable). No serious researcher would infer causation flowing from one unmanipulated variable to another on the basis of simple correlation coefficients. However, use of more sophisticated correlational methods have seduced some researchers, causing them to make seemingly causal statements. "Path analysis" is one relatively new method that has had a seductive effect on some researchers (a popular, sophisticated variation is called "Structural Equation Modeling"). Although this technique appears to be very complicated, its basic aim seems relatively simple. Pathways from some remote variables through other variables to some target variables are predicted (pathways can also be direct from remote to target variables). If the predicted pathways are observed, language may be used to suggest that a causal chain was revealed that extends from the remote variable to the target variables. The implication is that the remote variables somehow "caused" the observed variation in the intermediate variables, which, in turn, "caused" the variation in the target variable(s). In fact, the remote variable's variation does not in any reasonable sense occur *before* that observed in other variables. The prior occurrence of variation on one variable followed by subsequent variation in another variable is ordinarily required for causal statements to be made. Perhaps researchers should reverse their theoretical paths: look at the effects discovered along the reversed paths and factor these effects into interpretations (or even calculations) of their theoretical paths. Perhaps the reversed paths involve effects that rival theoretical effects in strength. "Cause" going the other way should be reconciled with "theoretical cause." In any case, the variation of the remote variables was not determined by some researcher or controlled by her or him. Lapsing into causal language in explaining the results of path analysis and its kin is clearly inappropriate. The problem, of course, is not with the technique but with its use by some researchers. The method is, in fact, a powerful alternative technique that is highly useful in cases wherein manipulations of variables are not possible. Bandura used a variety of this method in his Italian studies and was cautious about the conclusions he reported. Still, as indicated in Chapter 1, the experimental approach continues to be superior to the correlational method for testing causal hypotheses. However, correlational approaches have convincing defenders and advances in structural equation modeling are finessing some problems with earlier techniques.

In a similar vein, factor analysis, a long-established method, is correlational. It begins with a correlation matrix. Just because a variable is "loaded" on a particular factor does not mean that something about the factor caused variation in the variable. Also, no causal relationship among variables is implied by the observation that those variables all load on the same factor. Finally, just because two variables load on different factors does not imply that they are "caused" by different forces.

Where Have the Experiments Gone?

As I've indicated in this book, personologists rarely do real experiments: they rarely manipulate one variable and then observe whether there are any effects on some other variable(s). A possible reason for this neglect is that many personologists—especially trait theorists—assume that personality variables are set early in life and, thus, it is not possible to manipulate them. The major exception to this "rule" is Eysenck.

Suspending the assumption that personality variables are immutable could lead to a test of it. If a personality variable is truly set early in life (or at conception), attempts to manipulate it should fail. But what if experimental attempts to manipulate some personality variable—say, extraversion—succeeded? Let's assume that not only participants' levels of extraversion were changed, but also the gaps between them were closed so that most of them would have extreme extraversion scores. Would success at changing participants' extraversion necessarily mean that extraversion is highly malleable? In fact, such success has been reported in the personality literature and in this book. But does it necessarily mean that extraversion changes readily rather than being relatively stable? No, it does not. In the short term, it is possible to move extraverts in the direction of introversion (or the other way around). However, it may be likely that they would eventually move back approximately to their original positions on the extraversion scale. So why bother to move them? Moving people in the short term could allow for some interesting observations that might support some theory. For example, a theory that suggests that low extraversion in group members hampers group interaction might be supported if making people temporarily less extraverted reduces the level of social interaction when they are formed into groups.

The moral of this story is straightforward: avoiding experimentation in the study of personality makes no sense. Showing that supposedly immutable personality variables can be temporarily changed does no necessary damage to the assumption that these variables are relatively stable. Further, submitting personality variables to experimental manipulations might provide strong support for some theories. In sum, it seems obvious that conducting more experiments would advance the discipline of personality.

What We Know about Personality

Even with all the criticisms of theorists' assumptions and notions about personality, there is agreement concerning at least some of its qualities. Further, modern research has made it possible to state at least some strong conclusions about personality.

Personality Is Uniqueness

The one pronouncement about personality on which (almost) all personologists would probably agree (if they were asked) is that each human being's *unique* set of psychological characteristics (PCs) constitute her or his personality. But are PCs "cognitive processes," "traits," "needs," "constructs," or something else? While consensus on this issue seems unlikely in the near future, agreement on uniqueness could, *if generally acknowledged,* lead to greater theoretical flexibility. In turn, greater flexibility could lead to new theories that represent novel perspectives.

Personality Is Complex

Future personality theorists must understand what the classic personologists did not: personality is complex, not simplex. Classic theorists, such as Freud and Jung, attempted to characterize personality by use of only a few notions. Further, "personality" was described in vague, abstract terms as if it were something that transcended the brain. It was almost as if personality was an apparition that formed an aura about a person. People could not see, touch, or otherwise appreciate "personality" with their senses, but it was assumed that they could somehow apprehend its presence and nature. It is something that just *is;* no deeper comprehension is called for. What could be more simplex than that?

If personality is to be an entity that can be investigated and understood by scientific methods, it cannot be a nebulous thing that is described in only a few simple terms. It must become a concrete, complex phenomenon that scientists can relate to neurological and other biological processes. If personality theory evolves in this way, the day may come when its complexity is so great that it can no longer be considered only one thing. That is, global theories that attempt to account for all of personality within one frame of reference may become a thing of the past. Instead, we may see theories that deal with "interpersonal processes" (e.g., forming attachments to others) and "personal identity processes" (e.g., self-concept) and "daily functioning processes" (e.g., moral decision making) as well as other, more circumscribed theories.

What Will the Personality Theories of the Twenty-First Century Be Like?

Personality theories of the twenty-first century are likely to be more eclectic than the theories of the last two centuries, but not in the sense of tying together all theories in a grand attempt to explain everything about personality. They will be more eclectic in that they may use the best of previous theories' assumptions, conceptualizations, and methodologies to explain phenomena existing in some domain of the general personality arena (e.g., personal identity processes). In order to elaborate on this eclectic approach, we need to go back to the issues raised here and make some projections as to how they will play out in this new century.

Temporal Orientation.   Taking into account the explosive growth of cognitive psychology, it appears that people's orientation to the future, rather than to the past or the present, will be more emphasized during this century. This doesn't mean that future personality theories will not take into account people's attention to the past and the present. It does, however, mean that anticipation of the future may become more and more the focus of personality theories. Individuals under investigation by modern personologists have made it through the past and are surviving in the present, so what is it about them that will most facilitate attempts to understand them? It is intuitively obvious that whatever explains their anticipations of the future will provide the best means of understanding them. Such is true because anticipatory processes are proving to be good predictors of what people actually do, think, and feel on future occasions.

Consciousness and Unconsciousness. Solid research by psychologists such as Anthony Greenwald has made it clear that, yes, unconsciousness does exist, but no, it is not really what Freud and those who borrowed from him have said it is. Widespread acceptance of this research, along with the burgeoning cognitive movement, will likely make conscious processes more the focus in the future.

Developmental Stages. Casting development into *stages* has always been a part of both personality theories and child development theories. Such will be true in the future if the problems with stage conceptions are corrected. First, a given set of stages may apply only to people in certain cultures, not all cultures (e.g., Freud's psychosexual stages don't seem to apply to American Indians). Second, while a set of stages may apply to most people, some people may not go through the stages in the order proposed by the theorist who conceived them (e.g., Erikson's theory). A bit of flexibility and a willingness to custom fit stage conceptions to each broad, major culture will save the day for stage notions.

Humans: "Good" or "Bad"? Of course, it is philosophically impossible to decide whether all humans are "good" or all are "bad." Further, I think that it is unsatisfying and unproductive to simply assume "it's neither": there are both "good" and "bad" facets of people (or they are capable of "good" and "bad" actions). Such a default assumption leaves us struggling with discovering the "good" in people as well as the "bad." It seems better to do what the humanists have done, make a positive assumption about people: they are all worthy ("good"). Embracing this optimistic assumption will allow future personality theories to accentuate the positive and eliminate the negative. Modern theories that assume humans are "good" can focus on what promotes people's natural worthiness and on what causes them to betray their positive essence.

Internal or External Causation? (and) Genetic versus Environmental Causation. While it was an important issue during the nascent period of personality theory development, trying to decide between internal and external causation now seems almost ludicrous. Of course, both are important. The cognitive revolution and the burgeoning field of biological psychology ensure that only personality theories taking both internal and external events into account will survive in the future. "Cognition" is in part about the internal conception of external events. Cognitive processes both influence and are influenced by external events. Likewise, neurological, genetic, and other biological processes that function internally both influence and are influenced by external events. We cannot decide between external and internal causation of personality. Here is a debate we can call to a halt.

In a similar vein, we cannot decide between genetic and environmental causation. Genes unfold in environments that can change the expressions of the traits modulated by the genes. Under genetic influence, environments can be altered. So it is time to call an end to another debate. "The nature/nurture debate is over," and that is a virtual quote of a behavioral geneticist writing in one of psychology's most prestigious journals.

Bipolarity.   Bipolar notions have always been a part of personality theorizing and probably always will be. Trait theorists (Cattell, Eysenk, and Allport), classic theorists (Jung), cognitive–social personologists (Rotter), and "need" personologists (Murray) have embraced bipolar conceptions. As these diverse uses of bipolarity do not involve any contradictions—they are simply different ways to use the same idea—one can expect future personality theorists to use or not use bipolarity as it suits them.

Philosophical or Empirical?   During the premodern science era that existed at the time Freud, Jung, and Adler wrote their theories, it made some sense to speculate and "take ideas off the top of the head." After all, the scientific underpinnings of psychology were weak or nonexistent. It was a time when respected academics believed, based on nothing, that bumps on the head indicated various intellectual and personal characteristics. That bigger heads meant bigger brains, thus more intelligence, was extrapolated from the "bumps" notion and is still believed. But now we have modern scientific methods and results. It is time to reconsider premodern science ideas that came from nowhere and have not been practically useful or empirically supported. Why do we cling to these ideas? Because their nonscientific origins have been lost in time and no one has bothered to go in search of them. Not only the "bigger brain" notion and Freud's "dig up the past" assumption, but all ancient ideas that have never garnered any scientific support and/or have never proven practically useful should be laid aside. It is already true that ideas "taken off the top of the head" and presented without empirical support do not get into psychological journals. It will be truer in the future.

Idiographic versus Nomothetic Theory.   With the deaths of Kelly and Allport, idiographic theory has few proponents among major, living personologists. Only Mischel's theory qualifies as explicitly idiographic. Thus, the survival of the idiographic approach may depend on the prosperity of Mischel's view during this century.

Traits, Temperament, Behavioral, and Other Dispositions.   Will traits survive in the twenty-first century? They have been infused with such inertia during the past century it is very likely that they will survive, especially if trait theorists become more flexible. The notion, "trait," would shed many of the burdensome, excess baggage that weighed heavily on it during the last century if it came to be virtually synonymous with "temperament." Temperaments are broad orientations that, because of their wide scope, would not be expected to manifest themselves consistently across a spectrum of specific situations. They would also be more manageable because, each being broad, there would be relatively few of them to deal with. Further, their wide scope makes it more likely that genes relating to them might be discovered. The genetic system would crumble under its own weight if it generated genes for an indefinitely large number of narrow and specific characteristics.

Each temperament might give rise to a number of "behavioral dispositions," a phrase that is itself unburdened by trait assumptions: a "disposition" might be manifested in a given situation, but it would not necessarily. And why limit personality to behavioral dispositions? Temperaments might generate a number of cognitive and emotional dispositions. In sum, "traits" will survive if trait theorists become more broad-minded.

Cognitions and Constructs. The tentacles of cognitive science are stretching to almost all subdisciplines of psychology. "Cognitive processes" is a phrase that flows from the lips of scientists from many disciplines, not just psychology. For example, engineers working on artificial intelligence are heavily into "cognitive processes." Thus, in the field of personality, and in many others as well, the future of "cognitions" is very bright. The same cannot be said for "constructs" as Kelly conceived of the term. The notion as Kelly used it may die with his students. However, one never knows. Bolstered by the tenacious efforts of British psychologists, the roots of Kelly's theory may find fertile soil in the next century.

Situations. *Situation* is a murky concept. Rarely do those who use it define it. Probably because there is no consensus on its definition, attempts to develop taxonomies of situations have lost steam. How can something be classified if there is no agreement as to what it is? Unless at least most of the personologists who use the term agree on what it means, it is not likely to survive in the next century. Instead, each personologist will come up with her or his own conception of the social and physical environmental elements that interact with personality.

Reliance on Case Histories, Anecdotes, and Unsubstantiated Notions. Case histories will always be useful to illustrate important points. However, I have faith that anecdotes and notions materializing out of thin air are things of the past. We now have a solid scientific base from which to derive new conceptualizations. There is no longer any need to depend on cultural lore, mythology, or "off the top of the head" ideas.

Correlation Is Still Not Causation (and) Where Have the Experiments Gone? One reason that correlation will likely remain the most used technique for analyzing personality data is that experimental manipulations are often not feasible. If one wants to know how conscientiousness relates to grades in college, he or she is unlikely to come up with a conscientiousness manipulation powerful enough to influence grades. Further, this example suggests a second reason for the continued use of correlation. Attempting to "manipulate" people's basic characteristics, even temporarily, raises serious ethical questions. Still, I expect that increased flexibility on the part of this century's personologists will lead to an increased use of the experimental method. Much can be learned from creating variance along some personality dimension in order to observe effects on social behavior, cognition, or emotion.

Personality and Neuroscience

In the future, personality, like other psychological disciplines, is likely to rely more heavily on neuroscience. Ultimately what was learned in the last century about learning, memory, and perception will be translated into neuroscience ("brain") explanations. In fact, for those three disciplines, the process of translation is well underway. As Chapter 16 discloses, the study of personality traits is beginning to ascend to the level of neuroscience. Chapter 17 makes it clear that understanding personalities that are tainted by racism, and those that are relatively untainted, has already become a major neuroscience pursuit. Such will also be true of other personality sub-disciplines in the future.

In sum, there is every reason to expect that personality theories of the twenty-first century will include cognitive processes, will openly acknowledge that personality is uniqueness, will become more flexible, will be more future oriented, will concentrate on consciousness, will shed the false dichotomy "nature/nurture," will be more holistic, will pay more attention to developments in biological science (especially neuroscience), will abandon ideas plucked from nowhere, will broaden the notion "trait," will include experimentation, and, more generally, will acknowledge the complexity of personality.

Summary Points

1. "Future orientation" is likely to be more in focus in this century. Bandura's "personal agency" represents the "free will" movement of the present and, probably, the future. Conciousness has been emphasized by more modern personality theorists than classic theorists. "Stages of development" have been and will likely remain a pillar of personality psychology.

2. Deciding whether humans are "good" or "bad" is ultimately impossible and leads to unsatisfying solutions. Of course, personality theories must account for both external and internal determinants of thought, feeling, and behavior. The continued use of "bipolarity" seems unproblematic. Personality psychology will always have its philosophical underpinnings, but it is now possible to rely more on hard evidence.

3. There will always be a need to consider personality from a holistic perspective. Yet it is likely that considerations of the "organismic" side of people, just which aspects of personality are significantly influenced by the genes, and the spiritual side of people will be issues in the future. In the future psychologists will need to be trained in genetics.

4. Other biological contributions, such as developments in neuro-imaging, will play an important role in twenty-first century personality research. Nomothetic theories have ruled the roost in psychology, but the idiographic approach may fit the complexity of personality best. The problems with traits include how they are represented internally. "Genetics" seem one way to cast the internal representation of personality traits, but it has its own problems.

5. "Behavioral dispositions" seem attractive alternatives to traits, but they have their own limitations. Cognitive processes, on the other hand, have a bright future. The appeal of "temperament" rests in its breadth, which increases the likelihood of discovering a manageable number of genes relating to personality. "Constructs" seem to have few advocates today and may have fewer in the future. "Situation" is a murky concept, which, in any case, rarely exercises absolute control over behavior.

6. Reliance on case histories, anecdotes, and unsubstantiated notions once may have made sense, but no more. Correlation is still not causation, despite the development of new, sophisticated methods. Experimentation is still the best avenue to "casual statements" and is needed to support some hypotheses. Twenty-first century psychology will acknowledge "uniqueness" as the cornerstone of personality.

7. Personality is so complex that grand theories may give way to mini-theories. In the future, neuroscience will be prominent in the study of personality. The temporal orientation in the future will be "the future." Consciousness may eclipse unconsciousness in the future. Developmental stages are here to stay, but "good human"/"bad human" debate may be replaced by a positive assumption about humans. With regard to internal versus external, or more specifically, genes versus environment, the "nature/nurture" debate is over.

8. Empiricism will dominate philosophizing, but, in the future, the idiographic approach will need new advocates. Traits will survive, if they are broadened and made more flexible. Cognitions are here to stay, but constructs have an uncertain future. The era of heavy reliance on case histories, anecdotes, and unsubstantiated notions is over. Although correlation will always have its place in the study of personality, experimentation will likely increase in the future.

Running Comparison

Issue	*Theorists Who Endorse This Issue or Not*
Past, Present, Future	Freud, Rogers, and Bandura, respectively
Free Will	Maslow, Rogers, Bandura, and Kelly; partially: Horney, Fromm, Erikson, Adler, and Skinner (?) vs. Freud, Jung, Sullivan, and Murray
Unconsciousness/ Consciousness	Freud, Jung, Horney, and Sullivan vs. Allport, Rotter, Mischel, and Bandura
Developmental States	Freud, Jung, Erikson, Allport, and Sullivan
Humans: "Good" or "Bad"	Freud, Horney, Sullivan, and Murray vs. Rogers, Maslow, and Bandura
Internal vs. External Causation	Freud, Jung, Horney, Sullivan, Murray, Cattell, and Eysenck vs. Adler, Rotter, and Skinner
Bipolarity	wholly: Cattell, Eysenck, Murray, Allport, and Kelly; partially: Adler, Rotter, and Skinner
Philosophical vs. Empirical	Freud, Fromm, Horney, Murray, and Sullivan vs. Cattell, Eysenck, Skinner, Rotter, Mischel, and Bandura; partially: Rogers and Maslow
Holism vs. Fragmentation	Rogers, Maslow, and Murray (partially) vs. all others to varying degrees
Genetic vs. Environmental	Cattell and Eysenck (no true "environmentalists," except Skinner in a limited sense)
Idiographic vs. Nomothetic	Kelly, Mischel, and Allport (partially) vs. all of the others to varying degrees
Traits	Cattell, Eysenck, Murray, and Allport vs. Mischel, Bandura, and Rotter
Dispositions	Mischel, Rotter, and Bandura in some sense
Cognitions	Kelly, Mischel, and Bandura
Temperament	None of the theorists fully addresses temperament.
Constructs	Kelly
Situations	Mischel, Rotter, and Bandura use or imply "situations" in their work and theory.

Essay/Critical Thinking Questions _____

1. Argue that consciousness has been neglected.

2. Who is truly a holistic personologist?

3. When can you conclude "causation" based on correlational research?

4. Why is "uniqueness" so crucial to the conception of personality?

5. Argue for the increased use of experimentation in future personality research.

E-mail Interaction _____

Write the author at b-allen@wiu.edu. Forward one of the following or phrase your own.

1. Where do you stand on Free Will?

2. In the future, will there be a role for philosophy in the study of personality?

3. What will be the value of case histories in the future study of personality?

4. Whose present-day theories are most likely to carry over into the future?

5. Give me some more examples of "temperament."

Glossary

Abience is the name given to the negative need-promoting vectors that describe movements away from objects and people.

Ability trait is reflected in the kind of "response to the complexity of a situation, [that is selected after] the individual is clear on what goals he wants to achieve in that situation."

Abstracting across the cleavage line occurs when whole constructs fall under superordinate emergent and under superordinate implicit poles.

Accurate empathy is Rogers's term for the ability to correctly perceive the client's internal world in a nonevaluative way.

Activating stimuli are more complicated than simple stimuli in that they cause people to become engaged in productive activity for longer periods of time.

Active imagination is a method through which patients are encouraged to simulate dream experiences by actively engaging in imagination while fully awake.

Actone is a pattern of bodily movements in and of itself, divorced from its effect.

Actual self (Horney) is who one currently is.

Adience refers to the positive need-promoting vectors that describe movement toward objects and people.

Advantageous comparison is a cognitive mechanism by which " . . . deplored acts can be made to appear righteous by contrasting them with flagrant inhumanities."

Aesthetic needs are related to beauty, structure, and symmetry.

Alpha is press that actually exist, that is, are objectively verifiable.

Ambiverts show medium degrees of extraversion–introversion, with behaviors characteristic of both aspects.

Amphigenital refers to the case in which one or both members of a pair, who both may be homosexual or heterosexual, take on a role that is different from their usual role.

Amplification is broadening and enriching dream or other image content through a process of directed association.

Anal-expulsive is an adult personality type inclined to disregard widely accepted rules such as cleanliness, orderliness, and "appropriate behavior," a "diarrhetic" orientation.

Anal-retentive is an adult personality type that is characterized by delay of final satisfactions to the last possible moment; these people save, retain, show orderliness, stinginess, and stubbornness, a constipated orientation.

Anal stage is a period in which sexual gratification occurs when defecation relieves the tension of a full bowel and simultaneously stimulates the anus.

469

Anima is the representation of woman in man.

Animus is man in woman.

Anxiety (Freud) is a state of extremely unpleasant emotional discomfort.

Anxiety (Kelly) is what a person experiences when his or her construction system does not apply to critical events.

Anxiety gradient refers to "learning to discriminate increasing from diminishing anxiety and to alter activity in the direction of the latter."

Arbitrary rightness is the strategy of people who see life as a merciless battle and, therefore, feel they must be definite and "right" about everything lest "foreign influence" control them.

Archetypes, or ancient types, are preexistent forms that are innate and represent psychic predispositions that lead people to apprehend, experience, and respond to the world in certain ways.

Ascending reticular activating system (ARAS) acts as an arousal mechanism. The core of the system is the reticular formation of the brain stem.

Assimilation is how people acquire things.

Attitude (Cattell) is an expression of an ergic goal that is generally subsidiated to an erg(s).

Attitude (Jung) is a readiness of the psyche to act or react to experience in a certain way.

Attractors are stable end states resulting from multiple exposures to many situations; each represents a "state of mind," such as a set of beliefs or a set of affective states (e.g., states of security and resentment).

Authoritarians show high deference for authority figures, submission to the power of authority, and a need to command those seen as lower in the power than themselves.

Automaton conformity is the condition that occurs when the person, out of fear of aloneness, gives up freedom for union with society, and she or he bends over backwards to maintain the union by strict adherence to social norms and conventions.

Autonomy is independence stemming from the reasonable self-control that allows children to hold rather than restrain, to let be rather than lose.

Autophilic person is one who manifests no preadolescent development, because it has not oc-curred or was attempted without success, causing the continuation of self-directed love.

Basic anxiety is "an insidiously increasing, all-pervading feeling of being lonely and helpless in a hostile world."

Basic conflict involves contradictory orientations to move toward, away from, and against others, all existing within a neurotic.

Basic mistrust is the feeling of abandonment and helpless rage that accompanies uncertainty of satisfaction.

Basic trust results from the infant's sense that it can count on satisfaction of its needs; the world takes on the aura of a "trustworthy realm."

Behavioral dimension is a continuum of behavior analogous to a yardstick.

Behaviorism is a school of psychology for which the basic subject matter is "outside"; it is overt (observable) behavior.

Behavior therapy is psychological therapy employing behavioral techniques.

Belongingness and love needs orient the person toward affectionate relations with people, and a sense of place in family and groups.

Beta is press that are determined by the person's own interpretation, that is, subjectively determined.

Biophilia is love of life.

Birth order is the child's position relative to other siblings.

Blaming victims for their own fate is a self-exonerative process for escaping self-blame.

Blind spot is an area of contradiction about which the individual manages to remain unaware.

Bodily self is sensations that emanate from the muscles, joints, tendons, eyes, ears, and so on.

Brief therapy approach involves techniques that address and solve clients' problems in a specifiable and relatively small number of sessions.

B-values are ultimate or end-goals of meta-need fulfillment.

Cardinal p.d.s are pervasive and outstanding in the life of a person.

Care, the strength of maturity, is "the broadening concern for what has been generated by love, necessity, or accident—concern that overcome[s] . . . the narrowness of self-concern."

Case history method involves collecting background data about and making intensive observations on a single individual in order to discover how to treat that person or to obtain information that may apply to other people.

Castration anxiety is a generalized fear on the part of boys that they might lose their penises, the highly prized organs of pleasure (father may cut it off).

Catharsis is a process by which inner feelings are openly expressed in words or behaviors that can lead to relief of tensions.

Cathexes (Freud) are attachments of libidinous energy either to real external-world objects or to fantasized inner-world images.

Cathexis (Murray) is a process by which an object evokes a need.

Central p.d. is one of the entries on the relatively large list of traits we use to summarize an individual's personality.

Characterizing events associated with a situation is placing them into meaningful categories.

Childhood stage emerges with articulate speech and ends with the appearance of the need for peers (preschool years).

Choice is a decision between the alternatives provided by the construct that has preempted the situation.

Circumspection phase refers to a period of "trying on for size" the various constructs available in our personal repertory.

Cognitive Affective Personality System (CAPS; Mischel) "is characterized by . . . available cognitive and affective [or feeling] units" such that "when certain configurations of situation features are experienced by the individual a . . . subset of cognitions and affects becomes activated."

Cognitively complex people have construction systems containing constructs that are clearly differentiated, that is, distinguished one from the other.

Cognitively simple people have construction systems for which distinctions among constructs are blurred, a poorly differentiated system.

Cognitive needs are motivations to know, to understand, to explain, and to satisfy curiosity.

Collective unconscious is a storehouse of ancestral experiences dating to the dawn of humankind and common to all humans.

Commonality is a reference to the sharing of constructs by two or more people whose experiences are similar.

Common trait (Cattell) is "A trait which can be measured for all people by the same battery [of tests] and on which [the people] differ in degree rather than in form."

Common traits (Allport) "are . . . those aspects of personality in respect to which most people within a given culture can be profitably compared."

Compartmentalization is a mechanism by which individuals separate key aspects of themselves and their life situations into "logic-tight" compartments.

Compensate is to overcome weaknesses by striving to become superior in some way.

Compensation is the balancing of a conscious experience with an opposing unconscious representation as in observations that a dream's meaning is often just the opposite of the person's conscious experience.

Competence is "the free exercise (unimpaired by an infantile sense of inferiority) of dexterity and intelligence in the completion of serious tasks."

Competency embraces both the cognitive ability to size up a situation so that one understands how to operate effectively in it and the ability to perform behaviors that will lead to success in the situation.

Complexes are mental contents in the psyche that agglutinate or stick together like the clumping of red blood cells and eventually take up residence in the personal unconscious.

Conflicts of needs occur when needs oppose each other "within the personality, giving rise when prolonged to harassing spiritual dilemmas."

Congruence is a state in which a person's self-concept and actual experiences relating to self are consistent.

Conscience is the internal agent that punishes us when we do wrong.

Consequence is an event that occurs after a response has been performed and changes the probability that the response will occur again.

Construction system is an organization of many constructs with the more important, and often more abstract, at the top and the less important constructs at the bottom.

Constructive alternativism is the assumption that a person's present interpretations of her or his life situation are subject to revision and replacement.

Constructs are ways of construing events or "seeing the world" so that the future is anticipated.

Contentment is the perception that one's efforts result in the promotion of human well-being and that one is revered in the local community because of "good works."

Context of a construct is composed of all those elements to which the construct applies.

Contingent refers to a relationship in which the occurrence of event B depends on the prior occurrence of event A.

Continuous reinforcement involves a reinforcer following every response.

Contrafactions of needs are cases in which needs are related to their opposites in alternating phases.

Correlated refers to a condition that exists if variations in one variable correspond closely with variations in another.

Correlation coefficient is an index, designated by the letter *r*, of the degree to which variables are correlated.

Countertransference occurs when analysts project their own unconscious needs onto their patients.

Creative power of the individual is the process by which we each make original conceptions of ourselves and our world as we develop a style of life for pursuing the three great tasks.

Crystallized general ability (g_c) is "A general factor, largely . . . abilities learned at school, representing . . . applications of [g_f], and amount and intensity of schooling; it appears in vocabulary and numerical ability [tests]."

Cumulative records are graphs for which responses are accumulated and plotted against time.

Cynicism is "the denying or deriding of moral values" because of a deep-seated uncertainty with regard to morality.

Defense mechanisms are internal, unconscious, and automatic psychological strategies for coping with or regaining control over threatening id instincts.

Defensive behaviors are adopted in order to cope with unpleasant events that are anticipated on future occasions.

Deficiency needs or D-needs involve satisfactions that allow the person to avoid physical sickness and psychological maladjustment.

Dehumanization is a cognitive process that involves lowering the status of certain people from "human being" to "lesser being."

Delaying gratification is postponing some pleasure so that it can be enjoyed to the maximum degree or in its optimal form.

Denial (Freud) is the process by which we refuse to think about or address whatever is too hard to bear.

Denial (Rogers) involves the inability to recognize or accept the existence of an experience that has occurred.

Dependency constructs are special constructs that revolve around the child's survival needs, for example, a "mother" construct.

Dependent variables have values that are free to vary so that they are open to influence by the independent variables.

Despair is a feeling that time is too short for the achievement of integrity and the accompanying contribution to the connection between generations.

Diffusion of innovation occurs when models try something new and, thereby, display its benefits and advantages to others.

Dignity or worth is what we refer to when we give people credit for what they have done.

Directedness is having a goal or goals in life toward which one strives.

Discriminative facility is a sensitivity to the subtle cues in a situation that influence behavior, which amounts to a kind of social intelligence.

Displacement is finding a new target for some feelings, one that is less threatening than the original.

Displacement and diffusion of responsibility involves placing the blame for one's deplorable acts onto others, and spreading the responsibility for reprehensible behavior to others who are present, respectively.

Distortion involves a reinterpretation of an experience so as to make it consistent with how one wants things to be.

Diversity refers to the numerous cultures, along with gender and sexual orientations, that characterize the population in the United States and other countries.

Dream series analysis involves large numbers of dreams in succession, because Jung believed that one or a few dreams did not tell the whole story.

Dream symbol is an element of dream content that represents some person, thing, or activity involved in unconscious processes.

Dynamic lattice is "The tracing of the subsidiation of attitudes . . . ending in the satisfaction of a number of primary ergic goals."

Dynamic trait refers to motivations and interests.

Early adolescence erupts at puberty when the need for intimacy evolves toward lustful feelings of closeness and tenderness with a sexual partner.

Early infancy (Allport) is the first stage and involves no sense of self.

Early recollections (ERs) indicate how a person views her- or himself and other people and reveal what the person strives for in life, what he or she anticipates, and, more generally, his or her conception of life itself.

Effectiveness is the need to compensate for "being in a strange and overpowering world" by developing a sense of being able to do something that will "make a dent" in life.

Ego (Freud) is a coherent organization of mental processes that develops out of id energy, has access to consciousness, and is devoted to contacting reality for the purpose of satisfying id needs.

Ego (Jung) is what one thinks of oneself, the genuine me, and is the "centre of the total field of consciousness."

Ego ideal is positive standards in the form of internal representations of idealized parental figures that can result in feelings of pride and self-respect.

Ego-strength refers to the ability of the ego to successfully interact with reality on behalf of the id

and inhibit id impulses until "safe" satisfactions are found.

Elaborative choice is a selection of an alternative, aligned to a single construct dimension, that appears to provide the greatest opportunity for the further elaboration of a system.

Electra complex is based on the myth of Electra, who hated and participated in killing her mother.

Elusiveness is the ability to slither away from conflicts by refusing to take a stand.

Emergent pole is the primary and principle end of a construct, such as "good" in good–bad and "intelligent" in intelligent–stupid.

Empathy (Rogers) is sensing and participating in the emotions of others.

Empathy (Sullivan) is "the term that we use to refer to the peculiar emotional linkage [that exists between the] infant [and] other significant people. . . ."

Entropy is the equalization of differences in order to bring about a balance or equilibrium.

Epigenesis (*epi* means 'upon' and *genesis* means 'emergence') The life stages literally emerge "one on top of another in space and time."

Equivalence is the circumstance in which energy consumed to accommodate one intention—"say something nice"—is balanced by energy fueling an opposite intention—"say something nasty."

Erg is "An innate source of reactivity, such as is often described as a drive [or instinct], directed to a certain goal. . . ."

Erogenous zones are sensitive areas of the body from which instinctual satisfactions can be obtained.

Eros represents energy for preserving oneself (love of self) and one's species (love of others).

Esteem needs are of two kinds: (1) there are personal desires for adequacy, mastery, competence, achievement, confidence, independence, and freedom; and (2) there are desires for respect from other people, including attention, recognition, appreciation, status, prestige, fame, dominance, importance, and dignity.

Eugenics is the application of genetics to the improvement of human biological and psychological characteristics.

Euphemistic labeling is the cognitive process of assigning a name to deplorable behavior that makes it seem innocuous or even laudable.

Eupsychia (yew-sigh-key-ah) is a utopian society characterized by psychological health among all its members.

Excessive self-control arises in reaction to a flood of contradictory emotions and involves holding feelings and behavior in a vise-grip.

Excitation and stimulation is the need for the nervous system to be "exercised," that is, to experience a certain amount of excitation.

Existentialism is a philosophically based approach to understanding each person's most immediate experience and the conditions of his or her existence.

Existential needs are needs that must be met if one's existence is to be meaningful, one's inner being is to be developed, one's talents are to be fully exploited, and abnormality is to be avoided.

Expansive is to be "in control," to not admit that one is incorrect (or another person is correct), and to never give an inch in a conflict.

Expectancy (Mischel) is a belief based on past experience that provides a prediction of future outcomes.

Expectancy (Rotter) is "the probability held by the individual that a particular reinforcement will occur as a function of a specific behavior on his part in a specific situation or situations."

Experience (Kelly) is what one learns from the events of the past.

Experience (Rogers) is all that is going on within the organism at any given moment that is potentially available to awareness.

Experiment is a procedure whereby an experimenter first sets the variation in some independent variable(s) and then ascertains whether variation in some dependent variable(s) is influenced.

Exploitative orientation involves experiencing the source of all good as outside of oneself, and taking things through force or cunning, rather than expecting to receive from others.

Extension of self is expanding oneself to include all those significant aspects of one's environment, including people.

Extension of the cleavage line is a reference to the observation that the poles of a person's subordinate constructs fall directly under the corresponding emergent and implicit poles of his or her superordinate constructs.

Externalization is the tendency to experience internal processes as if they occurred outside oneself and to hold these "exterior" factors responsible for one's difficulties.

External locus of control refers to people's belief that reinforcement of their behaviors is due more to luck, chance, fate, powerful others, or complex and unpredictable environmental forces, rather than being determined by their own behaviors, efforts, or characteristics.

Extinction occurs when a previously reinforced response is no longer followed by the same reinforcer and the response eventually decreases in frequency.

Extraversion is an "outward-turning" of libido that involves a positive movement of interest away from one's inner experience toward outer experience.

Extrinsic (Allport) refers to an orientation to religion that is utilitarian and in the service of self-esteem maintenance.

Extrinsic rewards are rewards originating outside the individual (e.g., money).

Factor in *factor analysis* refers to a hypothetical construct that is applied to a data cluster (set of items) and suggests what it is measuring.

Factor analysis is a statistical procedure for determining the number and nature of factors underlying larger numbers of measures.

Favorable ratio refers to the idea that the greater the magnitude of the pull to the positive pole relative to the pull of the negative pole the better.

Fear is the experience one has when a new construct appears to be entering the system, and may become dominant.

Feature of a situation is some part of the total situation, such as a physical characteristic, or, more importantly, a factor associated with people who are present when the situation is unfolding.

Feeling evaluates how experiences strike us, whether they are suitable to us or not; it is a kind of judgment that is an entirely subjective process.

Fidelity is "the opportunity to fulfill personal potentialities . . . to be true to [oneself] and true to significant others . . . [and to] sustain loyalties . . . in spite of inevitable contradictions of value systems."

Fixation is the impairment of development at a particular stage because satisfactions appropriate for the stage are frustrated, resulting in permanent investment of libidinal energy in the stage.

Fixed-role therapy involves a client playing the role of an imaginary character who possesses constructs that are in contrast to his or her actual constructs.

Fluid general ability (g_f) is "that form of general intelligence which is largely innate and which adapts itself to all kinds of material, regardless of previous experience with it."

Forbidding gestures are negative, covert cues such as a wrinkled brow, a cold tone of voice, a too tight grasp, a hesitancy, reluctance, or even revulsion at having to interact with the infant.

Foresight is the capacity to look ahead in search of good experiences and in the interest of avoiding bad ones.

Forethought is anticipation of "likely consequences of . . . [future] actions."

Frame of orientation is a cognitive "map" of people's natural and social worlds that enables them to organize and make sense of puzzling matters and allows them to operate in the arena of rational understanding.

Free association is a process in which the person adopts a mental orientation that allows ideas, images, memories, and feelings to be expressed spontaneously.

Freedom refers to our belief that we can choose from various behaviors rather than having our actions controlled by an external force, the environment.

Frustration tolerance is exhibited when things go wrong; people who have it do not pitch a tantrum, blame others, or wallow in self-pity.

Functional autonomy is a process by which a new system of motivation evolves from an older one, but stems from tensions different from those of the original.

Fundamental postulate is the assumption that a person's psychological processes are routed through various channels or pathways by the ways in which she or he anticipates events.

Fusion of needs is the name Murray gave to a single "action pattern that satisfies two or more needs at the same time."

Futility is the perception that one is on the proverbial treadmill, merely keeping body and soul together, but doing nothing for the good of society or one's community.

"g" supposedly subsumes the so-called primary mental abilities and forms a common core of general intelligence.

Gambler's Fallacy is the expectation that a failure on one attempt means that success on a subsequent attempt becomes more likely.

General actualizing tendency is an inherent tendency of the organism to develop all its capacities in ways that serve to maintain or enhance the organism.

Generalized expectancy is an expectancy that holds for a number of situations that are similar to one another.

Generativity is "the concern with establishing and guiding the next generation."

Generic conscience is central to the development of personality and is a unifying force in personality: it lays down comprehensive guidelines for nearly all of a person's conduct.

Genital stage is the period of mature sexual love, beginning at puberty, that includes directing both feelings of lust and of affection toward another person.

Genuine sense of humor, as opposed to an appreciation of sexual and aggressive jokes, is being able "to laugh at the things one loves (including, of course, oneself and all that pertains to oneself), and still to love them."

Goals are anticipated achievements that are in line with current personal standards.

Gradualistic moral disengagement is a process during which people slowly slip unawares into what was normally unacceptable behavior.

Growth model emphasizes helping people to "remove whatever blocks to growth exist" so they can move beyond being normal or average.

Guilt (Erikson) is the harness that restrains pursuit of desires, urges, and potentials; the exercise of an overzealous conscience.

Guilt (Freud) is an intense feeling of regret over having done something wrong or evaluations of oneself as an undeserving, inadequate person.

Guilt (Kelly) is the result of the person's perception that he or she is being dislodged from some critical role.

Habitual responses (HR) are specific responses (Cattell's surface traits) that recur under similar circumstances, such as regularly saying "Hi" to a neighbor.

Heritability popularly refers to the proportion of the variability in a trait that is accounted for by the genes.

Heterophilic person "has . . . made the early adolescent change in which he has become intensely interested in achieving intimacy with members of . . . the other sex."

Hoarding orientation is embraced by people who believe the "goods" come from the inside not the outside, themselves not others, so security is based on an attitude of saving, of letting out as little as possible.

Hope is the enduring belief in the attainability of basic satisfactions.

Humanistic communitarian socialism is a political system embracing economic, social, and moral functions wherein ordinary citizens interact cooperatively and are actively involved in the various functions.

Humanistic psychoanalyst is one who believes in the essential worth and dignity of each person, and in the importance of helping each person to do the most with what she or he has.

Humanistic psychology is the school of psychology that emphasizes the present experience of the whole person, assumes the essential worth of the person, and fosters the belief that the person can solve his or her own psychological problems.

Hyper-competitiveness is the indiscriminate need by individuals to compete and win (and to avoid losing) at any cost as a means of maintaining or enhancing feelings of self-worth.

Hysterical neurosis is a condition in which a person displays symptoms of a disorder to avoid experiences too painful or threatening for conscious consideration, though physical evidence of the disorder is absent.

Id is beyond conscious awareness and comprises whatever is present at birth, including everything that relates to the satisfaction of physical drives, such as sex and hunger, or primitive psychological needs, such as for comfort and protection from danger.

Idealized image of self is an artificial pride system that the person creates to give the personality a sense of unity that does not exist.

Ideal self is the self a person most values and desires to be.

Identification (Freud) is the process of becoming like the same-sex parent.

Identity (Erikson) is accumulated confidence that the sameness and continuity one has previously cultivated are now appreciated by others, allowing, in turn, the promise of careers and lifestyles to come.

Identity (Fromm) is the need to be aware of oneself as a separate entity, and to sense oneself as the subject of one's own actions.

Identity confusion is the failure of previous identity developments to coalesce in such a way that it is clear what roles one is expected to play in the future.

Idiographic theorists are inclined to study each individual's unique traits without attempting to find a place for each along a few trait dimensions.

Impermeable refers to certain constructs that tend not to change in terms of range of convenience or place in the construction system.

Implicit pole is the contrasting end of a construct, like "uneducated" in educated–uneducated and "not admired" in admired–not admired.

Incentive is any circumstance, concrete or abstract, that creates an anticipation of positive outcome following the performance of a behavior.

Incongruence reflects an inconsistency between self-concept and experiences relating to the self.

Independent variables have variation that is arranged by the person who uses the experimental method, called the experimenter.

Individual character is the pattern of behavior characteristic of a given person, "the relatively permanent system of all noninstinctual strivings through which man relates himself to the human and natural world."

Individual differences (Introduction) refers to the observation that people differ in a variety of ways.

Individuality refers to differences among construction systems both in terms of the constructs comprising the systems and in terms of how the constructs are organized.

Individual psychology is an attempt to conceive of a unique human being as an interconnected whole, biologically, philosophically, and psychologically.

Individuation is the process by which a person becomes a psychological "in-dividual," that is, a separate, indivisible unity or 'whole'.

Inductive-hypothetico-deductive spiral refers to "the detecting of regularities in observational data [that] leads to a hypothesis from which experimental consequences are deduced, [leading] to further data from which new regularities are induced, and so on in an ever-expanding spiral."

Industry is children's absorption in the "tool world" of their culture—the workaday world—which prepares them "for a hierarchy of learning experiences which [they] will undergo with the help of cooperative peers and instructive adults."

Infancy stage (Sullivan) starts at birth and continues until the appearance of speech.

Inferiority (Adler) is the persistent feeling that one does not measure up to society's ideals or to one's own fictional standards.

Inferiority (Erikson) occurs if children perceive their skills or status among peers to be inadequate.

Inferiority complex is Adler's term for the consequences of an exaggerated, persistent form of inadequacy that is partly explained by a deficiency in social interest.

Initiative is acting on one's desires, urges, and potentials.

Insight is a method through which unacceptable and socially "taboo" experiences buried in the person's unconscious can be made conscious.

Instincts are inborn forces whose characteristics are both physical (bodily needs) and psychological (wishes).

Institutional safeguard is a cultural unit that protects and promotes products of crisis resolution.

Integrity is "an emotional integration faithful to the image bearers of the past and ready to take (and eventually renounce) leadership in the present."

Intellectualization involves talking and thinking at an academic rather than an emotional level about what we do or contemplate that is threatening to us (the smoker says "the link between cancer and smoking is unproven. I've seen the studies").

Interaction point of view is a position that emphasizes the interplay between internal entities or person factors and social situations, rather than either in isolation from the other.

Intermittent reinforcement is a process in which responses are reinforced every so often, or after some number of responses has occurred.

Internal locus of control is the belief that reinforcement is dependent on one's own behavior or characteristics, not fate, luck, or chance.

Interpersonal anxiety is a tension that is alleviated in relationships with significant others or in feelings of well-being.

Interpersonal relations are the relationships between a person and every other important person in his or her life.

Interpersonal security is "relaxation of the tension of anxiety" that is experienced as a return to a tranquil, untroubled state.

Interpersonal trust is a generalized expectancy that people's verbal promises are reliable.

Intimacy "is really the ability to fuse your identity with somebody else's without fear that you're going to lose something yourself."

Intolerance for ambiguity is the cognitive orientation requiring that everything be clearly distinguished from everything else, questions have definite answers, and problems have simple solutions.

Intrinsic (Allport) refers to religion being an end in itself, something that one surrenders to, not something to use.

Intrinsic motivation refers to the desire for intrinsic rewards, leading to the pursuit of the same.

Intrinsic rewards are rewards from within the individual (self-praise).

Introjection is a process by which the personality incorporates the norms and standards of its culture through identification with parents or other admired persons in society, such as clergy and teachers.

Introversion is an "inward-turning" of psychic energy and involves a negative movement or withdrawal of subjective interest away from outer objects and toward one's inner experience.

Intuiting suggests where something seems to have come from and where it may be going; it is a kind of "instinctive apprehension," of unconscious origin, with no tangible basis.

Isolation is the failure to secure close and cooperative relationships with the same and especially the opposite gender such that partners' identities are important to, but distinct from, one's own.

Isophilic refers to a person who " . . . has been unable to progress past preadolescence, and continues to regard as suitable for intimacy only people who are as like himself as possible . . . that is, members of his own sex."

Jealousy is the fear of losing a relationship that is seen as the best available means of satisfying an insatiable need for affection and incessant demands for unconditional love.

Juvenile era is ushered in with the child's need for peer companions, or "playmates rather like oneself."

Late adolescence begins with the acknowledgment of an orientation regarding genital behavior and how to fit that revelation into the rest of life, then ends with "the establishment of a fully

human or mature repertory of interpersonal relations."

Latency is a quiet period beginning about age six during which children repress their attraction to parents and their other infantile urges.

Latent content is the underlying meaning of each dream.

Law of movement is the direction taken by the person that originates in his or her ability to exercise free choice in fully exploiting personal capabilities and resources.

Learn by anxiety is a process that occurs when anxiety is not severe; individuals may become acquainted with the situations in which it is present so that those circumstances may be avoided.

Libido (Freud) is an energy variously described as "psychical desire," "erotic tendencies," "sexual desire in the broadest sense," and the "motive forces of sexual life."

Libido (Jung) is psychic energy.

Loadings are correlations of particular items with a given factor.

Locus of control refers to "the degree to which persons expect that . . . reinforcement [and other outcomes] of their behavior is [dependent on their] behavior or personal characteristics versus the degree to which [they expect it is due to] chance, luck, or fate, . . . powerful others, or is simply unpredictable."

Locus of evaluation refers to the source of evidence about values, whether it is inside oneself or outside, in others.

Long unit is the life cycle of the individual.

Loose constructs yield varying predictability.

Love "is the guardian of that elusive and yet all-pervasive power of cultural and personal style which binds . . . the affiliations of competition and cooperation, procreation and production" into a "way of life."

Lust is Sullivan's term for "certain tensions of or pertaining to the genitals," culminating in orgasm.

Make prompt statements of all that comes to mind is a task of the patient during the interview that is enabled by trusting the "situation to the extent of expressing the thoughts that it provokes."

Mandala, or magic circle, is a round object, often including an inner spiral, that draws the eyes to the center of its surface.

Manifest content is what the dreamer remembers about a dream when awakened.

Marketing orientation is unique to the modern historical era in which exchanging goods for money, other goods, or services became the backbone of a "supply and demand" economy.

Mature love "is union under the condition of preserving one's integrity, one's individuality . . . [it] is an active power of man."

Medical model refers to the idea that people with psychological problems are sick and need some sort of treatment, at least analogous to medication, that will make them normal again.

Mentalism is the belief that thoughts and feelings determine behavior, not external consequences.

Metagenital use does not involve one's own genitals, but another person's genitals are involved.

Meta-needs or growth needs (G-needs) are terms used "to describe the motivations of self-actualizing people."

Model refers to a person who performs some behavior for an audience, showing how it is done and what benefits accrue from it.

Modeling refers to the act of performing a behavior before one or more observers.

Morality principle is the code that concerns society's values regarding right and wrong.

Moral justification occurs when inhumane behavior is made "acceptable" because perpetrators claim it serves socially worthy or moral purposes.

Mothering one is a "significant, relatively adult personality whose cooperation is necessary to keep the infant alive."

Moving against people reflects compulsive cravings for power and prestige, as well as personal ambition.

Moving away from people reflects a person's concern with self, as seen in needs for admiration and perfectionism.

Moving toward people reflects neurotic needs for a partner and for affection; it also involves compulsive, exaggerated modesty.

n Abasement involves surrendering, complying, accepting punishment, apologizing, confessing, atoning, and generally being masochistic.

n Achievement indicates the drive to "overcome obstacles, to exercise power, to strive to do something difficult as well [and] as quickly as possible."

n Affiliation refers to the desire for friendships and associations; "To greet, join, and live with others."

n Aggression refers to an assaultive or injurious orientation to others, including to belittle, harm, blame, accuse, ridicule, punish severely, react sadistically toward, or even murder.

n Autonomy is the drive to resist influence or coercion, to defy authority, seek freedom, and strive for independence.

n Blamavoidance refers to avoiding blame, punishment, and ostracism by inhibiting asocial (or even unconventional) impulses and being a well-behaved, law-abiding citizen.

n Contrarience is the drive to act differently from others, to be unique, to take the opposite side, and to hold unconventional views.

n Dominance is the drive to influence, control, persuade, prohibit, dictate, lead, direct, restrain others, and to organize the behavior of a group.

n Exhibition is desiring to attract attention to one's person by exciting, amusing, stirring, shocking, or thrilling others.

n Infavoidance is an orientation to avoiding failure, shame, humiliation, or ridicule by concealing disfigurement and refraining from attempts at anything seen as beyond one's powers.

n Inviolacy is an attitude of attempting to prevent depreciation of self-respect, to preserve one's good name, to avoid criticism, and to maintain psychological distance.

n Order involves arranging, organizing, and putting away objects; to be tidy, clean, and scrupulously precise.

n Succorance is the dependent attitude of seeking aid, protection, and sympathy by crying for mercy and help from affectionate, nurturant parents.

Necrophilous character is engrossed by death, dwells on it, and glories in it.

Need (Murray) refers to "a . . . [physiochemical] force. . . in the brain . . . , [that] organizes perception, . . . intellection, . . . and action in such a way as to transform . . . an . . . unsatisfying situation [into a more satisfying one]."

Need for self-actualization is "the desire for self-fulfillment . . . the tendency for [one] to become actualized in what [one] is potentially."

Need for tenderness, distinguished from "love," refers to relief from various tensions.

Need integrate or complex is formed when images "of cathected objects . . . become integrated in the mind with the needs and emotions which they customarily excite. . . ."

Needs (Maslow) are desires for certain satisfactions that are sought by all humans, regardless of their culture, environment, or generation.

Negative correlation refers to high values on one variable corresponding to low values on the other variable.

Negative reinforcement is a process whereby the likelihood of a response increases when it is followed by the termination, reduction, or absence of an aversive stimulus.

Neuroses (Freud) are patterns of abnormal behavior related to an over-control of instincts.

Neuroses (Horney) are "psychic disturbance[s] brought about by fears and defenses against these fears, and by attempts to find compromise solutions for conflicting tendencies."

Neurosis (Adler) is an extreme form of reaction to shock, "a person's automatic, unknowing exploitation of the symptoms resulting from the effects of a shock."

Neurotic needs (Horney) are the coping techniques that are initiated in childhood, excessive, insatiable, and unrealistic demands developed in response to the basic anxiety that dominates the person.

Nomothetic theorists are inclined to derive general laws concerning how a relative few traits apply to all people.

Nonproductive types are those who yield, at best, pseudoconnection to others, and, at worst, destructive relations with others.

Notice changes in the body that signal decreases or increases in the tension; signifying anxiety is one of the interview tasks of the patient.

Notice marginal thoughts is paying attention to thoughts that monitor, critique, and alter speech in terms of formation and grammar, and in terms of errors that may cause incomplete or misunderstood communications to others (patient task during interview).

Objective tests are highly structured paper-and-pencil questionnaires such as true/false or multiple-choice, each of which can be scored with a key so that scorers all agree on the scores.

Object of devotion is a goal that gives meaning to people's existence and position in the world.

Observational learning is obtaining useful information that can be transformed into behavior by watching the performance of another person.

Oedipus complex is the constellation of feelings, desires, and strivings revolving around the boy's desire for his mother and his fearful/hateful orientation to his father.

Old age parallels childhood because of a return to submersion in the unconscious.

Operant conditioning is a process by which an organism operates on its environment with consequences that influence the likelihood that the operation, or behavior, will be repeated.

Operationalized refers to translation of concepts into a form that can be quantified or expressed in numbers.

Oral-aggressive is a type that is derived from childhood pleasures associated with the mouth, food, and eating, but with emphasis on chewing and biting.

Oral or *Narcissistic (self-centered) stage* is a phase that begins at birth and in which the organism's psychic activity focuses on satisfying the needs of the mouth and digestive tract, including the tongue and lips.

Oral-receptive is a personality type that results from childhood pleasurable experiences of food in the mouth and of ingestion; it is associated with adult dependency and suggestibility.

Organismic approach refers to a natural, biological, inborn predisposition reflected in the total functioning of every living being.

Orthogenital involves the integration of one's own genitals with the "natural receptor genitals" of the opposite sex, that is, heterosexual use of the genitals.

Overcompensate is to bend over backward to do or become whatever people's weaknesses have denied them.

Paragenital involves use of the sex organs such that one acts to seek contact with genitals opposite from one's own, but in such a way that impregnation will not occur.

Parataxic mode is experienced as the infant becomes a child who begins to use speech, but still makes few logical connections within the sequence of its experiences (approximately the preschool years).

Participant modeling occurs when a person with low self-efficacy imitates a model's efficacious behavior.

Peak experiences are intense mystical experiences associated with simultaneous feelings of limitless horizons, powerfulness and helplessness, a lost sense of time and place, and great ecstasy, wonder, and awe.

Penis envy refers to girls' feelings of inferiority over not having the male organ and compensatory wishes to someday obtain one of their own.

Periodicity refers to rhythms of activity and rest.

Persona, or mask, is the identities we assume because of the socially prescribed roles we play.

Personal agency is a condition in which people come to believe that they can make things happen that will be of benefit to themselves and to others.

Personal disposition (p.d.) is a trait that is unique to a particular individual.

Personal factors are memories of previous experiences, from the past history of an individual, that determine what the person employs for producing behavior at the present time.

Personality (Allport) "is the dynamic organization within the individual of those psychophysical systems that determine his characteristic behavior and thought."

Personality (Cattell) "[is] that which tells what a [person] will do when placed in a particular situation."

Personality (Fromm) is "the totality of inherited and acquired psychic qualities which are characteristic of one individual and which make the individual unique."

Personality (Introduction) is a set of degrees falling along many behavioral dimensions, each degree corresponding to a trait.

Personality (Kelly) consists of an organized system of constructs that may be ranked as to importance.

Personality (Sullivan) is "the relatively enduring pattern of recurrent interpersonal situations which characterize a human life."

Personality traits (Introduction) are internally based psychological characteristics that often correspond to adjectival labels such as *shy, kind, mean, outgoing, dominant,* and so forth.

Personal unconscious "is made up essentially of contents [that] have at one time been conscious but which have disappeared from consciousness through having been forgotten or repressed. . . ."

Personifications are investments of human attributes in persons or objects that do not actually possess the assigned traits, at least not in the degree to which they are applied.

Phallic stage is a phase in which satisfaction is gained primarily by stimulation of the penis or clitoris, through masturbation.

Phenomenology encompasses a search for essential issues, an emphasis on consciousness, the necessity of describing experience, and a desire to grasp reality as each individual uniquely perceives it.

Physiological needs encompass specific biological requirements for water, oxygen, proteins, vitamins, proper body temperature, sleep, sex, exercise, and so on.

Pleasure principle refers to the achievement of pleasurable feelings as quickly and immediately as possible through the reduction of discomfort, pain, or tension.

Positively correlated refers to a condition in which high values on one variable correspond to high values on the other, and low values correspond with low values.

Positive regard is experiencing oneself as making a positive difference in the life of another person and as receiving warmth, liking, respect, sympathy, acceptance, caring, and trust from others.

Positive reinforcement is a process whereby some event, usually a stimulus, increases the likelihood of a response on which its presentation is contingent.

Positive self-regard is a favorable attitude toward oneself.

Preadolescence is brief, beginning with the need for interpersonal intimacy in the form of a close relationship with another person "of comparable status."

Predictability refers to the ability to predict the future.

Preemption phase is a period during which one construct is allowed to preempt the situation and define the pair of alternatives between which the person must make his or her choice.

Prejudice is felt or expressed antipathy based on a faulty and inflexible generalization and may be directed toward a group as a whole or toward an individual because of membership in the group.

Press designates a directional tendency in an object or situation (*press* is also plural).

Primary factors are relatively pure and narrow in scope and it can be arranged statistically that they are independent.

Primary process is a continual flow of infantile images and wishes that demand immediate and direct satisfaction.

Productive orientation is an attitude of relatedness to the world and oneself that encompasses all realms of human experience: reasoning, loving, and working.

Productivity is people's perception that they are contributing to society through their careers and to their community through their personal involvement.

Projection protects us from threat by allowing us to see our own unacceptable characteristics only in other people.

Projective tests present people with test items that are unstructured, ambiguous, or open-ended, thus allowing them a wide range of freedom in making responses.

Propriate striving is planning for the future by setting long-range goals.

Proprium is "me as felt and known . . . the self as 'object' of knowledge and feeling."

Prospective or "anticipatory" refers to a process through which dreams may "foretell" future events and outcomes.

Prototaxic mode is the earliest (infancy), most primitive type of experience, a state of generalized sensation or feeling in the absence of thought.

Prototype is the "complete goal" of the style of life that is a fiction conceived as a means of adapting to life and includes a strategy for its achievement.

Psyche is total mentality, all of consciousness and unconsciousness.

Psychoanalysis refers to Freud's systematic procedures for providing a patient with the insight necessary to rid the personality of its neurotic conflicts.

Psychogenic needs are secondary to viscerogenic needs and may be derived from them, but, being one step away from the biological side of the organism, are psychological in nature.

Psychological determinism is a belief that nothing about human behavior occurs by accident or chance; everything about personality "is determined" or has a psychological cause.

Psychological situation is characterized in a way peculiar to a person, allowing the person to categorize it with certain other situations, as well as differentiate it from still others.

Psychosexual stages refer to phases that are *sexual* only in the broadest sense of the word, because some stages involve organs ordinarily seen as "sexual" and others organs not popularly regarded as "sexual."

Psychosocial development refers to a union of physical yearnings and the cultural forces that act on the individual.

Punishment is a process whereby the likelihood of a response *decreases* when it is followed by the *presentation* of an aversive stimulus.

Purpose is "the courage to envisage and pursue valued and tangible goals guided by conscience but not paralyzed by guilt and by fear of punishment."

R = f(S.P), where *R* stands for the "nature and magnitude of a person's behavioral response, . . . what he [or she] says, thinks, or does," which is some function (*f*) of S, the "stimulus situation in which [the person] is placed," and P, the nature of her or his personality.

Racism is negative sentiment directed toward people of color.

Radical behaviorism considers currently observable events and also potential, future events that can be observed and measured.

Range of convenience refers to the extent and breadth of the event-category to which a construct applies.

Range of focus refers to the events to which a construct is most readily applied.

Rate of responding, when it becomes stable, indicates that conditioning is completed and a new response acquired.

Rational coper is the sense of selfhood that is not merely able to solve problems, but also can reason them through "in the head" and come up with logical solutions.

Rationalization (Horney) allows us to excuse our destructive and unacceptable behavior and thoughts ("So I lost the money. Money is not what's important in life").

Rationalization (Freud) "may be defined as self-deception by reasoning."

Reality principle refers to the ego's capacity to delay satisfaction of id's demands until an appropriate object is found that will allow gratification without harmful side effects.

Real self is the potential for growth beyond the artificial idealized image of self.

Receptive refers to an orientation of people who experience the source of all good as being outside themselves.

Regnant was the name given to "dominant configurations in the brain" that correspond to internal representations.

Regression is retreating to behaviors, feelings, and thoughts characteristic of the earlier fixated stage (a 12-year-old frightened by a dog begins to suck his thumb).

Reinforcement (Rotter) refers to anything that has an influence on the occurrence, direction, or kind of behavior.

Reinforcement (Skinner) occurs when some event is contingent on the prior performance of some response, and the response changes in likelihood of occurrence on future occasions.

Reinforcement value is the degree of preference for any reinforcement to occur if the possibilities of many different reinforcements are all equal.

Relatedness is "the necessity to unite with other living beings . . . [that constitutes] an imperative need on the fulfillment of which man's sanity depends."

Reliability is the degree to which test results are repeatable.

Replacement is finding a new target for one's strong emotions that is less threatening than the original.

Replicate refers to repeating a test in the hope the results will be the same as before.

Repression refers to a selective type of memory mode in which threatening material is unavailable for recall, because it has been pressed down into the unconscious.

Resignation is to free oneself from the risks involved in approaching or attacking others by being an onlooker, a noncompetitor, an avoider, and a reactive person who is hypersensitive to influence attempts.

Resilience is the ability to absorb the slings and arrows of outrageous fortune and still believe that one can accomplish what one desires to do.

Response facilitation is a process in which nothing new is learned, but some old responses may be disinhibited as a result of watching a model's performance.

Role Construct Repertory (REP) Test is an assessment device designed to reveal an individual's construct system.

Roles involve behaving in ways that meet the expectations of important other people in one's life.

Rootedness is a deep craving to maintain one's natural ties and not be "separated."

Safety needs include security, protection, stability, structure, law and order, and freedom from fear and chaos.

Scientific refers to unbiased observations that are quantified so that systematic analyses can be performed.

Scientific model for studying personality involves two interlocking components: (1) description, which seeks to answer questions about "what" personality is, for example, what are the identifiable individual differences in traits and types?; and (2) explanation, which seeks to answer questions about "why" personality is the way it is, for example, "What are the causes of those individual differences?"

Secondary factors encompass several primary factors and are called "superfactors" or "second-order" factors.

Secondary p.d.s are dispositions that are "less conspicuous, less generalized, less consistent, . . . less often called into play . . . [and] more peripheral."

Secondary process refers to the intellectual operations such as thinking, evaluating, planning, and decision making that test reality to determine whether certain behaviors would be beneficial.

Secondary reinforcers are stimuli that come to have all the properties of primary reinforcers (such as food) through association with primary reinforcers.

Second-order traits are the "superfactors" that subsume the other traits ("secondary factors" define secondary traits).

Security operations involve skills that allow avoidance of forbidding gestures.

Seduction thesis refers to Freud's belief that his early female patients actually had been sexually molested by their fathers, as they allegedly claimed, and that these traumas were the source of their adult hysterical neuroses.

Self (Jung) is the "total personality," the unifying core of the psyche that ensures a balance of conscious and unconscious forces.

Self (Rogers) is the organized, consistent, conceptual whole composed of perceptions of the characteristics of the "I" or "me," the values attached to these perceptions, and the relationship of the "I" or "me" to various aspects of life.

Self-actualization (Rogers) is a person's lifelong process of realizing his or her potentialities to become a fully functioning person.

Self-actualizers (Maslow) are people who fulfill themselves by making complete use of their potentialities, capacities, and talents, who do the best they are capable of doing, and who develop themselves to the most complete stature possible for them.

Self-analysis is a process whereby people come to understand themselves better through their own efforts, often outside the context of psychotherapy.

Self-effacing is a mode of responding to others in which the person will seek accommodation at any price, including backing down whenever there is an interpersonal conflict in order to avoid loss of the friendship, support, or love of others.

Self-efficacy is a belief concerning one's ability to perform behaviors yielding an expected outcome that is desirable.

Self-esteem is pride in one's pursuits and accomplishments.

Self-evaluation is a process that involves assessing one's performance at various points along the way to task completion and issuing a vocal or "under the breath" judgment of its value.

Self-exonerative processes is the general name given to cognitive activities that allow people to dissociate themselves from the consequences of their actions.

Self-identity is the continuity of self over past, present, and future that results from the operation of memory.

Self-image is composed of the hopes and aspirations that develop from the perceptions and expectations that others have of oneself.

Self-recognition is coming to know one's neuroses, idealized self-image, and real self, including positive and negative attributes.

Self-regulatory plans are rules, established in advance of opportunity for behavioral performance, that act as guides for determining what behavior would be appropriate under particular conditions.

Self-regulatory processes are internal, cognitive–affective functions that guide and govern efforts toward goal attainment.

Self-system is "that part of personality which is born entirely out of the influences of significant others upon one's feeling of well-being."

Sensing determines that something is present; it is the same as sensory perceptions of sight, sound, smell, taste, and touch.

Sentiment is "a set of attitudes the strength of which has become correlated through their being all learnt by contact with a particular social institution [such as] sentiment to school, to home, to country."

Shadow is the underside of the personality, the inferiorities of the person that are emotional in nature and too unpleasant to willingly reveal.

Shame and doubt is the estrangement that results from the feeling of being controlled and of losing self-control.

Shaping is a process by which natural variability in behavior is exploited so that a new behavior is acquired by reinforcing successive approximations to it.

Shock may be experienced when a person's fiction runs head-on into reality.

Significant others are those people who are most meaningful to us in our lives.

Simple stimuli generate reflexes that call for reactions rather than actions, particularly surface reactions that are immediate and passive in nature.

16 PF (Personality Factors) is a test of adult personality measured in terms of 16 source traits.

Slips of the tongue are verbal errors that seem to replace neutral words with ones that supposedly emanate from the unconscious.

Social character represents "the core of a character structure common to most people of a given culture . . . [and] shows the degree to which character is formed by social and cultural patterns."

Social–cognitive learning theory proposes that important factors are cognitive and affective processes rather than traits.

Social comparison is determining how well one is doing in life by comparing oneself to those who share one's life situation.

Social desirability refers to the need to please others by displaying the characteristics that are valued in our society (for example, goodness, honesty, sincerity, and so forth).

Social Distance (SD) is a measure of discrimination that requires individuals to indicate how close to themselves they would allow members of some group to come.

Social feeling is a concern for the community of other human beings and a need to associate and cooperate with them.

Social interest (Gemeinschafsgefuhl) is individuals' efforts to develop social feeling.

Socialization is learning one's particular culture.

Social learning entails acquiring useful information through interactions with people and other elements of the environment.

Sociopsychological orientation is the sociological study of people that sheds light on their psychological nature.

Source trait is "A [primary] factor-dimension, stressing the proposition that variations in value along it are determined by a single unitary influence or source."

Specific responses (SR) are everyday behaviors or experiences that may or may not be characteristic of an individual, such as saying "Hi" to a neighbor.

Stagnation is the arrest of the ripening process that comes with inability to funnel previous development into the formation of the next generation.

State, or mood, is a psychological entity that fluctuates or varies over time and, thus, is "transitory," as distinguished from traits, which are "permanent."

Statistically significant is a condition that is reflected in a difference between conditions that is so large it is very unlikely to occur solely by chance.

Stereotype is an exaggerated belief that members of a group possess a certain trait; "Its function is to justify (rationalize) our conduct in relation to that [group]."

Stimulus is a very definite, well-defined component or event associated with a situation and can be either physical or behavioral.

Strength (Erikson) is a virtue arising from dominant movement toward the positive pole.

Strength (Murray) of a need is measured in terms of its frequency, intensity, and duration.

Striving for superiority is a universal psychological phenomenon that parallels physical growth and involves the goal of bringing about perfection, security, and strength.

Style of life is the individual's unique, but consistent, movement toward self-created goals and ideals developed beginning in childhood.

Sublimation is a process that reorients instinctual aims in new directions that are consistent with social norms.

Submerged pole is an implicit pole that either has never been put into word form, perhaps because the construct is new, or is being suppressed.

Subordinate refers to constructs that are at the bottom of the construction system.

Subsidization of needs occurs "When one or more needs are activated in the service of [one or more other needs]."

Success may be defined as effectively performing the behaviors that yield the outcomes that are valued by the performer.

Superego is the representation of society in personality that incorporates the norms and standards of the surrounding culture.

Superiority complex is Adler's term for an exaggerated, abnormal form of striving for superiority that involves "overcompensation" for personal weakness.

Superordinate refers to constructs that are at the top of the construction system.

Superstitious behavior is a response that is accidentally reinforced, as there is no prearranged contingency between the response and reinforcement.

Surface traits are "a set of personality characteristics which are correlated but do not form a factor, hence are believed to be determined by more than one influence or source."

Symbiotic union is a coupling of beings in which each meets the needs of the other while they "live 'together' " as "two, and yet one."

Symbol is one of the emergent elements to which a construct applies that illustrates the construct.

Symbolic modeling involves verbal and pictorial means used to convey information necessary for adoption of behaviors associated with rewards.

Synchronicity is the simultaneous occurrence of two happenings that are correlated but have no direct cause-and-effect connection.

Syntaxic mode becomes important when the meaning of words becomes shared with most other people so that experience, judgments, and observations can be shared (approximately the early elementary school years).

Systematic eclecticism takes the best and most effective methods and orientations from each school of thought and binds them into a comprehensive approach to understanding the person.

Teleological means to perform with a purpose.

Temperament trait is "a general personality trait [that] is usually stylistic, in the sense that it deals with tempo, persistence, [and so forth] covering a large variety of specific responses."

Thanatos is a class of instincts that is aimed at returning living things to their original nonliving state.

Thema is a combination of a particular need and a particular press or pressive object.

Thematic Apperception Test (TAT) is an instrument for assessing a person's self-reflective perceptions (apperceptions), revealing thema that are evoked by some ambiguous pictures.

Thinking determines what is present and interprets its meaning; it brings ideas into connection with one another to form concepts or reach solutions.

Threat is realization of the possibility that a person's entire construction system will be overhauled.

Tight constructs yield unvarying predictability.

Tolerance for ambiguity is a cognitive orientation which requires that everything be clearly distinguished from everything else: questions have definite answers and problems have simple solutions.

Trait (Allport) "is a neuropsychic structure having the capacity to render many stimuli functionally equivalent, and to initiate and guide equivalent . . . forms of adaptive and expressive behavior."

Trait (Cattell) is a permanent entity that does not fade in and out like a state; it is inborn or develops during the life course and regularly directs behavior.

Traits (Eysenck) are represented as statistical primary factors and defined as "theoretical constructs based on observed intercorrelations between a number of different habitual responses."

Transcendence is the act of transforming one's accidental and passive role of "creature" into that of an active and purposeful "creator."

Transference occurs when patients relate to the psychoanalyst as if he or she were a significant person from their past about whom they were continuing to experience mixed feelings.

Type (Jung) is a habitual attitude, or a person's characteristic way.

Types (Eysenck) are second-order dimensions made up of statistically intercorrelated primary traits. They can be thought of as superfactors, but Eysenck prefers "second-order."

Tyranny of the shoulds is the belief that one should do this and that, whatever a good person should do, whatever is expected by others, rather than what one feels it is his or her nature to do.

Unconditional positive regard is provided when other people communicate, with no strings attached, that one is accepted, valued, worthwhile, and trusted, simply for being who one is.

Undoing involves erasing "bad" behavior by displaying behavior designed to reverse the effects of undesirable acts ("Forgive me for hitting you! Let me grovel at your feet, and proclaim my undying love for you, and buy you flowers").

Unique trait is "so specific to an individual that no one else could be scored on [its dimension]."

Unitary trend refers to activity that is organized and directional in nature, not willy-nilly, trial-and-error.

Unity is a sense of oneness within one's self and with the "natural and human world outside."

Validity is the degree to which a test measures what it was designed to measure.

Values of outcomes refers to how much one prizes results of behavioral or stimulus occurrences in an ongoing situation.

Variable refers to variation in quantity specified by numbers.

Vicarious expectancy learning involves people adopting other peoples' expectancies concerning future events, especially expectancies of those with whom they share relevant experiences.

Vicarious reinforcement occurs when one observes another person being rewarded for performing a behavior.

Viscerogenic needs involve basic biological drives, and, though they form the foundation of the psychogenic needs, are relatively straightforward.

Will power is "the unbroken determination to exercise free choice as well as self-restraint in spite of the unavoidable experience of shame, doubt, and a certain rage over being controlled by others."

Wisdom is a "detached and yet active concern with life in the face of death," not magical access to "higher knowledge."

Word Association Test is a Jungian method in which people are instructed to say the first word that comes to mind after hearing each of 100 words from a standardized list.

References

Abramson, L., Seligman, M., & Teasdale, J. (1987). Learned helplessness in humans: Critique and reformulation. *Journal of Abnormal Psychology, 87,* 49–74.

Abt, L. E., & Bellak, L. (Eds.). (1950). *Projective Psychology: Clinical Approaches to the Total Personality.* New York: Grove Press.

Achterberg, J., & Lawlis, G. F. (1978). *Imagery of Cancer.* Champaign, IL: Institute for Personality and Ability Testing.

Ackerman, S. J., Clemence, A. J., Weatherill, R., & Hilsenroth, M. J. (1999). Use of the TAT in the assessment of *DSM-IV* Cluster B personality disorders. *Journal of Personality Assessment, 73,* 422–448.

Adams, P. (1994, Sept. 29). Changing their minds. *Peoria Journal Star,* p. A5.

Adler, A. (1907/1917). *Study of Organ Inferiority and its Psychical Compensation; A Contribution to Clinical Medicine.* New York: Nervous and Mental Diseases Publishing Company.

Adler, A. (1929/1971). *The Practice and Theory of Individual Psychology* (P. Radin, Trans.). London: Routledge & Kegan Paul.

Adler, A. (1932/1964). The structure of neurosis. In H. L. Ansbacher & R. R. Ansbacher (Eds.), *Alfred Adler: Superiority and Social Interest.* Evanston, IL: Northwestern University Press, pp. 204–215.

Adler, A. (1933/1964a). Advantages and disadvantages of the inferiority feeling. In H. L. Ansbacher & R. R. Ansbacher (Eds.), *Alfred Adler:*
Superiority and Social Interest. Evanston, IL: Northwestern University Press, pp. 178–189.

Adler, A. (1933/1965b). Religion and individual psychology. In H. L. Ansbacher & R. R. Ansbacher (Eds.), *Alfred Adler: Superiority and Social Interest.* Evanston, IL: Northwestern University Press, pp. 305–316.

Adler, A. (1956). In H. L. Ansbacher & R. R. Ansbacher (Eds.), *The Individual Psychology of Alfred Adler.* New York: Basic Books, pp. 170–179.

Adler, A. (1964). *Social Interest: A Challenge to Mankind.* New York: Capricorn Books.

Adler, A. (1982). In H. L. Ansbacher & R. R. Ansbacher (Trans.), *Co-Operation Between the Sexes.* New York: Norton, 1982.

Adler, K. (1994). Socialist influences on Adlerian psychology. *Individual Psychology Journal of Adlerian Theory, Research and Practice, 50,* 131–141.

Adler, N. E., & Snibbe, A. C. (2003). The role of psychosocial processes in explaining the gradient between socioeconomic status and health. *Current Directions in Psychological Science, 12,* 119–123.

Ainsworth, M. D. S. (1979). Infant-mother attachment. *American Psychologist, 34,* 932–937.

Alderfer, C. P. (1989). Theories reflecting my personal experience and life development. *Journal of Applied Behavioral Science, 25,* 351–365.

Alicke, M. D., & Klotz, M. L. (1993). Social roles and social judgment: How an impression conveyed influences an impression formed. *Personality and Social Psychology Bulletin, 1993, 19,* 185–194.

Allen, B. P. (1973). Perceived trustworthiness of attitudinal and behavioral expressions. *Journal of Social Psychology, 89,* 211–218.

Allen, B. P. (1975). Social distance and admiration reactions of "unprejudiced" whites. *Journal of Personality, 43,* 709–726.

Allen, B. P. (1976). Race and physical attractiveness as criteria for white subjects' dating choices. *Social Behavior and Personality, 4,* 289–296.

Allen, B. P. (1978). *Social Behavior: Fact and Falsehood.* Chicago: Nelson-Hall.

Allen, B. P. (1984). Harrower's and Miale-Selzer's use of Hjalmar Schacht in their characterizations of the Nazi leaders. *Journal of Personality Assessment, 48,* 257–258.

Allen, B. P. (1985). After the missiles: Sociopsychological effects of nuclear war. *American Psychologist, 40,* 927–937.

Allen, B. P. (1988a). Dramaturgical quality. *Journal of Social Psychology, 128,* 181–190.

Allen, B. P. (1998b). Beyond consistency in the definition of personality: Dramaturgical quality and value. *Imagination, Cognition and Personality, 7,* 201–213.

Allen, B. P. (1990). *Personal Adjustment.* Pacific Grove, CA: Brooks/Cole.

Allen, B. P. (1995). Gender stereotypes are not accurate: A replication of Martin (1987) using diagnostic, self-report, and behavioral criteria. *Sex Roles, 32,* 583–600.

Allen, B. P. (1996). African-Americans' and European-Americans' mutual attributions: Adjective Generation Technique (AGT) stereotyping. *Journal of Applied Social Psychology, 26,* 884–912.

Allen, B. P. (2000). World War II: 1939–1948, a Novel. New York: Writers Club Press (iUniversity.com).

Allen, B. P. (2001). *Coping with Life in the 21st Century.* New York: Writers Club Press (iUniversity.com).

Allen, B. P. (2002). "Race" and IQ. *The General Psychologist, 37*(1), 12–18.

Allen, B. P. (2003). If no "races," no relevance to brain size, and no consensus on intelligence, then no scientific meaning to relationships among these notions: Reply to Rushton. *The General Psychologist, 38*(2), 31–32.

Allen, B. P., & Adams, J. Q. (1992). The concept "race": Let's go back to the beginning. *Journal of Social Behavior and Personality, 7,* 163–168.

Allen, B. P., & Lindsay, D. S. (1998). Amalgamations of memories: Intrusions of information from one event into reports of another. *Applied Cognitive Psychology, 12,* 277–285.

Allen, B. P., & Potkay, C. R. (1973). Variability of self-description on a day-to-day basis: Longitudinal use of the adjective generation technique. *Journal of Personality, 41,* 638–652.

Allen, B. P., & Potkay, C. R. (1977b). Misunderstanding the Adjective Generation Technique (AGT): Comments on Bem's rejoinder. *Journal of Personality, 45,* 207–219.

Allen, B. P., & Potkay, C. R. (1977a). The relationship between AGT self-description and significant life events: A longitudinal study. *Journal of Personality, 45,* 334–342.

Allen, B. P., & Potkay, C. R. (1981). On the arbitrary distinction between states and traits. *Journal of Personality and Social Psychology, 41,* 916–928.

Allen, B. P., & Potkay, C. R. (1983a). *Adjective Generation Technique (AGT).* New York: Irvington.

Allen, B. P., & Potkay, C. R. (1983b). Just as arbitrary as ever: Comments on Zuckerman's rejoinder. *Journal of Personality and Social Psychology, 44,* 1087–1089.

Allen, B. P., & Smith, G. (1980). Traits, situations and their interaction as alternative "causes" of behavior. *Journal of Social Psychology, 111,* 99–104.

Allport, G. W. (1937). *Personality: A Psychological Interpretation.* New York: Henry Holt.

Allport, G. W. (1942). *The Use of Personal Documents in Psychological Science.* New York: Social Science Research Council.

Allport, G. W. (1954). *The Nature of Prejudice.* Reading, MA: Addison-Wesley.

Allport, G. W. (1955). *Becoming, Basic Considerations for a Psychology of Personality.* New Haven: Yale University Press.

Allport, G. W. (1961). *Pattern and Growth in Personality.* New York: Holt, Rinehart and Winston.

Allport, G. W. (1966). Traits revisited. *American Psychologist, 21,* 1–10.

Allport, G. W. (1967). Gordon W. Allport. In E. G. Boring & G. Lindzey (Eds.), *A History of Psychology in Autobiography* (Vol. 5). New York: Appleton-Century Crofts, pp. 259–265.

Allport, G. W. (1968). *The Person in Psychology: Selected Essays.* Boston: Beacon.

Allport, G. W. (1969). Comments on earlier chapters. In R. May (Ed.), *Existential Psychology.* New York: Random House, 93–98.

Allport, G. W., & Odbert, H. (1936). Trait-names: A psycho-lexical study. *Psychological Monographs 47,* Whole No. 211.

Allport, G. W., & Ross, J. M. (1967). Personal religious orientation and prejudice. *Journal of Personality and Social Psychology, 5,* 432–443.

Alpher, V. S. (1988). Comment on Skinner. *American Psychologist, 43,* 824–825.

Alvarado, N. (1994). Empirical validity of the Thematic Apperception Test. *Journal of Personality Assessment, 63,* 59–79.

American Psychologist. (1958). Award for distinguished scientific contributions to B. F. Skinner. *13,* 735–738.

American Psychologist. (1981). Award for distinguished scientific contributions to Albert Bandura *36,* 27–42.

American Psychologist. (1983). Award for distinguished scientific contributions to Walter Mischel, *38,* 9–14.

Ames, L. B., Learned, J., Metraux, R. W., & Walker, R. N. (1952). *Child Rorschach Responses: Developmental Trends from Two to Ten Years.* New York: Harper & Row.

Amirkhan, J. H., Risinger, R. T., & Swickert, R. J. (1995). Extraversion: A "hidden" personality factor in coping? *Journal of Personality, 63,* 189–212.

Amodio, D. M., Harmon-Jones, E., & Devine, P. (2003). Individual differences in the activation and control of affective race bias as assessed by startle eye-blink response and self-report. *Journal of Personality and Social Psychology, 84,* 738–753.

Amodio, D. M., Harmon-Jones, E., & Devine, P. (2004) Individual differences in the regulation of race bias among low-prejudice people: The role of conflict detection and neural signals for control. Unpublished manuscript.

Amodio, D. M., Harmon-Jones, E., Devine, P., Curtin, J. J., Hartley, S. L., & Covert, A. E. (2004). Neural signals for the detection of unintentional race bias. *Psychological Science, 15,* 88–93.

Anastasi, A. (1982). *Psychological Testing.* (5th ed.). New York: Macmillan.

Anch, A. M., Browman, C. P., Mitler, M. M., & Walsh, J. K. (1988). *Sleep: A Scientific Perspective.* Englewood Cliffs, NJ: Prentice-Hall.

Andersen, S. M., & Baum, A. (1994). Transference in interpersonal relations: Inferences and affect based on significant-other representations. *Journal of Personality, 62,* 459–497.

Anderson, C. F. (2002, August). Jealous lovers, cavemen, and psychologists. *Observer* (American Psychological Society), *15,* 25, 49.

Anderson, J. W. (1988). Henry A. Murray's early career: A psychobiographical exploration. *Journal of Personality, 56,* 137–171.

Anderson, J. W. (1990). The life of Henry A. Murray: 1893–1988. In A. I. Rabin, R. A. Zucker, R. A. Emmons, & S. Frank (Eds.), *Studying Persons and Lives.* New York: Springer Publishers, pp. 1–22.

Anderson, M. C., Ochsner, K. N., Kuhl, B., et al. (2004, January). Neural systems underlying suppression of unwanted memories. *Science, 303,* 232–235.

Anderson, S. M., & Cole, S. W. (1990). "Do I know you?": The role of significant others in general social perception. *Journal of Personality and Social Psychology, 59,* 384–399.

Andreasen, N. C. (1997). Linking mind and brain in the study of mental illnesses: A project for scientific psychopathology. *Science, 275,* 1586–1592.

Angyal, A. (1965). *Neurosis and Treatment: A Holistic Theory.* New York: Wiley.

Ansbacher, H. L. (1964). In A. Adler, *Problems of Neurosis: A Book of Case Histories.* P. Mairet (Ed.). New York: Harper & Row.

Ansbacher, H. L. (1990). Alfred Adler's influence on the three leading cofounders of humanistic psychology. *Journal of Humanistic Psychology, 30,* 45–53.

Ansbacher, H. L., & Ansbacher, R. R. (1956). *The Individual Psychology of Alfred Adler.* New York: Basic Books.

Ansbacher, H. L., & Ansbacher, R. R. (Eds.). (1964). *Alfred Adler: Superiority and Social Interest.* Evanston IL: Northwestern University Press.

APA Monitor. (1992, August). Bandura's childhood shaped life interests, p. 13.

APA Monitor. (1993, November). Opening addresses, p. 1, 12.

APA Monitor. (1999, July/August). Landmark events in psychology's history, p. 6.

APA Monitor. (1999, October). Landmark events in psychology's history, p. 6.

Artistico, D., Cervone, D., & Pezzuti, L. (2003). Perceived self-efficacy and everyday problem solving among young and older adults. *Psychology and Aging, 18,* 68–79.

Asch, S. E. (1952). *Social Psychology.* New York: Prentice-Hall.

Ashby, J. S., Kottman, T., & Draper, K. (2002). Social interest and locus of control: Relationships and implications. *Journal of Individual Psychology, 58,* 52–61.

Associated Press. (1981, September). Homosexuals may differ biologically, scientists say. *Peoria Journal Star,* p. 1A.

Associated Press. NCAA committee accused of racism. *Peoria Journal Star,* December 15, 1993, p. D5.

Astin, A. W. (1962). Productivity of undergraduate institutions. *Science, 136,* 129–135.

Astrachan, B. M. (1994, July/August). The "Seasons of a Man's Life" author Daniel J. Levinson (1920–1994). *Observer,* p. 36.

Ayduk, O., Mendoza-Denton, R., Mischel, W., Downey, G., Peake, P. K., & Rodriguez, M. (2000). Regulating the interpersonal self: Strategic self-regulation for coping with rejection sensitivity. *Journal of Personality and Social Psychology, 79,* 776–792.

Ayduk, O., Mischel, W., & Downey, G. (2002). Attentional mechanisms linking rejection to hostile reactivity: The role of "hot" versus "cool" focus. *Psychological Science, 13,* 443–448.

Azar, B. (1997a, October). From exotic to erotic: A new theory on sexuality. *Monitor on Psychology,* p. 29.

Azar, B. (1997b, October). Was Freud right: Maybe, maybe not. *Monitor,* pp. 28, 30.

Azar, B. (2002a, September). Searching for genes that explain our personalities. *Monitor on Psychology,* 44–45.

Azar, B. (2002b, October). Pigeons as baggage screeners, rats as rescuers. *Monitor on Psychology,* 42–44.

Baars, B. J. (2003). The double life of B. F. Skinner: Inner conflict, dissociation and the scientific taboo against consciousness. *Journal of Consciousness Studies, 10,* 5–25.

Bacciagaluppi, M. (1989). Eric Fromm's views on psychoanalytic "technique." *Contemporary Pyschoanalysis, 25,* 226–243.

Bailey, M. B., & Bailey, R. E. (1993). "Misbehavior": A case history. *American Psychologist, 48,* 1157–1158.

Bailey, M. J., Gaulin, S., Agyei, Y., Gladue, B. A. (1994). Effects of gender and sexual orientation on evolutionarily relevant aspects of human mating psychology. *Journal of Personality and Social Psychology, 66,* 1081–1093.

Baillargeon, J., & Danis, C. (1984). Barnum meets the computer: A critical test. *Journal of Personality Assessment, 48,* 415–419.

Bales, J. (1990). Skinner gets award, ovations at APA talk, *Monitor, 21*(10), pp. 1, 6.

Bandura, A. (1973). *Aggression: A Social Learning Analysis.* Englewood Cliffs, NJ: Prentice-Hall.

Bandura, A. (1977). *Social Learning Theory.* Englewood Cliffs, NJ: Prentice-Hall.

Bandura, A. (1982). The psychology of chance encounters and life paths. *American Psychologist, 37,* 747–755.

Bandura, A. (1989a). Social cognitive theory. *In Annals of Child Development* (Vol. 6, pp. 1–60). New York: Jai Press.

Bandura, A. (1989b). Human agency in social cognitive theory. *American Psychologist, 44,* 1175–1184.

Bandura, A. (1989c). Effect of perceived controllability and performance standards of self-regulation of complex decision making. *Journal of Personality and Social Psychology, 56,* 805–814.

Bandura, A. (1990a). Perceived self-efficacy in the exercise of personal agency. *Applied Sport Psychology, 2,* 128–163.

Bandura, A. (1990b). Mechanisms of moral disengagement. In W. Reich (Ed.), *Origins of Terrorism: Psychologies, Ideologies, States of Mind.* Cambridge, England: Cambridge University Press, (pp. 161–191).

Bandura, A. (1991a). Social cognitive theory of self-regulation. *Organizational Behavior and Human Decision Making Processes, 50,* 248–287.

Bandura, A. (1991b). Social cognitive theory of moral thought and action. In W. M. Kurtines & Jacob L. Gerwirtz (Eds.), *Handbook of Moral Behavior and Development, Vol. 1: Theory.* Hillsdale, NJ: Lawrence Erlbaum, pp. 45–103.

Bandura, A. (1993). Perceived self-efficacy in cognitive development and functioning. *Educational Psychologist, 28,* 117–148.

Bandura, A. (1994a). Social cognitive theory of mass communication. In J. Bryant & Dolf Zillmann (Eds.), *Media Effects: Advances in Theory and Research.* Hillsdale, NJ: Lawrence Erlbaum. pp. 61–90.

Bandura, A. (1994b). Self-efficacy. In V. S. Ramachaudran (Ed.), *Encyclopedia of Human Behavior,* Vol. 4. New York: Academic Press, pp. 71–81.

Bandura, A. (1995, July). Reflections on human agency. Keynote address presented at the IV European Congress of Psychology, Athens, Greece.

Bandura, A. (1997). *Self-Efficacy.* New York: W. H. Freeman.

Bandura, A. (1998a). Explorations of fortuitous determinants of life paths. *Psychological Inquiry, 9,* 95–99.

Bandura, A. (1998b). Personal and collective efficacy in human adaptation and change. In J. G. Adair, D. Belanger, & K. L. Dion (Eds.), *Advances in Psychological Science: Vol. 1. Personal, Social And Cultural Aspects.* Hove, UK: Psychology Press, pp. 51–71.

Bandura, A. (1999a). Social cognitive theory of personality. In L. Pervin & O. John (Eds.), *Handbook of Personality* (2nd ed.). New York: Guilfore, pp. 154–196.

Bandura, A. (1999b). A sociocognitive analysis of substance abuse: An agentic perspective. *Psychological Science, 10,* 214–217.

Bandura, A. (1999c). Moral disengagement in the perpetration of inhumanities. *Personality and Social Psychology Review, 3,* 193–209.

Bandura, A. (2000a). Exercise of human agency through collective efficacy. *Current Directions in Psychological Science,* 75–78.

Bandura, A. (2000b). Cultivate self-efficacy for personal and organizational effectiveness. In E. A. Lock (Ed.), *Handbook of Principles of Organization Behavior.* Oxford, UK: Blackwell, pp. 120–136.

Bandura, A. (2001a). Social cognitive theory: An agentic perspective. *Annual Review of Psychology, 52,* 1–23.

Bandura, A. (2001b). Social cognitive theory of mass communication. In J. Bryant & D. Zillmann (Eds.), *Media Effects: Advances in Theory and Research* (2nd ed.). Hillsdale, NJ: Lawrence Erlbaum, pp. 177–195.

Bandura, A. (2001c). The changing face of psychology at the dawning of a globalization era. *Canadian Psychology, 42,* 12–24.

Bandura, A. (2002). Environmental sustainability by sociocognitive deceleration of population growth. In P. Schmuck & W. Schultz (Eds.), *The psychology of sustainable development.* Dordrecht, The Netherlands: Kluwer.

Bandura, A., Barbaranelli, S., Caprara, G. V., & Pastorelli, C. (1996). Mechanisms of moral disengagement in the exercise of moral agency. *Journal of Personality and Social Psychology, 71,* 364–374.

Bandura, A., Barbaranelli, S., Caprara, G. V., & Pastorelli, C. (1996a). Multifaceted impact on self-efficacy beliefs on academic functioning. *Child Development, 67,* 1206–1222.

Bandura, A., Barbaranelli, S., Caprara, G. V., & Pastorelli, C. (2001). Self-efficacy beliefs as shapers of children's aspirations and career trajectories. *Child Development, 72,* 187–206.

Bandura, A., Barbaranelli, S., Caprara, G. V., Pastorelli, C. & Regalia, C. (2001). Sociocognitive self-regulatory mechanisms governing transgressive behavior. *Journal of Personality and Social Psychology, 80,* 125–135.

Bandura, A., & McDonald, F. (1963). The influence of social reinforcement and the behavior of models in shaping children's moral judgments. *Journal of Abnormal and Social Psychology, 67,* 274–281.

Bandura, A., Reese, L., & Adams, N. (1982). Microanalysis of action and fear arousal as a function of differential levels of perceived self-efficacy. *Journal of Personality and Social Psychology, 43,* 5–21.

Bandura, A., Ross, D., & Ross, S. (1963). Imitation of film-mediated aggressive models. *Journal of Abnormal and Social Psychology, 66,* 3–11.

Bandura, A., Underwood, B., & Fromson, M. E. (1975). Disinhibition of aggression through diffusion of responsibility and dehumanization of victims. *Journal of Research in Personality, 9,* 253–269.

Bandura, A., & Wood, R. (1989). Effect of perceived controllability and performance standards on self-regulation of complex decision making. *Journal of Personality and Social Psychology, 56,* 805–814.

Barber, T. X. (1978). "Hypnosis," suggestions, and psychosomatic phenomena: New look from the standpoint of recent experimental studies. In J. Fosshage & P. Olsen (Eds.), *Healing: Implications for Psychotherapy* New York: Human Sciences Press, pp. 269–297.

Barenbaum, N. B. (1997). The case(s) of Gordon Allport. *Journal of Personality, 65,* 743–755.

Barenbaum, N. B. (2003). Review of Ian A. M. Nicholson: "Inventing personality: Gordon Allport and the science of selfhood." *Journal of the History of the Behavioral Sciences, 39,* 408–409.

Barnes, H. E. (1953). Translator's introduction. In J-P. Sartre, *Being and Nothingness.* New York: Philosophical Library, pp. viii–xliii.

Barnet, H. S. (1990). Divorce stress and adjustment model: Locus of control and demographic predictors. *Journal of Divorce, 13,* 93–109.

Baron, R. A. (1977). *Human Aggression.* New York: Plenum.

Barry, H., Child, I., & Bacon, M. (1959). Relation of child rearing to subsistence economy. *American Anthropologist, 61,* 51–64.

Baum, W. M., & Heath, J. L. (1992). Behavioral explanations and intentional explanations in psychology. *American Psychologist, 47,* 1312–1317.

Baumeister, R. F. (1996, summer). Should schools try to boost self-esteem?: Beware of the dark side. *American Educator,* 14–19, 43.

Baumeister, R. F. (1999, January). Low self-esteem does not cause aggression. *Monitor of the American Psychological Association,* 7.

Baumeister, R. F., Campbell, J. D., Krueger, J. I., & Vohs, K. D. (2003). Does high self-esteem cause better performance, interpersonal success, happiness, or healthier lifestyles? *Psychological Science in the Public Interest, 4,* 1–44.

Beck, J. E. (1988). Testing a personal construct theory model of the experiential learning process—A. The impact of invalidation on the construing processes of participants in sensitivity training groups. *Small Group Behavior, 19,* 79–102.

Beer, J. M., & Horn, J. M. (2000). The influence of rearing order on personality development within two adoption cohorts. *Journal of Personality, 68,* 789–819.

Begley, S. (1998, July 13). You're OK, I'm terrific: 'Self-esteem' backfires. *Newsweek,* 69.

Bell, P. A., & Byrne, D. (1978). Repression-Sensitization. In H. London & J. E. Exner, Jr., (Eds.), *Dimensions of Personality.* New York: Wiley, pp. 449–485.

Belli, R. F., Lindsay, D. S., Gales, M. S., & McCarthy, T. T. (1994). Memory impairment and source misattribution in postevent misinformation experiments with short retention intervals. *Memory And Cognition, 22,* 40–54.

Bem, D. J. (1996). Exotic becomes erotic: A development theory of sexual orientation. *Psychological Review, 103,* 320–335.

Bem, D. J., & Allen, A. (1974). On predicting some of the people some of the time: The search for cross-situational consistencies in behavior. *Psychological Review, 81,* 506–520.

Bender, L. (1938). *A Visual Motor Gestalt Test and its Clinical Use.* New York: American Orthopsychiatric Association.

Benesch, K. F., & Page, M. M. (1989). Self-construct systems and interpersonal congruence. *Journal of Personality, 57,* 137–173.

Benjamin, L. T. (1988). A history of teaching machines. *American Psychologist, 43,* 703–712.

Benjamin, L. T., & Dixon, D. N. (1996). Dream analysis by mail: An American woman seeks Freud's advice. *American Psychologist, 51,* 461–468.

Benjamin, L. T., & Nielsen-Gammon, E. B. F. (1999). Skinner and psychotechnology: The case of the heir conditioner. *Review of General Psychology, 3,* 155–167.

Bennett, C. M. (1990). A Skinnerian view of human freedom. *The Humanist,* (July/August), 18–20, 30.

Benson, E. (2002, October). From the same planet after all. *Monitor on Psychology,* 34–36.

Bentler, P. M., Jackson, D. N., & Messick, S. (1971). Identification of content and style: A two-dimensional interpretation of acquiescence. *Psychological Bulletin, 76,* 186–204.

Bexton, W., Heron, W., & Scott, T. (1954). The effects of decreased variation in the sensory environment. *Canadian Journal of Psychology, 8,* 70–76.

Biancoli, R. (1992). Radical humanism in psychoanalysis or psychoanalysis as art. *Contemporary Psychoanalysis, 28,* 695–731.

Bieri, J. (1955). Cognitive complexity—simplicity and predictive behavior. *Journal of Abnormal and Social Psychology, 51,* 61–66.

Binswanger, L. (1958). The case of Ellen West: An anthropological-clinical study. In R. May, E. Angel, & H. F. Ellenberger (Eds.), *Existence: a New Dimension in Psychiatry and Psychology.* New York: Basic Books, pp. 237–364.

Binswanger, L. (1963). *Being-In-The-World: Selected Papers of Ludwig Binswanger* (J. Needleman, Trans.). New York: Harper and Row.

Bixler, R. H. (1990). Carl Rogers, "counseling," and the Minnesota point of view. *American Psychologist, 45,* 675.

Bjork, R. A. (2000). Different views of individual differences. *Observer, 13,* 3, 26.

Blake, M. J. F. (1967). Relationship between circadian rhythm of body temperature and introversion–extraversion. *Nature, 215,* 896–897.

Blake, M. J. F. (1971). Temperament and time of day. In W. P. Colquhoun (Ed.), *Biological Rhythms and Human Performance.* New York: Academic Press.

Blau, G. (1993). Testing the relationship of locus of control to different performance dimensions. *Journal of Occupational and Organizational Psychology, 66,* 125–138.

Blauner, R. (1992). The ambiguities of racial change. In M. L. Andersen & P. H. Collins (Eds.), *Race, Class, and Gender.* Belmont, CA: Wadsworth.

Blechner, M. J. (1994). Projective identification, countertransference, and the "maybe-me." *Contemporary Psychoanalysis, 30,* 619–631.

Bonanno, G. A. (2004). Loss, trauma, and human resilience: Have we underestimated the human capacity to thrive after extremely aversive events. *American Psychologist, 59,* 20–28.

Boring, E. (1957). *A History of Experimental Psychology* (2nd ed.). New York: Appleton-Century-Crofts.

Bornstein, R. F. (1998). Radical behaviorism, internal states, and the science of psychology: A reply to Skinner. *American Psychologist, 43,* 819–821.

Boss, M. (1963). *Psychoanalysis and Daseinsanalysis.* (L. B. LeFebre, Trans.) New York: Basic Books.

Bosselman, B. C. (1958). *Self-Destruction: A Study of the Suicidal Impulse.* Springfield, IL: Thomas.

Bottome, P. (1939). *Alfred Adler: Apostle of Freedom.* London: Faber & Faber.

Bower, B. (2003). Repeat after me: Imitation is the sincerest form of perception. *Science News, 163,* 330–332.

Bowers, K. (1973). Situationalism in psychology: An analysis and a critique. *Psychological Review, 80,* 307–336.

Bowlby, J. (1969). *Maternal Care and Mental Health.* New York: Schocken.

Bozarth, J. D. (1990). The evolution of Carl Rogers as a therapist. Special issue: Fiftieth anniversary of the person-centered approach. *Person Centered Review,* 387–393.

Bozarth, J. D., & Brodley, B. T. (1991). Actualization: A functional concept in client-centered therapy. Special issue: Handbook of self-actualization. *Journal of Social Behavior and Personality, 6,* 45–59.

Brackett, M. A., & Mayer, J. D. (2003). Convergent, discriminant, and incremental validity of competing measures of emotional intelligence. *Personality and Social Psychology Bulletin, 29,* 1147–1158.

Brakel, L. A., Kleinsorge, S., Snodgrass, M., & Shevrin, H. (2000). The primary process and the unconscious. Experimental evidence supporting two psychoanalytic presuppositions. *International Journal of Psychoanalysis, 81,* 563–569.

Breuer, J., & Freud, S. (1895/1950). *Studies in Hysteria.* Boston: Beacon Press.

Brody, B. (1970). Freud's case-load. *Psychotherapy: Theory, Research and Practice, 7,* 8–12.

Bromberg, P. M. (1993). "Obsessions and/or obsessionality: Perspectives on a psychoanalytic treatment": Comment and Erratum. *Contemporary Psychoanalysis, 29,* 372.

Bronfen, E. (1989). The lady vanishes: Sophie Freud and beyond the Pleasure Principle. *South Atlantic Quarterly, 88* (Fall), 961–991.

Brunner, H. G., Nelen, M., Breakefield, X. O., Ropers, B. A., & van Oost, B. A. (1993, October 22). Abnormal behavior associated with a point mutation in the structural gene for monoamine oxidase A. *Science, 262,* 578–570.

Buber, M. (1958). *I and Thou.* (2nd ed.). New York: Scribners.

Bugental, J. F. T. (1964). The third force in psychology. *Journal of Humanistic Psychology, 4,* 19–25.

Buhler, C. (1962). *Values in Psychotherapy.* New York: Free Press.

Buhler, C. (1965). Some observations on the psychology of the third force. *Journal of Humanistic Psychology, 5,* 54–55.

Bullock, W. A., & Gilliland, K. (1993). Eysenck's arousal theory of introversion-extraversion: A converging measures investigation. *Journal of Personality and Social Psychology, 64,* 113–123.

Burckle, M. A., Ryckman, R. M., Gold, J. A., Thornton, B., & Audesse, R. J. (1999). Forms of competitive attitude and achievement orientation in relation to disordered eating. *Sex Roles, 40,* 853–870.

Burris, C. T. (1994). Curvilinearity and Freligious types: A second look at intrinsic, extrinsic, and quest relations. *International Journal for the Psychology of Religion, 4,* 245–260.

Bushman, B. J., Bonacci, A. M., van Dijk, M., & Baumeister, R. F. (2003). Narcissism, sexual refusal, and aggression: Testing a narcissistic reactance model of sexual coercion. *Journal of Personality and Social Psychology, 84,* 1027–1040.

Buss, D. M., Larsen, R., Weston, D., & Semmelroth, J. (1992). Sex differences in jealousy: Evolution, physiology, and psychology. *Psychological Science,* 251–255.

Buss, D. M., & Schmitt, D. P. (1993). Sexual strategies theory: An evolutionary perspective on human mating. *Psychological Review, 100,* 204–232.

Buss, D. M., & Shackelford, T. K. (1997). From vigilance to violence: Mate retention tactics in married couples. *Journal of Personality and Social Psychology, 72,* 346–361.

Bussey, K., & Bandura, A. (1992). Self-regulatory mechanisms governing gender development. *Child Development, 63,* 1236–1250.

Bussey, K., & Bandura, A. (1999). Social cognitive theory of gender development and differentiation. *Psychological Review, 106.* 676–713.

Butler, J. M., & Haigh, G. V. (1954). Changes in the relation between self-concepts and ideal concepts consequent upon client-centered counseling. In C. R. Rogers & R. F. Dymond (Eds.), *Psychotherapy and Personality Change.* Chicago: University of Chicago Press, pp. 55–75.

Buttle, F. (1989). The social construction of needs. *Psychology and Marketing, 6,* 199–207.

Buunk, B. P., Angleitner, A., Oubaid, V., & Buss, D. M. (1996). Sex differences in jealousy, evolutionary and cultural perspective: Tests from the Netherlands, Germany, and the United States. *Psychological Science, 7,* 359–363.

Campbell, D. T. (1975). On the conflicts between biological and social evolution and between psychology and moral tradition. *American Psychologist, 30,* 1103–1126.

Campbell, D. T., & Fiske, D. W. (1959). Convergent and discriminant validation by the multitrait-multimethod matrix. *Psychological Bulletin, 56,* 81–105.

Campbell, F. A., & Ramey, C. T. (1994). Effects of early intervention on intellectual and academic achievement: A follow-up study of children from low-income families. *Child Development, 65,* 684–698.

Campbell, L., Simpson, J. A., Stewart, M., & Manning, J. (2003). Putting personality in social context: Extraversion, emergent leadership, and the availability of rewards. *Personality and Social Psychology Bulletin, 29,* 1547–1559.

Campbell, W. K., Foster, C. A., & Finkel, E. J. (2002). Does self-love lead to love for others? A story of narcissistic game playing. *Journal of Personality and Social Psychology, 83,* 340–354.

Canli, T., Sivers, H., Whitfield, W. L., Gotlib, I. H., & Gabrieli, J. D. E. (2002, June 21). Amygdala response to happy faces as a function of extraversion. *Science, 296,* 291.

Cannon, W. G. (1932). *Wisdom of the Body.* New York: Norton.

Cantor, N., & Mischel, W. (1977). Traits as prototypes: Effects on recognition memory. *Journal of Personality and Social Psychology, 35,* 38–48.

Cantor, N., Mischel, W., & Schwartz, J. C. (1982). A prototype analysis of psychological situations. *Cognitive Psychology, 14,* 45–77.

Cantril, H. (1960). *The morning notes of Adelbert Ames, Jr.; Including a correspondence with John Dewey.* New Brunswick, NJ: Rutgers University Press.

Caprara, G. V., Barbaranelli, C., Pastorelli, C., Bandura, A., & Zimbardo, P. G. (2000). Prosocial foundations of children's academic achievement. *Psychological Science, 11,* 302–306.

Caprara, G. V., Steca, P., Cervone, D., & Artistico, D. (2003). The contribution of self-efficacy beliefs to dispositional shyness: On social-cognitive systems and the development of personality dispositions. *Journal of Personality, 71,* 943–970.

Carlsmith, K. M., Darley, J. D., & Robinson, R. H. (2002). Why do we punish? Deterrence and just deserts as motives for punishment. *Journal of Personality and Social Psychology, 83,* 284–299.

Carlson, J. (1989). Brief therapy for health promotion. *Individual Psychology, 45,* 220–229.

Carlyn, M. (1977). An assessment of the Myers-Briggs Type Indicator. *Journal of Personality Assessment, 41,* 461–473.

Carpenter, S. (1999, July/August). Freud's dream theory gets boost from imaging work. *Monitor on Psychology,* 19.

Carpenter, S. (2001, February). Different dispositions, different brains. *Monitor on Psychology, 66–67*.

Carpenter, S. (2002, February). Plagiarism or memory glitch? *Monitor on Psychology, 25–26*.

Carskadon, T. G. (1978). Use of the Myers-Briggs Type Indicator in psychology courses and discussion groups. *Teaching of Psychology, 5, 140–142*.

Carson, R. C., & Butcher, F. N. (1992). *Abnormal Psychology and Modern Life*. New York: Harper-Collins.

Carson, R. C., Butcher, F. N., & Mineka, S. (1996). *Abnormal Psychology and Modern Life* (10 ed.). New York: HarperCollins.

Cartwright, D., DeBruin, J., & Berg, S. (1991). Some scales for assessing personality based on Carl Rogers' theory: Further evidence of validity. *Personality and Individual Differences, 12, 151–156*.

Caruso, D. R., Mayer, J. D., & Salovey, P. (2002). Relation of an ability measure of emotional intelligence to personality. *Journal of Personality Assessment, 79, 306–320*.

Caspi, A., McClay, J., Moffitt, T. E., Mill, J., Martin, J., Craig, I., Taylor, A., & Poulton, R. (2002, August 2). Role of genotype in the cycle of violence in maltreated children. *Science, 297, 851–853*.

Catanzaro, S. J., & Mearns, J. (1990). Measuring generalized expectancies for negative mood regulation: Initial scale development and implications. *Journal of Personality Assessment, 54, 546–563*.

Catina, A., & Tschuschke, V. (1993). A summary of empirical data from the investigation of two psychoanalytic groups by means of repertory grid technique. *Group Analysis, 26, 443–447*.

Cattell, H. E. P. (1993). Comment on Goldberg. *American Psychologist, 48, 1302–1303*.

Cattell, R. B. (1933). *Psychology and Social Progress*. London: C. W. Daniel.

Cattell, R. B. (1936–1937). "Is national intelligence declining?" *Eugenics Review, 28, 181–203*.

Cattell, R. B. (1937). *The Fight for Our National Intelligence*. London: P. S. King.

Cattell, R. B. (1946). *The Description and Measurement of Personality*. New York: World Book.

Cattell, R. B. (1949). *The Sixteen Personality Factor Questionnaire* (1st ed.). Champaign, IL: Institute for Personality and Ability Testing.

Cattell, R. B. (1950). *Personality: A Systematic, Theoretical and Factual Study*. New York: McGraw-Hill.

Cattell, R. B. (1963). The nature and measurement of anxiety. *Scientific American, 208, 96–104*.

Cattell, R. B. (1966). *The Scientific Analysis of Personality*. Baltimore, MD: Penguin.

Cattell, R. B. (1972). *A New Morality From Science: Beyondism*. New York: Pergamon.

Cattell, R. B. (1973). *Personality and Mood by Questionnaire*. San Francisco: Jossey-Bass.

Cattell, R. B. (1974a). Raymond B. Cattell. In G. Lindzey (Ed.), *A History of Psychology in Autobiography*. Englewood Cliffs, NJ: Prentice-Hall.

Cattell, R. B. (1974b). Travels in psychological hyperspace. In T. S. Krawiec (Ed.), *The Psychologists*. (Vol. 2). New York: Oxford University Press.

Cattell, R. B. (1979). *Personality and Learning Theory* (Vols. 1–2). New York: Springer.

Cattell, R. B. (1983). *Structured Personality-Learning Theory: A Wholistic Multivariate Research Approach*. New York: Praeger.

Cattell, R. B. (1984a). *Human Motivation and the Dynamic Calculus*. New York: Praeger.

Cattell, R. B. (1984b). The voyage of a laboratory, 1928–1984. *Multivariate Behavioral Research, 19, 121–174*.

Cattell, R. B. (1986). The 16 PF personality structure and Dr. Eysenck. *Journal of Social Behavior and Personality, 1, 153–160*.

Cattell, R. B. (1987). *Beyondism: Religion From Science*. New York: Praeger.

Cattell, R. B. (1994). Constancy of global, second-order personality factors over a twenty-year-plus period. *Psychological Reports, 75, 3–9*.

Cattell, R. B., & Brennan, J. (1984). The cultural types of modern nations, by two quantitative classification methods. *Sociology and Social Research, 68, 208–235*.

Cattell, R. B., Eber, H. W., & Tatsuoka, M. M. (1970). *Handbook for the Sixteen Personality Factor Questionnaire*. Champaign, IL: Institute for Personality and Ability Testing.

Cattell, R. B., & Kline, P. (1977). *The Scientific Analysis of Personality and Motivation*. New York: Academic Press.

Cattell, R. B., Rao, D. C., & Schuerger, J. M. (1985). Heritability in the personality control system: Ego strength (C), super ego strength (G) and the self-sentiment (Q_3), by the MAVA mode, Q-data, and Maximum likelihood analyses. *Social Behavior and Personality, 13, 33–41*.

Cattell, R. B., & Scheier, I. H. (1961). *The Meaning and Measurement of Neuroticism and Anxiety.* New York: Ronald Press.

Cattell, R. B., Schuerger, J. M., & Klein, T. W. (1982). Heritabilities of ego strength (factor C), super ego strength (factor G), and self-sentiment (factor Q_3) by multiple abstract variance analysis. *Journal of Clinical Psychology, 38,* 769–779.

Cattell, R. B., & Warburton, F. W. (1967). *Objective Personality & Motivation Tests: A Theoretical Introduction and Practical Compendium.* Urbana: University of Illinois Press.

Cautela, J. R., & Upper, D. (1976). *The Behavioral Inventory Battery: The Use of Self-Report Measures in Behavioral Analysis and Therapy.* In M. Hersen & A. S. Bellack (Eds.), *Behavioral Assessment: A Practical Handbook.* New York: Pergamon Press.

Cavalli-Sforza, L. L. (2000). *Genes, Peoples and Languages.* New York: North Point Press.

Cavalli-Sforza, L. L., Menozzi, P., & Piazza, A. (1994). *The History and Geography of Human Genes.* Princeton, NJ: Princeton University Press.

Ceci, S. J., Huffman, M. L. C., Smith, E., & Loftus, E. F. (1996). Repeatedly thinking about a non-event: Source misattributions among preschoolers. In K. Pezdek & W. P. Banks (Eds.), *The Recovered Memory/False Memory Debate.* New York: Academic Press.

Cervone, D. (2004). The architecture of personality. *Psychological Review, 111,* 183–204.

Cervone, D., Shadel, W. G., & Jencius, S. (2001) Social–cognitive theory of personality assessment. *Personality and Social Psychology Review, 5,* 33–51.

Cervone, D., & Shoda, Y. (1999). Beyond traits in the study of personality coherence. *Current Directions in Psychological Science, 8,* 27–31.

Cetola, H., & Prinkey, K. (1986). Introversion-extraversion and loud commercials. *Psychology and Marketing, 3,* 123–132.

Chapman, A. H. (1976). *Harry Stack Sullivan: His Life and His Work.* New York: Putnam.

Cherian, V. I. (1990). Birth order and academic achievement of children in Transkei. *Psychological Reports, 66,* 19–24.

Chiesa, M. (1992). Radical behaviorism and scientific frameworks: From mechanistic to relational accounts. *American Psychologist, 47,* 1287–1299.

Chomsky, N. (1959). A review of Verbal Behavior by B. F. Skinner. *Language, 35,* 26–58.

Christoper, J. C., Manaster, G. J., Campbell, R. L., & Weinfeld, M. B. (2002). Peak experiences, social interest, and moral reasoning: An exploratory study. *Journal of Individual Psychology, 58,* 35–51.

Churchill, J. C., Broida, J. P., & Nicholson, N. L. (1990). Locus of control and self-esteem of adult children of alcoholics. *Journal of Studies on Alcohol, 51,* 373–376.

Cialdini, R. B. (1985). *Influence: Science and Practice.* Glenview, IL: Scott, Foresman.

Cioffi, F. (1974). Was Freud a liar? *The Listener, 91,* 172–174.

Clark, K. B. (1965). The psychology of the ghetto. In *Dark Ghetto.* New York: Harper & Row, pp. 63–80.

Clark, R. E., & Squire, L. R. (1998). Classical conditioning and brain systems: The role of awareness. *Science, 280,* 77–81.

Clay, R. A. (2003, April). Researchers replace midlife myths with facts. *Monitor on Psychology,* 38–39.

Cohen, D. (1977). *Psychologists on Psychology.* New York: Taplinger.

Cohen, S., Evans, G. W., Krantz, D. S., & Stokols, D. (1980). Physiological, motivational, and cognitive effects of aircraft noise on children. *American Psychologist, 35,* 231–243.

Cohen, S., Tyrrell, D. A., & Smith, A. P. (1993). Negative life events, perceived stress, negative affect, and susceptibility to the common cold. *Journal of Personality and Social Psychology, 64,* 131–140.

Collins, B., & Hoyt, M. (1972). Personal responsibility for consequences: An integration and extension of the "forced" compliance literature. *Journal of Experimental Social Psychology, 8,* 558–593.

Conci, M. (1993). Harry Stack Sullivan and the training of the psychiatrist. *Contemporary Psychiatry, 29,* 530–540.

Conoley, J., & Impara, J. C. (1995). *Twelfth Mental Measurement Yearbook.* Lincoln, NE: Buros Institute of Mental Measurement.

Cook, W. L. (2000). Understanding attachment security in family context. *Journal of Personality and Social Psychology, 78,* 285–294.

Cooper, R., & Zubek, J. (1958). Effects of enriched and restricted environments on the learning ability of bright and dull rats. *Canadian Journal of Psychology, 12,* 159–164.

Corcoran, D. W. J. (1964).The relation between introversion and salivation. *American Journal of Psychology, 77,* 298–300.

Correll, J., Park, B., Judd, C. M., & Wittenbrink, B. (2002). The police officer's dilemma: Using ethnicity of disambiguate potentially threatening individuals. *Journal of Personality and Social Psychology, 83,* 1314–1349.

Cramer, P. (1968). *Word Association.* New York: Academic Press.

Crandall, J. E. (1980). Adler's concept of social interest: Theory, measurement, and implications for adjustment. *Journal of Personality and Social Psychology, 39,* 481–495.

Cresti, A. (2003). "The interpersonal perspective of Karen Horney" by Diego Garofalo. *American Journal of Psychoanalysis, 63,* 196–198.

Crews, F. (1996). The verdict on Freud. *Psychological Science, 7,* 63–68.

Crumbaugh, J., and Maholick, L. (1969). *Manual of Instructions for the Purpose in Life Test.* Munster, IN: Psychometric Affiliates.

Dahlberg, T. (2003, January 21). By, George! *Peoria Journal Star,* C2, C4.

Daley, T. C., Whaley, S. E., Sigman, M. D., Espinosa, M. P., & Neumann, C. (2003). IQ on the rise: The Flynn effect in rural Kenyan children. *Psychological Science, 14,* 215–220.

Dalton, P., & Dunnett, G. (1992). *A Psychology For Living: Personal Construct Theory for Professionals and Clients.* New York: John Wiley & Sons.

Daly, M., & Wilson, M. (1990). Is parent–offspring conflict sex-linked? Freudian and Darwinian models. *Journal of Personality, 58,* 163–190.

Danto, A., & Morgenbesser, S. (1960). *Philosophy of Science.* Cleveland: Meridan.

Darley, J., & Zanna, M. (1982). Making moral judgments. *American Scientist, 70,* 515–521.

Das, A. K. (1989). Beyond self-actualization. *International Journal for the Advancement of Counseling, 12,* 13–17.

David, J. P., Green, P. J., Martin, R., & Suls, J. (1997). Differential roles of neuroticism, extraversion, and event desirability for mood in daily life: An integrative model of top-down and bottom-up influences. *Journal of Personality and Social Psychology, 73,* 149–159.

Davidson, P. O., & Costello, C. G. (1969). (Eds.). N = 1: Experimental studies of single cases. New York: Van Nostrand Reinhold.

Davila, J., & Cobb, R. J. (2003). Predicting change in self-reported and interviewer-assessed adult attachment: Tests of the individual difference and life stress models of attachment change. *Personality and Social Psychology Bulletin, 29,* 859–870.

Davis, D., Shaver, P. R., & Vernon, M. L. (2003). Physical, emotional, and behavioral reactions to breaking up: The roles of gender, age, emotional involvement, and attachment style. *Personality and Social Psychology Bulletin, 29,* 871–884.

Davis, F. J. (1991). *Who Is Black?* University Park, PA: Pennsylvania State University Press.

Davis, W., & Phares, E. (1969). Parental antecedents of internal-external control of reinforcement. *Psychological Reports, 24,* 427–436.

Dawidowicz, L. S. (1975). *The War Against the Jews.* New York: Bantam.

DeAngelis, T. (1994a, July). Jung's theories keep pace and remain popular. *Monitor,* p. 41.

DeAngelis, T. (1994b, October). Loving styles may be determined in infancy. *Monitor,* p. 21.

DeAngelis, T. (1994c, October). Not Just a good theory: Transference is proven. *Monitor,* p. 56.

de Bonis, M., & Delgrange, C. (1977). A psycholinguistic approach to the measurement of anxiety. In C. D. Spielberger & I. G. Sarason (Eds.), *Stress and Anxiety* (Vol. 4). New York: Wiley, pp. 67–76.

deCarvalho, R. J. (1990). Contributions to the history of psychology: LXIX. Gordon Allport on the problem of method in psychology. *Psychological Reports, 67,* 267–275.

deCarvalho, R. J. (1991). Gordon Allport and humanistic psychology. *Journal of Humanistic Psychology, 31,* 8–13.

deCarvalho, R. J. (1991). The humanistic paradigm in education. *Humanistic Psychologist, 19,* 88–104.

deCarvalho, R. J. (1999). Otto Rank, The Rankian circle in Philadelphia, and the origins of Carl Rogers' person-centered psychotherapy. *History of Psychology, 2,* 132–148.

deCharms, R. (1972). Personal causation training in the schools. *Journal of Applied Social Psychology, 2,* 95–113.

deCharms, R., & Moeller, G. H. (1962). Values expressed in American children's readers: 1800–1950. *Journal of Abnormal Psychology, 64,* 136–142.

deCharms, R., & Muir, M. S. (1978). Motivation: Social approaches. In M. R. Rosenzweig & L. W. Porter (Eds.), *Annual Review of Psychology* (Vol. 29). Palo Alto, CA: Annual Reviews, 91–113.

DeGrandpre, R. J. (2000). A science of meaning: Can behaviorism bring meaning to psychological science? *American Psychologist, 55,* 721–739.

Dement, W. C. (1976). *Some Must Watch While Some Must Sleep.* New York: Norton.

Demorest, A. P., & Siegel, P. F. (1996). Personal influences on professional work: An empirical case study of B. F. Skinner. *Journal of Personality, 64,* 241–261.

DePaulo, B., & Rosenthal, R. (1979). Telling lies. *Journal of Personality and Social Psychology, 37,* 1713–1722.

DeSteno, D., Bartlett, M. Y., & Salovey, P. (2002). Sex differences in jealousy: Evolutionary mechanism or artifact of measurement? *Journal of Personality and Social Psychology, 83,* 1103–1116.

DeSteno, D. A., & Salovey, P. (1996). Evolutionary origins of sex differences in jealousy? Questioning the "Fitness" of the model. *Psychological Science, 7,* 367–372.

Detterman, D. K. (1998, May). The Cattell Award. *Monitor,* [Letters], p. 5.

Devine, P., Plant, W. A., Amodio, D. M., Harmon-Jones, E., & Vance, S. L. (2002). The regulation of explicit and implicit race bias: The role of motivations to respond without prejudice. *Journal of Personality and Social Psychology, 82,* 835–848.

Devlin, B., Daniels, M., & Roeder, K. (1997, July 31). The heritability of I.Q. *Nature, 388,* 468–471.

Dickens, W. T., & Flynn, J. R. (2001). Heritability estimates vs. environmental effects: The IQ paradox resolved. *Psychological Review, 108,* 346–369.

Diener, E., & Seligman, M. E. P. (2002). Very happy people. *Psychological Science, 13,* 81–86.

Diener, E., & Wallbom, M. (1976). Effects of self-awareness on antinormative behavior. *Journal of Research in Personality, 10,* 107–111.

Dinkmeyer, D., & Sherman, R. (1989). Brief Adlerian family therapy. *Individual Psychology, 45,* 148–158.

Dinsmoor, J. A. (1992). Setting the record straight: The social views of B. F. Skinner. *American Psychologist, 47,* 1454–1463.

Dittman, M. (2003b, January). Study explores how religion influences people's ability to cope. *Monitor on Psychology,* 16.

Dittman, M. (2003a, October). How 'emotional intelligence' emerged. *Monitor on Psychology,* 64.

Dixon, N. (1971). *Subliminal Perception: The Nature of a Controversy.* London: McGraw-Hill.

Doherty, W. (1983). Impact of divorce on locus of control orientation in adult women: A longitudinal study. *Journal of Personality and Social Psychology, 44,* 834–840.

Dolliver, R. H. (1994). Classifying the personality theories and personalities of Adler, Freud, and Jung with introversion/extroversion. *Individual Psychology Journal of Adlerian Theory, Research, and Practice, 50,* 192–202.

Domhoff, W. G. (2003, March 28). Making sense of dreaming. *Science, 299,* 1997–1998.

Don, N. W. (1999). "The Rhine-Jung letters: Distinguishing parapsychological from synchronistic events": Comments. *Journal of Parapsychology, 63,* 184–185.

Donn, J. (2000, March 30). Finger length may reflect sexual orientation. *Peoria Journal Star,* p. A14.

Donohue, M. J. (1985). Intrinsic and extrinsic religiousness: Review and meta-analysis. *Journal of Personality and Social Psychology, 48,* 400–419.

Dovidio, J. F., & Gaertner, L. S. (2000). Aversive racism and selective decisions: 1989–1999. *Psychological Science, 11,* 315–319.

Dovidio, J. F., Gaertner, S. L., & Validzic, A. (1998). Intergroup bias: Status, differentiation, and a common in-group identity. *Journal of Personality and Social Psychology, 75,* 109–120.

Dovidio, J. F., Kawakami, K., & Gaertner, S. L. (2002). Implicit and explicit prejudice and interracial interaction. *Journal of Personality and Social Psychology, 82,* 62–68.

Dreikurs, R. (1972a). Family counseling: A demonstration. *Journal of Individual Psychology, 28,* 207–222.

Dreikurs, R. (1972b). Technology of conflict resolution. *Journal of Individual Psychology, 28,* 203–206.

Dry, A. (1961). *The Psychology of Jung: A Critical Interpretation.* New York: Wiley.

Duckitt, J., Wagner, C., du Plessis, I., & Birum, I. (2002). The psychological bases of ideology and prejudice: Testing a dual process model. *Journal of Personality and Social Psychology, 83,* 75–93.

Duval, S., & Wicklund, R. A. (1972). *A Theory of Objective Self Awareness.* New York: Academic Press.

Duval, S., & Wicklund, R. A. (1973). Effects of objective self awareness on attribution of causality. *Journal of Experimental Social Psychology, 9,* 17–31.

Eagly, A. H. (1987). *Sex Differences in Social Behavior: A Social Role Interpretation.* Hillsdale, NJ: Erlbaum.

Eaves, L. J., & Eysenck, H. J. (1975). The nature of extraversion: A genetical analysis. *Journal of Personality and Social Psychology, 32,* 102–112.

Eckardt, M. H. (1980). Foreward. In K. Horney, *The Adolescent Diaries of Karen Horney.* New York: Basic Books.

Eckardt, M. H. (1991). Feminine psychology revisited: A historical perspective. [Special issue: Karen Horney]. *American Journal of Psychoanalysis, 51,* 235–243.

Eckardt, M. H. (1992). Fromm's concept of biophilia. *Journal of the American Academy of Psychoanalysis, 20,* 233–240.

Ekman, P., & Friesen, W. (1974). Detecting deception from the body and face. *Journal of Personality and Social Psychology, 29,* 288–298.

Eldredge, P. R. (1989). A granddaughter of violence: Doris Lessing's good girls as terrorists. [Special Issue: Interdisciplinary applications of Horney]. *American Journal of Psychoanalysis, 49,* 225–238.

Ellenberger, H. (1970). *The Discovery of the Unconscious: The History and Evolution of Dynamic Psychiatry.* New York: Basic Books.

Elliot, A. J., & Harackiewicz, J. M. (1996). Approach and avoidance achievement goals and intrinsic motivation: A mediational analysis. *Journal of Personality and Social Psychology, 70,* 461–465.

Ellis, A. (1974a). Rational-Emotive Theory. In A. Burton (Ed.), *Operational Theories of Personality.* New York: Brunner/Mazel, pp. 308–344.

Ellis, A. (1974b). Experience and rationality: The making of a Rational-Emotive therapist. *Psychotherapy: Theory, Research and Practice, 11,* 194–198.

Engelhard, G. (1990). Gender differences in performance on mathematics items: Evidence from the United States and Thailand. *Contemporary Educational Psychology, 15,* 13–26.

Engleman, E. (1976). *Berggasse 19: Sigmund Freud's Home and offices, Vienna 1938.* New York: Basic Books.

Enzle, M. E., & Wohl, M. J. A. (2002). Manipulating personal salience, redux: An occasion for recalling problems with the correlations approach for testing causal hypotheses. *Representative Research in Social Psychology, 26,* 15–25.

Epel, W. S., Bandura, A., & Zimbardo, P. G. (1999). Escaping homelessness: The influences of self-efficacy and time perspective on coping with homelessness. *Journal of Applied Social Psychology, 29,* pp. 575–596.

Epstein, R. (1991). Skinner, creativity, and the problems of spontaneous behavior. *Psychological Science, 2,* pp. 362–370.

Eric Erikson: The quest for identity. (1970, December 21). *Newsweek,* pp. 84–89.

Erikson, E. (1950). *Childhood and Society.* New York: W. W. Norton.

Erikson, E. (1968a). Womanhood and the inner space. In E. H. Erikson. *Identity, Youth and Crisis.* New York: Norton, pp. 261–294.

Erikson, E. (1968b). Life cycle. In D. Sills (Ed.), *International Encyclopedia of the Social Sciences.* Vol. 9. New York: Macmillan & Free Press, pp. 286–292.

Erikson, E. (1975). *Life History and the Historical Moment, Diverse Presentations.* New York: Norton.

Esterson, A. (1993). *Seductive Mirage: An Exploration of the Work of Sigmund Freud.* New York: Open Court.

Estes, K. (1944). An experimental study of punishment. *Psychological Monographs, 47,* No. 263.

Evans, R. I. (1964). *Conversations with Carl Jung, and Reactions From Ernest Jones.* Princeton, NJ: Van Nostrand.

Evans, R. I. (1967). *Dialogue with Erik Erikson.* New York: Harper & Row.

Evans, R. I. (1975). *Carl Rogers, the Man and His Ideas.* New York: E. P. Dutton.

Evans, R. I. (1976). *The Making of Psychology.* New York: A. A. Knoff.

Evans, R. I. (1988). Albert Bandura: A filmed interview. Videotape distributed by Pennsylvania State University.

Eysenck, H. J. (1952a). The effects of psychotherapy: An evaluation. *Journal of Consulting Psychology, 16,* 319–324.

Eysenck, H. J. (1952b). *The Scientific Study of Personality.* New York: Macmillan.

Eysenck, H. J. (1957). *Sense and Nonsense in Psychology.* Baltimore, MD: Penguin.

Eysenck, H. J. (1959). *Manual of the Maudsley Personality Inventory.* London: University of London Press.

Eysenck, H. J. (1962). *The Maudsley Personality Inventory Manual.* San Diego: Educational and Industrial Testing Service.

Eysenck, H. J. (1967). *The Biological Basis of Personality.* Springfield, IL: Charles C. Thomas.

Eysenck, H. J. (1970). A dimensional system of psychodiagnosis. In A. R. Mahrer (Ed.), *New Approaches to Personality Classification.* New York: Columbia University Press.

Eysenck, H. J. (1971). *The I.Q. Argument: Race, Intelligence and Education.* New York: Library Press.

Eysenck, H. J. (1974). *The Inequality of Man.* London: Temple Smith.

Eysenck, H. J. (1976). (Ed.). *The Measurement of Personality.* Baltimore, MD: University Park Press.

Eysenck, H. J. (1980). In G. Lindzey (Ed.), *A History of Psychology in Autobiography* (Vol. 7). San Francisco: W. H. Freeman, pp. 153–187.

Eysenck, H. J. (1981). (Ed.). *A Model for Personality.* New York: Springer-Verlag.

Eysenck, H. J. (1984). Cattell and the theory of personality. *Multivariate Behavioral Research, 19,* 323–336.

Eysenck, H. J. (1990). Genetic and environmental contributions to individual differences: The three major dimensions of personality. *Journal of Personality, 58,* 245–261.

Eysenck, H. J. (1993). Comment on Goldberg. *American Psychologist, 48,* 1299–1300.

Eysenck, H. J. (1997). Personality and experimental psychology: The unification of psychology and the possibility of a paradigm. *Personality and Social Psychology, 73,* 1224–1237.

Eysenck, H. J., & Eysenck, S. B. G. (1969). *Personality Structure and Measurement.* San Diego, CA: Robert R. Knapp.

Eysenck, H. J., & Eysenck, S. B. G. (1976). *Psychoticism as a Dimension of Personality.* New York: Crane, Russak.

Eysenck, H. J., & Levey, A. (1972). Conditioning, introversion-extraversion and the strength of the nervous system. In V. D. Nebylitsyn & J. A. Gray (Eds.), *Biological Bases of Individual Behavior.* New York: Academic Press, pp. 206–220.

Eysenck, S. B. G., & Eysenck, H. J. (1967). Salivary response to lemon juice as a measure of introversion. *Perceptual and Motor Skills 24,* pp. 1047–1053.

Eysenck, S. B. G., & Eysenck, H. J. (1968). The measurement of psychoticism: A study of factor analytic stability and reliability. *British Journal of Social and Clinical Psychology, 7,* 286–294.

Eysenck, S. B. G., & Eysenck, H. J. (1976). *Personality Structure and Measurement.* New York: Crane.

Fagen, J. W. (1993). Reinforcement is not enough: Learned expectancies and infant behavior. *American Psychologist 48,* 1153–1155.

Falbo, T. (1981). Relationships between birth category, achievement and interpersonal orientation. *Journal of Personality and Social Psychology, 41,* 121–131.

Falbo, T., & Polit, D. (1986). Quantitative review of the only child literature: Research evidence and theory development. *Psychological Bulletin, 100,* 176–189.

Fallon, D. (1992). An existential look at B. F. Skinner. *American Psychologist, 47,* 1433–1440.

Fancher, R. E. (2000). Snapshots of Freud in America, 1899–1999. *American Psychologist, 55,* 1025–1028.

Farber, A. (1978). Freud's love letters: Intimations of psychoanalytic theory. *Psychoanalytic Review, 65,* 167–189.

Farberow, N. L. (1970). A society by any other name. *Journal of Projective Techniques and Personality Assessment, 34,* 3–5.

Farley, R. C. (2002). Attachment stability from infancy to adulthood: Meta-analysis and dynamic modeling of developmental mechanisms. *Personality and Social Psychology Review, 6,* 123–151.

Farr, R. M. (2002). Psychology and astrophysics: Overcoming physics envy. *Dialogue, 17*(1), 17, 21.

Feldman, B. (1992). Jung's infancy and childhood and its influence upon the development of analytical psychology. *Journal of Analytical Psychology, 37,* 255–274.

Fenichel, O. (1945). *The Psychoanalytic Theory of Neurosis.* New York: Norton.

Ferenczi, S. (1916). *Contributions to Psychoanalysis.* Boston: Badger.

Ferguson, E. D. (1989). Adler's motivational theory: An historical perspective on belonging and the fundamental human striving. *Individual Psychology, 45,* 354–362.

Festinger, L. (1954). A theory of social comparison processes. *Human Relations, 2,* 117–140.

Finchilescu, G. (1988). Interracial contact in South Africa within the nursing context. *Journal of Applied Social Psychology, 18,* 1207–1221.

Findley, M., & Cooper, H. (1983). Locus of control and academic achievement: A literature review. *Journal of Personality and Social Psychology, 44,* 419–427.

Fischer, W. F. (1970). *Theories of Anxiety.* New York: Harper & Row.

Fischl, D., & Hoz, R. (1993). Stability and change of conceptions about teacher education held by teacher educators. [Special issue: International conference on teacher thinking: II.] *Journal of Structural Learning, 12,* 53–69.

Fleeson, W., Malanos, A. B., & Achille, N. M. (2002). An intraindividual process approach to the relationship between extraversion and positive affect: Is acting extraverted as "good" as being being extraverted? *Journal of Personality and Social Psychology, 83,* 1409–1422.

Fletcher, J. (1966). *Situation Ethics, The New Morality.* Philadelphia: Westminster Press.

Fliegel, Z. (1982). Half a century later: Current status of Freud's controversial view on women. *Psychoanalytic Review, 69,* 7–28.

Flynn, J. R. (1999). Searching for justice: The discovery of IQ gains over time. *American Psychologist, 54,* 5–20.

Flynn, J. R. (2000). IQ gains, WISC subtests and fluid g: g theory and the relevance of Spearman's hypotheses to race. In G. R. Bock & J. A. Goode (Eds.), *The Nature of Intelligence.* New York: Wiley, pp. 202–227.

Flynn, J. R. (2003). Movies about intelligence: The limitations of g. *Current Directions in Psychological Science, 12,* 95–99.

Forrester, J., & Cameron, L. (1999). 'A cure with a defect': a previously unpublished letter by Freud concerning 'Anna O.' *International Journal of Psychoanalysis, 80,* 929–942.

Frank, L. K. (1939). Projective methods for the study of personality. *Journal of Psychology, 8,* 389–413.

Frankl, V. E. (1960). *The Doctor and The Soul: An Introduction To Logotherapy.* New York: Knopf.

Frankl, V. E. (1961). Dynamics, existence and values. *Journal of Existential Psychiatry, 2,* 5–16.

Frankl, V. E. (1963). *Man's Search For Meaning: An Introduction To Logotherapy.* New York: Washington Square Press.

Frankl, V. E. (1968). *Psychotherapy and Existentialism: Selected Papers On Logotherapy.* New York: Simon & Schuster.

Fransella, F. (Ed.). (2003). *International Handbook of Personal Construct Psychology.* West Sussex, England: Wiley.

Franz, C. E., McClelland, D. C., & Weinberger, J. (1991).Childhood antecedents of conventional social accomplishment in midlife adults: A 36-year prospective study. *Journal of Personality and Social Psychology, 60,* 586–595.

Fredericksen, N. (1972). Toward a taxonomy of situations. *American Psychologist, 27,* 114–123.

Freeman, A. (1999). Will increasing our social interest bring about a loss of our innocence? *Journal of Individual Psychology, 55,* 130–145.

Freese, J., Powell, B., & Steelman, L. C. (1999). Rebel without a cause or effect: Birth order and social attitudes. *American Sociological Review, 64,* 207–231.

Fremont, T., Means, G. H., & Means, R. S. (1970). Anxiety as a function of task performance feedback and extraversion-introversion. *Psychological Reports, 27,* 455–458.

Freud, A. (1936/1967). *The Ego and The Mechanisms of Defense* (Rev. Ed.). New York: International University Press.

Freud, A. (1976). Changes in psychoanalytic practice and experience. *International Journal of Psychoanalysis, 57,* 257–260.

Freud, S. (1923). *The Ego and The Id.* London: Hogarth.

Freud, S. (1923/1936). *The Problem of Anxiety.* New York: Norton.

Freud, S. (1939a). *Moses and Monotheism.* (K. Jones, Trans.). New York: Knopf.

Freud, S. (1939b). *Civilization and Its Discontents.* London: Hogarth.

Freud, S. (1940/1949). *An Outline of Psychoanalysis.* New York: Norton.

Freud, S. (1920/1955). The psychogenesis of a case of homosexuality in a woman. *International Journal of Psycho-Analysis, 1,* 125–149.

Freud, S. (1910/1957). Leonardo da Vinci and a memory of his childhood. In J. Strachey (Ed.), *The Standard Edition of The Complete Psychological Works of Sigmund Freud* (Vol. 11). London: Hogarth Press.

Freud, S. (1900/1958). *The Interpretation of Dreams.* New York: Basic Books.

Freud, S. (1925/1959). Some psychological consequences of the anatomical distinction between the sexes. In J. Strachey (Ed.), *The Collected Papers of Sigmund Freud* (Vol. 5). New York: Basic Books, pp. 186–197.

Freud, S. (Ed.). (1961). *Letters of Sigmund Freud.* New York: Basic Books.

Freud, S. (1909/1963). Analysis of a phobia in a five-year-old boy. In S. Freud, *The Sexual Enlightenment of Children.* New York: Collier, pp. 47–138.

Freud, S. (1963). *Three Case Histories.* New York: Collier.

Freud, S. (1901/1965). *Psychopathology of Everyday Life.* New York: Mentor.

Freud, S. (1933/1965). *New Introductory Lectures On Psychoanalysis.* New York: Norton.

Freud, S. (1910/1977). *Five Lectures On Psychoanalysis.* New York: Norton.

Freud, S. (1920/1977). *Introductory Lectures On Psychoanalysis.* New York: Norton.

Freud, S. (1977). *Inhibition, Symptoms and Anxiety* (Alix Strachey, Trans., James Strachey, Ed.). New York: Norton.

Freud, S., & Bullit, W. C. (1966). *Thomas Woodrow Wilson: A Psychological Study.* New York: Avon.

Frey, D. L., & Gaertner, S. L. (1986). Helping and the avoidance of inappropriate interracial behavior: A strategy that perpetuates a nonprejudiced self-image. *Journal of Personality and Social Psychology, 50,* 1083–1090.

Friedman, R. C., & Downey, J. I. (1994, October 6). Homosexuality. *New England Journal of Medicine, 331,* 923–930.

Fromm, E. (1941). *Escape From Freedom.* New York: Holt, Rinehart and Winston.

Fromm, E. (1947). *Man For Himself: An Inquiry Into The Psychology of Ethics.* New York: Holt, Rinehart and Winston.

Fromm, E. (1955). *The Sane Society.* New York: Rinehart.

Fromm, E. (1956). *The Art of Loving.* New York: Harper & Brothers.

Fromm, E. (1959). Values, psychology and human existence. In A. H. Maslow (Ed.), *New Knowledge in Human Values.* New York: Harper & Brothers, pp. 151–164.

Fromm, E. (1961). *May Man Prevail?* Garden City: Doubleday.

Fromm, E. (1962). *Beyond The Chains of Illusion: My Encounter With Marx and Freud.* New York: Pocket Books.

Fromm, E. (1964). *The Heart of Man: Its Genius For Good and Evil.* New York: Harper & Row.

Fromm, E. (1968). On the sources of human destructiveness. In L. Ng (Ed.), *Alternatives To Violence.* New York: Time-Life Books, pp. 11–17.

Fromm, E. (1973). *The Anatomy of Human Destructiveness.* New York: Holt, Rinehart and Winston.

Fromm, E. (1976). *To Have Or To Be?* New York: Harper & Row.

Fromm, E. (1980). *The Greatness and Limitations of Freud's Thought.* New York: Harper and Row.

Fromm, E., & Maccoby, M. (1970). *Social Character in a Mexican Village: A Sociopsychoanalytic Study.* Englewood Cliffs, Prentice-Hall.

Frosch, J. (1991). The New York psychoanalytic civil war. *Journal of the American Psychoanalytic Association, 39,* 1037–1064.

Funk, R. (1982). *Erich Fromm: The Courage to Be Human.* New York: Continuum.

Gaertner, S. (1973). Helping behavior and racial discrimination among racial liberals and conservatives. *Journal of Personality and Social Psychology, 25,* 335–341.

Gaines, S. O., & Reed, E. S. (1994). Two social psychologies of prejudice: Gordon W. Allport,

W. E. B. DuBois and the legacy of Booker T. Washington. *Journal of Black Psychology, 20,* 8–29.

Gaines, S. O., & Reed, E. S. (1995). Prejudice: From Allport to DuBois. *American Psychologist, 50,* 96–103.

Garcia, J. (1993). Misrepresentations of my criticisms of Skinner. *American Psychologist, 48,* 1158.

Gardner, H. (1988). *Frames of mind: The theory of multiple intelligences.* New York: Basic Books.

Garfield, E. (1978). The hundred most cited authors. *Current Contents, 45,* 5–15.

Garrison, M. (1978). A new look at Little Hans. *Psychoanalytic Review, 65,* 523–532.

Gelman, D., & Hager, M. (1981, November 30). Finding the hidden Freud. *Newsweek,* 64–70.

Gendlin, E. T. (1961). Experiencing: A variable in the process of therapeutic change. *American Journal of Psychotherapy, 15,* 2.

Gendlin, E. T. (1962). *Experiencing and The Creation of Meaning.* New York: Free Press.

Gendlin, E. T. (1988). Carl Rogers (1902–1987). *American Psychologist, 43,* 127–128.

Gendlin, E. T., & Rychlak, J. F. (1970). Psychotherapeutic processes. In P. H. Mussen & M. R. Rosenzweig (Eds.), *Annual Review of Psychology, 21,* 155–190.

Gendlin, E. T., & Tomlinson, T. M. (1967). The process of conception and its measurement. In C. R. Rogers (Ed.), *The Therapeutic Relationship and Its Impact: A Study of Psychotherapy With Schizophrenics.* Madison: University of Wisconsin Press.

Genia, V. (1993). A psychometric evaluation of the Allport-Ross I/E scales in a religiously heterogeneous sample. *Journal for the Scientific Study of Religion, 32,* 284–290.

George, B. L., & Waehler, C. A. (1994). The ups and downs of TAT card 17BM. *Journal of Personality Assessment, 63,* 167–172.

Gerard, L. (1962). *Sigmund Freud: The Man and His Theories.* New York: Fawcett.

Gershoff, E. T. (2002). Parental corporal punishment and associated child behaviors and experiences: A meta-analysis and theoretical review. *Psychological Bulletin, 128,* 539–579.

Gibson, H. B. (1981). *Hans Eysenck: The Man and His Work.* London: Peter Owen.

Gieser, L., & Morgan, W. G. (1999). Look Homeward, Harry: Literary influence on the development of the Thematic Apperception Test. In L. Gieser & M. I. Stein (Eds.), *Evocative Images: The Thematic Apperception Test and The Art of Projection.* Washington, D.C.: American Psychological Association.

Gilberstadt, H., & Duker, J. (1965). *A Handbook For Clinical and Actuarial MMPI Interpretation.* Philadelphia: W. B. Saunders.

Gill, M. (1981). Special book review: A new perspective on Freud and psychoanalysis. *Psychoanalytic Review, 68,* 343–347.

Goble, F. G. (1970). *The Third Force: The Psychology of Abraham Maslow.* New York: Brossman.

Goetinck, S. (1999, October 31). Modern scientists still analyzing Freud's dream theory. *Peoria Journal Star,* p. A10.

Goldberg, L. R. (1993). Author's reactions to the six comments. *American Psychologist, 48,* 1303–1304.

Goldstein, K. (1939). *The Organism.* New York: American Book.

Goleman, D. (1995). *Emotional Intelligence: Why It May Matter More Than I.Q.* New York: Bantam.

Golub, S. (1981). Coping with cancer: Freud's experiences. *Psychoanalytic Review, 68,* 191–200.

Gordon, J. E. (1957). Interpersonal prediction of repressors and sensitizers. *Journal of Personality, 25,* 686–698.

Gorlow, L., Simonson, N. R., & Krauss, H. (1966). An empirical investigation of the Jungian typology. *British Journal of Social and Clinical Psychology, 5,* 108–117.

Gorman, C. (1991, September 9). Are gay men born that way? *Time,* pp, 60–61.

Gould, P., & White, R. (1974). *Mental Maps.* Baltimore, MD: Penguin,

Graf, C. (1994). On genuineness and the person-centered approach: A reply to Quinn. *Journal of Humanistic Psychology, 34,* 90–96.

Graham, W. K., & Balloun, J. (1973). An empirical test of Maslow's need hierarchy theory. *Journal of Humanistic Psychology, 13,* 97–108.

Gray, F. S. (1999). A model version of Freud's primal religious society in our own times: The psychological anthropology of Meyer Fortes among the Tallensi of West Africa. *Dissertation Abstracts International, 59*(8-A), *(Feb.),* 3056.

Greene, J. N., Plank, R. E., & Fowler, D. G. (1989). Compu-grid: A program for computing, sorting, categorizing, and graphing multiple Bieri grid measurements of cognitive complexity. *Educational and Psychological Measurement, 49,* 623–626.

Greenough, W. T., Black, J. E., & Wallace, C. S. (1987). Experience and brain development. *Child Development, 58,* 539–559.

Greenwald, A. G. (1992). New look 3: Unconscious cognition reclaimed. *American Psychologist, 47,* 766–779.

Greenwald, A. G., Drain, S. C., & Abrams, R. L. (1996). Three cognitive markers of unconscious semantic activation. *Science, 273,* 1699–1702.

Greenwald, A. G., Oakes, M. A., & Hoffman, H. G. (2003). Targets of discrimination: Effects of race on responses to weapons holders. *Journal of Experimental Social Psychology, 39,* 399–405.

Greenwood, C. R., Carta, J. J., Hart, B., Kamps, D., Terry, B., Arreaga-Mayer, C., Atwater, J., Walker, D., Risley, T., & Delquadri, J. C. (1992). Out of the laboratory and into the community: 26 years of applied behavior analysis at the Juniper Gardens Children's Project. *American Psychologist, 47,* 1464–1474.

Grey, A. L. (1993). The dialectics of psychoanalysis: A new synthesis of Fromm's theory and practice. *Contemporary Psychoanalysis, 29,* 645–672.

Griffin, D., & Bartholomew, K. (1994). Models of self and other: Fundamental dimensions underlying measures of adult attachment. *Journal of Personality and Social Psychology, 67,* 430–445.

Grivet-Shillito, M.-L. (1999). Carl Gustav before he became Jung. *Journal of Analytical Psychology, 44,* 87–100.

Gromly, J. (1982). Behaviorism and the biological viewpoint of personality. *Bulletin of The Psychonomic Society, 20,* 255–256.

Gross, O. (1981). Die zerebrale Sekundarfunktion. Leipzig, Germany: 1902. Referenced in H. J. Eysenck (Ed.), *A Model For Personality.* New York: Springer-Verlag.

Gruenfeld, D. H., & Preston, J. (2000). Upending the status quo: Cognitive complexity in U.S. Supreme Court Justices who overturn legal precedent. *Personality and Social Psychology Bulletin, 26,* 1013–1022.

Guastello, S. J. (1993). A two-(and-a-half)-tiered trait taxonomy. *American Psychologist, 48,* 1298–1299.

Guilford, J. P., & Zimmerman, W. S. (1956). Fourteen dimensions of temperament. *Psychological Monographs, 70,* Whole No. 417.

Guimond, S., Dambrun, M., Michinov, N., & Duarte, S. (2003). Does social dominance generate prejudice? Integrating individual and contextual determinants of intergroup cognitions. *Journal of Personality and Social Psychology, 84,* 697–721.

Guo, G., & VanWey, L. K. (1999a). Sibship size and intellectual development: Is the relationship causal? *American Sociological Review, 64,* 167–187.

Guo, G., & VanWey, L. K. (1999b). The effects of closely spaced and widely spaced sibship size on intellectual development: Reply to Phillips and to Downey et al. *American Sociological Review, 64,* 199–207.

Gupta, B. S., & Kaur, S. (1978). The effects of dextroamphetamine on kinesthetic figural after effects. *Psychopharmacology, 56,* 199–204.

Haan, N. (1978). Two moralities in action contexts. *Journal of Personality and Social Psychology, 36,* 286–305.

Hafner, J. L., Fakouri, M. E., & Labrentz, H. L. (1982). First memories of "normal" and alcoholic individuals. *Individual Psychology, 38,* 238–244.

Haggbloom, S. J., Warnick, R., Warnick, J. E., Jones, V. K., Yarbrough, B. L., Russell, T. M., Borecky, C. M., McGahhey, R., Powell III, J. L., Beavers, J., & Monte, E. (2002). The 100 most eminent psychologists of the 20th century. *Review of General Psychology, 6,* 139–152.

Hakmiller, K. L. (1966). Threat as a determinant of downward comparison. *Journal of Experimental Social Psychology, Supplement No. 1,* 32–39.

Hall, C., & Nordby, V. J. (1973). *A Primer of Jungian Psychology.* New York: Mentor.

Hall, C., & Van de Castle, R. (1965). An empirical investigation of the castration complex in dreams. *Journal of Personality, 33,* 20–29.

Hall, C. S., & Lindzey, G. (1978). *Theories of Personality.* (3rd ed.). New York: Wiley.

Hall, E. (1983). A conversation with Erik Erikson. *Psychology Today* (June), 35–42.

Hall, M. H. (1968). The psychology of universality. *Psychology Today, 2,* 34–37, 54–57.

Haney, D. O. (1990, August 20). Psychologist B. F. Skinner dies at 86. *Peoria Journal Star (Associated Press)*, p. B1.

Hanly, C. (1987). Review of *The Assault On Truth: Freud's Suppression of The Seduction Theory* by J. Masson. *International Journal of Psychoanalysis, 67,* 517–519.

Harber, K. D. (1998). Feedback to minorities: Evidence of positive bias. *Journal of Personality and Social Psychology, 74,* 622–628.

Harlow, H. F. (1958). The nature of love. *American Psychologist, 13,* 673–685.

Harlow, H. F. (1959). Love in monkeys. *Scientific American, 200,* 68–74.

Harper, F. K., Harper, J. A., & Stills, A. B. (2003). Counseling children in crisis based on Maslow's hierarchy of basic needs. *International Journal for the Advancement of Counseling, 25,* 10–25.

Harper, H., Oei, T. P. S., Mendalgio, S., & Evans, L. (1990). Dimensionality, validity, and utility of the I-E scale with anxiety disorders. *Journal of Anxiety Disorders, 4,* 89–98.

Harrington, D. M., Block, J. H., & Block, J. (1987). Testing aspects of Carl Rogers' theory of creative environments: Child-rearing antecedents of creative potential young adolescents. *Journal of Personality and Social Psychology, 52,* 851–856.

Harris, C. R. (2000). Psychophysiological responses to imagined infidelity: The specific innate modular view of jealousy reconsidered. *Journal of Personality and Social Psychology, 78,* 1082–1091.

Harris, C. R. (2003). A review of sex differences in sexual jealousy, including self-report data, psychophysiological responses, interpersonal violence, and morbid jealousy. *Personality and Social Psychology Review, 7,* 102–128.

Harris, C. R. (2004). The evolution of jealousy. *American Scientist, 92,* 62–71

Harris, C. R. & Christenfeld, N. (1996). Gender, jealousy, and reason. *Psychological Science, 7,* 364–366.

Harris, J. R. (2000). Context-specific learning, personality, and birth order. *Current Directions In Psychological Science, 9,* 174–177.

Hart, J. T., & Tomlinson, T. M. (1970). *New Directions In Client-Centered Therapy.* Boston: Houghton Mifflin.

Hartmann, H. (1958). *Ego Psychology and The Problem of Adaptation.* New York: International Universities Press.

Harvey, R. J., & Murry, W. D. (1994). Scoring the Myers-Briggs Type Indicator: Empirical comparison of preference score versus latent-trait methods. *Journal of Personality Assessment, 62,* 116–129.

Haslam, D. R. (1967). Individual differences in pain threshold and level of arousal. *British Journal of Psychology, 58,* 139–142.

Haslam, D. R., & Thomas, E. A. C. (1967). An optimum interval in the assessment of pain threshold. *Quarterly Journal of Experimental Psychology, 19,* 54–58.

Hastorf, A. H., Schneider, D. J., & Polefka, J. (1970). *Person Perception.* Menlo Park, CA: Addison-Wesley.

Hausdorff, D. (1972). *Eric Fromm.* New York: Twayne.

Havassy-De Avila, B. (1971). A critical review of the approach to birth order research. *Canadian Psychologist, 12,* 282–305.

Hayes, G. E. (1994). Empathy: A conceptual and clinical deconstruction. *Psychoanalytic Dialogues, 4,* 409–424.

Hayes, J. (1978). *Cognitive Psychology, Thinking and Creating.* Homewood, IL: Dorsey Press.

Hayes, S. C., & Hayes, L. J. (1992). Verbal relations and the evolution of behavior analysis. *American Psychologist, 47,* 1383–1395.

Hebb, D. O. (1949). *The Organization of Behavior.* New York: John Wiley.

Heckhausen, H., & Krug, S. (1982). Motive modification. In A. J. Stewart, (Ed.), *Motivation and Society.* San Francisco: Jossey-Bass, pp. 274–318.

Heidegger, M. (1949). *Existence and Being.* Chicago: Henry Regnery.

Heidegger, M. (1959). *An Introduction To Metaphysics* (R. Manheim, Trans.). New Haven: Yale University Press.

Heider, F. (1958). *The Psychology of Interpersonal Relations.* New York: Wiley.

Heitzmann, A. L. (2003). The plateau experience in context: An intensive in-depth psychobiographical case study of Abraham Maslow's "postmortem life." *Section B: The Sciences &*

Engineering, Vol. 64(1-B), 2003, 453, US: Univ Microfilms International.

Hempel, C., & Oppenheim, P. (1960). Problems of the concept of general law. In A. Danto & S. Morgenbesser (Eds.), *Philosophy of Science.* New York: World.

Henry, W. E. (1974). *The Analysis of Fantasy.* New York: Wiley.

Hermann, B. P., Whitman, S. W., Wyler, A. R., Anton, M. T., & Vanderzwagg, R. (1990). Psychosocial predictors of psychopathology in epilepsy. *British Journal of Psychiatry, 156,* 98–105.

Hermans, H. J. M., Kempen, H. J. G., & van Loon, R. J. P. (1992). The dialogical self: Beyond individualism and rationalism. *American Psychologist, 47,* 23–33.

Heron, W. (1957). The pathology of boredom. In S. Coopersmith (Ed.), *Frontiers of Psychological Research.* San Francisco: W. H. Freeman, 1966 (originally appeared in *Scientific American,* January).

Herrera, N. C., Zajonc, R. B., Wieczokowska, G., & Bogdan, C. (2003). Beliefs about birth order and their reflection in reality. *Journal of Personality and Social Psychology, 85,* 142–150.

Herrnstein, R. J., & Murray, C. (1994). *The Bell Curve: Intelligence and Class Structure in American Life.* New York: Free Press.

Heuer, G. (2001). Jung's twin brother. Otto Gross and Carl Gustav Jung. *Journal of Analytical Psychology, 46,* 655–688.

Hexel, M. (2003). Alexithymia and attachment style in relation to locus of control. *Personality and Individual Differences, 35,* 1261–1270.

Heylighen, F. (1992). A cognitive-systemic reconstruction of Maslow's theory of self-actualization. *Behavioral Science, 37,* 39–58.

Heymans, G. (1981). Uber einige psychische Korrelationen. *Z Angew Psychologie, 1908, 1,* 313–381. Referenced in H. J. Eysenck (Ed.), *A Model For Personality.* New York: Springer-Verlag.

Hibbard, S. (2003). A critique of Lilienfeld et al.'s (2000) "The scientific status of projective techniques." *Journal of Personality Assessment, 80,* 260–272.

Hibbard, S., Tang, P. C. Y., Latko, R., Park, J. H., Munn, S., Bolz, S., & Sommerville, S. (2000). Differential validity of the Defense Mechanism Manual for the TAT between Asian Americans

and whites. *Journal of Personality Assessment, 75,* 351–372.

Hill-Hain, A., & Rogers, C. R. (1988). A dialogue with Carl Rogers: Cross-cultural challenges of facilitating person-centered groups in South Africa. *Journal of Specialists in Group Work, 13,* 62–69.

Hilts, P. J. (1997, August 15). Group delays achievement award to psychologist accused of fascist and racist views. *The New York Times,* p. A10y.

Hineline, P. N. (1992). A self-interpretive behavior analysis. *American Psychologist, 47,* 1274–1286.

Hirsch, J. (1964). Genes and behavior: A reply. *Science, 144,* 891.

Hirsch, J. (1975). Jensenism: The bankruptcy of "science" without scholarship. *Educational Theory, 25 (1),* 1–27.

Hirsch, J. (1981). To "unfrock the charlatans." *Sage Race Relations Abstracts, 6,* (May), 1–67.

Hirsch, J. (1997). Some history of heredity-vs-environment, genetic inferiority at Harvard (?), and *The* (incredible) *Bell Curve. Genetica, 99,* 207–224.

Hobbis, I. C. A., Turpin G., & Read, N. W. (2003). Abnormal illness behaviour and locus of control in patients with functional bowel disorders. *British Journal of Health Psychology, 8,* 393–408.

Hoffman, E. (1988). *The Right To Be Human.* Los Angeles: Jeremy P. Tarcher.

Hoffman, L. E. (1993). Erikson on Hitler: The origins of "Hitler's imagery and German youth." *Psychohistory Review, 22,* 69–86.

Hogan, R. (1973). Moral conduct and moral character. *Psychological Bulletin, 79,* 217–232.

Hogan, R. (1983). A socioanalytic theory of personality. In M. Page & R. Dienstbier (Eds.), *Nebraska Symposium On Motivation, 1982: Personality—Current Theory and Research.* Lincoln: University of Nebraska Press.

Holden, C. (1998, September). A marker for female homosexuality? *Science, 279,* 1639.

Holland, J., & Skinner, B. (1961). *The Analysis of Behavior.* New York: McGraw-Hill.

Holmstrom, R. W., Karp, S. A., & Silber, D. E. (1991). The apperceptive personality test and Locus of Control. *Psychological Reports, 68,* 1071–1074.

Holtzman, W., Thorpe, J., Swartz, J., & Herron, E. (1961). *Inkblot Perception and Personality:*

Holtzman Inkblot Technique. Austin: University of Texas Press.

Hopkins, E. (1990, September 11). The impact of B. F. Skinner. *Peoria Journal Star,* p. A9.

Horn, J. (2001). Raymond Bernard Cattell (1905–1998). *American Psychologist, 56,* 71–72.

Horney, K. (1926). The flight from womanhood: The masculinity complex in women as viewed by men and by women. *International Journal of Psychoanalysis, 7,* 324–329.

Horney, K. (1937). *The Neurotic Personality of Our Time.* New York: Norton.

Horney, K. (1939). *New Ways in Psychoanalysis.* New York: Norton.

Horney, K. (1942). *Self Analysis.* New York: Norton.

Horney, K. (1945). *Our Inner Conflicts: A Constructive Theory of Neurosis.* New York: Norton.

Horney, K. (1946). *Are You Considering Psychoanalysis?* New York: Norton.

Horney, K. (1950). *Neurosis and Human Growth: The Struggle Toward Self-Realization.* New York: Norton.

Horney, K. (1967). *Feminine Psychology.* New York: Norton.

Horney, K. (1980). *The Adolescent Diaries of Karen Horney.* New York: Basic Books.

Horney, K. (2000). *The Unknown Karen Horney: Essays on Gender, Culture, and Psychoanalysis.* New Haven, CT: Yale University Press.

Houle, G. R. (1990). The diagnostic conference planning questionnaire for speech-language pathology. *Language, Speech, and Hearing Services in Schools, 21,* 118–119.

Huber, R. J., Widdifield, J. K., & Johnson, C. L. (1989). Frankenstein: An Adlerian odyssey. *Individual Psychology, 45,* 267–278.

Hunt, E. (1998). The Cattell affair: Do hard cases make poor lessons? *History and Philosophy of Psychology Bulletin, 10,* 26–29.

Hunt, J. Mc V. (1979). Psychological development: Early experience. In M. Rosenzweig & L. Porter (Eds.), *Annual Review, Vol. 30,* pp. 103–144.

Husserl, E. (1961). *Ideas* (Trans. W. R. Boyce Gibson). New York: Collier.

Hyer, L., Woods, M. G., & Boudewyns, P. A. (1989). Early recollections of Vietnam veterans with PTSD. *Individual Psychology, 45,* 300–312.

Iaccino, J. F. (1994). *Psychological Reflections On Cinematic Terror: Jungian Archetypes in Horror Films.* London: Praeger.

Iacoboni, M., Woods, R. P., Brass, M., Bekkering, H., Mazziotta, J. C., & Rizzolatti, G. (1999). Cortical mechanisms of human imitation. *Science, 286,* 2526–2528.

Impara, J. C., & Plake, B. S. (1998). *Thirteenth Mental Measurement Yearbook,* Lincoln, NE: Buros Institute of Mental Measurement.

Ionedes, N. S. (1989). Social interest psychiatry. *Individual Psychology, 45,* 416–422.

Ishiyama, F. I., Munson, P. A., & Chabassol, D. J. (1990). Birth order and fear of success among mid-adolescents. *Psychological Reports, 66,* 17–18.

Ittelson, W., & Kilpatrick, F. (1951). Experiments in perception. *Scientific American, 185,* 50–55.

Iversen, I.H, (1992). Skinner's early research: From reflexology to operant conditioning. *American Psychologist, 47,* 1318–1328.

Jackson, D., & Paunonen, S. V. (1980). Personality structure and assessment. In M. R. Rosenzweig & L. W. Porter (Eds.), *Annual Review of Psychology, 31,* 503–551.

Jackson, D. N. (1967). *Personality Research Form Manual.* Goshen, NY: Research Psychologists Press.

Jackson, D. N. (1984). *Personality Research Form Manual* (3rd ed.). Port Huron, MI: Sigma Assessment Systems.

Jackson, M., & Sechrest, L. (1962). Early recollections in four neurotic diagnostic categories. *Journal of Individual Psychology, 18,* 52–56.

Jacobi, J. (1962). *The Psychology of C. G. Jung.* (Rev. Ed.). New Haven: Yale University Press.

James, W. (1890/1950). *The Principles of Psychology* (Vol I). New York: Dover.

James, W. (1958). *The Varieties of Religious Experience.* New York: Mentor.

Jankowicz, A. D. (1987). Whatever became of George Kelly? Applications and implications. *American Psychologist, 42,* 481–487.

Jarman, T. L. (1961). *The Rise and Fall of Nazi Germany.* New York: Signet.

Jensen, A. R. (1969). How much can we boost IQ and scholastic achievement? *Harvard Educational Review, 39,* 1–123.

Jensen, A. R. (1978). Sir Cyril Burt in perspective. *American Psychologist, 33,* 499–503.

Johansson, B., Grant, J. D., Plomin, R., Pedersen, N. L., Ahern, F., Berg, S., & McClearn, G. E. (2001). Health locus of control in late life: A study of genetic and environmental influences in twins aged 80 years and older. *Health Psychology, 20,* 33–40.

Johnson, E. E., Nora, R. M., & Bustros, N. (1992). The Rotter I-E scale as a predictor of relapse in a population of compulsive gamblers. *Psychological Reports, 70,* 691–696.

Johnson, J. L. (1994). The Thematic Apperception Test and Alzheimer's Disease. *Journal of Personality Assessment, 62,* 314–319.

Johnson, K. R., & Layng, T. V. J. (1992). Breaking the structuralist barrier: Literacy and numeracy with fluency. *American Psychologist, 47,* 1475–1490.

Johnson, M. K., Hastroudi, S., & Lindsay, D. S. (1993). Source monitoring. *Psychological Bulletin, 114,* 3–29.

Jones, B. M. (1974). Cognition performance of introverts and extraverts following acute alcohol ingestion. *British Journal of Psychology, 65,* 35–42.

Jones, B. M., Hatcher, E., Jones, M. K., & Farris, J. J. (1978). The relationship of extraversion and neuroticism to the effects of alcohol on cognitive performance in male and female social drinkers. In F. A. Seixas (Ed.), *Currents in Alcoholism.* New York: Grune & Stratton.

Jones, E. (1953). *The Life and Work of Sigmund Freud.* (Vol. I). New York: Basic Books.

Jones, E. (1955). *The Life and Work of Sigmund Freud.* (Vol. II). New York: Basic Books.

Jones, E. (1957). *The Life and Work of Sigmund Freud.* (Vol. III.) New York: Basic Books.

Jones, R. A. (2000). On the empirical proof of archetypes: Commentary on Maloney. *Journal of Analytical Psychology, 45,* 599–605.

Jordan, E. W., Whiteside, M. M., & Manaster, G. J. (1982). A practical and effective research measure of birth order. *Individual Psychology, 38,* 253–260.

Joseph, E. (1980). Presidential address: Clinical issues in psychoanalysis. *International Journal of Psychoanalysis, 61,* 1–9.

Joseph, S. (2004). Client-centred (sic) therapy, post-traumatic stress disorder and post-traumatic growth: Theoretical perspectives and practical implications. *Psychology and Psychotherapy: Theory, Research and Practice, 77,* 101–119.

Jourden, F. J., Bandura, A., & Banfield, J. T. (1991). The impact of conceptions of ability on self-regulatory factors and motor skill acquisition. *Journal of Sport & Exercise Psychology, 8,* 213–226.

Jung, C. G. (1910). The association method. *American Journal of Psychology, 21,* 219–269.

Jung, C. G. (1954). *The Development of Personality.* (Trans., R. F. C. Hull). New York: Pantheon.

Jung, C. G. (1959a). *The Archetypes and the Collective Unconscious* (Trans., R. F. C. Hull,) Collected Works, Vol. 9, Part I. Princeton, NJ: Princeton University Press.

Jung, C. G. (1959b). *The Archetypes and the Collective Unconscious* (Trans., R. F. C. Hull), Collected Works Vol. IX, Part 2. Princeton, NJ: Princeton University Press.

Jung, C. G. (1963). *Memories, Dreams, Reflections* (Ed., A. Jaffe). New York: Pantheon.

Jung, C. G. (1964). *Man and His Symbols.* New York: Dell.

Jung, C. G. (1921/1971). *Psychological Types* (Trans., R. F. C. Hull). Collected Works Vol. 6. Princeton, NJ: Princeton University Press.

Jung, C. G. (1978). *Flying Saucers: A Modern Myth of Things Seen in the Skies.* (Trans., R. F. C. Hull) Princeton, NJ: Princeton University Press.

Jung, J. (1978). *Understanding Human Motivation.* New York: MacMillan.

Jussim, L. (2002). Intellectual imperialism. *Dialogue, 17*(1), 18–20.

Kaiser, W. (1994). Adler and C. G. Jung: The history of their meetings. *Zeitschrift Fur Individual Psychologie, 19,* 3–19.

Kal, E. F. (1972). Survey of contemporary Adlerian clinical practice. *Individual Psychology, 28,* 261–266.

Kanfer, F. H., & Goldstein, A. P. (Eds.). (1980). *Helping People Change: A Textbook of Methods* (2nd ed.). New York: Pergamon Press.

Kasser, R., & Ryan, R. M. (1996). Further examining the American Dream: Differential correlates of intrinsic and extrinsic goals. *Personality and Social Psychology Bulletin, 22,* 280–287.

Katz, S. H. (1995). Is race a legitimate concept for science? *Unesco Race Statement.* Available from S. H. Katz, Anthropology, University of Pennsylvania.

Kazdin, A. E., & Benjet, C. (2003). Spanking children: Evidence and issues. *Current Directions in Psychological Science, 12,* 99–103.

Kearins, J. M. (1981). Visual spatial memory in Australian Aboriginal children of desert regions. *Cognitive Psychology, 13,* 434–460.

Kearins, J. M. (1986). Visual spatial memory in Aboriginal and white Australian children. *Australian Journal of Psychology, 38,* 203–214.

Kelleher, K. (1992). The afternoon of life. Jung's view of the tasks of the second half of life. *Perspectives in Psychiatric Care, 28,* 25–28.

Kelley, H. H. (1967). Attribution theory in social psychology. In D. Levine (Ed.), *Nebraska Symposium on Motivation* (Vol. 15). Lincoln: University of Nebraska Press.

Kelley, H. H. (1973). The process of causal attribution. *American Psychologist, 28,* 107–128.

Kelly, G. (1955). *The Psychology of Personal Constructs* (Vols. 1–2). New York: Norton.

Kelly, G. (1963). *A Theory of Personality: The Psychology of Personal Constructs.* New York: Norton.

Kelly, G. (1969). The autobiography of a theory. In B. Maher (Ed.), *Clinical Psychology and Personality: The Selected Papers of George Kelly.* New York: Wiley.

Kelly, G. (1980). A psychology of the optimal man. In A. W. Landfield & L. M. Leitner (Eds.), *Personal Construct Psychology: Psychotherapy and Personality.* New York: Wiley.

Kelly, G. A. (2003). A brief introduction to personal construct theory. In F. Fransella (Ed.), *International Handbook of Personal Construct Psychology.* West Sussex, England: Wiley, pp. 3–20.

Kelman, H. (1967). Introduction. In K. Horney, *Feminine Psychology.* New York: Norton.

Kendler, H. H. (1988). Behavioral determinism: A strategic assumption? *American Psychologist, 43,* 822–823.

Keniston, K. (1983). Remembering Erikson at Harvard. *Psychology Today,* (June) 29.

Kerlinger, F. N. (1973). *Foundations of Behavioral Research* (2nd ed.). New York: Holt, Rinehart and Winston.

Kern, C. W., & Watts, R. E. (1993). Adlerian counseling. [Special Issue: Counselor educators' theories of counseling.] *TCA Journal, 21,* 85–95.

Kerns, H. G., Cohen, J. D., MacDonald III, A. W., Cho, R. Y., Stenger, V. A., & Carter, C. S. (2004, February, 13). Anterior cingulate conflict monitoring and adjustments in control. *Science, 303,* 1023–1026.

Kerr, J. (1993). *A Most Dangerous Method.* New York: A. A. Knopf.

Kesting, K. (2003, December). Religion and spirituality in the treatment room. *Monitor on Psychology,* 40–42.

Kiel, J. M. (1999). Reshaping Maslow's hierarchy of needs to reflect today's educational and managerial philosophies. *Journal of Instructional Psychology, 26,* 167–168.

Kierkegaard, S. (1954). *Fear and Trembling, and Sickness Unto Death* (W. Lowrie, Trans.). Garden City, NY: Doubleday.

Kihlstrom, J. F. (1994). Commentary: Psychodynamics and social cognition—notes on the fusion of psychoanalysis and psychology. *Journal of Personality, 62,* 681–696.

Kihlstrom, J. F. (2003). On B. F. Skinner—Who, had his theory been true, wouldn't have been B. F. Skinner. *Journal of Consciousness Studies, 10,* 48–54.

Kim, C. J. (2002). A comparison of Alfred North Whitehead's and Carl Gustav Jung's idea of religion. *Journal of Dharma, 27,* 417–428.

Kimble, G. A. (1961). *Hilgard and Marguis' Conditioning and Learning.* New York: Appleton-Century-Crofts.

Kimble, G. A. (2000). Behaviorism and the unity of psychology. *Current Directions in Psychological Science, 9,* 208–212.

Kinkade, K. (1973). Commune: A Walden Two experiment. *Psychology Today, 6,* 35.

Kirschenbaum, H. (1979). *On Becoming Carl Rogers.* New York: Delacorte Press.

Kirschenbaum, H. (1991). Denigrating Carl Rogers: William Coulson's last crusade. *Journal of Counseling & Development, 69,* 411–413.

Kirschenbaum, H., & Henderson, V. L. (Eds.). (1989). *The Carl Rogers Readers.* Boston: Houghton Mifflin.

Kitayama, S., Duffy, S., Kawamura, T., & Larsen, J. T. (2003). Perceiving an object and its context in different cultures: A cultural look at new look. *Psychological Science, 14,* 201–206.

Klein, G. (1970). *Perceptions, Motives and Personality.* New York: Knopf.

Klein, M. (1932). *The Psychoanalysis of Children.* London: Hogarth.

Klein, M. (1961). *Narrative of A Child Analysis.* New York: Delta.

Kline, P. (1972). *Fact and Fantasy in Freudian Theory.* London: Methuen.

Klopfer, B., Meyer, M. M., & Brawer, F. B. (Eds.). (1970). *Developments in The Rorschach Technique* (Vol. 3). New York: Harcourt Brace Jovanovich.

Knapp, R. R. (1976). *Handbook For The Personal Orientation Inventory.* San Diego: EDITS.

Knight, J. L. (2003, August). Consequences of person-environment fit across contexts: We are where we live. *Observer* (American Psychological Society), *28,* 36.

Knight, K. H., Elfenbein, M. H., Capozzi, L., Eason, H. A., Barnardo, M. F., & Ferus, K. S. (2000). Relationship of connected and separate knowing to parental style and birth order. *Sex Roles, 43,* 229–240.

Kochanska, G. (2002). Mutually responsive orientation between mothers and their young children: A context for the early development of conscience. *Current Directions in Psychological Science, 11,* 191–195.

Koenig, R. (1997, May, 9). Watson urges "Put Hitler behind us." *Science, 276,* 892.

Koestler, A. (1972). *The Roots of Coincidence.* New York: Vintage.

Koffka, K. (1935). *Principles of Gestalt Psychology.* New York: Harcourt.

Kohlberg, L. (1981). *The Meaning and Measurement of Moral Development.* Worchester, MA: Clark University Press.

Kohler, W. (1947). *Gestalt Psychology: An Introduction to New Concepts in Psychology.* New York: Liveright.

Kohn, A. (1990, January). The birth-order myth. *Health,* pp. 34–35.

Kohut, H. (1971). *The Analysis of The Self.* New York: International Universities Press.

Korn, J. H., Davis, R., & Davis, S. F. (1991). Historians' and chairpersons' judgments of eminence among psychologists. *American Psychologist, 46,* 789–792.

Kowaz, A. M., & Marcia, J. E. (1991). Development of and validation of a measure of Eriksonian industry. *Journal of Personality and Social Psychology, 60,* 390–397.

Krane, R., & Wagner, A. (1975). Taste aversion learning with a delayed shock US: Implications for the "generality of the laws of learning." *Journal of Comparative and Physiological Psychology, 88,* 882–889.

Krauss, S. W. (2003). Romanian authoritarianism 10 years after communism. *Personality and Social Psychology Bulletin, 28,* 1255–1264.

Kretschmer, E. (1921/1925). *Physique and Character.* (Trans., W. J. H. Spratt). New York: Harcourt.

Krippner, S., Achterberg, J., Bugental, J. F. T., Banathy, B., Collen, A., Jaffe, D. T., Hales, S., Kremer, J., Stigliano, A., Giorgi, A., May, R., Michael, D. N., & Salner, M. (1988). Whatever happened to scholarly discourse? A reply to B. F. Skinner. *American Psychologist, 43,* 819.

Kroger, R. O., & Wood, L. A. (1993). Reification, "Faking," and the Big Five. *American Psychologist, 48,* 1297–1298.

Krueger, R. F., Caspi, A., Moffitt, T. E., White, J., & Stouthamer-Loeber, M. (1996). Delay of gratification, psychopathology, and personality: Is low self-control specific to externalizing problems? *Journal of Personality, 64,* 107–129.

Kuhn, T. S. (1962). *The Structure of Scientific Revolutions.* Chicago: University of Chicago Press.

Labouvie-Vief, G. (2003). Dynamic integration: Affect, cognition, and the self in adulthood. *Current Directions in Psychological Science, 12,* 201–206.

Lakin, M. (1996). Carl Rogers and the culture of psychotherapy. *The General Psychologist, 32,* 62–68.

Lambert, A. J., Burroughs, T., & Nguyen, T. (1999). Perceptions of risk and the buffering hypothesis: The role of just world beliefs and right-wing authoritarianism. *Personality and Social Psychology Bulletin, 25,* 643–656.

Lamiell, J. (1981). Toward an idiothetic psychology of personality. *American Psychologist, 36,* 276–289.

Langer, W. C. (1972). *The Mind of Adolph Hitler: The Secret Wartime Report.* New York: Signet.

Las Heres, A. (1992). Psychosociology of Jung's parapsychological ability. *Journal of The Society For Psychical Research, 58,* 189–193.

Latane, B., & Darley, J. (1970). *The Unresponsive Bystander: Why Doesn't He Help?* New York: Appleton-Century-Crofts.

Lattal, K. A. (1992). B. F. Skinner and Psychology: Introduction to the special issue. *American Psychologist, 47,* 1269–1272.

Laungani, P. (1997). Hans Eysenck (1916–1996). *International Psychologist, 37,* 145.

Lawrence, A. (1938). The voice of Sigmund Freud, an audiotape. *Psychoanalytic Review.*

Learner, B. (1996, Summer). Self-esteem and excellence: The choice and the paradox. *American Educator,* 9–13, 41–42.

Lebowitz, M. (1990). Religious immoralism. *Kenyon Review,* (Spring), 154–156.

Ledoux, J. (2002). *Synaptic self.* New York: Viking.

Lee, D. E., & Ehrlich, H. J. (1977). Sensory alienation and interpersonal constraints as correlates of cognitive structure. *Psychological Reports, 40,* 840–842.

Lee, D. E., Hallahan, M., & Herzog, T. (1996). Explaining real life events: How culture and domain shape attributions. *Personality and Social Psychology Bulletin, 22,* 734–741.

Lee, V. (1992). Transdermal interpretation of the subject matter of behavior analysis. *American Psychologist, 47,* 1337–1343.

Leeper, A. M., Carwile, S., & Huber, R. J. (2002). An Adlerian analysis of the Unabomber. *Journal of Individual Psychology, 58,* 169–176.

Leiby, R. (1997, September). The magical mystery cure. *Esquire,* 99–103.

Leman, K. (2002). *The New Birth Order.* Chicago: Covenant.

Lesser, R. M. (1992). Frommian therapeutic practice: "A few rich hours." *Contemporary Psychoanalysis, 28,* 483–494.

Leupold-Lowenthal, H. (1989). The emigration of Freud's family. *Partisan Review, 56* (Winter), 57–64.

LeVay, S. (1991, September). A difference in hypothalamic structure between heterosexual and homosexual men. *Science, 253,* 1034–1037.

Leventhal, H. (1970). Findings and theory in the study of fear communications. In L. Berkowitz (Ed.), *Advances in Experimental Social Psychology* (Vol. 5). New York: Academic Press, pp. 119–186.

Levine-Ginsparg, S. (2000). Legends of the fall: A movie analysis. *Psychoanalytic Psychology, 17,* (Spring), 400–404.

Levinson, D. (1978). *The Seasons of A Man's Life.* New York: Knopf.

Levy, K. N., Blatt, S. J., & Shaver, P. R. (1998). Attachment styles and parental representations. *Journal of Personality and Social Psychology, 74,* 407–419.

Lewin, K. (1936). *Principles of Topological Psychology.* New York: McGraw-Hill.

Liddell, H. S. (1964). The role of vigilance in the development of animal neurosis. In P. H. Hoch & J. Zubin (Eds.), *Anxiety.* New York: Hafner, pp. 183–196.

Lieberman, M. D., & Rosenthal, R. (2001). Why introverts can't always tell who likes them: Multitasking and nonverbal decoding. *Journal of Personality and Social Psychology, 80,* 294–310.

Lilienfeld, S. O., Wood, J. M., & Garb, H. N. (2000a). The scientific status of projective techniques. *Psychological Science in The Public Interest, 1,* 27–65.

Lilienfeld, S. O., Wood, J. M., & Garb, H. N. (2000b). What's wrong with this picture? *Scientific American,* (May), 81–87.

Lilly, J. C. (1973). *The Center of The Cyclone.* New York: Bantam.

Lilly, J. C. (1977). *The Deep Self.* New York: Warner.

Lim, V. D. G., Thompson, S. H., Teo, S. H., & Loo, G. L. (2003). Sex, financial hardship and locus of control: An empirical study of attitudes towards money among Singaporean Chinese. *Personality and Individual Differences, 34,* 411–429.

Linder, D., Cooper, J., & Jones, E. E. (1967). Decision freedom as a determinant of the role of incentive magnitude in attitude change. *Journal of Personality and Social Psychology, 6,* 245–254.

Lindsay, D. S. (1990). Misleading suggestions can impair eyewitnesses' ability to remember event details. *Journal of Experimental Psychology: Learning, Memory, and Cognition, 16,* 1077–1083.

Lindsay, D. S., Allen, B. P., Chen, J., & Dhal, L. C. (2004) Eyewitness suggestibility and source similarity: Intrusions of detail from one event into memory reports of another event. *Journal of Memory and Language, 50,* 96–111.

Linville, P. (1982). The complexity-extremity effect and age-based stereotyping. *Journal of Personality and Social Psychology, 42,* 293–311.

Lippa, R. A. (2003). Are 2D:4D finger-length ratios related to sexual orientation? Yes for men, no for women. *Journal of Personality and Social Psychology, 85,* 179–188.

Liptzin, B. (1994). B. F. Skinner: An example of adaptive aging. *Journal of Geriatric Psychiatry, 27,* 35–40.

Loehlin, J. C. (1984). R. B. Cattell and behavior genetics. *Multivariate Behavioral Research, 19,* 337–343.

Loehlin, J. C., Horn, J. M., & Willerman, L. (1990). Heredity, environment, and personality change: Evidence from the Texas adoption project. *Journal of Personality, 58,* 221–244.

Loftus, E. F. (1979). *Eyewitness Testimony.* Cambridge, MA: Harvard University Press.

Loftus, E. F. (1993). The reality of repressed memories. *American Psychologist, 48,* 518–537.

Lopez Ibor, J. J. (1980). Basic anxiety as the core of neuroses. In G. D. Burrows & B. Davies (Eds.), *Handbook of Studies on Anxiety.* New York: Elsevier/North-Holland Biomedical Press, pp. 17–20.

Lopez, S. J., & Snyder, C. R. (2003). *Positive Psychological Assessment: A Handbook of Models and Measures.* Washington, DC: American Psychological Association.

Lorenz, K. (1966). *On Aggression.* New York: Harcourt, Brace and World.

Lothane, Z. (1981). Special book review: A new perspective on Freud and psychoanalysis. *Psychoanalytic Review, 68,* 348–361.

Loutitt, C. M., & Browne, C. G. (1947). Psychometric instruments in psychological clinics. *Journal of Consulting Psychology, 11,* 49–54.

Lucus, R. E., Diener, E., Grob, A., Suh, E. M., & Shao, L. (2000). Cross-cultural evidence for the fundamental features of extraversion. *Journal of Personality and Social Psychology, 79,* 452–468.

Lucus, R. E., & Fujita, F. (2000). Factors influencing the relation between extraversion and pleasant affect. *Journal of Personality and Social Psychology, 79,* 1039–1056.

Lynch, M. D., Norem-Hebeisen, A. A., & Gergen, K. J. (1981). *Self-Concept: Advances in Theory and Research.* Cambridge, MA: Ballinger.

Lynn, R., & Eysenck, H. J. (1961). Tolerance for pain, extraversion and neuroticism. *Perceptual and Motor Skills, 12,* 161–162.

MacDonald, A. P., Jr. (1971). Birth order and personality. *Journal of Consulting and Clinical Psychology, 36,* 171–176.

Maddi, S. (1968). *Personality Theories: A Comparative Analysis.* Homewood IL: Dorsey Press.

Maddox, K. B., & Gray, S. A. (2002). Cognitive representations of Black Americans: Reexploring the role of skin tone. *Personality and Social Psychology Bulletin, 28,* 250–259.

Magnus, K., Diener, E., Fujita, F., & Pavot, W. (1993). Extraversion and neuroticism as predictors of objective life events: A longitudinal analysis. *Journal of Personality and Social Psychology, 65,* 1046–1053.

Mahlberg, A. (1997). The rise in IQ scores. *American Psychologist, 52,* 71.

Maier, N. R. F. (1949). *Frustration: The Study of Behavior Without A Goal.* New York: McGraw-Hill.

Maloney, A. (1999). Preference ratings of images representing archetypal themes: An empirical study of the concept of archetypes. *Journal of Analytical Psychology, 44,* 101–116.

Maloney, A. (2000). Response to "On the empirical proof of archetypes": Commentary on Maloney. *Journal of Analytical Psychology, 45,* 607–612.

Maltz, R. (2002). Genesis of a femme and her Desire: Finding Mommy and Daddy in butch/femme. *Journal of Lesbian Studies, 6*(2), 61–71.

Mamlin, N., Harris, K. R., & Case, L. P. (2001). A methodological analysis of research on locus of control and learning disabilities: Rethinking a common assumption. *Journal of Special Education, 34,* 214–225.

Manaster, G. J., & Perryman, T. B. (1979). Manaster-Perryman Manifest Content. In H. A. Olson, *Early recollections: Their use in diagnosis and psychotherapy.* Springfield, IL: Charles Thomas, pp. 347–353.

Mandler, G., & Sarason, S. B. (1952). A study of anxiety and learning. *Journal of Abnormal and Social Psychology, 47,* 166–173.

Mann, L. (1981). The baiting crowd in episodes of threatened suicide. *Journal of Personality and Social Psychology, 41,* 703–709.

Mansager, E., & Gold, L. (2000). Three life tasks or five? *Journal of Individual Psychology, 56,* 155–171.

Mansfield, E., & McAdams, D. P. (1996). Generativity and themes of agency and communion in adult autobiography. *Personality and Social Psychology Bulletin, 22,* 721–731.

Martens, R., & Landers, D. M. (1970). Motor performance under stress: A test of the inverted-U hypothesis. *Journal of Personality and Social Psychology, 16,* 29–37.

Martin, A. R. (1975). Karen Horney's theory in today's world. *American Journal of Psychoanalysis, 35,* 297–302.

Mashek, D. J., Aron, A., & Boncimino, M. (2003). Confusions of self with close others. *Personality and Social Psychology Bulletin, 29,* 382–392.

Masling, J. M. (1997). On the nature and utility of projective and objective tests. *Journal of Personality Assessment, 69,* 257–270.

Maslow, A. H. (1951). Resistance to acculturation. *Journal of Social Issues, 7,* 26–29.

Maslow, A. H. (1954). *Motivation and Personality.* New York: Harper and Row.

Maslow, A. H. (1959). Psychological data and value theory. In A. H. Maslow (Ed.), *New Knowledge in Human Values.* New York: Harper and Row, pp. 119–136.

Maslow, A. H. (1962). Lessons from the peak experiences. *Journal of Humanistic Psychology, 2,* 9–18.

Maslow, A. H. (1965). *Eupsychian Management.* Homewood IL: Dorsey Press.

Maslow, A. H. (1966). *The Psychology of Science: A Reconnaissance.* New York: Harper and Row.

Maslow, A. H. (1967). A theory of metamotivation: The biological rooting of the value-life. *Journal of Humanistic Psychology, 7,* 93–127.

Maslow, A. H. (1968a). *Toward A Psychology of Being.* Princeton, NJ: D. Van Nostrand.

Maslow, A. H. (1968b). Toward the study of violence. In L. Ng (Ed.), *Alternatives To Violence.* New York: Time-Life, pp. 34–37.

Maslow, A. H. (1969a). Toward a humanistic biology. *American Psychologist, 24,* 724–735.

Maslow, A. H. (1969b). Existential psychology—what's in it for us? In Rollo May (Ed.), *Existential Psychology.* New York: Random House,

Maslow, A. H. (1970). *Motivation and Personality* (2nd ed.). New York: Harper and Row.

Maslow, A. H. (1971). *The Farther Reaches of Human Nature.* New York: Viking Press,

Maslow, B. G. (Ed.). (1972). *Abraham H. Maslow: A Memorial Volume.* Monterey, CA: Brooks/Cole.

Mason, B. J. (1997). A developmental examination of sex differences in jealousy: Fear of being cuckolded or immaturity? Masters Thesis, Western Illinois University, June.

Massey, R. F. (1989). The philosophical compatability of Adler and Berne. *Individual Psychology, 45,* 323–334.

Masson, J. M. (1984). *The Assault on Truth.* Toronto: Colins.

Mathes, E. W. (1981). *From Survival to the Universe: Values and Psychological Well-Being.* Chicago: Nelson-Hall.

Mathes, E. W., Adams, H., & Davies, R. (1985). Jealousy: Loss of relationship rewards, loss of self-esteem, depression, anxiety and anger. *Journal of Personality and Social Psychology, 48,* 1552–1556.

Mathes, E. W., & Smith, S. (1999). Are sex differences in jealousy a function of fear of being cuckolded or sexual strategies? Paper presented at the Midwestern Psychological Association, Chicago, May.

Mathes, E. W., Zevon, M. A., Roter, P. M., & Joerger, S. M. (1982). Peak experience tendencies: Scale development and theory testing. *Journal of Humanistic Psychology, 22,* 92–108.

Matlin, M. W., & Foley, H. J. (1997). *Sensation and Perception.* Boston: Allyn & Bacon.

Matthews, G., Davies, D. R., & Lees, J. L. (1990). Arousal, extraversion, and individual differences in resource availability. *Journal of Personality and Social Psychology, 59,* 150–168.

Matthews, G., Jones, D. M., & Chamberlin, A. G. (1989). Interactive effects of extraversion and arousal on attentional task performance: Multiple resources or encoding processes? *Journal of Personality and Social Psychology, 56,* 629–639.

Maurer, A. (1964). Did Little Hans really want to marry his mother? *Journal of Health Professions, 4,* 139–148.

May, R. (1950). *The Meaning of Anxiety.* New York: Ronald Press.

May, R. (1958). Contributions of existential psychotherapy. In R. May, E. Angel, & H. F. Ellenberger (Eds.), *Existence: A New Dimension In Psychiatry and Psychology.* New York: Basic Books, pp. 37–91.

May, R. (1969a). The emergence of existential psychology. In Rollo May (Ed.), *Existential Psychology.* New York: Random House, pp. 1–48.

May, R. (1969b). Existential bases of psychotherapy. In Rollo May (Ed.), *Existential Psychology.* New York: Random House, pp. 72–83.

May, R. (1983). *The Discovery of Being.* New York: W. W. Norton.

May, R., Angel, E., & Ellenberger, H. F. (Eds.). (1958). *Existence: A New Dimension in Psychiatry and Psychology.* New York: Basic Books.

McAdams, D. P. (2000). Attachment, intimacy, and generativity. *Psychological Inquiry, 11,* 117–120.

McAdams, D. P., Diamond, A., de St. Aubin, E., & Mansfield, E. (1997). Stories of commitment:

The psychological construction of generative lives. *Journal of Personality and Social Psychology, 72,* 678–694.

McAdams, D. P., Reynolds, J., Lewis, M., Patten, A. H., & Bowman, P. J. (2001). When bad things turn good and good things turn bad: Sequences of redemption and contamination in life narrative and their relation to psychosocial adaptation in midlife adults and in students. *Personality and Social Psychology Bulletin, 27,* 474–475.

McAdams, D. P., Ruetzel, K., & Foley, J. M. (1986). Complexity and generativity at mid-life: Relations among social motives, ego development, and adults' plans for the future. *Journal of Personality and Social Psychology, 50,* 800–807.

McCelland, D. C. (1961). *The Achieving Society.* New York: Free Press.

McClatchey, L. (1994). An investigation into the uniqueness of educational psychologist competences. *Educational and Child Psychology, 11,* 63–74.

McCullough, M. E., Emmons, R. A., Kilpatrick, S. D., & Mooney, C. N. (2003). Narcissists as "victims": The role of narcissism in the perception of transgressions. *Personality and Social Psychology Bulletin, 29,* 885–893.

McCullough, M. L. (2001). Freud's seduction theory and its rehabilitation: A saga of one mistake after another. *Review of General Psychology, 5,* 3–22.

McFatter, R. M. (1994). Interactions in predicting mood from extraversion and neuroticism. *Journal of Personality and Social Psychology, 66,* 570–578.

McGraw-Hill Films. (1971). *Personality.* New York: CRM Educational Films Collection.

McGuire, T. R., & Hirsch, J. (1977). General intelligence (g) and heritability (H^2, h^2). In I. C. Uzgiris & F. Weizmann (Eds.), *The Structuring of Experience.* New York: Plenum, pp. 25–72.

McGuire, W. (Ed.). (1974). *The Freud/Jung Letters* (R. Manheim & R. F. C. Hull, Trans.) Princeton, NJ: Princeton University Press.

McGuire, W., & Hull, R. F. C. (Eds.). (1977). *C. G. Jung Speaking: Interviews and Encounters.* Princeton, NJ: Princeton University Press.

McIntosh, D. (1979). The empirical bearing of psychoanalytic theory. *International Journal of Psychoanalysis, 60,* 405–431.

McMillan, M. (1997). *Freud Evaluated.* London: MIT Press.

Mead, M. (1974). On Freud's view of female psychology. In J. Strouse (Ed.), *Women and Analysis: Dialogues on Psychoanalytic Views of Femininity.* New York: Grossman, pp. 95–106.

Mead, M. (1975). *Blackberry Winter: My Earlier Years.* New York: PocketBooks.

Mearns, J. (1991). Coping with a breakup: Negative mood regulation expectancies and depression following the end of a romantic relationship. *Journal of Personality and Social Psychology, 60,* 327–334.

Mehler, B. (1997). Beyondism: Raymond B. Cattell and the new eugenics. *Genetica, 99,* 153–163.

Meltzoff, J., & Kornreich, M. (1970). *Research in Psychotherapy.* New York: Atherton Press.

Menninger, K. (1963). *The Vital Balance: The Life Process in Mental Health and Illness.* New York: Viking.

Menninger, W. C. (1948). *Psychiatry in a Troubled World.* New York: Macmillan.

Menon, Y., Morris, M. W., Chiu, C., & Hong, Y. (1999). Culture and the construal of agency: Attribution to individual versus group dispositions. *Journal of Personality and Social Psychology, 76,* 701–717.

Merkin, D. (2003, July 13). The literary Freud. *The New York Times Magazine,* NYTimes.com.

Merleau-Ponty, M. (1963). *The Structure of Behavior* (A. L. Fisher, Trans.). Boston: Beacon Press.

Mickelson, K. D., Kessler, R. C., & Shaver, P. R. (1997). Adult attachment in a nationally representative sample. *Journal of Personality and Social Psychology, 73,* 1092–1106.

Mikulincer, M. (1998). Adult attachment style and individual differences in functional versus dysfunctional experiences of anger. *Journal of Personality and Social Psychology, 74,* 513–524.

Miletic, M. P. (2002). The introduction of a feminine psychology to psychoanalysis. *Contemporary Psychoanalysis, 38,* 287–299.

Miley, C. H. (1969). Birth order research 1963–1967: Bibliography and index. *Journal of Individual Psychology, 25,* 64–70.

Milgram, S. (1974). *Obedience to Authority.* New York: Harper & Row.

Miller, L. C., Putcha-Bhagavatula, A., & Pedersen, W. C. (2002). Men's and women's mating preferences:

Distinct evolutionary mechanisms? *Current Directions in Psychological Science, 11,* 88–93.

Miller, P. C., Lefcourt, H. M., Holmes, J. G., Ware, E. E., & Saleh, W. E. (1986). Marital locus of control and marital problem solving. *Journal of Personality and Social Psychology, 51,* 161–169.

Miller, S. M., Riessman, R., & Seagull, A. A. (1968). Poverty and self-indulgence: A critique of the non-deferred gratification pattern. In A. Ferman, J. L. Kornbluh, & A. Haver (Eds.), *Poverty In America.* Ann Arbor, MI: The University of Michigan Press.

Mischel, W. (1968). *Personality and Assessment.* New York: Wiley.

Mischel, W. (1973). Toward a cognitive social learning reconceptualization of personality. *Psychological Review, 80,* 252–283.

Mischel, W. (1977). On the future of personality measurement. *American Psychologist, 32,* 246–254.

Mischel, W. (1984). Convergences and challenges in the search for consistency. *American Psychologist, 39,* 351–364.

Mischel, W. (1999). Personality coherence and dispositions in a cognitive-affective personality system (CAPS) approach. In D. Cervone & Y. Shoda (Eds.), *The Coherence of Personality.* New York: Guilford Press.

Mischel, W., & Ebbesen, E. (1973). Selective attention to the self: Situational and dispositional determinants. *Journal of Personality and Social Psychology, 27,* 129–142.

Mischel, W., Ebbesen, E., & Zeiss, A. (1972). Cognitive and attentional mechanisms in delay of gratification. *Journal of Personality and Social Psychology, 21,* 204–218.

Mischel, W., & Peake, P. (1982a). Analysing the construction of consistency in personality. In M. Page & R. Dienstbier, (Eds.), *Nebraska Symposium on Motivation, 1982: Personality—Current Theory and Research.* Lincoln: University of Nebraska Press.

Mischel, W., & Peake, P. (1982b). Beyond déjà vu in the search for cross-situational consistency. *Psychological Review, 89,* 730–733.

Mischel, W., & Shoda, Y. (1994). Personality psychology has two goals: Must it be two fields? *Psychological Inquiry, 5,* 156–158.

Mischel, W., & Shoda, Y. (1995). A cognitive-affective system theory of personality: Reconceptualizing situations, dispositions, dynamics, and invariance in personality structure. *Psychological Review, 102,* 246–268.

Mischel, W., & Shoda, Y. (1998). Reconciling processing dynamics and personality dispositions. *Annual Review of Psychology,* Vol. 49.

Mischel, W., & Shoda, Y. (2000). A cognitive-affective system theory of personality: Reconceptualizing situations, dispositions, dynamics, and invariance in personality structure. In E. T. Higgins & A. W. Kruglanski, (Eds.), *Motivational Science.* Philadelphia: Psychology Press.

Mischel, W., Shoda, Y., & Mendoza-Denton, R. (2002). Situation-behavior profiles as a locus of consistency in personality. *Current Directions in Psychological Science, 11,* 50–54.

Mischel, W., Shoda, Y., & Rodriguez, M. L. (1989). Delay of gratification in children. *Science,* 933–938.

Mischel, W., Shoda, Y., & Wright, J. C. (1994). Intraindividual stability in the organization and patterning of behavior: Incorporating psychological situations into the ideographic analysis of personality. *Journal of Personality and Social Psychology, 67,* 674–687.

Mitchell, J. V. (1985). *Ninth Mental Measurement Yearbook.* Lincoln, NE: Buros Institute of Mental Measurement.

Mitchell, K. M., Bozarth, J. D., and Krauft, C. C. (1977). A reappraisal of the therapeutic effectiveness of accurate empathy, nonpossessive warmth and genuineness. In A. S. Gurman & A. M. Razin (Eds.), *Effective Psychotherapy: A Handbook of Research.* New York: Pergamon, pp. 482–499.

Mittelman, W. (1991). Maslow's study of self-actualization: A reinterpretation. *Journal of Humanistic Psychology, 31,* 114–135.

Molière, J. (1928). *Le Bourgeois Gentilhomme* (1670). In I. A. Gregory (Ed.), *Three Last Plays.* New York: G. P. Putnam.

Monitor on Psychology. (1992, August). Bandura's childhood shaped life interests, p. 13.

Montagu, A. (1997). *Man's most dangerous myth: The fallacy of race* (6th ed.). London: AltaMira Press.

Morgan, W. G. (1995). Origin and history of the Thematic Apperception Test images. *Journal of Personality Assessment, 65,* 237–254.

Morgan, W. G. (1999). The 1943 images: Their origins and history. In L. Gieser & M. I. Stein (Eds.). *Evocative Images: The Thematic Apperception Test and The Art of Projection.* Washington, DC: American Psychological Association.

Morgan, W. G. (2000). Origin and history of an early TAT card: Picture C. *Journal of Personality Assessment, 74,* 88–94.

Morgan, W. G. (2002). Origin and history of the earliest Thematic Apperception Test pictures. *Journal of Personality Assessment, 79,* 422–445.

Morgan, W. G. (2003). Origin and history of the "Series B" and "Series C" TAT pictures. *Journal of Personality Assessment, 81,* 133–148.

Morris, M., & Peng, K. (1994). Culture and cause: American and Chinese attributions for social and physical events. *Journal of Personality and Social Psychology, 67,* 949–971.

Morrow, L. (1984). "I spoke . . . as a brother." *Time, 123*(2), 26–33.

Mosak, H. H. (1969). Early recollections: Evaluation of some recent research. *Journal of Individual Psychology, 25,* 56–63.

Mosak, H. H., & Kopp, R. R. (1973). The early recollections of Adler, Freud, and Jung. *Journal of Individual Psychology, 24,* 157–166.

Moss, P. D., & McEvedy, C. P. (1966). An epidemic of overbreathing among schoolgirls. *British Medical Journal, 2,* 1295–1300.

Motley, M. T. (1985). Slips of the tongue. *Scientific American, 253,* (March), 116–127.

Motley, M. T. (1987). What I mean to say. *Psychology Today,* (February), 24–28.

Mowrer, O. H. (1947). On the dual nature of learning—a reinterpretation of "conditioning" and "problem solving." *Harvard Educational Review, 17,* 102–148.

Moxley, R. A. (1992). From mechanistic to functional behaviorism. *American Psychologist, 47,* 1300–1311.

Mullahy, P. (1948). *Oedipus: Myth and Complex.* New York: Grove Press.

Mullahy, P. (Ed.). (1952). *The Contributions of Harry Stack Sullivan.* New York: Science House.

Mullahy, P. (1970). *The Beginnings of Modern American Psychiatry: The Ideas of Harry Stack Sullivan.* Boston: Houghton Mifflin.

Muller, R. (1993). Karen Horney's "resigned person" heralds DSM-III-R's borderline personality disorder. *Comprehensive Psychiatry, 34,* 264–272.

Murphy, L. L., Close, J., & Impara, J. C. (1994). *Tests in Print IV* (Vol. 1.) Lincoln, NE: Buros Institute of Mental Measurement.

Murray, B. (2002, November). Why we don't pick good quarterbacks. *Monitor On Psychology,* 22–23.

Murray, H. A. (1943). *Thematic Apperception Test Manual.* Cambridge: Harvard University Press.

Murray, H. A. (1938/1962). *Explorations in Personality.* New York: Science Editions.

Murray, H. A. (1981a). Proposals for a theory of personality. In E. S. Shneidman (Ed.), *Endeavors in Psychology: Selections from the Personology of Henry A. Murray.* New York: Harper & Row, pp. 125–203.

Murray, H. A. (1981b). Jung: Beyond the hour's most exacting expectation. In E. S. Shneidman (Ed.), *Endeavors in Psychology: Selections from the Personology of Henry A. Murray.* New York: Harper & Row, pp. 79–81.

Murray, H. A. (1981c). A note on the possible clairvoyance of dreams. In E. S. Shneidman (Ed.), *Endeavors in Psychology: Selections from the Personology of Henry A. Murray.* New York: Harper & Row, pp. 563–566.

Murray, H. A. (1981d). A method for investigating fantasies: The Thematic Apperception Test (with Christiana D. Morgan). In E. S. Shneidman (Ed.), *Endeavors in Psychology: Selections from the Personology of Henry A. Murray.* New York: Harper & Row, pp. 390–408.

Murstein, B. I. (Ed.). (1965). *Handbook of Projective Techniques.* New York: Basic Books.

Murstein, B. I. (1972). Normative written TAT responses for a college sample. *Journal of Personality Assessment, 36,* 109–147.

Mussen, P., Conger, J. & Kagan J. (1979). *Child Development and Personality.* New York: Harper & Row.

Myers, I. B. (1962). *Myers-Briggs Type Indicator Manual.* Palo Alto, CA: Consulting Psychologists Press.

Nail, P. R., Harton, H. C., & Decker, B. P. (2003). Political orientation and modern versus aversive racism: Tests of Dovidio and Gaertner's integrated model. *Journal of Personality and Social Psychology, 84,* 754–770.

Nash, H. (1983). Thinking about thinking about the unthinkable. *Bulletin of the Atomic Scientists, 39*(October), 39–42.

Nathan, P. E., & Harris, S. L. (1975). *Psychopathology and society.* New York: McGraw-Hill.

National Psychologist. (1998). Scientists, colleagues defend Cattell. Jan./Feb., p. 9.

Neher, A. (1991). Maslow's theory of motivation. A critique. *Journal of Humanistic Psychology, 31,* 89–112.

Neisser, U., Boodoo, G., Bouchard, T. J., Boykin, A. W., Brody, N., Ceci, S. J., Halpern, D. F., Loehlin, J. C., Perloff, R., Sternberg, R. J., & Urbina, S. (1996). Intelligence: Knowns and unknowns. *American Psychologist, 51,* 77–101.

Nesselroade, J. R. (1984). Concepts of intraindividual variability and change: Impressions of Cattell's influence on lifespan developmental psychology. *Multivariate Behavioral Research, 19,* 269–286.

Neuman, M. (1991). Was Jung an anti-Semite? *Sihotdialogue Israel Journal of Psychotherapy, 5,* 201–208.

Newman, L. S., Higgins, E. T., & Vookles, J. (1992). Self-guide strength and emotional vulnerability: Birth order as a moderator of self affect relations. *Personality and Social Psychology Bulletin, 18,* 402–411.

Newsweek. (1970). Erik Erikson: The quest for identity, December 21, 84–89.

New York Times Service. (1995). Scholar denied access to Jung papers. *Chicago Tribune,* (June 4), Sec. 1, p. 6.

Nicholson, I. A. M. (1997). To "correlate psychology and social ethics": Gordon Allport and the first course in American personality psychology. *Journal of Personality, 65,* 733–741.

Nisbett, R. E. (2003). *The geography of thought: How Asians and Westerners think differently . . . and why.* New York: The Free Press.

Nisbett, R. N. (1980). The trait construct in lay and professional psychology. In L. Festinger (Ed.), *Retrospections on Social Psychology.* New York: Oxford University Press.

Noll, R. (1994). *The Jung Cult: Origins of a Charismatic Movement.* Princeton, NJ: Princeton University Press.

Norman, W. T. (1963). Toward an adequate taxonomy of personality attributes: Replicated factor structure in peer nomination personality ratings. *Journal of Abnormal and Social Psychology, 66,* 574–583.

Norton, H. W. (1972). Blood groups and personality traits. *American Journal of Human Genetics, 23,* 225–226.

Nosek, B. A. (2004, January 30). Moderators of the relationship between implicit and explicit attitudes. Paper presented at the meeting of the Society for Personality and Social Psychology, Austin, Texas.

Nunnally, J. C. (1955). An investigation of some propositions of self-conception: The case of Miss Sun. *Journal of Abnormal and Social Psychology, 50,* 87–92.

Ochse, R., & Plug C. (1986). Cross-cultural investigation of the validity of Erikson's theory of personality development. *Journal of Personality and Social Psychology, 50,* 1240–1252.

O'Connor, K. P., Gareau, D., & Blowers, G. H. (1993). Changes in construals of tic-producing situations following cognitive and behavioral therapy. *Perceptual and Motor Skills, 77,* 776–778.

Oliviero, P. (1993). Social communication of biological materials: Blood, semen, organs, and cadaver. *Cahiers Internationaux de Psychologie Sociale, June (# 18),* 21–51.

Olson, H. A. (Ed.). (1979). *Early Recollections: Their Use in Diagnosis and Psychotherapy.* Springfield, IL: Charles C. Thomas.

Orlov, A. B. (1992). Carl Rogers and contemporary humanism. *Journal of Russian and East European Psychology, 30* (#1, January/February), 36–41.

Ormel, J., & Schaufeli, W. B. (1991). Stability and change in psychological distress and their relationship with self-esteem and locus of control: A dynamic equilibrium model. *Journal of Personality and Social Psychology, 60,* 288–299.

Ornduff, S. R., Freedenfeld, R. N., Kelsey, R. M., & Critelli, J. W. (1994). Object relations of sexually abused female subjects: A TAT analysis. *Journal of Personality Assessment, 63,* 223–238.

Ozer, E. M., & Bandura, A. (1990). Mechanisms governing empowerment effects: A self-efficacy analysis. *Personality and Social Psychology, 58,* 472–486.

Paige, K. E. (1973). Women learn to sing the menstrual blues. *Psychology Today,* (September), 65–68.

Palmer, D. C., & Donahoe, J. W. (1992). Essentialism and selectionism in cognitive science and behavior analysis. *American Psychologist, 47,* 1344–1358.

Palmer, E. M., & Hollin, C. R. (2001). Sociomoral reasoning: perceptions of parenting and self-reported delinquency in adolescents. *Applied Cognitive Psychology, 15,* 85–100.

Parisi, T. (1987). Why Freud failed: Some implications for neurophysiology and sociobiology. *American Psychologist, 42,* 235–245.

Park, B., Ryan, C. S., & Judd, C. (1992). Role of meaningful subgroups in explaining differences in perceived variability for in-groups and out-groups. *Journal of Personality and Social Psychology, 63,* 553–567.

Parrish, T. S. (1990). Examining teachers' perceptions of children's support systems. *Journal of Psychology, 124,* 113–118.

Patterson, C. H. (1961). The self in recent Rogerian theory. *Journal of Individual Psychology, 17,* 5–11.

Paunonen, S. V., Jackson, D. N., & Keinonen, M. (1990). The structured nonverbal assessment of personality. *Journal of Personality, 58,* 481–502.

Pavlov, I. P. (1927). *Conditioned Reflexes.* London: Oxford.

Pavlov, I. P. (1957). *Experimental Psychology.* New York: Philosophical Library.

Payne, B. K. (2001). Prejudice and perception: The role of automatic and controlled processes in misperceiving a weapon. *Journal of Personality and Social Psychology, 81,* 181–192.

Payne, B. K., Lambert, A. J., & Jacoby, L. L. (2002). Best laid plans: Effects of goals on accessibility bias and cognitive control in race-based misperceptions of weapons. *Journal of Experimental Social Psychology, 38,* 384–396.

Pelham, B. W. (1993). The idiographic nature of human personality: Examples of the idiographic self-concept. *Journal of Personality and Social Psychology, 64,* 665–677.

Pendergrast, M. (1995). *Victims of Memory: Incest Accusations and Shattered Lives.* Hinesburg, VT: Upper Access.

Pennypacker, H. S. (1992). Is behavior analysis undergoing selection by consequences? *American Psychologist, 47,* 1491–1498.

Perls, F. S. (1969). *Gestalt Therapy Verbatim.* Lafayette, CA: Real People Press.

Peoria Journal Star. (1994). Psychoanalyst Erik Erikson dead at 91. (May 13), p. C8.

Peoria Journal Star. (1998). Alberta won't pay off those forced sterilized. (March 12), p. 2A.

Perry, H. S. (1982). *Psychiatrist of America: The Life of Harry Stack Sullivan.* Cambridge: Harvard University Press.

Perry, W., Sprock, J., Schaible, D., McDougall, A., Minassian, A., Jenkins, M., & Braff, D. (1995). Amphetamine on Rorschach measures in normal subjects. *Journal of Personality Assessment, 64,* 456–465.

Pervin, L. A. (1985). Personality: Current controversies, issues, and directions. In M. R. Rosenzweig and L. W. Porter, (Eds.) *Annual Review of Psychology, 36,* 83–114.

Peterson, B. E., Doty, R. M., & Winter, D. G. (1993). Authoritarianism and attitudes toward contemporary social issues. *Personality and Social Psychology Bulletin, 19,* 174–184.

Peterson, B. E., & Lane, M. D. (2001). Implications of authoritarianism for young adulthood: Longitudinal analysis of college experiences and future goals. *Personality and Social Psychology Bulletin, 27,* 678–690.

Peterson, B. E., Smirles, K. A., & Wentworth, P. A. (1997). Generativity and authoritarianism: Implications for personality, political involvement, and parenting. *Journal of Personality and Social Psychology, 72,* 1202–1216.

Peterson, B. E., & Stewart, A. J. (1993). Generativity and social motives in young adults. *Journal of Personality and Social Psychology, 65,* 186–198.

Peterson, C., & Ulrey, L. M. (1994). Can explanatory style be scored from TAT protocols? *Personality and Social Psychology Bulletin, 20,* 102–106.

Petrides, K. V., Jackson, C. J., Furnham, A., & Levine, S. Z. (2003). Exploring issues of personality measurement and structure through the development of a short form of the Eysenck Pesonality Profiler. *Journal of Personality Assessment, 81,* 271–280.

Pezdek, K., & Banks, W. (1996). *The Recovered Memory/False Memory Debate.* New York: Academic Press.

Phares, E. (1962). Perceptual threshold decrements as a function of skill and chance expectancies. *Journal of Psychology, 53,* 399–407.

Phares, E. (1976). *Locus of Control in Personality.* Morristown, NJ: General Learning Press.

Phares, E. J., & Lamiell, J. T. (1977). Personality. In M. R. Rosenzweig & L. W, Porter, (Eds.) *Annual Review of Psychology, 28,* 113–140.

Phelps, E. A., O'Connor, K. J., Cunningham, W. A., Funayama, E. S., Gatenby, J. C., Gore, J. C., Banaji, M. R. (2000). Performance on indirect measures of race evaluation predicts amygdala activation. *Journal of Cognitive Neuroscience, 12,* 729–738.

Phillips, W. M., Watkins, J. T., & Noll, G. (1974). Self-actualization, self-transcendence, and personal philosophy. *Journal of Humanistic Psychology, 14,* 53–73.

Piaget, J. (1948). *The Moral Judgment of the Child.* Glencoe, IL: Free Press.

Pierce, D. L., Sewell, K. W., & Cromwell, R. L. (1992). Schizophrenia and depression: Construing and constructing empirical research. In R. A. Niemeyer & G. J. Neimeyer (Eds.), *Advances in Personal Construct Psychology.* (Vol. 2). Greenwich, CT: JAI Press.

Pietikainen, P. (2004). 'The sage knows you better than you know yourself': Psychological utopianism in Erich Fromm's work. *History of Political Thought, 25,* 86–115.

Pistole, D. R., & Ornduff, S. R. (1994). TAT assessment of sexually abused girls: An analysis of manifest content. *Journal of Personality Assessment, 63,* 211–222.

Plaks, J. E., Shafer, J. L., & Shoda, Y. (2003). Perceiving individuals and groups as coherent: How do perceivers make sense of variable behavior? *Social Cognition, 21,* 26–60.

Plant, E. A., & Devine, P. G. (1998). Internal and external motivation to respond without prejudice. *Journal of Personality and Social Psychology, 75,* 811–832.

Plant, E. A., & Devine, P. G. (2003). The antecedents and implications of interracial anxiety. *Personality and Social Psychology Bulletin, 29,* 790–801.

Pogrebin, L. (1980). *Growing Up Free.* New York: Bantam.

Polce-Lynch, M., & Lynch, J. R. (1998, September). Dangerous v. healthy self-esteem. *Monitor on Psychology,* 53.

Porcerelli, J., Abramsky, M. F., Hibbard, S., & Kamoo, R. (2001). Object relations and defense mechanisms of a psychopathic serial sexual homicide perpetrator: A TAT analysis. *Journal of Personality Assessment, 77,* 87–104.

Potkay, C. R., & Allen, B. P. (1988). The Adjective Generation Technique (AGT): Assessment via word descriptions of self and others. In C. D. Spielberger & J. N. Butcher (Eds.), *Advances in Personality Assessment.* Hillsdale, NJ: Lawrence Erlbaum.

Potkay, C. R., & Merrens, M. R. (1975). Sources of male chauvinism in the TAT. *Journal of Personality Assessment, 39,* 471–479.

Potkay, C. R., Merrens, M. R., & Allen, B. P. (1979). AGT descriptions of TAT figures: "Loving" females more favorable than "lonely" males. Paper presented at the Annual Meeting of the Midwestern Psychological Association, Chicago.

Potosky, D., & Bobko, P. (2000). A model for predicting computer experience from attitudes toward computers. *Journal of Business and Psychology 15,* 391–404.

Powell, G. E. (1981). A survey of the effects of brain lesions upon personality. In H. J. Eysenck (Ed.), *A Model For Personality.* New York: Springer-Verlag, pp. 65–87.

Powell, L. H., Shahabi, L., & Thoresen, C. E. (2003). Religion and spirituality: Linkages to physical health. *American Psychologist, 58,* 36–52.

Powell, R. A., & Boer, D. P. (1994). Did Freud mislead patients to confabulate memories of abuse? *Psychological Reports, 74,* 1283–1298.

Powell, R. A., & Boer, D. P. (1995). Did Freud misinterpret reported memories of sexual abuse as fantasies? *Psychological Reports, 77,* 563–570.

Pratt, M. W., Danso, H. A., Arnold, M. L., Norris, J. W., & Filyer, R. (2001). Adult generativity and the socialization of adolescents: Relations to mothers' and fathers' parenting beliefs, styles and practices. *Journal of Personality, 69,* 89–120.

Pratto, F., & Hegarty, P. (2000). The political psychology of reproductive strategies. *Psychological Science, 11,* 57–62.

Purton, C. (1989). The person-centered Jungian. *Person-Centered Review, 4,* 403–419.

Quinn, R. H. (1993). Confronting Carl Rogers: A developmental-interactional approach to person-centered therapy. *Journal of Humanistic Psychology, 33,* 7–23.

Quinn, S. (1988). *A Mind of Her Own: The Life of Karen Horney.* New York: Addison-Wesley.

Rank, O. (1945). *Will Therapy and Truth and Reality.* New York: Knopf.

Raskin, R., & Shaw, R. (1988). Narcissism and the use of personal pronouns. *Journal of Personality, 56,* 393–404.

Ravizza, K. (1977). Peak experiences in sport. *Journal of Humanistic Psychology, 17,* 35–40.

Recer, P. (2000, June, 27). Scientists decipher the human genetic code. *Peoria Journal Star* (Associated Press), pp. A1 & A5.

Revusky, S., & Garcia, J. (1970). Learned associations over long delays. In G. Bower (Ed.), *The Psychology of Learning and Motivation* (Vol. 4). New York: Academic Press.

Rice, G., Anderson, C., Risch, N., & Ebers, G. (1999, April). Male homosexuality: Absence of linkage to microsatellite markers at xq28. *Science, 284,* 665–667.

Roazen, P. (1974). *Freud and His Followers.* New York: Knopf.

Roazen, P. (1976). *Erik H. Erikson: The Power and Limits of a Vision.* New York: Free Press.

Roazen, P. (2003). Interviews on Freud and Jung with Henry A. Murray in 1965. *Journal of Analytical Psychology, 48,* 1–27.

Robbins, A. D. (1989). Harry Stack Sullivan: Neo-Freudian or not? *Contemporary Psychoanalysis, 25,* 624–640.

Robinson, F. G. (1992). *Love's Story Told: A Life of Henry A. Murray.* Cambridge, MA: Harvard University Press.

Robinson, M. D., Solberg, E. C., Vargas, P. T., & Tamir, M. (2003). Trait as default: Extraversion, subjective well-being, and distinction between neutral and positive events. *Journal of Personality and Social Psychology, 85,* 517–527.

Rockwell, W. T. (1994). Beyond determinism and indignity: A reinterpretation of operant conditioning. *Behavior and Philosophy, 22,* 53–66.

Rodgers, J. L., Cleveland, H. H., van den Oord, E., & Rowe, D. C. (2000). Resolving the debate over birth order, family size, and intelligence. *American Psychologist, 55,* 599–612.

Rodriquez, M. L., Mischel, W., & Shoda, Y. (1989). Cognitive variables in the delay of gratification of older children at risk. *Journal of Personality and Social Psychology, 57,* 358–367.

Rogers, C. R. (1942). *Counseling and Psychotherapy: Newer Concepts in Practice.* Boston: Houghton Mifflin.

Rogers, C. R. (1947). Some observations on the organization of personality. *American Psychologist, 2,* 358–368.

Rogers, C. R. (1954). The case of Mrs. Oak: A research analysis. In C. R. Rogers & R. F. Dymond (Eds.), *Psychotherapy and Personality Change.* Chicago: University of Chicago Press, pp. 259–348.

Rogers, C. R. (1957). The necessary and sufficient conditions of therapeutic personality change. *Journal of Consulting Psychology, 21,* 95–103.

Rogers, C. R. (1959). A theory of therapy, personality, and interpersonal relationships, as developed in the client-centered framework. In S. Koch (Ed.), *Psychology: A Study of a Science.* New York: Mc-Graw-Hill, pp. 184–256.

Rogers, C. R. (1961). *On Becoming a Person: A Therapist's View of Psychotherapy.* Boston: Houghton Mifflin.

Rogers, C. R. (1969a). Two divergent trends. In Rollo May (Ed.), *Existential Psychology.* New York: Random House.

Rogers, C. R. (1969b). *Freedom to Learn: A View of What Education Might Become.* Columbus, OH: Charles Merrill, pp. 84–92.

Rogers, C. R. (1970). *Carl Rogers on Encounter Groups.* New York: Harper and Row.

Rogers, C. R. (1972). *Becoming Partners: Marriage and Its Alternatives.* New York: Delacorte Press.

Rogers, C. R. (1973). My philosophy of interpersonal relationships and how it grew. *Journal of Humanistic Psychology, 13,* 3–15.

Rogers, C. R. (1974). In retrospect: Forty-six years. *American Psychologist, 29,* 115–123.

Rogers, C. R. (1977). *Carl Rogers on Personal Power.* New York: Delacorte Press.

Rogers, C. R. (1980). *A Way of Being.* Boston: Houghton Mifflin.

Rogers, C. R. (January 4, 1983). Personal communication.

Rogers, C. R. (1983). The foundations of the person-centered approach. *Education, 1979, 100,*

98–107. Reprinted in T. H. Carr & H. E. Fitzgerald (Eds.), *Psychology 83/84*. Guilford, CT: Dushkin, pp. 227–233.

Rogers, C. R. (1987a). The underlying theory: Drawn from experience with individuals and groups. *Counseling and Values, 32,* 38–46.

Rogers, C. R. (1987b). Inside the world of the Soviet professional. *Counseling and Values, 32,* 66.

Rogers, C. R. (1987c). Comments on the issue of equality in psychotherapy. *Journal of Humanistic Psychology, 27,* 38–39.

Rogers, C. R. (1987d). Steps toward Peace, 1948–1986: Tension reduction in theory and practice. *Counseling and Values, 32,* 12–15.

Rogers, C. R. (1989a). What I learned from two research studies. In H. Krischenbaum & V. L. Henderson (Eds.), *The Carl Rogers Reader.* Boston: Houghton Mifflin.

Rogers, C. R. (1989b). A psychologist looks at nuclear war. In H. Krischenbaum & V. L. Henderson (Eds.), *The Carl Rogers Reader.* Boston: Houghton Mifflin.

Rogers, C. R., & Dymond, R. F. (1954). (Eds.). *Psychotherapy and Personality Change.* Chicago: University of Chicago Press.

Rogers, C. R., & Malcolm, D. (1987). The potential contribution of the behavioral scientist to world peace. *Counseling and Values, 32,* 10–11.

Rogers, C. R., & Ryback, D. (1984). One alternative to nuclear planetary suicide. *Counseling Psychologist, 12,* 3–11.

Rogers, C. R., & Sanford, R. (1987), Reflections on our South African experience (January–February 1986). *Counseling and Values, 32,* 17–20.

Rogers, R., Flores, J., Ustad, K., & Sewell, K. W. (1995). Initial validation of the Personality Assessment Inventory-Spanish Version with clients from Mexican American communities. *Journal of Personality Assessment, 64,* 340–348.

Rom, E., & Mikulincer, M. (2003). Attachment theory and group processes: The association between attachment style and group-related representations, goals, memories, and functioning. *Journal of Personality and Social Psychology, 84,* 1220–1235.

Ronan, G. F., Date, A. L., & Weisbrod, M. (1995). Personal problem-solving scoring of the TAT: Sensitivity to training. *Journal of Personality Assessment, 64,* 119–131.

Rorer, L. G., & Widiger, T. A. (1983). Personality structure and assessment. In M. R. Rosenzweig and L. W. Porter (Eds.), *Annual Review of Psychology, 34,* 431–463.

Rorschach, H. (1942/1951). *Psychodiagnostics: A Diagnostic Test Based on Perception.* New York: Grune & Stratton.

Rosch, E. (1978). Principles of categorization. In E. Rosch & B. B. Lloyd (Eds.), *Cognition and Categorization.* Hillsdale, NJ: Erlbaum.

Rosenberg, S. D., Blatt, S. J., Oxman, T. E., McHugo, G. J., & Ford, R. Q. (1994). Assessment of object relatedness through a lexical content analysis of the TAT. *Journal of Personality Assessment, 63,* 345–362.

Rosenhan, D. L., & Seliaman, M. E. P. (1995). *Abnormal Psychology.* New York: W. W. Norton.

Rosenthal, R. (1979). The "file drawer problem" and tolerance for null results. *Psychological Bulletin, 86,* 638–641.

Ross, M., Xun, W. Q. E., & Wilson, A. E. (2002). Language and the bicultural self. *Personality and Social Psychology Bulletin, 28,* 1040–1050.

Rotter, J. (1954). *Social Learning and Clinical Psychology.* New York: Prentice-Hall.

Rotter, J. (1966). Generalized expectancies for internal versus external control of reinforcement. *Psychological Monographs: General and Applied, 80,* No. 1, [Whole No. 609], 1–28.

Rotter, J. (1967). A new scale for the measurement of interpersonal trust. *Journal of Personality, 35,* 651–665.

Rotter, J. (1975). Some problems and misconceptions related to the construct of internal versus external control of reinforcement. *Journal of Consulting and Clinical Psychology, 43,* 56–67.

Rotter, J. (1982). *The Development and Application of Social Learning Theory.* New York: Praeger.

Rotter, J. (1990). Internal versus external control of reinforcement. *American Psychologist, 45,* 489–493.

Rotter, J. (1992). Cognates of personal control: Locus of control, self-efficacy, and explanatory style. *Applied and Preventive Psychology, 1,* 127–129.

Rowan, J. (1999). Ascent and descent in Maslow's theory. *Journal of Humanistic Psychology, 39,* 125–133.

Royce, J. R., & Mos, L. P. (1981). *Humanistic Psychology: Concepts and Criticisms.* New York: Plenum Press.

Rubin, T. I. (1991). Horney, here and now: 1991. Special Issue: (Karen Horney). *American Journal of Psychoanalysis, 51,* 313–318.

Ruble, D. N. (1977). Premenstrual symptoms: A reinterpretation. *Science, 197,* 291–292.

Rudman, F. W., & Ansbacher, H. L. (1989). Anti-war psychologists: Alfred Adler. *Psychologists For Social Responsibility Newsletter, 8,* p. 8.

Rudnytsky, P. L. (1999). "Does the professor talk to God?" Countertransference and Jewish identity in the case of Little Hans. *Psychoanalysis & History, 1(2),* 175–194.

Rutherford, A. (2003). B. F. Skinner's technology of behavior in American life: From consumer culture to counterculture. *Journal of the History of the Behavioral Sciences, 39,* 1–23.

Rychlak, J. F. (1968). *A Philosophy of Science for Personality Theory.* Boston: Houghton Mifflin.

Rychlak, J. F. (1976). Is a concept of "self" necessary in psychological theory? In A. Wandersman, P. Poppen, & D. Ricks (Eds.), *Humanism and Behaviorism: Dialogue and Growth.* New York: Pergamon Press, pp. 121–143.

Rychlak, J. F. (1981). *Introduction to Personality and Psychotherapy.* Boston: Houghton Mifflin.

Ryckman, R. M., Libby, C. R., van den Borne, B., Gold, J. A., & Lindner, M. A. (1997). Values of hypercompetitive and personal development competitive individuals. *Journal of Personality Assessment, 69,* 271–283.

Ryckman, R. M., Thornton, B., & Butler, J. C. (1994). Personality correlates of the Hypercompetitive Attitude Scale: Validity tests of Horney's theory of neurosis. *Journal of Personality Assessment, 62,* 84–94.

Ryckman, R. M., Thornton, B., & Gold, J. A. (1999). Religious orientations of hypercompetitive individuals. Presentation at the Eastern Psychological Association.

Sabatelli, R., Buck, R., & Dreyer, A. (1983). Locus of control, interpersonal trust, and nonverbal communication accuracy. *Journal of Personality and Social Psychology, 44,* 399–409.

Sagan, C. (1995, September 17). Where did TV come from? *Parade Magazine,* pp. 10 & 12.

Salovey, P., & Mayer, J. D. (1990). Emotional intelligence. *Imagination, Cognition and Personality, 9,* 185–211.

Salovey, P., & Sluyster, D. (1997). *Emotional Development and Emotional Intelligence.* New York: Basic Books.

Salzinger, K. B. F. (1990, September) Skinner (1904–1990). *APA Observer, 3,* pp. 1, 3, 4.

Samuels, A. (1993). New material concerning Jung, anti-Semitism, and the Nazis. *Journal of Analytical Psychology, 38,* 463–470.

Sanchez-Burks, J., Lee, F., Choi, I., Nisbett, R., Zhao, S., & Koo, J. (2003). Conversing across cultures: East-West communication styles in work and nonwork contexts. *Journal of Personality and Social Psychology, 85,* 363–372.

Sanitioso, R., Kunda, Z., & Fong, G. T. (1990). Motivated recruitment of biographical memories. *Journal of Personality and Social Psychology, 59,* 229–241.

Sanna, L. J., & Pusecker, P. A. (1994). Self-efficacy, valence of self-evaluation, and performance. *Personality and Social Psychology Bulletin, 20,* 82–92.

Sapir, E. (1921). *Language: An Introduction to the Study of Speech.* New York: Harcourt, Brace and Company.

Sartre, J-P. (1956). *Being and Nothingness: An Essay on Phenomenological Ontology.* (H. Barnes, Trans.). New York: Philosophical Library.

Sartre, J-P. (1957). *Existentialism and Human Emotions.* New York: Philosophical Library.

Saucier, G. (2000). Isms and the structure of social attitudes. *Journal of Personality and Social Psychology, 78,* 366–385.

Scarberry, N. C., Ratcliff, C. D., Lord, C. G., Lanicek, D. L., & Desforges, D. M. (1997). Effects of individuating information on the generalization part of Allport's contact hypothesis. *Personality and Social Psychology Bulletin, 23,* 1291–1299.

Scarr, S., Webber, P., Weinberg, R., & Wittig, M. (1981). Personality resemblance among adolescents and their parents in biologically related and adoptive families. *Journal of Personality and Social Psychology, 40,* 885–898.

Schafer, R. (1976). *A New Language For Psychoanalysis.* New Haven: Yale University Press.

Schaller, M., Boyd, C., Yohannes, J., & O'Brien, M. (1995). The prejudiced personality revisited: Personal Need for Structure and formation of erroneous group stereotypes. *Journal of Personality and Social Psychology, 68,* 544–555.

Schimel, J., Greenberg, J., & Martens, A. (2003). Evidence that projection of a feared trait can serve a defensive function. *Personality and Social Psychology Bulletin, 29,* 969–979.

Schlinger, H. D. (1992). Theory in behavior analysis: An application to child development. *American Psychologist, 47,* 1396–1410.

Schmitz, B. & Skinner, E. (1993). Perceived control, effort, and academic performance: Interindividual, intraindividual, and multivariate time-series analyses. *Journal of Personality and Social Psychology, 64,* 1010–1028.

Schonemann, P. H. (1989). Some new results on the Spearman hypothesis artifact. *Bulletin of the Psychonomic Society, 27,* 462–464.

Schonemann, P. H. (1992). Extension of Guttman's result from g to PC1. *Multivariate Behavioral Research, 27,* 219–224.

Schooler, C. (1972). Birth order effects: Not here, not now! *Psychological Bulletin, 78,* 161–175.

Schwartz, B. (1978). *Psychology of Learning and Behavior.* New York: Norton.

Schwarzer, R. (2001). Social-cognitive factors in changing health-related behaviors. *Current Directions in Psychological Science, 10,* 47–51.

Sears, D. O., & Henry, P. J. (2003). The origins of symbolic racism. *Journal of Personality and Social Psychology, 85,* 259–275.

Sechrest, L., & Jackson, D. N. (1961). Social intelligence and accuracy of interpersonal predictions. *Journal of Personality, 29,* 167–182.

Seidenberg, M. S. (1997). Language acquisition and use: Learning and applying probabilistic constraints. *Science, 275,* 1599–1603.

Seiffge-Krenke, I., & Kirsch, H. S. (2002). The body in adolescent diaries: The case of Karen Horney. *Psychoanalytic Study of the Child, 57,* 400–410.

Selye, H. (1978). *The Stress of Life* (Rev. ed.). New York: McGraw-Hill.

Serbin, L., & Karp, J. (2003). Intergeneratonal studies of parenting and the transfer of risk from parent to child. *Current Directions in Psychological Science, 12,* 138–142.

Sethi, S., & Seligman, M. E. P. (1993). Optimism and fundamentalism. *Psychological Science, 4,* 256–260.

Shackelford, T. K., & Buss, D. M. (1997). Cues to infidelity. *Personality and Social Psychology Bulletin, 10,* 1034–1045.

Shadle, W. G., & Cervone, D. (1993). The Big Five versus nobody? *American Psychologist, 48,* 1300–1302.

Shafter, R. (1992). Women and masochism: An introduction to trends in psychoanalytic thinking. *Issues in Ego Psychology, 15,* 56–62.

Shaver, P. (1986). Being lonely, falling in love: Perspectives from attachment theory, 1986 (August). Paper presented at the American Psychological Association Convention, Washington, D.C., August.

Shaver, P. & Hazan, C. (1987). Being lonely and falling love: Perspectives from attachment theory. In M. Hojat & R. Crandall (Eds.), Loneliness: theory, research and applications, a special issue of *Journal of Social Behavior and Personality, 2*(2, Pt. 2), 105.

Sheehy, G. (1977). *Passages.* New York: Bantam.

Shelley, M. W. (1965). *Frankenstein: A Modern Prometheus.* New York: Dell.

Sherrill, C., Gench, B., Hinson, M., Gilstrap, T., Richir, K., & Mastro, J. (1990). Self-actualization of elite blind athletes: An exploratory study. *Journal of Visual Impairment & Blindness, 84,* 55–60.

Shirer, W. L. (1960). *The Rise and Fall of the Third Reich.* Greenwich, CT: Fawcett.

Shlien, J. M. (1970). Phenomenology and personality. In J. T. Hart & T. M. Tomlinson, (Eds.), *New Directions in Client-Centered Therapy.* Boston: Houghton Mifflin, pp. 95–128.

Shlien, J. M., & Zimring, F. M. (1970). Research directives and methods in client-centered therapy. In J. T. Hart & T. M. Tomlinson, (Eds.), *New Directions in Client-Centered Therapy.* Boston: Houghton Mifflin, pp. 33–57.

Shoda, Y., & Mischel, W. (1993). Cognitive social approach to dispositional inferences: What if the perceiver is a cognitive social theorist? *Personality and Social Psychology Bulletin, 19,* 574–585.

Shoda, Y., & Mischel, W. (2000). Reconciling contextualism with the core assumptions of personality psychology. *European Journal of Personality, 14,* 407–428.

Shoda, Y., Mischel, W., & Peake, P. K. (1990). Predicting adolescent cognitive and self-regulatory competencies from preschool delay of gratification: Identifying diagnostic conditions. *Developmental Psychology, 26,* 978–986.

Shoda, Y., Mischel, W., & Wright, J. C. (1989). Intuitive interactionism in person perception: Effects of situation-behavior relations on dispositional judgments. *Journal of Personality and Social Psychology, 56,* 41–53.

Shoda, Y., Mischel, W., & Wright, J. S. (1993). The role of situational demands and cognitive competencies in behavior organization and personality coherence. *Journal of Personality and Social Psychology, 65,* 1023–1035.

Shoda, Y., Tierman, S. L., & Mischel, W. (2002). Personality as a dynamical system: Emergence of stability and distinctiveness from intra-and interpersonal interactions. *Personality and Social Psychology Review, 6,* 316–325.

Shostrom, E. L. (Ed.). (1965). *Three Approaches To Psychotherapy: Rogers, Perls and Ellis.* Orange, CA: Psychological Films.

Shostrom, E. L. (1966). *Eits Manual for the Personal Orientation Inventory.* San Diego: Educational and Industrial Testing Service.

Shostrom, E. (1972). *Freedom To Be: Experiencing and Expressing Your Total Being.* New York: Bantam.

Shrauger, J. S., Ram, D., Greninger, S. A., & Mariano, E. (1996). Accuracy of self-predictions versus judgments by knowledgeable others. *Personality and Social Psychology Bulletin, 22,* 1229–1243.

Signell, K. (1966). Cognitive complexity in person perception and nation perception: A developmental approach. *Journal of Personality, 34,* 517–537.

Silva-Garcia, J. (1989). Fromm in Mexico, 1950–1973. *Contemporary Psychoanalysis, 25,* 244–257.

Silverman, L. (1971). An experimental technique for the study of unconscious conflict. *British Journal of Medical Psychology, 44,* 17–25.

Silverman, L. (1976). Psychoanalytic theory: "The reports of my death are greatly exaggerated." *American Psychologist, 31,* 621–637.

Simonton, O. C., & Simonton, S. (1975). Belief systems and management of the emotional aspects of malignancy. *Journal of Transpersonal Psychology, 7,* 29–48.

Simpson, P. W., Bloom, J. W., Newlon, B. J., & Arminio, L. (1994). Birth order proportions of the general population in the United States. *Individ-ual Psychology Journal of Adlerian Theory, Research and Practice, 50,* 173–182.

Singer, J. (1977). *Androgeny: Toward a New Theory of Sexuality.* Garden City, NY: Anchor.

Singer, J. A. (1990). Affective responses to autobiographical memories and their relationship to long-term goals. *Journal of Personality, 58,* 535–563.

Skinner, B. F. (1948). *Walden Two.* New York: McMillan.

Skinner, B. F. (1957). *Verbal Behavior.* New York: Appleton-Century-Crofts.

Skinner, B. F. (1971). *Beyond Freedom and Dignity.* New York: Knopf.

Skinner, B. F. (Ed.). (1972). *Cumulative Record: A Selection of Papers* (3rd ed.). New York: Appleton-Century-Crofts.

Skinner, B. F. (1972a). A lecture on "having" a poem. In B. F. Skinner (Ed.), *Cumulative Record: A Selection of Papers* (3rd ed.). New York: Appleton-Century-Crofts, pp. 345–358.

Skinner, B. F. (1972b). The design of cultures. In B. F. Skinner (Ed.), *Cumulative Record: A Selection of Papers* (3rd ed.). New York: Appleton-Century-Crofts, pp. 39–50.

Skinner, B. F. (1972c). Creating the creative artist. In B. F. Skinner (Ed.), *Cumulative Record: A Selection of Papers* (3rd ed.). New York: Appleton-Century-Crofts, pp. 333–344.

Skinner, B. F. (1972d). Freedom and the control of men. In B. F. Skinner (Ed.), *Cumulative Record: A Selection of Papers* (3rd ed.). New York: Appleton-Century-Crofts, pp. 3–24.

Skinner, B. F. (1972e). The operational analysis of psychological terms. In B. F. Skinner (Ed.), *Cumulative Record: A Selection of Papers* (3rd ed.). New York: Appleton-Century-Crofts, pp. 370–384.

Skinner, B. F. (1972f). Baby in a box. In B. F. Skinner (Ed.), *Cumulative Record: A Selection of Papers* (3rd ed.). New York: Appleton-Century-Crofts, pp. 567–573.

Skinner, B. F. (1972g). "Superstition" in the pigeon. In B. F. Skinner (Ed.), *Cumulative Record: A Selection of Papers* (3rd ed.). New York: Appleton-Century-Crofts, pp. 236–256.

Skinner, B. F. (1972h). Some relations between behavior modification and basic research. In B. F. Skinner (Ed.), *Cumulative Record: A Selection of Papers* (3rd ed.). New York: Appleton-Century-Crofts, pp. 276–282.

Skinner, B. F. (1972i). What is psychotic behavior? In B. F. Skinner (Ed.), *Cumulative Record: A Selection of Papers* (3rd ed.). New York: Appleton-Century-Crofts, pp. 257–275.

Skinner, B. F. (1972j). Reflection on a decade of teaching machines. In B. F. Skinner (Ed.), *Cumulative Record: A Selection of Papers* (3rd ed.). New York: Appleton-Century-Crofts, pp. 194–207.

Skinner, B. F. (1972k). Contingency management in the classroom. In B. F. Skinner (Ed.), *Cumulative Record: A Selection of Papers* (3rd ed.). New York: Appleton-Century-Crofts, pp. 225–235.

Skinner, B. F. (1972l). Why we need teaching machines. In B. Skinner (Ed.), *Cumulative Record: A Selection of Papers* (3rd ed.). New York: Appleton-Century-Crofts, pp. 171–193.

Skinner, B. F. (1976a). *Particulars of My Life*. New York: Knopf.

Skinner, B. F. (1976b). *About Behaviorism*. New York: Vintage Books.

Skinner, B. F. (1979). *The Shaping of a Behaviorist*. New York: Knopf.

Skinner, B. F. (1983a.) Origins of a behaviorist. *Psychology Today*, September, 22–33.

Skinner, B. F. (1983b). *A Matter of Consequences*. New York: Alfred A. Knopf.

Skinner, B. F. (1987a). *Upon Further Reflection*. Englewood Cliffs, NJ: Prentice-Hall.

Skinner, B. F. (1987b). Whatever happened to psychology as the science of behavior? *American Psychologist, 42*, 780–786.

Skinner, B. F. (1989). The origins of cognitive thought. *American Psychologist, 44*, 13–18.

Skinner, B. F., & Vaughan, M. E. (1983). *Enjoy Old Age*. New York: W. W. Norton.

Smith, B. (1973). On self-actualization: A transambivalent examination of a focal theme in Maslow's psychology. *Journal of Humanistic Psychology, 13*, 17–33.

Smith, D. (2002, October). The theory heard 'round the world. *Monitor on Psychology*, 30–32.

Smith, M. B., & Anderson, J. W. (1989). Henry A. Murray (1893–1988). *American Psychologist, 44*, 153–154.

Smith, M. L., & Glass, G. V. (1977). Meta-analysis of psychotherapy outcome studies. *American Psychologist, 32*, 752–760.

Smith, S. L. Extraversion and sensory threshold. (1968). *Psychophysiology, 5*, 293–299.

Solms, M. (1999, January 29). Wishes, perchance to dream. *Times Higher Education Supplement*, p. 16.

Solomon, R., & Wynne, L. (1953). Traumatic avoidance learning: Acquisition in normal dogs. *Psychological Monographs, 67*, No. 354, 19.

Sommers, S. R., & Ellsworth, P. C. (2001). An investigation of prejudice against black defendants in the American courtroom. *Psychology, Public Policy, & Law, 7*, 201–229.

Spain, J. S., Eaton, L. G., & Funder, D. C. (2000). Perspectives on personality: The relative accuracy of self versus others for the prediction of emotion and behavior. *Journal of Personality, 68*, 837–868.

Spearman, C. (1904). "General intelligence" objectively determined and measured. *American Journal of Psychology, 15*, 201–293.

Spearman, C. (1927). *Abilities of Man*. New York: Macmillan.

Speer, A. (1970). *Inside the Third Reich*. New York: Avon.

Spitz, R. A. (1946). Hospitalism: An inquiry into the genesis of psychotic conditions in early childhood. In *Psychoanalytic Study of the Child*, (Vol. 2). New York: International Universities Press.

Spivack, G., & Levine, M. (1964). The Devereux Child Behavior Rating Scales: A study of symptom behaviors in latency age atypical children. *American Journal of Mental Deficiency, 68*, 700–717.

Srivastava, S., John, O. P., Gosling, S. D., & Porter, J. (2003). Development of personality in early and middle adulthood: Set like plaster or persistent change? *Journal of Personality and Social Psychology, 84*, 1041–1053.

Standal, S. (1954). The need for positive regard: A contribution to client-centered theory. Unpublished doctoral dissertation, University of Chicago.

Stanovich, K. E. (1989). *How To Think Straight About Psychology* (2nd ed.). Glenview, IL: Scott, Foresman.

Station WQED (Pittsburgh). (1971). *Because That's My Way*. (film) Lincoln: GPI Television Library, University of Nebraska.

Staub, E. (1999, January). Aggression and self-esteem. *Monitor on Psychology*, 6.

Steel, P., & Ones, D. S. (2002). Personality and happiness: A national-level analysis. *Journal of Personality and Social Psychology, 83*, 767–781.

Steele, R. S. (1982). *Freud and Jung: Conflicts of Interpretation.* London: Routledge.

Steinem, G. (1994). Womb envy, testyria, and breast castration anxiety. *MS,* (March/April), 49–56.

Stelmack, R. M. (1990). Biological bases of extraversion: Psychopsychological evidence. *Journal of Personality, 58,* 291–311.

Stelmack, R. M. (1997). Toward a paradigm in personality: Comment on Eysenck's (1997) view. *Journal of Personality and Social Psychology, 73,* 1238–1241.

Stepansky, P. E. (1983). *In Freud's Shadow: Adler in Context.* Hillsdale, NJ: Erlbaum.

Stern, P. J. (1976). *C. G. Jung: The Haunted Prophet.* New York: Delta.

Sternberg, R. J. (1988). *The Triarchic Mind: A New Theory of Human Intelligence.* New York: Viking.

Sternberg, R. J. (2003, April). The other three Rs: Part two, reasoning. *Monitor on Psychology,* 5.

Stevens, R. (1983). *Erik Erikson: An Introduction.* New York: St. Martin's Press.

Stokes, D. (1986a). Chance can play key role in life, psychologist says. *Campus* (Stanford University), (June 4), (Profile).

Stokes, D. (1986b). It's no time to shun psychologists, Bandura says. *Campus* (Stanford University), (June 11), (Profile).

Stolorow, R. D., & Atwood, G. E. (1979). *Faces in a Cloud, Subjectivity in Personality Theory.* New York: Jason Aronson.

Strauser, D. R., Ketz, K., & Keim, J. (2002). The relationship between self-efficacy, locus of control and work personality. *Journal of Rehabilitation, 68,* 20–26.

Stuttaford, G. (1990). Review of "Freud on women: A reader" by Elisabeth Young-Bruehl. *Publisher's Weekly, 237* (June), p. 54.

Suh, E. M. (2002). Culture, identity consistency, and subjective well-being. *Journal of Personality and Social Psychology, 83,* 1378–1391.

Sullivan, H. S. (1947). *Conceptions of Modern Psychiatry.* New York: Norton.

Sullivan, H. S. (1953). *The Interpersonal Theory of Psychiatry* (H. S. Perry & M. L. Gawel, Eds.). New York: Norton.

Sullivan, H. S. (1954). *The Psychiatric Interview* (H. S. Perry & M. L. Gawel, Eds.). New York: Norton.

Sullivan, H. S. (1962). *Schizophrenia as a Human Process.* New York: Norton.

Sullivan, H. S. (1972). *Personal Psychopathology.* New York: Norton.

Sullivan, H. S. (1927/1994). The onset of schizophrenia. *American Journal of Psychiatry, 151,* (6, supplement), 135–139.

Sulloway, F. J. (1996). *Born To Rebel: Birth Order, Family Dynamics, and Creative Lives.* New York: Vintage.

Suls, J., Martin, R., & Wheeler, L. (2002). Social comparison: Why, with whom, and with what effect? *Current Directions in Psychological Science, 11,* 159–163.

Suomi, S. J., Collins, M. L., Harlow, H. F., & Ruppenthal, G. C. (1976). Effects of maternal and peer separations on young monkeys. *Journal of Child Psychology and Psychiatry, 17,* 101–112.

Suomi, S. J., & Harlow, H. F. (1972). Social rehabilitation of isolate-reared monkeys. *Developmental Psychology, 6,* 487–496.

Super, D. E. (1989). Comment on Carl Rogers' obituary. *American Psychologist, 44,* 1162–1163.

Sutich, A. J. (1968). Transpersonal psychology: An emerging force. *Journal of Humanistic Psychology, 7,* 77–78.

Suzuki, D. T. (1974). *An Introduction to Zen Buddhism.* New York: Causeway.

Symonds, A. (1991). Gender issues and Horney's theory. Special Issue: (Karen Horney). *American Journal of Psychoanalysis, 51,* 301–312.

Taylor, S. E. (1983). Adjustment to threatening events, a theory of cognitive adaptation. *American Psychologist, 38,* 1161–1173.

Taylor, S. E., Helgeson, V. S., Reed, B. M., & Skokan, L. A. (1991, Winter). Self-generated feelings of control and adjustment to physical illness. *Journal of Social Issues,* 91–110.

Teplov, B. M. (1964). Problems in the study of general types of higher nervous activity in man and animals. In J. A. Gray (Ed.), *Pavlov's Typology* (pp. 3–153). New York: Pergamon Press.

Tetlock, P. E., Armor, D., & Peterson, R. S. (1994). The slavery debate in antebellum America: Cognitive style, value conflict, and the limits of compromise. *Journal of Personality and Social Psychology, 66,* 115–126.

Tetlock, P. E., Peterson, R. S., & Berry, J. M. (1993). Flattering and unflattering personality portraits of integratively simple and complex managers. *Journal of Personality and Social Psychology, 64,* 500–511.

Thorne, A., & Gough, H. (1991). *Portraits of Type: An MBTI Research Compendium.* Palo Alto, CA: Consulting Psychologists Press.

Thorne, B. (1990). Carl Rogers and the doctrine of original sin. Special Issue: Fiftieth anniversary of the person-centered approach. *Person-Centered Review, 5,* 394–405.

Thunedborg, K., Allerup, P., Bech, P., & Joyce, C. R. (1993). Development of the Repertory Grid for measurement of individual quality of life in clinical trials. *International Journal of Methods in Psychiatric Research, 3,* 45–56.

Tiemann, J. (2001). An exploration of language-based personality differences in fluent bilinguals. Unpublished paper.

Tillich, P. (1952). *The Courage To Be.* New Haven: Yale University Press.

Todd, J. T., & Morris, E. K. (1992). Case histories in the great power of steady misrepresentation. *American Psychologist, 47,* 1441–1453.

Toffler, A. (1970). *Future Shock.* New York: Random House.

Toland, J. (1976). *Adolf Hitler.* New York: Ballantine Books.

Tolpin, M. (2000). "A cure with a defect": A previously unpublished letter by Freud concerning "Anna O": Commentary. *International Journal of Psychoanalysis, 81,* 357–359.

Tomkins, S. S., & Izard, C. E. (1965). *Affect, Cognition and Personality.* New York: Springer.

Tosi, D. J., & Hoffman, S. (1972). A factor analysis of the Personal Orientation Inventory. *Journal of Humanistic Psychology, 12,* 86–93.

Towles-Schwen, T., & Fazio, R. H. (2001). On the origins of racial attitudes: Correlates of childhood experiences. *Personality and Social Psychology Bulletin, 27,* 162–175.

Towles-Schwen, T., & Fazio, R. H. (2003). Choosing social situations: The relation between automatically activated racial attitudes and anticipated comfort interacting with African Americans. *Personality and Social Psychology Bulletin, 29,* 170–182.

Triandis, H., Loh, W., & Levine, L. (1966). Race, status, quality of spoken English, and opinion about civil rights as determinants of interpersonal attitudes. *Journal of Personality and Social Psychology, 3,* 468–472.

Tucker, W. H. (1994). *The Science and Politics of Racial Research.* Chicago: University of Illinois Press.

Tudge, J. R. H., & Winterhoff, P. A (1993). Vygotsky, Piaget, and Bandura: Perspectives on the relations between the social world and cognitive development. *Human Development, 36,* 61–81.

Tugade, M. M., & Fredrickson, B. L. (2004). Resilient individuals use positive emotions to bounce back from negative emotional experiences. *Journal of Personality and Social Psychology, 86,* 320–333.

Turco, R., Toon, T., Ackerman, T., Pollack, J., & Sagan, C. (1983). Nuclear winter: Global consequences of multiple nuclear explosions. *Science, 222,* 1283–1292.

Turkheimer, E., Haley, A., Waldron, M., D'Onofrio, B., & Gottesman, I. I. (2003). Socioeconomic status modifies heritability of IQ in young children. *Psychological Science, 14,* 623–628.

Tyler, K. (1994). The ecosystemic approach to personality. *Educational Psychology, 14,* 45–58.

Uhlemann, M. R., Lee, D. Y., & Hasse, R. F. (1989). The effects of cognitive complexity and arousal on client perception of counselor nonverbal behavior. *Journal of Clinical Psychology, 45,* 661–664.

Vaihinger, H. (1925). *The Philosophy of 'As If:' A System of the Theoretical, Practical and Religious Fictions of Mankind.* New York: Harcourt, Brace.

van Baaren, R. B., Holland, R. B., Kawakami, K., & van Knippenberg, A. (2004). Mimicry and prosocial behavior. *Psychological Science, 13,* 71–74

Vandenbergh, J. G. (2003). Prenatal hormone exposure and sexual variation. *American Scientist, 91,* 218–225.

Van der Kolk, B. A. (2000). Trauma, neuroscience, and the etiology of hysteria: An exploration of the relevance of Breuer and Freud's 1893 article in light of modern science. *Journal of the American Academy of Psychoanalysis, 28,* (Summer), 237–262.

VandeWoude, S., Richt, J. A., Zink, M. C., Rott, R., Narayan, O., & Clements J. E. (1990). A borna virus cDNA encoding a protein recognized by antibodies in humans with behavioral diseases. *Science, 250,* 1278–1281.

Van Kaam, A. (1963). Existential psychology as a comprehensive theory of personality. *Review of Existential Psychology and Psychiatry, 3,* 11–26.

Van Kaam, A. (1965). Existential and humanistic psychology. *Review of Existential Psychology and Psychiatry, 5,* 291–296.

Van Kaam, A. (1969). *Existential Foundations of Psychology.* New York: Image Books.

Vargas, J. S. (2003). On 'The Double Life of B. F. Skinner' by B. J. Baars. *Journal of Consciousness Studies, 10,* 67–73.

Vargas, J. S., & Chance, P. (2002, May/June). The depths of genius. *Psychology Today, 52*–55.

Viken, R. J., Rose, R. J., Kaprio, J., & Koskenvuo, M. (1994). A developmental genetic analysis of adult personality: Extraversion and neuroticism from 18 to 59 years of age. *Journal of Personality and Social Psychology, 66,* 722–730.

Viney, L. L., Benjamin, Y. N., & Preston, C. (1989). Mourning and reminiscence: Parallel psychotherapeutic processes for elderly people. *International Journal of Aging and Human Development, 28,* 239–249.

Vockell, E. L., Felker, D. W., & Miley, C. H. (1973). Birth order literature 1967–1971: Bibliography and index. *Journal of Individual Psychology, 29,* 39–53.

Wagner, S. H., Lavine, H., Christiansen, N., & Trudeau, M. (1997). Re-evaluating the structure of right-wing authoritarianism. Paper presented at the Midwestern Psychological Association Convention, Chicago.

Wasti, S. A., & Cortina, L. M. (2002). Coping in context: sociocultural determinants of responses to sexual harassment. *Journal of Personality and Social Psychology, 83,* 393–405.

Watkins, C. E. (1992). Adlerian-oriented early memory research: What does it tell us? *Journal of Personality Assessment, 59,* 248–263.

Watkins, C. E., Campbell, V. L., Nieberding, R., & Hallmark, R. (1995). Contemporary practice of psychological assessment by clinical psychologists. *Professional Psychology: Research and Practice, 26,* 54–60.

Watkins, M. M. (1976). *Waking Dreams.* New York: Harper.

Watson, D. L., & Tharp, R. G. (1977). *Self-Directed Behavior: Self-Modification for Personal Adjustment* (2nd ed.). Monterey, CA: Brooks/Cole.

Watson, J. (1930). *Behaviorism.* Chicago: University of Chicago Press.

Watson, J., & Rayner, R. (1920). Conditioned emotional reactions. *Journal of Experimental Psychology, 3,* 1–14.

Watson, N., & Watts, R. H. (2001). The predictive strength of personal constructs versus conventional constructs: Self-image disparity and neuroticism. *Journal of Personality, 69,* 121–145.

Watts, A. (1961). *Psychotherapy East and West.* New York: Pantheon.

Watts, R. E. (2000). Adlerian counseling: A viable approach for contemporary practice. *TCA Journal, 28,* 11–23.

Watts, R. E., & Holden, J. M. (1994). Why continue to use "fictional finalism"? *Individual Psychology, 50,* 161–163.

Weaver, B. L. (2003, August). Psychology that spans boundaries. *APS Observer, 16,* 9.

Wehr, G. (1989). *An Illustrated Biography of C. G. Jung.* Boston: Shambhala.

Weiner, E. J. (2003). Paths from Erich Fromm: Thinking authority pedagogically. *Journal of Educational Thought, 37,* 59–75.

Weiss, D., Mendelsohn, G., & Feimer, N. (1982). Reply to the comments of Block and Ozer. *Journal of Personality and Social Psychology, 42,* 1182–1184.

Weitz, S. (1972). Attitude, voice, and behavior: A repressed affect model of interaction. *Journal of Personality and Social Psychology, 24,* 14–21.

Weizmann, F., Wiener, N. I., Wiesenthal, D. L., & Ziegler, M. (1990). Differential K theory and racial hierarchies. *Canadian Psychology, 31,* 1–13.

Wexler, D. A., & Rice, L. N. (1974). *Innovations In Client-Centered Therapy.* New York: Wiley.

Wheeler, L. (1966). Motivation as a determinant of upward comparison. *Journal of Experimental Social Psychology,* Supplement No. 1.

Wheeler, L., Deci, E., Reis, H., & Zuckerman, M. (1978). *Interpersonal Influence.* Boston: Allyn and Bacon.

Whitley, B. E. (1999). Right-wing authoritarianism, social dominance orientation, and prejudice. *Journal of Personality and Social Psychology, 77,* 126–134.

Whitworth, R. H., & McBlaine, D. D. (1993). Comparison of the MMPI and MMPI-2 administered to Anglo- and Hispanic-American University Students. *Journal of Personality Assessment, 61,* 19–27.

Wichman, S. A., & Campbell, C. (2003a). The coconstruction of congruency: Investigating the conceptual metaphors of Carl Rogers and Gloria. *Counselor Education and Supervision, 43*, 15–24.

Wichman, S. A., & Campbell, C. (2003b). An analysis of how Carl Rogers enacted client-centered conversation with Gloria. *Journal of Counseling & Development, 81*, 178–184.

Wicker, F. W., Brown, G., Wiehe, J. A., Hagan, A. S., & Reed, J. L. (1993). On reconsidering Maslow: An examination of the deprivation/domination proposition. *Journal of Research in Personality, 27*, 118–133.

Wicker, F. W. & Wiehe, J. A. (1999). An experimental study of Maslow's deprivation-domination proposition. *Perceptual and Motor Skills, 88*, 1356–1358.

Wicker, F. W., Wiehe, J. A., Hagen, A. S., Brown, G. (1994). From wishing to intending: Differences in salience of positive versus negative consequences. *Journal of Personality, 62*, 347–368.

Wiedenfeld, S. A., O'Leary, A., Bandura, A., Brown, S., Levine, S., & Raska, K. (1990). Impact of perceived self-efficacy in coping with stressors on components of the immune system. *Journal of Personality and Social Psychology, 39*, 1082–1094.

Wiesel, E. *Night*. (1961). New York: Pyramid.

Wiggins, J. S. (1984). Cattell's system from the perspective of mainstream personality theory. *Multivariate Behavioral Research, 19*, 176–190.

Will, O. A. (1954). Introduction. In H. S. Sullivan, *The Psychiatric Interview*. New York: Norton, pp. ix–xxiii.

Williams, D. E., & Page, M. M. (1989). A multidimensional measure of Maslow's hierarchy of needs. *Journal of Research in Personality, 23*, 192–213.

Williams, J., & Morland, J. (1979). Comment on Bank's "White preference in blacks: A paradigm in search of a phenomenon." *Psychological Bulletin 86*, 28–32.

Wilson, G. D. (1981). Personality and social behavior. In H. J. Eysenck (Ed.), *A Model For Personality*. New York: Springer-Verlag, pp. 210–245.

Wilson, M. I., & Daly, M. (1996). Male sexual proprietariness and violence against wives. *Current Directions in Psychological Science, 5*, 2–7.

Winter, D. A. (1992). Repertory grid technique as a group psychotherapy research instrument. *Group Analysis, 25*, 449–462.

Winter, D. G. (1996). Gordon Allport and the legend of "Rinehart." *Journal of Personality, 64*, 263–273.

Winter, D. G. (1997). Allport's life and Allport's psychology. *Journal of Personality, 65*, 723–731.

Winterbrink, B., Judd, C. M., & Park, B. (1997). Evidence for racial prejudice at the implicit level and its relationship with questionnaire measures. *Journal of Personality and Social Psychology, 72*, 262–274.

Wood, R., & Bandura, A. (1989). Impact of conceptions of ability on self-regulatory mechanisms and complex decision making. *Journal of Personality and Social Psychology, 56*, 407–415.

Woodward, K. L. (1978, December 4). How they bend minds. *Newsweek, 92*, 72–77.

Woodward, K. L. (1994, May 23). An identity of wisdom. *Newsweek, 56*.

Wortis, J. (1954). *Fragments of an Analysis with Freud*. New York: Charter.

Wright, J. C., & Mischel, W. (1988). Conditional hedges and the intuitive psychology of traits. *Journal of Personality and Social Psychology, 55*, 454–469.

Wrosch, C., Scheier, M. F., Miller, G. E., Schulz, R., & Carver, C. S. (2003). Adaptive self-regulation of unattainable goals: Goal disengagement, goal reengagement, and subjective well-being. *Personality and Social Psychology Bulletin, 29*, 1494–1508.

Yee, A. H., Fairchild, H. H., Weizmann, F., & Wyatt, G. E. (1993). Addressing psychology's problems with race. *American Psychologist, 48*, 1132–1140.

Young, P. T. (1941). The experimental analysis of appetite. *Psychological Bulletin, 38*, 129–164.

Young, P. T. (1948). Appetite, palatability and feeding habit: A critical review. *Psychological Bulletin, 45*, 289–320.

Zajonc, R. B. (1986). The decline and rise of the Scholastic Aptitude Scores: A prediction derived from the confluence model. *American Psychologist, 41*, 862–867.

Zajonc, R. B., & Markus, G. B. (1975). Birth order and intellectual development. *Psychological Review, 82*, 74–88.

Zaragoza, M., & McCloskey, M. (1989). Misleading postevent information and the memory impairment hypothesis: Comments on Belli and reply to Tversky and Tuchin. *Journal of Experimental Psychology: General, 118,* 92–99.

Zaragoza, M., & Mitchell, K. J. (1996). Repeated exposure to suggestion and the creation of false memories. *Psychological Science, 118,* 294–300.

Zayas, V., Shoda, Y., & Ayduk, O. N. (2002). Personality in context: An interpersonal systems perspective. *Journal of Personality, 70,* 851–900.

Zelenski, H. M., & Larsen, R. J. (2002). Predicting the future: How affect-related personality traits influence likelihood judgments of future events. *Personality and Social Bulletin, 28,* 1000–1010.

Zentall, T. R. (2003). Imitation by animals: How do they do it? *Current Directions in Psychological Science, 12,* 91–94.

Zhang, J., & Norvilitis, J. M. (2002). Measuring Chinese psychological well-being with Western developed instruments. *Journal of Personality Assessment, 79,* 492–511.

Zhurbin, V. I. (1991). The notion of psychological defense in the conceptions of Sigmund Freud and Carl Rogers. *Soviet Psychology, 29,* 58–72.

Zimbardo, P. (1970). The human choice: Individuation, reason, and order versus deindividuation, impulse, and chaos. In W. Arnold & D. Levine (Eds.), *Nebraska Symposium on Motivation.* Lincoln, NE: University of Nebraska Press.

Zimmerman, B. J., Bandura, A., & Martinez-Pons, M. (1992). Self-motivation for academic attainment: The role of self-efficacy beliefs and personal goal setting. *American Educational Research Journal, 29,* 663–676.

Zuckerman, M. (1990). Some dubious premises in research and theory on racial differences: Scientific, social, and ethical issues. *American Psychologist, 12,* 1297–1303.

Zuroff, D. S. (1982). Person, situation, and person-by-situation interaction components in person perception. *Journal of Personality, 50,* 1–14.

Zuroff, D. S. (1986). Was Gordon Allport a trait theorist? *Journal of Personality and Social Psychology, 51,* 993–1000.

Zweig, S. (1962). Wider horizons on Freud. In L. Gerard, (Ed.), *Sigmund Freud: The Man and His Theories.* New York: Fawcett.

Zweigenhaft, R. L., & Von Ammon J. (2000). Birth order and civil disobedience: A test of Sulloway's "born to rebel" hypothesis. *The Journal of Social Psychology, 140,* 624–627.

Name Index

Subject Index